# Honda Accord Automotive Repair Manual

## by Jay Storer
## and John H Haynes
Member of the Guild of Motoring Writers

**Models covered:**
All Honda Accord models
1994 through 1997

(3F7 - 42013)                                    A

**Haynes Publishing Group**
Sparkford Nr Yeovil
Somerset BA22 7JJ England

**Haynes North America, Inc**
861 Lawrence Drive
Newbury Park
California 91320 USA

## Acknowledgements

Technical writers who contributed to this project include Rob Maddox and Larry Warren.

**A book in the Haynes Automotive Repair Manual Series**

**Printed in the U.S.A.**

**ISBN 1 56392 323 8**

**Library of Congress Catalog Card Number 98-85021**

# Contents

Haynes mechanic, author and photographer with 1994 Honda Accord

# About this manual

## Its purpose

The purpose of this manual is to help you get the best value from your vehicle. It can do so in several ways. It can help you decide what work must be done, even if you choose to have it done by a dealer service department or a repair shop; it provides information and procedures for routine maintenance and servicing; and it offers diagnostic and repair procedures to follow when trouble occurs.

We hope you use the manual to tackle the work yourself. For many simpler jobs, doing it yourself may be quicker than arranging an appointment to get the vehicle into a shop and making the trips to leave it and pick it up. More importantly, a lot of money can be saved by avoiding the expense the shop must pass on to you to cover its labor and overhead costs. An added benefit is the sense of satisfaction and accomplishment that you feel after doing the job yourself.

## Using the manual

The manual is divided into Chapters. Each Chapter is divided into numbered Sections, which are headed in bold type between horizontal lines. Each Section consists of consecutively numbered paragraphs.

At the beginning of each numbered Section you will be referred to any illustrations which apply to the procedures in that Section. The reference numbers used in illustration captions pinpoint the pertinent Section and the Step within that Section. That is, illustration 3.2 means the illustration refers to Section 3 and Step (or paragraph) 2 within that Section.

Procedures, once described in the text, are not normally repeated. When it's necessary to refer to another Chapter, the reference will be given as Chapter and Section number. Cross references given without use of the word "Chapter" apply to Sections and/or paragraphs in the same Chapter. For example, "see Section 8" means in the same Chapter.

References to the left or right side of the vehicle assume you are sitting in the driver's seat, facing forward.

Even though we have prepared this manual with extreme care, neither the publisher nor the author can accept responsibility for any errors in, or omissions from, the information given.

### NOTE

A **Note** provides information necessary to properly complete a procedure or information which will make the procedure easier to understand.

### CAUTION

A **Caution** provides a special procedure or special steps which must be taken while completing the procedure where the Caution is found. Not heeding a Caution can result in damage to the assembly being worked on.

### WARNING

A **Warning** provides a special procedure or special steps which must be taken while completing the procedure where the Warning is found. Not heeding a Warning can result in personal injury.

# Introduction to the Honda Accord

These models are available in two-door coupe, four-door sedan and station wagon body styles.

The transversely mounted inline four-cylinder or V6 engines used in these models are equipped with electronic fuel injection.

The engine drives the front wheels through either a five-speed manual or a four-speed automatic transaxle via independent driveaxles.

Independent suspension, featuring coil spring/shock absorber units, is used on all four wheels. The power-assisted rack-and-pinion steering unit is mounted behind the engine.

The brakes are disc at the front and either disc or drum at the rear, with power assist standard. Some models are equipped with Anti-lock Braking Systems (ABS).

# Vehicle identification numbers

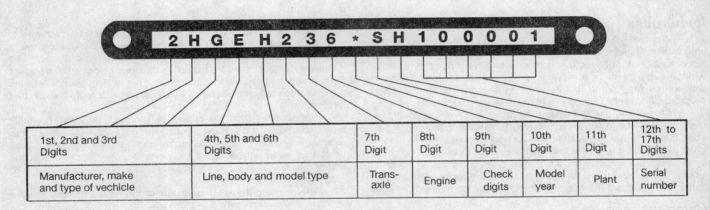

| | | 2 H G E H 2 3 6 ∗ S H 1 0 0 0 0 1 | | | | | |

| 1st, 2nd and 3rd Digits | 4th, 5th and 6th Digits | 7th Digit | 8th Digit | 9th Digit | 10th Digit | 11th Digit | 12th to 17th Digits |
|---|---|---|---|---|---|---|---|
| Manufacturer, make and type of vechicle | Line, body and model type | Trans-axle | Engine | Check digits | Model year | Plant | Serial number |

The Vehicle Identification Number (VIN) contains important information on the vehicle

Modifications are a continuing and unpublicized process in vehicle manufacturing. Since spare parts manuals and lists are compiled on a numerical basis, the individual vehicle numbers are essential to correctly identify the component required.

## Vehicle identification number (VIN)

This very important number is stamped on the firewall in the engine compartment and on a plate attached to the dashboard inside the windshield on the driver's side of the vehicle. The VIN also appears on the Vehicle Certificate of Title and Registration. It contains information such as where and when the vehicle was manufactured, the model year and the body style (see illustration).

### Model year
R = 1994
S = 1995

## Engine number

The engine code number, which is commonly needed when ordering engine parts, can be found near the right (passenger side) end of the engine, near the exhaust manifold on four-cylinder models (see illustration) or under the starter motor on V6 engines. The engine code is the first five digits of the number. The three engines covered by this manual are:

F22B1 - 2.2L SOHC 16-valve VTEC four-cylinder
F22B2 - 2.2L SOHC 16-valve four-cylinder
C27A4 - 2.7L SOHC V6

## Transaxle number

The transaxle number is commonly needed when ordering transaxle parts. On manual transaxles it's located on the bellhousing, near the starter motor. On automatic transaxles, it's located on the front of the transaxle case, above the dipstick.

The four-cylinder engine code number (arrow) is located near the exhaust manifold

# Buying parts

Replacement parts are available from many sources, which generally fall into one of two categories - authorized dealer parts departments and independent retail auto parts stores. Our advice concerning these parts is as follows:

*Retail auto parts stores:* Good auto parts stores will stock frequently needed components which wear out relatively fast, such as clutch components, exhaust systems, brake parts, tune-up parts, etc. These stores often supply new or reconditioned parts on an exchange basis, which can save a considerable amount of money. Discount auto parts stores are often very good places to buy materials and parts needed for general vehicle maintenance such as oil, grease, filters, spark plugs, belts, touch-up paint, bulbs, etc. They also usually sell tools and general accessories, have convenient hours, charge lower prices and can often be found not far from home.

*Authorized dealer parts department:* This is the best source for parts which are unique to the vehicle and not generally available elsewhere (such as major engine parts, transmission parts, trim pieces, etc.).

*Warranty information:* If the vehicle is still covered under warranty, be sure that any replacement parts purchased - regardless of the source - do not invalidate the warranty!

To be sure of obtaining the correct parts, have engine and chassis numbers available and, if possible, take the old parts along for positive identification.

# Maintenance techniques, tools and working facilities

## Maintenance techniques

There are a number of techniques involved in maintenance and repair that will be referred to throughout this manual. Application of these techniques will enable the home mechanic to be more efficient, better organized and capable of performing the various tasks properly, which will ensure that the repair job is thorough and complete.

## Fasteners

Fasteners are nuts, bolts, studs and screws used to hold two or more parts together. There are a few things to keep in mind when working with fasteners. Almost all of them use a locking device of some type, either a lockwasher, locknut, locking tab or thread adhesive. All threaded fasteners should be clean and straight, with undamaged threads and undamaged corners on the hex head where the wrench fits. Develop the habit of replacing all damaged nuts and bolts with new ones. Special locknuts with nylon or fiber inserts can only be used once. If they are removed, they lose their locking ability and must be replaced with new ones.

Rusted nuts and bolts should be treated with a penetrating fluid to ease removal and prevent breakage. Some mechanics use turpentine in a spout-type oil can, which works quite well. After applying the rust penetrant, let it work for a few minutes before trying to loosen the nut or bolt. Badly rusted fasteners may have to be chiseled or sawed off or removed with a special nut breaker, available at tool stores.

If a bolt or stud breaks off in an assembly, it can be drilled and removed with a special tool commonly available for this purpose. Most automotive machine shops can perform this task, as well as other repair procedures, such as the repair of threaded holes that have been stripped out.

Flat washers and lockwashers, when removed from an assembly, should always be replaced exactly as removed. Replace any damaged washers with new ones. Never use a lockwasher on any soft metal surface (such as aluminum), thin sheet metal or plastic.

## Fastener sizes

For a number of reasons, automobile manufacturers are making wider and wider use of metric fasteners. Therefore, it is important to be able to tell the difference between standard (sometimes called U.S. or SAE) and metric hardware, since they cannot be interchanged.

All bolts, whether standard or metric, are sized according to diameter, thread pitch and length. For example, a standard 1/2 - 13 x 1 bolt is 1/2 inch in diameter, has 13 threads per inch and is 1 inch long. An M12 - 1.75 x 25 metric bolt is 12 mm in diameter, has a thread pitch of 1.75 mm (the distance between threads) and is 25 mm long. The two bolts are nearly identical, and easily confused, but they are not interchangeable.

In addition to the differences in diameter, thread pitch and length, metric and standard bolts can also be distinguished by examining the bolt heads. To begin with, the distance across the flats on a standard bolt head is measured in inches, while the same dimension on a metric bolt is sized in millimeters (the same is true for nuts). As a result, a standard wrench should not be used on a metric bolt and a metric wrench should not be used on a standard bolt. Also, most standard bolts have slashes radiating out from the center of the head to denote the grade or strength of the bolt, which is an indication of the amount of torque that can be applied to it. The greater the number of slashes, the greater the strength of the bolt. Grades 0 through 5 are commonly used on automobiles. Metric bolts have a property class (grade) number, rather than a slash, molded into their heads to indicate bolt strength. In this case, the higher the number, the stronger the bolt. Property class numbers 8.8, 9.8 and 10.9 are commonly used on automobiles.

Strength markings can also be used to distinguish standard hex nuts from metric hex nuts. Many standard nuts have dots stamped into one side, while metric nuts are marked with a number. The greater the number of dots, or the higher the number, the greater the strength of the nut.

Metric studs are also marked on their ends according to property class (grade). Larger studs are numbered (the same as metric bolts), while smaller studs carry a geometric code to denote grade.

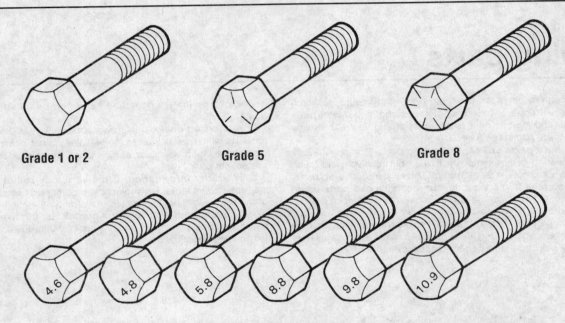

Grade 1 or 2      Grade 5      Grade 8

4.6   4.8   5.8   8.8   9.8   10.9

**Bolt strength markings (top - standard/SAE/USS; bottom - metric)**

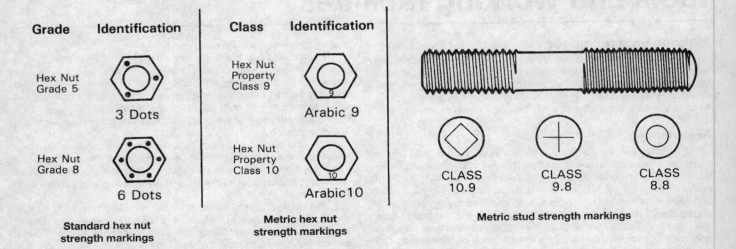

| Grade | Identification | Class | Identification |
|---|---|---|---|
| Hex Nut Grade 5 | 3 Dots | Hex Nut Property Class 9 | Arabic 9 |
| Hex Nut Grade 8 | 6 Dots | Hex Nut Property Class 10 | Arabic 10 |

**Standard hex nut strength markings**

**Metric hex nut strength markings**

CLASS 10.9     CLASS 9.8     CLASS 8.8

**Metric stud strength markings**

It should be noted that many fasteners, especially Grades 0 through 2, have no distinguishing marks on them. When such is the case, the only way to determine whether it is standard or metric is to measure the thread pitch or compare it to a known fastener of the same size.

Standard fasteners are often referred to as SAE, as opposed to metric. However, it should be noted that SAE technically refers to a non-metric fine thread fastener only. Coarse thread non-metric fasteners are referred to as USS sizes.

Since fasteners of the same size (both standard and metric) may have different strength ratings, be sure to reinstall any bolts, studs or nuts removed from your vehicle in their original locations. Also, when replacing a fastener with a new one, make sure that the new one has a strength rating equal to or greater than the original.

## Tightening sequences and procedures

Most threaded fasteners should be tightened to a specific torque value (torque is the twisting force applied to a threaded component such as a nut or bolt). Overtightening the fastener can weaken it and cause it to break, while undertightening can cause it to eventually come loose. Bolts, screws and studs, depending on the material they are made of and their thread diameters, have specific torque values, many of which are noted in the Specifications at the beginning of each Chapter. Be sure to follow the torque recommendations closely. For fasteners not assigned a specific torque, a general torque value chart is presented here as a guide. These torque values are for dry (unlubricated) fasteners threaded into steel or cast iron (not aluminum). As was previously mentioned, the size and grade of a fastener determine the amount of torque that can safely be applied to it. The

| Metric thread sizes | Ft-lbs | Nm |
|---|---|---|
| M-6 | 6 to 9 | 9 to 12 |
| M-8 | 14 to 21 | 19 to 28 |
| M-10 | 28 to 40 | 38 to 54 |
| M-12 | 50 to 71 | 68 to 96 |
| M-14 | 80 to 140 | 109 to 154 |
| **Pipe thread sizes** | | |
| 1/8 | 5 to 8 | 7 to 10 |
| 1/4 | 12 to 18 | 17 to 24 |
| 3/8 | 22 to 33 | 30 to 44 |
| 1/2 | 25 to 35 | 34 to 47 |
| **U.S. thread sizes** | | |
| 1/4 - 20 | 6 to 9 | 9 to 12 |
| 5/16 - 18 | 12 to 18 | 17 to 24 |
| 5/16 - 24 | 14 to 20 | 19 to 27 |
| 3/8 - 16 | 22 to 32 | 30 to 43 |
| 3/8 - 24 | 27 to 38 | 37 to 51 |
| 7/16 - 14 | 40 to 55 | 55 to 74 |
| 7/16 - 20 | 40 to 60 | 55 to 81 |
| 1/2 - 13 | 55 to 80 | 75 to 108 |

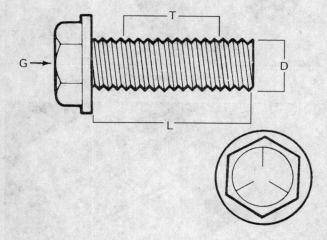

**Standard (SAE and USS) bolt dimensions/grade marks**

G    Grade marks (bolt length)
L    Length (in inches)
T    Thread pitch (number of threads per inch)
D    Nominal diameter (in inches)

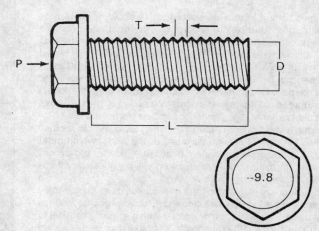

**Metric bolt dimensions/grade marks**

P    Property class (bolt strength)
L    Length (in millimeters)
T    Thread pitch (distance between threads in millimeters)
D    Diameter

figures listed here are approximate for Grade 2 and Grade 3 fasteners. Higher grades can tolerate higher torque values.

Fasteners laid out in a pattern, such as cylinder head bolts, oil pan bolts, differential cover bolts, etc., must be loosened or tightened in sequence to avoid warping the component. This sequence will normally be shown in the appropriate Chapter. If a specific pattern is not given, the following procedures can be used to prevent warping.

Initially, the bolts or nuts should be assembled finger-tight only. Next, they should be tightened one full turn each, in a criss-cross or diagonal pattern. After each one has been tightened one full turn, return to the first one and tighten them all one-half turn, following the same pattern. Finally, tighten each of them one-quarter turn at a time until each fastener has been tightened to the proper torque. To loosen and remove the fasteners, the procedure would be reversed.

### Component disassembly

Component disassembly should be done with care and purpose to help ensure that the parts go back together properly. Always keep track of the sequence in which parts are removed. Make note of special characteristics or marks on parts that can be installed more than one way, such as a grooved thrust washer on a shaft. It is a good idea to lay the disassembled parts out on a clean surface in the order that they were removed. It may also be helpful to make sketches or take instant photos of components before removal.

When removing fasteners from a component, keep track of their locations. Sometimes threading a bolt back in a part, or putting the washers and nut back on a stud, can prevent mix-ups later. If nuts and bolts cannot be returned to their original locations, they should be kept in a compartmented box or a series of small boxes. A cupcake or muffin tin is ideal for this purpose, since each cavity can hold the bolts and nuts from a particular area (i.e. oil pan bolts, valve cover bolts, engine mount bolts, etc.). A pan of this type is especially helpful when working on assemblies with very small parts, such as the carburetor, alternator, valve train or interior dash and trim pieces. The cavities can be marked with paint or tape to identify the contents.

Whenever wiring looms, harnesses or connectors are separated, it is a good idea to identify the two halves with numbered pieces of masking tape so they can be easily reconnected.

### Gasket sealing surfaces

Throughout any vehicle, gaskets are used to seal the mating surfaces between two parts and keep lubricants, fluids, vacuum or pressure contained in an assembly.

Many times these gaskets are coated with a liquid or paste-type gasket sealing compound before assembly. Age, heat and pressure can sometimes cause the two parts to stick together so tightly that they are very difficult to separate. Often, the assembly can be loosened by striking it with a soft-face hammer near the mating surfaces. A regular hammer can be used if a block of wood is placed between the hammer and the part. Do not hammer on cast parts or parts that could be easily damaged. With any particularly stubborn part, always recheck to make sure that every fastener has been removed.

Avoid using a screwdriver or bar to pry apart an assembly, as they can easily mar the gasket sealing surfaces of the parts, which must remain smooth. If prying is absolutely necessary, use an old broom handle, but keep in mind that extra clean up will be necessary if the wood splinters.

After the parts are separated, the old gasket must be carefully scraped off and the gasket surfaces cleaned. Stubborn gasket material can be soaked with rust penetrant or treated with a special chemical to soften it so it can be easily scraped off. A scraper can be fashioned from a piece of copper tubing by flattening and sharpening one end. Copper is recommended because it is usually softer than the surfaces to be scraped, which reduces the chance of gouging the part. Some gaskets can be removed with a wire brush, but regardless of the method used, the mating surfaces must be left clean and smooth. If for some reason the gasket surface is gouged, then a gasket sealer thick enough to fill scratches will have to be used during reassembly of the components. For most applications, a non-drying (or semi-drying) gasket sealer should be used.

### Hose removal tips

**Warning:** *If the vehicle is equipped with air conditioning, do not disconnect any of the A/C hoses without first having the system depressurized by a dealer service department or a service station.*

Hose removal precautions closely parallel gasket removal precautions. Avoid scratching or gouging the surface that the hose mates against or the connection may leak. This is especially true for radiator hoses. Because of various chemical reactions, the rubber in hoses can bond itself to the metal spigot that the hose fits over. To remove a hose, first loosen the hose clamps that secure it to the spigot. Then, with slip-joint pliers, grab the hose at the clamp and rotate it around the spigot. Work it back and forth until it is completely free, then pull it off. Silicone or other lubricants will ease removal if they can be applied between the hose and the outside of the spigot. Apply the same lubricant to the inside of the hose and the outside of the spigot to simplify installation.

As a last resort (and if the hose is to be replaced with a new one anyway), the rubber can be slit with a knife and the hose peeled from the spigot. If this must be done, be careful that the metal connection is not damaged.

If a hose clamp is broken or damaged, do not reuse it. Wire-type clamps usually weaken with age, so it is a good idea to replace them with screw-type clamps whenever a hose is removed.

### *Tools*

A selection of good tools is a basic requirement for anyone who plans to maintain and repair his or her own vehicle. For the owner who has few tools, the initial investment might seem high, but when compared to the spiraling costs of professional auto maintenance and repair, it is a wise one.

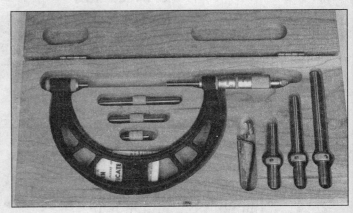

**Micrometer set**

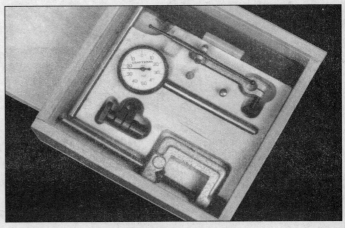

**Dial indicator set**

Dial caliper

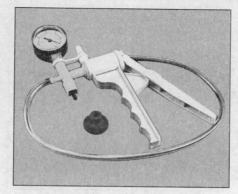

Hand-operated vacuum pump

Timing light

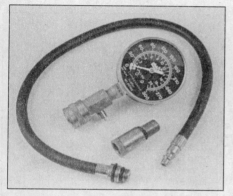

Compression gauge with spark plug
hole adapter

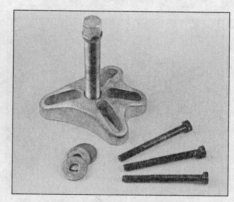

Damper/steering wheel puller

General purpose puller

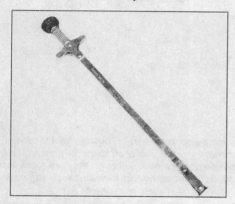

Hydraulic lifter removal tool

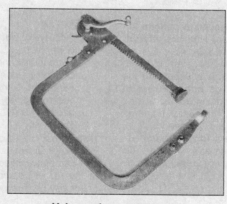

Valve spring compressor

Valve spring compressor

Ridge reamer

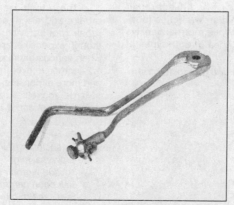

Piston ring groove cleaning tool

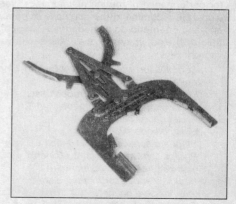

Ring removal/installation tool

**Ring compressor**

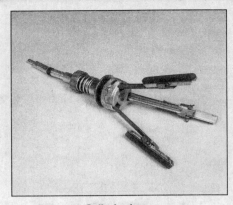

**Cylinder hone**

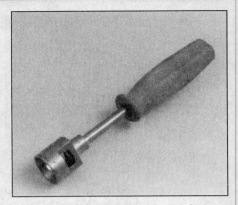

**Brake hold-down spring tool**

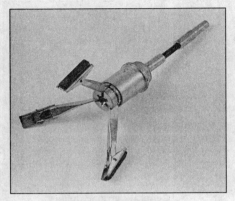

**Brake cylinder hone**

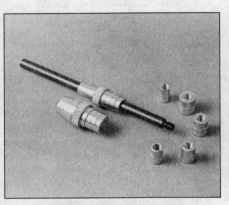

**Clutch plate alignment tool**

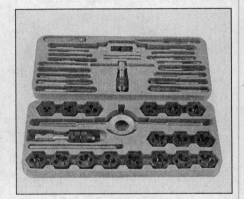

**Tap and die set**

To help the owner decide which tools are needed to perform the tasks detailed in this manual, the following tool lists are offered: *Maintenance and minor repair*, *Repair/overhaul* and *Special.*

The newcomer to practical mechanics should start off with the *maintenance and minor repair* tool kit, which is adequate for the simpler jobs performed on a vehicle. Then, as confidence and experience grow, the owner can tackle more difficult tasks, buying additional tools as they are needed. Eventually the basic kit will be expanded into the *repair and overhaul* tool set. Over a period of time, the experienced do-it-yourselfer will assemble a tool set complete enough for most repair and overhaul procedures and will add tools from the special category when it is felt that the expense is justified by the frequency of use.

## Maintenance and minor repair tool kit

The tools in this list should be considered the minimum required for performance of routine maintenance, servicing and minor repair work. We recommend the purchase of combination wrenches (box-end and open-end combined in one wrench). While more expensive than open end wrenches, they offer the advantages of both types of wrench.

*Combination wrench set (1/4-inch to 1 inch or 6 mm to 19 mm)*
*Adjustable wrench, 8 inch*
*Spark plug wrench with rubber insert*
*Spark plug gap adjusting tool*
*Feeler gauge set*
*Brake bleeder wrench*
*Standard screwdriver (5/16-inch x 6 inch)*
*Phillips screwdriver (No. 2 x 6 inch)*
*Combination pliers - 6 inch*
*Hacksaw and assortment of blades*
*Tire pressure gauge*
*Grease gun*

*Oil can*
*Fine emery cloth*
*Wire brush*
*Battery post and cable cleaning tool*
*Oil filter wrench*
*Funnel (medium size)*
*Safety goggles*
*Jackstands (2)*
*Drain pan*

**Note**: *If basic tune-ups are going to be part of routine maintenance, it will be necessary to purchase a good quality stroboscopic timing light and combination tachometer/dwell meter. Although they are included in the list of special tools, it is mentioned here because they are absolutely necessary for tuning most vehicles properly.*

## Repair and overhaul tool set

These tools are essential for anyone who plans to perform major repairs and are in addition to those in the maintenance and minor repair tool kit. Included is a comprehensive set of sockets which, though expensive, are invaluable because of their versatility, especially when various extensions and drives are available. We recommend the 1/2-inch drive over the 3/8-inch drive. Although the larger drive is bulky and more expensive, it has the capacity of accepting a very wide range of large sockets. Ideally, however, the mechanic should have a 3/8-inch drive set and a 1/2-inch drive set.

*Socket set(s)*
*Reversible ratchet*
*Extension - 10 inch*
*Universal joint*
*Torque wrench (same size drive as sockets)*
*Ball peen hammer - 8 ounce*
*Soft-face hammer (plastic/rubber)*
*Standard screwdriver (1/4-inch x 6 inch)*

Standard screwdriver (stubby - 5/16-inch)
Phillips screwdriver (No. 3 x 8 inch)
Phillips screwdriver (stubby - No. 2)
Pliers - vise grip
Pliers - lineman's
Pliers - needle nose
Pliers - snap-ring (internal and external)
Cold chisel - 1/2-inch
Scribe
Scraper (made from flattened copper tubing)
Centerpunch
Pin punches (1/16, 1/8, 3/16-inch)
Steel rule/straightedge - 12 inch
Allen wrench set (1/8 to 3/8-inch or 4 mm to 10 mm)
A selection of files
Wire brush (large)
Jackstands (second set)
Jack (scissor or hydraulic type)

**Note:** *Another tool which is often useful is an electric drill with a chuck capacity of 3/8-inch and a set of good quality drill bits.*

## Special tools

The tools in this list include those which are not used regularly, are expensive to buy, or which need to be used in accordance with their manufacturer's instructions. Unless these tools will be used frequently, it is not very economical to purchase many of them. A consideration would be to split the cost and use between yourself and a friend or friends. In addition, most of these tools can be obtained from a tool rental shop on a temporary basis.

This list primarily contains only those tools and instruments widely available to the public, and not those special tools produced by the vehicle manufacturer for distribution to dealer service departments. Occasionally, references to the manufacturer's special tools are included in the text of this manual. Generally, an alternative method of doing the job without the special tool is offered. However, sometimes there is no alternative to their use. Where this is the case, and the tool cannot be purchased or borrowed, the work should be turned over to the dealer service department or an automotive repair shop.

Valve spring compressor
Piston ring groove cleaning tool
Piston ring compressor
Piston ring installation tool
Cylinder compression gauge
Cylinder ridge reamer
Cylinder surfacing hone
Cylinder bore gauge
Micrometers and/or dial calipers
Hydraulic lifter removal tool
Balljoint separator
Universal-type puller
Impact screwdriver
Dial indicator set
Stroboscopic timing light (inductive pick-up)
Hand operated vacuum/pressure pump
Tachometer/dwell meter
Universal electrical multimeter
Cable hoist
Brake spring removal and installation tools
Floor jack

## Buying tools

For the do-it-yourselfer who is just starting to get involved in vehicle maintenance and repair, there are a number of options available when purchasing tools. If maintenance and minor repair is the extent of the work to be done, the purchase of individual tools is satisfactory. If, on the other hand, extensive work is planned, it would

be a good idea to purchase a modest tool set from one of the large retail chain stores. A set can usually be bought at a substantial savings over the individual tool prices, and they often come with a tool box. As additional tools are needed, add-on sets, individual tools and a larger tool box can be purchased to expand the tool selection. Building a tool set gradually allows the cost of the tools to be spread over a longer period of time and gives the mechanic the freedom to choose only those tools that will actually be used.

Tool stores will often be the only source of some of the special tools that are needed, but regardless of where tools are bought, try to avoid cheap ones, especially when buying screwdrivers and sockets, because they won't last very long. The expense involved in replacing cheap tools will eventually be greater than the initial cost of quality tools.

## Care and maintenance of tools

Good tools are expensive, so it makes sense to treat them with respect. Keep them clean and in usable condition and store them properly when not in use. Always wipe off any dirt, grease or metal chips before putting them away. Never leave tools lying around in the work area. Upon completion of a job, always check closely under the hood for tools that may have been left there so they won't get lost during a test drive.

Some tools, such as screwdrivers, pliers, wrenches and sockets, can be hung on a panel mounted on the garage or workshop wall, while others should be kept in a tool box or tray. Measuring instruments, gauges, meters, etc. must be carefully stored where they cannot be damaged by weather or impact from other tools.

When tools are used with care and stored properly, they will last a very long time. Even with the best of care, though, tools will wear out if used frequently. When a tool is damaged or worn out, replace it. Subsequent jobs will be safer and more enjoyable if you do.

## *Working facilities*

Not to be overlooked when discussing tools is the workshop. If anything more than routine maintenance is to be carried out, some sort of suitable work area is essential.

It is understood, and appreciated, that many home mechanics do not have a good workshop or garage available, and end up removing an engine or doing major repairs outside. It is recommended, however, that the overhaul or repair be completed under the cover of a roof.

A clean, flat workbench or table of comfortable working height is an absolute necessity. The workbench should be equipped with a vise that has a jaw opening of at least four inches.

As mentioned previously, some clean, dry storage space is also required for tools, as well as the lubricants, fluids, cleaning solvents, etc. which soon become necessary.

Sometimes waste oil and fluids, drained from the engine or cooling system during normal maintenance or repairs, present a disposal problem. To avoid pouring them on the ground or into a sewage system, pour the used fluids into large containers, seal them with caps and take them to an authorized disposal site or recycling center. Plastic jugs, such as old antifreeze containers, are ideal for this purpose.

Always keep a supply of old newspapers and clean rags available. Old towels are excellent for mopping up spills. Many mechanics use rolls of paper towels for most work because they are readily available and disposable. To help keep the area under the vehicle clean, a large cardboard box can be cut open and flattened to protect the garage or shop floor.

Whenever working over a painted surface, such as when leaning over a fender to service something under the hood, always cover it with an old blanket or bedspread to protect the finish. Vinyl covered pads, made especially for this purpose, are available at auto parts stores.

# Jacking and towing

## Jacking

**Warning:** *The jack supplied with the vehicle should only be used for changing a tire or placing jackstands under the frame. Never work under the vehicle or start the engine while this jack is being used as the only means of support.*

The vehicle should be on level ground. Place the shift lever in Park, if you have an automatic, or Reverse if you have a manual transaxle. Block the wheel diagonally opposite the wheel being changed. Set the parking brake.

Remove the spare tire and jack from stowage. Remove the wheel cover with the tapered end of the lug nut wrench by inserting and twisting the handle and then prying against the back of the wheel cover. **Caution:** *On some models the wheel cover can't be removed by prying; the wheel nuts must be removed first. Loosen, but do not remove, the lug nuts (one-half turn is sufficient).*

Place the scissors-type jack under the side of the vehicle and adjust the jack height until the slot in the jack head engages with the raised portion of the ridge on the vertical rocker panel flange nearest the wheel to be changed. There is a front and rear jacking point on each side of the vehicle **(see illustration).**

Turn the jack handle clockwise until the tire clears the ground. Remove the lug nuts and pull the wheel off. Replace it with the spare.

Install the lug nuts with the beveled edges facing in. Tighten them snugly. Don't attempt to tighten them completely until the vehicle is lowered or it could slip off the jack. Turn the jack handle counter-clockwise to lower the vehicle. Remove the jack and tighten the lug nuts in a criss-cross pattern.

Install the cover and be sure it's snapped into place all the way around.

Stow the tire, jack and wrench. Unblock the wheels.

## Towing

As a general rule, the vehicle should be towed with the front (drive) wheels off the ground (the best method is to have the vehicle placed on a flat-bed tow truck). If they can't be raised, place them on a dolly. The ignition key must be in the OFF position, since the steering lock mechanism isn't strong enough to hold the front wheels straight while towing.

Vehicles equipped with an automatic transaxle can be towed from the front with all four wheels on the ground, provided that speeds don't exceed 35 mph and the distance is not over 50 miles. Before towing,

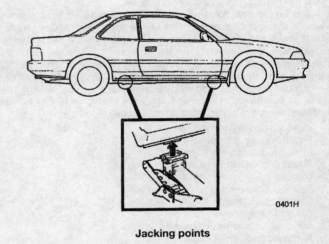

**Jacking points**

check the transmission fluid level (see Chapter 1). If the level is below the HOT line on the dipstick, add fluid or use a towing dolly. Additionally, perform the following steps:

a) *Release the parking brake*
b) *Start the engine*
c) *Move the transaxle gear selector into D4, then to Neutral*
d) *Turn off the engine*
e) *Place the ignition key in the OFF (not the LOCK position).*

**Caution:** *Never tow a vehicle with an automatic transaxle from the rear with the front wheels on the ground.*

When towing a vehicle equipped with a manual transaxle with all four wheels on the ground, be sure to place the shift lever in neutral and release the parking brake.

Equipment specifically designed for towing should be used. It should be attached to the main structural members of the vehicle, not the bumpers or brackets.

Safety is a major consideration when towing and all applicable state and local laws must be obeyed. A safety chain system must be used at all times. Remember that power steering and power brakes will not work with the engine off.

# Booster battery (jump) starting

Observe these precautions when using a booster battery to start a vehicle:

a) *Before connecting the booster battery, make sure the ignition switch is in the Off position.*

b) *Turn off the lights, heater and other electrical loads.*

c) *Your eyes should be shielded. Safety goggles are a good idea.*

d) *Make sure the booster battery is the same voltage as the dead one in the vehicle.*

e) *The two vehicles MUST NOT TOUCH each other!*

f) *Make sure the transaxle is in Neutral (manual) or Park (automatic).*

g) *If the booster battery is not a maintenance-free type, remove the vent caps and lay a cloth over the vent holes.*

Connect the red jumper cable to the positive (+) terminals of each battery **(see illustration)**.

Connect one end of the black jumper cable to the negative (-) terminal of the booster battery. The other end of this cable should be connected to a good ground on the vehicle to be started, such as a bolt or bracket on the body.

Start the engine using the booster battery, then, with the engine running at idle speed, disconnect the jumper cables in the reverse order of connection.

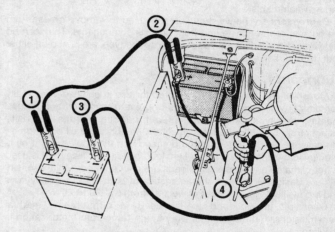

**Make the booster battery cable connections in the numerical order shown (note that the negative cable of the booster battery is NOT attached to the negative terminal of the dead battery)**

# Anti-theft audio system

1    All models were originally equipped with an audio system which includes an anti-theft feature that will render the stereo inoperative If the power source to the stereo is cut, the stereo will not work until a five-digit code (furnished with the vehicle when it was originally purchased from the dealer) is entered. Even if the power is immediately reconnected, the stereo will not function. If your vehicle is equipped win this anti-theft system, do not disconnect the battery, remove the number 32 (7.5a) fuse in the under-hood fuse block or remove the stereo unless you have the code number for the stereo.

2    Refer to your vehicle's owner's manual for more complete information on this audio system and it's anti-theft feature.

### Unlocking the stereo after a power loss

3    Turn on the radio. The word "CODE" should appear on the display.

4    Using the station reset selector buttons, enter the five-digit code. If you make a mistake when entering the code, continue the five digit sequence anyway - the radio will "beep" after the five digits are entered. **Note:** *You have three attempts to enter the correct code. If the correct code isn't entered in three tries you'll have to wait one hour, with the radio on, before you enter the code again.*

5    Once the code has been entered correctly, the wore "CODE" should disappear from the display and the radio should play (you'll have to tune in and enter your preset stations, however).

# Automotive chemicals and lubricants

A number of automotive chemicals and lubricants are available for use during vehicle maintenance and repair. They include a wide variety of products ranging from cleaning solvents and degreasers to lubricants and protective sprays for rubber, plastic and vinyl.

## Cleaners

*Carburetor cleaner and choke cleaner* is a strong solvent for gum, varnish and carbon. Most carburetor cleaners leave a dry-type lubricant film which will not harden or gum up. Because of this film it is not recommended for use on electrical components.

*Brake system cleaner* is used to remove grease and brake fluid from the brake system, where clean surfaces are absolutely necessary. It leaves no residue and often eliminates brake squeal caused by contaminants.

*Electrical cleaner* removes oxidation, corrosion and carbon deposits from electrical contacts, restoring full current flow. It can also be used to clean spark plugs, carburetor jets, voltage regulators and other parts where an oil-free surface is desired.

*Demoisturants* remove water and moisture from electrical components such as alternators, voltage regulators, electrical connectors and fuse blocks. They are non-conductive, non-corrosive and non-flammable.

*Degreasers* are heavy-duty solvents used to remove grease from the outside of the engine and from chassis components. They can be sprayed or brushed on and, depending on the type, are rinsed off either with water or solvent.

## Lubricants

*Motor oil* is the lubricant formulated for use in engines. It normally contains a wide variety of additives to prevent corrosion and reduce foaming and wear. Motor oil comes in various weights (viscosity ratings) from 5 to 80. The recommended weight of the oil depends on the season, temperature and the demands on the engine. Light oil is used in cold climates and under light load conditions. Heavy oil is used in hot climates and where high loads are encountered. Multi-viscosity oils are designed to have characteristics of both light and heavy oils and are available in a number of weights from 5W-20 to 20W-50.

*Gear oil* is designed to be used in differentials, manual transmissions and other areas where high-temperature lubrication is required.

*Chassis and wheel bearing grease* is a heavy grease used where increased loads and friction are encountered, such as for wheel bearings, balljoints, tie-rod ends and universal joints.

*High-temperature wheel bearing grease* is designed to withstand the extreme temperatures encountered by wheel bearings in disc brake equipped vehicles. It usually contains molybdenum disulfide (moly), which is a dry-type lubricant.

*White grease* is a heavy grease for metal-to-metal applications where water is a problem. White grease stays soft under both low and high temperatures (usually from -100 to +190-degrees F), and will not wash off or dilute in the presence of water.

*Assembly lube* is a special extreme pressure lubricant, usually containing moly, used to lubricate high-load parts (such as main and rod bearings and cam lobes) for initial start-up of a new engine. The assembly lube lubricates the parts without being squeezed out or washed away until the engine oiling system begins to function.

*Silicone lubricants* are used to protect rubber, plastic, vinyl and nylon parts.

*Graphite lubricants* are used where oils cannot be used due to contamination problems, such as in locks. The dry graphite will lubricate metal parts while remaining uncontaminated by dirt, water, oil or acids. It is electrically conductive and will not foul electrical contacts in locks such as the ignition switch.

*Moly penetrants* loosen and lubricate frozen, rusted and corroded fasteners and prevent future rusting or freezing.

*Heat-sink grease* is a special electrically non-conductive grease that is used for mounting electronic ignition modules where it is essential that heat is transferred away from the module.

## Sealants

*RTV sealant* is one of the most widely used gasket compounds. Made from silicone, RTV is air curing, it seals, bonds, waterproofs, fills surface irregularities, remains flexible, doesn't shrink, is relatively easy to remove, and is used as a supplementary sealer with almost all low and medium temperature gaskets.

*Anaerobic sealant* is much like RTV in that it can be used either to seal gaskets or to form gaskets by itself. It remains flexible, is solvent resistant and fills surface imperfections. The difference between an anaerobic sealant and an RTV-type sealant is in the curing. RTV cures when exposed to air, while an anaerobic sealant cures only in the absence of air. This means that an anaerobic sealant cures only after the assembly of parts, sealing them together.

*Thread and pipe sealant* is used for sealing hydraulic and pneumatic fittings and vacuum lines. It is usually made from a Teflon compound, and comes in a spray, a paint-on liquid and as a wrap-around tape.

## Chemicals

*Anti-seize compound* prevents seizing, galling, cold welding, rust and corrosion in fasteners. High-temperature ant-seize, usually made with copper and graphite lubricants, is used for exhaust system and exhaust manifold bolts.

*Anaerobic locking compounds* are used to keep fasteners from vibrating or working loose and cure only after installation, in the absence of air. Medium strength locking compound is used for small nuts, bolts and screws that may be removed later. High-strength locking compound is for large nuts, bolts and studs which aren't removed on a regular basis.

*Oil additives* range from viscosity index improvers to chemical treatments that claim to reduce internal engine friction. It should be noted that most oil manufacturers caution against using additives with their oils.

*Gas additives* perform several functions, depending on their chemical makeup. They usually contain solvents that help dissolve gum and varnish that build up on carburetor, fuel injection and intake parts. They also serve to break down carbon deposits that form on the inside surfaces of the combustion chambers. Some additives contain upper cylinder lubricants for valves and piston rings, and others contain chemicals to remove condensation from the gas tank.

## Miscellaneous

*Brake fluid* is specially formulated hydraulic fluid that can withstand the heat and pressure encountered in brake systems. Care must be taken so this fluid does not come in contact with painted surfaces or plastics. An opened container should always be resealed to prevent contamination by water or dirt.

*Weatherstrip adhesive* is used to bond weatherstripping around doors, windows and trunk lids. It is sometimes used to attach trim pieces.

*Undercoating* is a petroleum-based, tar-like substance that is designed to protect metal surfaces on the underside of the vehicle from corrosion. It also acts as a sound-deadening agent by insulating the bottom of the vehicle.

*Waxes and polishes* are used to help protect painted and plated surfaces from the weather. Different types of paint may require the use of different types of wax and polish. Some polishes utilize a chemical or abrasive cleaner to help remove the top layer of oxidized (dull) paint on older vehicles. In recent years many non-wax polishes that contain a wide variety of chemicals such as polymers and silicones have been introduced. These non-wax polishes are usually easier to apply and last longer than conventional waxes and polishes.

# Conversion factors

### Length (distance)

| | | | | | |
|---|---|---|---|---|---|
| Inches (in) | X | 25.4 | = Millimetres (mm) | X | 0.0394 | = Inches (in) |
| Feet (ft) | X | 0.305 | = Metres (m) | X | 3.281 | = Feet (ft) |
| Miles | X | 1.609 | = Kilometres (km) | X | 0.621 | = Miles |

Inches (in)   X 25.4 = Millimetres (mm)    X 0.0394 = Inches (in)
Feet (ft)   X 0.305 = Metres (m)    X 3.281 = Feet (ft)
Miles   X 1.609 = Kilometres (km)    X 0.621 = Miles

### Volume (capacity)

Cubic inches (cu in; $in^3$)   X 16.387 = Cubic centimetres (cc; $cm^3$)    X 0.061 = Cubic inches (cu in; $in^3$)
Imperial pints (Imp pt)   X 0.568 = Litres (l)    X 1.76 = Imperial pints (Imp pt)
Imperial quarts (Imp qt)   X 1.137 = Litres (l)    X 0.88 = Imperial quarts (Imp qt)
Imperial quarts (Imp qt)   X 1.201 = US quarts (US qt)    X 0.833 = Imperial quarts (Imp qt)
US quarts (US qt)   X 0.946 = Litres (l)    X 1.057 = US quarts (US qt)
Imperial gallons (Imp gal)   X 4.546 = Litres (l)    X 0.22 = Imperial gallons (Imp gal)
Imperial gallons (Imp gal)   X 1.201 = US gallons (US gal)    X 0.833 = Imperial gallons (Imp gal)
US gallons (US gal)   X 3.785 = Litres (l)    X 0.264 = US gallons (US gal)

### Mass (weight)

Ounces (oz)   X 28.35 = Grams (g)    X 0.035   Ounces (oz)
Pounds (lb)   X 0.454 = Kilograms (kg)    X 2.205 = Pounds (lb)

### Force

Ounces-force (ozf; oz)   X 0.278 = Newtons (N)    X 3.6 = Ounces-force (ozf; oz)
Pounds-force (lbf; lb)   X 4.448 = Newtons (N)    X 0.225 = Pounds-force (lbf; lb)
Newtons (N)   X 0.1 = Kilograms-force (kgf; kg)    X 9.81 = Newtons (N)

### Pressure

Pounds-force per square inch (psi; $lbf/in^2$; $lb/in^2$)   X 0.070 = Kilograms-force per square centimetre (kgf/cm²; kg/cm²)    X 14.223 = Pounds-force per square inch (psi; $lbf/in^2$; $lb/in^2$)
Pounds-force per square inch (psi; $lbf/in^2$; $lb/in^2$)   X 0.068 = Atmospheres (atm)    X 14.696 = Pounds-force per square inch (psi; $lbf/in^2$; $lb/in^2$)
Pounds-force per square inch (psi; $lbf/in^2$; $lb/in^2$)   X 0.069 = Bars    X 14.5 = Pounds-force per square inch (psi; $lbf/in^2$; $lb/in^2$)
Pounds-force per square inch (psi; $lbf/in^2$; $lb/in^2$)   X 6.895 = Kilopascals (kPa)    X 0.145 = Pounds-force per square inch (psi; $lbf/in^2$; $lb/in^2$)
Kilopascals (kPa)   X 0.01 = Kilograms-force per square centimetre (kgf/cm²; kg/cm²)    X 98.1 = Kilopascals (kPa)

### Torque (moment of force)

Pounds-force inches (lbf in; lb in)   X 1.152 = Kilograms-force centimetre (kgf cm; kg cm)    X 0.868 = Pounds-force inches (lbf in; lb in)
Pounds-force inches (lbf in; lb in)   X 0.113 = Newton metres (Nm)    X 8.85 = Pounds-force inches (lbf in; lb in)
Pounds-force inches (lbf in; lb in)   X 0.083 = Pounds-force feet (lbf ft; lb ft)    X 12 = Pounds-force inches (lbf in; lb in)
Pounds-force feet (lbf ft; lb ft)   X 0.138 = Kilograms-force metres (kgf m; kg m)    X 7.233 = Pounds-force feet (lbf ft; lb ft)
Pounds-force feet (lbf ft; lb ft)   X 1.356 = Newton metres (Nm)    X 0.738 = Pounds-force feet (lbf ft; lb ft)
Newton metres (Nm)   X 0.102 = Kilograms-force metres (kgf m; kg m)    X 9.804 = Newton metres (Nm)

### Power

Horsepower (hp)   X 745.7 = Watts (W)    X 0.0013 = Horsepower (hp)

### Velocity (speed)

Miles per hour (miles/hr; mph)   X 1.609 = Kilometres per hour (km/hr; kph)    X 0.621 = Miles per hour (miles/hr; mph)

### Fuel consumption*

Miles per gallon, Imperial (mpg)   X 0.354 = Kilometres per litre (km/l)    X 2.825 = Miles per gallon, Imperial (mpg)
Miles per gallon, US (mpg)   X 0.425 = Kilometres per litre (km/l)    X 2.352 = Miles per gallon, US (mpg)

### Temperature

Degrees Fahrenheit = (°C x 1.8) + 32      Degrees Celsius (Degrees Centigrade; °C) = (°F - 32) x 0.56

*It is common practice to convert from miles per gallon (mpg) to litres/100 kilometres (l/100km), where mpg (Imperial) x l/100 km = 282 and mpg (US) x l/100 km = 235

# Safety first

Regardless of how enthusiastic you may be about getting on with the job at hand, take the time to ensure that your safety is not jeopardized. A moment's lack of attention can result in an accident, as can failure to observe certain simple safety precautions. The possibility of an accident will always exist, and the following points should not be considered a comprehensive list of all dangers. Rather, they are intended to make you aware of the risks and to encourage a safety conscious approach to all work you carry out on your vehicle.

## Essential DOs and DON'Ts

**DON'T** rely on a jack when working under the vehicle. Always use approved jackstands to support the weight of the vehicle and place them under the recommended lift or support points.

**DON'T** attempt to loosen extremely tight fasteners (i.e. wheel lug nuts) while the vehicle is on a jack - it may fall.

**DON'T** start the engine without first making sure that the transmission is in Neutral (or Park where applicable) and the parking brake is set.

**DON'T** remove the radiator cap from a hot cooling system - let it cool or cover it with a cloth and release the pressure gradually.

**DON'T** attempt to drain the engine oil until you are sure it has cooled to the point that it will not burn you.

**DON'T** touch any part of the engine or exhaust system until it has cooled sufficiently to avoid burns.

**DON'T** siphon toxic liquids such as gasoline, antifreeze and brake fluid by mouth, or allow them to remain on your skin.

**DON'T** inhale brake lining dust - it is potentially hazardous (see *Asbestos* below).

**DON'T** allow spilled oil or grease to remain on the floor - wipe it up before someone slips on it.

**DON'T** use loose fitting wrenches or other tools which may slip and cause injury.

**DON'T** push on wrenches when loosening or tightening nuts or bolts. Always try to pull the wrench toward you. If the situation calls for pushing the wrench away, push with an open hand to avoid scraped knuckles if the wrench should slip.

**DON'T** attempt to lift a heavy component alone - get someone to help you.

**DON'T** rush or take unsafe shortcuts to finish a job.

**DON'T** allow children or animals in or around the vehicle while you are working on it.

**DO** wear eye protection when using power tools such as a drill, sander, bench grinder, etc. and when working under a vehicle.

**DO** keep loose clothing and long hair well out of the way of moving parts.

**DO** make sure that any hoist used has a safe working load rating adequate for the job.

**DO** get someone to check on you periodically when working alone on a vehicle.

**DO** carry out work in a logical sequence and make sure that everything is correctly assembled and tightened.

**DO** keep chemicals and fluids tightly capped and out of the reach of children and pets.

**DO** remember that your vehicle's safety affects that of yourself and others. If in doubt on any point, get professional advice.

## Asbestos

Certain friction, insulating, sealing, and other products - such as brake linings, brake bands, clutch linings, torque converters, gaskets, etc. - contain asbestos. Extreme care must be taken to avoid inhalation of dust from such products, since it is hazardous to health. If in doubt, assume that they do contain asbestos.

## Fire

Remember at all times that gasoline is highly flammable. Never smoke or have any kind of open flame around when working on a vehicle. But the risk does not end there. A spark caused by an electrical short circuit, by two metal surfaces contacting each other, or even by static electricity built up in your body under certain conditions, can ignite gasoline vapors, which in a confined space are highly explosive. Do not, under any circumstances, use gasoline for cleaning parts. Use an approved safety solvent.

Always disconnect the battery ground (-) cable at the battery before working on any part of the fuel system or electrical system. Never risk spilling fuel on a hot engine or exhaust component. It is strongly recommended that a fire extinguisher suitable for use on fuel and electrical fires be kept handy in the garage or workshop at all times. Never try to extinguish a fuel or electrical fire with water.

## Fumes

Certain fumes are highly toxic and can quickly cause unconsciousness and even death if inhaled to any extent. Gasoline vapor falls into this category, as do the vapors from some cleaning solvents. Any draining or pouring of such volatile fluids should be done in a well ventilated area.

When using cleaning fluids and solvents, read the instructions on the container carefully. Never use materials from unmarked containers.

Never run the engine in an enclosed space, such as a garage. Exhaust fumes contain carbon monoxide, which is extremely poisonous. If you need to run the engine, always do so in the open air, or at least have the rear of the vehicle outside the work area.

If you are fortunate enough to have the use of an inspection pit, never drain or pour gasoline and never run the engine while the vehicle is over the pit. The fumes, being heavier than air, will concentrate in the pit with possibly lethal results.

## The battery

Never create a spark or allow a bare light bulb near a battery. They normally give off a certain amount of hydrogen gas, which is highly explosive.

Always disconnect the battery ground (-) cable at the battery before working on the fuel or electrical systems.

If possible, loosen the filler caps or cover when charging the battery from an external source (this does not apply to sealed or maintenance-free batteries). Do not charge at an excessive rate or the battery may burst.

Take care when adding water to a non maintenance-free battery and when carrying a battery. The electrolyte, even when diluted, is very corrosive and should not be allowed to contact clothing or skin.

Always wear eye protection when cleaning the battery to prevent the caustic deposits from entering your eyes.

## Household current

When using an electric power tool, inspection light, etc., which operates on household current, always make sure that the tool is correctly connected to its plug and that, where necessary, it is properly grounded. Do not use such items in damp conditions and, again, do not create a spark or apply excessive heat in the vicinity of fuel or fuel vapor.

## Secondary ignition system voltage

A severe electric shock can result from touching certain parts of the ignition system (such as the spark plug wires) when the engine is running or being cranked, particularly if components are damp or the insulation is defective. In the case of an electronic ignition system, the secondary system voltage is much higher and could prove fatal.

# Troubleshooting

## Contents

This section provides an easy reference guide to the more common problems which may occur during the operation of your vehicle. These problems and their possible causes are grouped under headings denoting various components or systems, such as Engine, Cooling system, etc. They also refer you to the chapter and/or section which deals with the problem.

Remember that successful troubleshooting is not a mysterious black art practiced only by professional mechanics. It is simply the result of the right knowledge combined with an intelligent, systematic approach to the problem. Always work by a process of elimination, starting with the simplest solution and working through to the most complex - and never overlook the obvious. Anyone can run the gas tank dry or leave the lights on overnight, so don't assume that you are exempt from such oversights.

Finally, always establish a clear idea of why a problem has occurred and take steps to ensure that it doesn't happen again. If the electrical system fails because of a poor connection, check the other connections in the system to make sure that they don't fail as well. If a particular fuse continues to blow, find out why - don't just replace one fuse after another. Remember, failure of a small component can often be indicative of potential failure or incorrect functioning of a more important component or system.

## Engine

### 1   Engine will not rotate when attempting to start

1   Battery terminal connections loose or corroded (Chapter 1).
2   Battery discharged or faulty (Chapter 1).
3   Automatic transmission not completely engaged in Park (Chapter 7) or clutch not completely depressed (Chapter 8).
4   Broken, loose or disconnected wiring in the starting circuit (Chapters 5 and 12).
5   Starter motor pinion jammed in flywheel ring gear (Chapter 5).
6   Starter solenoid faulty (Chapter 5).
7   Starter motor faulty (Chapter 5).
8   Ignition switch faulty (Chapter 12).
9   Starter pinion or flywheel teeth worn or broken (Chapter 5).

### 2   Engine rotates but will not start

1   Fuel tank empty.
2   Battery discharged (engine rotates slowly) (Chapter 5).
3   Battery terminal connections loose or corroded (Chapter 1).
4   Leaking fuel injector(s), faulty fuel pump, pressure regulator, etc. (Chapter 4).
5   Fuel not reaching fuel rail (Chapter 4).
6   Ignition components damp or damaged (Chapter 5).
7   Worn, faulty or incorrectly gapped spark plugs (Chapter 1).
8   Broken, loose or disconnected wiring in the starting circuit (Chapter 5).
9   Loose distributor is changing ignition timing (Chapter 5).
10   Broken, loose or disconnected wires at the ignition coil or faulty coil (Chapter 5).
11   Broken or stripped timing belt (Shapter 2).

### 3   Engine hard to start when cold

1   Battery discharged or low (Chapter 1).
2   Malfunctioning fuel system (Chapter 4).
3   Injector(s) leaking (Chapter 4).
4   Distributor rotor carbon tracked (Chapter 5).

### 4   Engine hard to start when hot

1   Air filter clogged (Chapter 1).
2   Fuel not reaching the fuel injection system (Chapter 4).
3   Corroded battery connections, especially ground (Chapter 1).

### 5   Starter motor noisy or excessively rough in engagement

1   Pinion or flywheel gear teeth worn or broken (Chapter 5).
2   Starter motor mounting bolts loose or missing (Chapter 5).

### 6   Engine starts but stops immediately

1   Loose or faulty electrical connections at distributor, coil or alternator (Chapter 5).
2   Insufficient fuel reaching the fuel injector(s) (Chapters 1 and 4).
3   Vacuum leak at the gasket between the intake manifold and throttle body (Chapters 1 and 4).

### 7   Oil puddle under engine

1   Oil pan gasket and/or oil pan drain bolt washer leaking (Chapter 2).
2   Oil pressure sending unit leaking (Chapter 2).
3   Cylinder head covers leaking (Chapter 2).
4   Engine oil seals leaking (Chapter 2).

### 8   Engine lopes while idling or idles erratically

1   Vacuum leakage (Chapters 2 and 4).
2   Leaking EGR valve (Chapter 6).
3   Air filter clogged (Chapter 1).
4   Fuel pump not delivering sufficient fuel to the fuel injection system (Chapter 4).
5   Leaking head gasket (Chapter 2).
6   Timing belt and/or pulleys worn (Chapter 2).
7   Camshaft lobes worn (Chapter 2).

### 9   Engine misses at idle speed

1   Spark plugs worn or not gapped properly (Chapter 1).
2   Faulty spark plug wires (Chapter 1).
3   Vacuum leaks (Chapter 1).
4   Incorrect ignition timing (Chapter 1).
5   Uneven or low compression (Chapter 2).

### 10   Engine misses throughout driving speed range

1   Fuel filter clogged and/or impurities in the fuel system (Chapter 1).
2   Low fuel pressure (Chapter 4).
3   Faulty or incorrectly gapped spark plugs (Chapter 1).
4   Incorrect ignition timing (Chapter 5).
5   Cracked distributor cap, disconnected distributor wires or damaged distributor components (Chapters 1 and 5).
6   Leaking spark plug wires (Chapters 1 or 5).
7   Faulty emission system components (Chapter 6).
8   Low or uneven cylinder compression pressures (Chapter 2).
9   Weak or faulty ignition system (Chapter 5).
10   Vacuum leak in fuel injection system, intake manifold, air control valve or vacuum hoses (Chapter 4).

## 11 Engine stumbles on acceleration

1 Spark plugs fouled (Chapter 1).
2 Fuel injection system faulty (Chapter 4).
3 Fuel filter clogged (Chapters 1 and 4).
4 Incorrect ignition timing (Chapter 5).
5 Intake manifold air leak (Chapters 2 and 4).

## 12 Engine surges while holding accelerator steady

1 Intake air leak (Chapter 4).
2 Fuel pump faulty (Chapter 4).
3 Loose fuel injector wire harness connectors (Chapter 4).
4 Defective ECU or information sensor (Chapter 6).

## 13 Engine stalls

1 Idle speed incorrect (Chapter 1).
2 Fuel filter clogged and/or water and impurities in the fuel system (Chapters 1 and 4).
3 Distributor components damp or damaged (Chapter 5).
4 Faulty emissions system components (Chapter 6).
5 Faulty or incorrectly gapped spark plugs (Chapter 1).
6 Faulty spark plug wires (Chapter 1).
7 Vacuum leak in the fuel injection system, intake manifold or vacuum hoses (Chapters 2 and 4).
8 Valve clearances incorrectly set (Chapter 1).

## 14 Engine lacks power

1 Incorrect ignition timing (Chapter 5).
2 Excessive play in distributor shaft (Chapter 5).
3 Worn rotor, distributor cap or wires (Chapters 1 and 5).
4 Faulty or incorrectly gapped spark plugs (Chapter 1).
5 Fuel injection system malfunction (Chapter 4).
6 Faulty coil (Chapter 5).
7 Brakes binding (Chapter 9).
8 Automatic transaxle fluid level incorrect (Chapter 1).
9 Clutch slipping (Chapter 8).
10 Fuel filter clogged and/or impurities in the fuel system (Chapters 1 and 4).
11 Emission control system not functioning properly (Chapter 6).
12 Low or uneven cylinder compression pressures (Chapter 2).
13 Obstructed exhaust system (Chapter 4).

## 15 Engine backfires

1 Emission control system not functioning properly (Chapter 6).
2 Ignition timing incorrect (Chapter 5).
3 Faulty secondary ignition system (cracked spark plug insulator, faulty plug wires, distributor cap and/or rotor) (Chapters 1 and 5).
4 Fuel injection system malfunctioning (Chapter 4).
5 Vacuum leak at fuel injector(s), intake manifold, air control valve or vacuum hoses (Chapters 2 and 4).
6 Valve clearances incorrectly set and/or valves sticking (Chapter 1).

## 16 Pinging or knocking engine sounds during acceleration or uphill

1 Incorrect grade of fuel.
2 Ignition timing incorrect (Chapter 5).

3 Fuel injection system faulty (Chapter 4).
4 Improper or damaged spark plugs or wires (Chapter 1).
5 Worn or damaged distributor components (Chapter 5).
6 EGR valve not functioning (Chapter 6).
7 Vacuum leak (Chapters 2 and 4).

## 17 Engine runs with oil pressure light on

1 Low oil level (Chapter 1).
2 Short in wiring circuit (Chapter 12).
3 Faulty oil pressure sender (Chapter 2).
4 Worn engine bearings and/or oil pump (Chapter 2).

## 18 Engine diesels (continues to run) after switching off

1 Idle speed too high (Chapter 5)
2 Excessive engine operating temperature (Chapter 3).
3 Ignition timing in need of adjustment (Chapter 5).

# Engine electrical system

## 19 Battery will not hold a charge

1 Alternator drivebelt defective or not adjusted properly (Chapter 1).
2 Battery electrolyte level low (Chapter 1).
3 Battery terminals loose or corroded (Chapter 1).
4 Alternator not charging properly (Chapter 5).
5 Loose, broken or faulty wiring in the charging circuit (Chapter 5).
6 Short in vehicle wiring (Chapter 12).
7 Internally defective battery (Chapters 1 and 5).

## 20 Alternator light fails to go out

1 Faulty alternator or charging circuit (Chapter 5).
2 Alternator drivebelt defective or out of adjustment (Chapter 1).
3 Alternator voltage regulator inoperative (Chapter 5).

## 21 Alternator light fails to come on when key is turned on

1 Warning light bulb defective (Chapter 12).
2 Fault in the printed circuit, dash wiring or bulb holder (Chapter 12).

# Fuel system

## 22 Excessive fuel consumption

1 Dirty or clogged air filter element (Chapter 1).
2 Incorrectly set ignition timing (Chapter 5).
3 Emissions system not functioning properly (Chapter 6).
4 Fuel injection system malfunctioning (Chapter 4).
5 Low tire pressure or incorrect tire size (Chapter 1).

## 23 Fuel leakage and/or fuel odor

1 Leaking fuel feed or return line (Chapters 1 and 4).

2    Tank overfilled.
3    Evaporative canister filter clogged (Chapters 1 and 6).
4    Fuel injector internal parts excessively worn (Chapter 4).

## Cooling system

### 24  Overheating

1    Insufficient coolant in system (Chapter 1).
2    Radiator core blocked or grille restricted (Chapter 3).
3    Thermostat faulty (Chapter 3).
4    Electric coolant fan blades broken or cracked (Chapter 3).
5    Radiator cap not maintaining proper pressure (Chapter 3).
6    Ignition timing incorrect (Chapter 5).

### 25  Overcooling

1    Faulty thermostat (Chapter 3).
2    Inaccurate temperature gauge sending unit (Chapter 3)

### 26  External coolant leakage

1    Deteriorated/damaged hoses; loose clamps (Chapters 1 and 3).
2    Water pump defective (Chapter 3).
3    Leakage from radiator core or coolant reservoir bottle (Chapter 3).
4    Engine drain or water jacket core plugs leaking (Chapter 2).

### 27  Internal coolant leakage

1    Leaking cylinder head gasket (Chapter 2).
2    Cracked cylinder bore or cylinder head (Chapter 2).

### 28  Coolant loss

1    Too much coolant in system (Chapter 1).
2    Coolant boiling away because of overheating (Chapter 3).
3    Internal or external leakage (Chapter 3).
4    Faulty radiator cap (Chapter 3).

### 29  Poor coolant circulation

1    Inoperative water pump (Chapter 3).
2    Restriction in cooling system (Chapters 1 and 3).
3    Thermostat sticking (Chapter 3).

## Clutch

### 30  Pedal travels to floor - no pressure or very little resistance

1    No fluid in reservoir (Chapter 1)
2    Faulty clutch master cylinder, release cylinder or hydraulic line (Chapter 8).
3    Broken release bearing or fork (Chapter 8).

### 31  Unable to select gears

1    Faulty transaxle (Chapter 7).
2    Faulty clutch disc (Chapter 8).
3    Release lever and bearing not assembled properly (Chapter 8).
4    Faulty pressure plate (Chapter 8).
5    Pressure plate-to-flywheel bolts loose (Chapter 8).

### 32  Clutch slips (engine speed increases with no increase in vehicle speed)

1    Clutch plate worn (Chapter 8).
2    Clutch plate is oil soaked by leaking rear main seal (Chapter 8).
3    Clutch plate not seated. It may take 30 or 40 normal starts for a new one to seat.
4    Warped pressure plate or flywheel (Chapter 8).
5    Weak diaphragm spring (Chapter 8).
6    Clutch plate overheated. Allow to cool.

### 33  Grabbing (chattering) as clutch is engaged

1    Oil on clutch plate lining, burned or glazed facings (Chapter 8).
2    Worn or loose engine or transaxle mounts (Chapters 2 and 7).
3    Worn splines on clutch plate hub (Chapter 8).
4    Warped pressure plate or flywheel (Chapter 8).
5    Burned or smeared resin on flywheel or pressure plate (Chapter 8).

### 34  Transaxle rattling (clicking)

1    Release lever loose (Chapter 8).
2    Clutch plate damper spring failure (Chapter 8).
3    Low engine idle speed (Chapter 1).

### 35  Noise in clutch area

1    Fork shaft improperly installed (Chapter 8).
2    Faulty bearing (Chapter 8).

### 36  Clutch pedal stays on floor

1    Faulty clutch master or release cylinder (Chapter 8).
2    Broken release bearing or fork (Chapter 8).

### 37  High pedal effort

1    Piston binding in bore of clutch master or release cylinder (Chapter 8).
2    Pressure plate faulty (Chapter 8).

## Manual transaxle

### 38  Knocking noise at low speeds

1    Worn driveaxle constant velocity (CV) joints (Chapter 8).
2    Worn driveaxle bore in differential case (Chapter 7A).*

**39   Noise most pronounced when turning**

Differential gear noise (Chapter 7A).*

**40   Clunk on acceleration or deceleration**

1   Loose engine or transaxle mounts (Chapters 2 and 7A).
2   Worn differential pinion shaft in case.*
3   Worn driveaxle bore in differential case (Chapter 7A).*
4   Worn or damaged driveaxle inboard CV joints (Chapter 8).

**41   Clicking noise in turns**

Worn or damaged outboard CV joint (Chapter 8).

**42   Vibration**

1   Rough wheel bearing (Chapters 1 and 10).
2   Damaged driveaxle (Chapter 8).
3   Out of round tires (Chapter 1).
4   Tire out of balance (Chapters 1 and 10).
5   Worn CV joint (Chapter 8).

**43   Noisy in neutral with engine running**

1   Damaged input gear bearing (Chapter 7A).*
2   Damaged clutch release bearing (Chapter 8).

**44   Noisy in one particular gear**

1   Damaged or worn constant mesh gears (Chapter 7A).*
2   Damaged or worn synchronizers (Chapter 7A).*
3   Bent reverse fork (Chapter 7A).*
4   Damaged fourth speed gear or output gear (Chapter 7A).*
5   Worn or damaged reverse idler gear or idler bushing (Chapter 7A).*

**45   Noisy in all gears**

1   Insufficient lubricant (Chapter 7A).
2   Damaged or worn bearings (Chapter 7A).*
3   Worn or damaged input gear shaft and/or output gear shaft (Chapter 7A).*

**46   Slips out of gear**

1   Worn or improperly adjusted linkage (Chapter 7A).
2   Transaxle loose on engine (Chapter 7A).
3   Shift linkage does not work freely, binds (Chapter 7A).
4   Input gear bearing retainer broken or loose (Chapter 7A).*
5   Dirt between clutch cover and engine block (Chapter 7A).
6   Worn shift fork (Chapter 7A).*

**47   Leaks lubricant**

1   Driveaxle oil seals worn (Chapter 7).
2   Excessive amount of lubricant in transaxle (Chapters 1 and 7A).

3   Loose or broken input gear shaft bearing retainer (Chapter 7A).*
4   Input gear bearing retainer O-ring and/or lip seal damaged (Chapter 7A).*

**48   Locked in gear**

Lock pin or interlock pin missing (Chapter 7A).*
* Although the corrective action necessary to remedy the symptoms described is beyond the scope of the home mechanic, the above information should be helpful in isolating the cause of the condition so that the owner can communicate clearly with a professional mechanic.

## Automatic transaxle

**Note:** Due to the complexity of the automatic transaxle, it is difficult for the home mechanic to properly diagnose and service this component. For problems other than the following, the vehicle should be taken to a dealer or transmission shop.

**49   Fluid leakage**

1   Automatic transmission fluid is a deep red color. Fluid leaks should not be confused with engine oil, which can easily be blown onto the transaxle by air flow.
2   To pinpoint a leak, first remove all built-up dirt and grime from the transaxle housing with degreasing agents and/or steam cleaning. Then drive the vehicle at low speeds so air flow will not blow the leak far from its source. Raise the vehicle and determine where the leak is coming from. Common areas of leakage are:

a)  Pan (Chapters 1 and 7)
b)  Dipstick tube (Chapters 1 and 7)
c)  Transaxle oil lines (Chapter 7)
d)  Speed sensor (Chapter 7)

**50   Transaxle fluid brown or has a burned smell**

Transaxle fluid burned (Chapter 1).

**51   General shift mechanism problems**

1   Chapter 7, Part B, deals with checking and adjusting the shift linkage on automatic transaxles. Common problems which may be attributed to poorly adjusted linkage are:

a)  Engine starting in gears other than Park or Neutral.
b)  Indicator on shifter pointing to a gear other than the one actually being used.
c)  Vehicle moves when in Park.
2   Refer to Chapter 7B for the shift linkage adjustment procedure.

**52   Transaxle will not downshift with accelerator pedal pressed to the floor**

Throttle valve cable out of adjustment (Chapter 7B).

**53   Engine will start in gears other than Park or Neutral**

Neutral start switch malfunctioning (Chapter 7B).

## 54 Transaxle slips, shifts roughly, is noisy or has no drive in forward or reverse gears

There are many probable causes for the above problems, but the home mechanic should be concerned with only one possibility - fluid level. Before taking the vehicle to a repair shop, check the level and condition of the fluid as described in Chapter 1. Correct the fluid level as necessary or change the fluid and filter if needed. If the problem persists, have a professional diagnose the cause.

## Driveaxles

## 55 Clicking noise in turns

Worn or damaged outboard CV joint (Chapter 8).

## 56 Shudder or vibration during acceleration

1   Excessive toe-in (Chapter 10).
2   Incorrect spring heights (Chapter 10).
3   Worn or damaged inboard or outboard CV joints (Chapter 8).
4   Sticking inboard CV joint assembly (Chapter 8).

## 57 Vibration at highway speeds

1   Out of balance front wheels and/or tires (Chapters 1 and 10).
2   Out of round front tires (Chapters 1 and 10).
3   Worn CV joint(s) (Chapter 8).

## Brakes

**Note:** *Before assuming that a brake problem exists, make sure that:*

*a)  The tires are in good condition and properly inflated* (Chapter 1).
*b)  The front end alignment is correct* (Chapter 10).
*c)  The vehicle is not loaded with weight in an unequal manner.*

## 58 Vehicle pulls to one side during braking

1   Incorrect tire pressures (Chapter 1).
2   Front end out of line (have the front end aligned).
3   Front, or rear, tires not matched to one another.
4   Restricted brake lines or hoses (Chapter 9).
5   Malfunctioning drum brake or caliper assembly (Chapter 9).
6   Loose suspension parts (Chapter 10).
7   Loose calipers (Chapter 9).
8   Excessive wear of brake shoe or pad material or disc/drum on one side.

## 59 Noise (high-pitched squeal when the brakes are applied)

Front disc brake pads worn out. The noise comes from the wear sensor rubbing against the disc (does not apply to all vehicles). Replace pads with new ones immediately (Chapter 9).

## 60 Brake roughness or chatter (pedal pulsates)

1   Excessive lateral runout (Chapter 9).

2   Uneven pad wear (Chapter 9).
3   Defective disc (Chapter 9).

## 61 Excessive brake pedal effort required to stop vehicle

1   Malfunctioning power brake booster (Chapter 9).
2   Partial system failure (Chapter 9).
3   Excessively worn pads or shoes (Chapter 9).
4   Piston in caliper or wheel cylinder stuck or sluggish (Chapter 9).
5   Brake pads or shoes contaminated with oil or grease (Chapter 9).
6   New pads or shoes installed and not yet seated. It will take a while for the new material to seat against the disc or drum.

## 62 Excessive brake pedal travel

1   Partial brake system failure (Chapter 9).
2   Insufficient fluid in master cylinder (Chapters 1 and 9).
3   Air trapped in system (Chapters 1 and 9).

## 63 Dragging brakes

1   Incorrect adjustment of brake light switch (Chapter 9).
2   Master cylinder pistons not returning correctly (Chapter 9).
3   Restricted brakes lines or hoses (Chapters 1 and 9).
4   Incorrect parking brake adjustment (Chapter 9).

## 64 Grabbing or uneven braking action

1   Malfunction of proportioning valve (Chapter 9).
2   Malfunction of power brake booster unit (Chapter 9).
3   Binding brake pedal mechanism (Chapter 9).

## 65 Brake pedal feels spongy when depressed

1   Air in hydraulic lines (Chapter 9).
2   Master cylinder mounting bolts loose (Chapter 9).
3   Master cylinder defective (Chapter 9).

## 66 Brake pedal travels to the floor with little resistance

1   Little or no fluid in the master cylinder reservoir caused by leaking caliper piston(s) (Chapter 9).
2   Loose, damaged or disconnected brake lines (Chapter 9).

## 67 Parking brake does not hold

Parking brake linkage improperly adjusted (Chapters 1 and 9).

## Suspension and steering systems

**Note:** *Before attempting to diagnose the suspension and steering systems, perform the following preliminary checks:*

*a)  Tires for wrong pressure and uneven wear.*
*b)  Steering universal joints from the column to the steering gear for loose connectors or wear.*
*c)  Front and rear suspension and the steering gear assembly for loose or damaged parts.*
*d)  Out-of-round or out-of-balance tires, bent rims and loose and/or rough wheel bearings.*

## 68 Vehicle pulls to one side

1 Mismatched or uneven tires (Chapter 10).
2 Broken or sagging springs (Chapter 10).
3 Wheel alignment (Chapter 10).
4 Front brake dragging (Chapter 9).

## 69 Abnormal or excessive tire wear

1 Wheel alignment (Chapter 10).
2 Sagging or broken springs (Chapter 10).
3 Tire out of balance (Chapter 10).
4 Worn strut damper (Chapter 10).
5 Overloaded vehicle.
6 Tires not rotated regularly.

## 70 Wheel makes a thumping noise

1 Blister or bump on tire (Chapter 10).
2 Improper strut damper action (Chapter 10).

## 71 Shimmy, shake or vibration

1 Tire or wheel out-of-balance or out-of-round (Chapter 10).
2 Loose or worn front hub or wheel bearings (Chapters 1, 8 and 10).
3 Worn tie-rod ends (Chapter 10).
4 Worn lower balljoints (Chapters 1 and 10).
5 Excessive wheel runout (Chapter 10).
6 Blister or bump on tire (Chapter 10).

## 72 Hard steering

1 Lack of lubrication at balljoints and tie-rod ends (Chapters 1 and 10).
2 Front wheel alignment (Chapter 10).
3 Low tire pressure(s) (Chapters 1 and 10).

## 73 Poor returnability of steering to center

1 Lack of lubrication at balljoints and tie-rod ends (Chapters 1 and 10).
2 Binding in balljoints (Chapter 10).
3 Binding in steering column (Chapter 10).
4 Lack of lubricant in steering gear assembly (Chapter 10).
5 Front wheel alignment (Chapter 10).

## 74 Abnormal noise at the front end

1 Lack of lubrication at balljoints and tie-rod ends (Chapters 1 and 10).
2 Damaged strut mounting (Chapter 10).
3 Worn control arm bushings or tie-rod ends (Chapter 10).
4 Loose stabilizer bar (Chapter 10).
5 Loose wheel nuts (Chapters 1 and 10).
6 Loose suspension bolts (Chapter 10)

## 75 Wander or poor steering stability

1 Mismatched or uneven tires (Chapter 10).

2 Lack of lubrication at balljoints and tie-rod ends (Chapters 1 and 10).
3 Worn strut assemblies (Chapter 10).
4 Loose stabilizer bar (Chapter 10).
5 Broken or sagging springs (Chapter 10).
6 Wheels out of alignment (Chapter 10).

## 76 Erratic steering when braking

1 Front hub bearings worn (Chapter 10).
2 Broken or sagging springs (Chapter 10).
3 Leaking wheel cylinder or caliper (Chapter 10).
4 Warped discs or drums (Chapter 10).

## 77 Excessive pitching and/or rolling around corners or during braking

1 Loose stabilizer bar (Chapter 10).
2 Worn strut dampers or mountings (Chapter 10).
3 Broken or sagging springs (Chapter 10).
4 Overloaded vehicle.

## 78 Suspension bottoms

1 Overloaded vehicle.
2 Worn strut dampers (Chapter 10).
3 Incorrect, broken or sagging springs (Chapter 10).

## 79 Cupped tires

1 Front wheel or rear wheel alignment (Chapter 10).
2 Worn strut dampers (Chapter 10).
3 Wheel bearings worn (Chapter 10).
4 Excessive tire or wheel runout (Chapter 10).
5 Worn balljoints (Chapter 10).

## 80 Excessive tire wear on outside edge

1 Inflation pressures incorrect (Chapter 1).
2 Excessive speed in turns.
3 Front end alignment incorrect (excessive toe-in). Have professionally aligned.
4 Suspension arm bent or twisted (Chapter 10).

## 81 Excessive tire wear on inside edge

1 Inflation pressures incorrect (Chapter 1).
2 Front end alignment incorrect (toe-out). Have professionally aligned.
3 Loose or damaged steering or suspension components (Chapter 10).

## 82 Tire tread worn in one place

1 Tires out of balance.
2 Damaged or buckled wheel. Inspect and replace if necessary.
3 Defective tire (Chapter 1).

## 83 Excessive play or looseness in steering system

1    Front hub bearing(s) worn (Chapter 10).
2    Tie-rod end loose (Chapter 10).
3    Steering gear loose or worn (Chapter 10).
4    Worn or loose steering intermediate shaft (Chapter 10).

## 84 Rattling or clicking noise in steering gear

1    Steering gear loose (Chapter 10).
2    Steering gear defective.

# Chapter 1
# Tune-up and routine maintenance

## Contents

## Specifications

### Recommended lubricants and fluids

**Note:** *Listed here are manufacturer recommendations at the time this manual was written. Manufacturers occasionally upgrade their fluid and lubricant specifications, so check with your local auto parts store for current recommendations.*

| | |
|---|---|
| Engine oil | |
| Type | API grade SG or SH multigrade fuel efficient oil |
| Viscosity | 5W-30 or 10W-30 |
| Automatic transaxle fluid type | |
| 1994 through 1996 | Honda Premium Formula or Dexron II automatic transmission fluid |
| 1997 | Honda Premium Formula automatic transmission fluid |
| Manual transaxle | |
| 1994 through 1995 | |
| Lubricant type | API grade SG engine oil |
| Viscosity | 10W-30 or 10W-40 |
| 1996 and later | Honda Genuine Manual Transmission Fluid (MTF) |
| Brake fluid type | DOT 3 brake fluid |
| Power steering system fluid | Honda power steering fluid V or S, or equivalent (not ATF) |
| Fuel type | Unleaded gasoline, 87 octane or higher |

### Capacities*

| | |
|---|---|
| Engine oil | |
| V6 engine | 4.6 qts |
| F22B1 VTEC four-cylinder engine | 4.5 qts |
| F22B2 non-VTEC four-cylinder engine | 4 qts |
| Automatic transaxle (drain and refill) | |
| V6 engine | 3.1 qts |
| Four-cylinder engine | 2.5 qts |
| Manual transaxle | 2 qts |
| Coolant | |
| V6 engine | 7 qts |
| Four-cylinder engine | 5.7 qts |

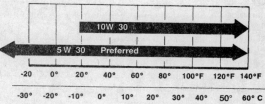

Engine oil viscosity chart

*All capacities approximate. Add as necessary to bring to appropriate level.*

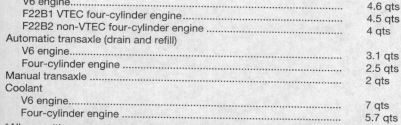

## Ignition system

Spark plug type and gap
    Type ................................................................... NGK ZFR5F-11 or equivalent
    Gap ..................................................................... 0.039 to 0.043-inch
Spark plug wire resistance ....................................... Less than 25,000 ohms
Engine firing order
    V6 engine............................................................ 1-4-2-5-3-6
    Four-cylinder engine ........................................ 1-3-4-2

**Four-cylinder engine**

## Cooling system

Thermostat rating
    Starts to open..................................................... 173-degrees F
    Fully open ............................................................ 194-degrees F

## Accessory drivebelt deflection

V6 engine
  Power steering pump
    New belt.............................................................. 3/8 to 1/2-inch
    Old belt ............................................................... 9/16 to 11/16-inch
  Alternator
    New belt.............................................................. 3/8 to 1/2-inch
    Old belt ............................................................... 9/16 to 11/16-inch
Four-cylinder engine
  Power steering pump
    New belt.............................................................. 7/16 to 1/2-inch
    Old belt ............................................................... 1/2 to 5/8-inch
  Alternator
    Without air-conditioning
      New belt ........................................................ 5/16 to 3/8-inch
      Old belt .......................................................... 3/8 to 1/2-inch
    With air-conditioning
      New belt ........................................................ 3/8 to 1/2-inch
      Old belt .......................................................... 1/4 to 9/32-inch

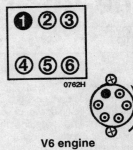

**V6 engine**

*The blackened terminal shown on the
distributor cap indicates the Number
One spark plug wire position*

**Cylinder location and
distributor rotation**

## Brakes

Disc brake pad lining thickness (minimum) ............... 1/16-inch
Drum brake shoe lining thickness (minimum)............. 3/32-inch
Parking brake adjustment
    Drum rear brake ................................................. 4 to 8 clicks
    Disc rear brake ................................................... 7 to 11 clicks

## Idle Speed

With IAC valve disconnected (for adjusting)............... 500 to 600 rpm
With IAC valve connected ......................................... 650 to 750 rpm

## Valve clearance (engine cold)

    Intake................................................................... 0.009 to 0.011-inch
    Exhaust................................................................. 0.011 to 0.013-inch

## Torque specifications

**Ft-lbs** (unless otherwise indicated)

Automatic transaxle
  V6 engine
    Filler plug ........................................................... 58
    Drain plug ........................................................... 36
  Four-cylinder engine drain plug ............................ 36
Manual transaxle
  Filler plug................................................................ 33
  Drain plug ............................................................... 29
Fuel filter banjo bolt
  V6 engine ............................................................... 9
  Four-cylinder engine .............................................. 16
Spark plugs
  V6 engine ............................................................... 16
  Four-cylinder engine .............................................. 13
Wheel lug nuts .......................................................... 80

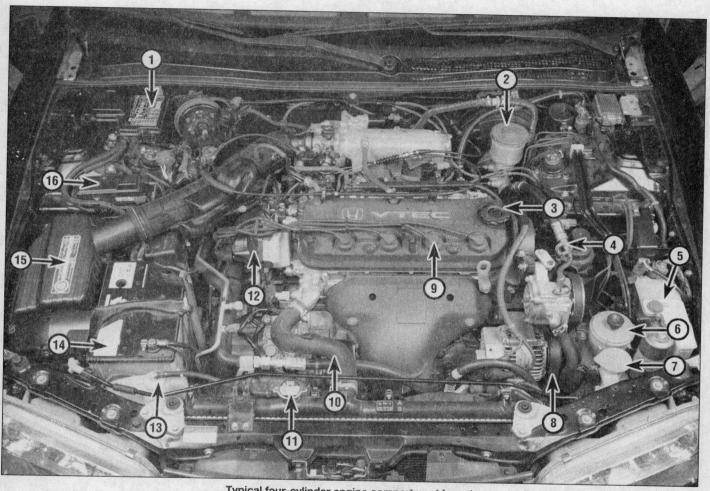

**Typical four-cylinder engine compartment layout**

1  Fuse block
2  Brake master cylinder reservoir
3  Engine oil filler cap
4  Engine oil dipstick
5  Anti-lock Brake System (ABS) unit
6  Power steering fluid reservoir

7  Windshield washer fluid reservoir
8  Alternator drivebelt
9  Spark plug and wire boot
10  Radiator hose
11  Radiator cap

12  Distributor cap
13  Engine coolant reservoir
14  Battery
15  Air filter housing
16  ABS fuse block

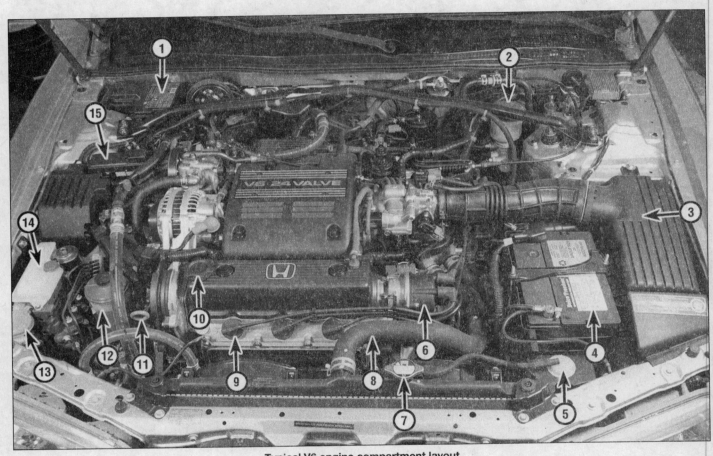

**Typical V6 engine compartment layout**

| | | |
|---|---|---|
| 1  Fuse block | 6  Distributor cap | 11  Engine oil dipstick |
| 2  Brake master cylinder reservoir | 7  Radiator cap | 12  Power steering fluid reservoir |
| 3  Air filter housing | 8  Radiator hose | 13  Windshield washer fluid reservoir |
| 4  Battery | 9  Spark plug and wire boot | 14  Anti-lock Brake System (ABS) unit |
| 5  Engine coolant reservoir | 10  Engine oil filler cap | 15  ABS fuse block |

**Typical engine compartment underside components**

| | | | |
|---|---|---|---|
| 1  Front brake caliper | 3  Brake line | 5  Engine oil drain plug | 7  Exhaust system |
| 2  Transaxle | 4  Outer driveaxle boot | 6  Exhaust system hanger | 8  Steering gear boot |

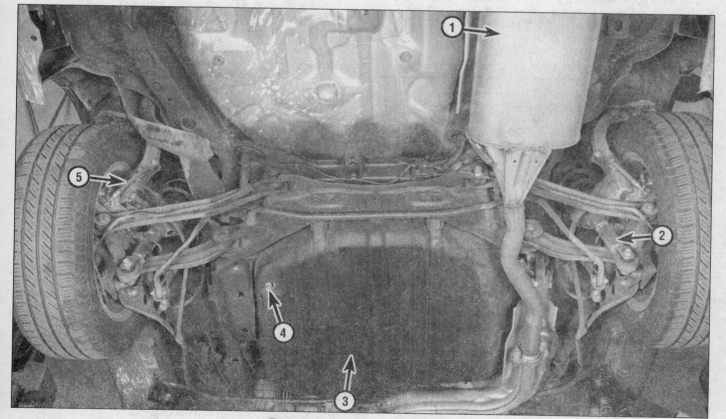

**Typical rear underside components**

| | | |
|---|---|---|
| 1  Muffler | 3  Fuel tank | 5  Brake hose |
| 2  Shock and spring assembly | 4  Tank drain plug | |

# 1 Honda Accord Maintenance schedule

The maintenance intervals in this manual are provided with the assumption that you, not the dealer, will be doing the work. These are the minimum maintenance intervals recommended by the factory for vehicles that are driven daily. If you wish to keep your vehicle in peak condition at all times, you may wish to perform some of these procedures even more often. Because frequent maintenance enhances the efficiency, performance and resale value of your car, we encourage you to do so. If you drive in dusty areas, tow a trailer, idle or drive at low speeds for extended periods or drive for short distances (less than four miles) in below freezing temperatures, shorter intervals are also recommended.

When your vehicle is new, it should be serviced by a factory authorized dealer service department to protect the factory warranty. In many cases, the initial maintenance check is done at no cost to the owner.

## Every 250 miles or weekly, whichever comes first

Check the engine oil level (Section 4)
Check the engine coolant level (Section 4)
Check the windshield washer fluid level (Section 4)
Check the brake and clutch fluid level (Section 4)
Check the tires and tire pressures (Section 5)

## Every 3000 miles or 3 months, whichever comes first

All items listed above plus:
Check the power steering fluid level (Section 6)
Check the automatic transaxle fluid level (Section 7)
Change the engine oil and oil filter (Section 8)

## Every 7500 miles or 6 months, whichever comes first

All items listed above plus:
Inspect and replace, if necessary, the windshield wiper blades (Section 9)
Check and service the battery (Section 10)
Check and adjust, if necessary, the engine drivebelts (Section 11)
Inspect and replace, if necessary, all underhood hoses (Section 12)
Check the cooling system (Section 13)
Rotate the tires (Section 14)

## Every 15,000 miles or 12 months, whichever comes first

All items listed above plus:
Inspect the brake system (Section 15)*
Replace the air filter (Section 16)*
Inspect the fuel system (Section 19)
Check the manual transaxle lubricant level (Section 20)*
Inspect the suspension and steering components (Section 21)*
Check the driveaxle boots (Section 22)
Check and adjust if necessary, the valve clearances (1994 four-cylinder models) (Section 23)

## Every 30,000 miles or 24 months, whichever comes first

All items listed above plus:
Check and adjust if necessary, the valve clearances (1995 four-cylinder models) (Section 23)

Replace the spark plugs (Section 17)
Inspect and replace, if necessary, the spark plug wires, distributor cap and rotor (Section 18)
Service the cooling system (drain, flush and refill) (Section 24)
Inspect the exhaust system (Section 25)
Change the automatic transaxle fluid (Section 26)**
Change the manual transaxle lubricant (Section 27)
Replace the brake fluid (Chapter 9)
Replace the fuel filter (Section 28)

## Every 60,000 miles or 72 months, whichever comes first

Check and, if necessary, replace the PCV valve (Section 29)
Check and adjust, if necessary, the engine idle speed (Section 30)

## Every 90,000 miles or 72 months, whichever comes first

Replace the timing and balance shaft belts (Chapter 2)***
* *This item is affected by "severe" operating conditions as described below. If your vehicle is operated under "severe" conditions, perform all maintenance indicated with a * at 3000 mile/3 month intervals. Severe conditions are indicated if you mainly operate your vehicle under one or more of the following conditions:*

Operating in dusty areas
Towing a trailer
Idling for extended periods and/or low speed operation
Operating when outside temperatures remain below freezing and when most trips are less than five miles

** *If operated under one or more of the following conditions, change the automatic transaxle fluid every 15,000 miles:*

In heavy city traffic where the outside temperature regularly reaches 90-degrees F (32-degrees C) or higher
In hilly or mountainous terrain

*** *This item is affected by "severe" operating conditions as described below. If operated under one or more of the following conditions, replace the timing and balance shaft belts every 60,000 miles:*

Operating in dusty areas
Towing a trailer
Idling for extended periods and/or low speed operation
Operating when outside temperatures remain below freezing and when most trips are less than five miles
In heavy city traffic or where the outside temperature regularly reaches 90-degrees F (32-degrees C) or higher

## 2   Introduction

This Chapter is designed to help the home mechanic maintain his/her car for peak performance, economy, safety and long life.

The following Sections deal specifically with each item on the maintenance schedule. Visual checks, adjustments, component replacement and other helpful items are included. Refer to the accompanying photos of the engine compartment and the underside of the vehicle for the location of various components.

Servicing your Honda in accordance with the mileage/time maintenance schedule and the following Sections will provide it with a planned maintenance program that should result in a long and reliable service life. This is a comprehensive plan, so maintaining some items but not others at the specified service intervals will not produce the same results.

As you service your car, you will discover that many of the procedures can - and should - be grouped together because of the nature of the particular procedure you're performing or because of the close proximity of two otherwise unrelated components to one another. For example, if the vehicle is raised for chassis lubrication, you should inspect the exhaust, suspension, steering and fuel systems while you're under the vehicle. When you're rotating the tires, it makes good sense to check the brakes and wheel bearings since the wheels are already removed.

Finally, let's suppose you have to borrow or rent a torque wrench. Even if you only need to tighten the spark plugs, you might as well check the torque of as many critical fasteners as time allows.

The first step of this maintenance program is to prepare yourself before the actual work begins. Read through all Sections pertinent to the procedures you're planning to do, then make a list of and gather together all the parts and tools you will need to do the job. If it looks as if you might run into problems during a particular segment of some procedure, seek advice from your local parts man or dealer service department.

## 3   Tune-up general information

The term tune-up is used in this manual to represent a combination of individual operations rather than one specific procedure.

If, from the time the vehicle is new, the routine maintenance schedule is followed closely and frequent checks are made of fluid levels and high wear items, as suggested throughout this manual, the engine will be kept in relatively good running condition and the need for additional work will be minimized.

More likely than not, however, there will be times when the engine is running poorly due to lack of regular maintenance. This is even more likely if a used vehicle, which has not received regular and frequent maintenance checks, is purchased. In such cases, an engine tune-up will be needed outside of the regular routine maintenance intervals.

The first step in any tune-up or engine diagnosis to help correct a poor running engine would be a cylinder compression check. A check of the engine compression (see Chapter 2 Part B) will give valuable information regarding the overall performance of many internal components and should be used as a basis for tune-up and repair procedures. If, for instance, a compression check indicates serious internal engine wear, a conventional tune-up will not help the running condition of the engine and would be a waste of time and money. Because of its importance, compression checking should be performed by someone with the proper compression testing gauge and the knowledge to use it properly.

The following series of operations are those most often needed to bring a generally poor running engine back into a proper state of tune.

### Minor tune-up

Check all engine related fluids (Section 4)

Clean, inspect and test the battery (Section 10)
Check and adjust the drivebelts (Section 11)
Check all underhood hoses (Section 12)
Check the cooling system (Section 13)
Check the air filter (Section 16)
Replace the spark plugs (Section 17)
Inspect the distributor cap and rotor (Section 18)
Inspect the spark plug and coil wires (Section 18)

### Major tune-up

All items listed under minor tune-up, plus . . .
Check the idle speed (Section 30)
Replace the air filter (Section 16)
Replace the distributor cap and rotor (Section 18)
Replace the spark plug wires (Section 18)
Check the fuel system (Section 19)

## 4   Fluid level checks (every 250 miles or weekly)

1   Fluids are an essential part of the lubrication, cooling, brake, clutch and other systems. Because these fluids gradually become depleted and/or contaminated during normal operation of the vehicle, they must be periodically replenished. See *Recommended lubricants, fluids and capacities* at the beginning of this Chapter before adding fluid to any of the following components. **Note:** *The vehicle must be on level ground before fluid levels can be checked.*

### Engine oil

*Refer to illustrations 4.2, 4.4 and 4.6*
2   The engine oil level is checked with a dipstick located at the front side of the engine **(see illustration)**. The dipstick extends through a metal tube from which it protrudes down into the engine oil pan.
3   The oil level should be checked before the vehicle has been driven, or about 15 minutes after the engine has been shut off. If the oil is checked immediately after driving the vehicle, some of the oil will remain in the upper engine components, producing an inaccurate reading on the dipstick.
4   Pull the dipstick from the tube and wipe all the oil from the end with a clean rag or paper towel. Insert the clean dipstick all the way back into its metal tube and pull it out again. Observe the oil at the end

4.2   **The engine oil dipstick has an orange loop handle and is located on the front (radiator) side of the engine**

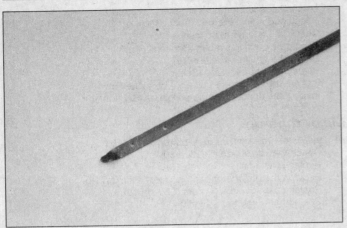

4.4  The oil level should be between the two holes in the dipstick - if it isn't, add enough oil to bring the level to or near the upper hole (it takes one quart to raise the level from the lower hole to the upper hole)

4.6  The threaded oil filler cap is located on the valve cover - to prevent dirt from contaminating the engine, always make sure the area around this opening is clean before unscrewing the cap

of the dipstick. At its highest point, the level should be between the upper and lower holes **(see illustration)**.

5    It takes one quart of oil to raise the level from the lower hole to the upper hole on the dipstick. Do not allow the level to drop below the lower hole or oil starvation may cause engine damage. Conversely, overfilling the engine (adding oil above the upper hole) may cause oil fouled spark plugs, oil leaks or oil seal failures.

6    Remove the threaded cap from the valve cover to add oil **(see illustration)**. Use an oil can spout or funnel to prevent spills. After adding the oil, install the filler cap hand tight. Start the engine and look carefully for any small leaks around the oil filter or drain plug. Stop the engine and check the oil level again after it has had sufficient time to drain from the upper block and cylinder head galleys.

7    Checking the oil level is an important preventive maintenance step. A continually dropping oil level indicates oil leakage through damaged seals, from loose connections, or past worn rings or valve guides. If the oil looks milky in color or has water droplets in it, a cylinder head gasket may be blown or the oil cooler could be leaking. The engine should be checked immediately. The condition of the oil should also be checked. Each time you check the oil level, slide your thumb and index finger up the dipstick before wiping off the oil. If you see small dirt or metal particles clinging to the dipstick, the oil should be changed (see Section 8).

### Engine coolant

*Refer to illustration 4.9*

**Warning:** *Do not allow antifreeze to come in contact with your skin or painted surfaces of the vehicle. Rinse off spills immediately with plenty of water. Antifreeze is highly toxic if ingested. Never leave antifreeze lying around in an open container or in puddles on the floor; children and pets are attracted by it's sweet smell and may drink it. Check with local authorities about disposing of used antifreeze. Many communities have collection centers which will see that antifreeze is disposed of safely.*

8    All vehicles covered by this manual are equipped with a pressurized coolant recovery system. A coolant reservoir located on the right side of the engine compartment is connected by a hose to the base of the radiator filler neck. If the coolant heats up during engine operation, coolant can escape through the pressurized filler cap, then through the connecting hose into the reservoir. As the engine cools, the coolant is automatically drawn back into the cooling system to maintain the correct level.

9    The coolant level in the reservoir should be checked regularly. It must be between the MAX and MIN lines on the tank. The level will vary with the temperature of the engine. When the engine is cold, the coolant level should be at or slightly above the MIN mark on the tank. Once the engine has warmed up, the level should be at or near the

4.9  Make sure the coolant level is between the MAX and MIN lines - if it's below the MIN line, unscrew the cap and add a sufficient quantity of the specified mixture of antifreeze and water

4.14  The windshield washer fluid reservoir is located at the left (four-cylinder models) or right (V6 models) front corner of the engine compartment - fluid can be added after flipping up the cap

4.15  A maintenance-free battery is sealed and does not need periodic refilling

4.17a  The brake fluid should be kept between the MIN and MAX marks on the reservoir - turn and lift up the cap to add fluid

MAX mark. If it isn't, allow the fluid in the tank to cool, then remove the cap from the reservoir **(see illustration)** and add coolant to bring the level up to the MAX line. **Warning:** *Do not remove the radiator cap to check the coolant level when the engine is warm! Use only ethylene glycol type coolant and water in the mixture ratio recommended by your owner's manual. Do not use supplemental inhibitors or additives. If only a small amount of coolant is required to bring the system up to the proper level, water can be used. However, repeated additions of water will dilute the recommended antifreeze and water solution. In order to maintain the proper ratio of antifreeze and water, it is advisable to top up the coolant level with the correct mixture. Refer to your owner's manual for the recommended ratio.*

10    If the coolant level drops within a short time after replenishment, there may be a leak in the system. Inspect the radiator, hoses, engine coolant filler cap, drain plugs, air bleeder bolt and water pump. If no leak is evident, have the radiator cap pressure tested . **Warning:** *Never remove the radiator cap or the coolant recovery reservoir cap when the engine is running or has just been shut down, because the cooling system is hot. Escaping steam and scalding liquid could cause serious injury.*

11    If it is necessary to open the radiator cap, wait until the system has cooled completely, then wrap a thick cloth around the cap and turn it to the first stop. If any steam escapes, wait until the system has cooled further, then remove the cap.

12    When checking the coolant level, always note its condition. It should be relatively clear. If it is brown or rust colored, the system should be drained, flushed and refilled. Even if the coolant appears to be normal, the corrosion inhibitors wear out with use, so it must be replaced at the specified intervals.

13    Do not allow antifreeze to come in contact with your skin or painted surfaces of the vehicle. Flush contacted areas immediately with plenty of water.

## Windshield washer fluid

*Refer to illustration 4.14*

14    Fluid for the windshield washer system is stored in a plastic reservoir which is located at the left (four-cylinder models) or right (V6 models) front corner of the engine compartment **(see illustration)**. Check the fluid level on four-cylinder models by detaching the cap and pulling up the dipstick while on V6 models the level markings are on the filler neck. In milder climates, plain water can be used to top up the reservoir, but the reservoir should be kept no more than 2/3 full to allow for expansion should the water freeze. In colder climates, the use of a specially designed windshield washer fluid, available at your dealer and any auto parts store, will help lower the freezing point of the fluid. Mix the solution with water in accordance with the manufac-

4.17b  Keep the level between the MIN and MAX lines on the clutch fluid reservoir

turer's directions on the container. Do not use regular antifreeze. It will damage the vehicle's paint.

## Battery electrolyte

*Refer to illustration 4.15*

15    The vehicles covered by this manual are equipped with a battery which is permanently sealed (except for vent holes) and has no filler caps. Water doesn't have to be added to these batteries at any time.

## Brake and clutch fluid

*Refer to illustrations 4.17a and 4.17b*

16    The brake master cylinder is mounted on the front of the power booster unit and the clutch master cylinder next to it on the firewall within the engine compartment. Models with an Anti-lock Brake System (ABS) also have a reservoir for the ABS modulator located on the right side of the engine compartment. ABS-equipped vehicles should be driven for a few minutes to equalize the fluid in the system before checking the fluid level in the reservoirs. If the level rises significantly above the MAX mark, have the system checked by a dealer because this could indicate a malfunction in the ABS system.

17    To check the fluid level of the brake or clutch master cylinder, simply look at the MAX and MIN marks on the reservoir **(see illustrations)**. The level should be between the two marks. If the vehicle is equipped with an Anti-lock Brake System (ABS), the fluid level in the

ABS unit reservoir must also be checked. It's located on the right (passenger) side of the engine compartment.

18   If the level is low, wipe the top of the reservoir cover with a clean rag to prevent contamination of the brake system before lifting the cap.

19   Add only the specified brake fluid to the brake, clutch or ABS reservoir (refer to *Recommended lubricants and fluids* at the front of this Chapter or to your owner's manual). Mixing different types of brake fluid can damage the system. Fill the brake master cylinder reservoir only to about 3/4-inch below the MAX line - this brings the fluid to the correct level when you put the cap back on. **Warning:** *Use caution when filling the reservoir - brake fluid can harm your eyes and damage painted surfaces. Do not use brake fluid that has been opened for more than one year or has been left open. Brake fluid absorbs moisture from the air. Excess moisture can cause a dangerous loss of braking.*

20   While the reservoir cap is removed, inspect the master cylinder reservoir for contamination. If deposits, dirt particles or water droplets are present, the system should be drained and refilled (see Chapters 8 or 9).

21   After filling the reservoir to the proper level, make sure the lid is properly seated to prevent fluid leakage and/or system pressure loss.

22   The brake fluid in the master cylinder will drop slightly as the brake pads at each wheel wear down during normal operation. If the master cylinder requires repeated replenishing to keep it at the proper level, this is an indication of leakage in the brake system, which should be corrected immediately. Check all brake lines and connections, along with the wheel cylinders and booster (see Section 15 for more information). A drop in the clutch reservoir level indicates a leak in the clutch hydraulic system (see Chapter 8).

23   If, upon checking the brake master cylinder fluid level, you discover an empty or nearly empty reservoir, the brake system should be bled (see Chapter 9).

## 5   Tire and tire pressure checks (every 250 miles or weekly)

*Refer to illustrations 5.2, 5.3, 5.4a, 5.4b and 5.8*

1   Periodic inspection of the tires may spare you from the inconve-

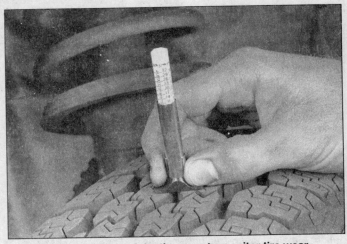

**5.2  Use a tire tread depth gauge to monitor tire wear - they are available at auto parts stores and service stations and cost very little**

nience of being stranded with a flat tire. It can also provide you with vital information regarding possible problems in the steering and suspension systems before major damage occurs.

2   Normal tread wear can be monitored with a simple, inexpensive device known as a tread depth indicator **(see illustration)**. When the tread depth reaches the specified minimum, replace the tire(s).

3   Note any abnormal tread wear **(see illustration)**. Tread pattern irregularities such as cupping, flat spots and more wear on one side than the other are indications of front end alignment and/or balance problems. If any of these conditions are noted, take the vehicle to a tire shop or service station to correct the problem.

4   Look closely for cuts, punctures and embedded nails or tacks. Sometimes a tire will hold its air pressure for a short time or leak down very slowly even after a nail has embedded itself into the tread. If a slow leak persists, check the valve core to make sure it is tight **(see**

| Condition | Probable cause | Corrective action | Condition | Probable cause | Corrective action |
|---|---|---|---|---|---|
| **Shoulder wear** | • Underinflation (both sides wear)<br>• Incorrect wheel camber (one side wear)<br>• Hard cornering<br>• Lack of rotation | • Measure and adjust pressure.<br>• Repair or replace axle and suspension parts.<br>• Reduce speed.<br>• Rotate tires. | Feathered edge<br>**Toe wear** | • Incorrect toe | • Adjust toe-in. |
| **Center wear** | • Overinflation<br>• Lack of rotation | • Measure and adjust pressure.<br>• Rotate tires. | **Uneven wear** | • Incorrect camber or caster<br>• Malfunctioning suspension<br>• Unbalanced wheel<br>• Out-of-round brake drum<br>• Lack of rotation | • Repair or replace axle and suspension parts.<br>• Repair or replace suspension parts.<br>• Balance or replace.<br>• Turn or replace.<br>• Rotate tires. |

**5.3  This chart will help you determine the condition of the tires, the probable cause(s) of abnormal wear and the corrective action necessary**

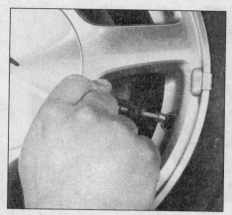

**5.4a  If a tire looses air on a steady basis, check the valve core first to make sure it's snug (special inexpensive wrenches are commonly available at auto parts stores)**

**5.4b  If the valve core is tight, raise the corner of the vehicle with the low tire and spray a soapy water solution onto the tread as the tire is turned slowly - leaks will cause small bubbles to appear**

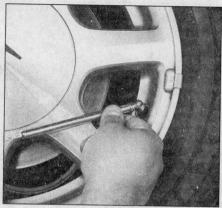

**5.8  To extend the life of the tires, check the air pressure at least once a week with an accurate gauge (don't forget the spare)**

illustration). Examine the tread for an object that may have embedded itself into the tire or for a "plug" that may have begun to leak (radial tire punctures are repaired with a plug that is installed in a puncture). If a puncture is suspected, it can be easily verified by spraying a solution of soapy water onto the puncture area **(see illustration)**. The soapy solution will bubble if there is a leak. Unless the puncture is inordinately large, a tire shop or gas station can usually repair the punctured tire.

5  Carefully inspect the inner side of each tire for evidence of brake fluid leakage. If you see any, inspect the brakes immediately.

6  Correct tire air pressure adds miles to the lifespan of the tires, improves mileage and enhances overall ride quality. Tire pressure cannot be accurately estimated by looking at a tire, particularly if it is a radial. A tire pressure gauge is therefore essential. Keep an accurate gauge in the glovebox. The pressure gauges fitted to the nozzles of air hoses at gas stations are often inaccurate.

7  Always check tire pressure when the tires are cold. "Cold," in this case, means the vehicle has not been driven over a mile in the three hours preceding a tire pressure check. A pressure rise of four to eight pounds is not uncommon once the tires are warm.

8  Unscrew the valve cap protruding from the wheel or hubcap and push the gauge firmly onto the valve **(see illustration)**. Note the reading on the gauge and compare this figure to the recommended tire

pressure shown on the tire placard on the left door jamb. Be sure to reinstall the valve cap to keep dirt and moisture out of the valve stem mechanism. Check all four tires and, if necessary, add enough air to bring them up to the recommended pressure levels.

9  Don't forget to keep the spare tire inflated to the specified pressure (consult your owner's manual). Note that the air pressure specified for the compact spare is significantly higher than the pressure of the regular tires.

## 6  Power steering fluid level check (every 3000 miles or 3 months)

*Refer to illustration 6.4*

1  The power steering system relies on fluid which may, over a period of time, require replenishing.

2  The fluid reservoir for the power steering pump is located on the inner fender panel near the left front of the engine compartment.

3  For the check, the front wheels should be pointed straight ahead and the engine should be off. The fluid should be cold when checking the level.

4  On all models, the reservoir is translucent plastic and the fluid level can be checked visually **(see illustration)**.

5  If additional fluid is required, pour the specified type directly into the reservoir, using a funnel to prevent spills.

6  If the reservoir requires frequent fluid additions, all power steering hoses, hose connections, the power steering pump and the steering gear should be carefully checked for leaks.

## 7  Automatic transaxle fluid level check (every 3000 miles or 3 months)

*Refer to illustration 7.5*

1  The level of the automatic transaxle fluid should be carefully maintained. Low fluid level can lead to slipping or loss of drive, while overfilling can cause foaming, loss of fluid and transaxle damage.

2  The transaxle fluid level should only be checked on level ground within one minute of the engine being shut off.

3  Remove the dipstick with the yellow loop handle - it's located down low on the front of the transaxle in the passenger's side of the engine compartment on four-cylinder models and on the driver's side on V6 models. Check the level of the fluid on the dipstick and note its condition.

4  Wipe the fluid from the dipstick with a clean rag and reinsert it.

**6.4  The power steering fluid reservoir is translucent so the fluid level can be checked without removing the cap - keep the fluid between the two lines**

**7.5  The automatic transaxle fluid level should be in the cross-hatched area on the dipstick**

5    Pull the dipstick out again and note the fluid level (**see illustration**). The level should be between the upper and lower marks on the dipstick. If the level is low, add the specified automatic transmission fluid through the dipstick opening with a funnel.
6    Add just enough of the specified fluid to fill the transaxle to the proper level. It takes about one pint to raise the level from the lower mark to the upper mark, so add the fluid a little at a time and keep checking the level until it is correct.
7    The condition of the fluid should also be checked along with the level. If the fluid at the end of the dipstick is black or a dark reddish brown color, or if it emits a burned smell, the fluid should be changed (see Section 26). If you are in doubt about the condition of the fluid, purchase some new fluid and compare the two for color and smell.

## 8    Engine oil and oil filter change (every 3000 miles or 3 months)

*Refer to illustrations 8.2, 8.7, 8.12 and 8.14*
1    Frequent oil changes are the best preventive maintenance the home mechanic can give the engine, because aging oil becomes diluted and contaminated, which leads to premature engine wear.
2    Make sure you have all the necessary tools before you begin this procedure (**see illustration**). You should also have plenty of rags or newspapers handy for mopping up any spills.
3    Access to the underside of the vehicle is greatly improved if the vehicle can be lifted on a hoist, driven onto ramps or supported by jackstands. **Warning:** *Do not work under a vehicle which is supported only by a bumper, hydraulic or scissors-type jack.*
4    If this is your first oil change, get under the vehicle and familiarize yourself with the locations of the oil drain plug and the oil filter. The engine and exhaust components will be warm during the actual work, so try to anticipate any potential problems before the engine and accessories are hot.
5    Park the vehicle on a level spot. Start the engine and allow it to reach its normal operating temperature. Warm oil and sludge will flow out more easily. Turn off the engine when it's warmed up. Remove the filler cap from the valve cover.
6    Raise the vehicle and support it securely on jackstands. **Warning:** *Never get beneath the vehicle when it is supported only by a jack. The jack provided with your vehicle is designed solely for raising the vehicle to remove and replace the wheels. Always use jackstands to support the vehicle when it becomes necessary to place your body underneath the vehicle.*
7    Being careful not to touch the hot exhaust components, place the drain pan under the drain plug in the bottom of the pan and remove the plug (**see illustration**). You may want to wear gloves while unscrewing the plug the final few turns if the engine is hot.
8    Allow the old oil to drain into the pan. It may be necessary to move the pan farther under the engine as the oil flow slows to a trickle.

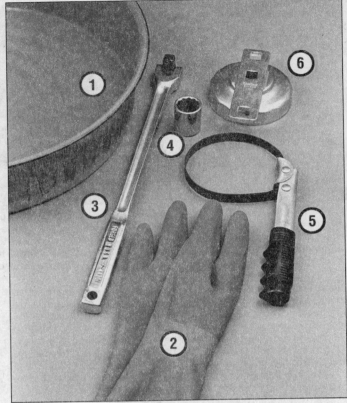

**8.2  These tools are required when changing the engine oil and filter**

1    **Drain pan** - It should be fairly shallow in depth, but wide to prevent spills
2    **Rubber gloves** - When removing the drain plug and filter, you will get oil on your hands (the gloves will prevent burns)
3    **Breaker bar** - Sometimes the oil drain plug is tight, and a long breaker bar is needed to loosen it
4    **Socket** - To be used with the breaker bar or a ratchet (must be the correct size to fit the drain plug)
5    **Filter wrench** - This is a metal band-type wrench, which requires clearance around the filter to be effective
6    **Filter wrench** - This type fits on the bottom of the filter and can be turned with a ratchet or breaker bar (different-size wrenches are available for different types of filters)

Inspect the old oil for the presence of metal shavings and chips.
9    After all the oil has drained, wipe off the drain plug with a clean rag. Even minute metal particles clinging to the plug would immediately contaminate the new oil.
10    Clean the area around the drain plug opening, reinstall the plug and tighten it securely, but do not strip the threads.
11    Move the drain pan into position under the oil filter.
12    Loosen the oil filter (**see illustration**) by turning it counterclockwise with an oil filter wrench. Once the filter is loose, use your hands to unscrew it from the block. Just as the filter is detached from the block, immediately tilt the open end up to prevent the oil inside the filter from spilling out. **Warning:** *The exhaust system may still be hot, so be careful.*
13    With a clean rag, wipe off the mounting surface on the block. If a residue of old oil is allowed to remain, it will smoke when the block is heated up. Also make sure that none of the old gasket remains stuck to the mounting surface. It can be removed with a scraper if necessary.
14    Compare the old filter with the new one to make sure they are the same type. Smear some clean engine oil on the rubber gasket of the new filter and screw it into place (**see illustration**). Because overtightening

8.7  Use the proper size box-end wrench or socket to remove the oil drain plug without rounding off the corners

8.12  The oil filter is usually on very tight and will require a special wrench for removal - DO NOT use the wrench to tighten the new filter

8.14  Lubricate the oil filter gasket with clean engine oil before installing the filter on the engine

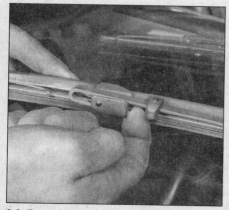

9.6  Press in on the tab and push the blade assembly out of the hook at the end to remove it

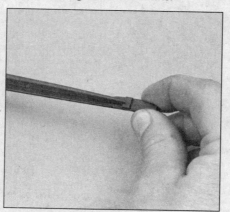

9.7  Squeeze the blade element tabs, then pull the element out of the metal frame and remove it

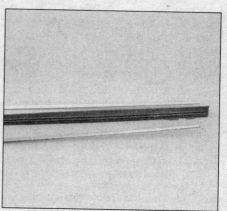

9.8  The metal retainers must be inserted into the slots in the rubber before installation

the filter will damage the gasket, do not use a filter wrench to tighten the filter. Tighten it by hand until the gasket contacts the seating surface. Then seat the filter by giving it an additional 3/4-turn.

15   Remove all tools, rags, etc. from under the vehicle, being careful not to spill the oil in the drain pan, then lower the vehicle.

16   Add new oil to the engine through the oil filler cap in the valve cover. Use a funnel, if necessary, to prevent oil from spilling onto the top of the engine. Pour three quarts of fresh oil into the engine. Wait a few minutes to allow the oil to drain into the pan, then check the level on the oil dipstick (see Section 4 if necessary). If the oil level is at or near the upper hole on the dipstick, install the filler cap hand tight, start the engine and allow the new oil to circulate.

17   Allow the engine to run for about a minute. While the engine is running, look under the vehicle and check for leaks at the oil pan drain plug and around the oil filter. If either is leaking, stop the engine and tighten the plug or filter.

18   Wait a few minutes to allow the oil to trickle down into the pan, then recheck the level on the dipstick and, if necessary, add enough oil to bring the level to the upper hole.

19   During the first few trips after an oil change, make it a point to check frequently for leaks and proper oil level.

20   Used motor oil cannot be re-used in its present state and should be discarded. Oil reclamation centers, auto repair shops and gas stations will normally accept the oil, which can be refined and used again. After the oil has cooled, it can be drained into a suitable container (capped plastic jugs, topped bottles, milk cartons, etc.) for transport to one of these disposal sites.

## 9   Windshield wiper blade inspection and replacement (every 7500 miles or 6 months)

*Refer to illustrations 9.6, 9.7 and 9.8*

1   The windshield wiper and blade assembly should be inspected periodically for damage, loose components and cracked or worn blade elements.

2   Road film can build up on the wiper blades and affect their efficiency, so they should be washed regularly with a mild detergent solution.

3   The action of the wiping mechanism can loosen bolts, nuts and fasteners, so they should be checked and tightened, as necessary, at the same time the wiper blades are checked.

4   If the wiper blade elements are cracked, worn or warped, or no longer clean adequately, they should be replaced with new ones.

5   Lift the arm assembly away from the glass for clearance.

6   Press in on the lock tab and push the blade assembly down the wiper arm, out of the hook at the end **(see illustration)**.

7   Squeeze the blade element tabs tightly and pull the element out of the metal frame **(see illustration)**.

8   Remove the metal retainers from the element and install them in the new element **(see illustration)**.

9   Insert the element into the frame and push it until the element tabs lock.

10   Place the metal arm assembly in the hook on the wiper arm and press it into place until the lock tab snaps into place.

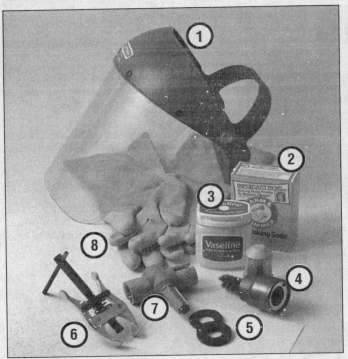

**10.1  Tools and materials required for battery maintenance**

1   ***Face shield/safety goggles*** - *When removing corrosion with a brush, the acidic particles can easily fly up into your eyes*
2   ***Baking soda*** - *A solution of baking soda and water can be used to neutralize corrosion*
3   ***Petroleum jelly*** - *A layer of this on the battery posts will help prevent corrosion*
4   ***Battery post/cable cleaner*** - *This wire brush cleaning tool will remove all traces of corrosion from the battery posts and cable clamps*
5   ***Treated felt washers*** - *Placing one of these on each post, directly under the cable clamps, will help prevent corrosion*
6   ***Puller*** - *Sometimes the cable clamps are very difficult to pull off the posts, even after the nut/bolt has been completely loosened. This tool pulls the clamp straight up and off the post without damage*
7   ***Battery post/cable cleaner*** - *Here is another cleaning tool which is a slightly different version of Number 4 above, but it does the same thing*
8   ***Rubber gloves*** - *Another safety item to consider when servicing the battery; remember that's acid inside the battery!*

---

**10   Battery check, maintenance and charging
       (every 7500 miles or 6 months)**

---

*Refer to illustrations 10.1, 10.6a, 10.6b, 10.7a, 10.7b and 10.11*
**Warning:** *Hydrogen gas is produced by the battery, so keep open flames and lighted tobacco away from it at all times. Always wear eye protection when working around the battery. Rinse off spilled electrolyte immediately with large amounts of water.*

## Check and maintenance

1   A routine preventive maintenance program for the battery in your vehicle is the only way to ensure quick and reliable starts. But before performing any battery maintenance, make sure that you have the proper equipment necessary to work safely around the battery **(see illustration)**.
2   There are also several precautions that should be taken whenever battery maintenance is performed. Before servicing the battery, always

**10.6a  Battery terminal corrosion usually appears as light, fluffy powder**

turn the engine and all accessories off and disconnect the cable from the negative terminal of the battery. **Caution:** *The radio in your vehicle is equipped with an anti-theft system, make sure you have the correct activation code before disconnecting the battery.*
3   The battery produces hydrogen gas, which is both flammable and explosive. Never create a spark, smoke or light a match around the battery. Always charge the battery in a ventilated area.
4   Electrolyte contains poisonous and corrosive sulfuric acid. Do not allow it to get in your eyes, on your skin on your clothes. Never ingest it. Wear protective safety glasses when working near the battery. Keep children away from the battery.
5   Note the external condition of the battery. If the positive terminal and cable clamp on your vehicle's battery is equipped with a rubber protector, make sure it's not torn or damaged. It should completely cover the terminal. Look for any corroded or loose connections, cracks in the case or cover or loose hold-down clamps. Also check the entire length of each cable for cracks and frayed conductors.
6   If corrosion, which looks like white, fluffy deposits **(see illustration)** is evident, particularly around the terminals, the battery should be removed for cleaning. Loosen the cable clamp nuts with a wrench, being careful to remove the negative cable first, and slide them off the terminals **(see illustration)**. Then disconnect the hold-down clamp nuts, remove the clamp and lift the battery from the engine compartment.
7   Clean the cable clamps thoroughly with a battery brush or a terminal cleaner and a solution of warm water and baking soda **(see illustration)**. Wash the terminals and the top of the battery case with the same solution but make sure that the solution doesn't get into the battery. When cleaning the cables, terminals and battery top, wear safety goggles and rubber gloves to prevent any solution from coming in contact with your eyes or hands. Wear old clothes too - even diluted, sulfuric acid splashed onto clothes will burn holes in them. If the terminals have been extensively corroded, clean them up with a terminal cleaner **(see illustration)**. Thoroughly wash all cleaned areas with plain water.
8   Before reinstalling the battery in the engine compartment, inspect the battery carrier. If it's dirty or covered with corrosion, clean it in the same solution of warm water and baking soda. Inspect the metal brackets which support the carrier to make sure that they are not covered with corrosion. If they are, wash them off. If corrosion is extensive, sand the brackets down to bare metal and spray them with a zinc-based primer (available in spray cans at auto paint and body supply stores).
9   Reinstall the battery back into the engine compartment. Make sure that no parts or wires are laying on the carrier during installation of the battery.
10  Install a pair of specially treated felt washers around the terminals (available at auto parts stores), then coat the terminals and the cable clamps with petroleum jelly or grease to prevent further corrosion. Install the cable clamps and tighten the nuts, being careful to install the negative cable last.

10.6b  Removing the cable from a battery post with a wrench - sometimes special battery pliers are required for this procedure if corrosion has caused deterioration of the nut hex (always remove the ground cable first and hook it up last!)

10.7a  When cleaning the cable clamps, all corrosion must be removed (the inside of the clamp is tapered to match the taper on the post, so don't remove too much material)

10.7b  Regardless of the type of tool used on the battery posts, a clean, shiny surface should be the result

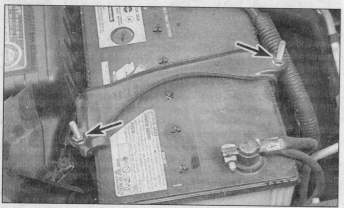

10.11  Make sure the battery hold-down nuts (arrows) are tight

11.2  A typical drivebelt layout

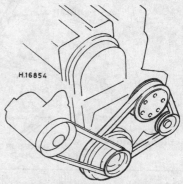

11  Install the hold-down clamp and nuts. Tighten the nuts only enough to hold the battery firmly in place (see illustration). Overtightening these nuts can crack the battery case.

## Charging

12  Remove all of the cell caps (if equipped) and cover the holes with a clean cloth to prevent spattering electrolyte. Disconnect the negative battery cable and hook the battery charger leads to the battery posts (positive to positive, negative to negative), then plug in the charger. Make sure it is set at 12 volts if it has a selector switch.

13  If you're using a charger with a rate higher than two amps, check the battery regularly during charging to make sure it doesn't overheat. If you're using a trickle charger, you can safely let the battery charge overnight after you've checked it regularly for the first couple of hours.

14  If the battery has removable cell caps, measure the specific gravity with a hydrometer every hour during the last few hours of the charging cycle. Hydrometers are available inexpensively from auto parts stores - follow the instructions that come with the hydrometer. Consider the battery charged when there's no change in the specific gravity reading for two hours and the electrolyte in the cells is gassing (bubbling) freely. The specific gravity reading from each cell should be very close to the others. If not, the battery probably has a bad cell(s).

15  Some batteries with sealed tops have built-in hydrometers on the top that indicate the state of charge by the color displayed in the hydrometer window. Normally, a bright-colored hydrometer indicates a full charge and a dark hydrometer indicates the battery still needs charging. Check the battery manufacturer's instructions to be sure you know what the colors mean.

16  If the battery has a sealed top and no built-in hydrometer, you can hook up a digital voltmeter across the battery terminals to check the charge. A fully charged battery should read 12.6 volts or higher.

17  Further information on the battery and jump starting can be found in Chapter 5 and at the front of this manual.

## 11  Drivebelt check, adjustment and replacement (every 7500 miles or 6 months)

*Refer to illustrations 11.2, 11.3a, 11.3b, 11.4, 11.6, 11.7 and 11.10*

## Check

1  The alternator and air conditioning compressor drivebelts are either V-belts or V-ribbed belts. Sometimes referred to as "fan" belts, the drivebelts are located at the left end of the engine. The good condition and proper adjustment of the alternator belt is critical to the operation of the engine. Because of their composition and the high stresses to which they are subjected, drivebelts stretch and deteriorate as they get older. They must therefore be periodically inspected.

2  The number of belts used on a particular vehicle depends on the accessories installed (see illustration).

3  With the engine off, open the hood and locate the drivebelts at the left end of the engine. With a flashlight, check each belt: On V-belts, check for cracks and separation of the belt plies (see illustration). On V-ribbed belts, check for separation of the adhesive rubber on both sides of the core, core separation from the belt side, a severed core, separation of the ribs from the adhesive rubber, cracking or separation of the ribs, and torn or worn ribs or cracks in the inner ridges of the ribs (see illustration). On both belt types, check for fraying and glazing, which gives the belt a shiny appearance. Both sides of the belt should be inspected, which means you will have to twist the belt to check the underside. Use your fingers to feel the belt where you can't see it. If any of the above conditions are evident, replace the belt (go to Step 8).

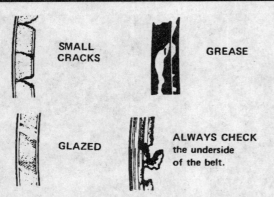

**11.3a  Here are some of the more common problems associated with drivebelts (check the belts very carefully to prevent an untimely breakdown)**

CRACKS RUNNING ACROSS "V" PORTIONS OF BELT

**ACCEPTABLE**

MISSING TWO OR MORE ADJACENT RIBS 1/2" OR LONGER

CRACKS RUNNING PARALLEL TO "V" PORTIONS OF BELT

**UNACCEPTABLE**

**11.3b  Check V-ribbed belts for signs of wear like these - if the belt looks worn, replace it**

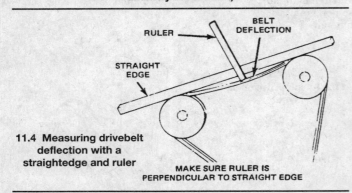

**11.4  Measuring drivebelt deflection with a straightedge and ruler**

MAKE SURE RULER IS PERPENDICULAR TO STRAIGHT EDGE

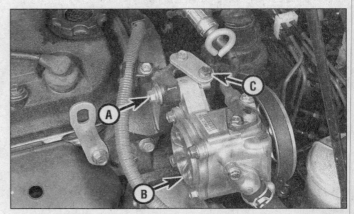

**11.6  Loosen the pivot nut (A) and the lower mounting nut (B), then turn the adjustment bolt (C) clockwise to tighten the belt, or counterclockwise to loosen the belt**

4     The tightness of each belt is checked by pushing on it at a distance halfway between the pulleys **(see illustration)**. Apply about 10 pounds of force with your thumb and see how much the belt moves down (deflects). Refer to the Specifications Section at the beginning of this Chapter for the amount of deflection allowed in each belt.

## Adjustment

5     If adjustment is necessary, it is done by moving the belt-driven accessory on the bracket.
6     For some components, there will be an adjusting bolt/nut and a pivot bolt. Both must be loosened slightly to enable you to move the component. After the two bolts have been loosened, move the component away from the engine (to tighten the belt) or toward the engine (to loosen the belt). After adjustment, tighten the bolts securely **(see illustration)**.
7     On other components, loosen the pivot bolt and locknut on the adjusting bolt. Turn the adjusting bolt to tension the belt **(see illustration)**.

## Replacement

8     To replace a belt, follow the above procedures for drivebelt adjustment but slip the belt off the crankshaft pulley and remove it. If you are replacing the alternator belt, you might have to remove another belt first because of the way they are arranged on the crankshaft pulley. Because of this and because belts tend to wear out more or less together, it is a good idea to replace both belts at the same time. Mark each belt and its appropriate pulley groove so the replacement belts can be installed in their proper positions. On some models, it may be necessary to remove the two left engine mount bolts to provide sufficient clearance for removal of the air conditioner compressor drivebelt.
9     Take the old belts to the parts store in order to make a direct comparison for length, width and design.
10    After replacing a V-ribbed drivebelt, make sure it fits properly in the ribbed grooves in the pulleys **(see illustration)**. It is essential that the belt be properly centered.
11    Adjust the belt(s) in accordance with the procedure outlined above.

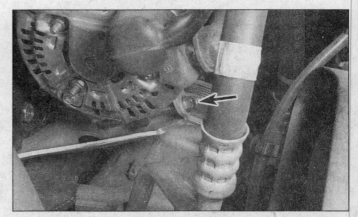

**11.7  Loosen the alternator through-bolt, loosen the adjuster locknut, then turn the adjusting bolt (arrow) to tighten or loosen the drivebelt**

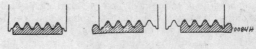

CORRECT          WRONG          WRONG

**11.10  When installing the V-ribbed belt, make sure it is centered on the pulley - it must not overlap either edge of the pulley**

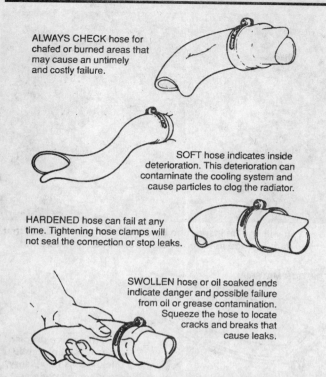

ALWAYS CHECK hose for chafed or burned areas that may cause an untimely and costly failure.

SOFT hose indicates inside deterioration. This deterioration can contaminate the cooling system and cause particles to clog the radiator.

HARDENED hose can fail at any time. Tightening hose clamps will not seal the connection or stop leaks.

SWOLLEN hose or oil soaked ends indicate danger and possible failure from oil or grease contamination. Squeeze the hose to locate cracks and breaks that cause leaks.

**13.4  Hoses, like drivebelts, have a habit of failing at the worst possible time - to prevent the inconvenience of a blown radiator or heater hose, inspect them carefully as shown here**

## 12  Underhood hose check and replacement (every 7500 miles or 6 months)

**Caution:** *Replacement of air conditioning hoses must be left to a dealer service department or air conditioning shop that has the equipment to depressurize the system safely. Never remove air conditioning components or hoses until the system has been depressurized.*

### General

1    High temperatures in the engine compartment can cause the deterioration of the rubber and plastic hoses used for engine, accessory and emission systems operation. Periodic inspection should be made for cracks, loose clamps, material hardening and leaks.

2    Information specific to the cooling system hoses can be found in Section 13.

3    Some, but not all, hoses are secured to the fittings with clamps. Where clamps are used, check to be sure they haven't lost their tension, allowing the hose to leak. If clamps aren't used, make sure the hose has not expanded and/or hardened where it slips over the fitting, allowing it to leak.

### Vacuum hoses

4    It's quite common for vacuum hoses, especially those in the emissions system, to be color coded or identified by colored stripes molded into them. Various systems require hoses with different wall thickness, collapse resistance and temperature resistance. When replacing hoses, be sure the new ones are made of the same material.

5    Often the only effective way to check a hose is to remove it completely from the vehicle. If more than one hose is removed, be sure to label the hoses and fittings to ensure correct installation.

6    When checking vacuum hoses, be sure to include any plastic T-fittings in the check. Inspect the fittings for cracks and the hose where it fits over the fitting for distortion, which could cause leakage.

7    A small piece of vacuum hose (1/4-inch inside diameter) can be used as a stethoscope to detect vacuum leaks. Hold one end of the hose to your ear and probe around vacuum hoses and fittings, listening for the "hissing" sound characteristic of a vacuum leak. **Warning:** *When probing with the vacuum hose stethoscope, be very careful not to come into contact with moving engine components such as the drivebelts, cooling fan, etc.*

### Fuel hose

**Warning:** *Gasoline is extremely flammable, so take extra precautions when you work on any part of the fuel system. Don't smoke or allow open flames or bare light bulbs near the work area, and don't work in a garage where a natural gas-type appliance (such as a water heater or clothes dryer) with a pilot light is present. Since gasoline is carcinogenic, wear latex gloves when there's a possibility of being exposed to fuel, and, if you spill any fuel on your skin, rinse it off immediately with soap and water. Mop up any spills immediately and do not store fuel-soaked rags where they could ignite. The fuel system is under constant pressure, so, if any fuel lines are to be disconnected, the fuel pressure in the system must be relieved first (see Chapter 4 for more information). When you perform any kind of work on the fuel system, wear safety glasses and have a Class B type fire extinguisher on hand.*

8    Check all rubber fuel lines for deterioration and chafing. Check especially for cracks in areas where the hose bends and just before fittings, such as where a hose attaches to the fuel filter.

9    When replacing hose, use only hose that is specifically designed for your fuel injection system.

### Metal lines

10    Sections of metal line are often used for fuel line between the fuel pump and fuel injection unit. Check carefully to be sure the line has not been bent or crimped and that cracks have not started in the line.

11    If a section of metal fuel line must be replaced, only seamless steel tubing should be used, since copper and aluminum tubing don't have the strength necessary to withstand normal engine vibration.

12    Check the metal brake lines where they enter the master cylinder and brake proportioning unit (if used) for cracks in the lines or loose fittings. Any sign of brake fluid leakage calls for an immediate thorough inspection of the brake system.

## 13  Cooling system check (every 7500 miles or 6 months)

*Refer to illustration 13.4*

1    Many major engine failures can be attributed to a faulty cooling system. If the vehicle is equipped with an automatic transaxle, the cooling system also cools the transmission fluid and thus plays an important role in prolonging transaxle life.

2    The cooling system should be checked with the engine cold. Do this before the vehicle is driven for the day or after the engine has been shut off for at least three hours.

3    Remove the radiator cap by turning it to the left until it reaches a stop. If you hear a hissing sound (indicating there is still pressure in the system), wait until it stops. Now press down on the cap with the palm of your hand and continue turning to the left until the cap can be removed. Thoroughly clean the cap, inside and out, with clean water. Also clean the filler neck on the radiator. All traces of corrosion should be removed. The coolant inside the radiator should be relatively transparent. If it's rust colored, the system should be drained and refilled (see Section 24). If the coolant level isn't up to the top, add additional antifreeze/coolant mixture (see Section 4).

4    Carefully check the large upper and lower radiator hoses along with the smaller diameter heater hoses which run from the engine to the firewall. Inspect each hose along its entire length, replacing any hose which is cracked, swollen or shows signs of deterioration. Cracks may become more apparent if the hose is squeezed **(see illustration)**. Regardless of condition, it's a good idea to replace hoses with new ones every two years.

5    Make sure that all hose connections are tight. A leak in the cooling system will usually show up as white or rust colored deposits on the areas adjoining the leak. If wire-type clamps are used at the ends of the hoses, it may be a good idea to replace them with more secure screw-type clamps.

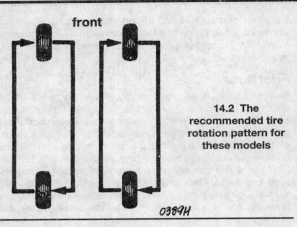

front

**14.2 The recommended tire rotation pattern for these models**

0389H

6     Use compressed air or a soft brush to remove bugs, leaves, etc. from the front of the radiator or air conditioning condenser. Be careful not to damage the delicate cooling fins or cut yourself on them.
7     Every other inspection, or at the first indication of cooling system problems, have the cap and system pressure tested. If you don't have a pressure tester, most gas stations and repair shops will do this for a minimal charge.

## 14   Tire rotation (every 7500 miles or 6 months)

*Refer to illustration 14.2*
1     The tires should be rotated at the specified intervals and whenever uneven wear is noticed. Since the vehicle will be raised and the tires removed anyway, check the brakes (see Section 15) at this time.
2     Radial tires must be rotated in a specific pattern **(see illustration)**.
3     Refer to the information in *Jacking and towing* at the front of this manual for the proper procedures to follow when raising the vehicle and changing a tire. If the brakes are to be checked, do not apply the parking brake as stated. Make sure the tires are blocked to prevent the vehicle from rolling.
4     Preferably, the entire vehicle should be raised at the same time. This can be done on a hoist or by jacking up each corner and then lowering the vehicle onto jackstands placed under the frame rails. Always use four jackstands and make sure the vehicle is firmly supported.
5     After rotation, check and adjust the tire pressures as necessary and be sure to check the lug nut tightness.
6     For further information on the wheels and tires, refer to Chapter 10.

## 15   Brake check (every 7500 miles or 6 months)

*Refer to illustrations 15.6, 15.9 and 15.14*
**Note:** *For detailed photographs of the brake system, refer to Chapter 9.*
1     In addition to the specified intervals, the brakes should be inspected every time the wheels are removed or whenever a defect is suspected. Any of the following symptoms could indicate a potential brake system defect: The vehicle pulls to one side when the brake pedal is depressed; the brakes make squealing or dragging noises when applied; brake travel is excessive; the pedal pulsates; brake fluid leaks, usually onto the inside of the tire or wheel.
2     The disc brake pads have built-in wear indicators which should make a high pitched squealing or scraping noise when they are worn to the replacement point. When you hear this noise, replace the pads immediately or expensive damage to the discs can result.
3     Loosen the wheel lug nuts.
4     Raise the vehicle and place it securely on jackstands.
5     Remove the wheels (see *Jacking and towing* at the front of this book, or your owner's manual, if necessary).

**15.6 You will find an inspection hole like this in each caliper that you can view the inner and outer brake pad lining through**

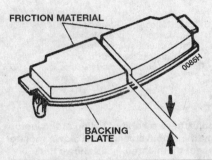

FRICTION MATERIAL

BACKING PLATE

0085H

**15.9 If a more precise measurement of pad thickness is necessary, remove the pads and measure the remaining friction material**

### Disc brakes

**Note:** *All models covered by this manual have front disc brakes. Some models are also equipped with disc brakes at the rear.*
6     There are two pads - an outer and an inner - in each caliper. The pads are visible through an inspection hole in each caliper **(see illustration)**.
7     Check the pad thickness by looking at each end of the caliper and through the inspection hole in the caliper body. If the lining material is less than the specified thickness (see this Chapter's Specifications), replace the pads. **Note:** *Keep in mind that the lining material is riveted or bonded to a metal backing plate and the metal portion is not included in this measurement.*
8     If it is difficult to determine the exact thickness of the remaining pad material by the above method, or if you are at all concerned about the condition of the pads, remove the caliper(s), then remove the pads from the calipers for further inspection (see Chapter 9).
9     Once the pads are removed from the calipers, clean them with brake system cleaner and remeasure them with a ruler or a vernier caliper **(see illustration)**.
10    Measure the disc thickness with a micrometer to make sure that it still has service life remaining. If any disc is thinner than the specified minimum thickness, replace it (see Chapter 9). Even if the disc has service life remaining, check its condition. Look for scoring, gouging and burned spots. If these conditions exist, have the disc resurfaced (see Chapter 9).
11    Before installing the wheels, check all brake lines and hoses for damage, wear, deformation, cracks, corrosion, leakage, bends and twists, particularly in the vicinity of the rubber hoses at the calipers. Check the clamps for tightness and the connections for leakage. Make sure all hoses and lines are clear of sharp edges, moving parts and the exhaust system. If any of the above conditions are noted, repair, reroute or replace the lines and/or fittings as necessary (see Chapter 9).

### Rear drum brakes

12    Refer to Chapter 9 and remove the rear brake drums.
13    **Warning:** *Brake dust produced by lining wear and deposited on*

brake components may contain asbestos, which is hazardous to your health. DO NOT blow it out with compressed air and DO NOT inhale it! DO NOT use gasoline or petroleum-based solvents to remove the dust. Brake system cleaner should be used to flush the dust into a drain pan. After the brake components are wiped clean, dispose of the contaminated rag(s) and cleaner in a covered and labeled container. Try to use non-asbestos replacement parts whenever possible.

14    Note the thickness of the lining material on the rear brake shoes **(see illustration)** and look for signs of contamination by brake fluid and grease. If the lining material is within 3/32-inch of the recessed rivets or metal shoes, replace the brake shoes with new ones. The shoes should also be replaced if they are cracked, glazed (shiny lining surfaces) or contaminated with brake fluid or grease. See Chapter 9 for the replacement procedure.

15    Check the shoe return and hold-down springs and the adjusting mechanism to make sure they're installed correctly and in good condition. Deteriorated or distorted springs, if not replaced, could allow the linings to drag and wear prematurely.

16    Check the wheel cylinders for leakage by carefully peeling back the rubber boots. If brake fluid is noted behind the boots, the wheel cylinders must be replaced (see Chapter 9).

17    Check the drums for cracks, score marks, deep scratches and hard spots, which will appear as small discolored areas. If imperfections cannot be removed with emery cloth, the drums must be resurfaced by an automotive machine shop (see Chapter 9 for more detailed information).

18    Refer to Chapter 9 and install the brake drums.

19    Install the wheels and tighten the wheel lug nuts finger tight.

20    Remove the jackstands and lower the vehicle.

21    Tighten the wheel lug nuts to the torque listed in this Chapter's Specifications.

### Brake booster check

22    Sit in the driver's seat and perform the following sequence of tests.

23    With the brake fully depressed, start the engine - the pedal should move down a little when the engine starts.

24    With the engine running, depress the brake pedal several times - the travel distance should not change.

25    Depress the brake, stop the engine and hold the pedal in for about 30 seconds - the pedal should neither sink nor rise.

26    Restart the engine, run it for about a minute and turn it off. Then firmly depress the brake several times - the pedal travel should decrease with each application.

27    If your brakes do not operate as described above when the preceding tests are performed, the brake booster is either in need of repair or has failed. Refer to Chapter 9 for the removal procedure.

### Parking brake

28    Slowly pull up on the parking brake and count the number of

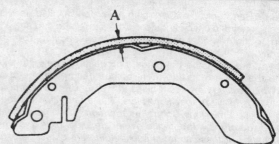

**15.14  If the lining is bonded to the brake shoe, measure the lining thickness from the outer surface to the metal shoe, as shown here; if the lining is riveted to the shoe, measure from the lining outer surface to the rivet head**

clicks you hear until the handle is up as far as it will go. The adjustment is correct if you hear the specified number of clicks (see this Chapter's Specifications). If you hear more or fewer clicks, it's time to adjust the parking brake (see Chapter 9).

29    An alternative method of checking the parking brake is to park the vehicle on a steep hill with the parking brake set and the transmission in Neutral. If the parking brake cannot prevent the vehicle from rolling, it is in need of adjustment (see Chapter 9).

### 16    Air filter replacement (every 15,000 miles or 12 months)

*Refer to illustrations 16.2a, 16.2b and 16.4*

1    At the specified intervals, the air filter should be replaced with a new one.

2    Loosen the air cleaner cover screws **(see illustrations)**.

3    Lift the cover up.

4    Lift the air filter element out of the housing and wipe out the inside of the air cleaner housing with a clean rag **(see illustration)**.

5    While the air cleaner cover is off, be careful not to drop anything down into the air cleaner assembly.

6    Place the new filter in the air cleaner housing. Make sure it seats properly in the lower half of the housing.

7    Install the air cleaner cover and tighten the screws securely.

### 17    Spark plug replacement (every 30,000 miles or 24 months)

*Refer to illustrations 17.1, 17.4a, 17.4b, 17.6, 17.8, 17.10 and 17.11*

1    Spark plug replacement requires a spark plug socket which fits onto a ratchet wrench. This socket is lined with a rubber grommet to protect the porcelain insulator of the spark plug and to hold the plug

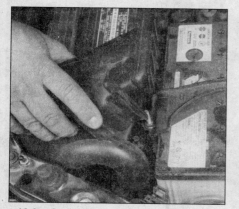

**16.2a  On four-cylinder models, remove the battery air duct for access to the air cleaner screws**

**16.2b  Remove the air cleaner cover screws with either a socket and extension or a screwdriver**

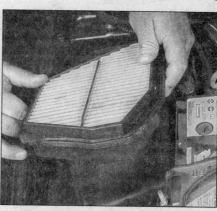

**16.4  Move the cover out of the way and remove the filter**

while you insert it into the spark plug hole. You will also need a wire-type feeler gauge to check and adjust the spark plug gap and a torque wrench to tighten the new plugs to the specified torque **(see illustration)**.

2    If you are replacing the plugs, purchase the new plugs, adjust them to the proper gap and then replace each plug one at a time. **Note:** *When buying new spark plugs, it's essential that you obtain the correct plugs for your specific vehicle. This information can be found on the Vehicle Emissions Control Information (VECI) label located on the underside of the hood, in the owner's manual or in this Chapter's Specifications. If these sources specify different plugs, purchase the spark plug type listed on the VECI label because that information is provided specifically for your engine.*

3    Inspect each of the new plugs for defects. If there are any signs of cracks in the porcelain insulator of a plug, don't use it.

4    Check the electrode gaps of the new plugs. Check the gap by inserting the wire gauge of the proper thickness between the electrodes at the tip of the plug **(see illustration)**. The gap between the electrodes should be identical to that specified on the VECI label. If the gap is incorrect, use the notched adjuster on the feeler gauge body to bend the curved side electrode slightly **(see illustration)**.

5    If the side electrode is not exactly over the center electrode, use the notched adjuster to align them. **Caution:** *If the gap of a new plug must be adjusted, bend only the base of the ground electrode. Do not touch the tip.*

## Removal

6    To prevent the possibility of mixing up spark plug wires, work on one spark plug at a time. Remove the wire and boot from one spark plug. Grasp the boot - not the cable - as shown, give it a half twisting motion and pull straight out **(see illustration)**.

7    If compressed air is available, blow any dirt or foreign material away from the spark plug area before proceeding.

8    Remove the spark plug **(see illustration)**.

9    Whether you are replacing the plugs at this time or intend to re-use the old plugs, compare each old spark plug with the chart on the inside back cover of this manual to determine the overall running condition of the engine.

## Installation

10    It's a good idea to lightly coat the threads of the spark plugs with anti-seize compound **(see illustration)** to insure that the spark plugs do not seize in the aluminum cylinder head.

11    It's often difficult to insert spark plugs into their holes without cross-threading them. To avoid this possibility, fit a piece of 3/8-inch ID rubber hose over the end of the spark plug **(see illustration)**. The

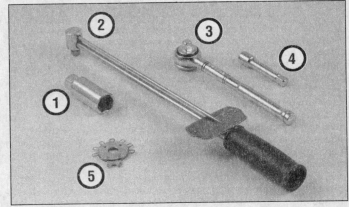

**17.1  Tools required for changing spark plugs**

1    **Spark plug socket** - *This will have special padding inside to protect the spark plug's porcelain insulator*
2    **Torque wrench** - *Although not mandatory, using this tool is the best way to ensure the plugs are tightened properly*
3    **Ratchet** - *Standard hand tool to fit the spark plug socket*
4    **Extension** - *Depending on model and accessories, you may need special extensions and universal joints to reach one or more of the plugs*
5    **Spark plug gap gauge** - *This gauge for checking the gap comes in a variety of styles. Make sure the gap for your engine is included*

flexible hose acts as a universal joint to help align the plug with the plug hole. Should the plug begin to cross-thread, the hose will slip on the spark plug, preventing thread damage. Tighten the plug securely.

12    Attach the plug wire to the new spark plug, again using a twisting motion on the boot until it is firmly seated on the end of the spark plug.

13    Follow the above procedure for the remaining spark plugs, replacing them one at a time to prevent mixing up the spark plug wires.

## 18    Spark plug wire, distributor cap and rotor check and replacement (every 30,000 miles or 24 months)

*Refer to illustrations 18.11 and 18.12*

1    The spark plug wires should be checked whenever new spark plugs are installed.

**17.4a  Spark plug manufacturers recommend using a wire-type gauge when checking the gap - if the wire does not slide between the electrodes with a slight drag, adjustment is required**

**17.4b  To change the gap, bend the side electrode only, as indicated by the arrows, and be very careful not to crack or chip the porcelain insulator surrounding the center electrode**

**17.6  When removing spark plug wires, pull only on the boot using a twisting/pulling motion**

**17.8  Because they are deeply recessed, an extension will be required when removing or installing the spark plugs**

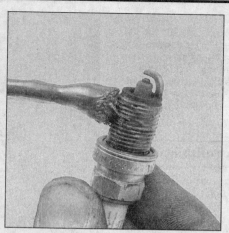

**17.10  A light coat of anti-seize compound applied to the threads of the spark plugs will keep the threads in the cylinder head from being damaged the next time the plugs are removed**

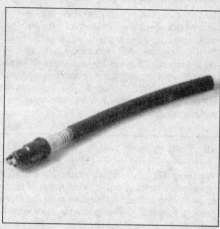

**17.11  A piece of 3/8-inch rubber hose will aid in getting the spark plug started in the hole**

2    Begin this procedure by making a visual check of the spark plug wires while the engine is running. In a darkened garage (make sure there is ventilation) start the engine and observe each plug wire. Be careful not to come into contact with any moving engine parts. If there is a break in the wire, you will see arcing or a small spark at the damaged area. If arcing is noticed, make a note to obtain new wires, then allow the engine to cool and check the distributor cap and rotor.

3    The spark plug wires should be inspected one at a time to prevent mixing up the order, which is essential for proper engine operation. Each original plug wire should be numbered to help identify its location. If the number is illegible, a piece of tape can be marked with the correct number and wrapped around the plug wire.

4    Disconnect the plug wire from the spark plug. A removal tool can be used for this purpose or you can grasp the rubber boot, twist the boot half a turn and pull the boot free. Do not pull on the wire itself.

5    Check inside the boot for corrosion, which will look like a white crusty powder.

6    Push the wire and boot back onto the end of the spark plug. It should fit tightly onto the end of the plug. If it doesn't, remove the wire and use pliers to carefully crimp the metal connector inside the wire boot until the fit is snug.

7    Using a clean rag, wipe the entire length of the wire to remove built-up dirt and grease. Once the wire is clean, check for burns, cracks and other damage. Do not bend the wire sharply, because the conductor might break.

8    Disconnect the wire from the distributor. Again, pull only on the rubber boot. Check for corrosion and a tight fit. Replace the wire in the distributor.

9    Inspect the remaining spark plug wires, making sure that each one is securely fastened at the distributor and spark plug when the check is complete.

10   If new spark plug wires are required, purchase a set for your specific engine model. Pre-cut wire sets with the boots already installed are available. Remove and replace the wires one at a time to avoid mix-ups in the firing order.

11   Detach the distributor cap by removing the cap retaining screws. Look inside it for cracks, carbon tracks and worn, burned or loose contacts **(see illustration)**.

12   Remove the retaining screw and pull the rotor off the distributor shaft. It may be necessary to use a small screwdriver to gently pry off the rotor and examine it for cracks and carbon tracks **(see illustration)**. Replace the cap and rotor if any damage or defects are noted.

**18.11  Check the distributor cap for cracks, carbon tracks, broken tower, or damaged or worn rotor button (if in doubt about its condition, install a new one)**

**18.12  The ignition rotor should be checked for wear and corrosion (if in doubt about its condition, buy a new one)**

13   It is common practice to install a new cap and rotor whenever new spark plug wires are installed, but if you wish to continue using the old cap, check the resistance between the spark plug wires and the cap first. If the indicated resistance is more than the specified maximum value (see this Chapter's Specifications), replace the cap and/or wires.

14   When installing a new cap, remove the wires from the old cap one at a time and attach them to the new cap in the exact same location - do not simultaneously remove all the wires from the old cap or firing order mix-ups may occur.

## 19   Fuel system check (every 15,000 miles or 12 months)

**Warning:** *Gasoline is extremely flammable, so take extra precautions when you work on any part of the fuel system. Don't smoke or allow open flames or bare light bulbs near the work area, and don't work in a garage where a natural gas-type appliance (such as a water heater or clothes dryer) with a pilot light is present. Since gasoline is carcinogenic, wear latex gloves when there's a possibility of being exposed to fuel, and, if you spill any fuel on your skin, rinse it off immediately with soap and water. Mop up any spills immediately and do not store fuel-soaked rags where they could ignite. The fuel system is under constant pressure, so, if any fuel lines are to be disconnected, the fuel pressure in the system must be relieved first (see Chapter 4 for more information). When you perform any kind of work on the fuel system, wear safety glasses and have a Class B type fire extinguisher on hand.*

1   If you smell gasoline while driving or after the vehicle has been sitting in the sun, inspect the fuel system immediately.

2   Remove the fuel filler cap and inspect it for damage and corrosion. The gasket should have an unbroken sealing imprint. If the gasket is damaged or corroded, remove it and install a new one.

3   Inspect the fuel feed and return lines for cracks. Make sure all fuel line connections are tight. **Warning:** *It is necessary to relieve the fuel system pressure before servicing fuel system components. The correct procedure for fuel system pressure relief is outlined in Chapter 4.*

4   Since some components of the fuel system - the fuel tank and part of the fuel feed and return lines, for example - are underneath the vehicle, they can be inspected more easily with the vehicle raised on a hoist. If that's not possible, raise the vehicle and support it securely on jackstands.

5   With the vehicle raised and safely supported, inspect the gas tank and filler neck for punctures, cracks and other damage. The connection between the filler neck and the tank is particularly critical. Sometimes a rubber filler neck will leak because of loose clamps or deteriorated rubber. These are problems a home mechanic can usually rectify. **Warning:** *Do not, under any circumstances, try to repair a fuel tank (except rubber components). A welding torch or any open flame can easily cause fuel vapors inside the tank to explode.*

6   Carefully check all rubber hoses and metal lines leading away from the fuel tank. Check for loose connections, deteriorated hoses, crimped lines and other damage. Carefully inspect the lines from the tank to the fuel injection system. Repair or replace damaged sections as necessary.

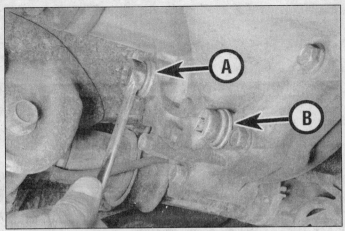

20.1  The manual transaxle fill plug (A) and drain plug (B) is located on the passenger side of the transaxle

## 20   Manual transaxle lubricant level check (every 15,000 miles or 12 months)

*Refer to illustrations 20.1, 20.2a and 20.2b*

1   The manual transaxle does not have a dipstick. To check the fluid level, raise the vehicle and support it securely on jackstands. The check/fill and drain plugs are on the right side of the transaxle housing **(see illustration)**. Remove it. If the lubricant level is correct, it should be up to the lower edge of the hole.

2   If the transaxle needs more lubricant (if the level is not up to the hole), use a funnel to add more **(see illustrations)**. Stop filling the transaxle when the lubricant begins to run out the hole.

3   Install the plug and tighten it securely. Drive the vehicle a short distance, then check for leaks.

## 21   Steering and suspension check (every 15,000 miles or 12 months)

*Refer to illustrations 21.8 and 21.9*
**Note:** *For detailed illustrations of the steering and suspension components, refer to Chapter 10.*

## With the wheels on the ground

1   With the vehicle stopped and the front wheels pointed straight ahead, rock the steering wheel gently back and forth. If freeplay is

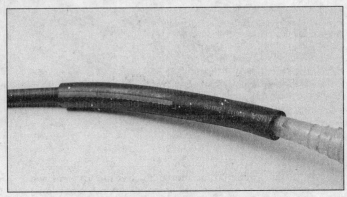

20.2a  Use two different size pieces of hose to make an adapter on the funnel . . .

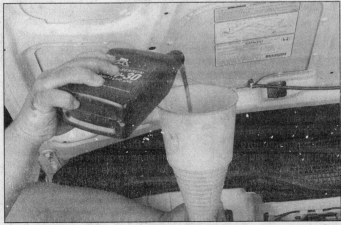

20.2b  . . . so you can easily add lubricant to the transaxle from above

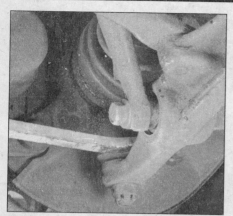

**21.8 Pry between the balljoint and the lower control arm to check for movement indicating balljoint wear**

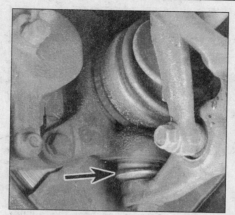

**21.9 Push on the balljoint boot (arrow) to check for tears and grease leaks**

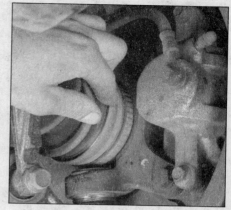

**22.2 Flex the driveaxle boots by hand to check for tears, cracks and leaking grease**

excessive, a front wheel bearing, main shaft yoke, intermediate shaft yoke, lower arm balljoint or steering system joint is worn or the steering gear is out of adjustment, loose on its mounts or broken. Refer to Chapter 10 for the appropriate repair procedure.

2    Other symptoms, such as excessive vehicle body movement over rough roads, swaying (leaning) around corners and binding as the steering wheel is turned, may indicate faulty steering and/or suspension components.

3    Check the shock absorbers by pushing down and releasing the vehicle several times at each corner. If the vehicle does not come back to a level position within one or two bounces, the shocks/struts are worn and must be replaced. When bouncing the vehicle up and down, listen for squeaks and noises from the suspension components. Additional information on suspension components can be found in Chapter 10.

4    Note whether the vehicle looks canted to one side or corner. If it is, try to level it by rocking it down. If this doesn't work, look for bad springs or worn or loose suspension parts.

## Under the vehicle

5    Raise the vehicle with a floor jack and support it securely on jackstands. See *Jacking and towing* at the front of this book for the proper jacking points.

6    Check the tires for irregular wear patterns (see Section 5) and proper inflation.

7    Inspect the universal joint between the steering shaft and the steering gear housing. Check the steering gear housing for grease leakage or oozing. Make sure that the dust seals and boots are not damaged and that the boot clamps are not loose. Check the steering linkage for looseness or damage. Check the tie-rod ends for excessive play. Look for loose bolts, broken or disconnected parts and deteriorated rubber bushings on all suspension and steering components. While an assistant turns the steering wheel from side to side, check the steering components for free movement, chafing and binding. If the steering components do not seem to be reacting with the movement of the steering wheel, try to determine where the slack is located.

8    Check the balljoints for wear by prying between each balljoint and lower control arm **(see illustration)** to ensure the balljoint has no play. If any balljoint does have play, replace it. Refer to Chapter 10 for the front balljoint replacement procedure.

9    Inspect the balljoint boots for tears and leaking grease **(see illustration)**. Replace the boots with new ones if they are damaged (see Chapter 10).

## 22   Driveaxle boot check (every 15,000 miles or 12 months)

*Refer to illustration 22.2*

1    The driveaxle boots are very important because they prevent dirt, water and foreign material from entering and damaging the constant velocity (CV) joints. Oil and grease can cause the boot material to deteriorate prematurely, so it's a good idea to wash the boots with soap and water.

2    Inspect the boots for tears and cracks as well as loose clamps **(see illustration)**. If there is any evidence of cracks or leaking grease, they must be replaced as described in Chapter 8.

## 23   Valve clearance check and adjustment (four-cylinder engines only) (every 15,000 miles or 12 months)

*Refer to illustrations 23.4 and 23.5*

1    The valve clearances must be checked and adjusted with the engine cold.

2    Place the number one piston (closest to the drivebelt end of the engine) at Top Dead Center (TDC) on the compression stroke. This is accomplished by rotating the crankshaft pulley clockwise until the timing pointer on the block lines up with the TDC mark on the front pulley. The distributor rotor should be pointing toward the number one spark plug wire terminal on the distributor cap. If it isn't, rotate the engine one complete turn and realign the marks.

3    Remove the valve cover (see Chapter 2A).

4    With the engine in this position, the number one cylinder valve adjustment can be checked and adjusted **(see illustration)**.

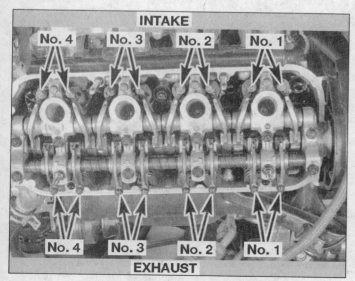

**23.4 Valve layout - four-cylinder engine**

23.5 Insert a feeler gauge between the valve stem and rocker arm, loosen the lock-nut with a box-end wrench and adjust the clearance with a screwdriver

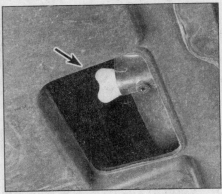

24.4 On most models you will have to remove a cover for access to the radiator drain fitting located at the bottom of the radiator (arrow)

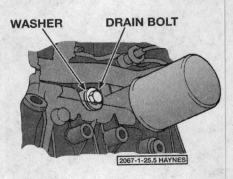

24.5 The coolant drain plug is located the back side of the block near the oil filter on four-cylinder models

5    Start with the intake valve clearance. Insert a feeler gauge of the correct thickness (see this Chapter's Specifications) between the valve stem and the rocker arm **(see illustration)**. Withdraw it; you should feel a slight drag. If there's no drag or a heavy drag, loosen the adjuster nut and back off the adjuster screw. Carefully tighten the adjuster screw until you can feel a slight drag on the feeler gauge as you withdraw it.

6    Hold the adjuster screw with a screwdriver (to keep it from turning) and tighten the locknut. Recheck the clearance to make sure it hasn't changed. Repeat the procedure in this Step and the previous Step on the other intake valve, then on the two exhaust valves.

7    Rotate the crankshaft pulley 180-degrees counterclockwise (the camshaft pulley will turn 90-degrees) until the number three cylinder is at TDC. With the number three cylinder at TDC, the UP mark on the camshaft sprocket should be at the exhaust side (nine O'clock position) and the distributor rotor should point at the number three spark plug wire terminal. Check and adjust the number three cylinder valves.

8    Rotate the crankshaft pulley 180-degrees counterclockwise until the number four cylinder is at TDC. With the number four cylinder at TDC, the UP mark on the camshaft sprocket should be pointed straight down. The distributor rotor should point at the number four spark plug wire terminal. Check and adjust the number four cylinder valves.

9    Rotate the crankshaft pulley 180-degrees counterclockwise to bring the number two cylinder to TDC. The UP mark on the camshaft sprocket should be on the intake side (three o'clock position). The distributor rotor should point at the number two spark plug wire. Check and adjust the number two cylinder valves.

10   Install the valve cover.

## 24  Cooling system servicing (draining, flushing and refilling) (every 30,000 miles or 24 months)

*Refer to illustrations 24.4, 24.5, 21.13a and 24.13b*

**Warning 1:** *Do not allow antifreeze to come in contact with your skin or painted surfaces of the vehicle. Rinse off spills immediately with plenty of water. Antifreeze is highly toxic if ingested. Never leave antifreeze lying around in an open container or in puddles on the floor; children and pets are attracted by it's sweet smell and may drink it. Check with local authorities about disposing of used antifreeze. Many communities have collection centers which will see that antifreeze is disposed of safely.*

**Warning 2:** *Wait until the engine has completely cooled before beginning this procedure.*

1    Periodically, the cooling system should be drained, flushed and refilled to replenish the antifreeze mixture and prevent formation of rust and corrosion, which can impair the performance of the cooling system and cause engine damage. When the cooling system is serviced, all hoses and the radiator cap should be checked and replaced if necessary.

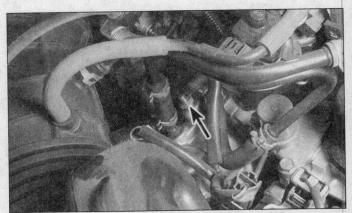

24.13a The air bleed bolt (arrow) is located on the thermostat housing - use a wrench to open it during the filling process to bleed air out of the system (four-cylinder engine)

## Draining

2    Apply the parking brake and block the wheels. If the vehicle has just been driven, wait several hours to allow the engine to cool down before beginning this procedure.

3    Once the engine is completely cool, remove the radiator cap.

4    Move a large container under the radiator drain fitting to catch the coolant. Then open the drain fitting (a pair of pliers may be required to turn it) **(see illustration)**.

5    After the coolant stops flowing out of the radiator, move the container under the engine block drain plug(s) **(see illustration)** (the V6 engine has two drain plugs, one on each side of the block). Loosen the plug(s) and allow the coolant in the block to drain.

6    While the coolant is draining, check the condition of the radiator hoses, heater hoses and clamps (refer to Section 13 if necessary).

7    Replace any damaged clamps or hoses.

## Flushing

8    Once the system is completely drained, flush the radiator with fresh water from a garden hose until water runs clear at the drain. The flushing action of the water will remove sediments from the radiator but will not remove rust and scale from the engine and cooling tube surfaces.

9    These deposits can be removed by the chemical action of a cleaner. Follow the procedure outlined in the manufacturer's instructions. If the radiator is severely corroded, damaged or leaking, it should be removed (see Chapter 3) and taken to a radiator repair shop.

10   Remove the overflow hose from the coolant recovery reservoir. Drain the reservoir and flush it with clean water, then reconnect the hose.

24.13b V6 engine air bleed bolt location (arrow)

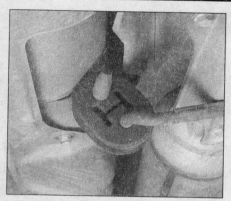

25.4 Inspect the exhaust system rubber hangers for cracks and damage

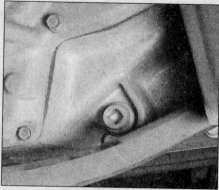

26.7 Use a 3/8-inch ratchet to remove the automatic transaxle drain plug

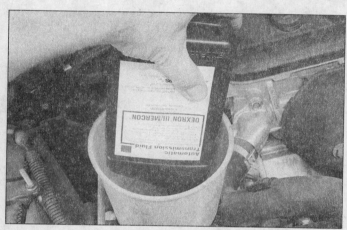

26.9 Use a funnel to add fluid to the transaxle

## Refilling

11   Close and tighten the radiator drain. Install and tighten the block drain plug(s).
12   Place the heater temperature control in the maximum heat position.
13   Loosen the air bleed bolt, located on the top of the thermostat housing (four-cylinder models) or water passage (V6 models) **(see illustrations)**.
14   Slowly add new coolant (a 50/50 mixture of water and antifreeze) to the radiator until a steady, bubble-free stream flows from the air bleed bolt, then tighten the bolt securely. Add coolant to the reservoir until the level is at the upper mark.
15   Leave the radiator cap off and run the engine in a well-ventilated area until the thermostat opens (coolant will begin flowing through the radiator and the upper radiator hose will become hot).
16   Turn the engine off and let it cool. Add more coolant mixture to bring the level back up to the lip on the radiator filler neck.
17   Squeeze the upper radiator hose to expel air, then add more coolant mixture if necessary. Install the radiator cap.
18   Start the engine, allow it to reach normal operating temperature and check for leaks.

## 25   Exhaust system check (every 30,000 miles or 24 months)

*Refer to illustration 25.4*
1   With the engine cold (at least three hours after the vehicle has been driven), check the complete exhaust system from its starting point at the engine to the end of the tailpipe. This should be done on a hoist where unrestricted access is available.

2   Check the pipes and connections for evidence of leaks, severe corrosion or damage. Make sure that all brackets and hangers are in good condition and tight.
3   At the same time, inspect the underside of the body for holes, corrosion, open seams, etc. which may allow exhaust gases to enter the passenger compartment. Seal all body openings with silicone sealant or body putty.
4   Rattles and other noises can often be traced to the exhaust system, especially the mounts and hangers **(see illustration)**. Try to move the pipes, muffler and catalytic converter. If the components can come in contact with the body or suspension parts, secure the exhaust system with new mounts.
5   Check the running condition of the engine by inspecting inside the end of the tailpipe. The exhaust deposits here are an indication of engine state-of-tune. If the pipe is black and sooty or coated with white deposits, the engine is in need of a tune-up, including a thorough fuel system inspection.

## 26   Automatic transaxle fluid change (every 30,000 miles or 24 months)

*Refer to illustrations 26.7 and 26.9*
1   At the specified time intervals, the automatic transaxle fluid should be drained and replaced.
2   Before beginning work, purchase the specified transmission fluid (see *Recommended fluids and lubricants* at the front of this Chapter).
3   Other tools necessary for this job include jackstands to support the vehicle in a raised position, a 3/8-inch drive ratchet and extension, a drain pan capable of holding at least eight pints, newspapers and clean rags.
4   The fluid should be drained immediately after the vehicle has been driven. Hot fluid is more effective than cold fluid at removing built-up sediment. **Warning:** *Fluid temperature can exceed 350-degrees F in a hot transaxle. Wear protective gloves.*
5   After the vehicle has been driven to warm up the fluid, raise it and place it on jackstands for access to the transaxle drain plug.
6   Move the necessary equipment under the vehicle, being careful not to touch any of the hot exhaust components.
7   Place the drain pan under the transaxle drain plug and remove the drain plug. It's located near the bottom of the transaxle on the right side on four-cylinder models or the left side on V6 modes **(see illustration)**. Be sure the drain pan is in position, as fluid will come out with some force. Once the fluid is drained, clean the drain plug and reinstall it securely.
8   Lower the vehicle.
9   Pull out the dipstick (four-cylinder models) or remove the filler bolt marked ATF (V6 models), and add new fluid to the transaxle through the dipstick or bolt hole (see *Recommended fluids and lubricants* for the recommended fluid type and capacity). Use a funnel to prevent spills **(see illustration)**. It is best to add a little fluid at a time,

**28.4a  Working in the engine compartment, hold the fitting (A) and unscrew the filter banjo bolt (B)**

**28.4b  From underneath the engine compartment, use a flare nut wrench, if possible, to loosen the fuel line - unscrew the fitting (arrow) from the bottom of the filter**

continually checking the level with the dipstick (see Section 7). Allow the fluid time to drain into the pan.
10    Install the dipstick or filler bolt.
11    Start the engine and shift the selector into all positions from P through 2, then shift into P and apply the parking brake.
12    Turn off the engine and check the fluid level. Add fluid to bring the level into the cross-hatched area on the dipstick.

## 27    Manual transaxle lubricant change (every 30,000 miles or 24 months)

1    Remove the filler and drain plugs (see Section 20) and drain the lubricant into a drain pan.
2    Reinstall the drain plug securely.
3    Add new lubricant until it begins to run out of the filler hole (see Section 20) and install the filler plug. See *Recommended lubricants and fluids* for the specified lubricant type.

## 28    Fuel filter replacement (every 30,000 miles or 24 months)

*Refer to illustrations 28.4a and 28.4b*
**Warning:** *Gasoline is extremely flammable, so take extra precautions when you work on any part of the fuel system. Don't smoke or allow open flames or bare light bulbs near the work area, and don't work in a garage where a natural gas-type appliance (such as a water heater or clothes dryer) with a pilot light is present. Since gasoline is carcinogenic, wear latex gloves when there's a possibility of being exposed to fuel, and, if you spill any fuel on your skin, rinse it off immediately with soap and water. Mop up any spills immediately and do not store fuel-soaked rags where they could ignite. The fuel system is under constant pressure, so, if any fuel lines are to be disconnected, the fuel pressure in the system must be relieved first (see Chapter 4 for more information). When you perform any kind of work on the fuel system, wear safety glasses and have a Class B type fire extinguisher on hand.*
1    *Disconnect the negative battery cable.* **Caution:** *The stereo in your vehicle is equipped with an anti-theft system. Make sure you have the correct activation code before disconnecting the battery.*
2    The fuel filter is located on the firewall in the engine compartment.
3    Relieve the fuel system pressure as described in Chapter 4.
4    Place shop towels around and under the filter. Remove the banjo bolt, unscrew the threaded fitting, remove the clamp bolt(s) and remove the filter from the engine compartment **(see illustrations)**.

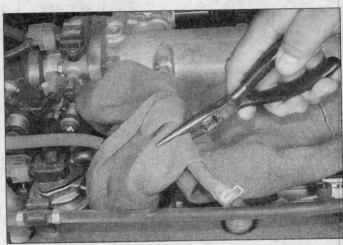

**29.2  Squeeze the PVC hose gently with a pair of pliers - use rag to protect the hose surface**

**Note:** *If available, use a flare-nut wrench when disconnecting the fuel line fitting at the filter.*
5    Installation is the reverse of removal. Use new sealing washers on either side of the banjo fitting and tighten the banjo bolt to the torque listed in this Chapter's Specifications. Tighten the threaded line fitting securely. Start the engine and check for leaks.

## 29    Positive Crankcase Ventilation (PCV) valve check and replacement (every 15,000 miles or 12 months)

*Refer to illustrations 29.2 and 29.4*
**Note:** *For a detailed description of the PCV system, refer to Chapter 6.*
1    The PCV valve is located in a breather hose that connects the crankcase and intake manifold.

### Check

2    With the engine idling at normal operating temperature, gently squeeze shut the PCV hose located at the top of the engine with a pair of pliers, using a rag to protect the surface of the hose **(see illustration)**.
3    If the PCV valve is operating properly, it will make a clicking sound when the hose is pinched shut. If it doesn't, replace the valve.

**29.4  The PCV valve is located in the valve cover - to remove, simply pull it out of the rubber grommet**

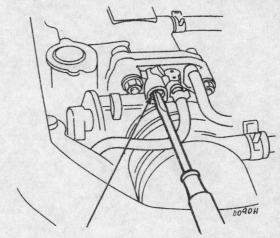

**30.8  Use a screwdriver to turn the adjusting screw until the idle speed is correct**

**31.1  Press the reset button (arrow) to reset the Maintenance Required Indicator**

## Replacement

4    The PCV valve is located in the intake manifold below the fuel injector rail **(see illustration)**. Detach the hose and remove the valve, noting its installed position and direction.

5    When purchasing a replacement PCV valve, make sure it's for your particular vehicle and engine size. Compare the old valve with a new one to make sure they're the same.

6    Installation is the reverse of removal.

## 30   Idle speed check and adjustment (60,000 miles or 72 months)

## Check

1    Engine idle speed is the speed at which the engine operates when no accelerator pedal pressure is applied, as when stopped at a traffic light. The speed is critical to the performance of the engine itself, as well as many subsystems.

2    Start the engine and run it at 3000 rpm until it warms up to normal operating temperature (the cooling fan comes on).

3    Stop the engine. Hook up a hand-held tachometer in accordance with the tool manufacturer's instructions.

4    Set the parking brake firmly and block the wheels to prevent the vehicle from rolling. On Canadian models equipped with Daytime Running Lights, the parking brake must be applied so the headlights are off during the procedure. Place the transaxle in Neutral (manual transaxle) or Park (automatic transaxle).

5    Disconnect the electrical connector from the Idle Air Control (IAC) valve (see Chapter 4).

6    Start the engine with the accelerator slightly depressed and stabilize the idle at 1000 rpm. Slowly release the accelerator until the idle drops to normal speed. Make sure all accessories are turned off and the transaxle is in Neutral (manual transaxle) or Park (automatic transaxle).

7    Note the idle speed on the tachometer and compare it to that listed on the VECI label or in this Chapter's Specifications. **Note:** *If the idle speed listed on the VECI label is different than that listed in this Chapter's Specifications, use the specification shown on the VECI label.*

## Adjustment

*Refer to illustration 30.8*

8    If the idle speed is too low or too high turn the screw to obtain the specified idle speed **(see illustration)**.

9    Turn the engine off and plug in the electrical connector to the IAC valve. On four-cylinder models, remove the 7.5 amp BACK UP fuse from the underhood fuse block for ten seconds. This will clear the ECM memory.

10   Turn on the engine, let it idle for one minute, recheck the idle speed and compare it to the speed listed on the VECI label or in this Chapter's Specifications.

11   Turn off the engine and disconnect the tachometer.

## 31   Maintenance Required Indicator resetting

*Refer to illustration 31.1*

1    The Maintenance Required Indicator will glow yellow every 7,500 miles, reminding you its time for scheduled maintenance. If you exceed 7,500 miles between service, it will glow red. After performing the required maintenance (see the maintenance schedule), reset the Maintenance Required Indicator by inserting the ignition key into the slot in the dash **(see illustration)**.

# Notes

# Chapter 2 Part A
# Four-cylinder engines

## Contents

## Specifications

### General

| | |
|---|---|
| Firing order | 1-3-4-2 |
| Cylinder numbers (front-to-rear) | 1-2-3-4 |
| Bore | 3.35 inches |
| Stroke | 3.74 inches |
| Displacement | 131.6 cubic inches (2.2 liters) |
| Intake/exhaust manifold warpage limit | 0.006 inch |

### Camshaft

| | |
|---|---|
| Endplay | |
| Standard | 0.002 to 0.006 inch |
| Maximum | 0.020 inch |
| Runout | 0.002 inch (maximum) |
| Journal oil clearance | |
| Standard | 0.002 to 0.0035 inch |
| Maximum | 0.006 inch |
| Camshaft lobe height | |
| F22B1 (VTEC) | |
| Intake | |
| primary | 1.4872 inches |
| mid | 1.5640 inches |
| secondary | 1.3575 inches |
| Exhaust | 1.5105 inches |
| F22B2 | |
| Intake | 1.5168 inches |
| Exhaust | 1.5267 inches |

*The blackened terminal shown on the distributor cap indicates the Number One spark plug wire position*

**Cylinder location and distributor rotation**

## Oil pump

| | |
|---|---|
| Inner-to-outer rotor tip clearance | |
|    Standard | 0.001 to 0.006 inch |
|    Service limit | 0.008 inch |
| Outer rotor-to-pump body clearance | |
|    Standard | 0.004 to 0.007 inch |
|    Service limit | 0.008 inch |
| Pump housing-to-rotor, axial clearance | |
|    Standard | 0.001 to 0.003 inch |
|    Service limit | 0.005 inch |

## Torque specifications

| | Ft-lbs (unless otherwise indicated) |
|---|---|
| Air intake plenum | 16 |
| Camshaft bearing cap bolts | |
|    6.0 x 1.0 mm | 108 in-lbs |
|    8.0 x 1.25 mm | 16 |
| Valve cover bolts/nuts | 86 in-lbs |
| Balance shafts tensioner bolt | 33 |
| Timing belt tensioner bolt | 33 |
| Camshaft sprocket bolt | 27 |
| Crankshaft pulley bolt | 181 |
| Cylinder head bolts | |
|    First step | 29 |
|    Second step | 51 |
|    Third step | 73 |
| Flywheel-to-crankshaft bolts | 76 |
| Driveplate-to-crankshaft bolts | 54 |
| Intake manifold bolts | 16 |
| Exhaust manifold nuts | 23 |
| Balance shaft (front) sprocket bolt | 22 |
| Balance shaft (rear) sprocket bolt | 18 |
| Oil pan-to-engine bolts | 120 in-lbs |
| Oil pump pick-up tube bolts | 108 in-lbs |
| Oil pump housing bolts | 108 in-lbs |
| Rear main oil seal housing bolts | 108 in-lbs |
| Timing belt cover bolts (upper and lower) | 108 in-lbs |
| Water pump bolts | See Chapter 3 |

## 1   General information

This Part of Chapter 2 is devoted to in-vehicle repair procedures for the 2.2L engine. All information concerning engine removal and installation and engine block and cylinder head overhaul can be found in Chapter 2, Part C.

There are two versions of the 2.2L engine in the models covered by this manual. The F22B2 is the base engine, and the F22B1 is virtually the same engine with the addition of the VTEC valve train (see Section 6).

The following repair procedures are based on the assumption that the engine is installed in the vehicle. If the engine has been removed from the vehicle and mounted on a stand, many of the steps outlined in this Part of Chapter 2 will not apply.

The Specifications included in this Part of Chapter 2 apply only to the procedures contained in this chapter. Chapter 2C contains the Specifications necessary for cylinder head and engine block rebuilding.

The Accord models covered in this manual are equipped with a 2.2L fuel-injected, four-cylinder engine with a single overhead camshaft that controls four valves per cylinder (total 16-valves). It is a compact and lightweight engine with an aluminum block and cylinder head. The engine is also equipped with two balance shafts that help smooth out vibration created by the opposing force of the pistons and crankshaft. The crankshaft is supported by the main bearing caps, which are tied into a unit by the main cap "bridge", with the number four bearing (the thrust bearing) assigned the additional task of controlling crankshaft endplay.

The pistons have two compression rings and one oil control ring. The semi-floating piston pins are press fitted into the small end of the connecting rod. The connecting rod big ends are also equipped with renewable insert-type plain bearings.

The engine is liquid-cooled, utilizing a centrifugal impeller-type pump, driven by a toothed belt, to circulate coolant around the cylinders and combustion chambers and through the intake manifold.

Lubrication is handled by a rotor-type oil pump mounted on the front of the engine under the timing belt cover. It's inner rotor is driven by two flats on the front of the crankshaft. The oil is filtered continuously by a cartridge-type filter mounted on the firewall side of the engine.

## 2   Repair operations possible with the engine in the vehicle

Clean the engine compartment and the exterior of the engine with some type of degreaser before any work is done. It will make the job easier and help keep dirt out of the internal areas of the engine.

Depending on the components involved, it may be helpful to remove the hood to improve access to the engine as repairs are performed (refer to Chapter 11 if necessary). Cover the fenders to prevent damage to the paint. Special pads are available, but an old bedspread or blanket will also work.

If vacuum, oil or coolant leaks develop, indicating a need for gasket or seal replacement, the repairs can generally be made with the engine in the vehicle. The intake and exhaust manifold gaskets, oil pan gasket, crankshaft oil seals and cylinder head gasket are all accessible with the engine in place.

Exterior engine components, such as the intake and exhaust manifolds, the oil pan, the water pump, the starter motor, the alternator,

**3.7 Mark the distributor housing directly beneath the number one spark plug wire terminal (double check the distributor cap to verify that the rotor points to the number 1 spark plug wire)**

the distributor and the fuel system components can be removed for repair with the engine in place.

Since the cylinder head can be removed without pulling the engine, camshaft and valve component servicing can also be accomplished with the engine in the vehicle. Replacement of the timing chain and sprockets is also possible with the engine in the vehicle.

In extreme cases caused by a lack of necessary equipment, repair or replacement of piston rings, pistons, connecting rods and rod bearings is possible with the engine in the vehicle. However, this practice is not recommended because of the cleaning and preparation work that must be done to the components involved.

## 3   Top Dead Center (TDC) for number one piston - locating

*Refer to illustrations 3.7 and 3.8*

**Note:** *The following procedure is based on the assumption that the spark plug wires and distributor are correctly installed. If you are trying to locate TDC to install the distributor correctly, piston position must be*

**3.8 Align the white mark on the crankshaft pulley with the notch in the pointer then check to see if the distributor rotor is pointing to the number 1 cylinder (if not, the camshaft is 180-degrees out of time [number 4 is at TDC] - the crankshaft will have to be rotated 360-degrees) - the second mark (arrow) is usually red and is for ignition timing**

determined by feeling for compression at the number one spark plug hole, then aligning the ignition timing marks as described in Step 8.

1   Top Dead Center (TDC) is the highest point in the cylinder that each piston reaches as it travels up-and-down when the crankshaft turns. Each piston reaches TDC on the compression stroke and again on the exhaust stroke, but TDC generally refers to piston position on the compression stroke.

2   Positioning the piston(s) at TDC is an essential part of many procedures such as camshaft and timing belt/sprocket removal and distributor removal.

3   Before beginning this procedure, be sure to place the transaxle in Neutral and apply the parking brake or block the rear wheels. Also, disable the ignition system by detaching the primary (low voltage) electrical connectors from the ignition coil. Remove the spark plugs (see Chapter 1).

4   In order to bring any piston to TDC, the crankshaft must be turned using one of the methods outlined below. When looking at the front of the engine, normal crankshaft rotation is counterclockwise.

   a)  *The preferred method is to turn the crankshaft with a socket and ratchet attached to the bolt threaded into the front of the crankshaft.*

   b)  *A remote starter switch, which may save some time, can also be used. Follow the instructions included with the switch. Once the piston is close to TDC, use a socket and ratchet as described in the previous paragraph.*

   c)  *If an assistant is available to turn the ignition switch to the Start position in short bursts, you can get the piston close to TDC without a remote starter switch. Make sure your assistant is out of the vehicle, away from the ignition switch, then use a socket and ratchet as described in Paragraph a) to complete the procedure.*

5   Note the position of the terminal for the number one spark plug wire on the distributor cap. If the terminal isn't marked, follow the plug wire from the number one cylinder spark plug to the cap.

6   Detach the cap from the distributor and set it aside (see Chapter 1 if necessary).

7   Mark the distributor cover directly under the rotor terminal **(see illustration)** for the number 1 cylinder.

8   Turn the crankshaft (see Paragraph 3 above) until the TDC mark (white mark) on the crankshaft pulley is aligned with the groove in the pointer **(see illustration).**

9   Look at the distributor rotor - it should be pointing directly at the mark you made on the distributor body (cover). If the rotor is pointing at the mark, go to Step 12. If it isn't, go to Step 10.

10   If the rotor is 180-degrees off, the number one piston is at TDC on the exhaust stroke.

11   To get the piston to TDC on the compression stroke, turn the crankshaft one complete turn (360-degrees) clockwise. The rotor should now be pointing at the mark on the distributor. When the rotor is pointing at the number one spark plug wire terminal in the distributor cap and the crankshaft pulley timing marks are aligned, the number one piston is at TDC on the compression stroke.

12   After the number one piston has been positioned at TDC on the compression stroke, TDC for any of the remaining pistons can be located by turning the crankshaft and following the firing order. Mark the remaining spark plug wire terminal locations on the distributor body just like you did for the number one terminal, then number the marks to correspond with the cylinder numbers. As you turn the crankshaft, the rotor will also turn. When it's pointing directly at one of the marks on the distributor, the piston for that particular cylinder is at TDC on the compression stroke.

## 4   Valve cover - removal and installation

*Refer to illustrations 4.4 and 4.7*

### Removal

1   Detach the cable from the negative battery terminal. **Caution:** *The radio in your vehicle is equipped with an anti-theft system. Make sure you have the correct activation code before disconnecting the battery.*

**4.4 Remove the vacuum hose from the valve cover**

**4.7 Remove the ground strap (arrow) at the timing belt end of the cover**

**5.3 Push down on the mid-rocker of cylinder number 1 to check the action of the VTEC rocker assembly - it should move independently of the primary and secondary intake rockers**

2    Pull the spark plug wires from their plugs (see Chapter 1). Be sure to mark each wire for correct installation.

3    Mark and detach any hoses or wires that will interfere with the removal of the valve cover.

4    Disconnect the vacuum hose from the valve cover **(see illustration)**.

5    Wipe off the valve cover thoroughly to prevent debris from falling onto the exposed cylinder head or camshaft/valve train assembly.

6    Remove the valve cover bolts and their sealing washers.

7    Remove the bolt holding the ground strap at the timing belt end of the cover **(see illustration)**.

8    Carefully lift off the valve cover and gasket. If the gasket is stuck to the cylinder head, tap it with a rubber mallet to break the seal. Do not pry between the cover and cylinder head or you'll damage the gasket mating surfaces.

## Installation

9    The one-piece valve cover gasket can be re-used if it isn't damaged. Peel the gasket carefully out of the groove in the cover and clean the mating surfaces of the cylinder head and the valve cover with a rag soaked in lacquer thinner or acetone.

10    Apply beads of RTV sealant to the corners where the cylinder head mates with the rocker arm assembly. Wait five minutes or so and let the RTV "set-up" (slightly harden) before installation.

11    Install a new rubber gasket into the valve cover. Install the molded rubber gasket onto the cover by pushing it into the slot that circles the valve cover perimeter. Apply RTV to the four corners where the covers goes over the front and rear camshaft caps. Install the valve cover, sealing grommets and nuts and tighten them to the torque listed in this Chapter's Specifications. **Note:** *Make sure the RTV sealant has slightly hardened before installing the valve cover. If the weather is damp and cold, the sealant will take some extra time to harden. The valve cover bolt sealing washers can be lubed with soapsuds for easy installation.*

12    On VTEC engines, check the condition of the spark plug sealing washers before installing the valve cover.

13    The remainder of installation is the reverse of removal.

## 5    Rocker arm assembly - removal, inspection and installation

## Removal

*Refer to illustrations 5.3 and 5.6*

1    Remove the valve cover (see Section 4).

2    Position the number one piston at Top Dead Center (see Section 3).

3    On VTEC engines, push on the mid-intake rocker arm for

**5.6 Leave the camshaft bearing cap bolts in place as you remove the rocker arm assembly**

cylinder number 1 to see that it moves independently of the primary and secondary intake rockers **(see illustration)**. Check the rockers for the other cylinders at their own TDC positions.

4    Return to TDC for number 1 piston and remove the timing belt (see Section 11).

5    Loosen the camshaft bearing cap bolts 1/4-turn at a time, in the correct order, until the spring pressure is relieved. **Note:** *Refer to illustration 5.12 and reverse the order shown to loosen the rocker arm assembly. Do not remove the bolts from the bearing caps.*

6    Lift the rocker arms and shaft assembly from the cylinder head **(see illustration)**.

## Inspection

*Refer to illustrations 5.7a, 5.7b, 5.8 and 5.9*

7    If you wish to disassemble and inspect the rocker arm assembly, (a good idea as long as you have them off), remove the retaining bolts and slip the rocker arms, springs and bearing caps off the shafts **(see illustrations)**. Mark the relationship of the shafts to the bearing caps and keep the parts in order so you can reassemble them in the same positions. **Note:** *On VTEC engines, keep the three intake rockers for each cylinder together by wrapping them with a heavy rubber band.*

8    Thoroughly clean the parts and inspect them for wear and damage. Check the rocker arm faces that contact the camshaft and the rocker arm tips **(see illustration)**. Check the surfaces of the shafts that the rocker arms ride on, as well as the bearing surfaces inside the rocker arms, for scoring and excessive wear. Replace any parts that

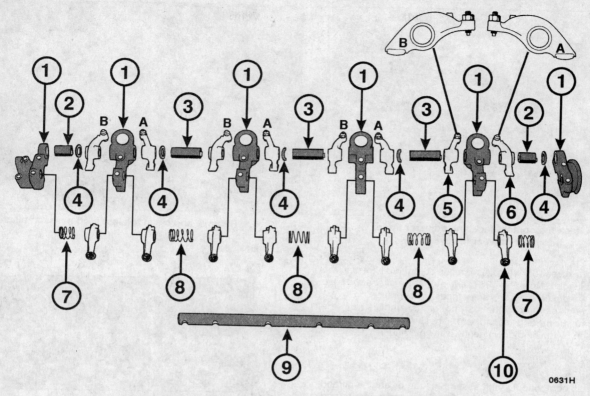

**5.7a An exploded view of the rocker arms and shafts (non-VTEC engine)**

| 1 | Camshaft holder | 5 | Intake rocker arm B | 8 | Spring A |
|---|---|---|---|---|---|
| 2 | Intake rocker shaft | 6 | Intake rocker arm A | 9 | Exhaust rocker shaft |
| 3 | Intake rocker shaft B | 7 | Spring B | 10 | Exhaust rocker arm |
| 4 | Wave washer | | | | |

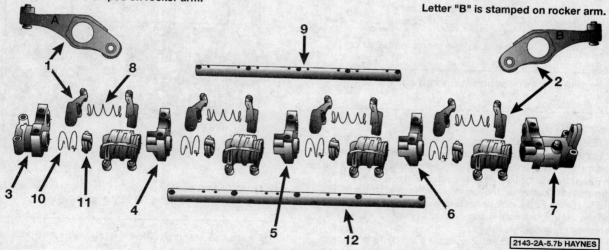

Letter "A" is stamped on rocker arm.

Letter "B" is stamped on rocker arm.

**5.7b Layout of rocker arm assembly - VTEC engines**

| 1 | Exhaust rocker arm A | 7 | No. 5 camshaft holder |
|---|---|---|---|
| 2 | Exhaust rocker arm B | 8 | Spring |
| 3 | No. 1 camshaft holder | 9 | Exhaust rocker shaft |
| 4 | No. 2 camshaft holder | 10 | Spring |
| 5 | No. 3 camshaft holder | 11 | Timing plate |
| 6 | No. 4 camshaft holder | 12 | Intake rocker shaft |

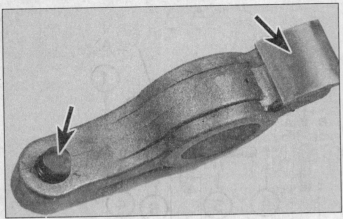

**5.8  Check the contact face and adjuster tip for damage or wear (arrows)**

**5.9  Remove and clean the lost motion assemblies**

are damaged or excessively worn. Also, make sure the oil holes in the shafts are not plugged. **Note:** *On VTEC engines, the rocker arms have roller tips, check them for wear and smoothness of operation.*

9    On VTEC engines remove the lost motion assemblies from the head **(see illustration)**, and clean them. Check for smoothness of plunger operation by pushing down gently with your finger.

## Installation

*Refer to illustrations 5.12a and 5.12b*

10    Lubricate all components with assembly lube or engine oil and reassemble the shafts. When installing the rocker arms, shafts and springs, note the markings and the difference between the left and right side parts.

11    Coat the cam lobes and journals with camshaft installation lubricant. Apply anaerobic-type sealant to the cylinder head contact surfaces of bearing caps 1 and 6 and install the rocker arm assembly.

12    Tighten the camshaft bearing cap bolts a little at a time, in the proper sequence **(see illustrations)** to the torque listed in this Chapter's Specifications.

13    The remainder of installation is the reverse of removal.

14    Check the valve clearances and adjust to Specifications (see Chapter 1).

15    Run the engine and check for oil leaks and proper operation.

## 6    VTEC engine system - description and component checks

*Refer to illustration 6.7*

1    The VTEC system stands for Honda's design for Variable Valve Timing and Lift Electronic Control. Engines equipped with this system are identified by the VTEC lettering cast into the valve cover, and the designation F22B1 on the radiator side of the block (see Chapter 1).

2    The differences between the base engines and their VTEC counterparts is strictly in the components and operation of the valve train. The engine short block, oiling and cooling systems are identical, as are all attached components.

3    The engine management computer has the ability to physically change which camshaft intake lobes are being used to operate the intake valves. The computer turns the system ON or OFF, depending on sensor input.

4    The following are used to determine VTEC operation:

   a)  *Engine speed (rpm)*
   b)  *Vehicle speed (mph)*
   c)  *Throttle position sensor (TPS)*
   d)  *Engine load measured by Manifold Absolute Pressure (MAP) sensor*
   e)  *Coolant temperature*

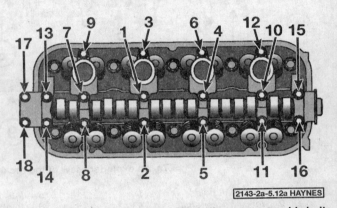

**5.12a  TIGHTENING sequence for the rocker arm assembly bolts - F22B2 engine**

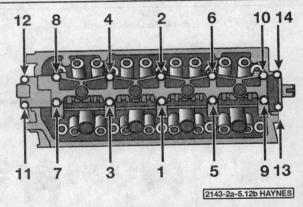

**5.12b  TIGHTENING sequence for the rocker arm assembly bolts - F22B1 (VTEC) engine**

5    The camshaft has three different intake valve lobe profiles (lift and duration specifications).

6    At low speeds, the secondary intake valve operates on its own camshaft lobe, which has very low lift and duration (compared to the primary valve). The opening is intended to be just enough to keep atomized fuel from building up, "puddling", at the valve head. This limited valve operation is designed to provide good low end torque and responsiveness, by inducing swirl in the combustion chamber from the primary intake valve, which operates with a normal profile.

7    When performance is needed, the primary and secondary rocker arms are locked together through the use of an electrically controlled

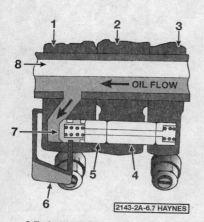

1 Primary rocker arm
2 Mid rocker arm
3 Secondary rocker arm
4 Synchronizing piston B
5 Synchronizing piston A
6 Timing plate
7 Timing piston
8 Intake rocker shaft

6.7 At high engine speeds, oil flow through the rocker shaft pushes on the synchronizing piston A to lock all three intake rocker arms together

6.18 To remove the oil control orifice for cleaning, thread a machine screw into the top and pull up on the orifice (arrow)

hydraulic system (see illustration). Hydraulically operated synchronizing pistons lock all three rocker arms together. When activated, both intake valves open to the higher lift and duration of the middle rocker arm, which has its own camshaft lobe. **Note:** *The secondary rocker arm no longer contact its own camshaft lobe, until the system is disengaged.*

## Component checks
**Note:** *Some checks and inspections of the VTEC components requires removal of the rocker arm assembly (see Section 5).*

### Lost motion assembly
8    The four lost motion assemblies sit in pockets in the cylinder head.
9    Remove the individual lost motion assemblies from the head.
10   Test each lost motion assembly by pushing the plunger with your finger. A light pressure should move the plunger slightly, and firmer pressure will move it further. If the assembly doesn't move smoothly, replace it.

### Timing plate, collar and return spring
*Refer to illustration 6.11*
11   The timing plate and return spring (see illustration) are assembled to the camshaft holder on the intake rocker shaft (four required). **Note:** *As shown in the illustration, the collar used with the return spring and timing plate has a shoulder to hold the spring.*
12   Inspect the spring, making sure the spring is connected to the camshaft holder and timing plate.

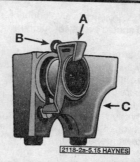

6.11 Timing plate synchronizing assembly

a    Timing plate
b    Return spring
c    Cam holder

6.20 The VTEC lock-up solenoid (arrow) and pressure switch are located at the right rear of the cylinder head

13   Look for signs of scoring, broken parts or overheating (discoloration, bluish color).
14   Replace parts as necessary.
15   Reassemble as shown (see illustration 5.7b).

### Synchronizing assembly
*Refer to illustration 6.18*
16   Once the rocker arm assemblies have been removed and disassembled (see Section 5), separate the rocker arms and synchronizing components (see illustrations 5.7b and 6.7).

**VTEC components:**
a)   Primary rocker arm
b)   Secondary rocker arm
c)   Mid rocker arm
d)   Synchronizing piston A
e)   Synchronizing piston B
f)   Timing piston

17   Inspect the timing spring, making sure it's not broken or collapsed. Replace it if necessary.
18   Inspect all other parts (rocker arms and synchronizing pistons) for wear, galling, scoring or signs of overheating (bluish in color). Replace any parts necessary. Remove the oil control orifice from the number 3 camshaft holder (see illustration), clean and reinstall it.
19   Reassembly is the reverse of removal. **Note:** *Reassemble and hold together (rubber bands work well) each cylinder's components before trying to assemble on the rocker shaft (see Section 5).*

### VTEC lock-up control solenoid valve
*Refer to illustrations 6.20, 6.21, 2.22, 2.25 and 2.26*
**Note 1:** *A problem in the VTEC solenoid valve circuit will set a diagnostic* **trouble code (DTC) 21**, *and light the Check Engine light on the dash. Refer to Chapter 6 for accessing trouble codes.*
**Note 2:** *A problem in the VTEC pressure switch circuit will set a diagnostic* **trouble code (DTC) 22**, *and light the Check Engine light on the dash.*
20   The lock-up VTEC solenoid valve (see illustration) is located on the right rear of the cylinder head (firewall side of head).

21   Check for continuity between VTEC solenoid valve connector and body ground **(see illustration)**. There should be 14-to-30 ohms; if not, replace the VTEC solenoid valve.

22   With the ignition off, pull the harness plug from the pressure switch and check for continuity between the two oil pressure switch terminals on the VTEC solenoid **(see illustration)**. There should be continuity. If not, replace the oil pressure switch.

23   Turn the ignition on and check for voltage between oil pressure switch harness blue/black wire and ground. There should be approximately 12 volts. If not, inspect for an open or short to ground in the blue/black wire between the connector and the ECM.

24   With the ignition still in the ON position, measure the voltage across the blue/black and brown/black terminals of the oil pressure switch harness. There should be approximately 12 volts. If not, repair the open in the brown/black wire.

25   Remove the solenoid and push the plunger to check for free movement **(see illustration)**. Use a new O-ring when reinstalling the solenoid.

26   Remove the whole solenoid assembly from the cylinder head and check the filter/O-ring for clogging **(see illustration)**. Clean and reinstall with a new O-ring.

---

## 7   Valve springs, retainers and seals - replacement

*Refer to illustrations 7.5, 7.8 and 7.16*

**Note:** *Broken valve springs and defective valve stem seals can be replaced without removing the cylinder heads. Two special tools and a compressed air source are normally required to perform this operation, so read through this Section carefully and rent or buy the tools before beginning the job.*

1   Remove the valve cover (see Section 4).

2   Remove the spark plug from the cylinder which has the defective component. If all of the valve stem seals are being replaced, all of the spark plugs should be removed.

3   Turn the crankshaft until the piston in the affected cylinder is at Top Dead Center on the compression stroke (refer to Section 3 for instructions). If you're replacing all of the valve stem seals, begin with cylinder number one and work on the valves for one cylinder at a time. Move from cylinder-to-cylinder following the firing order sequence (see this Chapter's Specifications).

4   Remove the rocker arms and shafts (see Section 5).

5   Thread an adapter into the spark plug hole and connect an air hose from a compressed air source to it **(see illustration)**. Most auto parts stores can supply the air hose adapter. **Note:** *Because of the length of the spark plug tubes, it will be necessary to use a spark plug adapter with a length of hose attached (as used on many cylinder compression gauges) utilizing a quick-disconnect fitting to hook to your air source.*

6   Apply compressed air to the cylinder. **Warning:** *The piston may*

**6.21  There should be continuity between the solenoid valve connector and body ground**

**6.22  Check for continuity between the two terminals of the VTEC oil pressure switch**

*be forced down by the compressed air, causing the crankshaft to turn suddenly. If the wrench used when positioning the number one piston at TDC is still attached to the bolt in the crankshaft nose, it could cause damage or injury when the crankshaft moves.*

7   The valves should be held in place by the air pressure. If the valve faces or seats are in poor condition, leaks may prevent air pressure from retaining the valves. If the valves cannot hold air, the cylinder

**6.25  With your finger, check for free movement of the solenoid plunger (arrow)**

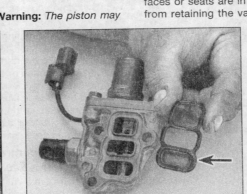

**6.26  Whenever the cylinder head is torn down or problems are suspected in the VTEC system, check the O-ring and filter (arrow) behind the VTEC solenoid**

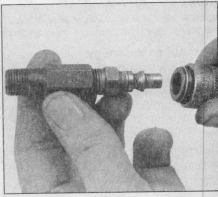

**7.5  This is what the air hose adapter that threads into the spark plug hole looks like - they're commonly available from auto parts stores**

**7.8 Use a valve spring compressor to compress the springs, then remove the keepers from the valve stem with a magnet or small needle-nose pliers**

**7.16 Apply a small dab of grease to each keeper as shown here before installation - it'll hold them in place on the valve stem as the spring is released**

**8.9 Looking up at the bottom of the intake manifold, remove the bolts on the intake-to-block brace (upper arrow), and the two bolts (lower arrows) holding the wiring harness to the manifold**

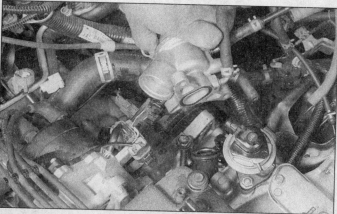

**8.10 Remove the bolts from the thermostat assembly and pull it away from the intake manifold**

head should be removed for a valve job at a machine shop.

8    Stuff shop rags into the cylinder head holes around the valves to prevent parts and tools from falling into the engine, then use a valve spring compressor to compress the spring **(see illustration)**. Remove the keepers with small needle-nose pliers or a magnet.

9    Remove the spring retainer, shield and valve spring, then remove the umbrella type guide seal.

10    Wrap a rubber band or tape around the top of the valve stem so the valve won't fall into the combustion chamber, then release the air pressure.

11    Inspect the valve stem for damage. Rotate the valve in the guide and check the end for eccentric movement, which would indicate that the valve is bent.

12    Move the valve up-and-down in the guide and make sure it doesn't bind. If the valve stem binds, either the valve is bent or the guide is damaged. In either case, the head will have to be removed for repair.

13    Reapply air pressure to the cylinder to retain the valve in the closed position, then remove the tape or rubber band from the valve stem.

14    Lubricate the valve stem with engine oil and install a new guide seal.

15    Install the spring(s) in position over the valve, with the more closely wound spring coils toward the head.

16    Install the valve spring retainer. Compress the valve spring and carefully position the keepers in the groove. Apply a small dab of grease to the inside of each keeper to hold it in place **(see illustration)**.

17    Remove the pressure from the spring tool and make sure the keepers are seated.

18    Disconnect the air hose and remove the adapter from the spark plug hole.

19    Refer to Section 5 and install the rocker arm assembly.

20    Refer to Section 4 and install the valve cover.

21    Install the spark plug(s) and hook up the wire(s).

22    Start and run the engine, then check for oil leaks and unusual sounds coming from the valve cover area.

## 8    Intake manifold - removal and installation

**Warning:** *Gasoline is extremely flammable, so take extra precautions when you work on any part of the fuel system. Don't smoke or allow open flames or bare light bulbs near the work area, and don't work in a garage where a natural gas-type appliance (such as a water heater or clothes dryer) with a pilot light is present. Since gasoline is carcinogenic, wear latex gloves when there's a possibility of being exposed to fuel, and, if you spill any fuel on your skin, rinse it off immediately with soap and water. Mop up any spills immediately and do not store fuel-soaked rags where they could ignite. The fuel system is under constant pressure, so, if any fuel lines are to be disconnected, the fuel pressure in the system must be relieved first (see Chapter 4 for more information). When you perform any kind of work on the fuel system, wear safety glasses and have a Class B type fire extinguisher on hand.*

### Removal

*Refer to illustrations 8.9, 8.10 and 8.11*

1    Detach the cable from the negative battery terminal. **Caution:** *The radio in your vehicle is equipped with an anti-theft system. Make sure you have the correct activation code before disconnecting the battery.*

2    Drain the cooling system (see Chapter 1).

3    Remove the intake air ducts from the air cleaner assembly (see Chapter 4).

4    Clearly label and detach any vacuum lines and electrical connectors which will interfere with removal of the manifold.

5    Detach the accelerator cable from the throttle lever (see Chapter 4).

6    Remove the air intake plenum (see Chapter 4).

7    Remove the coolant hoses from the intake manifold.

8    Relieve the fuel pressure and disconnect the fuel feed and return lines at the fuel rail (see Chapter 4).

9    Working under the engine compartment, remove the brace that supports the intake manifold and the bolts securing the wiring harness under the manifold **(see illustration)**.

10    Remove the thermostat housing assembly from the intake manifold **(see illustration)**.

11    Remove the intake manifold nuts and remove the manifold from the engine **(see illustration)**.

## Installation

*Refer to illustration 8.14*

12    Clean the manifold components with solvent and dry them with compressed air, if available. **Warning:** *Wear eye protection!*

13    Check the mating surfaces of the manifold for flatness with a precision straightedge and feeler gauges. Refer to this Chapter's Specifications for the warpage limit.

14    Unbolt the EGR passage cover and clean out any deposits with solvent and a small wire brush **(see illustration)**.

15    Inspect the manifold for cracks and distortion. If the manifold is cracked or warped, replace it or see if it can be resurfaced at an automotive machine shop.

16    Check carefully for any stripped or broken intake manifold bolts/studs. Replace any defective bolts with new parts.

17    Using a scraper, remove all traces of old gasket material from the cylinder head and manifold mating surfaces. Clean the surfaces with lacquer thinner or acetone.

18    Install the intake manifold with a new gasket and tighten the bolts finger tight. Starting at the center and working out in both directions, tighten the bolts in a criss-cross pattern until the torque listed in this Chapter's Specifications is reached.

19    The remainder of the installation procedure is the reverse of removal. Refer to Chapter 1 and refill the cooling system.

---

## 9    Exhaust manifold - removal and installation

*Refer to illustrations 9.2, 9.3 and 9.4*

## Removal

1    Disconnect the negative battery cable from the battery. **Caution:** *The radio in your vehicle is equipped with an anti-theft system. Make sure you have the correct activation code before disconnecting the battery.*

2    Raise the front of the vehicle and support it securely on jackstands. Detach the exhaust pipe **(see illustration)** from the exhaust manifold. Apply penetrating oil to the fastener threads if they are difficult to remove.

3    Remove the heat shield from the exhaust manifold **(see illustration)**. Be sure to soak the bolts and nuts with penetrating oil before attempting to remove them from the manifold.

4    Remove the exhaust manifold nuts **(see illustration)** and detach the exhaust manifold from the cylinder head. **Note:** *Be sure to remove the bolts from the lower brace located near the flange of the exhaust manifold.*

## Installation

5    Discard the old gasket and use a scraper to clean the gasket mating surfaces on the manifold and head, then clean the surfaces

**8.11  Remove the nuts from the intake manifold, pull it to the rear to clear the studs and remove it from the engine**

with a rag soaked in lacquer thinner or acetone.

6    Place the exhaust manifold in position on the cylinder head and install the nuts. Starting at the center, tighten the nuts in a criss-cross pattern until the torque listed in this Chapter's Specifications is reached.

7    The remainder of installation is the reverse of removal.

8    Start the engine and check for exhaust leaks between the manifold and the cylinder head and between the manifold and the exhaust pipe.

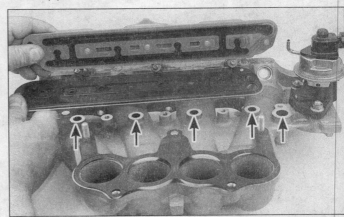

**8.14  Unbolt the EGR cover from the intake manifold and clean out the EGR passages (arrows)**

**9.2  Remove the flange nuts and lower the exhaust pipe. Be sure to spray the nuts with penetrating lubricant before attempting to remove them**

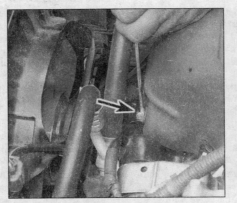

**9.3  The two upper heat shield mounting bolts are obvious, but there is one (arrow) at the bottom as well**

**9.4  Remove the exhaust manifold mounting nuts - don't forget the lower brace (arrow)**

## 10 Balance shafts belt/sprockets - removal, inspection and installation

**Note:** *When a loose balance shaft drivebelt is suspected as the cause of excessive noise, the tension must be adjusted. It is possible to do this procedure without removing the timing belt cover (see Step 19). The tensioner simultaneously exerts tension upon the balance shafts belt as well as the timing belt.*

### Removal

*Refer to illustrations 10.5, 10.8, 10.9, 10.10a, 10.10b and 10.11*

1    Position the number one cylinder at top dead center on the compression stroke (see Section 3). Disconnect the cable from the negative terminal of the battery. **Caution:** *The radio in your vehicle is equipped with an anti-theft system. Make sure you have the correct activation code before disconnecting the battery.*

2    Remove the power steering belt and disconnect the power steering pump from the mounting bracket (see Chapter 10). Position the power steering pump off to one side.

3    Remove the alternator and brackets from the timing belt cover (see Chapter 5).

4    Raise the vehicle and support it securely on jackstands. Working under the vehicle, remove the splash pan (see Chapter 11) and the left side wheel well cover.

5    Remove the large bolt at the front of the crankshaft and slide the pulley off. **Note:** *To keep the crankshaft from turning while you're removing this bolt, wedge a large screwdriver into the flywheel/driveplate ring gear* **(see illustration)**. *If the pulley won't slide off, pullers are available at auto parts stores that will make removal*

**10.5 With a screwdriver wedged in the flywheel, use a breaker bar to unbolt the crank pulley**

easy.

6    Support the engine with a floor jack and a block of wood. Remove the left side engine mount and bracket (see Section 19).

7    Remove the oil dipstick and the tube from the engine block.

8    Remove the bolts attaching the timing belt covers (upper and lower) to the engine block **(see illustration)**. Draw a simple diagram showing the location and length of each of the bolts so they can be

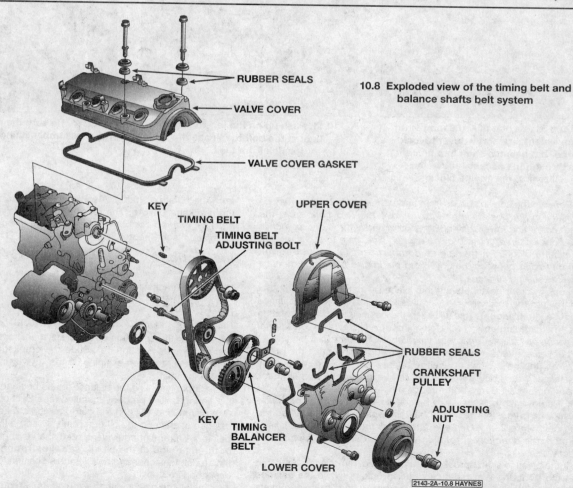

**10.8 Exploded view of the timing belt and balance shafts belt system**

RUBBER SEALS

VALVE COVER

VALVE COVER GASKET

KEY

TIMING BELT

TIMING BELT ADJUSTING BOLT

UPPER COVER

RUBBER SEALS

CRANKSHAFT PULLEY

ADJUSTING NUT

KEY

TIMING BALANCER BELT

LOWER COVER

2143-2A-10.8 HAYNES

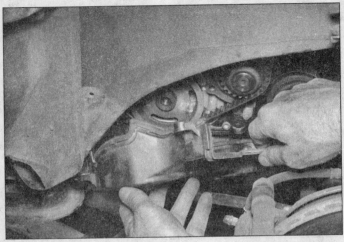

**10.9  It may be necessary to unbolt one of the engine mounts and lower the engine in order to make clearance for removing the lower timing belt cover**

**10.10a  Remove the access bolt from the rear side of the engine**

**10.10b  Use a bolt (6 X 100 mm) or an equivalent size screwdriver to lock the rear balance shaft into place through the access hole at the rear of the engine block**

**10.11  Push up on the tensioner and tighten the bolt to release the tension from the belts**

**10.16a  Be sure the rear balance shaft gear assembly timing marks are aligned**

9      Remove the splash shields from under the vehicle **Note:** *It may be necessary in some installations to remove the two bolts from the engine mount and lower the engine approximately three or four inches with a floor jack in order to provide enough clearance to pull the lower timing belt cover from the engine compartment* **(see illustration)**. **Caution:** *Prying between the cover and the engine block can damage the gasket sealing surfaces.*

10     Lock the rear balance shaft into place by installing one bolt (6 x 100 mm) into the block in the designated access hole for the balance shaft **(see illustrations)**. This will keep the balance shaft from rotating while the adjustments are being made. **Note:** *For additional information on balance shaft removal refer to Chapter 2C.*

11     Loosen the tensioner bolt **(see illustration)** and push the pulley away from the balance shafts belt to release any tension. When only the balancer belt is being worked on, the tensioner can be held back by inserting a 6 x 1.0 mm bolt through a hole in the tensioner into the block. Remove the balance shaft belt. **Note 1:** *The tensioner simultaneously exerts tension upon the balance shafts belt as well as the timing belt.* **Note 2:** *If you intend to reinstall the same balance shafts belt, mark the direction of rotation on the belt so it can be installed correctly.*

12     If the balance shaft sprockets are damaged, remove the bolts that retain the front and rear balance shaft sprockets (while the balance shafts are held with 6 x10mm bolts in the block) and lift the sprockets

from the balance shafts). Also, remove the crankshaft sprocket from the crankshaft. **Note:** *The rear balance shaft has a set of gears that must be marked correctly before they are removed to ensure proper installation* (see Chapter 2C).

## Inspection

13     Check the balance shafts belt, tensioner and sprockets for wear, damage or cracks. Replace parts as necessary.

## Installation

*Refer to illustrations 10.16a, 10.16b and 10.18*

14     Check the condition of the crankshaft front seal and replace it if necessary (see Section 12). Slide the crankshaft sprocket onto the front of the crankshaft by lining up the keyway in the sprocket with the key on the shaft.

15     Before installing the balance shafts belt and sprockets, make sure the timing belt is properly installed (see Section 11) and the Number One piston is at TDC on the compression stroke (see Section 3). Both balance shafts and the oil pump must also be in place. Make sure the bolt (6 x 100mm) or equivalent sized shaft is in place in the access hole at the rear side of the block **(see illustration 10.10b)**. Retract the timing belt tensioner and hold it in this position following the procedure described in Step 11.

16     Install the balance shafts sprockets, if removed (see Chapter 2C).

**10.16b  Timing marks for the balance shafts (note the front balance shaft has two sets of timing marks; one on the side of the oil pump cover and sprocket and one on the top of the balance shaft and pump cover)**

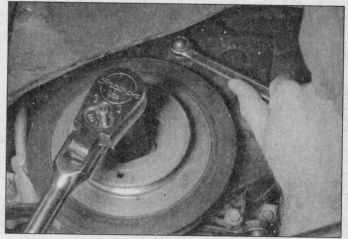

**10.18  Working under the engine compartment in the wheel well area, it is possible to adjust the belt tension with the timing belt covers assembled**

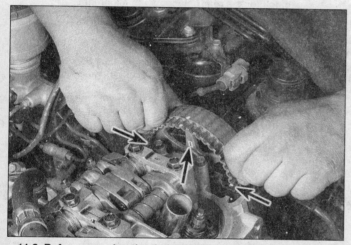

**11.2  Before removing the timing belt, make a mark on the belt and the cam sprocket at the top - Line up the two timing dots on the sprocket (outer arrows) with the head and keep the cast arrow on the sprocket (center arrow here) pointing straight up**

Double-check the position of the marks on the rear balance shaft gear case and sprocket **(see illustration)**. Install the balance shafts belt **(see illustration)** onto the sprockets.

17    Recheck the position of the match marks, then install the balance shaft sprocket bolts and tighten them to the torque listed in this Chapter's Specifications. **Note:** *Be sure to double-check the timing marks on the rear balance shaft sprocket by referring to Chapter 2C.*

18    Adjust the belt slack as follows: Make sure the tensioner adjuster nut is loose and rotate the crankshaft counterclockwise three teeth on the camshaft sprocket to create tension on the timing belt and the balance shafts belt and tighten the tensioner nut to the torque listed in this Chapter's Specifications. **Note 1:** *The tensioner applies tension to the timing belt and the balance shafts belt at the same time. Check to make sure the belt is properly tensioned by pressing the belt with the tip of your finger near the camshaft sprocket. The belt should be tensioned on both sides of the sprocket.* **Note 2:** *It is possible to adjust the tension of the timing belt and balance shafts belt with the timing covers in place* **(see illustration)**. *It is a good idea to make the tensioning adjustments with the cover OFF and then check all the timing marks before reassembling the covers.*

19    Install the timing belt covers onto the engine block and cylinder

head **(see illustration 10.8)**. Tighten the bolts to the torque listed in this Chapter's Specifications. Make sure the rubber gaskets do not pop out of the gasket rails inside the edge of the timing belt covers.

20    When reinstalling the crankshaft pulley, lubricate the threads and underside of the crankshaft pulley bolt's head. Install the bolt and tighten it to the torque listed in this Chapter's Specifications.

## 11  Timing belt and sprockets - removal, inspection and installation

*Refer to illustrations 11.2, 11.6a and 11.6b*

**Note:** *When a loose timing belt is suspected as the cause of excessive noise, the tension must be adjusted. It is possible to do this procedure without removing the timing belt cover (see Section 10, Step 18). The tensioner simultaneously exerts tension on the balance shafts belt as well as the timing belt.*

### Removal

1    With the engine at TDC for number 1 cylinder, remove the timing belt covers and the balance shafts belt for access to the timing belt (see Section 10).

2    With the balance shafts belt removed (see Section 10) and the tension relieved from the tensioner, the timing belt can be slipped off the sprockets. **Note:** *If you intend to reinstall the same timing belt, mark the direction of rotation on the belt so it can be installed correctly* **(see illustration)**. The camshaft sprocket can be removed by placing a screwdriver or large punch between the cylinder head and the sprocket casting hole and carefully removing the bolt with a breaker bar and socket.

### Inspection

3    Inspect the sprocket teeth for wear and damage. Check the timing belt for any cracks or excessive oil coating. Also check the camshaft for excessive endplay (see Chapter 2C). Check the timing belt tensioner for smooth operation. Replace any worn parts with new ones. **Note:** *Because of the work involved in getting at the water pump on the Accord engine, most dealerships routinely replace the water pump when they do a timing belt (see Chapter 3).*

### Installation

4    If the camshaft sprocket was removed, install it and tighten the bolt to the torque listed in this Chapter's Specifications.

5    Check to make sure the number one piston is still at Top Dead Center (TDC) (see Section 3).

**11.6a  Looking from the wheel well area, observe the alignment marks on the crankshaft sprocket and the oil pump cover (arrows)**

6    Align all the timing marks on the engine block with the marks on the crankshaft and camshaft sprockets **(see illustrations)**. Make sure the bolt (6 x 100mm) or equivalent is in place in the access hole at the rear side of the block **(see illustration 10.10b)**. Install the timing belt onto the sprockets.

7    Since the tensioner applies tension to the balance shafts belt as well as the timing belt, it is necessary to install the balance shafts belt before tensioning the timing belt (see Section 10, Steps 15 through 20).

8    After the timing belt and balance shafts belt have been tensioned, it is a good idea to rotate the crankshaft 90-degrees to both sides of the TDC mark and then back to TDC just to make sure the timing belt returns to all the original timing marks (use the crankshaft pulley bolt for this test).

9    The remainder of installation is the reverse of removal. When reinstalling the crankshaft pulley, lubricate the threads and underside of the crankshaft pulley bolt's head. **Caution:** *Do not use an impact wrench on the crank pulley bolt.*

## 12  Crankshaft front oil seal - replacement

*Refer to illustration 12.4*

1    Remove the drivebelts (see Chapter 1).

2    Remove the crankshaft pulley (see Section 10).

3    Remove the balance shafts belt and the timing belt (see Sections 10 and 11).

4    On 1996 and later models, disconnect the CKP/TDC electrical connector from the main harness. Remove the CKP/TDC sensor's four mounting bolts and remove the sensor assembly from the oil pump housing.

**12.5  Use two screwdrivers and carefully pry the sprocket off the crankshaft**

**11.6b  Alignment marks for the timing belt and the balance shafts belt (arrows). Be sure the word UP is on the upper section of the camshaft sprocket and a bolt (6 X 100mm) or equivalent is placed through the access hole at the rear of the engine block for the rear balance shaft alignment**

5    Remove the crankshaft sprocket from the crankshaft **(see illustration)**, then remove the concave washer.

6    Carefully pry the seal out of the oil pump housing with a seal removal tool or a screwdriver. Don't scratch the seal bore or damage the crankshaft in the process (if the crankshaft is damaged, the new seal will end up leaking).

7    Clean the bore in the oil pump housing and coat the outer edge of the new seal with engine oil or multi-purpose grease. Using a socket with an outside diameter slightly smaller than the outside diameter of the seal, carefully drive the seal into place squarely with a hammer. If a socket is not available, a short section of a large diameter pipe will work. Check the seal after installation to be sure the spring did not pop out.

8    Install the concave washer and the crankshaft sprocket.

9    Lubricate the threads and underside of the head of the crankshaft bolt, then reinstall the crankshaft pulley. The remainder of installation is the reverse of removal.

10    Run the engine and check for leaks.

## 13  Camshaft - removal, inspection and installation

### Removal

*Refer to illustration 13.7*

1    Remove the valve cover (see Section 4).

2    Set the engine at TDC for cylinder number one (see Section 3).

3    Remove the distributor (see Chapter 5).

4    Remove the balance shafts belt and the timing belt (see Sections 10 and 11).

5    If it is necessary to separate the sprocket from the camshaft, remove the camshaft sprocket bolt. **Note:** *Prevent the camshaft from turning by inserting a screwdriver through one of the holes in the sprocket.*

6    Remove the rocker arm assembly (see Section 5). If the camshaft bearing caps must be removed from the assembly and they don't have numbers on them, number them before removal. Be sure to put the marks on the same ends of all the caps to prevent incorrect orientation of the caps during installation.

7    Lift out the camshaft **(see illustration)**, wipe it off with a clean shop towel and set it aside.

### Inspection

*Refer to illustrations 13.8, 13.10 and 13.11*

8    To check camshaft endplay:

a)  Install the camshaft and secure it with the caps.

13.7 Lift the camshaft from the cylinder head

13.8 To check camshaft endplay, mount a dial indicator like this, with the gauge plunger touching the nose of the camshaft

b) *Mount a dial indicator on the head* (see illustration).
c) *Using a large screwdriver as a lever at the opposite end, move the camshaft forward-and-backward and note the dial indicator reading.*
d) *Compare the reading with the endplay listed in this Chapter's Specifications.*
e) *If the indicated reading is higher, either the camshaft or the head is worn. Replace parts as necessary.*

9   To check camshaft runout requires a pair of precision-ground V-blocks and a dial indicator. Only a machine shop would generally have such equipment, so if in doubt about the straightness of a camshaft, have it checked at your local machine shop and compare the runout to this Chapter's Specifications. Replace the camshaft if it is out-of-specifications.
10   Check the camshaft bearing journals and caps for scoring and signs of wear. If they are worn, replace the cylinder head with a new or rebuilt unit. Measure the journals on the camshaft with a micrometer (see illustration). Check the oil clearance of each camshaft journal with plastigage, comparing your readings with this Chapter's Specifications. If the oil clearance of any of the journals is out-of-specification, replace the camshaft and check the oil clearance again. If it's still out-of-specification replace the cylinder head. **Note:** *For instructions on the use of plastigage, see Chapter 2, Part B, Sections 23 or 25.*
11   Check the cam lobes for wear:

a) *Check the toe and ramp areas of each cam lobe for score marks and uneven wear. Also check for flaking and pitting.*

b) *If there's wear on the toe or the ramp, replace the camshaft, but first try to find the cause of the wear. Look for abrasive substances in the oil and inspect the oil pump and oil passages for blockage. Lobe wear is usually caused by inadequate lubrication or dirty oil.*
c) *Using a micrometer, measure the cam lobe height* (see illustration). *If the lobe wear is greater than listed in this Chapter's Specifications, replace the camshaft.*

12   Inspect the rocker arms for wear, galling and pitting of the contact surfaces.
13   If any of the conditions described above are noted, the cylinder head is probably getting insufficient lubrication or dirty oil, so make sure you track down the cause of this problem (low oil level, low oil pump capacity, clogged oil passage, etc.) before installing a new head, camshaft or rocker arms.

## Installation

*Refer to illustration 13.15*

14   Thoroughly clean the camshaft, the bearing surfaces in the head and caps and the rocker arms. Remove all sludge and dirt. Wipe off all components with a clean, lint-free cloth.
15   Lubricate the camshaft bearing surfaces in the head and the bearing journals and lobes on the camshaft with camshaft installation lube (see illustration). Carefully lower the camshaft into position with the "**UP** mark" stamped on the camshaft sprocket pointing UP. **Caution:** *Failure to adequately lubricate the camshaft and related components can cause serious damage to bearing and friction*

13.10 Check the diameter of each camshaft bearing journal, in several locations, to pinpoint excessive wear and out-of-round conditions

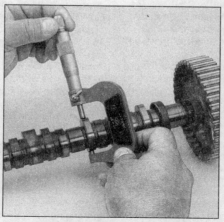

13.11 Measure the camshaft lobe heights with a micrometer

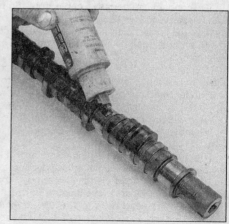

13.15 Be sure to apply camshaft lube to the cam lobes and bearing journals before installing the camshaft

14.8 Remove the hose clamp (arrow) and hose connected to the head under the distributor area

14.10a If the cylinder head sticks to the block, pry between the power steering pump bracket and the engine block

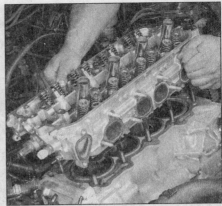

14.10b Lift the cylinder head off - this can be done either with or without the intake and exhaust manifolds attached

surfaces during the first few seconds after engine start-up, when the oil pressure is low or nonexistent.

16   Install the rocker arm assembly (see Section 5 or 6). **Note:** On VTEC engines, clean the oil control orifice **(see illustration 6.18)**.

17   Rotate the camshaft as necessary to align the two marks on the camshaft sprocket parallel with the cylinder head. Install the timing belt, balance shafts belt and related components (see Sections 10 and 11). **Note:** If the valve timing was disturbed, align the sprockets and install the belt as described in Section 11.

18   Remove the spark plugs and rotate the crankshaft by hand to make sure the valve timing is correct. After two revolutions, the timing marks on the sprockets should still be aligned. If they're not, remove the timing belt and set all the timing marks again (see Section 10). **Note:** If you feel resistance while rotating the crankshaft, stop immediately and check the valve timing by referring to Section 11.

19   The remainder of installation is the reverse of removal.

## 14  Cylinder head - removal and installation

*Refer to illustrations 14.8, 14.10a, 14.10b, 14.11 and 14.17*
**Caution:** *Allow the engine to cool completely before beginning this procedure.*

### Removal

1   Position the number one piston at Top Dead Center (see Section 3).
2   Disconnect the negative cable from the battery. **Caution:** *The radio in your vehicle is equipped with an anti-theft system. Make sure you have the correct activation code before disconnecting the battery.*
3   Drain the cooling system and remove the spark plugs (see Chapter 1).
4   Remove the intake manifold brace and exhaust manifold flange bolts (see Sections 8 and 9). It isn't necessary to remove the manifolds for cylinder head removal, but their absence will certainly make the head easier to lift off the block.
5   Remove the valve cover (see Section 4).
6   Remove the distributor (see Chapter 5), including the cap and wires.
7   Remove the timing belt (see Section 11), rocker arm assembly (see Section 5) and the camshaft (see Section 13).
8   Squeeze the hose clamp and remove the water hose located under the distributor area **(see illustration)**.
9   Loosen the head bolts in 1/4-turn increments until they can be removed by hand. Work in a pattern that's the reverse of the tightening sequence **(see illustration 14.17)** to avoid warping the head. Note where each bolt goes so it can be returned to the same location on installation.
10   Lift the head off the engine **(see illustrations)**. If resistance is felt,

don't pry between the head and block gasket mating surfaces - damage to the mating surfaces will result. Instead, pry between the power steering pump bracket and the engine block. Set the head on blocks of wood to prevent damage to the gasket sealing surfaces.

11   Cylinder head disassembly and inspection procedures are covered in detail in Chapter 2, Part C. It's a good idea to check the head for warpage, even if you're just replacing the gasket **(see illustration)**.

### Installation

12   The mating surfaces of the cylinder head and block must be perfectly clean when the head is installed.

13   Use a gasket scraper to remove all traces of carbon and old gasket material, then clean the mating surfaces with lacquer thinner or acetone. If there's oil on the mating surfaces when the head is installed, the gasket may not seal correctly and leaks may develop. When working on the block, stuff the cylinders with clean shop rags to keep out debris. Use a vacuum cleaner to remove material that falls into the cylinders. Since the head and block are made of aluminum, aggressive scraping can cause damage. Be extra careful not to nick or gouge the mating surfaces with the scraper.

14   Check the block and head mating surfaces for nicks, deep scratches and other damage. If damage is slight, it can be removed with a file; if it's excessive, machining may be the only alternative.

15   Use a tap of the correct size to chase the threads in the head bolt holes in the block. Mount each head bolt in a vise and run a die down the threads to remove corrosion and restore the threads. Dirt, corrosion, sealant and damaged threads will affect torque readings. On F22B2 engines (non-VTEC), remove the oil control orifice from the block, clean it and reinstall before replacing the cylinder head.

16   Place a new gasket on the block. Check to see if there are any markings (such as "TOP") on the gasket that indicate how it is to be installed. Those identification marks must face UP. Also, apply sealant to the edges of the timing belt cover where it mates with the engine block. Set the cylinder head in position.

17   Lubricate the threads and the seats of the cylinder head bolts, then install them. They must be tightened in a specific sequence **(see illustration)**, in three stages and to the torque listed in this Chapter's Specifications.

18   Attach the camshaft sprocket to the camshaft (see Section 13).

19   Reinstall the remaining parts in the reverse order of removal.

20   Be sure to refill the cooling system and check all fluid levels.

21   Rotate the crankshaft clockwise slowly by hand through two complete revolutions. **Caution:** *If you feel any resistance while turning the engine over, stop and re-check the camshaft timing. The valves may be hitting the pistons.*

22   Start the engine and check the ignition timing (see Chapter 1).

23   Run the engine until normal operating temperature is reached. Check for leaks and proper operation.

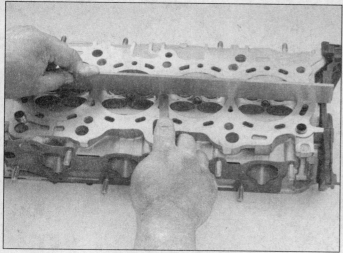

**14.11 Check for cylinder head warpage with a precision straightedge and a feeler gauge - check lengthwise and diagonally across the head**

**14.17 Cylinder head bolt TIGHTENING sequence**

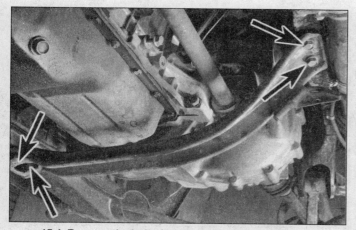

**15.4 Remove the bolts (arrows) from the center beam and lower it from the chassis**

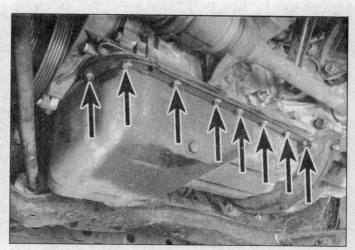

**15.5 Remove the oil pan bolts (arrows) from the oil pan**

## 15 Oil pan - removal and installation

*Refer to illustrations 15.4 and 15.5*

1    Warm up the engine, then drain the oil and replace the oil filter (see Chapter 1). Allow the engine to cool off before proceeding.

2    Detach the cable from the negative battery terminal. **Caution:** *The radio in your vehicle is equipped with an anti-theft system. Make sure you have the correct activation code before disconnecting the battery.*

3    Raise the vehicle and support it securely on jackstands.

4    Remove the center beam from under the engine **(see illustration)**.

5    Remove the bolts securing the oil pan to the engine block **(see illustration)**.

6    Tap on the pan with a soft-face hammer to break the gasket seal, then detach the oil pan from the engine. Don't pry between the block and oil pan mating surfaces.

7    Using a gasket scraper, remove all traces of old gasket and/or sealant from the engine block and oil pan. Remove the seals from each end of the engine block or oil pan. Clean the mating surfaces with lacquer thinner or acetone. Make sure the threaded bolt holes in the block are clean.

8    Clean the oil pan with solvent and dry it thoroughly. Check the gasket flanges for distortion, particularly around the bolt holes. If necessary, place the pan on a block of wood and use a hammer to flatten and restore the gasket surfaces.

9    Apply a small bead of RTV sealant to the mating points of the oil pump-to-block and the rear main seal retainer plate-to-block. Apply RTV sealant to the rear of the one-piece pan gasket at the corners of the semi-circle at the rear.

10   Carefully place the oil pan and gasket in position.

11   Install the two front, two rear and two center nuts finger tight. Install the rest of the bolts and tighten them all in small increments to the torque listed in this Chapter's Specifications. Start with the fasteners closest to the center of the pan and work out in a spiral pattern. Don't overtighten them or leakage may occur.

12   Add oil (see Chapter 1), run the engine and check for oil leaks.

## 16 Oil pump - removal, inspection and installation

### Removal

*Refer to illustrations 16.3, 16.4a, 16.4b and 16.5*

1    Remove the balance shafts belt and the timing belt (see Sections 10 and 11). Also, remove the front balance shaft sprocket and the rear balance shaft gear case assembly (see Chapter 2C). On 1996 and later models, also disconnect the CKP/TDC electrical connector from the main harness. Remove the CKP/TDC sensor's four mounting bolts and remove the sensor assembly from the oil pump housing.

**16.3  Remove the oil pick-up tube bolts (arrows) from the oil pump and main bearing cap bridge**

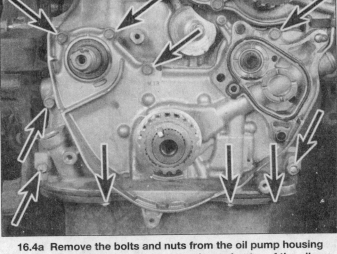

**16.4a  Remove the bolts and nuts from the oil pump housing (arrows). Don't forget the nuts along the perimeter of the oil pan**

**16.4b  Lift the oil pump housing from the engine block**

**16.5  Remove the oil pump cover screws (arrows)**

2    Remove the oil pan (see Section 15).

3    Remove the oil pickup tube and screen from the pump housing and the main bearing cap bridge **(see illustration)**.

4    Remove the bolts **(see illustration)** from the oil pump housing and lift the assembly from the engine **(see illustration)**.

5    Remove the screws and disassemble the oil pump **(see illustration)**. You may need to use an impact screwdriver to loosen the pump cover screws without stripping the heads out.

## Inspection

*Refer to illustrations 16.6a, 16.6b and 16.6c*

6    Check the inner-to-outer rotor tip clearance, the rotor-to-pump body clearance and the pump housing-to-rotor axial clearance **(see illustrations)**. Compare your measurements to the figures listed in this Chapter's Specifications. Replace the pump if any of the measurements are outside of the specified limits.

7    Remove the pressure relief valve plug and extract the spring and pressure relief valve plunger from the pump housing. Check the spring for distortion and the relief valve plunger for scoring. Replace parts as necessary.

8    Install the pump rotors. Pack the spaces between the rotors with petroleum jelly (this will prime the pump).

9    Install the pump cover screws and tighten them securely, using

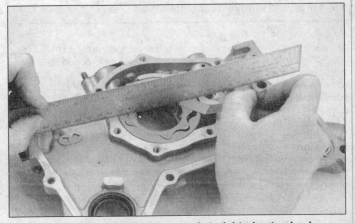

**16.6a  Using a feeler gauge and straightedge to check the axial clearance**

thread-locking compound on the screws. Install the oil pressure relief valve and spring assembly. Use a new sealing washer on the plug and tighten the plug securely.

16.6b  Using a feeler gauge to check the tooth tip clearance between the inner and outer rotors

16.6c  Using a feeler gauge to check the outer rotor-to-pump body clearance

17.3  Remove the flywheel/driveplate bolts (arrows) from the crankshaft

## Installation

10   Apply a thin coat of RTV sealant to the pump housing-to-block sealing surface. Making sure the dowel pin is in place, install the pump housing using new O-rings. Apply RTV sealant to the bolt threads and tighten the bolts to the torque listed in this Chapter's Specifications. **Note:** *Install the oil pump within five minutes of applying the RTV sealant, and make sure the flats on the oil pump rotor are aligned with the flats on the crankshaft as you install it.*
11   Install the rear balance shaft sprocket-and-gear case assembly and the balance shafts belt and timing belt (see Sections 10 and 11).
12   On 1996 and later models, install the CKP/TDC sensor assembly and the four mounting bolts onto the oil pump housing. Tighten the bolts to the torque listed in this Chapter's Specifications. Connect the CKP/TDC electrical connector to the main harness.
13   Install the oil pick-up tube and screen, using a new gasket. Tighten the bolts to the torque listed in this Chapter's Specifications.
14   Install the oil pan (see Section 15).
15   The remainder of installation is the reverse of removal. Add the specified type and quantity of oil and coolant (see Chapter 1), run the engine and check for leaks.

## 17   Flywheel/driveplate - removal and installation

### Removal

*Refer to illustration 17.3*
1   Raise the vehicle and support it securely on jackstands, then refer to Chapter 7 and remove the transaxle.

2   Remove the pressure plate and clutch disc (see Chapter 8) (manual transaxle-equipped models). Now is a good time to check/replace the clutch components and pilot bearing.
3   Remove the bolts that secure the flywheel/driveplate to the crankshaft **(see illustration)**. If the crankshaft turns, remove the starter (see Chapter 5) and wedge a screwdriver in the ring gear teeth (manual transaxle models), or insert a long punch through one of the holes in the driveplate and allow it to rest against a projection on the engine block (automatic transaxle models).
4   Remove the flywheel/driveplate from the crankshaft. Since the flywheel is fairly heavy, be sure to support it while removing the last bolt. **Caution:** *The teeth on the flywheel/driveplate may be sharp; wear gloves or handle the flywheel with rags while removing it.*
5   Clean the flywheel with brake cleaner or lacquer thinner to remove grease and oil. Inspect the surface for cracks, rivet grooves, burned areas and score marks. Light scoring can be removed with emery cloth. Check for cracked and broken ring gear teeth. Lay the flywheel on a flat surface and use a straightedge to check for warpage.
6   Clean and inspect the mating surfaces of the flywheel/driveplate and the crankshaft. If the rear main oil seal is leaking, replace it before reinstalling the flywheel/driveplate (see Section 18).

### Installation

7   Position the flywheel/driveplate against the crankshaft. Note that some engines have an alignment dowel or staggered bolt holes to ensure correct installation. Before installing the bolts, apply thread-locking compound to the threads.
8   Prevent the flywheel/driveplate from turning by using one of the methods described in Step 3. Using a diagonal-crossing pattern, tighten the bolts to the torque listed in this Chapter's Specifications.
9   The remainder of installation is the reverse of the removal procedure.

## 18   Rear main oil seal - replacement

*Refer to illustrations 18.4a and 18.4b*
1   The transaxle must be removed from the vehicle for this procedure (see Chapter 7).
2   Remove the flywheel/driveplate (see Section 17).
3   Before removing the seal, it is very important that the clearance between the seal and the outside edge of the retainer is checked. Use a small ruler or caliper and record the distance, which should be between 0.020 to 0.030-inch (approximately 1/64 to 1/32-inch). The new seal must not be driven in past this measurement (refer to Chapter 2C for more details).

**18.4a  Carefully pry the oil seal out with a removal tool or a screwdriver - don't nick or scratch the crankshaft or the new seal will be damaged and leaks will develop**

**18.4b  Because the seal lip is stiff, it won't slide over the end of the crankshaft easily - if you lubricate the journal and the seal lip with multi-purpose grease and carefully work the seal over the journal with a smooth, blunt object, it should go on without damage**

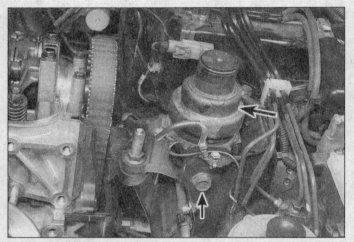

**19.7  The side engine mount (upper arrow) is just in front of the timing belt - the lower arrow indicates the through-bolt**

**19.8a  Front engine mount - large arrow indicates location of through-bolt, smaller arrows indicate bracket-to-block bolts (upper three) and bracket to chassis bolts (lower two)**

4    The seal can be replaced without removing the oil pan or seal retainer. Use a screwdriver and a rag to carefully pry the seal out of the housing **(see illustration)**. Use the rag to be sure no nicks are made in the crankshaft seal surface. Apply a film of clean oil to the crankshaft seal journal and the lip of the new seal and carefully tap the seal into place **(see illustration)**. The lip is stiff so carefully work it onto the seal journal of the crankshaft with a smooth object like the end of a socket extension. Tap the seal into the retainer with a seal driver. If a seal driver isn't available, a large socket or piece of pipe, with an outside diameter slightly smaller than that of the seal, can be used. Don't rush it or you may damage the seal. **Note:** *Removal of the oil seal retainer and replacement of the seal are covered in Chapter 2, Part C.*
5    The remaining steps are the reverse of removal.
6    Run the engine and check for oil leaks.

## 19   Engine mounts - check and replacement

*Refer to illustrations 19.7, 19.8a and 19.8b*

### Check

1    During the check, the engine must be raised slightly to remove the weight from the mounts.
2    Raise the vehicle and support it securely on jackstands, then position a jack under the engine oil pan. Place a large block of wood between the jack head and the oil pan, then carefully raise the engine just enough to take the weight off the mounts. **Warning:** *DO NOT place any part of your body under the engine when it's supported only by a jack!*
3    Check the mounts to see if the rubber is cracked, hardened or separated from the metal plates. Sometimes the rubber will split right down the center.
4    Check for relative movement between the mount plates and the engine or frame (use a large screwdriver or prybar to attempt to move the mounts). If movement is noted, lower the engine and tighten the mount fasteners.
5    Rubber preservative should be applied to the mounts to slow deterioration.
6    Disconnect the negative battery cable from the battery, then set the parking brake, block the rear wheels, raise the front of the vehicle and support it securely on jackstands (if not already done). **Caution:** *The stereo in your vehicle is equipped with an anti-theft system. Make sure you have the correct activation code before disconnecting the battery.*

19.8b The rear engine mount (shown here with intake manifold removed) is of the Engine Mount Control System type on automatic transaxle models - which has a vacuum line connected to a solenoid (arrow) on the firewall

19.25 Disconnect the connector (arrow) at the solenoid and check for batter voltage at the black/yellow wire

## Replacement

7   The side mount is attached to the engine near the timing belt **(see illustration)**. The transaxle mount is sandwiched between the center fore-and-aft crossmember and the engine below the bellhousing area (see Chapter 7).

8   The front and rear mounts, which bear the majority of the engine/transaxle weight, are bolted to the respective crossmembers. They are located low between the engine and firewall and between the engine and radiator **(see illustrations)**.

9   Automatic transaxle models also have an upper transaxle mount.

10   To ensure maximum bushing life and prevent excessive noise and vibration, the vehicle should be level and the engine weight should be on the mounts during the final tightening stage. **Note:** *Use thread locking compound on the nuts/bolts.* Ensure that the bushings are not twisted or offset. If you intend to replace more than one mount, or when you are installing the engine, tighten the mounts in the following order:

   a) *Side mount - do not tighten bolt and nut on engine side yet.*
   b) *Transmission mount - do not tighten the nuts on the transmission side yet.*
   c) *Rear mount - bracket-to-block bolts first, then the through-bolt, then the mount-to-chassis bolts.*
   d) *Tighten the side mount bolt/nut.*
   e) *Tighten the nuts on transmission mount.*

11   To remove the mounts one at a time, support the engine with a floor jack under the oil pan. Place a block of wood between the jack head and the oil pan to protect it from damage. **Warning:** *DO NOT place any part of your body under the engine when it's supported only by a jack!*

### Transaxle (passenger-side) mount

12   Remove the nuts/bolts (see Chapter 7) and slip the mount out of the vehicle.

13   Install the mount and tighten the fasteners securely.

### Front mount

14   Loosen the through-bolt, raise the engine slightly and remove the through-bolt **(see illustration 19.8a).**

15   Raise the engine more, unbolt the mount from the chassis and lift it from the vehicle.

16   Install the mount on the crossmember, and lower the engine until the through-bolt can be installed. Be sure all fasteners are tightened securely.

### Side (driver's side) mount

17   The upper mount carries little weight and seldom fails in service.

18   Whenever the engine is removed, the mounts should be inspected and replaced as necessary. To change the mount, remove the through-bolt **(see illustration 19.7)** and pull the mount out of its bracket.

19   Installation is the reverse of removal. Tighten the bolts securely.

### Rear mount (conventional)

20   Unless the intake manifold is removed, access to this mount is tight and only from the bottom. Loosen the through-bolt and raise the engine enough to take the weight off the rear mount.

21   Remove the four bolts (three bolts on F22B2 engines) holding the mount to the chassis, remove the through-bolt, and raise the engine enough to pull out the mount. Installation is the reverse of removal.

### Rear mount (Engine Mount Control System)

#### Description

22   All automatic transaxle models have a special rear engine mount that is computer-controlled to reduce idle speed vibrations from the engine. The interior of the liquid-filled mount has two chambers. When the engine is idling, the computer (ECM) signals a firewall-mounted engine mount control solenoid valve, which allows manifold vacuum to go to the rear mount. There a diaphragm actuator pulls a rod that changes the flow of liquid between the two chambers, to cancel vibrations at idle speeds. At engine speeds over 1000 rpm, the vacuum is shut off and the motor mount changes to its normal mode.

#### Check

*Refer to illustrations 19.25, 19.28 and 19.31*

23   If abnormal vibration is noticed at idle, check the vacuum hoses to the engine mount control solenoid for signs of damage or leakage.

24   With the car idling warm (less than 800 rpm), have an assistant put the car in gear with their foot on the brake and the emergency brake on, while you connect and disconnect the connector on the solenoid valve. There should be a noticeable change in smoothness.

25   Put the transmission in PARK or NEUTRAL, disconnect the connector and test the Black/Yellow wire for battery voltage **(see illustration)**. If there is no voltage, check the circuit from the connector to the number 4 fuse in the under-dash fuse panel (see Chapter 12).

26   Raise the engine rpm over 1000, and there should **not** be battery voltage at the Black/Yellow wire. If there is, look for a short in the wire to the ECM.

27   Measure between the two wires of the connector at idle speed. Battery voltage should be present, if not, check the circuit between the connector and the ECM.

28   Disconnect the vacuum hose from the diaphragm/actuator on the

**19.28  Apply 9 inches of vacuum to the diaphragm/actuator - it should hold vacuum for at least 20 seconds**

**19.31  Use a small mirror (arrow) to check the movement of the actuator rod when vacuum is applied to the diaphragm**

mount and apply 9 inches of vacuum with a hand pump **(see illustration)**. The vacuum should hold for 20 seconds or more. If not, replace the vacuum hose to the rear engine mount or the engine mount itself.

29    With the engine still running, release and reapply vacuum. The engine should change in smoothness.

30    Pull the lower vacuum hose from the solenoid and test for manifold vacuum with a gauge. If vacuum isn't present, check for a bad hose. If vacuum is present, but the engine failed to change in smoothness in Step 28, replace the solenoid.

31    With the engine OFF, connect a vacuum pump to the actuator on the rear motor mount **(see illustration)**. With nine inches of vacuum applied, the actuator rod should arc 80 degrees. If not, replace the actuator. **Note:** *The movement of the actuator is difficult to see when the intake manifold is in place. Even with the intake removed, it will be helpful to use a small, hand-held mirror to see the actuator movement.*

# Chapter 2 Part B
# V6 engine

## Contents

## Specifications

### General

Cylinder numbers (timing belt end-to-transaxle end)
Rear (firewall) side........................................................................ 1-2-3
Front (radiator) side ..................................................................... 4-5-6
Firing order ................................................................................... 1-4-2-5-3-6

### Camshaft and rocker arms

Camshaft bearing oil clearance
    Standard......................................................................... 0.0018 to 0.0032 inch
    Service limit .................................................................... 0.004 inch
Camshaft lobe height
    Intake ............................................................................ 1.5537 inches
    Exhaust.......................................................................... 1.5515 inches
Camshaft endplay
    Standard......................................................................... 0.002 to 0.006 inch
    Service limit .................................................................... 0.020 inch
Camshaft runout limit (total indicator reading) ............................ 0.0006 inch
Rocker arm-to-shaft oil clearance service limit ........................... 0.003 inch

2143-2b-specs HAYNES

**Cylinder locations and distributor rotor rotation**

## Oil pump clearances

| | |
|---|---|
| Outer rotor to body | 0.004 to 0.008 inch |
| Outer rotor to inner rotor | 0.002 to 0.008 inch |
| Housing-to-rotor clearance | 0.001 to 0.005 inch |

## Torque specifications

| | Ft-lbs |
|---|---|
| Camshaft bearing cap bolts | |
| 6mm | 104 in-lbs |
| 8mm | 20 |
| Camshaft sprocket bolts | 23 |
| Crankshaft pulley bolt | 181 |
| Cylinder head bolts | |
| Step one | 29 |
| Step two | 56 |
| Valve cover bolts | |
| Top | 132 in-lbs |
| Side | 104 in-lbs |
| Driveplate bolts | 54 |
| EGR chamber cover bolts | 104 in-lbs |
| Exhaust manifold nuts | 22 |
| Exhaust heat shield bolts | 192 in-lbs |
| Intake manifold bolts/nuts | 192 in-lbs |
| Oil pan bolts/nuts | 120 in-lbs |
| Oil pan drain plug | 33 |
| Oil pick-up screen mounting bolts | 104 in-lbs |
| Oil pump mounting bolts | |
| 6mm bolts | 104 in-lbs |
| 8mm bolts | 192 in-lbs |
| Rocker arm guide plate bolts | 104 in-lbs |
| Rocker arm shaft sealing plug | 33 |
| Timing belt tensioner bolt | 31 |
| Timing belt cover bolts | 104 in-lbs |
| Rear main oil seal retainer bolts | 104 in-lbs |

## 1   General information

This Part of Chapter 2 is devoted to in-vehicle repair procedures for the V6 engine. All information concerning engine removal and installation and engine block and cylinder head overhaul can be found in Part C of this Chapter.

The following repair procedures are based on the assumption that the engine is installed in the vehicle. If the engine has been removed from the vehicle and mounted on a stand, many of the steps outlined in this Part of Chapter 2 will not apply.

The Specifications included in this Part of Chapter 2 apply only to the procedures contained in this Part. Part C of Chapter 2 contains the Specifications necessary for cylinder head and engine block rebuilding.

## 2   Repair operations possible with the engine in the vehicle

Many major repair operations can be accomplished without removing the engine from the vehicle.

Clean the engine compartment and the exterior of the engine with some type of degreaser before any work is done. It will make the job easier and help keep dirt out of the internal areas of the engine.

Depending on the components involved, it may be helpful to remove the hood to improve access to the engine as repairs are performed (refer to Chapter 11 if necessary). Cover the fenders to prevent damage to the paint. Special pads are available, but an old bedspread or blanket will also work.

If vacuum, exhaust, oil or coolant leaks develop, indicating a need for gasket or seal replacement, the repairs can generally be made with the engine in the vehicle. The intake and exhaust manifold gaskets, oil pan gasket, crankshaft oil seals and cylinder head gaskets are all accessible with the engine in place.

Exterior engine components, such as the intake and exhaust manifolds, the oil pan, the oil pump, the water pump (see Chapter 3), the starter motor, the alternator, the distributor (see Chapter 5) and the fuel system components (see Chapter 4) can be removed for repair with the engine in place.

Since the cylinder heads can be removed without pulling the engine, valve component servicing can also be accomplished with the engine in the vehicle. Replacement of the camshafts, timing belt and sprockets is also possible with the engine in the vehicle.

In extreme cases caused by a lack of necessary equipment, repair or replacement of piston rings, pistons, connecting rods and rod bearings is possible with the engine in the vehicle. However, this practice is not recommended because of the cleaning and preparation work that must be done to the components involved.

## 3   Top Dead Center (TDC) for number one piston - locating

*Refer to illustrations 3.6 and 3.8*
**Note:** *The following procedure is based on the assumption that the distributor is correctly installed. If you are trying to locate TDC to install the distributor correctly, piston position must be determined by feeling for compression at the number one spark plug hole, then aligning the ignition timing marks as described in Step 8.*

1    Top Dead Center (TDC) is the highest point in the cylinder that each piston reaches as it travels up-and-down when the crankshaft turns. Each piston reaches TDC on the compression stroke and again on the exhaust stroke, but TDC generally refers to piston position on the compression stroke.

2    Positioning the piston(s) at TDC is an essential part of several procedures such as camshaft and timing belt/sprocket removal and distributor removal.

**3.6 Mark the distributor below the number one terminal (arrow)**

**3.8 Align the white TDC mark (top arrow) with the pointer - the red mark (lower arrow here) is for setting ignition timing only**

**4.4 Remove the retaining bolts (arrows) - front top valve cover shown, rear cover similar**

3    Before beginning this procedure, be sure to place the transaxle in Neutral and apply the parking brake or block the rear wheels. Also, disable the ignition system by detaching the coil wire from its terminal on the distributor cap and grounding it on the block with a jumper wire. Remove the spark plugs (see Chapter 1).

4    In order to bring any piston to TDC, the crankshaft must be turned using one of the methods outlined below. When looking at the timing belt end of the engine, normal crankshaft rotation is counter-clockwise.

  *a) The preferred method is to remove the lower splash shield on the driver's side and turn the crankshaft with a socket and ratchet attached to the bolt threaded into the front of the crankshaft.*

  *b) A remote starter switch, which may save some time, can also be used. Follow the instructions included with the switch. Once the piston is close to TDC, use a socket and ratchet as described in the previous paragraph.*

  *c) If an assistant is available to turn the ignition switch to the Start position in short bursts, you can get the piston close to TDC without a remote starter switch. Make sure your assistant is out of the vehicle, away from the ignition switch, then use a socket and ratchet as described in Paragraph a) to complete the procedure.*

5    Note the position of the terminal for the number one spark plug wire on the distributor cap. If the plug wire isn't marked, follow the plug wire from the number one cylinder spark plug to the cap.

6    Use a felt-tip pen or chalk to make a mark on the distributor body directly under the terminal **(see illustration)**.

7    Detach the cap from the distributor and set it aside (see Chapter 1 if necessary).

8    Turn the crankshaft (see Step 4) until the TDC mark in the crankshaft pulley is aligned with the forked pointer on the timing belt cover **(see illustration)**. **Note:** *There are two marks on the pulley, the white mark is for TDC, the red mark is only for setting ignition timing with a timing light.*

9    Look at the distributor rotor - it should be pointing directly at the mark you made on the distributor body.

10    If the rotor is 180-degrees off, the number one piston is at TDC on the exhaust stroke.

11    To get the piston to TDC on the compression stroke if the rotor is 180-degrees off, turn the crankshaft one complete turn (360-degrees) clockwise. The rotor should now be pointing at the mark on the distributor. When the rotor is pointing at the number one spark plug wire terminal in the distributor cap and the ignition timing marks are aligned, the number one piston is at TDC on the compression stroke.

12    After the number one piston has been positioned at TDC on the compression stroke, TDC for any of the remaining pistons can be located by turning the crankshaft and following the firing order. Mark the remaining spark plug wire terminal locations on the distributor body just like you did for the number one terminal, then number the

marks to correspond with the cylinder numbers. As you turn the crankshaft, the rotor will also turn. The crankshaft must be turned 120-degrees to move from one cylinder to the next one in the firing order. When it's pointing directly at one of the marks on the distributor, the piston for that particular cylinder is at TDC on the compression stroke.

## 4    Valve covers - removal and installation

*Refer to illustrations 4.4 and 4.6*

### Top covers

1    Disconnect the negative cable from the battery. **Caution:** *The radio in your vehicle is equipped with an anti-theft system. Make sure you have the correct activation code before disconnecting the battery.*

2    Remove the spark plug connectors, wires and brackets from the spark plugs and set them aside. Unplug the oil temperature sensor located on top of the rear cover, at the timing belt end.

3    Detach the breather hose from the cover fitting.

4    Remove the retaining bolts **(see illustration)**, then detach the valve cover. If the cover is stuck to the head, bump the end with a block of wood and a hammer to jar it loose. **Caution:** *Don't pry at the cover-to-head joint or damage to the sealing surfaces may occur, leading to oil leaks after the cover is reinstalled.*

5    Remove the old gasket and seal washers and clean the mating surfaces of the cylinder head and cover. Remove the PCV valve from the front valve cover to clean and inspect it (see Chapter 1) and replace the seals.

6    Position a new gasket in the groove **(see illustration)** and install new seal washers on the bolts.

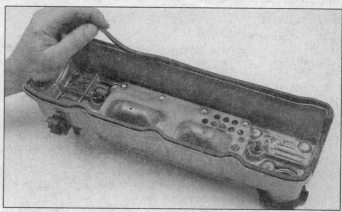

**4.6 Position a new gasket in the groove**

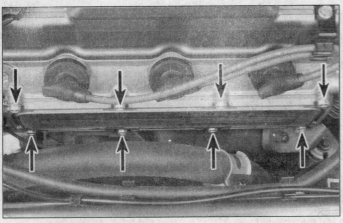

**4.10  Remove the side cover bolts (arrows)**

**5.4  Remove the four Allen bolts for the center cover plate first, then the four bolts holding the intake manifold cover (arrows)**

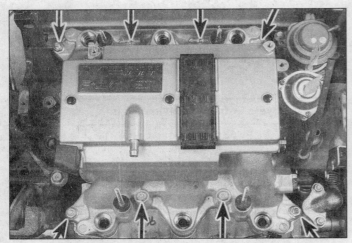

**5.10a  Remove the mounting nuts/bolts (arrows)**

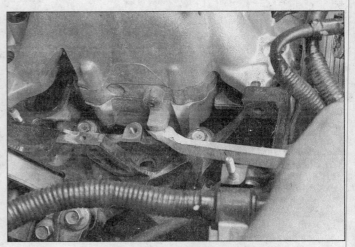

**5.10b  Pry against external tabs such as this**

7    Apply a small amount of RTV sealant at the four corners of the gaskets, where the flat area meets the round openings at each of the covers.

8    Within 5 minutes of applying the sealant, install the cover and tighten the bolts to the torque listed in this Chapter's Specifications in three equal steps. The sealing washers, and the areas of the covers they sit on, should be lubed with soapsuds before installation.

9    Reinstall the remaining parts, run the engine and check for oil leaks. **Note:** *Wait 20 minutes after installation for the sealant to cure before adding oil to the engine.*

### Side covers

*Refer to illustration 4.10*

10    Remove the bolts around the perimeter of the cover **(see illustration)**. On the front cover, detach and set aside the ground cable. On both the front and rear covers, detach any wiring harness brackets.

11    Detach the cover from the engine. If the cover is stuck to the head, bump the end with a block of wood and a hammer to jar it loose. **Caution:** *Don't pry at the cover-to-head joint or damage to the sealing surfaces may occur, leading to oil leaks after the cover is reinstalled.*

12    Remove the old O-ring gasket and clean the mating surfaces of the cylinder head and cover.

13    Position a new O-ring gasket in the groove.

14    Install the cover and tighten the bolts to the torque listed in this Chapter's Specifications in two equal steps.

15    Reinstall the remaining parts, run the engine and check for oil leaks.

## 5    Intake manifold - removal and installation

*Refer to illustrations 5.4, 5.10a, 5.10b, 5.12 and 5.13*

1    Relieve the fuel pressure (see Chapter 4) and then disconnect the negative cable from the battery. **Caution:** *The radio in your vehicle is equipped with an anti-theft system. Make sure you have the correct activation code before disconnecting the battery.*

2    Drain the coolant into a clean container (see Chapter 1).

3    Remove the intake air duct (see Chapter 4).

4    Remove the intake manifold cover **(see illustration)**.

5    Clearly label, then detach all wires, hoses and brackets attached to the intake manifold.

6    Remove the alternator and power steering pump (see Chapters 5 and 10).

7    Detach the spark plug wires from the spark plugs and wire holders (leave them connected at the distributor).

8    Disconnect the accelerator cable from the throttle body and remove the fuel injectors, lines and hoses (see Chapter 4).

9    Detach the EGR pipe from the front exhaust manifold.

10    Remove the mounting nuts/bolts **(see illustration)**, then detach the manifold from the engine. If it's stuck, don't pry between the gasket mating surfaces or damage may result **(see illustration)**.

11    Carefully use a scraper to remove all traces of old gasket material and sealant from the manifold and cylinder heads, then clean the mating surfaces with lacquer thinner or acetone.

12    If necessary, remove the bolts/nuts **(see illustration)** and separate the manifold and bypass valve body. Clean the valve body

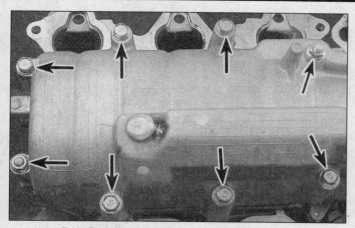

5.12 Remove the bolts/nuts (arrows) from the
air bypass valve body

5.13 Slip new gaskets over the studs

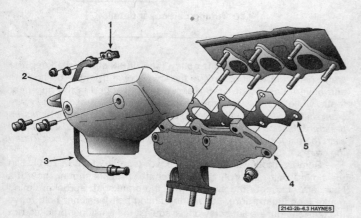

6.3 Exhaust manifold details (rear manifold shown)

1   Gasket              4   Exhaust manifold
2   Cover               5   Gasket
3   EGR pipe

6.5a Front exhaust pipe nut locations (arrows)

6.5b Rear exhaust pipe nut locations (arrows)

and reassemble with new gaskets and tighten securely.

13   Install new gaskets **(see illustration)**, then position the manifold on the engine. Make sure the gaskets haven't shifted and install the nuts/bolts.

14   Tighten the nuts/bolts, in three equal steps, to the torque listed in this Chapter's Specifications. Work from the center out towards the ends to avoid warping the manifold.

15   Install the remaining parts in the reverse order of removal.

16   Refill the cooling system. Run the engine and check for fuel, vacuum and coolant leaks.

## 6   Exhaust manifolds - removal and installation

*Refer to illustrations 6.3, 6.5a and 6.5b*

**Note:** *The engine must be completely cool before starting this procedure.*

1   Disconnect the negative cable from the battery. **Caution:** *The radio in your vehicle is equipped with an anti-theft system. Make sure you have the correct activation code before disconnecting the battery.*

2   Spray penetrating oil on the exhaust manifold fasteners and allow it to soak in.

3   Unbolt the heat shield from the manifold(s) being removed **(see illustration)**.

4   Block the rear wheels to prevent the vehicle from rolling. Set the

parking brake and place the transaxle in Park. Raise the front of the vehicle and support it securely on jackstands. Remove the lower splash guard.

5   Disconnect the exhaust pipes from the manifolds **(see illustrations)** and lower the pipes.

6   Remove the EGR pipe from the rear manifold **(see illustration 6.3)**.

7   Remove the self-locking nuts retaining the manifold to the cylinder head and slip it off the mounting studs.

8    Carefully inspect the manifold and fasteners for cracks and damage. If the manifold is cracked, replace it with a new one.

9    Use a scraper to remove any traces of old gasket material and carbon deposits from the manifold and cylinder head mating surfaces. If the gasket was leaking, have the manifold checked for warpage at an automotive machine shop and resurfaced if necessary.

10    Position a new gasket over the cylinder head studs.

11    Install the manifold and thread the mounting nuts into place.

12    Working from the center out, tighten the nuts to the torque listed in this Chapter's Specifications in three equal steps.

13    Reinstall the remaining parts in the reverse order of removal. Use anti-seize compound on all bolts, nuts and the EGR pipe fitting.

14    Run the engine and check for exhaust leaks.

## 7   Timing belt and sprockets - removal, inspection and installation

### *Removal*

*Refer to illustrations 7.10, 7.12, 7.13a, 7.13b, 7.14, 7.15a, 7.15b, 7.16 and 7.17*

1    Disconnect the negative cable from the battery. **Caution:** *The radio in your vehicle is equipped with an anti-theft system. Make sure you have the correct activation code before disconnecting the battery.*

2    Loosen the lug nuts on the right front wheel, but don't remove them yet.

3    Place the transaxle in Park.

4    Apply the parking brake and block the rear wheels. Raise the front of the vehicle and support it securely on jackstands. Remove the right front wheel.

5    Remove the right front inner fender splash guard.

6    Remove the drivebelts (see Chapter 1).

7    Remove the alternator and power steering pump (see Chapters 5 and 10).

8    Support the engine by placing a floor jack under the oil pan (with a block of wood on the jack to protect the pan).

9    Remove the three bolts holding the passenger-side engine mount to the block, and rotate the mount away from the engine.

10    Remove the upper timing belt covers **(see illustration)**.

11    Remove the spark plugs to make it easier to turn the crankshaft (see Chapter 1). Position the number one piston at TDC (see Section 3).

12    If you intend to re-use the belt, mark the belt to indicate the direction of rotation **(see illustration)**.

13    Make sure the timing marks are properly aligned **(see illustrations)**.

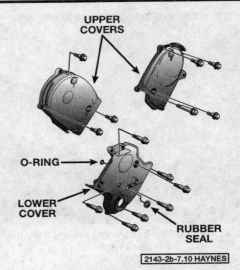

**7.10  Timing belt cover details**

14    Remove the crankshaft pulley **(see illustration)**. To keep the crankshaft from turning, remove the lower cover from the bellhousing and have an assistant keep a screwdriver wedged in the ring-gear teeth while you loosen the crank pulley bolt. **Note:** *When the crankshaft pulley bolt is loosened, the position of the timing marks on the crankshaft pulley and the camshafts may be disturbed. Check and align them again. Temporarily reinstall the crankshaft pulley bolt to turn the crankshaft.*

15    Remove the lower timing belt cover **(see illustration 7.10)**. Slip the timing belt guide off the crankshaft sprocket, noting how it's installed. Also note the alignment of the crankshaft sprocket timing marks **(see illustration)**. Loosen the timing belt tensioner bolt, move the tensioner (use a flat screwdriver against the tensioner bracket, **not** the belt) to relieve tension on the belt and retighten the bolt. Remove the timing belt **(see illustration)**.

16    The camshaft sprockets can be removed at this point, if they are damaged or to replace the oil seals **(see illustration)**. On the rear sprocket, remove the lower bolt last. Remove the keys from the shafts so they don't fall out and get lost.

17    If it's worn or damaged, or if you're replacing the crankshaft front oil seal, the crankshaft sprocket can now be removed. If it won't come off by hand, carefully pry it off **(see illustration)**. Also remove the inner timing belt guide, noting how it's installed.

**7.12  Mark the direction of rotation on the timing belt**

**7.13a  Front camshaft timing marks (arrows) - the pointer on the housing is colored yellow, while the TDC mark on the sprocket is green**

**7.13b  Rear camshaft timing marks (arrows) - the TDC mark is green and the pointer is a groove on the housing**

**7.14  Remove the crankshaft pulley bolt (arrow)**

**7.15a  Crankshaft sprocket timing marks**

**7.15b  Loosen the timing belt tensioner bolt (arrow)**

**7.16  Prevent the camshaft from turning by inserting a screwdriver through a hole in the sprocket while you loosen the bolts, then pull the sprocket off**

**7.17  Carefully work the crankshaft sprocket off without damaging anything.**

**7.25  Install the outer timing belt guide (arrow) as shown**

## Inspection

18   Refer to Chapter 2, Part A for the timing belt inspection procedure.
19   If the engine has high mileage, now is the best time to remove and inspect/replace the water pump (see Chapter 3).

## Installation

*Refer to illustration 7.25*

20   Remove all dirt and oil from the timing belt area.
21   If any of the timing belt sprockets were removed, install them now with their keys and tighten the bolts to the torque listed in this Chapter's Specifications.
23   If removed, install the inner timing belt guide over the crankshaft sprocket with the chamfered edge facing away from the belt. Also install the crankshaft sprocket.
24   Recheck the position of the timing marks **(see illustrations 7.13a, 7.13b and 7.15a)**. Install the timing belt, starting at the crankshaft sprocket and tensioner pulley, then front camshaft sprocket, water pump, and rear camshaft sprocket. For ease of installation, temporarily advance the rear camshaft sprocket about one-half tooth. If you're re-using the original belt, the arrow you made in Step 12 should point in the normal direction of rotation.
25   Install the outer timing belt guide over the crankshaft sprocket with the chamfered edge facing away from the belt **(see illustration)**.
26   Loosen the tensioner adjustment bolt, allow the tensioner to move into position and retighten the bolt.
27   Turn the crankshaft slowly six revolutions clockwise using a socket and breaker bar on the crankshaft pulley bolt to seat the belt,

then return to TDC. Recheck the alignment of cam and crank timing marks. **Caution:** *If you feel any resistance, back up and recheck the belt timing. Do not force the crankshaft to turn or engine damage will occur!*
28   Install the lower timing belt cover.
29   Slip the drivebelt pulley onto the crankshaft, aligning the pulley keyway with the crankshaft key. Install the bolt and tighten it to the specified torque. Use the method described in Step 14 to keep the crankshaft from turning.
30   Loosen the tensioner bolt again, allow the tensioned to settle against the belt, and retighten the bolt.
31   Recheck the timing marks **(see illustrations 7.13a and 7.13b)**.
**Caution:** *If the timing marks are not aligned exactly as shown, repeat the timing belt installation procedure. DO NOT start the engine until you're absolutely certain that the timing belt is installed correctly. Serious and costly engine damage could occur if the belt is installed wrong.*
**Note:** *Both upper timing belt covers have inspection holes (remove the rubber plugs) that allows checking the camshaft sprocket timing marks even when the covers are in place.*
32   Reinstall the remaining parts in the reverse order of removal.

## 8   Crankshaft front oil seal - replacement

*Refer to illustrations 8.2 and 8.4*

1   Remove the timing belt and crankshaft sprocket (see Section 7).
2   Carefully pry the seal out of the engine with a screwdriver or seal

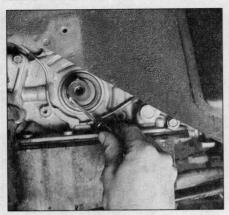

8.2  Carefully pry out the oil seal

8.4  Lubricate the seal lip and tap the new crankshaft seal into place with a large socket or piece of pipe and a hammer

9.2  Remove the oil seal from its bore (arrow)

9.4  If a seal driver is not available, use a hammer and a section of pipe or a large socket to tap the new seal into place

10.3  Remove the camshaft holder bolts (arrows)

removal tool (see illustration). If you use a screwdriver, don't scratch the housing bore or damage the crankshaft (if the crankshaft is damaged, the new seal will end up leaking).

3    Clean the oil seal bore and coat the outer edge of the new seal with a small amount of engine oil to ease installation. Apply multi-purpose grease to the seal lip.

4    Using Honda tool no. 07GAD-PH70200 or a socket with an out-side diameter slightly smaller than the outside diameter of the seal, carefully drive the new seal into place with a hammer (see illustration). Make sure it's installed squarely and driven in to the same depth as the original. If a socket isn't available, a short section of large-diameter pipe will also work. Check the seal after installation to make sure the garter spring didn't pop out of place.

5    Reinstall the crankshaft sprocket and timing belt (see Section 7).

6    Run the engine and check for oil leaks at the front seal.

### 9   Camshaft oil seals - replacement

*Refer to illustrations 9.2 and 9.4*

**Note:** *The following procedure is for replacing camshaft seals without removing the camshafts. The seals are also replaced very easily anytime the camshafts are removed for other cylinder head or valvetrain work. Both camshaft oil seals should be replaced at the same time, even if only one is leaking.*

1    Remove the timing belt and camshaft sprockets (see Section 7).

2    Note how far each seal is seated in the bore, then carefully pry it out with a screwdriver (see illustration). Wrap the screwdriver tip with

tape - don't scratch the bore or damage the camshaft (if the camshaft is damaged, the new seal will end up leaking).

3    Clean the bore and coat the outer edge of the new seal with engine oil or multi-purpose grease. Apply multi-purpose grease to the seal lip.

4    Using a socket with an outside diameter slightly smaller than the outside diameter of the seal, carefully drive the new seal into place with a hammer (see illustration). Make sure it's installed squarely and driven in to the same depth as the original. If a socket of the correct size isn't available, a short section of pipe will also work. After the seal is installed, make sure the garter spring did not pop loose.

5    Reinstall the camshaft sprocket and timing belt (see Section 7).

6    Run the engine and check for oil leaks at the camshaft seals.

### 10   Camshafts and valve components - removal, inspection and installation

*Removal*

*Refer to illustrations 10.3, 10.4, 10.5, 10.7, 10.9a, 10.9b, 10.9c, 10.9d, 10.10a and 10.10b*

**Note:** *To remove all the rocker arm components, it is necessary to remove the exhaust rocker arm shafts, which is difficult with the cylinder head installed in the vehicle. Therefore, if the rocker arm shafts must be removed, we recommend first removing the cylinder head from the vehicle (see the next Section).*

1    Remove the valve covers (see Section 4) and the timing belt, sprockets and inner covers (see Section 7).

10.4  Carefully lift off the camshaft holders and plates

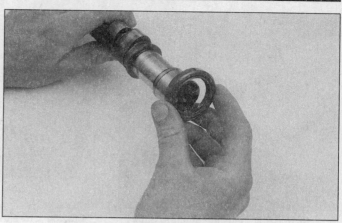

10.5  Slip the oil seal off the end of the camshaft

10.7  Remove the rocker arm guide plate bolts (arrows), then remove the rocker arms from the top of the cylinder head

10.9a  Unscrew the end caps . . .

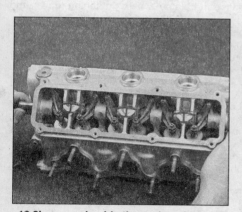

10.9b  . . . and guide the rocker shaft out

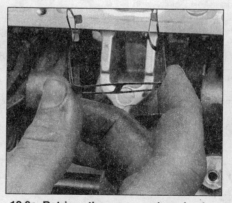

10.9c  Retrieve the wave washers (spring clips) as the shaft is removed

10.9d  The rocker arms will be released when the wave washers are removed

2    Remove the distributor (see Chapter 5).
3    Working in a sequence around the bolt pattern, loosen the camshaft holder bolts (see illustration) in 1/3-turn increments until they can be removed by hand.
4    Remove the camshaft holder plates and camshaft holders (see illustration). Remove the rear camshaft sealing plug. Note the position of the sprocket locating dowel pin for reassembly and lift out the camshaft. Be sure to keep it level during removal.
5    Remove the oil seal by slipping it off the end of the camshaft (see illustration).
6    Mark the holder plates and holders to indicate which cylinder

head they came from.
7    Remove the rocker arm guide plates, then lift out the rocker arms (see illustration). Be sure to keep them separate so they can be reinstalled in their original locations. Label egg cartons to store and organize them.
8    Working in the lower cylinder head cover openings, loosen the exhaust rocker arm lock nuts and back off the adjustment screws. Lift out the pushrods. Push them through holes in a cardboard box and label their positions so they can be reinstalled in their original locations.
9    Remove the end caps and slide the exhaust rocker arm shaft out (see illustrations). If the shaft is stuck, install a long 12 x 1.25 mm bolt

**10.10a  Pull the lash adjusters out**

**10.10b  Store the lash adjusters in an organized manner**

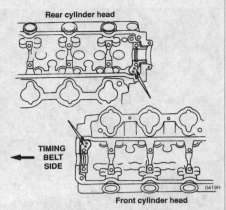

**10.15  Pour oil into the holes marked with arrows**

and use it as a handle. Remove the spring clips and lift the exhaust rocker arms out. Store them in order so they can be returned to their original locations. **Note:** *Rocker shaft removal is difficult with the engine in the vehicle. Several components must be removed for clearance and rear cylinder head access is limited. Therefore, we recommend removing the cylinder head (see the next Section) when the rocker arm shaft must be removed.*

10   Remove the lash adjusters by pulling them out **(see illustration)**. Store them in order so they may be reinstalled in the same position **(see illustration)**.

## Inspection

11   Roll the pushrods on a piece of glass to check for bent ones. Replace as necessary.

12   Visually inspect the rocker arms for excessive wear. Slip the exhaust rockers over the rocker shaft and check for excess clearance and/or shaft wear. Check all the rockers for wear and damage, especially where the rockers contact the rocker shaft, pushrods and camshaft.

13   Check the lash adjusters for wear and damage, especially where the rockers contact them.

14   Refer to Chapter 2, Part A for camshaft checking procedures. Be sure to use the Specifications in this Part of Chapter 2 for the V6 engine.

## Installation

*Refer to illustrations 10.15, 10.17, 10.21 and 10.22*

15   Pour engine oil into the lash adjuster holes in the cylinder heads, then insert the lash adjusters into the heads in the same locations they were originally in. Do not rotate the lash adjusters during installation. If you suspect any of the lash adjusters are faulty, take them to a dealer for air bleeding and inspection using Honda tool no. 07GAJ-PH70100 or equivalent. Pour oil into the oil filler holes **(see illustration)**.

16   Apply moly-base grease or engine assembly lube to the contact surfaces of all moving parts. Install the exhaust rocker arms, wave washers and shafts into their original locations in the heads.

17   Install the inside exhaust rocker arms, pushrods and intake rocker arms (cam followers) in their original positions over the lash adjusters **(see illustration)**.

18   Lubricate the lips with engine oil, then install a new camshaft oil seal by slipping it over the end of the camshaft. Be sure the spring side faces in. Install the rear camshaft sealing plug.

19   Rotate the crankshaft to 30-degrees after TDC, to avoid any valve-to-piston clearance problems when tightening down the camshafts.

20   If the cylinder heads had been removed for this procedure, reinstall them at this time (see Section 11). Set the camshaft in place in the cylinder head, being sure the seal is positioned correctly. **Note:** *The front camshaft has a groove for driving the distributor.* Locate the front camshaft dowel pin at the one o'clock position and the rear camshaft dowel pin at the 11 o'clock position.

21   Apply a thin coat of non-hardening sealant to the outer edges of the bearing cap-to-cylinder head mating surfaces **(see illustration)**. Install the camshaft holders, camshaft holder plates and dowel pins with their bolts.

22   Tighten the camshaft holder bolts in 1/3-turn increments until the torque listed in this Chapter's Specifications is reached. Follow the

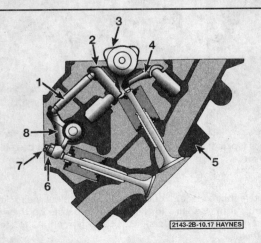

2143-2B-10.17 HAYNES

**10.17  Relationship of the rocker arms, camshafts and pushrods**

| | | | |
|---|---|---|---|
| 1 | Pushrod | 5 | Cylinder head |
| 2 | Exhaust inside rocker arm | 6 | Locknut |
| 3 | Camshaft | 7 | Adjusting screw |
| 4 | Intake rocker arm | 8 | Exhaust rocker arm |

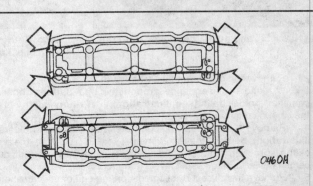

**10.21  Apply sealant at these locations (arrows)**

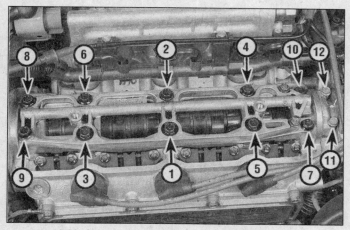

**10.22  Camshaft holder bolt tightening sequence**

**11.8a  Bolt locations for the front inner timing belt cover (arrows)**

factory-recommended sequence **(see illustration)**.
23   Apply camshaft installation lube to the camshaft lobes, bearing journals and thrust faces.
24   Install the other camshaft in the same manner.
25   Turn the engine back 30-degrees counterclockwise until TDC is reached again.
26   Reinstall the timing belt rear covers, camshaft sprockets and timing belt (see Section 7).
27   With the engine at Top Dead Center for number one cylinder (see Section 3) and the camshaft timing marks aligned (see Section 7), adjust the exhaust valves for cylinders number one, two and four. Loosen the locknut, tighten the adjusting screw until the tip contacts the valve, then turn it 1-1/8 turns more and tighten the locknut securely.
28   Turn the crankshaft one full turn (360-degrees). Adjust the exhaust valves for cylinders three, five and six as described in the previous Step.
29   Reinstall the remaining components in the reverse order of removal.
30   Remove the spark plugs and crank the engine. Check for compression at each cylinder. If any cylinder lacks compression, it may be necessary to disassemble the head and check for faulty lash adjusters.
31   Run the engine at low speed for five minutes to allow the hydraulic lash adjusters to settle, then check for leaks and proper operation. **Note:** *There will be some tappet noise during the first few minutes of operation. If the noise continues, it may indicate a problem with one of the lash adjusters.*

## 11   Cylinder heads - removal and installation

**Caution:** *Allow the engine to cool completely before beginning this procedure.*

### *Removal*

*Refer to illustrations 11.8a, 11.8b, 11.10 and 11.12*
1   Relieve the fuel pressure (see Chapter 4).
2   Disconnect the negative cable from the battery. **Caution:** *The radio in your vehicle is equipped with an anti-theft system. Make sure you have the correct activation code before disconnecting the battery.*
3   Drain the cooling system, including both block drains (see Chapter 1).
4   Remove the alternator and distributor (see Chapter 5).
5   Remove the intake manifold (see Section 5).
6   Remove the exhaust manifold (see Section 6).
7   Detach the timing belt and camshaft sprockets (see Section 7).
8   Remove the inner timing belt cover **(see illustrations)**.
9   Remove the camshaft(s) from the head(s) you intend to remove (see Section 10).
10   Detach the coolant passage assembly **(see illustration)**.
11   Using a socket, loosen the cylinder head bolts in 1/4-turn increments until they can be removed by hand. Loosen them in a sequence opposite that of the tightening sequence **(see illustration 11.22)**
12   Lift the cylinder head off the engine block. If the head is stuck, pry against an external casting protrusion **(see illustration). Caution:** *Don't*

**11.8b  Bolt locations for the rear inner timing belt cover (arrows)**

**11.10  Remove the coolant passage assembly bolts (arrows indicate two - the other two aren't visible in this photo)**

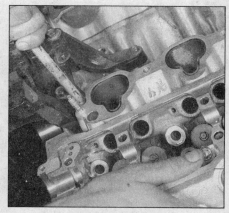

**11.12  Pry up carefully on a casting protrusion**

**11.15  Use a scraper to remove all traces of old gasket material**

**11.19  Fit the new gasket over the oil control orifice (top arrow, one per head) and locating dowels (arrows)**

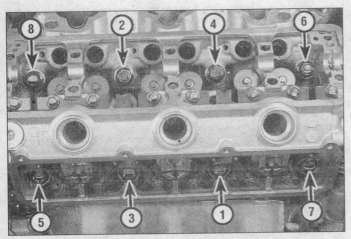

**11.22  Cylinder head bolt TIGHTENING sequence**

pry between the head and block. The gasket surfaces may be damaged and leaks could result.

13    Repeat Steps 6, 8, 11 and 12 for the other head. Check the cylinder heads for warpage as shown in Chapter 2C.

## Installation

*Refer to illustrations 11.15, 11.19 and 11.22*

14    The mating surfaces of the cylinder heads and block must be perfectly clean when the heads are installed.

15    Use a gasket scraper to remove all traces of carbon and old gasket material **(see illustration)**. Be careful not to gouge the delicate aluminum. Clean the mating surfaces with lacquer thinner or acetone. If there's oil on the mating surfaces when the head is installed, the gasket may not seal correctly and leaks could develop. When working on the block, stuff the cylinders with clean shop rags to keep out debris. Use a vacuum cleaner to remove material that falls into the cylinders.

16    Check the block and head mating surfaces for nicks, deep scratches and other damage. If damage is slight, it can be removed with a file; if it's excessive, machining may be the only alternative.

17    Use a tap of the correct size to chase the threads in the head bolt holes, then clean the holes with compressed air - make sure that nothing remains in the holes. **Warning:** *Wear eye protection when using compressed air!*

18    Mount each bolt in a vise and run a die down the threads to remove corrosion and restore the threads. Dirt, corrosion, sealant and damaged threads will affect torque readings.

19    Clean the oil-control jets thoroughly and reinstall them with new O-rings. Position the new gaskets over the oil-control jets and locating dowels in the block **(see illustration)**.

20    Carefully set the head on the block without disturbing the gasket.

21    Before installing the head bolts, apply a small amount of clean engine oil to the threads.

22    Install the bolts and special washers and tighten them finger tight. Following the recommended sequence **(see illustration)**, tighten the bolts to the torque listed in this Chapter's Specifications in two steps.

23    Repeat the entire procedure to install the other cylinder head, if necessary.

24    The remaining installation steps are the reverse of removal.

25    Refill the cooling system, change the oil and filter (see Chapter 1), run the engine and check for leaks. Run the engine at low speed for five minutes to allow the hydraulic lash adjusters to settle, then check for leaks and proper operation. **Note:** *There will be some tappet noise during the first few minutes of operation. If the noise continues, it may indicate a problem with one of the lash adjusters.*

## 12   Oil pan - removal and installation

## Removal

*Refer to illustrations 12.5a, 12.5b, 12.8a and 12.8b*

1    Disconnect the negative cable from the battery. **Caution:** *The radio in your vehicle is equipped with an anti-theft system. Make sure you have the correct activation code before disconnecting the battery.*

2    Block the rear wheels and set the parking brake. Raise the front of the vehicle and support it securely on jackstands.

3    Remove the lower splash shields.

4    Drain the engine oil and remove the oil filter (see Chapter 1).

5    Unbolt the longitudinal crossmember **(see illustrations)**.

6    Unbolt the exhaust pipes from the manifolds (see Section 6).

7    Detach the lower bellhousing cover, if equipped.

8    Remove the bolts/nuts **(see illustration)** and lower the oil pan. The bolts adjacent to the driveaxle can be removed with a 1/4-inch drive socket, extension and ratchet. If the pan is stuck, break it loose with a soft-face hammer **(see illustration)**. Don't damage the mating surfaces of the pan and block or oil leaks could develop.

## Installation

9    Use a scraper to remove all traces of old sealant from the block and oil pan. Be careful not to gouge the delicate aluminum block. Clean the mating surfaces with lacquer thinner or acetone.

10    Make sure the threaded bolt holes in the block are clean.

11    Check the oil pan flange for distortion, particularly around the bolt

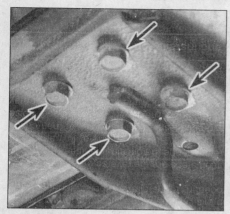

12.5a  Remove the bolts (arrows) . . .

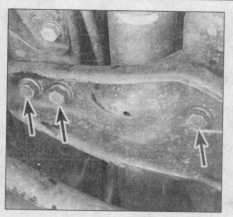

12.5b  . . . from the ends of
the crossmember

12.8a  Remove the bolts from around the
perimeter of the oil pan

12.8b  Use a soft-face hammer to break the oil pan loose

13.2  Oil pickup screen bolt locations (arrows)

holes. If necessary, place the pan on a block of wood and use a
hammer to flatten and restore the gasket surface.
12    Inspect the oil pump pick-up screen assembly for damage and a
blocked strainer. If the pick-up and/or baffle was removed, install it
now. Use a new O-ring on the pick-up. Tighten the fasteners to the
torque listed in this Chapter's Specifications.
13    Position a new gasket on the oil pan.
14    Carefully position the oil pan on the engine block and install the
bolts/nuts. Working from the center out, tighten them to the torque
listed in this Chapter's Specifications in three steps.
15    The remainder of installation is the reverse of removal. Be sure to
add oil and install a new oil filter. **Note:** *If the oil pump has been
replaced, wait 20 minutes (to allow the sealant to cure) before adding
oil.*
16    Run the engine and check for oil pressure and leaks.

## 13    Oil pump - removal and installation

### Removal

*Refer to illustrations 13.2, 13.4, 13.5 and 13.6*

1    Remove the timing belt and crankshaft sprocket (see Section 7).
**Note:** *Leave the engine mount on the timing belt end of the engine
connected to support the engine. It's not necessary to completely
remove the belt.*
2    Remove the oil pan (see Section 12) and oil pickup screen **(see
illustration)**. If equipped, remove the oil level sensor.

13.4  Oil pump housing bolt locations (arrows)

3    Remove the CKP sensor and timing belt tensioner (see Section 7).
At the bottom left of the oil pump case ( when facing the oil pump),
remove the timing belt stopper plate.
4    Remove the bolts and detach the oil pump housing from the
engine **(see illustration)**. You may have to pry carefully between the
main bearing cap and the pump housing with a screwdriver.

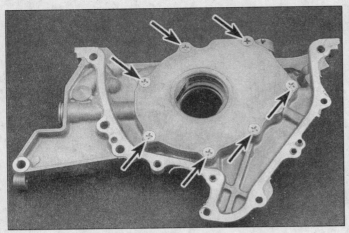

**13.5  Remove the screws from the pump cover (arrows)**

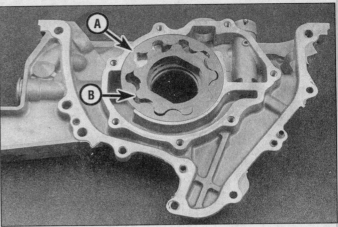

**13.6  Inspect the condition of the rotors and the inside of the cover - with feeler gauges, measure the clearances at A (outer rotor to housing) and B (inner rotor to outer rotor), lay a straightedge across the face of the pump housing and measure the housing-to-rotor axial clearance and compare to Specifications**

5    Use a large Phillips screwdriver to remove the screws holding the pump cover to the rear of the housing (see illustration).
6    Lift the cover off and inspect the pump rotors (see illustration). If any wear or damage is evident, replace the pump. Check the rotor clearances with feeler gauges and compare to this Chapter's Specifications.
7    Use a scraper to remove any traces of old sealant from the pump body and engine block, being careful not to damage the delicate aluminum.

## Installation

8    Replace the old crankshaft oil seal (see Section 8). Apply multi-purpose grease to the seal lip.
9    Pack the pump cavity with petroleum jelly and install the cover. Apply Loctite to the threads and tighten the screws securely following a criss-cross pattern.
10   Use acetone or lacquer thinner and a clean rag to remove all traces of oil from the gasket surfaces.
11   Apply a bead of sealant (Honda no. 08718-5500000 OE or equivalent) to the oil pump flange and the 8-mm x 1.25 x 45-mm bolt. Avoid using an excessive amount of sealant, especially around oil passages and bolt holes. Parts must be assembled within five minutes of sealant application, otherwise the material must be removed and reapplied. Wherever O-rings are employed, use new ones.
12   If removed, position the oil pass pipe for installation. Be sure to use a new seal.
13   Engage the flat surfaces on the oil pump drive rotor with the matching flats on the crankshaft and slide the pump into place.
14   Install the pump mounting bolts in their original locations and tighten them to the torque listed in this Chapter's Specifications in a criss-cross pattern.
15   Using a new O-ring, install the oil pick-up screen and tighten the fasteners to the torque listed in this Chapter's Specifications.
16   Reinstall the remaining parts in the reverse order of removal.
17   Wait 20 minutes (to allow the sealant to cure), then add oil, start the engine and check for oil leaks and pressure.
18   Recheck the engine oil level.

## 14   Driveplate - removal and installation

*Refer to illustrations 14.2 and 14.7*

1    Remove the transaxle (see Chapter 7). If it's leaking, now would be a very good time to replace the front pump seal/O-ring.
2    Remove the bolts that secure the driveplate to the crankshaft (see illustration). Hold the crankshaft from turning with a large screwdriver wedged into the ring-gear to jam the driveplate.
3    Remove the spacer washer and driveplate from the crankshaft. Since it's fairly heavy, be sure to support it while removing the last bolt. **Warning:** *The ring gear teeth can be sharp, so wear gloves or handle*

**14.2  Remove the bolts (arrows) with a 12-point socket**

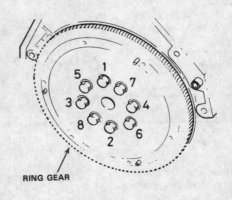

**14.7  Flywheel/driveplate bolt tightening sequence**

RING GEAR

**15.2  Carefully pry the rear main seal out - don't damage the surface of the crankshaft or the new seal will leak**

15.3  Drive the new seal in squarely

16.1a  The V6 transaxle mount (arrow) is located right behind the battery on the driver's side

16.1b  The V6 side mount (arrow) is at the timing belt end of the engine, between the alternator and power steering pump

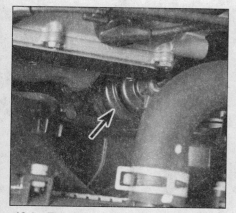

16.1c  The V6 front engine mount (arrow) is between the engine and radiator, near the transaxle/engine juncture

16.1d  The V6 rear mount (lower arrow) is vacuum-controlled to reduce idle vibrations - The upper arrow indicates where the engine's bracket attaches to the top stud of the mount

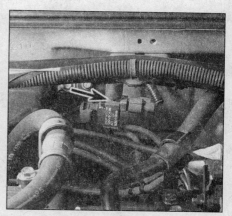

16.e  The control solenoid (arrow) for the rear motor mount on V6 models is located near the center of the firewall

the driveplate with rags.

4    Clean the driveplate and inspect the surface for cracks. Check for worn, cracked or broken ring-gear teeth. Lay the driveplate on a flat surface and use a straightedge to check for warpage.

5    Clean and inspect the mating surfaces of the driveplate and the crankshaft. If the crankshaft oil seal is leaking, replace it before reinstalling the driveplate.

6    Position the driveplate against the crankshaft. Note that offset bolt holes ensure correct installation. Be sure to install the spacer washer with the driveplate.

7    Hold the crankshaft from turning as described above. Working in several stages, following the tightening sequence (see illustration), tighten the bolts to the torque listed in this Chapter's Specifications.

8    The remainder of installation is the reverse of the removal procedure.

## 15  Crankshaft rear oil seal - replacement

*Refer to illustrations 15.2 and 15.3*

1    The transaxle must be removed from the vehicle for this procedure and the driveplate must be separated from the engine. Refer to Chapter 7 and Section 14 as necessary.

2    The seal can be replaced without dropping the oil pan or removing the seal retainer. However, the lip of the seal is quite stiff and

it's possible to cock the seal in the retainer bore or damage it during installation. If you want to take the chance, pry out the old seal with a screwdriver (see illustration).

3    Apply multi-purpose grease to the crankshaft seal journal and the lip of the new seal and carefully drive the new seal into place (see illustration). Install the seal with the spring side in. Use a socket, section of pipe or Honda special tool no. 07749-0010000. The lip is stiff so carefully work it onto the seal journal of the crankshaft. Don't rush it or you may damage the seal.

4    The crankshaft seal replacement method described in Chapter 2C is recommended but requires removal of the oil pan and the seal retainer. If you use this method, you can also measure the clearance between the seal and the bottom of the seal bore, which should be 0.008 to 0.020 inch. The seal should not bottom out. This clearance can't be easily measured with the cover in place on the block.

5    The remaining steps are the reverse of removal.

## 16  Engine mounts - check and replacement

*Refer to illustrations 16.1a, 16.1b, 16.1c, 16.1d and 16.e*

Refer to Chapter 2, Part A for information on engine mount replacement procedures and testing of the special rear mount used in the Honda Engine Mount Control System. See the illustrations here for V6 mount configurations.

# Notes

# Chapter 2  Part C
# General engine overhaul procedures

## Contents

## Specifications

## Four-cylinder engines

### General

| | |
|---|---|
| Displacement | 132 cu in (2.2 liters) |
| Cylinder compression pressure | |
| Standard | 178 psi |
| Minimum | 135 psi |
| Maximum variation between cylinders | 28 psi |
| | |
| Oil pressure (engine warm) | |
| At 3000 rpm | 50 psi |
| At idle | 10 psi minimum |
| Cylinder head warpage service limit | 0.002 inch |

### Valves and related components

| | |
|---|---|
| Minimum valve margin width | |
| Intake | |
| Standard | 0.033 to 0.045 inch |
| Service limit | 0.026 inch |

## Four-cylinder engines (continued)

### Valves and related components

Minimum valve margin width
    Exhaust
        Standard ................................................................. 0.041 to 0.053 inch
        Service limit............................................................. 0.037 inch
Valve stem diameter
    Intake
        Standard ................................................................. 0.2159 to 0.2163 inch
        Service limit............................................................. 0.2148 inch
    Exhaust
        Standard ................................................................. 0.2146 to 0.2150 inch
        Service limit............................................................. 0.2134 inch
Valve stem-to-guide clearance
    Intake
        Standard ................................................................. 0.0008 to 0.0018 inch
        Service limit............................................................. 0.003 inch
    Exhaust
        Standard ................................................................. 0.0022 to 0.0031 inch
        Service limit............................................................. 0.005 inch
Valve spring free length
    F22B1 engine (V-TEC)
        Intake ................................................................. 2.011 inches
        Exhaust ............................................................... 2.188 inches
    F22B2 engine
        Intake
            Associated Spring* ....................................... 2.158 inches
            Other manufacture* ...................................... 2.103 inches
        Exhaust
            Associated Spring* ....................................... 2.216 inches
            Other manufacture* ...................................... 2.152 inches

*See text in Section 10*

### Crankshaft and connecting rods

Connecting rod journal
    Diameter................................................................... 1.8888 to 1.8898 inches
    Taper and out-of-round (maximum)........................... 0.0002 inch
Rod bearing oil clearance
    Standard................................................................... 0.0008 to 0.0019 inch
    Service limit.............................................................. 0.0024 inch
Connecting rod side clearance (endplay)
    Standard................................................................... 0.006 to 0.012 inch
    Service limit.............................................................. 0.016 inch
Main bearing journal
    Diameter
        No. 1 and 4 journals............................................ 1.9679 to 1.9688 inch
        No. 2 journal....................................................... 1.9676 to 1.9685 inch
        No. 3 journal....................................................... 1.9674 to 1.9683 inch
        No. 5 journal....................................................... 1.9680 to 1.9690 inch
    Taper and out-of-round (maximum)........................... 0.0002 inch
    Runout
        Standard............................................................. 0.001 inch
        Service limit........................................................ 0.002 inch
Bearing oil clearance
    No. 1 and 4 journals
        Standard............................................................. 0.0005 to 0.0015 inch
        Service limit........................................................ 0.002 inch
    No. 2 journal
        Standard............................................................. 0.0008 to 0.0018 inch
        Service limit........................................................ 0.002 inch
    No. 3 journal
        Standard............................................................. 0.0010 to 0.0019 inch
        Service limit........................................................ 0.0022 inch
    No. 5 journal
        Standard............................................................. 0.0004 to 0.0013 inch
        Service limit........................................................ 0.0016 inch
Crankshaft endplay
    Standard................................................................... 0.004 to 0.0014 inch
    Service limit.............................................................. 0.018 inch
Crankshaft rear oil seal clearance ................................. 0.02 to 0.03 inch

## Balance shafts
### Front shaft
Number 1 journal
    Standard .................................................................... 1.6820 to 1.6824 inches
    Service limit................................................................. 1.681 inches
    Bearing-to-shaft oil clearance
        Standard ............................................................... 0.0026 to 0.0039 inch
        Service limit .......................................................... 0.005 inch
Number 2 journal
    Standard .................................................................... 1.5241 to 1.5246 inches
    Service limit................................................................. 1.524 inches
    Bearing-to-shaft oil clearance
        Standard ............................................................... 0.0030 to 0.0043 inch
        Service limit .......................................................... 0.005 inch
Number 3 journal
    Standard .................................................................... 1.3670 to 1.3675 inches
    Service limit................................................................. 1.367 inches
    Bearing-to-shaft oil clearance
        Standard ............................................................... 0.0026 to 0.0039 inch
        Service limit .......................................................... 0.005 inch

### Rear shaft
Number 1 journal
    Standard .................................................................... 0.8243 to 0.8248 inch
    Service limit................................................................. 0.824 inch
    Bearing-to-shaft oil clearance
        Standard ............................................................... 0.002 to 0.003 inch
        Service limit .......................................................... 0.004 inch
Number 2 journal
    Standard .................................................................... 1.5241 to 1.5246 inches
    Service limit................................................................. 1.524 inches
    Bearing-to-shaft oil clearance
        Standard ............................................................... 0.0030 to 0.0043 inch
        Service limit .......................................................... 0.005 inch
Number 3 journal
    Standard .................................................................... 1.3670 to 1.3675 inches
    Service limit................................................................. 1.367 inches
    Bearing-to-shaft oil clearance
        Standard ............................................................... 0.0026 to 0.0039 inch
        Service limit .......................................................... 0.005 inch

## Cylinder block
Cylinder block deck warpage
    Standard.................................................................... 0.003 inch
    Service limit................................................................. 0.004 inch
Cylinder bore
    Diameter
        Marked A or I (standard) ........................................ 3.3468 to 3.3472 inches
        Marked B or II (standard) ....................................... 3.3465 to 3.3468 inches
        Service limit .......................................................... 3.3492 inches
    Taper and out-of-round, service limit............................ 0.002 inch

## Pistons and rings
Piston diameter (measured at 0.80-inch from bottom of skirt)
    No marking
        Standard ............................................................... 3.3457 to 3.3461 inches
        Service limit .......................................................... 3.3453 inches
    Letter B
        Standard ............................................................... 3.3453 to 3.3457 inches
        Service limit .......................................................... 3.3449 inches
Piston-to-bore clearance
    Standard.................................................................... 0.0008 to 0.0016 inch
    Service limit................................................................. 0.002 inch
Piston ring end gap
    Top ring
        Standard ............................................................... 0.008 to 0.014 inch
        Service limit .......................................................... 0.024 inch
    Middle ring
        Standard ............................................................... 0.016 to 0.022 inch
        Service limit .......................................................... 0.028 inch

## Four-cylinder engines (continued)
### Pistons and rings (continued)
Piston ring end gap
  Oil ring
    Standard ........................................................................ 0.008 to 0.028 inch
    Service limit................................................................... 0.031 inch
Piston ring side clearance
  Top ring
    Standard ........................................................................ 0.0014 to 0.0024 inch
    Service limit................................................................... 0.005 inch
  Middle ring
    Standard ........................................................................ 0.0012 to 0.0022 inch
    Service limit................................................................... 0.005 inch

### Torque specifications*    **Ft-lbs** (unless otherwise indicated)
Rear balance shaft gear case bolts ...................................... 18
Main bearing cap bolts
  Step 1 ............................................................................. 22
  Step 2 ............................................................................. 54
Connecting rod cap nuts ........................................................ 34
Rear main oil seal retainer bolts ........................................... 104 in-lbs
*Refer to Part A for additional torque specifications.*

## V6 engine

### General
Displacement ...................................................................... 164 cu in. (2.7 Liters)
Cylinder compression pressure at 200 rpm with wide open throttle
  Standard........................................................................... 171 psi
  Minimum........................................................................... 142 psi
Maximum variation between cylinders ................................... 28 psi
Oil pressure (coolant temperature 178 degrees F.)
At 3000 rpm ......................................................................... 63 psi minimum
At idle .................................................................................. 12 psi minimum
Cylinder head warpage limit ................................................. 0.002 inch

### Valves and related components
Minimum valve margin width
  Intake
    Standard ........................................................................ 0.053 to 0.065 inch
    Service limit................................................................... 0.045 inch
  Exhaust
    Standard ........................................................................ 0.065 to 0.077 inch
    Service limit................................................................... 0.057 inch
Valve stem diameter
  Intake
    Standard ........................................................................ 0.2591 to 0.2594 inch
    Service limit................................................................... 0.258 inch
  Exhaust
    Standard ........................................................................ 0.2579 to 0.2583 inch
    Service limit................................................................... 0.257 inch
Valve stem-to-guide clearance
  Intake
    Standard ........................................................................ 0.0008 to 0.002 inch
    Service limit................................................................... 0.003 inch
  Exhaust
    Standard ........................................................................ 0.002 to 0.003 inch
    Service limit................................................................... 0.004 inch
Valve guide inside diameter (all)
  Standard ........................................................................... 0.260 to 0.261 inch
  Service limit...................................................................... 0.262 inch
Valve spring free length
  Intake
    Standard ........................................................................ 2.043 inches
    Service limit................................................................... 2.004 inches
  Exhaust
    Standard ........................................................................ 1.823 inches
    Service limit................................................................... 1.784 inches

## Crankshaft and connecting rods

Connecting rod journal
  Diameter ............................................................................... 2.0463 to 2.0472 inches
  Taper and out-of-round
    Standard ........................................................................... 0.0002 inch
    Service limit...................................................................... 0.0004 inch
  Bearing oil clearance
    Standard ........................................................................... 0.001 to 0.002 inch
    Service limit...................................................................... 0.002 inch
Connecting rod side clearance (endplay)
  Standard................................................................................ 0.006 to 0.012 inch
  Service limit ......................................................................... 0.016 inch
Main bearing journal
  Diameter ............................................................................... 2.5187 to 2.5197 inches
  Taper and out-of-round
    Standard ........................................................................... 0.0002 inch
    Service limit...................................................................... 0.0004 inch
  Bearing oil clearance
    Standard ........................................................................... 0.0009 to 0.0019 inch
    Service limit...................................................................... 0.002 inch
Crankshaft endplay
  Standard................................................................................ 0.004 to 0.014 inch
  Service limit ......................................................................... 0.018 inch
Crankshaft rear oil seal clearance ........................................ 0.008 to 0.020 inch

## Cylinder block

Cylinder block warpage
  Standard................................................................................ 0.003 inch
  Service limit ......................................................................... 0.004 inch
Cylinder bore
  Diameter
    Marked A or I (standard) ................................................. 3.4256 to 3.4260 inches
    Marked B or II (standard) ................................................ 3.4252 to 3.4256 inches
  Taper and out-of-round, service limit................................ 0.002 inch

## Pistons and rings

Piston diameter (measured at 0.7-inch above bottom of skirt)
  No mark
    Standard ........................................................................... 3.4244 to 3.4248 inches
    Service limit...................................................................... 3.4240 inches
  Marked "B"
    Standard ........................................................................... 3.4240 to 3.4244 inches
    Service limit...................................................................... 3.4236 inches
Piston-to-bore clearance
  Standard................................................................................ 0.0008 to 0.0016 inch
  Service limit ......................................................................... 0.003 inch
Piston ring end gap
  No. 1 (top) compression ring
    Standard ........................................................................... 0.008 to 0.014 inch
    Service limit...................................................................... 0.024 inch
  No. 2 (middle) compression ring
    Standard ........................................................................... 0.014 to 0.020 inch
    Service limit...................................................................... 0.028 inch
  Oil ring
    Standard ........................................................................... 0.008 to 0.028 inch
    Service limit...................................................................... 0.031 inch
Piston ring side clearance
  No. 1 (top)
    Standard ........................................................................... 0.0018 to 0.0030 inch
    Service limit...................................................................... 0.0057 inch
  No. 2 (middle)
    Standard ........................................................................... 0.0024 to 0.0035 inch
    Service limit...................................................................... 0.0063 inch

## Torque specifications*

**Ft-lbs (unless otherwise indicated)**

Main bearing bolts
  Cap bolt................................................................................ 29
  Cap bridge bolt .................................................................... 48
  Side bolt .............................................................................. 36
Connecting rod cap nuts ........................................................ 33
Rear main oil seal retainer bolts ........................................... 104 in-lbs

*Refer to Part B for additional torque specifications.*

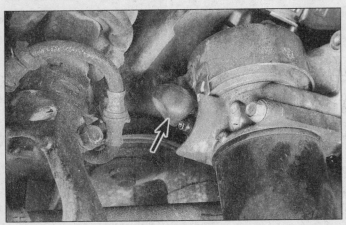

**2.4a  The oil pressure sending unit (arrow) is located above the oil filter on V6 models**

**2.4b  Oil pressure sending unit location (arrow) - four-cylinder model**

# 1    General information

This chapter covers three engines available in the vehicles covered by this manual, the 2.2L four-cylinder (F22B2), the V-TEC version of this same four-cylinder (F22B1), and the 2.7L V6 designated the C27A4.

Included in this portion of Chapter 2 are the general overhaul procedures for the cylinder head(s) and internal engine components.

The information ranges from advice concerning preparation for an overhaul and the purchase of replacement parts to detailed, step-by-step procedures covering removal and installation of internal engine components and the inspection of parts.

The following Sections have been written based on the assumption that the engine has been removed from the vehicle. For information concerning in-vehicle engine repair, as well as removal and installation of the external components necessary for the overhaul, see Part A or B of this Chapter.

The Specifications included in this Part are only those necessary for the inspection and overhaul procedures which follow. Refer to Parts A and B for additional Specifications.

# 2    Engine overhaul - general information

*Refer to illustrations 2.4a and 2.4b*

It's not always easy to determine when, or if, an engine should be completely overhauled, as a number of factors must be considered. High mileage is not necessarily an indication that an overhaul is needed, while low mileage doesn't preclude the need for an overhaul. Frequency of servicing is probably the most important consideration. An engine that's had regular and frequent oil and filter changes, as well as other required maintenance, will most likely give many thousands of miles of reliable service. Conversely, a neglected engine may require an overhaul very early in its life.

Excessive oil consumption is an indication that piston rings, valve seals and/or valve guides are in need of attention. Make sure that oil leaks aren't responsible before deciding that the rings and/or guides are bad. Test the cylinder compression (see Section 3) or have a leak down test performed by an experienced tune-up mechanic to determine the extent of the work required. Further diagnosis of overall engine condition can be made by testing with a simple vacuum gauge (see Section 4).

Check the engine oil pressure with a gauge installed in place of the oil pressure sending unit **(see illustrations)** and compare it to that listed in this Chapter's specifications. If it's extremely low, the bearings and/or oil pump are probably worn out.

Loss of power, rough running, knocking or metallic engine noises,

excessive valvetrain noise and high fuel consumption rates may also point to the need for an overhaul, especially if they're all present at the same time. If a complete tune-up doesn't remedy the situation, major mechanical work is the only solution.

An engine overhaul involves restoring the internal parts to the specifications of a new engine. During an overhaul, the piston rings are replaced and the cylinder walls are reconditioned (rebored and/or honed). If a rebore is done by an automotive machine shop, new oversize pistons will also be installed. The main bearings, connecting rod bearings and camshaft bearings are generally replaced with new ones and, if necessary, the crankshaft may be reground to restore the journals. Generally, the valves are serviced as well, since they're usually in less-than-perfect condition at this point. While the engine is being overhauled, other components, such as the distributor, starter and alternator, can be rebuilt as well. The end result should be a like-new engine that will give many trouble free miles.

**Note:** *Critical cooling system components such as the hoses, drivebelts, thermostat and water pump MUST be replaced with new parts when an engine is overhauled. The radiator should be checked carefully to ensure that it isn't clogged or leaking (see Chapter 3). Many professional rebuilders will not warranty their engines unless you have written proof that the vehicle's radiator was professionally cleaned before the new engine was installed. Also, we don't recommend overhauling the oil pump - always install a new one when an engine is rebuilt.*

Before beginning the engine overhaul, read through the entire procedure to familiarize yourself with the scope and requirements of the job. Overhauling an engine isn't difficult, but it is time consuming. Plan on the vehicle being tied up for a minimum of two weeks, especially if parts must be taken to an automotive machine shop for repair or reconditioning. Check on availability of parts and make sure that any necessary special tools and equipment are obtained in advance. Most work can be done with typical hand tools, although a number of precision measuring tools are required for inspecting parts to determine if they must be replaced. Often an automotive machine shop will handle the inspection of parts and offer advice concerning reconditioning and replacement. **Note:** *Always wait until the engine has been completely disassembled and all components, especially the engine block, have been inspected before deciding what service and repair operations must be performed by an automotive machine shop.* Since the block's condition will be the major factor to consider when determining whether to overhaul the original engine or buy a rebuilt one, never purchase parts or have machine work done on other components until the block has been thoroughly inspected. As a general rule, time is the primary cost of an overhaul, so it doesn't pay to install worn or substandard parts.

As a final note, to ensure maximum life and minimum trouble from a rebuilt engine, everything must be assembled with care in a spotlessly-clean environment.

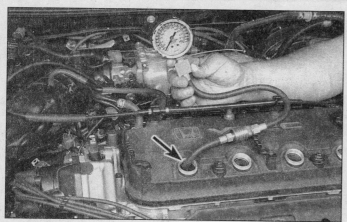

**3.6  To use a compression gauge, you must have a gauge with a hose long enough to reach down the spark-plug tubes (arrow) - be sure to open the throttle as far as possible during the compression check**

**4.5  A simple vacuum gauge can be very handy in diagnosing engine condition and performance**

## 3  Cylinder compression check

*Refer to illustration 3.6*

1    A compression check will tell you what mechanical condition the upper end of your engine (pistons, rings, valves, head gaskets) is in. Specifically, it can tell you if the compression is down due to leakage caused by worn piston rings, defective valves and seats or a blown head gasket. **Note:** *The engine must be at normal operating temperature and the battery must be fully charged for this check.*

2    Begin by cleaning the area around the spark plugs before you remove them (compressed air should be used, if available, otherwise a small brush or even a bicycle tire pump will work). The idea is to prevent dirt from getting into the cylinders as the compression check is being done.

3    Remove all of the spark plugs from the engine (see Chapter 1).

4    Block the throttle wide open.

5    Detach the coil wire from the center of the distributor cap and ground it on the engine block. Use a jumper wire with alligator clips on each end to ensure a good ground. The fuel pump circuit should also be disabled (see Chapter 4).

6    Install the compression gauge in the spark plug hole **(see illustration)**.

7    Crank the engine over at least seven compression strokes and watch the gauge. The compression should build up quickly in a healthy engine. Low compression on the first stroke, followed by gradually increasing pressure on successive strokes, indicates worn piston rings. A low compression reading on the first stroke, which doesn't build up during successive strokes, indicates leaking valves or a blown head gasket (a cracked head could also be the cause). Deposits on the undersides of the valve heads can also cause low compression. Record the highest gauge reading obtained.

8    Repeat the procedure for the remaining cylinders and compare the results to this Chapter's Specifications.

9    Add some engine oil (about three squirts from a plunger-type oil can) to each cylinder, through the spark plug hole, and repeat the test.

10    If the compression increases after the oil is added, the piston rings are definitely worn. If the compression doesn't increase significantly, the leakage is occurring at the valves or head gasket. Leakage past the valves may be caused by burned valve seats and/or faces or warped, cracked or bent valves.

11    If two adjacent cylinders have equally low compression, there's a strong possibility that the head gasket between them is blown. The appearance of coolant in the combustion chambers or the crankcase would verify this condition.

12    If one cylinder is slightly lower than the others, and the engine has a slightly rough idle, a worn lobe on the camshaft could be the cause.

13    If the compression is unusually high, the combustion chambers are probably coated with carbon deposits. If that's the case, the cylinder head(s) should be removed and decarbonized.

14    If compression is way down or varies greatly between cylinders, it would be a good idea to have a leak-down test performed by an automotive repair shop. This test will pinpoint exactly where the leakage is occurring and how severe it is.

## 4  Vacuum gauge diagnostic checks

*Refer to illustration 4.5*

A vacuum gauge provides valuable information about what is going on in the engine at a low-cost. You can check for worn rings or cylinder walls, leaking head or intake manifold gaskets, incorrect carburetor adjustments, restricted exhaust, stuck or burned valves, weak valve springs, improper ignition or valve timing and ignition problems.

Unfortunately, vacuum gauge readings are easy to misinterpret, so they should be used in conjunction with other tests to confirm the diagnosis.

Both the absolute readings and the rate of needle movement are important for accurate interpretation. Most gauges measure vacuum in inches of mercury (in-Hg). The following references to vacuum assume the diagnosis is being performed at sea level. As elevation increases (or atmospheric pressure decreases), the reading will decrease. For every 1,000 foot increase in elevation above approximately 2000 feet, the gauge readings will decrease about one inch of mercury.

Connect the vacuum gauge directly to intake manifold vacuum, not to ported (throttle body) vacuum **(see illustration)**. Be sure no hoses are left disconnected during the test or false readings will result.

Before you begin the test, allow the engine to warm up completely. Block the wheels and set the parking brake. With the transmission in Park, start the engine and allow it to run at normal idle speed. **Warning:** *Carefully inspect the fan blades for cracks or damage before starting the engine. Keep your hands and the vacuum gauge clear of the fan and do not stand in front of the vehicle or in line with the fan when the engine is running.*

Read the vacuum gauge; an average, healthy engine should normally produce about 17 to 22 inches of vacuum with a fairly steady needle. Refer to the following vacuum gauge readings and what they indicate about the engine's condition:

a)    *A low steady reading usually indicates a leaking gasket between the intake manifold and carburetor or throttle body, a leaky vacuum hose, late ignition timing or incorrect camshaft timing. Check ignition timing with a timing light and eliminate all other possible causes, utilizing the tests provided in this Chapter before you remove the timing chain cover to check the timing marks.*

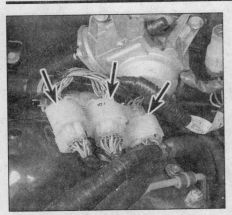

6.6a  Disconnect the electrical connectors (arrows)

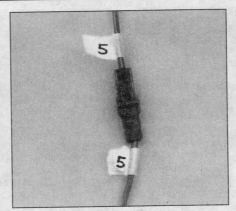

6.6b  Label each wire before disconnecting the connector

6.14  Attach a lifting sling to fixtures (arrow) on the engine and take up the slack

b) *If the reading is three to eight inches below normal and it fluctuates at that low reading, suspect an intake manifold gasket leak at an intake port or a faulty fuel injector.*

c) *If the needle has regular drops of about two-to-four inches at a steady rate, the valves are probably leaking. Perform a compression check or leak-down test to confirm this.*

d) *An irregular drop or down-flick of the needle can be caused by a sticking valve or an ignition misfire. Perform a compression check or leak-down test and read the spark plugs.*

e) *A rapid vibration of about four in.-Hg vibration at idle combined with exhaust smoke indicates worn valve guides. Perform a leak-down test to confirm this. If the rapid vibration occurs with an increase in engine speed, check for a leaking intake manifold gasket or head gasket, weak valve springs, burned valves or ignition misfire.*

f) *A slight fluctuation, say one inch up and down, may mean ignition problems. Check all the usual tune-up items and, if necessary, run the engine on an ignition analyzer.*

g) *If there is a large fluctuation, perform a compression or leak-down test to look for a weak or dead cylinder or a blown head gasket.*

h) *If the needle moves slowly through a wide range, check for a clogged PCV system, incorrect idle fuel mixture, carburetor/throttle body or intake manifold gasket leaks.*

i) *Check for a slow return after revving the engine by quickly snapping the throttle open until the engine reaches about 2,500 rpm and let it shut. Normally the reading should drop to near zero, rise above normal idle reading (about 5 in.-Hg over) and then return to the previous idle reading. If the vacuum returns slowly and doesn't peak when the throttle is snapped shut, the rings may be worn. If there is a long delay, look for a restricted exhaust system (often the muffler or catalytic converter). An easy way to check this is to temporarily disconnect the exhaust ahead of the suspected part and redo the test.*

## 5   Engine removal - methods and precautions

If you've decided that an engine must be removed for overhaul or major repair work, several preliminary steps should be taken.

Locating a suitable place to work is extremely important. Adequate work space, along with storage space for the vehicle, will be needed. If a shop or garage isn't available, at the very least a flat, level, clean work surface made of concrete or asphalt is required. Cleaning the engine compartment and engine before beginning the removal procedure will help keep tools clean and organized.

An engine hoist or A-frame will also be necessary. Make sure the equipment is rated in excess of the combined weight of the engine and transaxle. Safety is of primary importance, considering the potential hazards involved in lifting the engine out of the vehicle.

If the engine is being removed by a novice, a helper should be

available. Advice and aid from someone more experienced would also be helpful. There are many instances when one person cannot simultaneously perform all of the operations required when lifting the engine out of the vehicle.

Plan the operation ahead of time. Arrange for or obtain all of the tools and equipment you'll need prior to beginning the job. Some of the equipment necessary to perform engine removal and installation safely and with relative ease are (in addition to an engine hoist) a heavy-duty floor jack, complete sets of wrenches and sockets as described in the front of this manual, wooden blocks and plenty of rags and cleaning solvent for mopping up spilled oil, coolant and gasoline. If the hoist must be rented, make sure that you arrange for it in advance and perform all of the operations possible without it beforehand. This will save you money and time.

Plan for the vehicle to be out of use for quite a while. A machine shop will be required to perform some of the work which the do-it-yourselfer can't accomplish without special equipment. These shops often have a busy schedule, so it would be a good idea to consult them before removing the engine in order to accurately estimate the amount of time required to rebuild or repair components that may need work.

Always be extremely careful when removing and installing the engine. Serious injury can result from careless actions. Plan ahead, take your time and a job of this nature, although major, can be accomplished successfully.

## 6   Engine - removal and installation

*Refer to illustrations 6.6a, 6.6b, 6.14, 6.17a, 6.17b, 6.17c, 6.17d and 6.18*

**Warning 1:** *The air conditioning system is under high pressure. Do not loosen any hose fittings or remove any components until after the system has been discharged. Air conditioning refrigerant should be properly discharged into an EPA-approved recovery/recycling unit at a dealer service department or an automotive air conditioning repair facility. Always wear eye protection when disconnecting air conditioning system fittings.*

**Warning 2:** *Gasoline is extremely flammable, so take extra precautions when you work on any part of the fuel system. Don't smoke or allow open flames or bare light bulbs near the work area, and don't work in a garage where a natural gas-type appliance (such as a water heater or a clothes dryer) with a pilot light is present. Since gasoline is carcinogenic, wear latex gloves when there's a possibility of being exposed to fuel, and, if you spill any fuel on your skin, rinse it off immediately with soap and water. Mop up any spills immediately and do not store fuel-soaked rags where they could ignite. The fuel system is under constant pressure, so, if any fuel lines are to be disconnected, the fuel pressure in the system must be relieved first (see Chapter 4 for more information). When you perform any kind of work on the fuel*

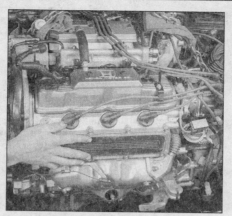

**6.17a  Lift the engine/transaxle clear of its mounts (V6 shown)**

**6.17b  Turn the engine as necessary to clear obstructions**

**6.17c  If the engine or transaxle gets caught on something (arrow), stop and free it before proceeding**

system, wear safety glasses and have a Class B type fire extinguisher on hand.

**Note:** *Read through the entire Section before beginning this procedure. The engine and transaxle are removed as a unit and then separated outside the vehicle.*

## Removal

1    Relieve the fuel system pressure. Remove the air cleaner assembly and ducts (see Chapter 4).

2    Disconnect the cable from the negative battery terminal. **Caution:** *The radio in your vehicle is equipped with an anti-theft system. Make sure you have the correct activation code before disconnecting the battery.*

3    Place protective covers on the fenders and cowl and remove the hood (see Chapter 11).

4    Remove the alternator, distributor and spark plug wires (see Chapter 5).

5    Block the rear wheels and set the parking brake. Raise the vehicle and support it securely on jackstands. Remove the oil filter, drain the cooling system, transaxle and engine oil and remove the drivebelts (see Chapter 1).

6    Clearly label and disconnect all vacuum lines, coolant and emissions hoses, electrical connectors **(see illustration)**, ground straps and fuel lines. Masking tape and/or a touch-up paint applicator work well for marking items **(see illustration)**. Take instant photos or sketch the locations of components and brackets as necessary.

7    Remove the cooling fan(s) and radiator (see Chapter 3).

8    Release any residual pressure in the fuel tank by removing the gas cap, then undo the fuel lines connecting the engine to the chassis (see Chapter 4). Plug or cap all open fittings.

9    Disconnect the throttle linkage, TV linkage and speed control

cable, if equipped, from the engine (see Chapter 4).

10    Unbolt the power steering pump. If clearance allows, tie the pump aside without disconnecting the hoses. If necessary, remove the pump (see Chapter 10).

11    On air-conditioned vehicles, unbolt the compressor and set it aside. Don't disconnect the refrigerant hoses.

12    Detach the exhaust pipe(s) from the manifold(s) (see Chapter 4).

13    Remove the driveaxles (see Chapter 8) and refer to Chapter 7 for information on how to disconnect the wire harness, shift linkage and speedometer cable from the transaxle prior to removal.

14    Attach a lifting sling to the brackets on the engine **(see illustration)**. Position a hoist and connect the sling to it. Take up the slack until there is slight tension on the hoist

15    Recheck to be sure nothing except the mounts are still connecting the engine/transaxle to the vehicle. Disconnect anything still remaining.

16    Support the transaxle with a floor jack. Place a block of wood on the jack head to prevent damage to the transaxle. Remove the nuts/bolts from the engine and transaxle mounts (see the appropriate engine mount procedure in Chapter 2A or 2B). **Warning:** *DO NOT place any part of your body under the engine/transaxle when it's supported only by a hoist or other lifting device.*

17    Slowly lift the engine/transaxle out of the vehicle **(see illustrations)**. It may be necessary to pry the mounts away from the frame brackets.

18    Move the engine/transaxle away from the vehicle and carefully lower the hoist until the transaxle is supported on the floor or a sturdy workbench **(see illustration)**.

19    Remove the engine block-to-transaxle brace.

20    On automatic transaxle equipped models, remove the torque converter-to-driveplate fasteners (see Chapter 7) and push the

**6.17d  Lift the engine/transaxle clear of the vehicle**

**6.18  Lower the engine/transaxle onto a work surface, then remove the transaxle and mount the engine on a stand**

converter back slightly into the bellhousing.

21   Remove the engine-to-transaxle bolts and separate the engine from the transaxle. The torque converter should remain in the transaxle.

22   Place the engine on the floor or remove the flywheel/driveplate and mount the engine on an engine stand.

## Installation

23   Check the engine/transaxle mounts. If they're worn or damaged, replace them. Refer to Chapter 2A, Section 18 for testing the Engine Mount Control System used on automatic-transaxle-equipped vehicles.

24   On manual transaxle-equipped models, inspect the clutch components (see Chapter 8) and apply a dab of high temperature grease to the pilot bearing.

25   On automatic transaxle-equipped models, inspect the converter seal and bushing, and apply a dab of grease to the nose of the converter and to the seal lips.

26   Carefully guide the transaxle into place, following the procedure outlined in Chapter 7. **Caution:** *Do Not use the bolts to force the engine and transaxle into alignment. It may crack or damage major components.*

27   Install the engine-to-transaxle bolts and tighten them securely.

28   Attach the hoist to the engine and carefully lower the engine/transaxle assembly into the engine compartment.

29   Install the mount bolts and tighten them securely (refer to Chapter 2A, Section 18).

30   Reinstall the remaining components and fasteners in the reverse order of removal.

31   Add coolant, oil, power steering and transmission fluids and an oil filter as needed (see Chapter 1).

32   Run the engine and check for proper operation and leaks. Shut off the engine and recheck the fluid levels.

## 7   Engine rebuilding alternatives

The do-it-yourselfer is faced with a number of options when performing an engine overhaul. The decision to replace the engine block, piston/connecting rod assemblies and crankshaft depends on a number of factors, with the number one consideration being the condition of the block. Other considerations are cost, access to machine-shop facilities, parts availability, time required to complete the project and the extent of prior mechanical experience on the part of the do-it-yourselfer.

Some of the rebuilding alternatives include:

**Individual parts** - If the inspection procedures reveal that the engine block and most engine components are in reusable condition, purchasing individual parts may be the most economical alternative. The block, crankshaft and piston/connecting rod assemblies should all be inspected carefully. Even if the block shows little wear, the cylinder bores should be surface-honed.

**Short-block** - A short-block consists of an engine block with a crankshaft and piston/connecting rod assemblies already installed. All new bearings are incorporated and all clearances will be correct. The existing camshaft, valvetrain components, cylinder head(s) and external parts can be bolted to the short block with little or no machine-shop work necessary.

**Long-block** - A long-block consists of a short-block plus an oil pump, oil pan, cylinder head(s), cylinder head covers or valve cover(s), camshaft and valvetrain components, timing sprockets, belt and timing cover. All components are installed with new bearings, seals and gaskets incorporated throughout. The installation of manifolds and external parts is all that's necessary.

Give careful thought to which alternative is best for you and discuss the situation with local automotive machine shops, auto parts dealers and experienced rebuilders before ordering or purchasing replacement parts.

## 8   Engine overhaul - disassembly sequence

1   It's much easier to disassemble and work on the engine if it's mounted on a portable engine stand. A stand can often be rented quite cheaply from an equipment-rental yard. Before the engine is mounted on a stand, the flywheel/driveplate and rear oil seal retainer should be removed from the engine.

2   If a stand isn't available, it's possible to disassemble the engine with it blocked up on the floor. Be extra careful not to tip or drop the engine when working without a stand.

3   If you're going to obtain a rebuilt engine, all external components must come off first, to be transferred to the replacement engine, just as they will if you're doing a complete engine overhaul yourself. These include:

> *Alternator and brackets*
> *Emissions control components*
> *Distributor, spark plug wires and spark plugs*
> *Thermostat and housing cover*
> *Water pump*
> *Fuel injection components*
> *Intake and exhaust manifolds*
> *Oil filter*
> *Engine mounts*
> *Clutch and flywheel/driveplate*
> *Engine rear plate*

**Note:** *When removing the external components from the engine, pay close attention to details that may be helpful or important during installation. Note the installed position of gaskets, seals, spacers, pins, brackets, dowels, washers, bolts and other small items.*

4   If you're going to obtain a short-block, which consists of the engine block, crankshaft, pistons and connecting rods all assembled, then the cylinder head(s), oil pan and oil pump will have to be removed as well. See *Engine rebuilding alternatives* for additional information regarding the different possibilities to be considered.

5   If you're planning a complete overhaul, the engine must be disassembled and the internal components removed in the following order:

> *Valve cover(s)*
> *Intake and exhaust manifolds*
> *Timing belt covers*
> *Timing belt and sprockets*
> *CKP/TDC sensor (1996 and later four-cylinder models)*
> *Balance shafts belt (four-cylinder models)*
> *Cylinder head(s)*
> *Oil pan*
> *Balance shafts (four-cylinder models)*
> *Oil pump*
> *Piston/connecting rod assemblies*
> *Crankshaft rear oil seal retainer*
> *Crankshaft and main bearings*

6   Before beginning the disassembly and overhaul procedures, make sure the following items are available. Also, refer to *Engine overhaul - reassembly sequence* for a list of tools and materials needed for engine reassembly.

> *Common hand tools*
> *Small cardboard boxes or plastic bags for storing parts*
> *Gasket scraper*
> *Ridge reamer*
> *Micrometers*
> *Telescoping gauges*
> *Dial-indicator set*
> *Valve spring compressor*
> *Cylinder surfacing hone*
> *Piston-ring-groove cleaning tool*
> *Electric drill motor*
> *Tap and die set*
> *Wire brushes*
> *Oil gallery brushes*
> *Cleaning solvent*

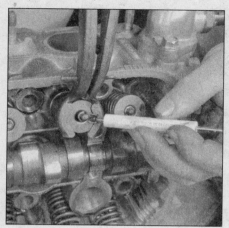

**9.2  Use a valve spring compressor to compress the spring, then remove the keepers from the valve stem with a magnet or small pliers**

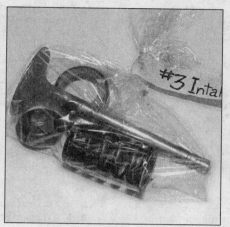

**9.3  A small plastic bag, with an appropriate label, can be used to store the valve train components so they can be kept together and reinstalled in the original location**

**9.4  If the valve won't pull through the guide, deburr the edge of the stem end and the area around the top of the keeper groove with a file or whetstone**

## 9  Cylinder head - disassembly

*Refer to illustrations 9.2, 9.3 and 9.4*

**Note 1:** *New and rebuilt cylinder heads are commonly available for most engines at dealerships and auto parts stores. Due to the fact that some specialized tools are necessary for the disassembly and inspection procedures, and some replacement parts may not be readily available, it may be more practical and economical for the home mechanic to purchase replacement head(s) rather than taking the time to disassemble, inspect and recondition the original(s).*

**Note 2:** *On F22B2 four-cylinder engines, remove the oil-control-orifice from the block immediately after cylinder head removal. Clean it and store in a plastic bag for reassembly.*

1    Cylinder head disassembly involves removal of the intake and exhaust valves and related components. It's assumed that the rocker arms and camshaft(s) have already been removed (see Part A or B of this Chapter as needed).

2    Compress the spring on the first valve with a spring compressor and remove the keepers **(see illustration)**. Carefully release the valve spring compressor and remove the retainer, the spring and the spring seat (if used).

3    After the valves are removed, label and store them, along with their related components, so they can be kept separate and reinstalled in the same valve guides they are removed from **(see illustration)**.

4    Pull the valve out of the head, then remove the oil seal from the guide. If the valve binds in the guide (won't pull through), push it back into the head and deburr the area around the keeper groove with a fine file or whetstone **(see illustration)**.

5    Repeat the procedure for the remaining valves. Remember to keep all the parts for each valve together so they can be reinstalled in the same locations.

6    Once the valves and related components have been removed and stored in an organized manner, the head should be thoroughly cleaned and inspected. If a complete engine overhaul is being done, finish the engine disassembly procedures before beginning the cylinder head cleaning and inspection process.

## 10  Cylinder head - cleaning and inspection

*Refer to illustrations 10.13, 10.15, 10.16, 10.17, 10.18 and 10.19*

1    Thorough cleaning of the cylinder head(s) and related valvetrain components, followed by a detailed inspection, will enable you to decide how much valve service work must be done during the engine overhaul. **Note:** *If the engine was severely overheated, the cylinder head is probably warped* (see Steps 12 and 13).

### Cleaning

2    Scrape all traces of old gasket material and sealing compound off the head gasket, intake manifold and exhaust manifold sealing surfaces. Be very careful not to gouge the cylinder head. Special gasket-removal solvents that soften gaskets and make removal much easier are available at auto parts stores.

3    Remove all built up scale from the coolant passages.

4    Run a stiff wire brush through the various holes to remove deposits that may have formed in them.

5    Run an appropriate-size tap into each of the threaded holes to remove corrosion and thread sealant that may be present. If compressed air is available, use it to clear the holes of debris produced by this operation. **Warning:** *Wear eye protection when using compressed air!*

6    Clean the exhaust and intake manifold stud threads with a wire brush.

7    Clean the cylinder head with solvent and dry it thoroughly. Compressed air will speed the drying process and ensure that all holes and recessed areas are clean. **Note:** *Decarbonizing chemicals are available and may prove very useful when cleaning cylinder heads and valvetrain components. These chemicals are very caustic and should be used with caution. Wear rubber gloves, goggles, and be sure to follow the instructions on the container.*

8    Clean the rocker arms with solvent and dry them thoroughly (don't mix them up during the cleaning process). Compressed air will speed the drying process and can be used to clean out the oil passages. **Note:** *On V-TEC engines, keep the three intake rockers for each cylinder bundled together with rubber bands.*

9    Clean all the valve springs, spring seats, keepers and retainers with solvent and dry them thoroughly. Work on the components from one valve at a time to avoid mixing up the parts.

10    Scrape off any heavy deposits that may have formed on the valves, then use a motorized wire brush to remove deposits from the valve heads and stems. Again, make sure the valves don't get mixed up.

11    Remove, clean, and store in order the hydraulic tappets or lost-motion assemblies (V-TEC four-cylinder). **Note:** *The oil-control orifice should be removed, cleaned and put away at this time. It is located in the top of the head on V-TEC four-cylinder engines, and in the block (under the head) on V6 models and F22B2 four-cylinder engines.*

**10.13 Check the cylinder head gasket surface for warpage by trying to slip a feeler gauge under the straightedge (see the Specifications for the maximum warpage allowed and use a feeler gauge of that thickness)**

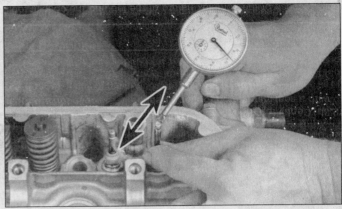

**10.15 A dial indicator can be used to measure valve stem-to-guide clearance (move the valve stem back and forth as shown)**

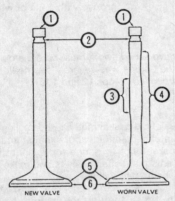

**10.16 Check for valve wear at the points shown here:**

| | | | |
|---|---|---|---|
| 1 | Valve tip | 4 | Stem (most worn area) |
| 2 | Keeper groove | 5 | Valve face |
| 3 | Stem (least worn area) | 6 | Margin |

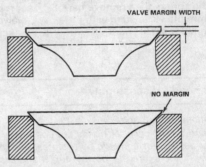

**10.17 The margin width on each valve must be as specified (if no margin exists, the valve cannot be reused)**

## Inspection

**Note:** *Be sure to perform all of the following inspection procedures before concluding that machine shop work is required. Make a list of the items that need attention. The inspection procedures for the lifters and rocker arms, as well as the camshafts, can be found in Part A.*

### Cylinder head

12   Inspect the head very carefully for cracks, evidence of coolant leakage and other damage. If cracks are found, check with an automotive machine shop concerning repair. If repair isn't possible, a new cylinder head should be obtained.
13   Using a straightedge and feeler gauge, check the head-gasket mating surface for warpage **(see illustration)**. If the warpage exceeds the specified limit, it can be resurfaced at an automotive machine shop.
14   Examine the valve seats in each of the combustion chambers. If they're pitted, cracked or burned, the head will require valve service that's beyond the scope of the home mechanic.
15   Check the valve stem-to-guide clearance with a small hole gauge and micrometer. Also check the valve stem deflection crosswise (parallel to the rocker arm) with a dial indicator attached securely to the head **(see illustration)**. The valve must be in the guide and approximately 1/16-inch off the seat. The total valve stem movement indicated by the gauge needle must be noted. If it exceeds the stem-to-guide clearance limit listed in this Chapter's specifications, the valve guides should be replaced. After this is done, if there's still some doubt

regarding the condition of the valve guides, they should be checked by an automotive machine shop (the cost should be minimal).

### Valves

16   Carefully inspect each valve face for uneven wear **(see illustration)**, deformation, cracks, pits and burned areas. Check the valve stem for scuffing and galling and the neck for cracks. Rotate the valve and check for any obvious indication that it's bent. Look for pits and excessive wear on the end of the stem. The presence of any of these conditions indicates the need for valve service by an automotive machine shop.
17   Measure the margin width on each valve **(see illustration)**. Any valve with a margin narrower than that listed in this Chapter's Specifications will have to be replaced with a new one.

### Valve components

18   Check each valve spring for wear (on the ends) and pits. Stand each spring on a flat surface and check it for squareness **(see illustration)**. If any of the springs are distorted or sagged, replace all of them with new parts.
19   Measure the free length of each valve spring with a dial or vernier caliper **(see illustration)**. The tension of springs decreases with age and usage. We recommend replacing the valve springs during an overhaul.
20   Check the spring retainers and keepers for obvious wear and cracks. Any questionable parts should be replaced with new ones, as extensive damage will occur if they fail during engine operation.
21   Any damaged or excessively worn parts must be replaced with new ones.
22   If the inspection process indicates that the valve components are in generally poor condition and worn beyond the limits specified, which is usually the case in an engine that's being overhauled, reassemble the valves in the cylinder head and refer to Section 11 for valve servicing recommendations.

10.18  Check each valve spring for squareness

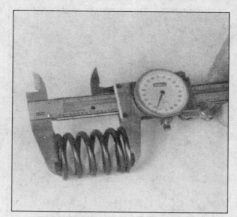

10.19  Measure the free length of each valve spring with a dial or vernier caliper

12.3a  Drop the spring seats over the valve guides

12.3b  Gently tap the valve seals into place with a seal installation tool or a deep socket and hammer

12.5  Install the spring (closely-wound coils toward the head) and retainer over the valve stem

12.6  Apply a small dab of grease to each keeper before installation to hold them in place on the valve stem until the spring is released

## 11  Valves - servicing

1    Because of the complex nature of the job and the special tools and equipment needed, servicing of the valves, the valve seats and the valve guides, commonly known as a valve job, should be done by a professional.

2    The home mechanic can remove and disassemble the head, do the initial cleaning and inspection, then reassemble and deliver it to a dealer service department or an automotive machine shop for the actual service work. Doing the inspection will enable you to see what condition the head and valvetrain components are in and will ensure that you know what work and new parts are required when dealing with an automotive machine shop.

3    The dealer service department, or automotive machine shop, will remove the valves and springs, recondition or replace the valves and valve seats, recondition the valve guides, check and replace the valve springs, spring retainers and keepers (as necessary), replace the valve seals with new ones, reassemble the valve components and make sure the installed spring height is correct. The cylinder head gasket surface should also be resurfaced if it's warped. If you're working on a V6 model and one of the heads is warped, have both of them resurfaced.

4    After the valve job has been performed by a professional, the head will be in like new condition. When the head is returned, be sure to clean it again before installation on the engine to remove any metal particles and abrasive grit that may still be present from the valve service or head resurfacing operations. Use compressed air, if available, to blow out all the oil holes and passages.

## 12  Cylinder head - reassembly

*Refer to illustrations 12.3a, 12.3b, 12.5 and 12.6*

1    Regardless of whether or not the head was sent to an automotive repair shop for valve servicing, make sure it's clean before beginning reassembly.

2    If the head was sent out for valve servicing, the valves and related components will already be in place. Begin the reassembly procedure with Step 8.

3    Slip the spring seats over the guides **(see illustration)**, then install new seals on each of the valve guides. **Note:** *Intake and exhaust valves require different seals - DO NOT mix them up! Exhaust seals have black springs and intake seals have white or silver springs.* Gently tap each valve seal into place with Honda tool no. 07GAD-PH70100 or KD tool no. 2899 until it's seated on the guide **(see illustration)**. **Caution:** *Don't hammer on the valve seals once they're seated or you may damage them. Don't twist or cock the seals during installation or they won't seat properly on the valve stems.*

4    Beginning at one end of the head, lubricate and install the first valve. Apply moly-base grease or clean engine oil to the valve stem.

5    Set the valve spring and retainer in place **(see illustration)**, with the more-closely-wound spring coils toward the head.

6    Compress the springs with a valve spring compressor and carefully install the keepers in the upper groove, then slowly release the compressor and make sure the keepers seat properly. Apply a small dab of grease to each keeper to hold it in place if necessary **(see illustration)**.

**13.1  To remove the front balance shaft sprocket, the shaft must be held with a bolt or screwdriver through this maintenance hole behind the sprocket**

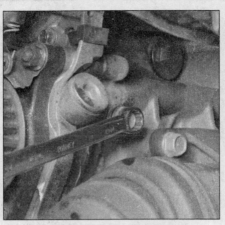

**13.3a  Remove this access bolt on the side of the engine . . .**

**13.3b  . . . and insert a bolt or tool of the correct diameter through the balance shaft to keep the rear balance shaft from turning - The tool will only go in when the balance shaft marks are aligned**

**13.5  Remove the two bolts (arrows) retaining the front balance shaft thrust plate**

**14.1  A ridge reamer is required to remove the ridge from the top of each cylinder - do this before removing the pistons!**

**14.4  Check the connecting rod side clearance with a feeler gauge as shown here**

7    Repeat the procedure for the remaining valves. Be sure to return the components to their original locations - don't mix them up!

8    The camshaft(s) and rocker arm assemblies can be installed after the cylinder head is assembled to the finished short-block.

## 13  Balance shafts - removal and inspection (four-cylinder models)

### *Removal*

*Refer to illustrations 13.1, 13.3a, 13.3b and 13.5*

1    Insert a 6 x 100-mm bolt or a suitable-size screwdriver through the access hole in the front balance shaft (just behind the sprocket) and unbolt the front balance shaft sprocket **(see illustration)**.

2    Remove the cover over the rear balance shaft gear case.

3    Insert the bolt or screwdriver in the access hole in the rear of the block to secure the rear balance shaft, and unbolt the rear balance shaft gear case **(see illustrations)**. With the shaft secured by the bolt or screwdriver, unbolt the rear balance shaft driven gear from the shaft and remove the gear.

4    Remove the oil pump housing (see Chapter 2A).

5    Remove the two bolts retaining the thrust plate from the front balance shaft **(see illustration)**. Withdraw the balance shafts carefully to avoid nicking the bearings.

### *Inspection*

6    Clean the balance shafts and inspect the journals for signs of wear, discoloration or scoring. Normally, the wear points exhibit a mirror-like surface.

7    With a micrometer, measure the front and rear edges of each journal. If the difference in measurements (taper) exceeds this Chapter's Specifications, replace the balance shaft.

8    Measure the journal diameters and compare to this Chapter's Specifications. When your block goes to the machine shop, have them measure the inside-diameter of the balance shaft bearings in the block and by subtracting the journal diameter from each bearing diameter, the shaft-to-bearing oil clearance can be calculated. Compare these measurements to the Specifications. If the shafts are in good condition, have new balance shaft bearings installed in the block at the machine shop.

## 14  Pistons/connecting rods - removal

*Refer to illustrations 14.1, 14.4, 14.5a, 14.5b and 14.7*

**Note:** *Prior to removing the piston/connecting rod assemblies, remove the cylinder head(s), the oil pan, oil pump pick-up tube and bearing cap bridge by referring to* **Chapter 2A or 2B**.

1    Use your fingernail to feel if a ridge has formed at the upper limit

14.5a DO NOT confuse the stamped numbers on the parting surface, such as this 3 (arrow) with cylinder numbers - this number indicates big-end bore size

14.5b Before they're removed, the connecting rods and caps should be marked with a center punch to indicate in which cylinder they're installed

14.7 To prevent damage to the crankshaft journals and cylinder walls, slip sections of hose over the rod bolts before removing the pistons

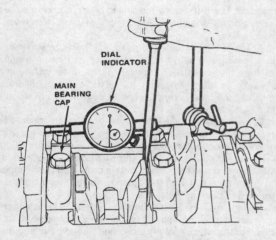

15.1 Position the dial indicator as shown and move the crankshaft back and forth with a screwdriver

rod and cap (1, 2, 3, etc., depending on the engine type and cylinder they're associated with) (see illustration).

6    Loosen each of the connecting rod cap nuts 1/2-turn at a time until they can be removed by hand. Remove the number one connecting rod cap and bearing insert. Don't drop the bearing insert out of the cap.

7    Slip a short length of plastic or rubber hose over each connecting rod cap bolt to protect the crankshaft journal and cylinder wall as the piston is removed (see illustration).

8    Remove the bearing insert and push the connecting rod/piston assembly out through the top of the engine. Use a wooden hammer handle to push on the upper bearing surface in the connecting rod. If resistance is felt, double-check to make sure that all of the ridge was removed from the cylinder.

9    Repeat the procedure for the remaining cylinders.

10    After removal, reassemble the connecting rod caps and bearing inserts in their respective connecting rods and install the cap nuts finger tight. Leaving the old bearing inserts in place until reassembly will help prevent the connecting rod bearing surfaces from being accidentally nicked or gouged.

11    Don't separate the pistons from the connecting rods (see Section 19 for additional information).

## 15  Crankshaft - removal

Refer to illustrations 15.1, 15.3 and 15.4

Note: The crankshaft can be removed only after the engine has been removed from the vehicle. It's assumed that the flywheel or driveplate, timing belt, oil pan, oil pick-up tube, oil pump and piston/connecting rod assemblies have already been removed. The rear main oil seal retainer must be unbolted and separated from the block before proceeding with crankshaft removal.

1    Before the crankshaft is removed, check the endplay. Mount a dial indicator with the stem in line with the crankshaft and just touching one of the crank throws (see illustration). Note: The main caps and main-cap bridge should be in place and torqued to Specifications.

2    Push the crankshaft all the way to the rear and zero the dial indicator. Next, pry the crankshaft to the front as far as possible and check the reading on the dial indicator. The distance that it moves is the endplay. If it's greater than specified, check the crankshaft thrust surfaces for wear. If no wear is evident, new thrust washers should correct the endplay.

3    If a dial indicator isn't available, feeler gauges can be used. Gently pry or push the crankshaft all the way to the front of the engine. Slip feeler gauges between the crankshaft and the back face of the front

of ring travel (about 1/4-inch down from the top of each cylinder). If carbon deposits or cylinder wear have produced ridges, they must be completely removed with a special tool (see illustration). Follow the manufacturer's instructions provided with the tool. Failure to remove the ridges before attempting to remove the piston/connecting rod assemblies may result in piston breakage.

2    After the cylinder ridges (if any) have been removed, turn the engine upside-down so the crankshaft is facing up.

3    On V6 engines, the oil baffle plate must be removed first to access the connecting rods.

4    Before the connecting rods are removed, check the side clearance (endplay) with feeler gauges. Slide them between the first connecting rod and the crankshaft throw until the play is removed (see illustration). The endplay is equal to the thickness of the feeler gauge(s). If the endplay exceeds the service limit, new connecting rods will be required. If new rods (or a new crankshaft) are installed, the endplay may fall under the specified minimum (if it does, the rods will have to be machined to restore it - consult an automotive machine shop for advice if necessary). Repeat the procedure for the remaining connecting rods.

5    The existing numbers on the connecting rods indicate the rod bore size, not the position in the engine (see illustration). Use a small center punch to make the appropriate number of indentations on each

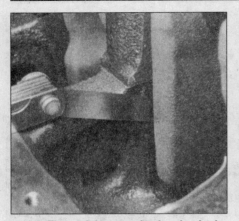

**15.3  The endplay can also be checked with a feeler gauge at the thrust bearing journal**

**15.4  The main bearing caps should have numbers and arrows - this number indicates it is the second cap from the timing belt end and the arrows point toward the timing belt end**

**16.7  All bolt holes in the block - particularly the main bearing cap and head bolt holes - should be cleaned and restored with a tap (be sure to remove debris from the holes after this is done)**

thrust bearing to determine the clearance **(see illustration)**. The thrust bearing on four-cylinder engines is journal number four, while on the V6 engine it's number three.

4    Check the main bearing caps to see if they're marked to indicate their locations. They should be numbered consecutively from the front of the engine to the rear **(see illustration)**. If they aren't, mark them with number-stamping dies or a center punch. Main bearing caps generally have a cast-in arrow, which points to the front of the engine. Loosen the main bearing cap bridge bolts 1/4-turn at a time each, working around the engine until they can be removed by hand.

5    Pull the main bearing cap bridge off, then gently tap the caps with a soft-face hammer and separate them from the engine block. If necessary, use the bolts as levers to remove the caps. Try not to drop the bearing inserts if they come out with the caps.

**Note:** *On V6 engines, there are additional main cap bolts beside the ones holding the bridge. Each main cap has an extra bolt on either side of the bridge, as well as bolts that enter from the side through the engine block ( for a total of six bolts per main cap). Make sure all bolts are removed before trying to remove the caps.*

6    Carefully lift the crankshaft out of the engine. It may be a good idea to have an assistant available, since the crankshaft is quite heavy. With the bearing inserts in place in the engine block, return the caps to their respective locations on the engine block, install the main bearing cap bridge and tighten the bolts finger tight.

## 16   Engine block - cleaning

*Refer to illustration 16.7*

1    Using a gasket scraper, remove all traces of gasket material from the engine block. Be very careful not to nick or gouge the gasket sealing surfaces.

2    Remove the main bearing caps and bridge and separate the bearing inserts from the caps and the engine block. Tag the bearings, indicating which cylinder they were removed from. The oil groove identifies the upper bearings.

3    Remove all of the threaded oil gallery plugs from the block. The plugs are usually very tight - they may have to be drilled out and the holes retapped. Use new plugs when the engine is reassembled.

4    If the block is extremely dirty it should be taken to an automotive machine shop to be steam cleaned or tanked.

5    After the block is returned, clean all oil holes and oil galleries one more time. Brushes specifically designed for this purpose are available at most auto parts stores. Flush the passages with warm water until the water runs clear, dry the block thoroughly and wipe all machined surfaces with a light, rust preventive oil. If you have access to

compressed air, use it to speed the drying process and to blow out all the oil holes and galleries. **Warning:** *Wear eye protection when using compressed air!*

6    If the block isn't extremely dirty or sludged up, you can do an adequate cleaning job with hot soapy water and a stiff brush. Take plenty of time and do a thorough job. Regardless of the cleaning method used, be sure to clean all oil holes and galleries very thoroughly, dry the block completely and coat all machined surfaces with light oil.

7    The threaded holes in the block must be clean to ensure accurate torque readings during reassembly. Run the proper size tap into each of the holes to remove rust, corrosion, thread sealant or sludge and restore damaged threads **(see illustration)**. If possible, use compressed air to clear the holes of debris produced by this operation. Now is a good time to clean the threads on the head bolts and the main bearing cap bolts as well.

8    Reinstall the main bearing caps and tighten the bolts finger tight.

9    Apply non-hardening sealant (such as Permatex no. 2 or Teflon pipe sealant) to the new oil gallery plugs and thread them into the holes in the block. Make sure they're tightened securely.

10   If the engine isn't going to be reassembled right away, cover it with a large plastic trash bag to keep it clean.

## 17   Engine block - inspection

*Refer to illustrations 17.4a, 17.4b, 17.4c, 17.12a and 17.12b*

1    Before the block is inspected, it should be cleaned as described in Section 16.

2    Visually check the block for cracks, rust and corrosion. Look for stripped threads in the threaded holes. It's also a good idea to have the block checked for hidden cracks by an automotive machine shop that has the special equipment to do this type of work. If defects are found, have the block repaired, if possible, or replaced.

3    Check the cylinder bores for scuffing and scoring.

4    Check the cylinders for taper and out-of-round conditions as follows **(see illustrations)**:

5    Measure the diameter of each cylinder at the top (just under the ridge area), center and bottom of the cylinder bore, parallel to the crankshaft axis.

6    Next, measure each cylinder's diameter at the same three locations perpendicular to the crankshaft axis.

7    The taper of the cylinder is the difference between the bore diameter at the top and the diameter at the bottom.

8    The out-of-round specification of the cylinder bore is the difference between the parallel and the perpendicular readings.

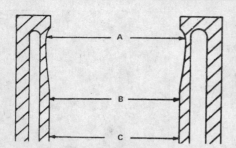

17.4a  Measure the diameter of each cylinder just under the wear ridge (A), at the center (B) and at the bottom (C)

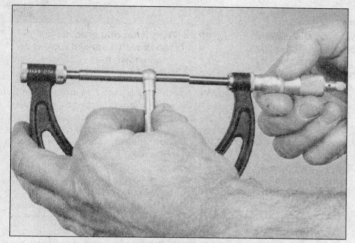

17.4c  The gauge is then measured with a micrometer to determine the bore size

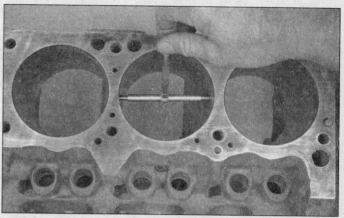

17.4b  The ability to "feel" when the telescoping gauge is at the correct point will be developed over time, so work slowly and repeat the check until you're satisfied the bore measurement is accurate

resurfaced by an automotive machine shop.

13    If the cylinders are in reasonably good condition and not worn to the outside of the limits, and if the piston-to-cylinder clearances can be maintained properly (see Section 19), then they don't have to be rebored. Honing is all that's necessary (see Section 18).

## 18  Cylinder honing

*Refer to illustrations 18.3a and 18.3b*

1    Prior to engine reassembly, the cylinder bores must be honed so the new piston rings will seat correctly and provide the best possible combustion chamber seal. **Note:** *If you don't have the tools or don't want to tackle the honing operation, most automotive machine shops will do it for a reasonable fee.*

2    Before honing the cylinders, install the main bearing caps or cap assembly (without bearing inserts) and tighten the bolts to the torque listed in this Chapter's Specifications.

3    Two types of cylinder hones are commonly available - the flex hone or "bottle brush" type and the more traditional surfacing hone with spring-loaded stones. Both will do the job, but for the less experienced mechanic the "bottle brush" hone will probably be easier to use. You'll also need some kerosene or honing oil, rags and an electric drill motor. Proceed as follows:

9    Compare the results to those listed in this Chapter's Specifications.

10    If the cylinder walls are badly scuffed or scored, or if they're out-of-round or tapered beyond the limits given in this Chapter's Specifications, have the engine block rebored and honed at an automotive machine shop.

11    If a rebore is done, oversize pistons and rings will be required.

12    Using a precision straightedge and feeler gauge, check the block deck (the surface that mates with the cylinder head[s]) for distortion **(see illustrations)**. If it's distorted beyond the specified limit, it can be

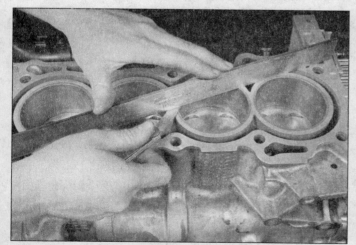

17.12a  Check the block deck for distortion with a precision straightedge and feeler gauges

17.12b  Lay the straightedge across the block, diagonally and from end-to-end when making the check

**18.3a  The home mechanic can use either the stone-type (shown) or the bottle-brush type**

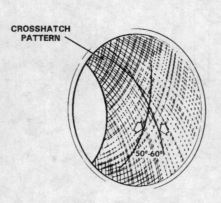

CROSSHATCH PATTERN

50°-60°

**18.3b  The cylinder hone should leave a smooth, crosshatch pattern with the lines intersecting at approximately a 60-degree angle**

**19.4a  The piston ring grooves can be cleaned with a special tool, as shown here, . . .**

**19.4b  . . . or a section of a broken ring**

a) *Mount the hone in the drill motor, compress the stones and slip it into the first cylinder (see illustration). Be sure to wear safety goggles or a face shield!*

b) *Lubricate the cylinder with plenty of honing oil, turn on the drill and move the hone up-and-down in the cylinder at a pace that will produce a fine crosshatch pattern on the cylinder walls. Ideally, the crosshatch lines should intersect at approximately a 60-degree angle (see illustration). Be sure to use plenty of lubricant and don't take off any more material than is absolutely necessary to produce the desired finish.* **Note:** *Piston ring manufacturers may specify a smaller crosshatch angle than the traditional 60-degrees - read and follow any instructions included with the new rings.*

c) *Don't withdraw the hone from the cylinder while it's running. Instead, shut off the drill and continue moving the hone up-and-down in the cylinder until it comes to a complete stop, then compress the stones and withdraw the hone. If you're using a "bottle brush" type hone, stop the drill motor, then turn the chuck in the normal direction of rotation while withdrawing the hone from the cylinder.*

d) *Wipe the oil out of the cylinder and repeat the procedure for the remaining cylinders.*

4    After the honing job is complete, chamfer the top edges of the cylinder bores with a small file so the rings won't catch when the pistons are installed. Be very careful not to nick the cylinder walls with the end of the file.

5    The entire engine block must be washed again very thoroughly with warm, soapy water to remove all traces of the abrasive grit produced during the honing operation. **Note:** *The bores can be considered clean when a lint-free white cloth - dampened with clean engine oil and used to wipe them out - doesn't pick-up any more honing residue, which will show up as gray areas on the cloth.* Be sure to run a brush through all oil holes and galleries and flush them with running water.

6    After rinsing, dry the block and apply a coat of light rust preventive oil to all machined surfaces. Wrap the block in a plastic trash bag to keep it clean and set it aside until reassembly.

## 19  Pistons/connecting rods - inspection

*Refer to illustrations 19.4a, 19.4b, 19.10, 19.11 and 19.12*
1    Before the inspection process can be carried out, the piston/connecting rod assemblies must be cleaned and the original piston rings removed from the pistons. **Note:** *Always use new piston rings when the engine is reassembled.*
2    Using a piston ring tool, carefully remove the rings from the pistons. Be careful not to nick or gouge the pistons in the process.
3    Scrape all traces of carbon from the top of the piston. A hand-held wire brush or a piece of fine emery cloth can be used once the majority of the deposits have been scraped away. Do not, under any circumstances, use a wire brush mounted in a drill motor to remove deposits from the pistons. The piston material is soft and may be eroded away by the wire brush.
4    Use a piston-ring groove cleaning tool to remove carbon deposits from the ring grooves. If a tool isn't available, a piece broken off the old ring will do the job. Be very careful to remove only the carbon deposits - don't remove any metal and do not nick or scratch the sides of the ring grooves **(see illustrations)**.
5    Once the deposits have been removed, clean the piston/rod assemblies with solvent and dry them with compressed air (if available). Make sure the oil return holes in the back sides of the ring grooves and the oil hole in the lower end of each rod are clear. **Warning:** *Wear eye protection when using compressed air.*
6    If the pistons and cylinder walls aren't damaged or worn excessively, and if the engine block is not rebored, new pistons won't be necessary. Normal piston wear appears as even vertical wear on the piston thrust surfaces and slight looseness of the top ring in its groove. New piston rings, however, should always be used when an engine is rebuilt.
7    Carefully inspect each piston for cracks around the skirt, at the pin bosses and at the ring lands.
8    Look for scoring and scuffing on the thrust faces of the skirt, holes in the piston crown and burned areas at the edge of the crown. If the skirt is scored or scuffed, the engine may have been suffering from overheating and/or abnormal combustion, which caused excessively-

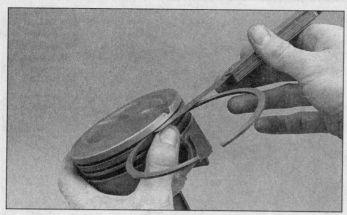

19.10  Check the ring side clearance with a feeler gauge at several points around the groove

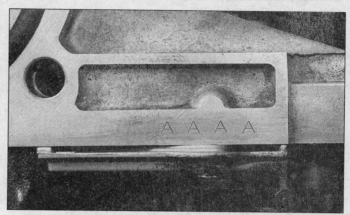

19.11  Match the marks with the letters on the pistons - the marks are located on a pad at the rear of the engine and read from left to right, on V6 engines, the mark is in the same area, with cylinders 1 through 3 on top and 4 through 6 on the bottom row

19.12  Measure the piston diameter at a 90-degree angle to the piston pin and in line with it

high operating temperatures. The cooling and lubrication systems should be checked thoroughly. A hole in the piston crown is an indication that abnormal combustion (preignition) was occurring. Burned areas at the edge of the piston crown are usually evidence of spark knock (detonation). If any of the above problems exist, the causes must be corrected or the damage will occur again. The causes may include intake air leaks, incorrect fuel/air mixture, incorrect ignition timing and EGR system malfunctions.

9    Corrosion of the piston, in the form of small pits, indicates that coolant is leaking into the combustion chamber and/or the crankcase. Again, the cause must be corrected or the problem may persist in the rebuilt engine.

10   Measure the piston ring side clearance by laying a new piston ring in each ring groove and slipping a feeler gauge in beside it **(see illustration)**. Check the clearance at three or four locations around each groove. Be sure to use the correct ring for each groove - they are different. If the side clearance is greater than specified, new pistons will have to be used.

11   Check the piston-to-bore clearance by measuring the bore (see Section 15) and the piston diameter. Make sure the pistons and bores are correctly matched. **Note:** *There are two standard size pistons (marked A or I and B or II on the piston). Additionally, the engine block is marked* **(see illustration)** *to indicate which size piston was originally fitted to each bore.*

12   Measure the piston across the skirt, at a 90-degree angle to the piston pin, the distance listed in this Chapter's Specifications from the bottom edge of the piston skirt **(see illustration)**. Subtract the piston diameter from the bore diameter to obtain the clearance. If it's greater than specified, the block will have to be rebored and new pistons and rings installed.

13   Check the piston pin-to-rod clearance by twisting the piston and rod in opposite directions. Any noticeable play indicates excessive wear, which must be corrected. The piston/connecting rod assemblies should be taken to an automotive machine shop to have the pistons and rods resized and new pins installed.

14   If the pistons must be removed from the connecting rods for any reason, they should be taken to an automotive machine shop. While they are there have the connecting rods checked for bend and twist, since automotive machine shops have special equipment for this purpose. **Note:** *Unless new pistons and/or connecting rods must be installed, do not disassemble the pistons and connecting rods.*

15   Check the connecting rods for cracks and other damage. Temporarily remove the rod caps, lift out the old bearing inserts, wipe the rod and cap bearing surfaces clean and inspect them for nicks, gouges and scratches. After checking the rods, replace the old bearings, slip the caps into place and tighten the nuts finger tight. **Note:** *If the engine is being rebuilt because of a connecting rod knock, be sure to install new rods.*

## 20  Crankshaft - inspection

*Refer to illustration 20.1, 20.3 and 20.5*

1    Remove all burrs from the crankshaft oil holes with a stone, file **(see illustration)** or scraper.

2    Check the main and connecting rod bearing journals for uneven wear, scoring, pits and cracks.

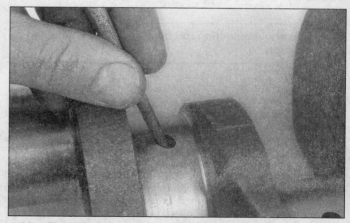

20.1  The oil holes should be chamfered so sharp edges don't gouge or scratch the new bearings

**20.3  Use a wire or stiff plastic bristle brush to clean the oil passages in the crankshaft**

**20.5  Measure the diameter of each crankshaft journal at several points to detect taper and out-of-round conditions**

3    Clean the crankshaft with solvent and dry it with compressed air (if available). Be sure to clean the oil holes with a stiff brush **(see illustration)** and flush them with solvent.

4    Check the rest of the crankshaft for cracks and other damage. It should be magnafluxed to reveal hidden cracks - an automotive machine shop will handle the procedure.

5    Using a micrometer, measure the diameter of the main and connecting rod journals and compare the results to this Chapter's Specifications **(see illustration)**. By measuring the diameter at a number of points around each journal's circumference, you'll be able to determine whether or not the journal is out-of-round. Take the measurement at each end of the journal, near the crank throws, to determine if the journal is tapered. Crankshaft runout should be checked also, but large V-blocks and a dial indicator are needed to do it correctly. If you don't have the equipment, have a machine shop check the runout.

6    If the crankshaft journals are damaged, tapered, out-of-round or worn beyond the limits given in this Chapter's Specifications, have the crankshaft reground by an automotive machine shop. Be sure to use the correct size bearing inserts if the crankshaft is reconditioned.

7    Check the oil seal journals at each end of the crankshaft for wear and damage. If the seal has worn a groove in the journal, or if it's nicked or scratched, the new seal may leak when the engine is reassembled. In some cases, an automotive machine shop may be able to repair the journal by pressing on a thin sleeve. If repair isn't feasible, a new or different crankshaft should be installed.

8    Refer to Section 19 and examine the main and rod bearing inserts.

## 21   Main and connecting rod bearings - inspection and selection

### Inspection

*Refer to illustration 21.1*

1    Even though the main and connecting rod bearings should be replaced with new ones during the engine overhaul, the old bearings should be retained for close examination, as they may reveal valuable information about the condition of the engine **(see illustration)**.

2    Bearing failure occurs because of lack of lubrication, the presence of dirt or other foreign particles, overloading the engine and corrosion. Regardless of the cause of bearing failure, it must be corrected before the engine is reassembled to prevent it from happening again.

3    When examining the bearings, remove them from the engine block, the main bearing caps, the connecting rods and the rod caps

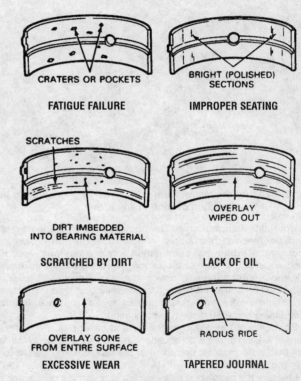

**21.1  Typical bearing failures**

and lay them out on a clean surface in the same general position as their location in the engine. This will enable you to match any bearing problems with the corresponding crankshaft journal.

4    Dirt and other foreign particles get into the engine in a variety of ways. It may be left in the engine during assembly, or it may pass through filters or the PCV system. It may get into the oil, and from there into the bearings. Metal chips from machining operations and normal engine wear are often present. Abrasives are sometimes left in engine components after reconditioning, especially when parts are not thoroughly cleaned using the proper cleaning methods. Whatever the source, these foreign objects often end up embedded in the soft bearing material and are easily recognized. Large particles will not embed in the bearing and will score or gouge the bearing and journal. The best prevention for this cause of bearing failure is to clean all parts

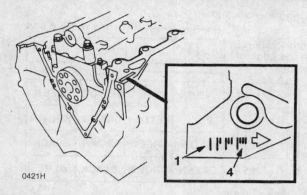

**21.10  On V6 models, the main journal bore codes are stamped on the block adjacent to the oil pan surface (codes for mains 1 through 4) - codes are in the same place on four-cylinder models with codes for mains 1 through 5**

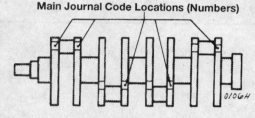

**21.11b  On four-cylinder models, the main bearing journal grade numbers are also stamped adjacent to their respective journals**

thoroughly and keep everything spotlessly clean during engine assembly. Frequent and regular engine oil and filter changes are also recommended.

5  Lack of lubrication (or lubrication breakdown) has a number of interrelated causes. Excessive heat (which thins the oil), overloading (which squeezes the oil from the bearing face) and oil leakage or throw off (from excessive bearing clearances, worn oil pump or high engine speeds) all contribute to lubrication breakdown. Blocked oil passages, which usually are the result of misaligned oil holes in a bearing shell, will also oil starve a bearing and destroy it. When lack of lubrication is the cause of bearing failure, the bearing material is wiped or extruded from the steel backing of the bearing. Temperatures may increase to the point where the steel backing turns blue from overheating.

6  Driving habits can have a definite effect on bearing life. Full throttle, low speed operation (lugging the engine) puts very high loads on bearings, which tends to squeeze out the oil film. These loads cause the bearings to flex, which produces fine cracks in the bearing face (fatigue failure). Eventually the bearing material will loosen in pieces and tear away from the steel backing. Short-trip driving leads to corrosion of bearings because insufficient engine heat is produced to drive off the condensed water and corrosive gases. These products collect in the engine oil, forming acid and sludge. As the oil is carried to the engine bearings, the acid attacks and corrodes the bearing material.

7  Incorrect bearing installation during engine assembly will lead to bearing failure as well. Tight-fitting bearings leave insufficient bearing oil clearance and will result in oil starvation. Dirt or foreign particles trapped behind a bearing insert result in high spots on the bearing which lead to failure.

## Selection

*Refer to illustrations 21.10, 21.11a, 21.11b, 21.12, 21.15a, 21.15b, 21.16a and 21.16b*

8  If the original bearings are worn or damaged, or if the oil

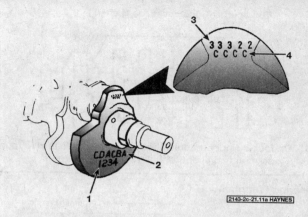

**21.11a  On the V6, the main journal grade numbers are stamped on the number 1 crank counterweight, and on the four-cylinder, they are in front of the number 1 throw:**

1  V6 main journal codes, 1 through 4 (left-to-right)
2  V6 rod journal codes, 1 through 6 (left-to-right)
3  Four-cylinder main journal codes, 5 through 1 (left-to-right)
4  Four-cylinder rod journal codes, 4 through 1 (left-to-right)

clearances are incorrect (see Section 24 or 26), the following procedures should be used to select the correct new bearings for engine reassembly. However, if the crankshaft has been reground, new undersize bearings must be installed - the following procedure should not be used if undersize bearings are required! The automotive machine shop that reconditions the crankshaft will provide or help you select the correct-size bearings. Regardless of how the bearing sizes are determined, use the oil clearance, measured with Plastigage, as a guide to ensure the bearings are the right size.

### Main bearings

9  If you need to use a STANDARD-size main bearing, install one that has the same color code as the original bearing.
10  If the color code on the original main bearing has been obscured, locate the codes stamped into the block for the corresponding cap location (see illustration).
11  Locate the main journal grade numbers on the crankshaft as well (see illustrations).
12  Use the accompanying chart to determine the correct bearings for each journal (see illustration).

### Bearing Identification

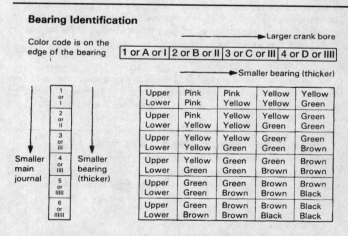

| Color code is on the edge of the bearing | | 1 or A or I | 2 or B or II | 3 or C or III | 4 or D or IIII |
|---|---|---|---|---|---|
| | | → Larger crank bore | | | |
| | | → Smaller bearing (thicker) | | | |
| | 1 or I | Upper | Pink | Pink | Yellow | Yellow |
| | | Lower | Pink | Yellow | Yellow | Green |
| | 2 or II | Upper | Pink | Yellow | Yellow | Green |
| | | Lower | Yellow | Yellow | Green | Green |
| | 3 or III | Upper | Yellow | Yellow | Green | Green |
| | | Lower | Yellow | Green | Green | Brown |
| Smaller main journal | 4 or IIII | Upper | Yellow | Green | Green | Brown |
| | | Lower | Green | Green | Brown | Brown |
| | 5 or IIIII | Upper | Green | Green | Brown | Brown |
| | | Lower | Green | Brown | Brown | Black |
| | 6 or IIIIII | Upper | Green | Brown | Brown | Black |
| | | Lower | Brown | Brown | Black | Black |

Smaller bearing (thicker)

**21.12  Find the correct main bearing color code for V6 and Four-cylinder models by using the number/letter on the block and the Arabic number on the crankshaft - example: C3 would be green**

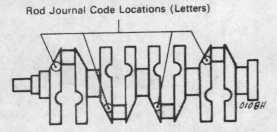

Rod Journal Code Locations (Letters)

**21.15  On four-cylinder models, the rod journal code is also found stamped adjacent to their respective journals**

## Bearing Identification

Color code is on the edge of the bearing

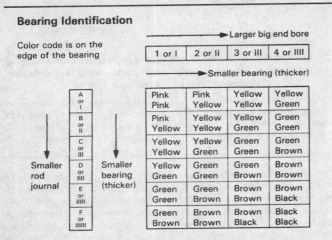

|  | 1 or I | 2 or II | 3 or III | 4 or IIII |
|---|---|---|---|---|
| A or I | Pink Pink | Pink Yellow | Yellow Yellow | Yellow Green |
| B or II | Pink Yellow | Yellow Yellow | Yellow Green | Green Green |
| C or III | Yellow Yellow | Yellow Green | Green Green | Green Brown |
| D or IIII | Yellow Green | Green Green | Green Brown | Brown Brown |
| E or IIIII | Green Green | Green Brown | Brown Brown | Brown Black |
| F or IIIIII | Green Brown | Brown Brown | Brown Black | Black Black |

Larger big end bore → (above columns)
Smaller bearing (thicker) →

Smaller rod journal        Smaller bearing (thicker)

**21.16b  Find the correct connecting rod bearing color code for V6 models by using the letter on each crankshaft throw and the number on the respective connecting rod - example: D4 would be brown (note that some call for different upper and lower bearing codes)**

## Connecting rod bearings

13   If you need to use a STANDARD-size rod bearing, install one that has the same color code as the original.

14   If the color code has been obscured, locate the number stamped on each connecting rod cap **(see illustration 14.5a)**. This code indicates the connecting rod big-end-bearing bore size, **not** the cylinder number it came from.

15   Locate the letters stamped on the crankshaft **(see illustration)**. These denote the size of their respective connecting rod journals.

16   Use the accompanying chart **(see illustrations)** to determine the correct bearings for each journal.

## All bearings

17   Remember, the oil clearance is the final judge when selecting new bearing sizes. If you have any questions or are unsure which bearings to use, get help from your dealer parts or service department.

## 22   Engine overhaul - reassembly sequence

1   Before beginning engine reassembly, make sure you have all the necessary new parts, gaskets and seals as well as the following items on hand:

*Common hand tools*
*A 1/2-inch drive torque wrench*
*Piston ring installation tool*
*Piston ring compressor*
*Short lengths of rubber or plastic hose to fit over connecting rod bolts*

Bearing Identification

Color code is on the edge of the bearing

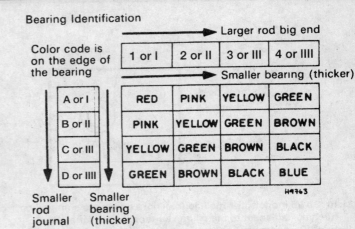

|  | 1 or I | 2 or II | 3 or III | 4 or IIII |
|---|---|---|---|---|
| A or I | RED | PINK | YELLOW | GREEN |
| B or II | PINK | YELLOW | GREEN | BROWN |
| C or III | YELLOW | GREEN | BROWN | BLACK |
| D or IIII | GREEN | BROWN | BLACK | BLUE |

Larger rod big end →
Smaller bearing (thicker) →

Smaller rod journal        Smaller bearing (thicker)

H9763

**21.16a  Find the correct connecting rod bearing color code for four-cylinder models by using the letter on each crankshaft throw and the number on the respective connecting rod - example: D4 would be blue**

*Plastigage*
*Feeler gauges*
*A fine-tooth file*
*New engine oil*
*Engine assembly lube or moly-base grease*
*Gasket sealer*
*Thread locking compound*

2   In order to save time and avoid problems, engine reassembly must be done in the following general order:

### *Four-cylinder engine*

*Piston rings*
*Crankshaft and main bearings*
*Piston/connecting rod assemblies*
*Rear main (crankshaft) oil seal*
*Main cap bridge*
*Balance shafts*
*Oil pump (see Part A)*
*Oil pick-up (see Part A)*
*Oil pan (see Part A)*
*Cylinder head (see Part A)*
*Camshaft and rockers (see Part A)*
*Timing belt and sprockets (see Part A)*
*Timing belt cover (see Part A)*
*Valve cover (see Part A)*
*Intake and exhaust manifolds (see Part A)*
*Flywheel/driveplate (see Part A)*

### *V6 engine*

*Piston rings*
*Crankshaft and main bearings*
*Piston/connecting rod assemblies*
*Rear main oil seal/retainer*
*Crankshaft main bridge*
*Oil baffle plate*
*Oil pump (see Part B)*
*Oil pan (see Part B)*
*Cylinder heads (see Part B)*
*Camshafts and valve components (see Part B)*
*Timing belt and sprockets (see Part B)*
*Timing belt covers (see Part B)*
*Intake and exhaust manifolds (see Part B)*
*Valve covers (see Part B)*
*Flywheel/driveplate (see Part B)*

**23.3  When checking piston ring end gap, the ring must be square in the cylinder bore (this is done by pushing the ring down with the top of a piston as shown)**

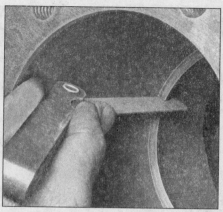

**23.4  With the ring square in the cylinder, measure the end gap with a feeler gauge**

**23.9a  Installing the spacer/expander in the oil control ring groove**

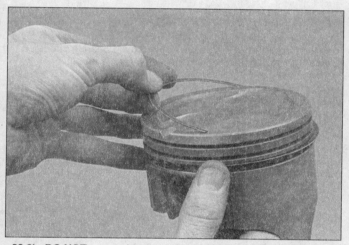

**23.9b  DO NOT use a piston ring installation tool when installing the oil ring side rails**

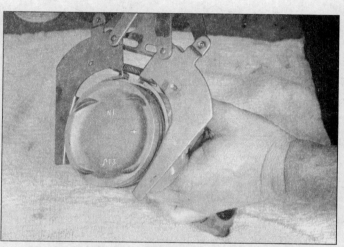

**23.12  Installing the compression rings with a ring expander - the mark must face up**

## 23  Piston rings - installation

*Refer to illustrations 23.3, 23.4, 23.9a, 23.9b and 23.12*

1    Before installing the new piston rings, the ring end gaps must be checked. It's assumed that the piston ring side clearance has been checked and verified correct (see Section 19).

2    Lay out the piston/connecting rod assemblies and the new ring sets so the ring sets will be matched with the same piston and cylinder during the end-gap measurement and engine assembly.

3    Insert the top (number one) ring into the first cylinder and square it up with the cylinder walls by pushing it in with the top of the piston **(see illustration)**. The ring should be near the bottom of the cylinder, at the lower limit of ring travel.

4    To measure the end gap, slip feeler gauges between the ends of the ring until a gauge equal to the gap width is found **(see illustration)**. The feeler gauge should slide between the ring ends with a slight amount of drag. Compare the measurement to this Chapter's Specifications. If the gap is larger or smaller than specified, double-check to make sure you have the correct rings before proceeding.

5    If the gap is too small, try another set of rings - DO NOT file the ends to increase the clearance.

6    Excess end gap isn't critical unless it's greater than 0.040-inch. Again, double-check to make sure you have the correct rings for your engine.

7    Repeat the procedure for each ring that will be installed in the first cylinder and for each ring in the remaining cylinders. Remember to keep rings, pistons and cylinders matched up.

8    Once the ring end gaps have been checked/corrected, the rings can be installed on the pistons.

9    The oil control ring (lowest one on the piston) is usually installed first. It's composed of three separate components. Slip the spacer/expander into the groove **(see illustration)**. If an anti-rotation tang is used, make sure it's inserted into the drilled hole in the ring groove. Next, install the lower side rail. Don't use a piston-ring installation tool on the oil ring side rails, as they may be damaged. Instead, place one end of the side rail into the groove between the spacer/expander and the ring land, hold it firmly in place and slide a finger around the piston while pushing the rail into the groove **(see illustration)**. Next, install the upper side rail in the same manner.

10    After the three oil ring components have been installed, check to make sure that both the upper and lower side rails can be turned smoothly in the ring groove.

11    The number two (middle) ring is installed next. It's usually stamped with a mark which must face up, toward the top of the piston. **Note:** *Always follow the instructions printed on the ring package or box - different manufacturers may require different approaches.* Do not mix up the top and middle rings, as they have different cross-sections.

12    Use a piston-ring installation tool and make sure the ring's identification mark is facing the top of the piston, then slip the ring into the middle groove on the piston **(see illustration)**. Don't expand the ring

**24.10 Lay the Plastigage strips (arrow) on the main bearing journals, parallel to the crankshaft centerline**

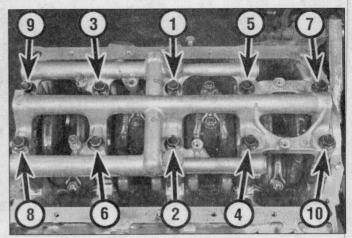

**24.12a Bolt tightening sequence for the main bearing caps/bridge on four-cylinder models**

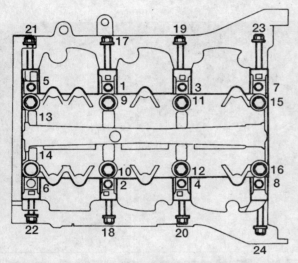

**24.12b Bolt tightening sequence for the main bearing caps/bridge on V6 models**

---

any more than necessary to slide it over the piston.

13    Install the number one (top) ring in the same manner. Make sure the mark is facing up. Be careful not to confuse the number one and number two rings.

14    Repeat the procedure for the remaining pistons and rings.

---

**24    Crankshaft - installation and main bearing oil clearance check**

*Refer to illustrations 24.10, 24.12a, 24.12b and 24.14*

1    Crankshaft installation is the first major step in engine reassembly. It's assumed at this point that the engine block and crankshaft have been cleaned, inspected and repaired or reconditioned.

2    Position the engine with the bottom facing up.

3    Remove the main bearing cap bolts and lift out the caps and bridge. Lay the caps out in the proper order to ensure correct installation.

4    If they're still in place, remove the old bearing inserts from the block and the main bearing caps. Wipe the main bearing surfaces of the block and caps with a clean, lint free cloth. They must be kept spotlessly clean!

*Main bearing oil clearance check*

5    Clean the back sides of the new main bearing inserts and lay the bearing half with the oil groove in each main bearing saddle in the block. Lay the other bearing half from each bearing set in the corresponding main bearing cap. Make sure the tab on each bearing insert fits into the recess in the block or cap. Also, the oil holes in the block must line up with the oil holes in the bearing insert. **Caution:** *Do not hammer the bearings into place and don't nick or gouge the bearing faces. No lubrication should be used at this time.*

6    If you're working on a V6 engine, the thrust bearings (washers) must be installed in the number three position. On four-cylinder engines, the thrust bearings (washers) must be installed in the number four position.

7    Clean the faces of the bearings in the block and the crankshaft main bearing journals with a clean, lint free cloth. Check or clean the oil holes in the crankshaft, as any dirt here can go only one way - straight through the new bearings.

8    Once you're certain the crankshaft is clean, carefully lay it in position in the main bearings.

9    Before the crankshaft can be permanently installed, the main bearing oil clearance must be checked.

10    Trim several pieces of the appropriate size Plastigage (they must be slightly shorter than the width of the main bearings) and place one piece on each crankshaft main bearing journal, parallel with the journal axis **(see illustration)**.

11    Clean the faces of the bearings in the caps and install the caps in their respective positions (don't mix them up) with the arrows pointing toward the front of the engine. Carefully lay the main bearing caps/bridge in place. Don't disturb the Plastigage. Apply a light coat of oil to the bolt threads and the under sides of the bolt heads, then install them.

12    Tighten the main bearing cap bolts, in three steps, to the torque listed in this Chapter's Specifications. Don't rotate the crankshaft at any time during this operation! Follow the recommended tightening sequence for each engine type **(see illustrations)**.

13    Remove the bolts and carefully lift off the main bearing caps. Keep them in order. Don't disturb the Plastigage or rotate the crankshaft. If any of the main bearing caps are difficult to remove, tap them gently from side-to-side with a soft-face hammer to loosen them.

14    Compare the width of the crushed Plastigage on each journal to the scale printed on the Plastigage envelope to obtain the main bearing oil clearance **(see illustration)**. Check this Chapter's Specifications to make sure it's correct.

15    If the clearance is not as specified, the bearing inserts may be the wrong size (which means different ones will be required - see Section 21). Before deciding that different inserts are needed, make sure that no dirt or oil was between the bearing inserts and the caps or

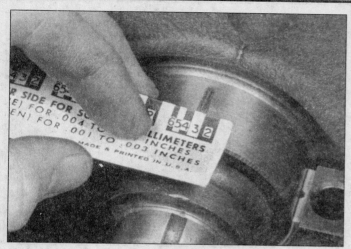

**24.14 Compare the width of the crushed Plastigage to the scale on the envelope to determine the main bearing oil clearance (always take the measurement at the widest point of the Plastigage); be sure to use the correct scale - standard and metric ones are included**

block when the clearance was measured. If the Plastigage is noticeably wider at one end than the other, the journal may be tapered (see Section 20).

16    Carefully scrape all traces of the Plastigage material off the main bearing journals and/or the bearing faces. Don't nick or scratch the bearing faces.

### Final crankshaft installation

17    Carefully lift the crankshaft out of the engine. Clean the bearing faces in the block, then apply a thin, uniform layer of clean moly-base grease or engine assembly lube to each of the bearing surfaces. Coat the thrust washers as well.

18    Lubricate the crankshaft surfaces that contact the oil seals with moly-base grease, engine assembly lube or clean engine oil.

19    Make sure the journals are clean, then lay the crankshaft back in place in the block. Clean the faces of the bearings in the caps, then apply lubricant to them.

20    With the engine block positioned so the crankshaft is at the top, install the pistons and connecting rods (see Section 26).

21    Install the caps and bridge in their respective positions with the arrows pointing toward the front of the engine. **Note:** *Be sure to install the thrust washers.*

22    Apply a light coat of oil to the bolt threads and the under sides of

the bolt heads, then install them. Start the bolts by hand. Tap the ends of the crankshaft forward and backward with a lead or brass hammer to line up the thrust washer and crankshaft surfaces before the bolts are tightened. Tighten all main bearing cap and bridge bolts to the torque listed in this Chapter's Specifications. Be sure to follow the recommended sequence **(see illustration 24.12)** and don't forget the side bolts on V6 models.

23    Rotate the crankshaft a number of times by hand to check for any obvious binding.

24    Check the crankshaft endplay with a feeler gauge or a dial indicator as described in Section 15. The endplay should be correct if the crankshaft thrust faces aren't worn or damaged and new thrust washers have been installed.

25    Install a new rear main oil seal, then bolt the retainer to the block (see Section 25).

### 25    Rear main oil seal - installation

*Refer to illustrations 25.3, 25.4 and 25.5*

1    The crankshaft must be installed first and the main bearing caps and bridge bolted in place, then the new seal should be installed in the retainer and the retainer bolted to the block.

2    Check the seal contact surface on the crankshaft very carefully for scratches and nicks that could damage the new seal lip and cause oil leaks. If the crankshaft is damaged, the only alternative is a new or different crankshaft.

3    The old seal can be removed from the retainer by driving it out from the back side with a hammer and punch **(see illustration)**. Be sure to note how far it's recessed into the bore before removing it (measure the clearance with feeler gauges); the new seal will have to be recessed an equal amount. Be very careful not to scratch or otherwise damage the bore in the retainer or oil leaks could develop.

4    Make sure the retainer is clean, then apply a thin coat of engine oil to the outer edge of the new seal. The seal must be pressed squarely into the bore, so hammering it into place isn't recommended. If you don't have access to a press, sandwich the housing and seal between two smooth pieces of wood and press the seal into place with the jaws of a large vise. The pieces of wood must be thick enough to distribute the force evenly around the entire circumference of the seal. Work slowly and make sure the seal enters the bore squarely **(see illustration)**.

5    If a vise in not available, the seal can be tapped into the retainer with a hammer. Use a block of wood to distribute the force evenly and make sure the seal is driven in squarely If the clearance measured with the feeler gauges is the same all around the seal, it is square to the bore **(see illustration)**.

6    The seal lips must be lubricated with clean engine oil or grease

**25.3 Drive the old seal out using a blunt punch and a small hammer**

**25.4 Drive the new seal into the retainer with a block of wood or a section of pipe - make sure that you don't cock the seal in the retainer bore**

**25.5 The depth the oil seal seats in the retainer must be checked as shown with feeler gauges and compared to this Chapter's Specifications**

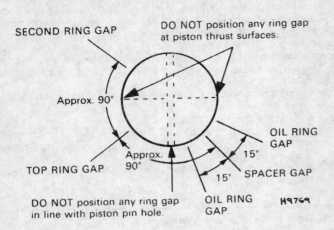

SECOND RING GAP

DO NOT position any ring gap at piston thrust surfaces.

Approx. 90°

Approx. 90°

TOP RING GAP

OIL RING GAP

15°

15°     SPACER GAP

OIL RING GAP

DO NOT position any ring gap in line with piston pin hole.

H9769

**26.5  Position the piston ring gaps as shown here before installing the piston/connecting rod assemblies in the engine**

**26.9  When installing pistons, the arrow (arrow) must point to the front (timing belt end) of the engine - pliers-type ring compressors like this are the easiest to use**

before the seal/retainer is slipped over the crankshaft and bolted to the block. No gasket is required. Instead, clean the surface and then apply a 2-mm wide bead of RTV sealant to the retainer-to-block surface just prior to installation.

7    Tighten the bolts a little at a time to the torque listed in this Chapter's Specifications.

## 26  Pistons/connecting rods - installation and rod bearing oil clearance check

*Refer to illustrations 26.5, 26.9, 26.11, 26.13 and 26.17*

1    Before installing the piston/connecting rod assemblies, the cylinder walls must be perfectly clean, the top edge of each cylinder must be chamfered, and the crankshaft must be in place.

2    Remove the cap from the end of the number one connecting rod (refer to the marks made during removal). Remove the original bearing inserts and wipe the bearing surfaces of the connecting rod and cap with a clean, lint-free cloth. They must be kept spotlessly-clean.

### *Connecting rod bearing oil clearance check*

3    Clean the back side of the new upper bearing insert, then lay it in place in the connecting rod. Make sure the tab on the bearing fits into the recess in the rod so the oil holes line up. Don't hammer the bearing

insert into place and be very careful not to nick or gouge the bearing face. Don't lubricate the bearing at this time.

4    Clean the back side of the other bearing insert and install it in the rod cap. Again, make sure the tab on the bearing fits into the recess in the cap, and don't apply any lubricant. It's critically important that the mating surfaces of the bearing and connecting rod are perfectly clean and oil-free when they're assembled.

5    Position the piston ring gaps at staggered intervals around the piston **(see illustration)**.

6    Slip a section of plastic or rubber hose over each connecting rod cap bolt.

7    Lubricate the piston and rings with clean engine oil and attach a piston ring compressor to the piston. Leave the skirt protruding about 1/4-inch to guide the piston into the cylinder. The rings must be compressed until they're flush with the piston.

8    Rotate the crankshaft until the number one connecting rod journal is at BDC (bottom dead center) and apply a coat of engine oil to the cylinder walls.

9    With the arrow on top of the piston **(see illustration)** facing the timing belt end of the engine, gently insert the piston/connecting rod assembly into the number one cylinder bore and rest the bottom edge of the ring compressor on the engine block.

10   Tap the top edge of the ring compressor to make sure it's contacting the block around its entire circumference.

11   Gently tap on the top of the piston with the end of a wooden

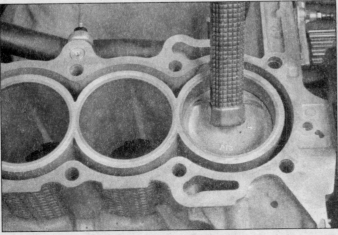

**26.11  The piston can be driven (gently) into the cylinder bore with the end of a wooden or plastic hammer handle**

**26.13  Lay the Plastigage strips on each rod bearing journal, parallel to the crankshaft centerline**

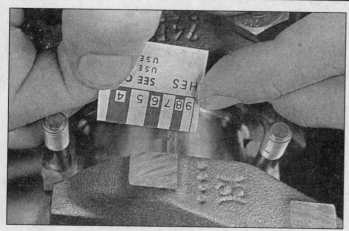

**26.17 Measuring the width of the crushed Plastigage to determine the rod bearing oil clearance (be sure to use the correct scale - standard and metric ones are included)**

hammer handle **(see illustration)** while guiding the end of the connecting rod into place on the crankshaft journal. The piston rings may try to pop out of the ring compressor just before entering the cylinder bore, so keep some down pressure on the ring compressor. Work slowly, and if any resistance is felt as the piston enters the cylinder, stop immediately. Find out what's hanging up and fix it before proceeding. Do not, for any reason, force the piston into the cylinder - you might break a ring and/or the piston.

12  Once the piston/connecting rod assembly is installed, the connecting rod bearing oil clearance must be checked before the rod cap is permanently bolted in place.

13  Cut a piece of the appropriate-size Plastigage slightly shorter than the width of the connecting rod bearing and lay it in place on the number one connecting rod journal, parallel with the journal axis **(see illustration)**.

14  Clean the connecting rod cap bearing face, remove the protective hoses from the connecting rod bolts and install the rod cap. Make sure the mating mark on the cap is on the same side as the mark on the connecting rod. If you're working on a four cylinder engine, make sure the connecting rod oil hole is facing the intake manifold side of the engine If you're working on a V6 make sure the connecting rod oil hole is facing the firewall side of the engine.

15  Apply a light coat of oil to the under sides of the nuts, then install and tighten them to the torque listed in this Chapter's Specifications, working up to it in three steps. Use a thin-wall socket to avoid erroneous torque readings that can result if the socket is wedged between the rod cap and nut. If the socket tends to wedge itself between the nut and the cap, lift up on it slightly until it no longer contacts the cap. Do not rotate the crankshaft at any time during this operation.

16  Remove the nuts and detach the rod cap, being very careful not to disturb the Plastigage.

17  Compare the width of the crushed Plastigage to the scale printed on the Plastigage envelope to obtain the oil clearance **(see illustration)**. Compare it to the Specifications to make sure the clearance is correct.

18  If the clearance is not as specified, the bearing inserts may be the wrong size (which means different ones will be required). Before deciding that different inserts are needed, make sure that no dirt or oil was between the bearing inserts and the connecting rod or cap when the clearance was measured. Also, recheck the journal diameter. If the Plastigage was wider at one end than the other, the journal may be tapered (refer to Section 20).

## Final connecting rod installation

19  Carefully scrape all traces of the Plastigage material off the rod journal and/or bearing face. Be very careful not to scratch the bearing - use your fingernail or the edge of a credit card.

20  Make sure the bearing faces are perfectly clean, then apply a uniform layer of clean moly-base grease or engine assembly lube to both of them. You'll have to push the piston into the cylinder to expose the face of the bearing insert in the connecting rod - be sure to slip the protective hoses over the rod bolts first.

21  Slide the connecting rod back into place on the journal, remove the protective hoses from the rod cap bolts, install the rod cap and tighten the nuts to the torque listed in this Chapter's Specifications. Again, work up to the torque in three steps.

22  Repeat the entire procedure for the remaining pistons/connecting rods.

23  The important points to remember are :

a)  *Keep the back sides of the bearing inserts and the insides of the connecting rods and caps perfectly clean when assembling them.*

b)  *Make sure you have the correct piston/rod assembly for each cylinder.*

c)  *The arrow on the piston must face the timing belt end of the engine.*

d)  *Be sure the stamped marks on the rod and rod cap are on the same side.*

e)  *Lubricate the cylinder walls with clean oil.*

f)  *Lubricate the bearing faces when installing the rod caps after the oil clearance has been checked.*

24  After all the piston/connecting rod assemblies have been properly installed, rotate the crankshaft a number of times by hand to check for any obvious binding.

25  As a final step, the connecting rod endplay must be checked. Refer to Section 14 for this procedure.

26  Compare the measured endplay to the Specifications to make sure it's correct. If it was correct before disassembly and the original crankshaft and rods were reinstalled, it should still be right. If new rods or a new crankshaft were installed, the endplay may be inadequate. If so, the rods will have to be removed and taken to an automotive machine shop for resizing.

## 27  Balance shafts - installation (four-cylinder models)

*Refer to illustrations 27.4a and 27.4b*

1  Install the cleaned and lubricated balance shafts into the block, guiding them in carefully to avoid nicking the bearings.

2  Secure the front balance shaft in place with its retainer and bolts and install the oil pump (see Chapter 2A).

3  Install the front balance shaft sprocket, and with the rear shaft secured by a bolt or screwdriver (see Section 13), install the rear balance shaft driven gear and bolt.

4  Lubricate the thrust faces of the balance shaft drive and driven gears with clean moly-base grease or engine assembly lube. Align the groove on the rear sprocket flange with the pointer on the gear case **(see illustration)**. Install the gear case to the block meshing the drive

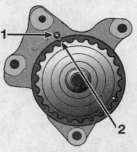

2143-2c-27.04a HAYNES

**27.4a  When installing the rear balance shaft gear case, align the groove in the sprocket flange (2) with the pointer on the gear case (1) and install the gear case to the block**

and driven gears. As you install the gear case and the gears mesh, the sprocket will rotate slightly clockwise. When the gear case is fully seated against the block, check that the mark on the sprocket is aligned with the pointer on the oil pump cover **(see illustration)**. If the marks are properly aligned, install the bolts and tighten them to the torque listed in this Chapter's Specifications.

5      Refer to Chapter 2A for balance shaft belt installation.

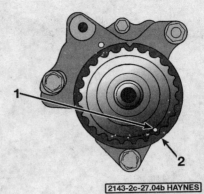

27.4b  With the gear case fully seated, the mark on the sprocket (1) should align with the pointer on the oil pump cover (2)

---

## 28   Initial start-up and break-in after overhaul

**Warning:** *Have a fire extinguisher handy when starting the engine for the first time.*

1      Once the engine has been installed in the vehicle, double-check the engine oil and coolant levels.

2      With the spark plugs out of the engine and the ignition system disabled (see Section 3), crank the engine until oil pressure registers on the gauge or the light goes out.

3      Install the spark plugs, connect the plug wires and restore the ignition system functions (see Section 3).

4      Start the engine. It may take a few moments for the fuel system to build up pressure, but the engine should start without a great deal of effort.

5      After the engine starts, allow it to warm up to normal operating temperature. While the engine is warming up, make a thorough check for fuel, oil and coolant leaks. When all new bearings, rings and camshaft(s) are installed, the engine should run for 15 minutes at normal operating temperature on the first start-up to help break in the new components.

6      Shut the engine off and recheck the engine oil and coolant levels.

7      Drive the vehicle to an area with minimum traffic, accelerate from 30 to 50 mph, then allow the vehicle to slow to 30 mph with the throttle closed. Repeat the procedure 10 or 12 times. This will load the piston rings and cause them to seat properly against the cylinder walls. Check again for oil and coolant leaks.

8      Drive the vehicle gently for the first 500 miles (no sustained high speeds) and keep a constant check on the oil level. It is not unusual for an engine to use oil during the break-in period.

9      At approximately 500 to 600 miles, change the oil and filter.

10     For the next few hundred miles, drive the vehicle normally. Do not pamper it or abuse it.

11     After 2000 miles, change the oil and filter again and consider the engine broken in.

# Chapter 3
# Cooling, heating and air conditioning systems

**Contents**

**Specifications**

## General
| | |
|---|---|
| Coolant capacity........................... | See Chapter 1 |
| Drivebelt tension........................... | See Chapter 1 |
| Radiator pressure cap rating ........................... | 14 to 18 psi |
| Thermostat rating (fully open)........................... | 194-degrees F |

## Torque specifications
| | |
|---|---|
| Thermostat housing cover bolts........................... | 104 in-lbs |
| Water pump retaining bolts | |
| Four-cylinder engine ........................... | 104 in-lbs |
| V6 engine | |
| 6mm bolts........................... | 104 in-lbs |
| 8mm bolts........................... | 192 in-lbs |

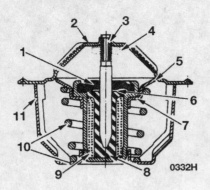

**1.2 Pellet type thermostat**

| | | | |
|---|---|---|---|
| 1 | Flange seal | 7 | Valve |
| 2 | Flange | 8 | Rubber diaphragm |
| 3 | Piston | 9 | Wax pellet |
| 4 | Nut | 10 | Coil spring |
| 5 | Valve seat | 11 | Frame |
| 6 | Teflon seal | | |

## 1   General information

*Refer to illustrations 1.2 and 1.3*

### Engine cooling system

All vehicles covered by this manual employ a pressurized engine cooling system with thermostatically controlled coolant circulation. An impeller-type water pump mounted on the engine block pumps coolant through the engine. The coolant flows around each cylinder and toward the rear of the engine. Cast-in coolant passages direct coolant around the intake and exhaust ports, near the spark plug areas and in close proximity to the exhaust valve guides.

A wax-pellet type thermostat controls engine coolant temperature. During warm up, the closed thermostat prevents coolant from circulating through the radiator. As the engine nears normal operating temperature, the thermostat opens and allows hot coolant to travel through the radiator, where it's cooled before returning to the engine **(see illustration)**.

The cooling system is sealed by a pressure-type radiator cap, which raises the boiling point of the coolant and increases the cooling efficiency of the radiator. If the system pressure exceeds the cap pressure relief value, the excess pressure in the system forces the spring-loaded valve inside the cap off its seat and allows the coolant to escape through the overflow tube into a coolant reservoir. When the system cools the excess coolant is automatically drawn from the reservoir back into the radiator **(see illustration)**.

The coolant reservoir serves as both the point at which fresh coolant is added to the cooling system to maintain the proper fluid level and as a holding tank for overheated coolant.

This type of cooling system is known as a closed design because coolant that escapes past the pressure cap is saved and reused.

### Heating system

The heating system consists of a blower fan and heater core located in the heater box, the hoses connecting the heater core to the engine cooling system and the heater/air conditioning control head on the dashboard. Hot engine coolant is circulated through the heater core. When the heater mode is activated, a flap door opens to expose the heater box to the passenger compartment. A fan switch on the control head activates the blower motor, which forces air through the core, heating the air.

### Air conditioning system

The air conditioning system consists of a condenser mounted in

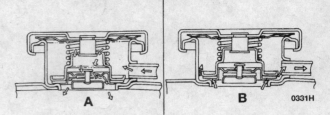

**1.3 Pressure-type radiator cap**

front of the radiator, an evaporator mounted adjacent to the heater core, a compressor mounted on the engine, a receiver-drier which contains a high pressure relief valve and the plumbing connecting all of the above components.

A blower fan forces the warmer air of the passenger compartment through the evaporator core (sort of a radiator-in-reverse), transferring the heat from the air to the refrigerant. The liquid refrigerant boils off into low pressure vapor, taking the heat with it when it leaves the evaporator.

## 2   Antifreeze - general information

**Warning:** *Do not allow antifreeze to come in contact with your skin or painted surfaces of the vehicle. Rinse off spills immediately with plenty of water. Antifreeze is highly toxic if ingested. Never leave antifreeze lying around in an open container or in puddles on the floor; children and pets are attracted by it's sweet smell and may drink it. Check with local authorities about disposing of used antifreeze. Many communities have collection centers which will see that antifreeze is disposed of safely. Never dump used anti-freeze on the ground or into drains.*
**Note:** *Non-Toxic coolant is available at local auto parts stores. Although the coolant is non-toxic when fresh, proper disposal is still required.*

The cooling system should be filled with a water/ethylene glycol based antifreeze solution, which will prevent freezing down to at least -20-degrees F, or lower if local climate requires it. It also provides protection against corrosion and increases the coolant boiling point.

The cooling system should be drained, flushed and refilled at the specified intervals (see Chapter 1). Old or contaminated antifreeze solutions are likely to cause damage and encourage the formation of rust and scale in the system. Use distilled water with the antifreeze.

Before adding antifreeze, check all hose connections, because antifreeze tends to leak through very minute openings. Engines don't normally consume coolant, so if the level goes down, find the cause and correct it.

The exact mixture of antifreeze-to-water which you should use depends on the relative weather conditions. The mixture should contain at least 50-percent antifreeze, but should never contain more than 70-percent antifreeze. Consult the mixture ratio chart on the antifreeze container before adding coolant. Hydrometers are available at most auto parts stores to test the coolant. Use antifreeze which meets the vehicle manufacturer's specifications.

## 3   Thermostat - check and replacement

**Warning:** *Do not remove the radiator cap, drain the coolant or replace the thermostat until the engine has cooled completely.*

### Check

1   Before assuming the thermostat is to blame for a cooling system problem, check the coolant level, drivebelt tension (see Chapter 1) and temperature gauge operation.

2   If the engine seems to be taking a long time to warm up (based on heater output or temperature gauge operation), the thermostat is

3.10  To replace the thermostat, remove the hose, remove the two cover bolts, pull off the cover and remove the thermostat from the housing

3.13  Install a new rubber seal over the thermostat

3.14  Install the new thermostat in the housing with the spring towards the engine and the jiggle pin (arrow) at the top

probably stuck open. Replace the thermostat with a new one.

3    If the engine runs hot, use your hand to check the temperature of the upper radiator hose. If the hose isn't hot, but the engine is, the thermostat is probably stuck closed, preventing the coolant inside the engine from escaping to the radiator. Replace the thermostat. **Caution:** *Don't drive the vehicle without a thermostat. The computer may stay in open loop and emissions and fuel economy will suffer.*

4    If the upper radiator hose is hot, it means that the coolant is flowing and the thermostat is open. Consult the *Troubleshooting* section at the front of this manual for cooling system diagnosis.

## Replacement

*Refer to illustrations 3.10, 3.13 and 3.14*

5    Disconnect the negative battery cable from the battery. **Caution:** *The radio in your vehicle is equipped with an anti-theft system. Make sure you have the correct activation code before disconnecting the battery.*

6    Drain the cooling system (see Chapter 1). If the coolant is relatively new or in good condition (see Chapter 1), save it and reuse it. Read the **Warning** in Section 2.

7    Locate the thermostat housing cover.

8    Loosen the hose clamp, then detach the hose from the fitting. If it's stuck, grasp it near the end with a pair of adjustable pliers and twist it to break the seal, then pull it off. If the hose is old or deteriorated, cut it off and install a new one.

9    If the outer surface of the large fitting that mates with the hose is deteriorated (corroded, pitted, etc.) it may be damaged further by hose removal. If it is, the thermostat housing cover will have to be replaced.

10    Remove the thermostat cover bolts **(see illustration)** and detach the housing cover. If the cover is stuck, tap it with a soft-face hammer to jar it loose. Be prepared for some coolant to spill as the gasket seal is broken.

11    Note how it's installed - with the jiggle pin up - then remove the thermostat.

12    Remove all traces of old gasket material and/or sealant from the housing and cover.

13    Install a new rubber gasket over the thermostat **(see illustration)**.

14    Install the new thermostat in the housing without using sealant. Make sure the jiggle pin is at the top and the spring end is directed into the engine **(see illustration)**.

15    Install the housing cover and bolts. Tighten the bolts to the torque listed in this Chapter's Specifications.

16    Reattach the hose and tighten the hose clamp securely. Install all components that were removed for access.

17    Refill the cooling system (see Chapter 1).

18    Start the engine and allow it to reach normal operating temperature, then check for leaks and proper thermostat operation (as described in Steps 2 through 4).

## 4    Cooling fans and circuit - check and replacement

**Warning:** *To avoid possible injury or damage, DO NOT operate the engine with a damaged fan. Do not attempt to repair fan blades - replace a damaged fan with a new one.*

**Note:** *All air conditioned models have two complete fan circuits - one for the condenser and one for the radiator. The following procedures apply to both.*

## Check

*Refer to illustrations 4.1a, 4.1b, 4.3a, 4.3b, 4.3c, 4.4a, 4.4b, 4.5a, 4.5b, 4.5c, 4.6a and 4.6b*

1    To test a fan motor, disconnect the electrical connector at the motor **(see illustrations)** and use fused jumper wires to connect the fan directly to the battery. If the fan still doesn't work, replace the motor.

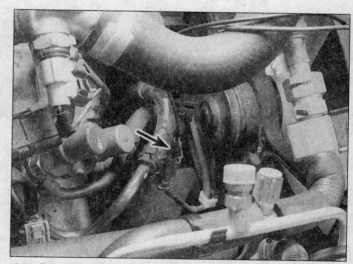

4.1a  To test either fan motor disconnect the electrical connector (arrow) and use jumper wires to connect the fan directly to the battery - if the fan still doesn't work, replace the motor

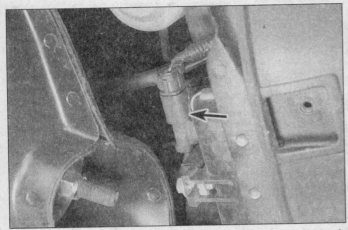

4.1b  It's easier to get at the radiator fan motor connector (arrow), which is behind the lower right rear corner of the fan shroud, from underneath the vehicle

4.3a  The ECT switch A (arrow) controls the radiator fan, and is located on the thermostat housing at the right/rear side of the engine (four-cylinder engine)

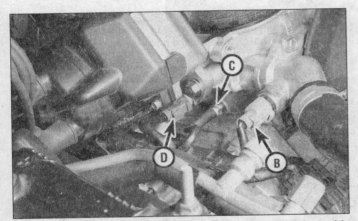

4.3b  Switch B (arrow) is for the condenser fan; switch C (arrow) is the coolant temperature gauge sending unit and switch D (arrow) is the coolant temperature sensor for the ECM; to test either fan switch, disconnect the connector, warm up the engine and note the resistance across the terminals as the temperature rises to the range indicated in the text

2    If the motor tests OK, check the fuses (located in the engine compartment fuse box), the coolant temperature switch, the radiator fan relay (located in the engine compartment fuse box) and the condenser fan relay (located at the left front corner of the engine compartment on four-cylinder models or at the right rear of the engine compartment on V6 models). Also check the wiring which connects the components.

3    To test either coolant temperature switch, remove the electrical connector at the switch **(see illustrations)**. Start the engine and measure the resistance across the terminals of the switch as the engine warms up. Neither switch should have continuity while the coolant is cold. The radiator fan switch (ECT switch A) should close between 196 and 203 degrees F. The condenser fan switch (ECT switch B) should close between 217 and 228 degrees F. If a switch fails to show continuity within this range, replace it. Each switch should open at 37 to 48 degrees F below the temperature it closed. **Caution:** *Don't run the engine any longer than necessary with the switch disconnected. As soon as you've verified that the switch is good or bad, plug in the connector and let the fan run awhile, then turn off the engine.*

4    On V6 models, there is one coolant temperature switch and an engine oil temperature switch **(see illustrations)**. The specifications and testing are the same as the A and B switch tests in Step 3, with the V6 coolant switch being A and the oil switch being B.

4.3c  Test the continuity of the ECT switches with an ohmmeter

4.4a  On V6 models, the coolant temperature switch (arrow) is located on the firewall side of the coolant transfer passage and has the same test specifications as ECT switch A on a four-cylinder engine

4.4b  The V6 oil temperature switch (arrow) is located on the rear valve cover and has the same test specifications as ECT switch B on a four-cylinder engine

4.5a  The radiator fan relay (arrow) is located in the main fuse panel on the right side of the firewall

4.5b  There are two relays (arrows) mounted on the condenser fan housing on the left side of the vehicle - the one nearest the radiator is the air conditioning compressor clutch relay and the other is the condenser fan relay

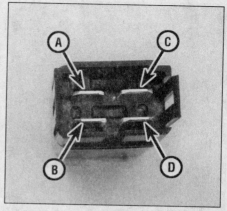

4.5c  Terminal identification for cooling fan relay testing

5    To test the cooling fan relays **(see illustrations),** remove the relay and apply battery power to terminal B and ground terminal D. This should close the relay and create continuity between terminals A and C. When the battery power is removed, there should be no continuity between A and C.

## Fan control module check

6    Both V6 and four-cylinder models have a radiator fan control module located behind the glove compartment. Check each wire with the module connected, the ignition switch ON, and the air conditioning OFF (backprobe the wires with a paper clip inserted from the harness side, do not puncture any insulation) **(see illustrations).**

7    Check for voltage at the black wire. If there is more than 1 volt, check for an open to ground.

8    Check for battery voltage at the following wires: white, black/yellow-1, black-yellow-2, yellow/white, and yellow. If you don't get battery voltage, check the fuses in both the underdash fuse panel and the underhood fuse panel. If the fuses are good, the module should be replaced.

9    Before trying a new module, disconnect both fan relays and check for continuity between the yellow or yellow/white wires and ground (20K ohms scale). There should be no continuity, if these circuits are grounded the new module will be damaged when connected.

10   Again with ignition ON and everything connected, connect the green wire to ground. If the fans don't come on, check for opens in the green, yellow and yellow/white circuits.

11   Check the white/green wire (four-cylinder models) or orange wire (V6 models) for voltage. There should be 11-12 volts when the engine is below 223 degrees F. If not, check for shorts to body ground, a bad module, or bad temperature switch (ECT switch B on 4-cylinder models, oil temperature switch on V6 models).

## Replacement

*Refer to illustrations 4.15, 4.16, 4.17, 4.18 and 4.19*
**Note:** *This procedure applies to either fan.*

12   Disconnect the negative battery cable from the battery. **Caution:** *The radio in your vehicle is equipped with an anti-theft system. Make sure you have the correct activation code before disconnecting the battery.*

13   Set the parking brake and block the rear wheels to prevent the vehicle from rolling. Raise the front of the vehicle and support it securely with jackstands. Remove the lower splash pan, if equipped, from under the radiator.

14   Insert a small screwdriver into the connector to lift the lock tab and disconnect the fan wiring connector.

15   Remove the fan lower mounting bolt(s) **(see illustration).**

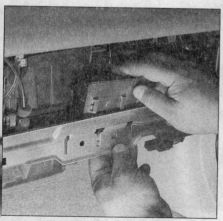

4.6a  The radiator fan control module is located behind the glovebox (removed here for clarity) - push it upward to release it from the bracket

4.6b  Backprobe the module connector with the ignition ON and the air conditioning OFF

4.15  Remove the lower fan mounting bolt (arrow)

**4.16 Remove the upper fan mounting bolts (arrows)**

**4.17 To remove the condenser fan assembly (shown), simply unbolt it and pull it out - to remove the radiator fan, remove the air conditioning line bracket bolts, push the bracket aside, then carefully lift the fan out of the engine compartment;**

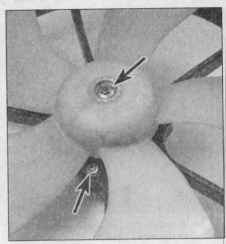

**4.18 To remove the fan, unscrew the nut in the center (upper arrow), then pull the fan blade from the motor shaft (the lower arrow points to one of the motor mounting screws)**

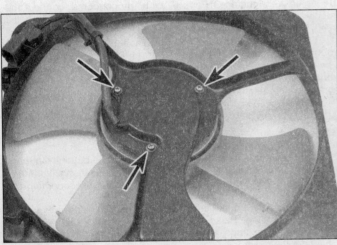

**4.19 To detach the condenser fan motor from the shroud, remove these screws (arrows)**

16   Unbolt the fan from the radiator at the top **(see illustration)**.
17   Carefully lift the fan out of the engine compartment **(see illustration)**.
18   To detach the fan from the motor, remove the motor shaft nut **(see illustration)**.
19   To detach the fan motor from the shroud, remove the mounting screws **(see illustration)**.
20   Installation is the reverse of removal.

---

## 5   Radiator - removal and installation

**Warning:** *Wait until the engine is completely cool before beginning this procedure.;;*

### Removal

*Refer to illustrations 5.2. 5.4, 5.6, 5.8 and 5.9*
1   Disconnect the negative battery cable from the battery. **Caution:** *The radio in your vehicle is equipped with an anti-theft system. Make*

**5.2  With the vehicle securely supported, remove the bolts retaining the lower splash pan**

**5.4  If the vehicle is equipped with an automatic transaxle, disconnect the cooler lines from the radiator (outer arrows) - center arrow indicates coolant drain fitting**

**5.6  Loosen the hose clamps and detach the upper and lower radiator hoses - marking one end of each hose with paint makes reassembly easier**

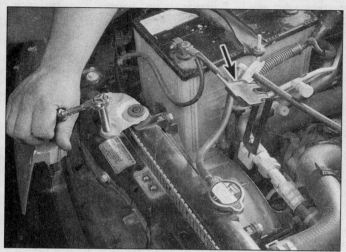

**5.8  Remove the two bolts that attach the upper/right radiator mount to the front crossmember, then remove the two bolts that attach the bracket (arrow) for the air conditioning refrigerant line**

**5.9  Carefully lift the radiator from the vehicle**

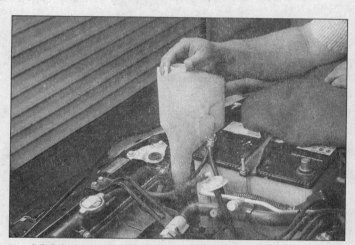

**6.2  Lift the coolant reservoir straight up out of its bracket**

sure you have the correct activation code before disconnecting the battery.

2     Set the parking brake and block the rear wheels. Raise the front of the vehicle and support it securely on jackstands. Remove the splash pan beneath the radiator **(see illustration)**.

3     Drain the cooling system (see Chapter 1). If the coolant is relatively new or in good condition, save it and reuse it. Read the **Warning** in Section 2.

4     If the vehicle is equipped with an automatic transaxle, disconnect the cooler lines from the radiator **(see illustration)**. Use a drip pan to catch spilled fluid and plug the lines and fittings.

5     Disconnect the electrical connector for the cooling fan switch (see Section 4).

6     Loosen the hose clamps, then detach the radiator hoses from the fittings **(see illustration)**. If they're stuck, grasp each hose near the end with a pair of slip joint pliers and twist it to break the seal, then pull it off - be careful not to damage the radiator fittings! If the hoses are old or deteriorated, cut them off and install new ones. Also disconnect the small hose to the coolant reservoir.

7     Remove the engine cooling fans (see Section 4).

8     Unbolt the small brackets that attach the upper end of the radiator to the front crossmember and unbolt the bracket for the air conditioning refrigerant line **(see illustration)**.

9     Carefully lift out the radiator **(see illustration)**. Don't spill coolant on the vehicle or scratch the paint.

10    Inspect the radiator for leaks and damage. If it needs repair, have a radiator shop or dealer service department perform the work as special techniques are required.

11    Bugs and dirt can be removed from the radiator by spraying with a garden hose nozzle from the back side.

12    Check the radiator mounts for deterioration and replace if necessary.

*Installation*

13    Installation is the reverse of the removal procedure. Guide the radiator into the mounts until they seat properly.

14    After installation, fill the cooling system with the proper mixture of antifreeze and water. Refer to Chapter 1 if necessary, and be sure to use the bleeder screw to bleed air out of the system.

15    Start the engine and check for leaks. Allow the engine to reach normal operating temperature, indicated by the upper radiator hose becoming hot. Recheck the coolant level and add more if required.

16    If you're working on an automatic-transaxle equipped vehicle, check and add fluid as needed.

## 6    Coolant reservoir - removal and installation

*Refer to illustration 6.2*

**Warning:** *The engine must be completely cool before removing the reservoir. Read the warning at the beginning of Section 2.*

1     The coolant reservoir is mounted adjacent to the radiator in the right front corner of the engine compartment, just in front of the battery.

2     Unscrew the cap with the hose still attached. Lift the reservoir straight up out of the bracket **(see illustration)**.

3     Pour the coolant into a container.

4     After washing the reservoir inside and out (use a household "bottle" brush to clean inside), inspect the reservoir for cracks and chafing. If it's damaged or so obscured by age as to make reading the water level difficult, replace it.

5     Installation is the reverse of removal.

## 7    Water pump - check

*Refer to illustrations 7.3a and 7.3b*

1     A failure in the water pump can cause serious engine damage due to overheating.

2     There are two ways to check the operation of the water pump while it's installed on the engine. If the pump is defective, it should be

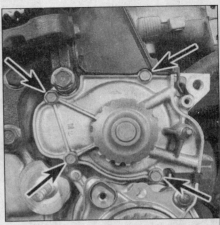

7.3a  The four-cylinder weep holes (arrows) are located on the rear side of the water pump

7.3b  The weep hole (arrow) on V6 models is on the underside of the pump - you'll need a flashlight and small mirror to inspect it (with the timing belt cover removed)

8.6a  Remove the water pump bolts (arrows) and detach the water pump from the engine (four-cylinder models)

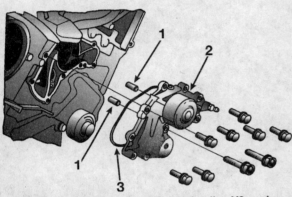

8.6b  Water pump installation details - V6 engine

| 1 | Dowel pins | 3 | O-ring |
|---|------------|---|--------|
| 2 | Water pump |   |        |

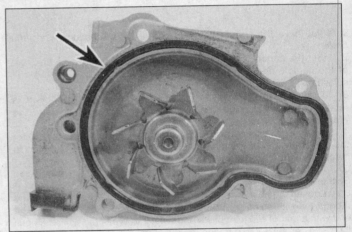

8.11  Apply a thin layer of RTV sealant to the O-ring groove of the new pump, then carefully set a new O-ring in the groove

replaced with a new or rebuilt unit.

3     Water pumps are equipped with weep (or vent) holes **(see illustrations)**. If a failure occurs in the pump seal, coolant will leak from the hole. With the timing belt cover removed, you'll need a flashlight and small mirror to find the hole on the water pump from underneath to check for leaks.

4     If the water pump shaft bearings fail, there may be a howling sound at the pump while it's running. Shaft wear can be felt with the timing belt removed if the water pump pulley is rocked up and down (with the engine off). Don't mistake drivebelt slippage, which causes a squealing sound, for water pump bearing failure.

5     Even a pump that exhibits no outward signs of a problem, such as noise or leakage, can still be due for replacement. Removal for close examination is the only sure way to tell. Sometimes the fins on the back of the impeller can corrode to the point that cooling efficiency is hampered.

## 8     Water pump - replacement

*Refer to illustrations 8.6a, 8.6b and 8.11*

**Warning:** *Wait until the engine is completely cool before beginning this procedure.*

1     Disconnect the negative battery cable from the battery. **Caution:** *The radio in your vehicle is equipped with an anti-theft system. Make*

*sure you have the correct activation code before disconnecting the battery.*

2     Drain the cooling system (see Chapter 1). If the coolant is relatively new or in good condition, save it and reuse it. Read the **Warning** in Section 2.

3     Remove the drivebelts (see Chapter 1).

4     Remove the timing belt (see Chapter 2A or 2B), and remove the timing belt tensioner.

5     On four-cylinder models, remove the camshaft sprocket and the upper belt back cover (see Chapter 2A).

6     Remove the bolts **(see illustrations)** and detach the water pump from the engine. Note the location of the longer bolt(s). Check the impeller on the backside for evidence of corrosion or missing fins.

7     Clean the bolt threads and the threaded holes in the engine to remove corrosion and sealant.

8     Compare the new pump to the old one to make sure they're identical.

9     Remove all traces of old gasket sealant and O-ring from the engine.

10    Clean the engine and new water pump mating surfaces with lacquer thinner or acetone.

11    Apply a thin layer of RTV sealant to the O-ring groove of the new pump, then carefully set a new O-ring in the groove **(see illustration)**.

12    Carefully attach the pump to the engine and thread the bolts into

9.1 On V6 models, the temperature sending unit (arrow) is in the water passage next to the distributor, just behind it is the ECT sensor for the computer

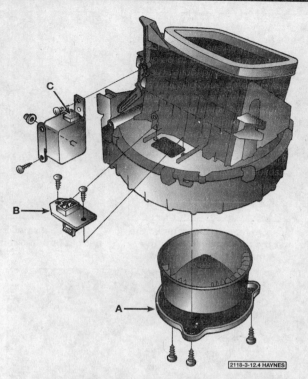

10.2 Blower motor  housing and components

a)  Blower motor
b)  Blower motor resistor

c)  Recirculation control motor

the holes finger tight. Use a small amount of RTV sealant on the bolt threads, and make sure that the dowel pins are in their original locations.

13    Install the remaining bolts. Tighten the bolts to the torque listed in this Chapter's Specifications in 1/4-turn increments. Don't overtighten the bolts or the pump may be distorted.

14    Reinstall all parts removed for access to the pump.

15    Refill and bleed the cooling system and check the drivebelt tension (see Chapter 1). Run the engine and check for leaks.

## 9    Coolant temperature sending unit - check and replacement

*Refer to illustration 9.1*

**Warning:** *Wait until the engine is completely cool before beginning this procedure.*

### Check

1    The coolant temperature indicator system consists of a temperature gauge mounted in the instrument panel and a coolant temperature sending unit mounted on the engine **(see illustration and illustration 4.3b)**. Some vehicles have more than one sending unit, but only one is used for the indicator system. **Warning:** *This vehicle is equipped with electric cooling fans. Stay clear of the fan blades, which can come on even when the engine is not running, as long as the ignition is ON.*

2    If an overheating indication occurs even when the engine is cold, check the wiring between the dash and the sending unit for a short circuit to ground.

3    If the gauge is inoperative, test the circuit by briefly grounding the wire to the sending unit while the ignition is On (engine not running for safety). If the gauge deflects full scale, replace the sending unit.

4    If the gauge doesn't respond in the test outlined in Step 3, check for an open circuit in the gauge wiring.

### Replacement

5    If the sending unit must be replaced, simply unscrew it from the engine and quickly install the replacement. Use sealant on the threads. Make sure the engine is cool before removing the defective sending unit. There will be some coolant loss as the unit is removed, so be prepared to catch it. Check the coolant level after the replacement part has been installed.

## 10    Blower motor - removal and installation

*Refer to illustrations 10.2, 10.3 and 10.5*

1    Disconnect the negative cable from the battery. **Caution:** *The radio in your vehicle is equipped with an anti-theft system. Make sure you have the correct activation code before disconnecting the battery.*

2    The blower unit is located under the dash, behind the glovebox. The blower motor unit or housing incorporates the blower motor, the blower motor resistor and the recirculation control motor **(see illustration)**.

3    Disconnect the electrical connector from the blower motor and remove the three retaining screws **(see illustration)**. Remove the

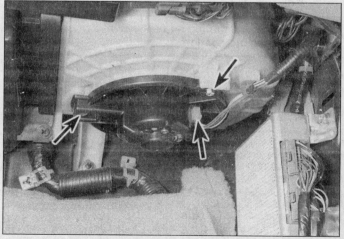

10.3 Arrows indicate the location of the blower motor electrical connector and the mounting screws - one screw is not visible here

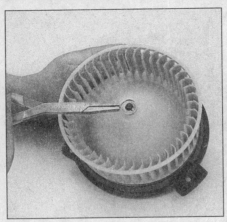

**10.5  Use pliers to release and remove the clamp, and the blower fan lifts off the motor shaft**

**11.2  Use a small screwdriver to pop the defrost button out of the instrument panel**

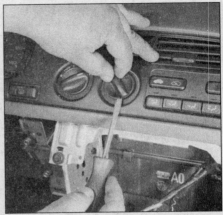

**11.3  Pry the blower speed and temperature control knobs gently off with a small screwdriver**

**11.4  Remove the screws and pull out the instrument panel bezel far enough to disconnect the two electrical connectors (arrows) from the heater/air conditioning control assembly**

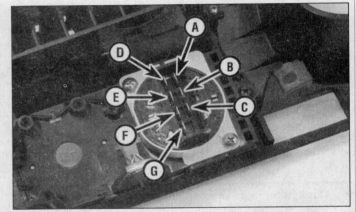

**11.7  Blower fan switch terminal guide for continuity checks**

blower motor.

4    If you're replacing the blower motor itself, separate the blower motor from the fan wheel and place the fan on the new blower motor.

5    Remove the clip **(see illustration)** to separate the fan wheel from the blower motor.

6    Installation is the reverse of removal. Check for proper operation.

---

## 11   Heater/air conditioning control assembly - check, removal and installation

### Removal and installation

*Refer to illustrations 11.2, 11.3, 11.4, 11.7 and 11.8*

1    Disconnect the negative cable from the battery. **Caution:** *The radio in your vehicle is equipped with an anti-theft system. Make sure you have the correct activation code before disconnecting the battery.*

2    Carefully pry the defrost button from the instrument panel **(see illustration)** and disconnect the electrical connector from the back.

3    Remove the blower speed and temperature control knobs by prying carefully outward with a small screwdriver **(see illustration)**.

4    Remove the six self-tapping screws on the instrument panel, pull the bezel forward and disconnect the two wiring connectors behind the control assembly **(see illustration)**.

5    Remove the five self-tapping screws from behind the instrument panel bezel and separate the heater/air conditioning control assembly from the bezel.

6    Installation is the reverse of the disassembly procedure.

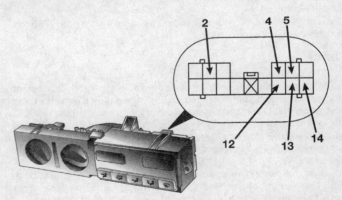

**11.8  Mode control switch terminal guide for continuity checks**

### Check

7    Check the indicated terminals on the back of the heater fan switch for continuity in each position **(see illustration)**:

a) *In the OFF position, there should be no continuity between any terminals.*
b) *In position 1, continuity should exist between B, A and D.*
c) *In position 2, continuity should exist between B, A and E.*
d) *In position 3, continuity should exist between B, A and F.*
e) *In position 4, continuity should exist between B, A and G.*

If the switch fails the continuity check in any position, replace the switch.

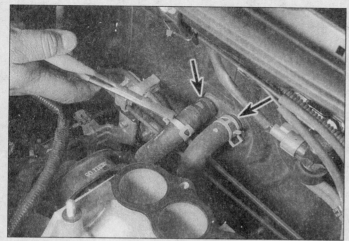

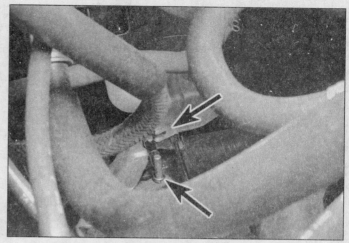

**12.4  Loosen the two heater hose clamps and disconnect the heater hoses (arrows) from the heater core inlet and outlet pipes at the firewall**

**12.5  To disconnect the heater valve cable, pry open this clip (upper arrow) with a small screwdriver and lift the cable end off the pin (lower arrow) on the heater valve lever arm**

8　Check the indicated terminals on the back of the mode control switch for continuity in each position **(see illustration)**:

 a) *In the Heat position, there should be continuity between terminals 2 and 14.*

 b) *In the Heat/Defrost position, continuity should exist between 2 and 13.*

 c) *In the Defrost position, continuity should exist between 2 and 12.*

 d) *In the Vent position, continuity should exist between 2 and 4.*

 e) *In the Heat/Vent position, continuity should exist between 2 and 5.*

If the switch fails the continuity check in any position, replace the switch.

## 12  Heater core - removal and installation

*Refer to illustrations 12.4, 12.5, 12.10, 12.11 and 12.15*

**Warning 1:** *The vehicles covered by this manual are equipped with airbags. Always disable the airbag system before working in the vicinity of the steering column, instrument panel or console to avoid the possibility of accidental deployment of the airbag, which could cause personal injury (see Chapter 12). The yellow wiring harness and connectors routed through the console and instrument panel are used for the airbag system. Do not use electrical test equipment on the system wiring or connectors or tamper with them in any way.*

**Warning 2:** *The air conditioning system is under high pressure. Do not loosen any hose fittings or remove any components until after the system has been discharged. Air conditioning refrigerant should be properly discharged into an EPA-approved recovery/recycling unit at a dealer service department or an automotive air conditioning repair facility. Always wear eye protection when disconnecting air conditioning system fittings.*

### Removal

1　**Note:** *Heater core removal on this vehicle is a difficult task for the home mechanic. It can be done with slow, careful attention to detail, but many fasteners and wiring connectors are difficult to get at behind the dash. The air conditioning must be discharged and the entire dash panel must be removed to allow the heater/air conditioning unit to be removed from the car. The driver and passenger airbags must be disabled, and the steering-column support must be removed. The following is a synopsis of the factory procedure, but we recommend having this job done at a dealership.*

2　If equipped with air conditioning, have the refrigerant discharged and recycled by an air conditioning technician. Disconnect the

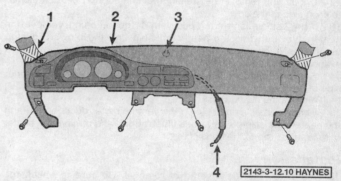

**12.10  Dashboard installation details**

| | | |
|---|---|---|
| 1 | *Protective tape* | 3 | *Guide pin* |
| 2 | *Dashboard* | 4 | *Air mix control cable* |

negative cable from the battery. **Caution:** *The radio in your vehicle is equipped with an anti-theft system. Make sure you have the correct activation code before disconnecting the battery.*

3　Drain the cooling system (see Chapter 1). Read the **Warning** in Section 2.

4　Working in the engine compartment, disconnect the heater hoses from the inlet and outlet tubes where they enter the firewall **(see illustration)**. Place a drain pan underneath the hoses to catch any coolant that runs out when the hoses are disconnected.

5　Disconnect the heater valve cable **(see illustration)**.

6　Remove the console, glove box, instrument panel lower cover and knee bolster (see Chapter 11).

7　Remove the lower steering joint cover. Remove the two bolts and the two nuts retaining the steering column to the support beam and lower the steering column.

8　Disconnect the steering column electrical connector, the instrument panel electrical connectors at the fuse box and under the left side of the dash and remove the harness clips from the dashboard.

9　Disconnect the air mix cable and the blower motor electrical connectors from the heater unit.

10　Remove the left and right defogger trim pieces, remove the six dashboard retaining bolts and lift the dashboard off the guide pins **(see illustration)**. **Note:** *Before removing the dash entirely, wrap masking tape around the bottom of the interior windshield posts to prevent marking them as the dash is removed.* Carefully remove the dashboard from the vehicle.

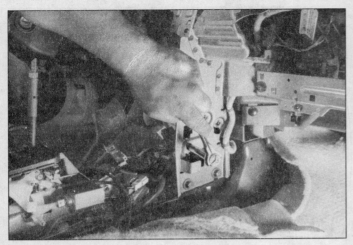

**12.11  Unbolt the two metal side panels of the console**

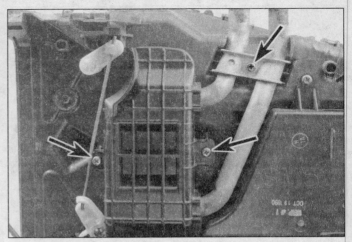

**12.15  To remove the heater core from the housing, remove the three screws on the cover (two lower arrows; lower screw at lower end of cover not visible in this photo), remove the screw (upper arrow) that attaches the clamp for the inlet and outlet pipes and pull the core out of the housing (this view is looking down on the top of the housing)**

11    Remove the center support panels **(see illustration)**.
12    Unbolt and remove the steering-column support beam attached to each side of the cowl.
13    If the vehicle isn't equipped with air conditioning, remove the heater duct between the heater housing and the blower housing assemblies. If the vehicle is equipped with air conditioning, remove the evaporator (see Section 17).
14    Remove the upper fasteners holding the heater unit to the interior side of the firewall, and the two nuts on the engine side of the firewall, then remove the heater unit.
15    Remove the clamps holding the vent/defroster ducts on top and the heater pipe clamp screw **(see illustration)**, and remove the heater core from the top of the housing.

## Installation

16    Installation is the reverse of removal. Be sure to check the operation of the air control flaps. If any parts bind, correct the problem before installation. Double-check all of your electrical connections.
17    Refill and bleed the cooling system (see Chapter 1), reconnect the battery and run the engine. Check for leaks and proper system operation. If equipped with air conditioning have the system evacuated, charged and leak-tested by an air conditioning technician.

---

## 13   Air conditioning and heating system - check and maintenance

---

## Air conditioning system

*Refer to illustration 13.5*
**Warning:** *The air conditioning system is under high pressure. Do not loosen any hose fittings or remove any components until after the system has been discharged. Air conditioning refrigerant should be properly discharged into an EPA-approved recovery/recycling unit at a dealer service department or an automotive air conditioning repair facility. Always wear eye protection when disconnecting air conditioning system fittings.*
**Caution:** *When replacing entire components, additional refrigerant oil should be added equal to the amount that is removed with the component being replaced. Be sure to read the can before adding any oil to the system, to make sure it is compatible with the R-134a system.*
1    The following maintenance checks should be performed on a regular basis to ensure that the air conditioning continues to operate at peak efficiency.
  a) *Inspect the condition of the compressor drivebelt. If it is worn or deteriorated, replace it (see Chapter 1).*

  b) *Check the drivebelt tension and, if necessary, adjust it (see Chapter 1).*
  c) *Inspect the system hoses. Look for cracks, bubbles, hardening and deterioration. Inspect the hoses and all fittings for oil bubbles or seepage. If there is any evidence of wear, damage or leakage, replace the hose(s).*
  d) *Inspect the condenser fins for leaves, bugs and any other foreign material that may have embedded itself in the fins. Use a "fin comb" or compressed air to remove debris from the condenser.*
  e) *Make sure the system has the correct refrigerant charge.*
  f) *If you hear water sloshing around in the dash area or have water dripping on the carpet, slip off the evaporative housing condensation drain tube (located in the lower right forward corner of the housing) and insert a piece of wire into both openings to check for blockage.*
2    It's a good idea to operate the system for about ten minutes at least once a month. This is particularly important during the winter months because long term non-use can cause hardening, and subsequent failure, of the seals. Note that using the Defrost function operates the compressor.
3    Because of the complexity of the air conditioning system and the special equipment necessary to service it, in-depth troubleshooting and repairs are beyond the scope of this manual. However, simple component replacement procedures are provided in this Chapter.
4    First make sure the compressor clutch is operating. If it doesn't engage the compressor (it clicks when it turns on and off) when the air conditioning is turned on, then check the number 4 and number 8 fuses in the underdash fuse panel. If they are OK, check the air conditioning relay **(see illustration 4.5b)**, which can be checked for continuity just like the fan relays in Section 4.
5    The most common cause of poor cooling is simply a low system refrigerant charge. If a noticeable drop in system cooling ability occurs **(see illustration)**, one of the following quick checks will help you determine whether the refrigerant level is low.
6    With the air conditioning operating, inspect the sight glass, if equipped. The sight glass is located near the high and low-side service connections near the center of the passenger-side fenderwell, although some models do not have a sight glass. If the vents aren't as cold as they were and the refrigerant looks foamy in the sight glass, the refrigerant is low. If you watch the compressor clutch while the engine is operating with the air conditioning ON, and the clutch is constantly clicking on and off, this also indicates a low refrigerant charge. Have the system charged by a dealer service department or an EPA-certified

**13.5 Insert a thermometer in the center duct while operating the air conditioning system - the output air should be 35-40 degrees F less than the ambient temperature, depending on humidity (but not lower than 40-degrees F)**

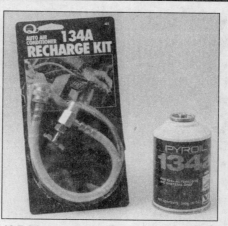

**13.7 A basic charging kit for 134a systems is available at most auto parts stores - it must say 134a (not R-12) and so should the 12-ounce can of refrigerant**

**13.10 Attach the refrigerant kit to the low-side charging port (arrow)**

automotive air conditioning repair shop. It is also possible with R-134a systems to add some refrigerant at home.

## Adding refrigerant

*Refer to illustrations 13.7, 13.10 and 13.11*

7    Buy an automotive charging kit at an auto parts store. A charging kit includes a 12-ounce can of refrigerant, a tap valve and a short section of hose that can be attached between the tap valve and the system low side service valve **(see illustration)**. Because one can of refrigerant may not be sufficient to bring the system charge up to the proper level, it's a good idea to buy a couple of additional cans. Make sure that one of the cans contains red refrigerant dye. If the system is leaking, the red dye will leak out with the refrigerant and help you pinpoint the location of the leak. **Warning:** *Never add more than two cans of refrigerant to the system.*

8    Hook up the charging kit by following the manufacturer's instructions. **Warning:** *DO NOT hook the charging kit hose to the system high side!* The fittings on the charging kit are designed to fit **only** on the low side of the system.

9    Back off the valve handle on the charging kit and screw the kit onto the refrigerant can, making sure first that the O-ring or rubber seal inside the threaded portion of the kit is in place. **Warning:** *Wear protective eyewear when dealing with pressurized refrigerant cans.*

10    Remove the dust cap from the low-side charging port (near the center of the passenger-side fenderwell) and attach the quick-connect fitting on the kit hose **(see illustration)**.

11    Warm up the engine and turn on the air conditioning. Keep the charging kit hose away from the fan and other moving parts. **Note:** *The charging process requires the compressor to be running. If the clutch cycles off, you can put the air conditioning switch on High and leave the car doors open to keep the clutch on and compressor working.* **Note:** *The compressor can be kept on during the charging by removing the connector from the low-pressure switch* **(see illustration)**, *and bridging it with a paper clip or jumper wire.*

12    Turn the valve handle on the kit until the stem pierces the can, then back the handle out to release the refrigerant. You should be able to hear the rush of gas. Add refrigerant to the low side of the system, keeping the can upright at all times, but shaking it occasionally. Allow stabilization time between each addition.

13    If you have an accurate thermometer, you can place it in the center air conditioning duct inside the vehicle and keep track of the output air temperature. A charged system that is working properly should cool down to approximately 40-degrees F. If the ambient (outside) air temperature is very high, say 110 degrees F, the duct air temperature may be as high as 60 degrees F, but generally the air

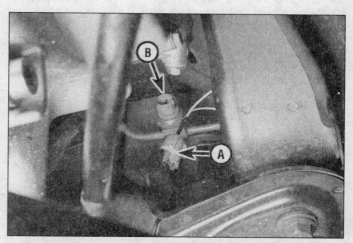

**13.11 Looking up from underneath the passenger-side of the engine compartment, disconnect the electrical connector (A) from the low-pressure switch (B), and connect a jumper wire to keep the compressor on during recharging**

conditioning is 30-40 degrees F cooler than the ambient air.

14    When the can is empty, turn the valve handle to the closed position and release the connection from the low-side port. Replace the dust cap.

15    Remove the charging kit from the can and store the kit for future use with the piercing valve in the UP position, to prevent inadvertently piercing the can on the next use.

## Heating systems

16    If the carpet under the heater core is damp, or if antifreeze vapor or steam is coming through the vents, the heater core is leaking. Remove it (see Section 12) and install a new unit (most radiator shops will not repair a leaking heater core).

17    If the air coming out of the heater vents isn't hot, the problem could stem from any of the following causes:

a) *The thermostat is stuck open, preventing the engine coolant from warming up enough to carry heat to the heater core. Replace the thermostat* (see Section 3).

b) *There is a blockage in the system, preventing the flow of coolant through the heater core. Feel both heater hoses at the firewall. They should be hot. If one of them is cold, there is an obstruction in one of the hoses or in the heater core, or the heater control*

**13.22  Backprobe the blower motor harness connector (arrow) with a voltmeter and check for varying voltage at different blower switch positions with the key ON**

**13.23  If varying voltages were received at the harness but the motor does not operate, check the motor by applying chassis ground and fused voltage - if it doesn't operate, replace it**

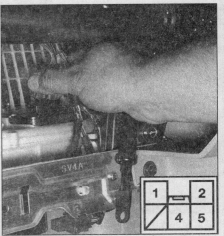

**13.25  Remove the harness connector from the blower resistor assembly and check for continuity on the resistor itself - there should be continuity between all terminals and 2 to 3 ohms resistance between terminals 1 and 5**

*valve is shut. Detach the hoses and back flush the heater core with a water hose. If the heater core is clear but circulation is impeded, remove the two hoses and flush them out with a water hose.*

c) *If flushing fails to remove the blockage from the heater core, the core must be replaced (see Section 12).*

### Blower motor circuit check

*Refer to illustrations 13.22, 13.23 and 13.25*

18   Check the fuse and all connections in the circuit for looseness and corrosion. Make sure the battery is fully charged.

19   With the transmission in Park, the parking brake securely set, turn the ignition switch to the ON position. It isn't necessary to start the vehicle.

20   The blower motor is located under the glove compartment area of the dash, near the firewall (see illustration 10.3).

21   Connect a voltmeter to the blower motor connector. First hook the red lead to the yellow/black wire and the black lead to a chassis ground. There should be full battery voltage when the ignition is ON. If not, check the fuses and blower motor relay, located in the underdash fuse panel (see Chapter 12).

22   Reconnect the harness electrical connector to the blower motor and backprobe each side of the connector, i.e. push the meter's red probe in alongside the yellow/black wire, and the black probe at the blue/red wire. With the ignition key ON, move the blower switch through each of its positions and note the voltage readings (see illustration). Changes in voltage indicates that the motor speeds will also vary as the switch is moved to the different positions. Slower speeds will deliver less voltage to the blower, and the HIGH position will bypass the resistor to supply close to full voltage. A typical range would be 3.6 volts in position 1, 5.5 volts in position 2, 8.0 volts in position 3, and 10.4 on high (more when the engine is running).

23   If there is voltage, but the blower motor does not operate, connect a jumper wire between the motor ground terminal and a good chassis ground. Connect a fused jumper wire between the battery positive terminal and the positive terminal on the motor (see illustration). If the motor still doesn't work, the blower motor is faulty.

24   If voltages did not vary in Step 22, check the blower resistor, located on the blower motor housing unit case. There are several resistance elements mounted on the resistor board to provide four blower speeds. The glove compartment must be removed to access the blower resistor (see Chapter 11).

25   Remove the blower resistor from the blower case mounting location and visually check for damage. Check the resistor block for

continuity between all terminals. Check for 2 to 3 ohms resistance between terminals 1 and 5 (see illustration). Replace the resistor if it fails these tests.

26   With an ohmmeter (one side grounded to the chassis, the other side probing the terminals) check for continuity at each of the indicated terminals on the resistor harness electrical connector with the switch in each of the following positions:

a) *Position 1 should have continuity to ground on the blue wire.*
b) *Position 2 should have continuity to ground on the blue/yellow wire.*
c) *Position 3 should have continuity to ground on the blue/black wire.*
d) *Position 4 should have continuity to ground on the blue/red wire.*

Lack of continuity at any terminal means there is an open in either that wire from the resistor to the switch, or a portion of the switch itself. Repair the open wire or replace the switch.

---

### 14  Air conditioning receiver-driver - removal and installation

*Refer to illustration 14.4*

**Warning:** *The air conditioning system is under high pressure. Do not loosen any hose fittings or remove any components until after the system has been discharged. Air conditioning refrigerant should be properly discharged into an EPA-approved recovery/recycling unit at a dealer service department or an automotive air conditioning repair facility. Always wear eye protection when disconnecting air conditioning system fittings.*

**Caution:** *When replacing entire components, additional refrigerant oil should be added equal to the amount that is removed with the component being replaced. Be sure to read the can before adding any oil to the system, to make sure it is compatible with the R-134a system.*

1   Have the refrigerant discharged and recycled by an air conditioning technician.

2   Disconnect the ground cable from the negative terminal of the battery. **Caution:** *The radio in your vehicle is equipped with an anti-theft system. Make sure you have the correct activation code before disconnecting the battery.*

3   Remove the radiator coolant overflow tank (see Section 6).

4   Disconnect the refrigerant lines (see illustration) from the receiver and cap the open fittings to prevent dirt and moisture entry.

5   Loosen the receiver bracket clamping screw and lift the receiver

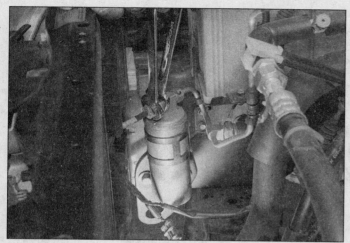

**14.4  Holding the top of the receiver/drier body with a back-up wrench, use another wrench to remove the refrigerant lines from the receiver/drier**

**15.8  To remove the compressor, disconnect the electrical connector (arrow), remove the refrigerant line fittings, plug the open fittings to prevent entry of dirt and moisture, and remove the four bolts (two upper bolts indicated here with arrows, two lower bolts not visible here)**

out of the vehicle.

6    Installation is the reverse of removal.

7    Have the system evacuated, charged and leak tested by an air conditioning technician. If the receiver was replaced, add 1/3 ounce of refrigerant oil.

## 15  Air conditioning compressor - removal and installation

*Refer to illustration 15.8*

**Warning:** *The air conditioning system is under high pressure. Do not loosen any hose fittings or remove any components until after the system has been discharged. Air conditioning refrigerant should be properly discharged into an EPA-approved recovery/recycling unit at a dealer service department or an automotive air conditioning repair facility. Always wear eye protection when disconnecting air conditioning system fittings.*

**Caution:** *When replacing entire components, additional refrigerant oil should be added equal to the amount that is removed with the component being replaced. Be sure to read the can before adding any oil to the system, to make sure it is compatible with the R-134a system.*

**Note:** *The receiver-drier should be replaced whenever the compressor is replaced.*

### Removal

1    Have the air conditioning system refrigerant discharged and recycled by an air conditioning technician.

2    Disconnect the negative battery cable from the battery. **Caution:** *The radio in your vehicle is equipped with an anti-theft system. Make sure you have the correct activation code before disconnecting the battery.*

3    Set the parking brake, block the rear wheels and raise the front of the vehicle, supporting it securely on jackstands.

4    Remove the drivebelt (see Chapter 1).

5    On four-cylinder models, remove the power steering pump (see Chapter 10), cruise control actuator (if equipped), and alternator (see Chapter 5).

6    Remove the condenser fan/motor (see Section 4).

7    Disconnect the compressor clutch wiring harness.

8    Disconnect the refrigerant lines from the compressor. Plug the open fittings to prevent entry of dirt and moisture **(see illustration)**.

9    Unbolt the compressor from the mounting bracket and remove it from the vehicle.

### Installation

10    The clutch may have to be transferred from the old compressor to the new unit.

11    Add the proper amount of refrigerant oil to the new compressor using the following calculations:

  a)  *Drain the refrigerant oil from the old compressor through the suction fitting and measure it in ounces.*

  b)  *Subtract this number from 4-1/3 fluid ounces (V6 models) or 5-1/3 ounces (four-cylinder models).*

  c)  *The difference between these two figures is equal to the amount you should drain from the new compressor.*

12    Installation is the reverse of removal.

13    Have the system evacuated, recharged and leak tested by an air conditioning technician.

## 16  Air conditioning condenser - removal and installation

*Refer to illustrations 16.7 and 16.8*

**Warning:** *The air conditioning system is under high pressure. Do not loosen any hose fittings or remove any components until after the system has been discharged. Air conditioning refrigerant should be properly discharged into an EPA-approved recovery/recycling unit at a dealer service department or an automotive air conditioning repair facility. Always wear eye protection when disconnecting air conditioning system fittings.*

**Caution:** *When replacing entire components, additional refrigerant oil should be added equal to the amount that is removed with the component being replaced. Be sure to read the can before adding any oil to the system, to make sure it is compatible with the R-134a system.*

### Removal

1    Have the refrigerant discharged and recycled by an air conditioning technician.

2    Disconnect the negative cable from the battery. **Caution:** *The radio in your vehicle is equipped with an anti-theft system. Make sure you have the correct activation code before disconnecting the battery.*

3    Remove the coolant reservoir (see Section 6).

4    Remove the grille (see Chapter 11).

5    Remove the radiator and condenser fans (see Section 4).

6    Remove the radiator upper mounting brackets (see Section 5).

7    Disconnect the condenser line and discharge line from the

**16.7 Disconnect the condenser line and discharge line attaching bolts from the condenser - arrow indicates the condenser-to-compressor (discharge) connection**

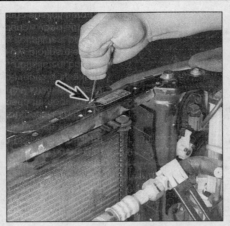

**16.8 Remove the condenser retaining nuts (arrow) (right nut shown, left nut in same location on driver's side of crossmember)**

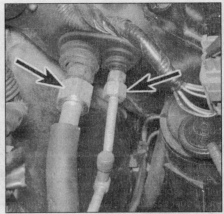

**17.3 Disconnect the suction line (left arrow) and the receiver line (right arrow) from the evaporator - plug both lines to prevent contaminants and moisture from entering the air conditioning system**

condenser **(see illustration)**.

8     Remove the condenser retaining bolts **(see illustration)**.

9     Remove the condenser.

## *Installation*

10     Installation is the reverse of removal. Assemble all connections with new O-rings, lightly lubricated with R-134a compressor oil.

11     Have the system evacuated, charged and leak tested by an air conditioning technician. If a new condenser was installed, add 1/3-ounce (V6 models) or 5/6-ounce (four-cylinder models) of refrigerant oil.

## 17   Air conditioning evaporator - removal and installation

*Refer to illustrations 17.3 and 17.7*

**Warning:** *The air conditioning system is under high pressure. Do not loosen any hose fittings or remove any components until after the system has been discharged. Air conditioning refrigerant should be properly discharged into an EPA-approved recovery/recycling unit at a dealer service department or an automotive air conditioning repair facility. Always wear eye protection when disconnecting air conditioning system fittings.*

**Caution:** *When replacing entire components, additional refrigerant oil should be added equal to the amount that is removed with the component being replaced. Be sure to read the can before adding any oil to the system, to make sure it is compatible with the R-134a system.*

## *Removal*

1     Have the air conditioning system discharged and recycled by an air conditioning technician.

2     Disconnect the cable from the negative battery cable. **Caution:** *The radio in your vehicle is equipped with an anti-theft system. Make sure you have the correct activation code before disconnecting the battery.*

3     Disconnect the receiver line and suction line from the evaporator **(see illustration)**.

4     Plug both lines to prevent contaminants and moisture from entering the air conditioning system.

5     Remove the glovebox and the glovebox frame (see Chapter 11).

6     Disconnect the electrical connector from the thermostat.

7     Remove the four self-tapping screws, two nuts and one bolt **(see**

**illustration)** retaining the evaporator housing to the firewall and dash structure.

8     Disconnect the drain hose and remove the evaporator unit from the vehicle.

9     Remove the thermostat sensor from the evaporator.

10     Remove the screws, separate the housing and remove the evaporator. If necessary remove the expansion valve.

## *Installation*

11     Installation is the reverse of removal. Install new O-rings and coat them with R-134a refrigerant oil. Tape the expansion valve capillary tube to the suction line and install the thermostat sensor in its original location.

12     Have the system evacuated, charged and leak tested by an air conditioning technician. If a new evaporator was installed, add one ounce (V6 models) or 1 1/3 ounce (four-cylinder models) of refrigerant oil.

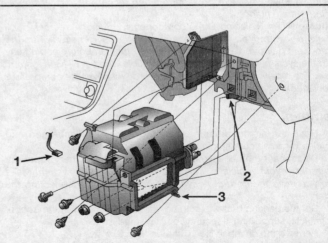

**17.7 After removing the glove box and frame, remove the screws, nuts and bolt that retain the evaporator housing to the dash and firewall**

| | | |
|---|---|---|
| *1* | *Thermostat connector* | *3*  *Evaporator* |
| *2* | *Drain hose* | |

# Chapter 4
# Fuel and exhaust systems

## Contents

## Specifications

### General

| | |
|---|---|
| Fuel pressure | |
| Four-cylinder engines | |
| With regulator vacuum hose attached | 31 to 38 psi |
| With regulator vacuum hose disconnected | |
| 1995 and 1996 | 40 to 47 psi |
| 1997 | 38 to 46 psi |
| V6 engines | |
| With regulator vacuum hose attached | 36 to 43 psi |
| With regulator vacuum hose disconnected | 44 to 51 psi |
| Fuel injector resistance | 1.5 to 2.5 ohms |
| Injector resistor resistance | 5 to 7 ohms |
| Idle Air Control valve resistance | 8 to 15 ohms |

### Torque specifications

**Ft-lbs** (unless otherwise indicated)

| | |
|---|---|
| Fuel injection service bolt | 96 in-lbs |
| Throttle body mounting nuts | 16 |
| Fuel rail mounting nuts | 108 in-lbs |

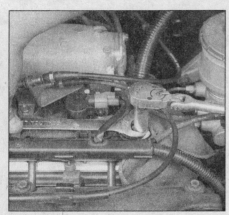

2.2a  Be sure to use a back-up wrench to obtain a secure grip - before the bolt is loosened, cover the wrenches with a shop rag to catch the escaping fuel (four-cylinder engine shown)

2.2b  To relieve the fuel pressure on a V6 engine loosen the service bolt located on the top fuel filter fitting (arrow)

3.4a  For the four-cylinder engines with the test port located on the fuel rail, purchase a 12 X 1.25 mm bolt and nut from a hardware store . . .

## 1    General information

The vehicles covered by this manual are equipped with the Programmed Fuel Injection (PGM-FI) system. This system uses timed impulses to sequentially inject the fuel directly into the intake ports of each cylinder. The injectors are controlled by the Engine Control Module (ECM). The ECM monitors various engine parameters and delivers the exact amount of fuel, in the correct sequence, into the intake ports.

All models are equipped with an electric fuel pump, mounted in the fuel tank. It is necessary to remove the fuel tank for access to the fuel pump. The fuel level sending unit can be removed through the access hole under the rear seat with the fuel tank in the vehicle.

The exhaust system consists of a header pipe, exhaust manifold, a catalytic converter, an exhaust pipe and a muffler. Each of these components is replaceable. For further information regarding the catalytic converter, refer to Chapter 6.

## 2    Fuel pressure relief procedure

*Refer to illustrations 2.2a and 2.2b*
**Warning:** *Gasoline is extremely flammable, so take extra precautions when you work on any part of the fuel system. Don't smoke or allow open flames or bare light bulbs near the work area, and don't work in a garage where a natural gas-type appliance (such as a water heater or a clothes dryer) with a pilot light is present. Since gasoline is carcinogenic, wear latex gloves when there's a possibility of being exposed to fuel, and, if you spill any fuel on your skin, rinse it off immediately with soap and water. Mop up any spills immediately and do not store fuel-soaked rags where they could ignite. The fuel system is under constant pressure, so, if any fuel lines are to be disconnected, the fuel pressure in the system must be relieved first. When you perform any kind of work on the fuel system, wear safety glasses and have a Class B type fire extinguisher on hand.*
1    Detach the cable from the negative battery terminal. Unscrew the fuel filler cap to relieve pressure built up in the fuel tank. **Caution:** *The stereo in your vehicle is equipped with an anti-theft system. Make sure you have the correct activation code before disconnecting the battery.*
2    You'll need two wrenches for this procedure, one to loosen the service bolt and another to hold the special banjo bolt into which the service bolt is installed. On four-cylinder engines, the service bolt is located at the fuel rail, on V6 engines its located at the fuel filter **(see illustrations)**.
3    Place a shop rag over the service bolt to catch any escaping fuel. While holding the special banjo bolt, slowly loosen the service bolt one complete turn - fuel will begin to flow from the fitting. Allow the

pressure to be relieved completely, then remove the bolt and install a new sealing washer.
4    After all work to the fuel system has been performed, install the service bolt and tighten it to the torque listed in this Chapter's Specifications.

## 3    Fuel pump/fuel pressure - check

**Warning:** *Gasoline is extremely flammable, so take extra precautions when you work on any part of the fuel system. Don't smoke or allow open flames or bare light bulbs near the work area, and don't work in a garage where a natural gas-type appliance (such as a water heater or a clothes dryer) with a pilot light is present. Since gasoline is carcinogenic, wear latex gloves when there's a possibility of being exposed to fuel, and, if you spill any fuel on your skin, rinse it off immediately with soap and water. Mop up any spills immediately and do not store fuel-soaked rags where they could ignite. The fuel system is under constant pressure, so, if any fuel lines are to be disconnected, the fuel pressure in the system must be relieved first (see Section 2 for more information). When you perform any kind of work on the fuel system, wear safety glasses and have a Class B type fire extinguisher on hand.*

### Preliminary check

**Note:** *On all models, the fuel pump is located inside the fuel tank (see Section 4).*
1    If you suspect insufficient fuel delivery, first inspect all fuel lines to ensure that the problem is not simply a leak in a line. Check the fuel filter (see Chapter 1) and replace it if necessary. Also, check the fuel pump fuse **(see illustration 3.22)**.
2    Set the parking brake and have an assistant turn the ignition switch to the ON position while you listen to the fuel pump. You should hear a whirring sound, lasting for a couple of seconds. Start the engine. The whirring sound should now be continuous (although harder to hear with the engine running). If there is no whirring sound, either the fuel pump or the fuel main relay circuit is defective (proceed to Step 12).

### Pressure check

*Refer to illustrations 3.4a, 3.4b, 3.4c and 3.4d*
3    Relieve the fuel pressure (see Section 2).
4    On 1995 and 1996 four-cylinder engines, remove the service bolt from the top of the service fitting located on the fuel rail and, on 1997 four-cylinder engines, remove the sealing nut from the end of the fuel rail. On V6 engines, remove the service bolt from the top of the fuel filter. Attach a fuel pressure gauge, using a special adapter which can be purchased at a tool store or dealer service department. If you can't locate the proper adapter, you can  fabricate one from a bolt and nut **(see illustrations)**. If you choose this route on V6 engines, also remove

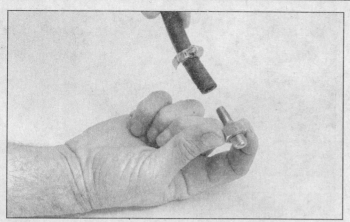

3.4b ... cut the bolt head off, drill a hole through the center and then grind down the cut-off end for the fuel gauge hose

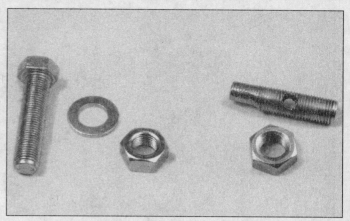

3.4c For the V6 engines, cut the head off the bolt (12 mm diameter/1.25 thread pitch) and drill a hole directly through the center. Grind the end to form a slight taper and drill a vertical hole to allow system pressure to flow. It is important that the vertical hole is drilled in the correct location. The easiest method is to use the banjo bolt that was removed from the fuel filter and place it directly next to the tool for the correct alignment of the vertical passage for fuel flow

3.4d Install a fuel pressure gauge on the service port

the fitting on the fuel filter that the service bolt screws into.

5    Start the engine and check the pressure on the gauge with the pressure regulator vacuum hose disconnected and connected, comparing your readings with the pressure listed in this Chapter's Specifications.

6    If the pressure is not within specifications, check the following:

a) *If the pressure is within specifications when the vacuum hose is connected to the pressure regulator but does not increase when*

the vacuum hose is disconnected, check for vacuum at the hose (see Step 9). If there is vacuum present, replace the pressure regulator (see Section 14). If there is no vacuum, check the hose for a break or an obstruction.

b) *If the pressure is higher than specified, check for a pinched or clogged fuel return hose or pipe. If the return line is not obstructed, replace the fuel pressure regulator (see Section 14).*

c) *If the pressure is lower than specified:*

1) *Inspect the fuel filter - make sure it's not clogged (see Chapter 1).*

2) *Look for a pinched or clogged fuel hose between the fuel tank and the fuel rail.*

3) *Check the pressure regulator for a malfunction (see below).*

4) *Look for leaks in the fuel line.*

7    If there are no problems with any of the above-listed components, check the fuel pump.

### Fuel pressure regulator check

*Refer to illustrations 3.8a, 3.8b, 3.9a and 3.9b*

8    Connect a vacuum pump to the fuel pressure regulator **(see illustrations)**. Read the fuel pressure gauge without vacuum applied to the fuel pressure regulator and also with vacuum applied. The fuel

3.8a Install a vacuum pump to the fuel pressure regulator and check for fuel pressure without vacuum applied ...

3.8b ... next, apply vacuum and check the fuel pressure - the fuel pressure should decrease as vacuum is applied, then increase as the vacuum is released

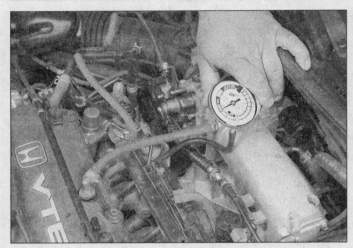

**3.9a  Remove the vacuum hose from the fuel pressure regulator and attach a vacuum pressure gauge. Start the engine and make sure the fuel pressure regulator is receiving vacuum (four-cylinder engine shown)**

**3.9b  Checking for vacuum to the fuel pressure regulator on the V6 engine**

pressure should decrease as vacuum increases. Compare your readings with the values listed in this Chapter's Specifications.

9    Reconnect the vacuum hose to the regulator and check the fuel pressure at idle, comparing your reading with the value listed in this Chapter's Specifications. Disconnect the hose and watch the gauge - the pressure should jump up to the maximum specified pressure as soon as the hose is disconnected. If the pressure at idle was too high (with the hose disconnected), connect a vacuum gauge to the hose and check for vacuum **(see illustrations)**.

10    If the fuel pressure is LOW, pinch the fuel return line shut and watch the gauge. If the pressure doesn't rise, the fuel pump is defective or there is a restriction in the fuel feed line. If the pressure rises sharply, replace the fuel pressure regulator (see Section 14).

11    If the indicated fuel pressure is too high, disconnect the fuel return line and blow through it to check for blockage. If there is no blockage, replace the fuel pressure regulator (see Section 14).

### Fuel pump operational check

*Refer to illustrations 3.16 and 3.17*

12    Remove the rear seat (see Chapter 11).

13    Remove the protective covering from the chassis to expose the fuel level sending unit access cover (see Section 4).

14    If you suspect a problem with the fuel pump, verify the pump actually runs. Have an assistant turn the ignition switch to ON - you should hear a brief whirring noise as the pump comes on and pressurizes the system. Have the assistant start the engine. This time you should hear a constant whirring sound from the pump (but it's more difficult to hear with the engine running).

15    If the pump does not come on (makes no sound), proceed to the next step.

16    Disconnect the main fuel pump relay connector and with the ignition key ON (engine not running), check for battery voltage on the green/white wire (terminal number 4) **(see illustration)**.

17    If battery voltage is present at the relay, install the relay into the connector and check for battery voltage present at the fuel pump. Remove the rear seat (see Chapter 11) and backprobe the three-pin connector (make sure the ignition switch is turned off before inserting the pin into the connector. Battery voltage should be present when the ignition key is turned ON **(see illustration)**.

18    If battery voltage is available to the fuel pump but there is still no sound, disconnect the electrical connector and using a jumper wire, apply battery voltage to the fuel pump (green/red wire middle terminal) and listen for fuel pump operation.

19    If battery voltage is available, but the fuel pump doesn't run when connected, replace the fuel pump (see Section 5). If no voltage is available, check the main relay (see below).

**3.16  The main relay is located under the dash on the driver's side. Check for battery voltage at the fuel pump electrical connector on the green/white wire**

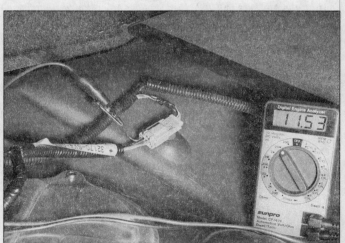

**3.17  Working near the trunk area, check for battery voltage (black/yellow wire) on the fuel pump/sending unit electrical connector**

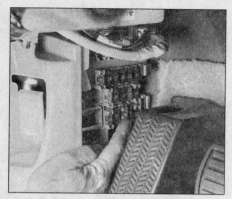

**3.22  Check the fuel pump fuse (15A) located in the fuse panel on the driver's side kick panel**

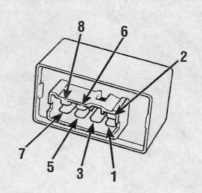

**3.23  Remove the main relay and test it on the bench - refer to the terminal numbers when testing the relay**

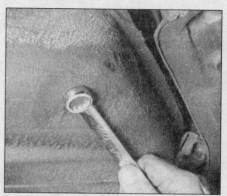

**4.4  Remove the drain bolt from the fuel tank**

## Main relay check

*Refer to illustration 3.22 and 3.23*

20   To test the main relay, first remove it from its location next to the under-dash fuse panel.

21   Remove the relay from the connector and verify that there is battery voltage (ignition switch ON) at the black/yellow wire of the connector (terminal number 4) **(see illustration 3.16)**.

22   If there is no voltage, check the fuel pump fuse **(see illustration)**. If battery voltage is present, check the relay.

23   Working on the bench **(see illustration)**, using a pair of jumper wires, connect battery voltage to the no. 6 terminal of the relay, ground the no. 8 terminal, then check for continuity between the no. 5 and no. 7 terminals. If there's no continuity, replace the relay.

24   Connect battery voltage to the no. 5 terminal, ground the no. 2 terminal and verify there's continuity between the no. 1 and no. 3 terminals. If there isn't, replace the relay.

25   Connect battery voltage to the no. 3 terminal, ground the no. 8 terminal. Verify there's continuity between the no. 5 and no. 7 terminals. If there is no continuity, replace the relay. If there is continuity, the relay is OK. Check the wiring harness from the fuses to the relay and the pump.

## 4   Fuel tank - removal and installation

*Refer to illustrations 4.4, 4.5, 4.6, 4.7a, 4.7b, 4.7c, 4.8a, 4.8b, 4.8c, 4.10a, 4.10b, 4.10c and 4.11*

**Warning:** *Gasoline is extremely flammable, so take extra precautions when you work on any part of the fuel system. Don't smoke or allow open flames or bare light bulbs near the work area, and don't work in a garage where a natural gas-type appliance (such as a water heater or a clothes dryer) with a pilot light is present. Since gasoline is carcinogenic, wear latex gloves when there's a possibility of being exposed to fuel, and, if you spill any fuel on your skin, rinse it off immediately with soap and water. Mop up any spills immediately and do not store fuel-soaked rags where they could ignite. The fuel system is under constant pressure, so, if any fuel lines are to be disconnected, the fuel pressure in the system must be relieved first (see Section 2 for more information). When you perform any kind of work on the fuel system, wear safety glasses and have a Class B type fire extinguisher on hand.*

**Note:** *The following procedure is much easier to perform if the fuel tank is empty. Some tanks have a drain plug for this purpose. If the tank does not have a drain plug, the fuel can be siphoned from the tank using a siphoning kit, available at most auto parts stores. NEVER start the siphoning action with your mouth!*

1   Remove the fuel tank filler cap to relieve fuel tank pressure.

2   Relieve the fuel system pressure (see Section 2).

3   Detach the cable from the negative terminal of the battery.

**Caution:** *The stereo in your vehicle is equipped with an anti-theft system. Make sure you have the correct activation code before disconnecting the battery.*

4   If the tank has a drain plug, remove it and drain the fuel into an approved gasoline container **(see illustration)**. If it doesn't have a drain plug, siphon the fuel into an approved gasoline container, using a siphoning kit (available at most auto parts stores).

5   Remove the rear seat (see Chapter 11) and disconnect the fuel gauge and fuel pump electrical connectors **(see illustration)**.

6   Remove the fuel level sending unit access cover **(see illustration)**.

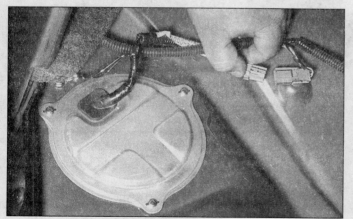

**4.5  Disconnect the fuel pump/sending unit harness connector**

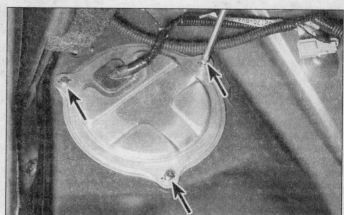

**4.6  Remove the screws (arrows) from the fuel level sending unit access cover**

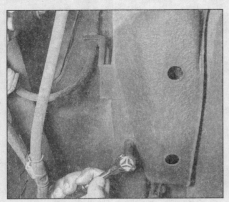

4.7a  Remove the lower splash shield from the fuel tank

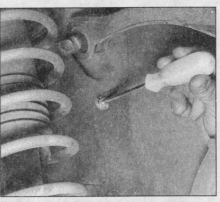

4.7b  Remove the retainers from the inner splash shield and . . .

4.7c  . . . lift the shield from the fenderwell area

4.8a  Disconnect the clamps and fuel hoses from the metal lines

4.8b  Loosen the clamp and remove the fuel filler hose from the bracket assembly. Remove the bracket, if necessary

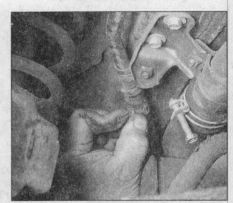

4.8c  Remove the clamp and separate the fuel tank vent line from the metal tubing

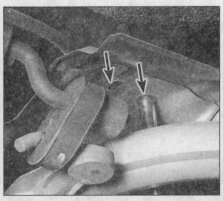

4.10a  Remove the bolts (arrows) from the exhaust shield and . . .

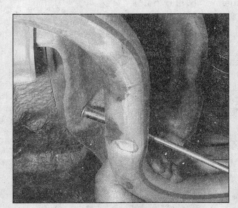

4.10b  . . . separate the complete assembly from the exhaust system

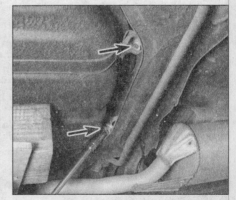

4.10c  Remove the fuel tank strap nuts (arrows)

7    Remove the splash panels that protect the fuel tank and the fuel lines **(see illustrations)**.

8    Label and disconnect the fuel supply and return hoses from the metal fuel lines. Disconnect the fuel filler hose and vent hose **(see illustrations)**.

9    Support the fuel tank with a floor jack. Position a wood block between the jack head and the fuel tank to protect the tank.

10   Disconnect both fuel tank retaining straps and pivot them down until they are hanging out of the way **(see illustration)**.

11   Remove the tank from the vehicle **(see illustration)**.

12   Installation is the reverse of removal.

## 5    Fuel tank cleaning and repair - general information

1    All repairs to the fuel tank or filler neck should be carried out by a professional who has experience in this critical and potentially dangerous work. Even after cleaning and flushing of the fuel system, explosive fumes can remain and ignite during repair of the tank.

2    If the fuel tank is removed from the vehicle, it should not be placed in an area where sparks or open flames could ignite the fumes coming out of the tank. Be especially careful inside garages where a natural gas-type appliance is located, because the pilot light could cause an explosion.

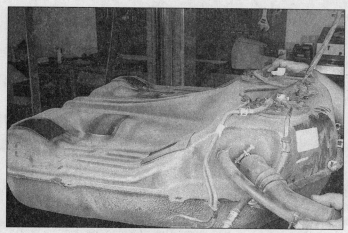

4.11  Remove the fuel tank from the vehicle

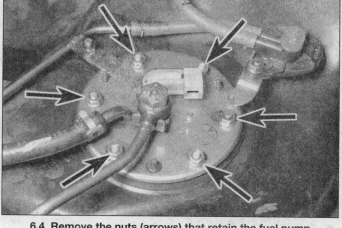

6.4  Remove the nuts (arrows) that retain the fuel pump assembly to the fuel tank

6.6  Lift the pump from the fuel tank. Be sure to angle it slightly to avoid damaging the pump screen attached to the bottom

6.7  Remove the nut and electrical connector from the terminal on the fuel pump

## 6    Fuel pump - removal and installation

*Refer to illustrations 6.4, 6.6, 6.7, 6.8, 6.9 and 6.10*

**Warning:** *Gasoline is extremely flammable, so take extra precautions when you work on any part of the fuel system. Don't smoke or allow open flames or bare light bulbs near the work area, and don't work in a garage where a natural gas-type appliance (such as a water heater or a clothes dryer) with a pilot light is present. Since gasoline is carcinogenic, wear latex gloves when there's a possibility of being exposed to fuel, and, if you spill any fuel on your skin, rinse it off immediately with soap and water. Mop up any spills immediately and do not store fuel-soaked rags where they could ignite. The fuel system is under constant pressure, so, if any fuel lines are to be disconnected, the fuel pressure in the system must be relieved first (see Section 2 for more information). When you perform any kind of work on the fuel system, wear safety glasses and have a Class B type fire extinguisher on hand.*

1    Detach the cable from the negative battery terminal. **Caution:** *The stereo in your vehicle is equipped with an anti-theft system. Make sure you have the correct activation code before disconnecting the battery.*
2    Relieve the fuel system pressure (see Section 2).
3    Remove the fuel tank from the vehicle (see Section 4).
4    Remove the nuts that retain the fuel pump cover **(see illustration)**.
5    Disconnect the electrical connector from the fuel pump and detach the fuel lines.

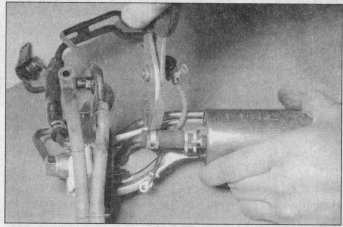

6.8  Squeeze the clamps and slide them up the hose . . .

6    Remove the fuel pump from the tank **(see illustration)**.
7    Remove the nut and detach the electrical connector from the terminal **(see illustration)**.
8    Squeeze the hose clamps with a pair of pliers- remove the upper clamp from the hose and slide the lower clamp halfway up the hose, off the fuel pump inlet **(see illustration)**.

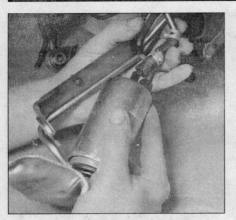

6.9  . . . and separate the pump from the bracket

6.10  Pry off the retaining clip with a small screwdriver and detach the filter (sock) from the pump

7.2  Test the fuel level sending unit in the fuel tank by attaching the positive probe of the ohmmeter onto the red wire and the negative probe onto the outside terminal

9     Separate the pump from the fuel pump bracket **(see illustration)**.
10    Remove the sock filter from the end of the pump **(see illustration)**.
11    Installation is the reverse of removal. Be sure to use a new gasket on the cover flange and new washers on the Banjo bolt.

## 7   Fuel level sending unit - check and replacement

*Refer to illustrations 7.2, 7.5, 7.8 and 7.9*
**Warning:** *Gasoline is extremely flammable, so take extra precautions when you work on any part of the fuel system. Don't smoke or allow open flames or bare light bulbs near the work area, and don't work in a garage where a natural gas-type appliance (such as a water heater or a clothes dryer) with a pilot light is present. Since gasoline is carcinogenic, wear latex gloves when there's a possibility of being exposed to fuel, and, if you spill any fuel on your skin, rinse it off immediately with soap and water. Mop up any spills immediately and do not store fuel-soaked rags where they could ignite. The fuel system is under constant pressure, so, if any fuel lines are to be disconnected, the fuel pressure in the system must be relieved first (see Section 2 for more information). When you perform any kind of work on the fuel system, wear safety glasses and have a Class B type fire extinguisher on hand.*

### Check

1     Remove the fuel pump/fuel level sending unit access cover **(see illustration 4.4)**.
2     Position the ohmmeter probes onto the electrical connector terminals and check for resistance **(see illustration)**.
3     First, check the resistance of the sending unit with the fuel tank completely full. The resistance of the sending unit should be about 4 to 5 ohms.
4     Now check the resistance of the unit with the fuel tank almost empty. The resistance should be 100 to 110 ohms.
5     If the readings are incorrect or there is very little change in resistance as the float travels from full to empty, replace the sending unit.
**Note:** *The fuel level sending unit can also be checked by removing the unit (see Steps 6 through 10). Check the resistance while moving the float from full (arm at highest point of travel) to empty (arm at lowest point of travel* **(see illustration)**.

### Replacement

6     Remove the rear seat (see Chapter 11).
7     Remove the fuel level sending unit access cover **(see illustration 4.6)** and lift the access cover from the floor of the vehicle.
8     Remove the nuts that retain the sending unit assembly to the fuel tank **(see illustration)**.

7.5  If the test results are inconclusive, remove the fuel tank sending unit and check the complete range of the sensor as you rotate the float level from completely empty to full. The resistance should vary from approximately 120 ohms (empty) to 5 ohms (full)

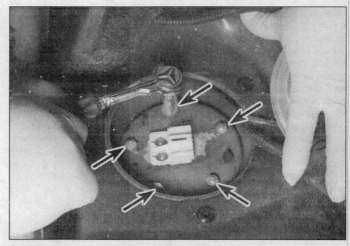

7.8  Remove the nuts (arrows) that retain the fuel level sending unit cover located under the rear seat

7.9  Lift the fuel level sending unit through the access hole

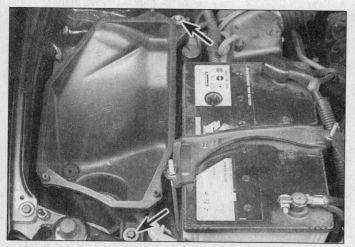

9.4  Remove the bolts (arrows) from the air cleaner housing
(four-cylinder engine shown)

9    Lift the fuel level sending unit from the tank **(see illustration)**. Be careful not to damage the float arm.
10    Installation is the reverse of removal. Be sure to use a new gasket under the sealing flange.

---

## 8    Fuel lines and fittings - repair and replacement

**Warning:** *Gasoline is extremely flammable, so take extra precautions when you work on any part of the fuel system. Don't smoke or allow open flames or bare light bulbs near the work area, and don't work in a garage where a natural gas-type appliance (such as a water heater or a clothes dryer) with a pilot light is present. Since gasoline is carcinogenic, wear latex gloves when there's a possibility of being exposed to fuel, and, if you spill any fuel on your skin, rinse it off immediately with soap and water. Mop up any spills immediately and do not store fuel-soaked rags where they could ignite. The fuel system is under constant pressure, so, if any fuel lines are to be disconnected, the fuel pressure in the system must be relieved first (see Section 2 for more information). When you perform any kind of work on the fuel system, wear safety glasses and have a Class B type fire extinguisher on hand.*
1    Always relieve the fuel pressure before servicing fuel lines or fittings (see Section 2).
2    The fuel feed, return and vapor lines extend from the fuel tank to the engine compartment. The lines are secured to the underbody with clip and screw assemblies. These lines must be occasionally inspected for leaks, kinks and dents.

3    If evidence of dirt is found in the system or fuel filter during disassembly, the line should be disconnected and blown out. Check the fuel strainer on the fuel gauge sending unit (see Section 5) for damage and deterioration.

### Steel tubing

4    If replacement of a fuel line or emission line is called for, use welded steel tubing meeting the manufacturer's specifications or its equivalent.
5    Don't use copper or aluminum tubing to replace steel tubing. These materials cannot withstand normal vehicle vibration.
6    Because fuel lines used on fuel-injected vehicles are under high pressure, they require special consideration.
7    Some fuel lines have threaded fittings with O-rings. Any time the fittings are loosened to service or replace components:
   a)  *Use a backup wrench while loosening and tightening the fittings.*
   b)  *Check all O-rings for cuts, cracks and deterioration. Replace any that appear hardened, worn or damaged.*
   c)  *If the lines are replaced, always use original equipment parts, or parts that meet the original equipment standards specified in this Section.*

### Flexible hose

**Warning:** *Use only original equipment replacement hoses or their equivalent. Others may fail from the high pressures of this system.*
8    Don't route fuel hose within four inches of any part of the exhaust system or within ten inches of the catalytic converter. Metal lines and rubber hoses must never be allowed to chafe against the frame. A minimum of 1/4-inch clearance must be maintained around a line or hose to prevent contact with the frame.

#### Removal and installation
9    Relieve the fuel pressure.
10    Remove all fasteners attaching the lines to the vehicle body.
11    **Note:** *On 1996 and later models, some of the fuel lines are equipped with a quick-disconnect type fitting at each end of the fuel line.* **Caution:** *The quick-disconnect fittings cannot be serviced separately. Do not attempt to service these types of fuel lines in the event the retainer tabs or the line becomes damaged. Replace the entire fuel line as an assembly. On fuel lines so equipped, detach the clamp(s) that attach the fuel hoses to the metal lines, then pull the hose off the fitting. Twisting the hoses back and forth will allow them to separate more easily. On quick-disconnect fittings, hold the connector with one hand and depress the retaining tabs with the other hand, then separate the connector from the pipe.*
12    Installation is the reverse of removal. Be sure to use new O-rings at the threaded fittings (if equipped). On quick-disconnect fittings, align the retainer locking pawls with the connector grooves. Push the connector onto the pipe until both retaining pawls lock with a clicking sound.

#### Repair
13    In the event of any fuel line damage (metal or flexible lines) it is necessary to replace the damaged lines with factory replacement parts. Others may fail from the high pressures of this system.

---

## 9    Air cleaner assembly - removal and installation

*Refer to illustrations 9.4*
1    Detach the cable from the negative battery terminal. **Caution:** *The stereo in your vehicle is equipped with an anti-theft system. Make sure you have the correct activation code before disconnecting the battery.*
2    Remove the air cleaner cover and filter element (see Chapter 1).
3    Remove the clamps that hold the air intake duct to the air cleaner housing.
4    Remove the bolts that hold the air cleaner housing to the engine compartment **(see illustration)**.
5    Lift the assembly up and detach it from the fresh air intake duct, then remove it from the engine compartment.
6    Installation is the reverse of removal.

10.2  Hold the adjusting nut with a back-up wrench while loosening the locknut

10.3  Remove the cable end from the throttle valve

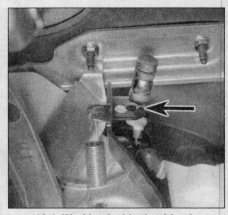

10.4  Working inside the driver's compartment, pull the accelerator cable end out and then lift the cable out of the recess (arrow) in the pedal

## 10   Accelerator cable - replacement and adjustment

*Refer to illustrations 10.2, 10.3, 10.4 and 10.7*

### Replacement

1    Detach the cable from the negative battery terminal. **Caution:** *The stereo in your vehicle is equipped with an anti-theft system. Make sure you have the correct activation code before disconnecting the battery.*
2    Loosen the locknut and remove the accelerator cable from its bracket **(see illustration).**
3    Rotate the throttle shaft bellcrank until the cable is out of its guide groove in the bellcrank and detach the cable from the bellcrank **(see illustration).**
4    Working underneath the dash, detach the cable from the accelerator pedal **(see illustration).**
5    Pull the grommet from the firewall and pull the cable through the firewall from the engine compartment side.
6    Installation is the reverse of removal.

### Adjustment

7    To adjust the cable **(see illustration):**
  a) *Lift up on the cable to remove any slack.*
  b) *Turn the adjusting nut until it is 1/8-inch (3 mm) away from the cable bracket.*
  c) *Tighten the locknut and check cable deflection at the throttle linkage. Deflection should be 3/8 to 1/2-inch. If deflection is not within specifications, loosen the locknut and turn the adjusting nut until the deflection is as specified.*
  d) *After you have adjusted the throttle cable, have an assistant help you verify that the throttle valve opens all the way when you depress the accelerator pedal to the floor and that it returns to the idle position when you release the accelerator. Verify the cable operates smoothly. It must not bind or stick.*
  e) *If the vehicle is equipped with an automatic transaxle, adjust the transaxle Throttle Valve (TV) cable (see Chapter 7B).*

## 11   Fuel injection system - general information

*Refer to illustration 11.1a and 11.1b*

The Programmed Fuel Injection (PGM-FI) system **(see illustrations)** consists of three sub-systems: air intake, electronic control and fuel delivery. The system uses an Engine Control Module (ECM) along with the sensors (coolant temperature sensor, Throttle Position Sensor (TPS), Manifold Absolute Pressure (MAP) sensor etc.) to determine the proper air/fuel ratio under all operating conditions.

The fuel injection system and the emissions control system are

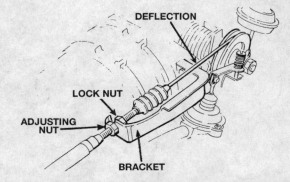

10.7  Lift up the cable to remove the slack, turn the adjusting nut until it is 1/8-inch from the cable bracket, then tighten the locknut

closely linked in function and design. For additional information, refer to Chapter 6.

### Air intake system

The air intake system consists of the air cleaner, the air intake ducts, the throttle body, the idle control system and the intake manifold. A resonator in the air intake tube provides silencing as air is drawn into the system.

The throttle body is a single barrel, side-draft design. The lower portion of the throttle body is heated by engine coolant to prevent icing in cold weather. The idle adjusting screw is located on top of the throttle body. A throttle position sensor is attached to the throttle shaft to monitor changes in the throttle opening.

When the engine is idling, the air/fuel ratio is controlled by the idle air control (IAC) system, which consists of the Engine Control Module (ECM), the fast idle thermo valve, the IAC valve and the starting valve. The IAC valve is activated by the ECM depending upon the running conditions of the engine (air conditioning system, power steering, cold and warm running etc.). This valve regulates the amount of airflow past the throttle plate and into the intake manifold. The ECM receives information from the sensors (vehicle speed, coolant temperature, air conditioning, power steering mode etc.) and adjusts the idle according to the demands of the engine and driver. Finally, to prevent rough running after the engine starts, the starting valve is opened during cranking and immediately after starting to provide additional air into the intake manifold.

Some models are equipped with the Intake Air Bypass (IAB) system. The IAB system allows the intake manifold to divert the path of intake air into the combustion chamber. Two air intake paths are provided in the intake manifold to allow the option of the intake volume

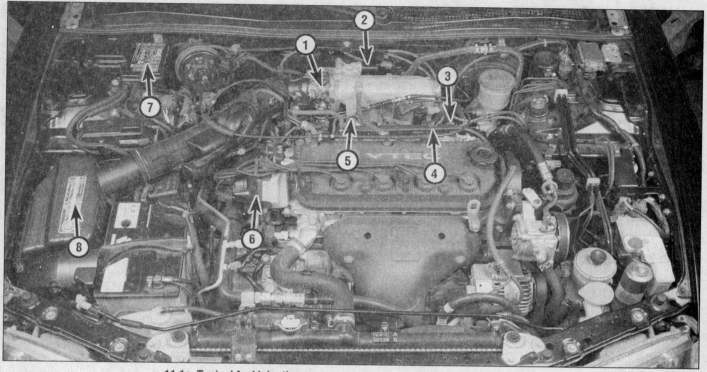

**11.1a  Typical fuel injection system components on a four-cylinder engine**

| | | | | | |
|---|---|---|---|---|---|
| 1 | Throttle body | 4 | Fuel rail | 7 | Fuse and relay control center |
| 2 | IAC motor | 5 | Fuel pressure regulator | 8 | Air cleaner housing |
| 3 | Fuel pressure service fitting | 6 | Distributor | | |

**11.1b  Typical fuel injection system components on a V6 engine**

| | | | | | |
|---|---|---|---|---|---|
| 1 | Fuel pressure service fitting (on fuel filter) | 4 | Distributor | 7 | Fuel rail (under intake manifold cover) |
| 2 | Throttle body | 5 | IAC motor | 8 | Fuse and relay control center |
| 3 | Air cleaner housing | 6 | Fuel pressure regulator | | |

**13.13a  Remove the four nuts (arrows) and separate the throttle body from the air intake plenum (four-cylinder engine shown)**

**13.13b  Location of the throttle body mounting nuts on the V6 engine**

most favorable for the particular engine speed. Optimum performance is achieved by switching the valves from either the closed position (for high torque at low rpm) or the open position (for maximum horsepower at high rpm).

## Electronic control system

The Electronic control system and the Engine Control Module (ECM) are explained in detail in Chapter 6.

## Fuel delivery system

The fuel delivery system consists of these components: The fuel pump, the pressure regulator, the fuel injectors, the injector resistor and the main relay.

The fuel pump is an in-line, direct drive type. Fuel is drawn through a filter into the pump, flows past the armature through the one-way valve, passes through another filter and is delivered to the injectors. A relief valve prevents excessive pressure build-up by opening in the event of a blockage in the discharge side and allowing fuel to flow from the high to the low pressure side.

The pressure regulator maintains a constant fuel pressure to the injectors. Excess fuel is routed back to the fuel tank through the return line.

The injectors are solenoid-actuated, constant stroke, pintle types consisting of a solenoid, plunger, needle valve and housing. When current is applied to the solenoid coil, the needle valve raises and pressurized fuel fills the injector housing and squirts out the nozzle. The injection quantity is determined by the length of time the valve is open (the length of time during which current is supplied to the solenoid coils).

Because it determines opening and closing intervals - which in turn determines the air-fuel mixture ratio - injector timing must be quite accurate. To attain the best possible injector response, the current rise time, when voltage is being applied to each injector coil, must be as short as possible. The number of windings in the coil has therefore been reduced to lower the inductance in the coil. However, this creates low coil resistance, which could compromise the durability of the coil. The flow of current in the coil is therefore restricted by a resistor installed in the injector wire harness.

The main relay, which is installed adjacent to the fuse box, is a direct coupler type which contains the relays for the Engine Control Module power supply and the fuel pump power supply.

## 12  Fuel injection system - preliminary check

**Note**: *The following procedure is based on the assumption that the fuel pressure is adequate* (see Section 3).

1    Check the ground wire connections on the intake manifold for

tightness. Check all wiring harness connectors that are related to the system. Loose connectors and poor grounds can cause many problems that resemble more serious malfunctions.

2    Check to see that the battery is fully charged, as the control unit and sensors depend on an accurate supply voltage in order to properly meter the fuel.

3    Check the air filter element - a dirty or partially blocked filter will severely impede performance and economy (see Chapter 1).

4    If a blown fuse is found, replace it and see if it blows again. If it does, search for a grounded wire in the harness to the fuel pump.

5    Check the air intake duct to the intake manifold for leaks, which will result in an excessively lean mixture. Also check the condition of all vacuum hoses connected to the intake manifold.

6    Remove the air intake duct from the throttle body and check for dirt, carbon or other residue build-up. If it's dirty, clean it with aerosol carburetor cleaner, a shop rag and a toothbrush.

7    The remainder of the system checks can be found in the following Sections.

## 13  Throttle body - check, removal and installation

*Refer to illustrations 13.13a and 13.13b*

### Check

1    On top of the throttle body, locate the vacuum hose that goes to the fuel pressure regulator (**see illustrations 3.9a and 3.9b**). Detach it from the throttle body and attach a vacuum gauge in its place.

2    Start the engine and warm it to its normal operating temperature (wait until the cooling fan comes on twice). Verify the gauge indicates no vacuum.

3    Open the throttle slightly from idle and verify that the gauge indicates vacuum. If the gauge indicates no vacuum, check the port to make sure it is not clogged. Clean it with aerosol carburetor cleaner if necessary.

4    Stop the engine and verify the accelerator cable and throttle valve operate smoothly without binding or sticking.

5    If the accelerator cable or throttle valve binds or sticks, check for a build-up of sludge on the cable or throttle shaft.

6    If a build-up of sludge is evident, try removing it with aerosol carburetor cleaner or a similar solvent.

7    If cleaning fails to remedy the problem, replace the throttle body.

### Removal and installation

**Warning:** *Wait until the engine is completely cool before beginning this procedure.*

8    Detach the cable from the negative battery terminal. **Caution:** *The stereo in your vehicle is equipped with an anti-theft system. Make sure you have the correct activation code before disconnecting the battery.*

**14.5  Remove the fuel pressure regulator bolts (arrows)**

**15.2  Use a mechanics stethoscope to determine if the injectors are working properly - they should make a steady clicking sound that rises and falls as engine speed changes**

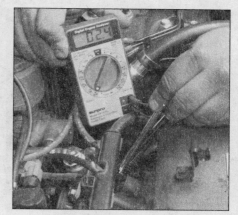

**15.3  Disconnect the fuel injector electrical connector and measure the resistance across the terminals of each injector**

9    Remove the air duct that connects the air cleaner assembly to the throttle body.

10    Disconnect the throttle position sensor connector from the throttle body. Also label and detach all vacuum hoses from the throttle body.

11    Detach the accelerator cable (see Section 10) and, if equipped, the transaxle Throttle Valve (TV) cable (see Chapter 7B).

12    Detach the coolant hoses from the throttle body. Plug the lines to prevent coolant loss.

13    Remove the four mounting nuts **(see illustrations)** and remove the throttle body and gasket. Remove all traces of old gasket material from the throttle body and air intake plenum.

14    Installation is the reverse of removal. Be sure to use a new gasket. Adjust the accelerator cable (see Section 10) and, if equipped, the Throttle Valve (TV) cable (see Chapter 7B). Check the coolant level and add, if necessary (see Chapter 1).

## 14  Fuel pressure regulator - check and replacement

**Warning:** *Gasoline is extremely flammable, so take extra precautions when you work on any part of the fuel system. Don't smoke or allow open flames or bare light bulbs near the work area, and don't work in a garage where a natural gas-type appliance (such as a water heater or a clothes dryer) with a pilot light is present. Since gasoline is carcinogenic, wear latex gloves when there's a possibility of being exposed to fuel, and, if you spill any fuel on your skin, rinse it off immediately with soap and water. Mop up any spills immediately and do not store fuel-soaked rags where they could ignite. The fuel system is under constant pressure, so, if any fuel lines are to be disconnected, the fuel pressure in the system must be relieved first (see Section 2 for more information). When you perform any kind of work on the fuel system, wear safety glasses and have a Class B type fire extinguisher on hand.*

### Check

*Refer to illustrations 14.5*

1    Relieve the fuel system pressure (see Section 2) and install a fuel pressure gauge (see Section 3). Check for leakage around the gauge connections when the engine is started.

2    Follow the fuel pressure checks and the fuel pressure regulator checks in Section 3.

### Replacement

*Refer to illustration 14.5*

3    Relieve the system fuel pressure (see Section 2).

4    Detach the cable from the negative battery terminal. **Caution:** *The*

*stereo in your vehicle is equipped with an anti-theft system. Make sure you have the correct activation code before disconnecting the battery.*

5    Detach the vacuum hose and fuel hose from the pressure regulator, then unscrew the mounting bolts **(see illustration)**.

6    Remove the pressure regulator.

7    Installation is the reverse of removal. Be sure to use a new O-ring. Lubricate the O-ring with a light coat of clean engine oil before installation.

8    Check for fuel leaks after installing the pressure regulator.

## 15  Fuel injectors - check, removal and installation

**Warning:** *Gasoline is extremely flammable, so take extra precautions when you work on any part of the fuel system. Don't smoke or allow open flames or bare light bulbs near the work area, and don't work in a garage where a natural gas-type appliance (such as a water heater or a clothes dryer) with a pilot light is present. Since gasoline is carcinogenic, wear latex gloves when there's a possibility of being exposed to fuel, and, if you spill any fuel on your skin, rinse it off immediately with soap and water. Mop up any spills immediately and do not store fuel-soaked rags where they could ignite. The fuel system is under constant pressure, so, if any fuel lines are to be disconnected, the fuel pressure in the system must be relieved first (see Section 2 for more information). When you perform any kind of work on the fuel system, wear safety glasses and have a Class B type fire extinguisher on hand.*

### Check

**Refer to illustrations 15.2, 15.3 and 15.5**

1    Start the engine and warm it to its normal operating temperature.

2    With the engine idling, place an automotive stethoscope against each injector, one at a time, and listen for a clicking sound, indicating operation **(see illustration)**. If you don't have a stethoscope, place the tip of a screwdriver against the injector and listen through the handle. Disconnect each injector one-at-a-time, note the change in idle speed then reconnect the injector. If the idle speed drop is almost the same for each cylinder, the injectors are operating correctly. If unplugging a particular injector fails to change the idle speed, proceed to the next step. **Note:** *It is necessary to remove the nuts from the wiring harness straps and lift up on the harness rail to make clearance for removal of the connectors from the injectors.*

3    Turn the engine off. Remove the connector from the injector, and measure the resistance between the two terminals of the injector **(see illustration)**.

4    The resistance should be between approximately 1.5 and 2.5 ohms. If not, replace the fuel injector.

**15.5 Install the injector test light or "noid" light into each injector harness electrical connector and confirm that it blinks when the engine is cranking or running**

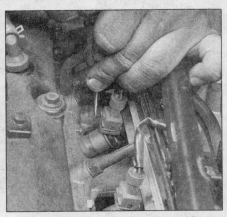

**15.8a Use a small screwdriver or sharp pick to remove the bail from the fuel injector electrical connector (four-cylinder engine shown)**

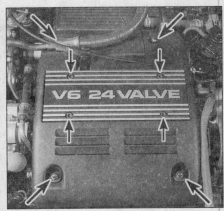

**15.8b Remove the intake manifold cover bolts (arrows) from the engine (V6 engine shown)**

**15.9 Remove the fuel return line from the fuel rail (four-cylinder engine shown)**

**15.11 Remove the banjo fitting (fuel inlet line) from the fuel rail**

**15.12a Remove the fuel rail mounting nuts (arrows)**

5    If the resistance is as specified, connect a special injector harness test light (available at some auto parts stores) to the harness electrical connector **(see illustration)**.

  a)  *If the battery voltage is present (if the light flashes when the starter is activated), the injector is receiving proper voltage.*
  b)  *If there is no voltage, check the wiring harness for damage.*
  c)  *If the wiring harness is not damaged or shorted, check the wiring between the PGM-FI main relay and the injector(s) for an open or short circuit or a bad connection.*

## Removal

*Refer to illustrations 15.8a, 15.8b, 15.9, 15.11, 15.12a, 15.12b, 15.13a, 15.13b and 15.13c*

6    Detach the cable from the negative battery terminal. **Caution:** *The stereo in your vehicle is equipped with an anti-theft system. Make sure you have the correct activation code before disconnecting the battery.*
7    Relieve the fuel pressure (see Section 2).
8    Disconnect the injector connectors. On V6 engines, remove the intake manifold cover to gain access to the electrical connectors **(see illustrations)**.
9    Detach the fuel return hose from the fuel rail **(see illustration)**.
10    Detach any ground cables from the fuel rail.
11    Detach the fuel feed line from the fuel rail **(see illustration)**.
12    Remove the mounting nuts and lift the fuel rail from the engine **(see illustrations)**.
13    Remove the injector(s) from the bore(s) in the fuel rail **(see**

illustration) and remove and discard the O-ring, cushion ring and seal ring **(see illustrations)**. **Note:** *Whether you're replacing an injector or a leaking O-ring, it's a good idea to remove all the injectors from the fuel rail and replace all the O-rings, seal rings and cushion rings.*

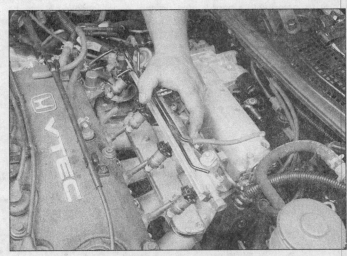

**15.12b Lift the fuel rail and injector assembly from the intake manifold**

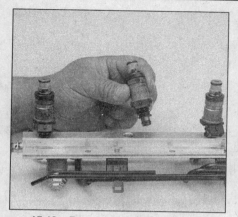

15.13a Remove the injectors from the fuel rail

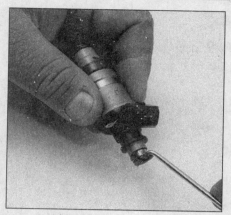

15.13b Carefully remove the injector O-rings

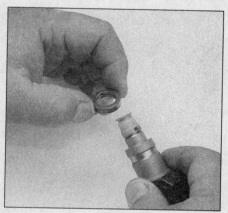

15.13c Remove the seal ring and cushion ring from the injector

16.2 Remove the coolant hose (arrow) from the throttle body

16.3a Loosen the hose clamp and remove the intake duct from the throttle body

## Installation

14 Coat the new cushion rings with clean engine oil and slide them onto the injectors.

15 Coat the new O-rings with clean engine oil and install them on the injector(s), then insert each injector into its corresponding bore in the fuel rail.

16.3b After removing the intake duct from the air cleaner assembly, lift one end and remove the lower section of the duct from the vacuum chamber

16 Coat the new seal rings with clean engine oil and press them into the injector bore(s) in the intake manifold.

17 Install the injector and fuel rail assembly on the intake manifold. Tighten the fuel rail mounting nuts to the torque listed in this Chapter's Specifications.

18 The remainder of installation is the reverse of removal.

19 After the injector/fuel rail assembly installation is complete, turn the ignition switch to ON, but don't operate the starter (this activates the fuel pump for about two seconds, which builds up fuel pressure in the fuel lines and the fuel rail). Repeat this about two or three times, then check the fuel lines, rail and injectors for fuel leakage.

## 16 Intake air plenum (four-cylinder engines) - removal and installation

*Refer to illustrations 16.2, 16.3a, 16.3b, 16.4 and 16.5*
**Note:** *The V6 engine is not equipped with an air intake plenum. Instead, the V6 engines utilizes an intake manifold that houses the throttle body, fast idle thermo valve, EGR components and the Intake Air Bypass valve. Refer to Chapter 2B for intake manifold removal.*

1 Drain the coolant from the radiator and engine block (see Chapter 1).

2 Remove the coolant lines from the fast idle thermo valve **(see illustration)**.

3 Remove the air intake duct from the throttle body and air cleaner housing and lift it from the engine compartment **(see illustrations)**.

4 Disconnect all vacuum hoses, electrical connectors and coolant

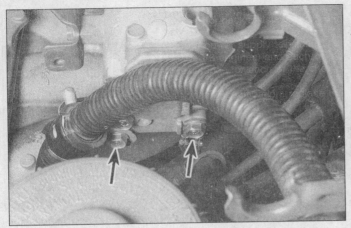

16.4  Remove the ground strap bolts (arrows) from the
air intake plenum

16.5  Air intake plenum mounting bolts (arrows)

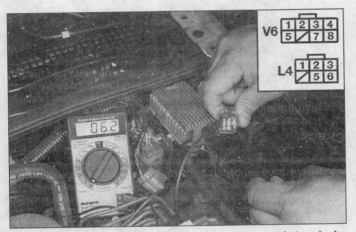

17.4  Check the resistance between the power supply terminal
number 1 (four-cylinder engines) or number 5 (V6 engines)
and each of the other terminals. It should be
approximately 5 to 7 ohms

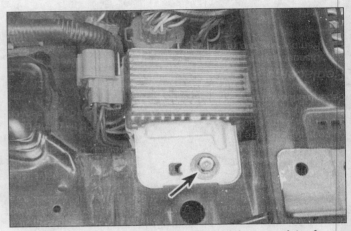

17.8  Remove the bolt (arrow) and lift the injector resistor from
the engine compartment (four-cylinder engine shown,
V6 engines similar)

lines from the air intake plenum **(see illustration)**. Be sure to label everything with masking tape.

5    Remove the air intake plenum mounting nuts and lift the plenum from the engine **(see illustration)**.

6    Installation is the reverse of removal. Be sure to clean the surface of the air intake plenum and the intake manifold and install a new gasket.

## 17   Injector resistor - check and replacement

*Refer to illustrations 17.4 and 17.8*

### Check

1    Detach the cable from the negative battery terminal. **Caution:** *The stereo in your vehicle is equipped with an anti-theft system. Make sure you have the correct activation code before disconnecting the battery.*

2    Locate the injector resistor. It's on the firewall in the engine compartment **(see illustration 17.8)**.

3    Trace the wire harness from the resistor back to its connector and disconnect it.

4    Check the resistance between the power supply terminal (1 for the four-cylinder engines) or (5 for the V6 engines) and each of the other terminals in the connector. Resistance for each of the checks should be about 5 to 7 ohms **(see illustration)**.

5    If the indicated resistance isn't within specification, replace the resistor.

### Replacement

6    Detach the cable from the negative battery terminal. **Caution:** *The stereo in your vehicle is equipped with an anti-theft system. Make sure you have the correct activation code before disconnecting the battery.*

7    Disconnect the electrical connector from the injector resistor.

8    Remove the bolt that attaches the resistor to the body and remove the unit **(see illustration)**.

9    Installation is the reverse of removal.

## 18   Idle Air Control (IAC) valve - check and replacement

*Refer to illustrations 18.3, 18.4, 18.7a and 18.7b*

1    The idle speed is controlled by the IAC valve. This valve changes the amount of air that will bypass into the intake manifold. The IAC valve is activated by the ECM depending upon the running conditions of the engine (air conditioning system, power steering, cold and warm running etc.). A malfunction in the IAC system will normally set a Code 14 in the self-diagnosis system (see Chapter 6).

### Check

2    Apply the parking brake, block the wheels and place the transaxle in Neutral (manual) or Park (automatic). Connect a tachometer, according to the manufacturer's instructions, to the engine. Start the engine and hold the accelerator steady at 3,000 rpm until the coolant fan comes on. Return the engine to idle and disconnect the electrical

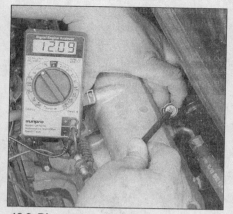

**18.3  Disconnect the electrical connector from the IAC valve and with the ignition key ON (engine not running), check for battery voltage at the connector (four-cylinder engine shown)**

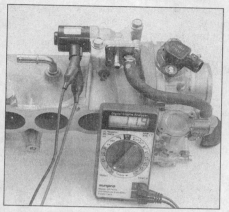

**18.4  Check the resistance of the IAC valve using an ohmmeter - it should be approximately 8 to 15 ohms**

**18.7a  Remove the bolts from the IAC valve and separate it from the air intake plenum (four-cylinder engine)**

**18.7b  Remove the bolts (arrows) and separate the IAC motor from the throttle body (V6 engine)**

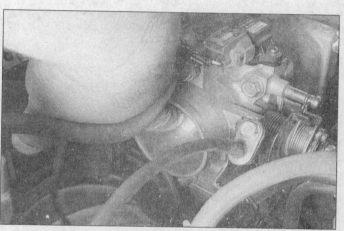

**19.3  With the finger blocking the lower port inside the throttle body, make sure air flows into the fast idle thermo valve**

connector to the IAC valve. **Warning:** *Keep hands, loose clothing, etc. away from any moving engine parts while working on a running engine or personal injury may result.* There should be a noticeable reduction in idle speed when the IAC valve is disconnected. If there isn't, the IAC valve is probably defective. If there was a drop in idle with the IAC valve disconnected and an intermittent idle problem still persists, check the wiring harness from the IAC valve to the ECM for poor connections or damaged wires.

3    If a code 14 was indicated by the self-diagnosis system, disconnect the electrical connector from the IAC valve, turn the ignition key ON (engine not running) and measure the voltage between the positive yellow/black terminal of the wiring harness connector and body ground **(see illustration)**. There should be battery voltage. If no voltage is present, check for an open circuit in the yellow/black wire from the IAC valve to the PGM-FI main relay.

4    Using an ohmmeter, measure the resistance of the IAC valve **(see illustration)**. It should be between 8 and 15 ohms. Check for continuity between each terminal of the IAC valve and ground. There should be no continuity. If there is, replace the IAC valve.

5    If the voltage and resistance readings are correct, have the ECM and electrical circuit for the IAC valve diagnosed by a dealer service department or other qualified repair shop.

### Replacement

6    Disconnect the electrical connector from the IAC valve.

7    Remove the two mounting screws from the valve and lift it from

the air intake plenum **(see illustrations)**.

8    Installation is the reverse of removal. Be sure to install a new O-ring.

___

## 19    Fast idle thermo valve - check and replacement

*Refer to illustrations 19.3 and 19.9*

1    The fast idle thermo valve is a device attached to the throttle body that controls erratic running when the engine is cold. Engine rpm levels are raised using a wax plunger that expands and contracts during warm and cold cycles. Coolant from the engine is directed through hoses to the area around the thermowax plunger thereby heating or cooling the thermo valve. When cold, the thermo valve contracts thereby allowing more air into the intake and raising the engine rpm. When the engine reaches operating temperature, the valve closes reducing the amount of recirculated air into the manifold thereby lowering the idle.

### Check

2    Remove the air intake duct from the throttle body (see Section 9).

3    Start the engine and position a finger over the lower port in the throttle body **(see illustration)**. **Warning:** *Keep hands, loose clothing, etc. away from any moving engine parts while working on a running engine or personal injury may result.* Make sure air flows into the fast idle thermo valve when the engine is cold.

4    If air does not flow, replace the valve.

5    Next, hold the engine rpm at 3,000 with no load until the radiator fan activates (warm engine). Allow the engine to return to idle.
6    Position your finger over the lower port and observe the rpm change. If the rpm remains steady, the fast idle thermo valve is working properly. If the rpm drops, the fast idle thermo valve is leaking and must be replaced.

## Replacement

7    Drain the coolant from the radiator (see Chapter 3).
8    Remove the throttle body from the air intake plenum (see Section 13).
9    Remove the bolts that retain the fast idle thermo valve to the throttle body **(see illustration)**.
10    Remove the valve from the throttle body.
11    Installation is the reverse of removal. Be sure to use new gaskets when reassembling the fast idle thermo valve onto the throttle body.

## 20   Intake Air Resonator (IAR) control system (four-cylinder engines) - component check and replacement

*Refer to illustrations 20.1, 20.3, 20.5, 20.6, 20.10 and 20.11*
1    This system provides intake air into the manifold while silencing the air charge. The IAR control solenoid is activated by the ECM during 2,900 and 3,700 rpm (mid-range) **(see illustration)**.

## Check

2    Start the engine and allow it to idle.
3    Remove the upper vacuum hose from the IAR control solenoid and connect a vacuum gauge **(see illustration)**. There should be NO vacuum.
4    If vacuum exists, disconnect the electrical connector from the IAR control solenoid. If vacuum still exists, there is a leak in the solenoid.
5    If there originally was no vacuum (Step 3), raise the engine rpm to 3,000 and check for vacuum **(see illustration)**. There should be vacuum.
6    If there is NO vacuum at 3,000 rpm, disconnect the lower vacuum hose on the IAR control solenoid and connect a vacuum gauge **(see illustration)**. There should be vacuum.
7    If vacuum does not exist, check the vacuum hose from the air intake plenum for cracks, damage or disconnected hoses.
8    If vacuum exists (see Step 6), measure the voltage between the black/yellow wire (+) and the orange/green wire (-). If battery voltage exists, then the IAR control solenoid is defective.
9    If there is no voltage, check the harness for opens, shorts or damage.

**19.9  Remove the bolts (arrows) from the fast idle thermo valve (four-cylinder engine shown)**

10    If there is vacuum (see Step 5), connect a vacuum pump to the IAR control diaphragm and apply vacuum. It should hold without leaks **(see illustration)**.
11    Install a vacuum gauge in place of the vacuum pump and raise the engine rpm to 4,500 and observe the gauge. There should be no vacuum over 3,700 rpm **(see illustration)**. If there is, have the ECM checked by a dealer service department.

## Replacement

12    Remove the air cleaner assembly (see Section 8).
13    Disconnect the electrical connectors and vacuum hoses to the IAR control valve and IAR control diaphragm.
14    Remove the bolts and lift the assembly from the engine compartment. Replace the defective components and install the assembly.

## 21   Fuel Injection Air (FIA) control system (four-cylinder engines) - component check and replacement

*Refer to illustrations 21.1, 21.3, 21.6 and 21.9*
1    This system supplies manifold air directly next to each individual fuel injector between 1,300 and 4,500 rpm **(see illustration)**. This additional air charge helps lean the mixture and provide complete combustion during acceleration.

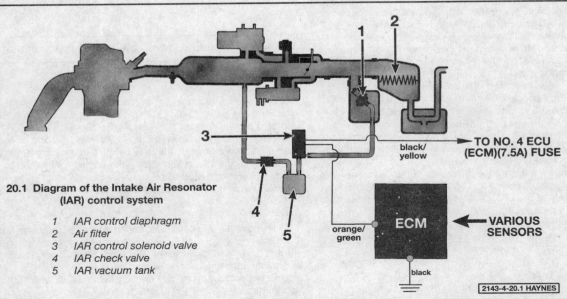

**20.1  Diagram of the Intake Air Resonator (IAR) control system**

1    *IAR control diaphragm*
2    *Air filter*
3    *IAR control solenoid valve*
4    *IAR check valve*
5    *IAR vacuum tank*

TO NO. 4 ECU (ECM)(7.5A) FUSE

black/yellow

ECM

VARIOUS SENSORS

orange/green

black

2143-4-20.1 HAYNES

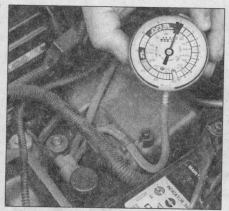

20.3  With the engine idling, there should be no vacuum from the IAR control valve

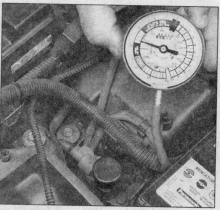

20.5  Raise the engine speed and observe that the IAR control valve switches to vacuum at approximately 3,000 rpm

20.6  There should be vacuum to the IAR control valve at 3,000 rpm

20.10  Apply vacuum to the IAR control diaphragm and observe that vacuum holds and does not leak down

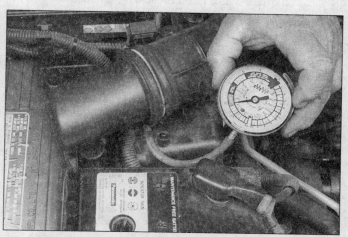

20.11  There should be NO vacuum at the IAR control diaphragm over 3,700 rpm

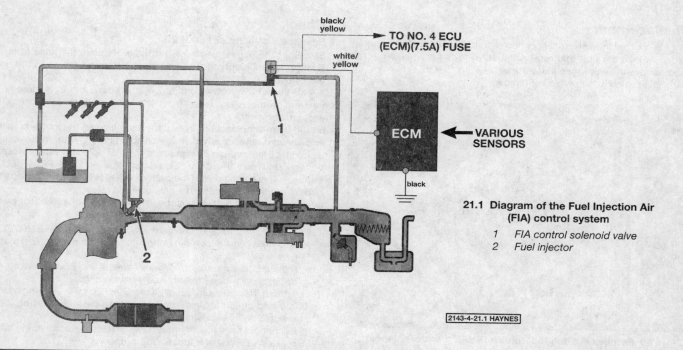

21.1  Diagram of the Fuel Injection Air (FIA) control system

1   FIA control solenoid valve
2   Fuel injector

2143-4-21.1 HAYNES

**21.3  There should be no vacuum present at the
FIA control solenoid at idle**

**21.6  Raise the engine rpm to 3,000 and observe that
vacuum is present**

## Check

2    Start the engine and hold it at 3,000 rpm until the radiator fan
activates. Allow the engine to idle.
3    Remove the vacuum hose from the intake air supply manifold and
install a vacuum gauge to the hose **(see illustration)**. Plug the vacuum
fitting at the supply manifold. There should be no vacuum at the FIA
control solenoid valve at idle.
4    If there is vacuum, disconnect the electrical connector from the
FIA control solenoid valve and check for vacuum. If there's vacuum
present, replace the FIA control solenoid.
5    Check for power to the FIA control solenoid with the ignition key
ON (engine not running). There should be battery voltage at the
connector.
6    If there is no vacuum (see Step 4), raise the engine rpm to approximately 1,500 and check for vacuum **(see illustration)**. There should
be vacuum.
7    Raise the engine to 5,000 rpm. There should be NO vacuum. If the
FIA control valve does not operate as described, the ECM or circuits
could be defective.

## Replacement

8    Disconnect the electrical connector from the FIA control solenoid.
9    Remove the bolt that retains the valve to the air intake plenum
and remove the valve **(see illustration)**.
10   Installation is the reverse of removal.

**21.9  Remove the bolt that retains the FIA control solenoid**

## 22  Intake Air Bypass (IAB) control system (V6 engines) -
component check and replacement

*Refer to illustration 22.1*
1    The Intake Air Bypass (IAB) system allows the intake manifold to
divert the path of intake air into the combustion chamber **(see illustration)**. Two air intake paths are provided in the intake manifold to
allow the option of the intake volume most favorable for the particular
engine speed. Optimum performance is achieved by switching the
valves from either the closed position (for high torque at low rpm) or
the open position (for maximum horsepower at high rpm).
2    The bypass control solenoids are controlled by the ECM. Any
failure with the solenoids can lead to problems with the system,
resulting in poor driveability. Follow the simple checks to help
diagnose any system defects. **Note:** *The Intake Air Bypass (IAB)
system does not have any self diagnostic codes directly relating to this
system.*

## Check

*Refer to illustrations 22.1 and 22.3*
3    Start the engine and allow it to idle. Remove the hose from the
bypass control diaphragm and connect a vacuum gauge to the hose
**(see illustration)**.
4    If there is vacuum, continue with Steps 7 and 8. If there is no
vacuum, remove the hose from the vacuum tank and check for
vacuum at the tank.
5    If there is no vacuum, check the line between the intake manifold
and vacuum tank for any damage or obstructions. If there is vacuum,
disconnect the two-pin connector at the IAB solenoid valve. Measure
voltage between the BLK/YEL (+) terminal and the PINK/BLU (-)
terminal. There should NOT be battery voltage. If there is, replace the
bypass control solenoid with a new unit and retest.
6    If there is no battery voltage, measure the voltage between the
BLK/YEL (+) and ground. There should be voltage.

   a)  *If there is no voltage, check for an open circuit in the BLK/YEL (+)
       wire between the two-pin connector and the number 2 (15 amp)
       fuse.*
   b)  *If there is voltage, have the wire harness and ECM checked at a
       dealer service department or other repair shop.*

7    If there was vacuum initially (see Step 2), raise the engine rpm
to 5,000 and check for vacuum at the hose **(see illustration 22.3)**.
There should be no vacuum.
8    Reconnect the vacuum hose. If all the tests are correct, the Intake
Air Bypass (IAB) system is functioning properly.

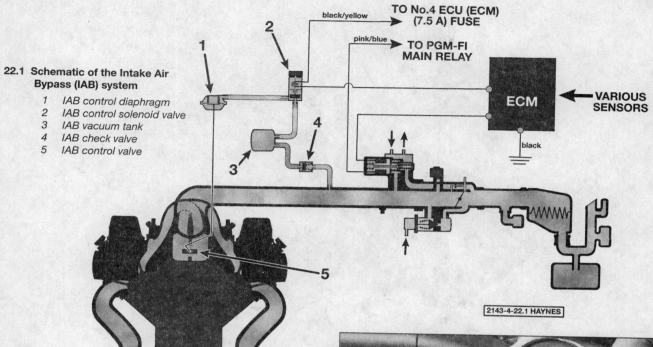

**22.1  Schematic of the Intake Air Bypass (IAB) system**

1   IAB control diaphragm
2   IAB control solenoid valve
3   IAB vacuum tank
4   IAB check valve
5   IAB control valve

TO No.4 ECU (ECM) (7.5 A) FUSE

black/yellow

pink/blue

TO PGM-FI MAIN RELAY

ECM

VARIOUS SENSORS

black

## Bypass valve test

*Refer to illustrations 22.10 and 22.11*

9    Check the bypass valve shaft and linkage for binding or any obvious damage.

10   With the engine idling, check that the bypass valve linkage is in contact with the stopper when the vacuum hose is disconnected from the diaphragm **(see illustration)**.

11   Check that the bypass valve linkage is in contact with the full close screw when the vacuum hose is connected **(see illustration)**.

12   If there are any problems, clean the bypass valves and shafts with aerosol carburetor cleaner. If the shafts still bind, remove the intake manifold (see Chapter 2B) and inspect the bypass valve body assembly.

13   If the diaphragm doesn't hold vacuum, replace the diaphragm assembly.

**22.3  Remove the hose from the Bypass Control Diaphragm (arrow) and check for vacuum. Vacuum should be present when the engine is idling**

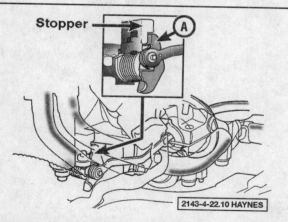

**22.10  Observe the location of the stopper and the lever (A) when the hoses are disconnected - they should be contacting each other**

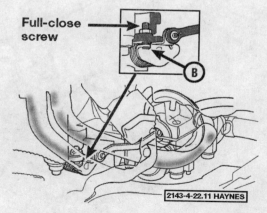

**22.11  Observe the location of the full close screw (1) - when vacuum is applied to both diaphragms the lever should contact the screw (B)**

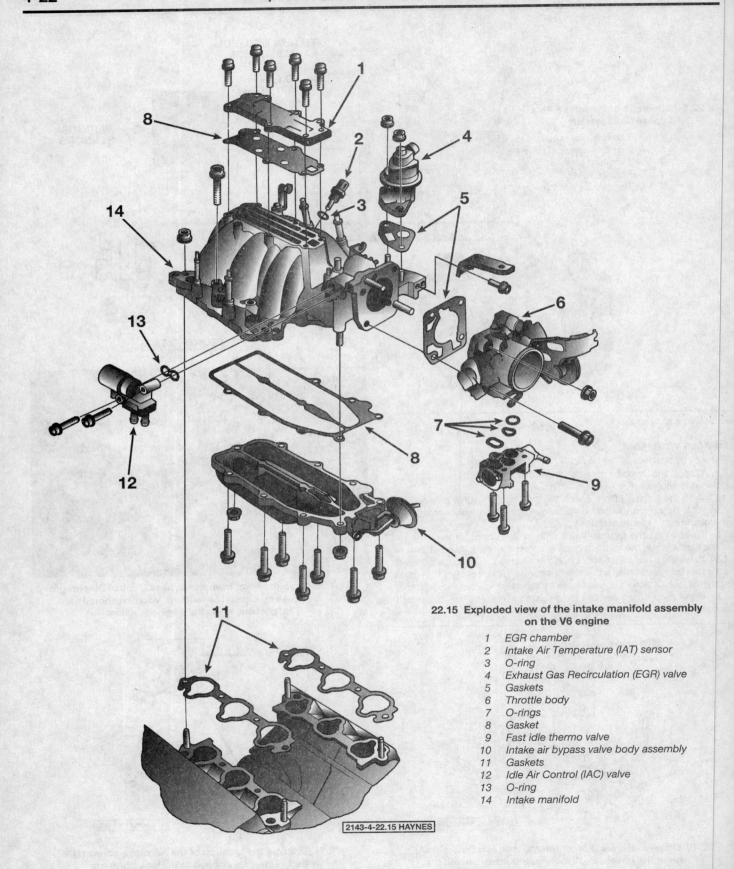

**22.15  Exploded view of the intake manifold assembly
on the V6 engine**

1   EGR chamber
2   Intake Air Temperature (IAT) sensor
3   O-ring
4   Exhaust Gas Recirculation (EGR) valve
5   Gaskets
6   Throttle body
7   O-rings
8   Gasket
9   Fast idle thermo valve
10  Intake air bypass valve body assembly
11  Gaskets
12  Idle Air Control (IAC) valve
13  O-ring
14  Intake manifold

2143-4-22.15 HAYNES

**23.1  Check the condition of the rubber hangers that secure the muffler to the body**

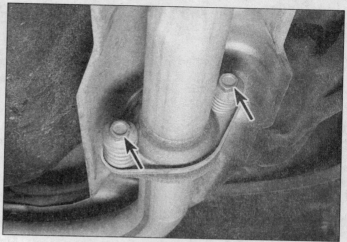

**23.4  Be sure to use penetrating spray to lubricate the flange bolts (arrows) before removing them**

## Replacement

*Refer to illustration 22.15*

14    Remove the intake manifold (see Chapter 2B).

15    Remove the bypass valve body from the intake manifold **(see illustration).**

16    Scrape all remaining traces of the gasket material from the plenum and valve body without damaging the aluminum material.

17    Installation is the reverse of removal. Be sure to use new gaskets.

## 23   Exhaust system servicing - general information

*Refer to illustrations 23.1 and 23.4*

**Warning:** *Inspection and repair of exhaust system components should be done only after enough time has elapsed after driving the vehicle to allow the system components to cool completely. Also, when working under the vehicle, make sure it is securely supported on jackstands.*

1    The exhaust system consists of the exhaust manifold(s), the catalytic converter, the muffler, the tailpipe and all connecting pipes, brackets, hangers and clamps. The exhaust system is attached to the body with mounting brackets and rubber hangers **(see illustration).** If any of the parts are improperly installed, excessive noise and vibration will be transmitted to the body.

## Muffler and pipes

2    Conduct regular inspections of the exhaust system to keep it safe and quiet. Look for any damaged or bent parts, open seams, holes, loose connections, excessive corrosion or other defects which could allow exhaust fumes to enter the vehicle. Also check the catalytic converter when you inspect the exhaust system (see below). Deteriorated exhaust system components should not be repaired; they should be replaced with new parts.

3    If the exhaust system components are extremely corroded or rusted together, welding equipment will probably be required to remove them. The convenient way to accomplish this is to have a muffler repair shop remove the corroded sections with a cutting torch. If, however, you want to save money by doing it yourself (and you don't have a welding outfit with a cutting torch), simply cut off the old components with a hacksaw. If you have compressed air, special pneumatic cutting chisels can also be used. If you do decide to tackle the job at home, be sure to wear safety goggles to protect your eyes from metal chips and work gloves to protect your hands.

4    Here are some simple guidelines to follow when repairing the exhaust system:

a)  *Work from the back to the front when removing exhaust system components.*

b)  *Apply penetrating oil to the exhaust system component fasteners to make them easier to remove* **(see illustration).**

c)  *Use new gaskets, hangers and clamps when installing exhaust systems components.*

d)  *Apply anti-seize compound to the threads of all exhaust system fasteners during reassembly.*

e)  *Be sure to allow sufficient clearance between newly installed parts and all points on the underbody to avoid overheating the floor pan and possibly damaging the interior carpet and insulation. Pay particularly close attention to the catalytic converter and heat shield.*

## Catalytic converter

**Warning:** *The converter gets very hot during operation. Make sure it's cooled down before you touch it.*

**Note:** *See Chapter 6 for more information on the catalytic converter.*

5    Periodically, inspect the heat shield for cracks, dents and loose or missing fasteners.

6    Remove the heat shield and inspect the converter for cracks or other damage.

7    If the converter must be replaced, remove the mounting nuts from the flanges at each end, detach the rubber mounts and separate the converter from the exhaust system (you should be able to push the exhaust pipes at each end out of the way to clear the converter studs.

8    Installation is the reverse of removal. Be sure to use new gaskets.

# Notes

# Chapter 5
# Engine electrical systems

## Contents

## Specifications

### Ignition system

Externally mounted coil
  Primary resistance
    Non VTEC four-cylinder engine ............................................................. 0.6 to 0.8 ohms
    V6 engine ............................................................. 0.3 to 0.4 ohms
  Secondary resistance ............................................................. 14 to 22 K-ohms
Internally mounted coil (VTEC engine)
  Primary resistance ............................................................. 0.4 to 0.6 ohms
  Secondary resistance ............................................................. 22 to 34 K-ohms

### Charging system

Alternator brush length (minimum) ............................................................. 1/4-inch

### Ignition timing

All models ............................................................. 15 degrees BTDC (RED) at 650 to 750 rpm

## 1  General information

The engine electrical systems include all ignition, charging and starting components. Because of their engine-related functions, these components are discussed separately from chassis electrical devices such as the lights, the instruments, etc. (which are included in Chapter 12).

Always observe the following precautions when working on the electrical systems:

a) *Be extremely careful, when servicing engine electrical components. They are easily damaged if checked, connected or handled improperly.*
b) *Never leave the ignition switch on for long periods of time with the engine off.*
c) *Don't disconnect the battery cables while the engine is running.*
d) *Maintain correct polarity when connecting a battery cable from another vehicle during jump starting.*
e) *Always disconnect the negative cable first and hook it up last or the battery may be shorted by the tool being used to loosen the cable clamps.*

It's also a good idea to review the safety-related information regarding the engine electrical systems located in the *Safety First* section near the front of this manual before beginning any operation included in this Chapter.

## 2  Battery - emergency jump starting

Refer to the *Booster battery (jump) starting* procedure at the front of this manual.

## 3  Battery cables - check and replacement

1    Periodically inspect the entire length of each battery cable for damage, cracked or burned insulation and corrosion. Poor battery cable connections can cause starting problems and decreased engine performance.

2    Check the cable-to-terminal connections at the ends of the cables for cracks, loose wire strands and corrosion. The presence of white, fluffy deposits under the insulation at the cable terminal connection is a sign that the cable is corroded and should be replaced. Check the terminals for distortion, missing mounting bolts and corrosion.

3    When removing the cables, always disconnect the negative cable first and hook it up last or the battery may be shorted by the tool used to loosen the cable clamps. Even if only the positive cable is being replaced, be sure to disconnect the negative cable from the battery first (see Chapter 1 for further information regarding battery cable removal). **Caution:** *The radio in your vehicle is equipped with an anti-theft system, make sure you have the correct activation code before disconnecting the battery.*

4    Disconnect the old cables from the battery, then trace each of them to their opposite ends and detach them from the starter solenoid and ground terminals. Note the routing of each cable to ensure correct installation.

5    If you are replacing either or both of the old cables, take them with you when buying new cables. It is vitally important that you replace the cables with identical parts. Cables have characteristics that make them easy to identify: positive cables are usually red and larger in cross-section; ground cables are usually black and smaller in cross section.

6    Clean the threads of the solenoid or ground connection with a wire brush to remove rust and corrosion. Apply a light coat of battery terminal corrosion inhibitor, or petroleum jelly, to the threads to prevent future corrosion.

7    Attach the cable to the solenoid or ground connection and tighten the mounting nut/bolt securely.

8    Before connecting a new cable to the battery, make sure that it reaches the battery post without having to be stretched.

**4.2  Remove the two nuts (arrows) and detach the hold-down clamps**

9    Connect the positive cable first, followed by the negative cable.

## 4  Battery - removal and Installation

*Refer to illustration 4.2*

1    Disconnect both cables from the battery terminals. **Caution 1:** *Always disconnect the negative cable first and hook it up last or the battery may be shorted by the tool being used to loosen the cable clamps.* **Caution 2:** *The radio in your vehicle is equipped with an anti-theft system, make sure you have the correct activation code before disconnecting the battery.*

2    Remove the battery hold-down clamp (**see Illustration**).

3    Lift out the battery. Be careful - it's heavy. **Note:** *Battery straps and handlers are available at most auto parts stores for a reasonable price. They make it easier to remove and carry the battery.*

4    While the battery is out, remove and inspect the carrier (tray) for corrosion.

5    If corrosion has leaked down to the battery support, remove the bolts and lift the support out. Clean the deposits from the metal to prevent the support from further oxidation.

6    If you are replacing the battery, make sure you get one that's identical, with the same dimensions, amperage rating, cold cranking rating, etc.

7    Installation is the reverse of removal.

## 5  Ignition system - general information

**Warning:** *The transistorized electronic ignition systems used on the models covered by this manual generate considerably higher voltage than conventional systems . Be extra careful when servicing these ignition systems.*

The Programmed Ignition (PGM-IG) system provides complete control of the ignition timing by determining the optimum timing using a micro computer in response to engine speed, coolant temperature, throttle position and vacuum pressure in the intake manifold. These parameters are relayed to the ECM by the TDC/CKP/CYP Sensors, Throttle Position sensor, Coolant Temperature sensor and MAP sensor. Ignition timing is altered during warm-up, idling and warm running conditions by the PGM-IG system. This electronic ignition system also consists of the ignition switch, battery, coil, distributor, spark plug wires and spark plugs.

All distributors are driven by the camshaft. Distributors are advanced and retarded by the Engine Control Module. All models employ a crankshaft position sensor. On four-cylinder models the sensors are located inside the distributor; these distributors must be replaced as a single unit if they become defective. Refer to a dealer parts department or auto parts store for any questions concerning the availability of the distributor parts and assemblies. Testing the TDC/CKP/CYP sensors are covered in Chapter 6.

## 6    Ignition system - check

*Refer to illustration 6.1*

**Warning:** *Because of the high voltage generated by the ignition system, extreme care should be taken whenever an operation involving ignition components is performed.*

1    If the engine will not start even though it turns over, check for spark at the spark plug by installing a calibrated ignition system tester to the end of the plug wire **(see illustration)**. The tool is available at most auto parts stores. Be sure to order the correct tool for your particular ignition system ( high energy electronic).

2    Connect the clip on the tester to a ground such as a metal bracket or valve cover bolt, crank the engine and watch the end of the tester for a bright blue, well defined spark.

3    If sparks occur, sufficient voltage is reaching the plugs to fire the engine. However the plugs themselves may be fouled, so remove and check them as described in Chapter 1 or replace them with new ones.

4    If no spark occurs, remove the distributor cap and check the cap and rotor as described in Chapter 1. If moisture is present, use WD-40 or something similar to dry out the cap and rotor, then reinstall the cap and repeat the spark test.

5    If there is still no spark, attach the tester to the high-tension wire from the coil and repeat the test again. If there is still no spark, the coil to cap wire may be bad, check it for an open with an ohmmeter.

6    If the coil-to-cap wire tests good, check the primary wire connections at the coil to make sure they are clean and tight. Make any necessary repairs, then check for voltage to the ignition coil with the ignition key ON (engine not running). Also, check the primary and secondary resistance of the ignition coil (see Section 7).

7    If sparks now occur, the distributor cap, rotor, plug wires or spark plugs may be defective.

8    If still no sparks occur, check the ignition module. Attach a 12 volt test light between body ground and terminal C (green wire) on the V6 engines or terminal B (green wire) on the NON-VTEC four cylinder engines or terminal B (blue wire) on the VTEC engines. Remove the coil wire from the ignition coil and use a suitable wire to ground the secondary terminal. Crank the engine and observe that the test light flashes evenly. This test checks the ignition module signal to the coil. If there still is no flash (spark), perform additional checks on the ignition module (see Section 8). **Note:** *It is preferable to use the LED style automotive test light over the bulb type test light. The LED is sensitive to lower voltage signals and will better illuminate the ignition module pulse signals.* **Note:** *Although this module check works best with a vehicle with the EXTERNAL ignition coil, it is possible to perform this check using jumper wires installed properly into the backside of the electrical terminals on the outside of the distributor on INTERNAL coil types (see Section 7).*

**6.1  To use a calibrated ignition tester, simply disconnect a spark plug wire, connect it to the tester, clip the tester to a convenient ground and operate the starter with the ignition on - if there's enough power to fire the plug, sparks will be visible between the electrode tip and the tester body**

## 7    Ignition coil - check and replacement

### *Internally mounted coils (four-cylinder VTEC models)*

#### Check

*Refer to illustrations 7.5 and 7.6*

1    Make sure the ignition switch is turned OFF for the following checks.

2    Detach the high tension lead from the secondary terminal (coil tower).

3    Remove the distributor cap, rotor and the cover.

4    Remove the two electrical connectors from the ignition coil primary terminals.

5    Using an ohmmeter, touch the probes to the primary terminals (A and B) of the coil, measure the primary resistance and compare your reading to the value listed in this Chapter's Specifications **(see illustration)**.

6    Touch the probes to the secondary winding terminal and the positive primary terminal (A) **(see illustration)**, measure the secondary resistance and compare your reading to the resistance value listed in this Chapter's Specifications.

7    The figures in the specifications will vary somewhat with the temperature of the coil. The specified resistance values are for a coil temperature of about 70-degrees F.

8    If the coil fails either check, replace it with a new part.

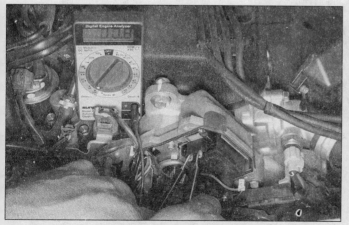

**7.5  Checking the resistance between the coil primary terminals. Remove the electrical connectors from the coil before testing**

**7.6  Checking the resistance between the coil positive terminal (A) and the high-tension (secondary) terminal**

**7.11  Remove the two bolts (arrows) and slide the coil from the distributor housing (internal type coil)**

## Replacement

*Refer to illustration 7.11*

9    Detach the cable from the negative terminal of the battery. **Caution:** *The radio in your vehicle is equipped with an anti-theft system, make sure you have the correct activation code before disconnecting the battery.*

10    Remove the distributor cap (see Chapter 1) and leak cover (if equipped). Remove the screws and detach the wires from the primary terminals.

11    Remove the two screws and slide the coil out **(see illustration)**.

12    Installation is the reverse of removal.

## *Externally mounted coils (non-VTEC four cylinder and V6 models)*

### Check

*Refer to illustration 7.16*

13    Make sure the ignition switch is turned OFF for the following checks.

14    Detach the high-tension lead from the secondary winding terminal (coil tower).

15    Remove the 4-pin electrical connector from the ignition coil primary terminals.

16    Using an ohmmeter, touch the probes to the primary terminals (A and C) of the coil, measure the primary resistance and compare your reading to the value listed in this Chapter's Specifications **(see illustration)**.

17    Touch the probes to the secondary winding terminal and the positive primary terminal (A) **(see illustration 7.16)**, measure the secondary resistance and compare your reading to the resistance value listed in this Chapter's Specifications.

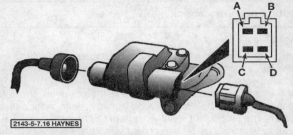

2143-5-7.16 HAYNES

**7.16  Check the primary resistance between terminals A and C on external coils**

18    The figures in the specifications will vary somewhat with the temperature of the coil. The specified resistance values are for a coil temperature of about 70-degrees F.

19    If the coil fails either check, replace it with a new part.

## Replacement

*Refer to illustration 7.22*

20    Detach the cable from the negative terminal of the battery. **Caution:** *The radio in your vehicle is equipped with an anti-theft system, make sure you have the correct activation code before disconnecting the battery.*

21    Disconnect all electrical connections from the ignition coil.

22    Remove the bolts that retain the coil **(see illustration)**.

23    Installation is the reverse of removal.

## 8    Ignition Control Module (ICM) - check and replacement

### *Check*

*Refer to illustrations 8.3a, 8.3b and 8.5*

1    Remove the distributor cap, rotor and the ICM cover

2    Disconnect the wires from the ICM unit.

3    With the ignition key turned ON (engine not running), check for voltage between the black/yellow wire (four-cylinder) or yellow wire (V6) and body ground **(see illustrations)**. There should be battery voltage.

4    If there is no voltage, check the circuit between the corresponding wire and the ignition switch. Make sure the ignition switch delivers battery voltage to the ICM with the key ON.

5    With the ignition key turned ON (engine not running), check for voltage between the blue wire (VTEC four-cylinder) or green wire (non-VTEC four-cylinder and V6) and body ground **(see illustration)**. There should be battery voltage. This test checks battery voltage from the ignition coil.

**7.22  The ignition coil is located under the distributor on V6 engines**

**8.3a  Check for battery voltage from the ignition switch on the black/yellow wire (four-cylinder engine)**

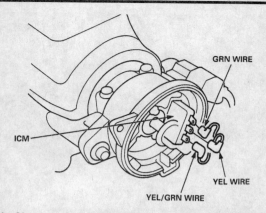

8.3b  Check for battery voltage from the ignition switch on the YELLOW wire (V6 engine)

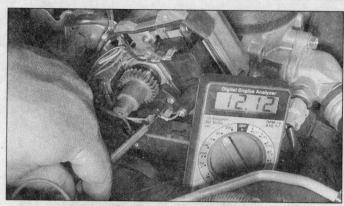

8.5  With the ignition key ON (engine not running), check for battery voltage from the ignition coil on the blue wire (VTEC four-cylinder engine)

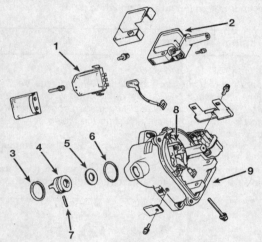

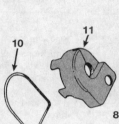

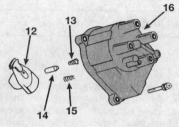

8.10  Exploded view of the internal coil distributor assembly

| | | | |
|---|---|---|---|
| 1 | ICM | 6 | O-ring | 11 | Leak cover |
| 2 | Coil | 7 | Pin | 12 | Rotor |
| 3 | Pin retainer | 8 | CKP/TDC/CYP | 13 | Carbon point spring |
| 4 | Coupling | | sensor (typical) | 14 | Carbon point |
| 5 | Thrust washer | 9 | Distributor | 15 | Contact point spring |
| | | 10 | Cap seal | 16 | Cap |

6    If there is no voltage, check the circuit between the corresponding wire and the ignition coil. Also check for an open circuit inside the ignition coil by checking for continuity between terminals A and B of the ignition coil **(see illustration 7.16)**

7    If the ignition coil and circuits are good and there is still no spark, replace the ICM.

## Replacement

*Refer to illustration 8.10, 8.11a and 8.11b*

8    Disconnect the negative battery cable from the battery terminal.

**Caution:** *The radio in your vehicle is equipped with an anti-theft system, make sure you have the correct activation code before disconnecting the battery.*

9    Remove the distributor cap and cover from the distributor (see Chapter 1).

10   Remove all the electrical connectors from the ICM unit **(see illustration)**.

11   Remove the two set screws from the ICM body and pull the ICM unit straight out **(see illustrations)**.

12   Installation is the reverse of removal.

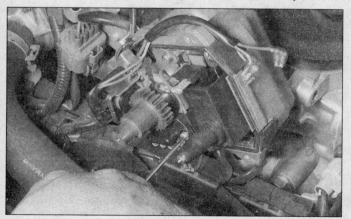

8.11a  Remove the two screws from the Ignition Control Module

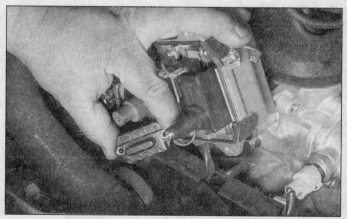

8.11b  Lift the module from the distributor

**9.5a  Make one mark directly underneath the rotor tip and another between the distributor base and the cylinder head**

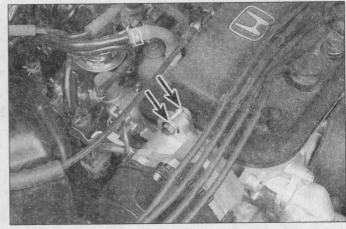

**9.5b  Mark the position of the distributor body in relation to the cylinder head (arrows) using white paint**

## 9    Distributor - removal and installation

### Removal

*Refer to illustration 9.5a and 9.5b*

1    Detach the cable from the negative battery terminal. **Caution:** *The radio in your vehicle is equipped with an anti-theft system, make sure you have the correct activation code before disconnecting the battery.*

2    Detach any clamps and electrical connectors on the distributor. Mark the wires and hoses so they can be returned to their original locations.

3    Look for a raised number or letter on the distributor cap. This marks the location for the number-one cylinder spark plug wire terminal. If the cap does not have a mark for the number-one terminal, locate the number-one spark plug and trace the wire back to the terminal on the cap.

4    Remove the distributor cap (see Chapter 1) and turn the engine over until the rotor is pointing toward the number-one spark plug terminal (see the locating TDC procedure in Chapter 2A).

5    Make a mark on the edge of the distributor base directly below the rotor tip **(see illustration)** and in line with it. Also, mark the distributor base and the cylinder head to ensure the distributor is installed correctly **(see Illustration).**

6    If not already done, unplug the ICM wires.

7    Remove the distributor hold-down bolt(s) and pull out the distributor. **Caution:** *Do not turn the crankshaft while the distributor is out of the engine, or the alignment marks will be useless.*

### Installation

**Note:** *If the crankshaft has been moved while the distributor is out, the number-one piston must be repositioned at TDC. This can be done by feeling for compression pressure at the number-one plug hole as the crankshaft is turned. Once compression is felt, align the ignition timing zero mark with the pointer.*

8    Install a new O-ring on the distributor housing.

9    Insert the distributor into the cylinder head in exactly the same relationship to the head that it was when removed. **Note:** *The lugs on the end of the distributor and the corresponding grooves in the camshaft end are offset to eliminate the possibility of installing the distributor 180-degrees out of phase.*

10    Recheck the alignment marks between the distributor base and the cylinder head to verify the distributor is in the same position it was in before removal. Also check the rotor to see if it's aligned with the mark you made on the distributor.

11    Loosely install the hold-down bolt(s).

12    The remainder of installation is the reverse of removal. Check the ignition timing and tighten the distributor hold-down bolt(s) securely.

## 10    Ignition timing - adjustment

*Refer to illustrations 10.2, 10.4 and 10.5*

**Note:** *It is imperative that the procedures included on the Vehicle Emissions Control Information (VECI) label be followed when adjusting the ignition timing. The label will include all information concerning preliminary steps to be performed before adjusting the timing, as well as the timing specifications.*

1    Start the engine and allow it to reach normal operating temperature.

2    With the ignition off, locate the VECI label under the hood and read through and perform all preliminary instructions concerning igni-

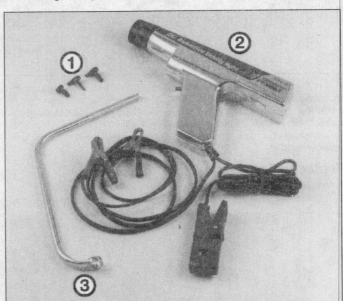

**10.2  Tools needed to check and adjust the ignition timing**

1    ***Vacuum plugs*** - *Vacuum hoses will, in most cases, have to be disconnected and plugged. Molded plugs in various shapes and sizes are available for this*

2    ***Inductive pick-up timing light*** - *Flashes a bright, concentrated beam of light when the number-one spark plug fires. Connect the leads according to the instructions supplied with the light*

3    ***Distributor wrench*** - *On some models, the hold-down bolt for the distributor is difficult to reach and turn with conventional wrenches or sockets. A special wrench like this must be used*

**10.4 Be sure when viewing the timing mark on the pulley (arrow) that you are directly above the pointer aiming the timing light down so as not to create an extreme angle**

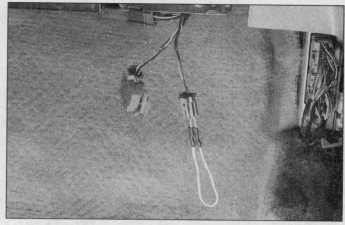

**10.5 The service check-connector is located behind the kick-panel next to the ECM; connect the two terminals together with a jump wire**

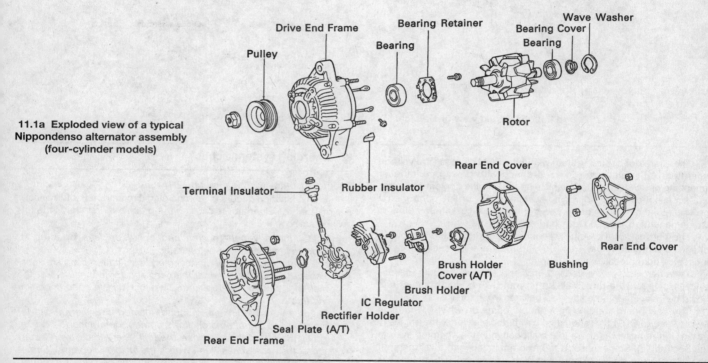

**11.1a Exploded view of a typical Nippondenso alternator assembly (four-cylinder models)**

ignition timing. Several special tools will be needed for this procedure **(see illustration)**.

3    With the ignition off, hook up an inductive pick-up timing light in accordance with the manufacturer's instructions. Connect the inductive pick-up lead of the timing light to the number-one spark plug wire. On all models, number-one is the one closest to the drivebelt end of the engine.

4    Locate the timing marks on the front pulley **(see illustration)**.

5    Locate the service check-connector **(see illustration)**, it's the green/blue and red, two-terminal electrical connector under the dash in the far right (passenger's side) corner. With the ignition off, connect the two terminals together with a jumper wire.

6    With the engine at normal operating temperature, start the engine and point the timing light at the timing pointer.

7    The appropriate mark on the pulley (refer to the VECI label or this Chapter's Specifications) will appear stationary and be aligned with the pointer if the timing is correct.

8    If an adjustment is required, loosen the hold-down bolt(s) and

rotate the distributor slightly until the timing is correct.

9    Tighten the hold-down bolt(s) and recheck the timing.

10    Turn off the engine and remove the timing light.

11    Replace inspection plug and remove the jumper wire from the service check connector.

## 11   Charging system - general information and precautions

*Refer to illustrations 11.1a and 11.1b*

The charging system includes the alternator **(see illustrations)**, an internal voltage regulator, a charge indicator light, the battery, a fusible link and the wiring between all the components. The charging system supplies electrical power for the ignition system, the lights, the radio, etc. The alternator is driven by a drivebelt at one end of the engine.

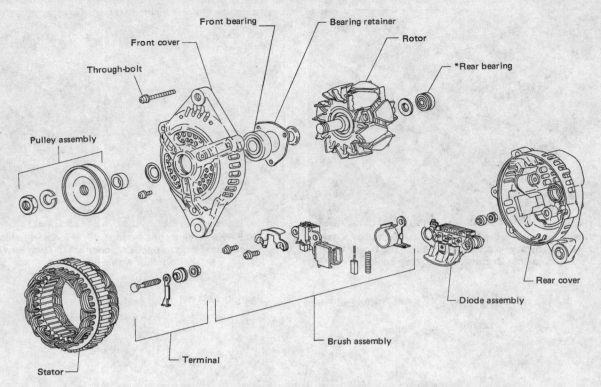

Through-bolt
Front cover
Front bearing
Bearing retainer
Rotor
*Rear bearing
Pulley assembly
Stator
Terminal
Brush assembly
Diode assembly
Rear cover

**11.1b Exploded view of a typical Mitsubishi alternator assembly (V6 models)**

The alternator control system within the ECM changes the voltage generated at the alternator in accordance with driving conditions. Depending upon electric load, vehicle speed, engine coolant temperature, accessories (air conditioning system, radio, cruise control etc.) and the intake air temperature, the system will adjust the amount of voltage generated, creating less load on the engine.

The purpose of the voltage regulator is to limit the alternator's voltage to a preset value. This prevents power surges, circuit overloads, etc., during peak voltage output.

The charging system doesn't ordinarily require periodic maintenance. However, the drivebelt, battery and wires and connections should be inspected at the intervals outlined in Chapter 1.

The dashboard warning light should come on when the ignition key is turned to ON, but it should go off immediately after the engine is started. If it remains on, there is a malfunction in the charging system (see Section 12). Some vehicles are also equipped with a voltmeter. If the voltmeter indicates abnormally high or low voltage, check the charging system (see Section 12).

Be very careful when making electrical circuit connections to a vehicle equipped with an alternator and note the following:

a) When reconnecting wires to the alternator from the battery, be sure to note the polarity.
b) Before using arc welding equipment to repair any part of the vehicle, disconnect the wires from the alternator and the battery terminals.
c) Never start the engine with a battery charger connected.
d) Always disconnect both battery leads before using a battery charger.
e) The alternator is turned by an engine drivebelt which could cause serious injury it your hands, hair or clothes become entangled in it with the engine running.
f) Because the alternator is connected directly to the battery, it could arc or cause a fire if overloaded or shorted out.
g) Wrap a plastic bag over the alternator and secure it with rubber bands before steam cleaning the engine.

## 12   Charging system - check

*Refer to illustrations 12.1a through 12.1f*

1    If a malfunction occurs in the charging circuit, don't automatically assume that the alternator is causing the problem. First check the following items:

a) *Check the drivebelt tension and condition (see Chapter 1). Replace it if it's worn or deteriorated.*
b) *Make sure the alternator mounting and adjustment bolts are tight.*
c) *Inspect the alternator wiring harness and the connectors at the alternator and voltage regulator. They must be in good condition and tight.*
d) *Check the fusible link (if equipped) located between the starter solenoid and the alternator. If it's burned, determine the cause, repair the circuit and replace the link (the vehicle won't start and/or the accessories won't work if the fusible link blows). Sometimes a fusible link may look good, but still be bad. If in doubt, remove it and check for continuity.*
e) *Start the engine and check the alternator for abnormal noises (a shrieking or squealing sound indicates a bad bearing).*
f) *Check the specific gravity of the battery electrolyte. if it's low, charge the battery (doesn't apply to maintenance-free batteries).*
g) *Make sure the battery is fully charged (one bad cell in a battery can cause overcharging by the alternator).*
h) *Disconnect the battery cables (negative first, then positive).* **Caution:** *The radio in your vehicle is equipped with an anti-theft system, make sure you have the correct activation code before disconnecting the battery. Inspect the battery posts and the cable clamps for corrosion. Clean them thoroughly if necessary (see Chapter 1). Reconnect the cable to the positive terminal.*
i) *With the key OFF, connect a test light between the negative battery post and the disconnected negative cable clamp.*
   *1) It the test light does not come on, reattach the clamp and proceed to the next step.*
   *2) If the test light comes on brightly (it will glow dimly because of*

12.1a  Disconnect the 3-pin connector from the back of the alternator

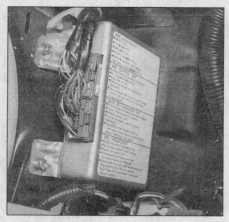

12.1b  The ABS Control Unit is located directly above the ECM under the passenger's dash

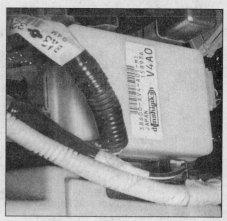

12.1c  The Integrated Control Unit is located near the driver's side fuse panel behind the kickpanel

12.1d  The alternator fuse (7.5 AMP) is located in the driver's side fuse panel

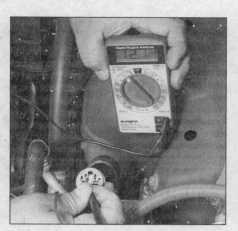

12.1e  Probe the black/yellow wire and check for battery voltage

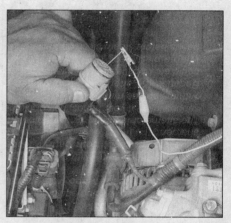

12.1f  Ground the white/blue wire and check that the charge warning light is ON

normal draws from the ECM, radio and clock), there is a short (drain) in the electrical system of the vehicle. The short must be repaired before the charging system can be checked. If the light stays on bright, pull each fuse until the light dims (this will tell you which circuit is shorted).

j)  Disconnect the alternator wiring harness from the backside of the alternator **(see illustration)**. Turn the ignition key to ON (engine not running).

k)  If the charging light goes out, install the connector onto the alternator and proceed to Step 3.

l)  Disconnect the ABS control unit and the Integrated Control Unit **(see illustrations)**. If the charging light remains ON, repair the short to ground in the white/blue wire.

m)  Check the number 4 (7.5 amp) fuse in the dash fuse box **(see illustration)**. If it is blown, the charge warning light will remain ON even though the system is charging.

n)  With the ignition key ON (engine not running), there should be battery voltage between the black/yellow wire and body ground **(see illustration)**. If there is no voltage, check for an open in the circuit.

o)  Now check the bulb itself. Turn the ignition key ON (engine not running) - the charge warning light should be ON. If it does not light, unplug the alternator connector and short the pin of the white/blue terminal to ground (see illustration). The light should come ON. If it does not, check for a bad bulb, an open circuit in the white/blue wire between the warning light and the dash fuse

box, an open circuit in the black/yellow wire between the warning light and the dash fuse box or an open circuit between the dash fuse box and the ignition switch. Note: Consult Chapter 6 and test the ELD (Electric Load Detector) for additional information concerning the charging system.

2    Using a voltmeter, check the battery voltage with the engine off. It should be approximately 12-volts.

3    Start the engine and check the battery voltage again. It should now be approximately 14 to 15 volts.

4    Turn on the headlights. The voltage should drop, and then come back up, if the charging system is working properly.

5    If the voltage reading is more than the specified charging voltage, replace the voltage regulator (see Section 14). If the voltage is less, the alternator diode(s), stator or rectifier may be bad or the voltage regulator may be malfunctioning.

## 13  Alternator - removal and installation

Refer to illustration 13.3a and 13.3b

### Removal

1    Detach the cable from the negative terminal of the battery. **Caution:** *The radio in your vehicle is equipped with an anti-theft system, make sure you have the correct activation code before disconnecting the battery.*

13.3a  Loosen the pivot bolt located at the top of the alternator (four-cylinder engine shown)

13.3b  Then loosen the adjustment bolt located at the bottom of the alternator (four-cylinder engine shown)

14.2  Remove the three nuts (arrows) and detach the rear cover from the alternator

14.3  Once the rear cover is removed, remove the two screws (arrows) that retain the brush holder

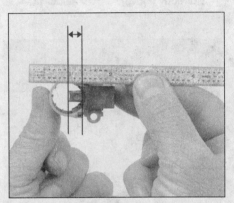

14.5  Measure the exposed length of the brushes and compare your measurements to the specified minimum length to determine if they should be replaced

14.12  Remove the voltage regulator screws (arrows) . . .

2      Mark and detach the electrical connector and any ground straps from the alternator.
3      Loosen the alternator adjusting bolt and pivot bolt, then detach the drivebelt **(see illustrations).**
4      Remove the adjusting and pivot bolts and separate the alternator from the engine. **Note:** *To remove the adjustment bolt and assembly, it is necessary to remove the bracket bolt located next to the adjustment bolt as well as the mounting bolt located lower and at a 90-degree angle.*
5      If you are replacing the alternator, take the old one with you when purchasing a replacement unit. Make sure the new/rebuilt unit looks identical to the old alternator. Look at the terminals - they should be the same in number, size and location as the terminals on the old alternator. Finally, look at the identification numbers - they will be stamped into the housing or printed on a tag attached to the housing. Make sure the numbers are the same on both alternators.
6      Many new/rebuilt alternators DO NOT have a pulley installed, so you may have to switch the pulley from the old unit to the new/rebuilt one. When buying an alternator, find out the shop's policy regarding pulleys; some shops will perform this service free of charge.

## Installation

7      Installation is the reverse of removal.
8      After the alternator is installed, adjust the drivebelt tension (see Chapter 1).
9      Check the charging voltage to verify proper operation of the alternator (see Section 12).

## 14   Alternator components - check and replacement

1      Remove the alternator (see Section 13) and place it on a clean workbench.

### Nippondenso alternators (four-cylinder models)

#### Brushes

*Refer to illustrations 14.2, 14.3 and 14.5*
2      Remove the three rear cover nuts, the nut and terminal insulator and the rear cover **(see Illustration).**
3      Remove the two brush holder retaining screws **(see illustration).**
4      Remove the brush holder from the rear end frame.
5      Measure the exposed length of the brush **(see Illustration)** and compare it to the specified minimum length. If the length of the brush is less than the minimum listed in this Chapter's Specifications, replace the brush.
6      Make sure that each brush moves smoothly in the brush holder.
7      Install the brush holder by depressing the brush with a small screwdriver to clear the shaft.
8      Install the brush holder screws into the rear frame.
9      Install the rear cover and tighten the three nuts securely.
10     Install the terminal insulator and tighten it with the nut.
11     Install the alternator (see Section 13).

#### Voltage regulator

*Refer to illustrations 14.12 and 14.13*
12     Remove the three retaining screws from the rear end frame **(see illustration).**

14.13 ... and remove the regulator from the alternator assembly

14.15 Remove the mounting screws (arrows) that retain the rectifier assembly

14.20a Continuity should exist between the rotor slip rings

14.20b Check the continuity between the rotor frame and the slip rings. There should be no continuity

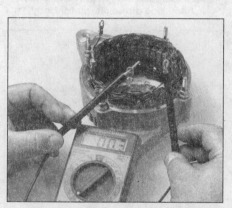

14.21 Check for continuity between the stator windings

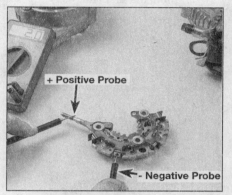

14.22a Position the positive probe of the ohmmeter onto the rectifier assembly positive post and the negative probe to a diode terminal. Continuity should exist

13   Lift the voltage regulator from the alternator assembly **(see illus-tration)**.

14   Installation is the reverse of removal.

## Rotor, stator and rectifier

*Refer to illustrations 14.15, 14.20a, 14.20b, 14.21, 14.22a and 14.22b*

15   Remove the rectifier assembly **(see illustration)**. Remove the four rubber insulators and the seal plate.

16   Scribe or paint marks on the front and rear end frame housings of the alternator to facilitate reassembly.

17   Remove the nut retaining the pulley to the rotor shaft and remove the pulley.

18   Remove the four nuts retaining the front and rear end frame together, then separate the rear end frame assembly from the front end frame **(see illustration 11.1a)**.

19   Remove the thrust washer and separate the rotor from the end frame.

20   Check the rotor for an open between the two slip rings **(see illus-tration)**. There should be 2 to 4 ohms resistance between the slip rings. Check for grounds between each slip ring and the rotor frame or shaft **(see illustration)**. There should be no continuity (infinite resis-tance) between the rotor frame or shaft and either slip ring. If the rotor fails either test, or if the slip rings are excessively worn, the rotor is defective.

21   Check for opens between each end terminal of the stator wind-ings **(see illustration)**. If either reading is high (infinite resistance), the stator is defective. Check for a grounded stator winding between each stator terminal and the frame. If there's continuity between any stator winding and the frame the stator is defective.

22   Start the checks on the rectifier by touching one probe (positive +)

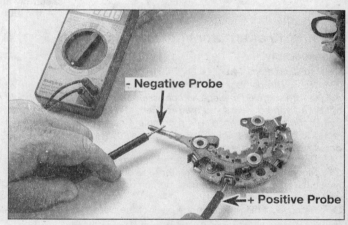

14.22b Switch the polarity of the ohmmeter probes and observe that now there is NO continuity within the diode. Check each diode (four pairs total) individually

of the ohmmeter onto the positive post and the other probe (neg-ative -) onto one of the other designated diode terminals **(see illustra-tion)**. Then reverse the probes and check again **(see illustration)**. The diode should have continuity with the ohmmeter one way and no conti-nuity when the probes are reversed. Check each of the diode terminals in this manner. Check each diode again, this time testing between each diode terminal and ground (the frame), reversing the polarity after each test. If any of the diodes fail the test (a total of sixteen tests), the rectifier assembly is defective.

**14.24  Remove the through bolts (arrows) from the alternator body**

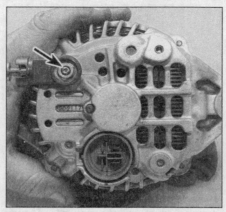

**14.26  Remove the nut (arrow) from the back side of the alternator body**

**14.27  Use a heat gun to warm the bearing surface of the alternator**

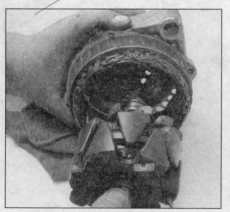

**14.28  Separate the rotor assembly from the alternator body**

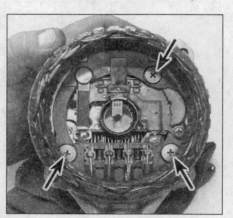

**14.29  Remove the screws (arrows) and separate the stator, regulator/brush assembly and rectifier from the alternator body**

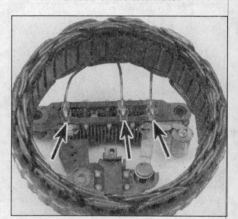

**14.30  To separate the stator from the rectifier assembly, unsolder the connections (arrows)**

## Mitsubishi alternators (V6 models)

### Disassembly

*Refer to illustrations 14.24, 14.26, 14.27, 14.28, 14.29 and 14.30*

23   **Note:** *The components of the Mitsubishi alternator, used on V6 models, are soldered in place and disassembly of the alternator should not be attempted unless you are proficient in electrical soldering. This unit is commonly replaced with a complete new or rebuilt unit when found to be defective. If you wish to disassemble the unit, the procedures are as follows:*

24   Remove the nuts from the alternator body **(see illustrations).**

25   Mount the front of the alternator face down in a vice. Using rags as a cushion, clamp the front case portion of the alternator in the jaws of the vice.

26   Remove all the nuts from the back of the alternator **(see illustration).**

27   Insert two standard screwdrivers into the two halves of the alternator (not too deep or you will damage the stator) and pry the rear case off the alternator. **Caution:** *Pry gently or you will break the aluminum case.* **Note:** *If necessary, use a heat gun to warm the case bearings from the outside of the alternator body* **(see illustration).** *This will allow easier separation of the two halves.*

28   Separate the rotor from the alternator body **(see illustration).**

29   Remove the screws and separate the stator and rectifier/regulator/brush assembly from the alternator body **(see illustration).**

30   If necessary, unsolder the stator from the rectifier assembly **(see illustration). Note:** *While applying heat to electrical components, it's a good idea to use a pair of needle nose pliers as a heat sink. Don't apply*

heat for more than about five seconds.

### Check

*Refer to illustrations 14.31a, 14.31b and 14.32*

31   Measure the length of the brushes **(see illustration).** Replace them if necessary by unsoldering them **(see illustration).**

32   When installing new brushes, solder the pigtails so the brush limit line will be about 0.079 to 0.118 inches above the end of the brush holder **(see illustration).**

### Reassembly

*Refer to illustration 14.33*

33   To reassemble, compress the brushes into their holder and retain them with a straight piece of wire that can be pulled from the back of the alternator when reassembled **(see illustration).**

34   The remainder of installation is the reverse of removal.

---

## 15   Starting system - general information and precautions

The sole function of the starting system is to turn over the engine quickly enough to allow it to start.

The starting system consists of the battery, the starter motor, the starter solenoid and the wires connecting them. The solenoid is mounted directly on the starter motor.

The solenoid/starter motor assembly is installed on the upper part of the engine, next to the transmission bellhousing.

When the ignition key is turned to the Start position, the starter

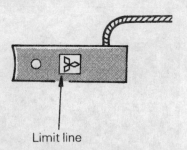

**14.31a If the brushes are worn past the wear limit line, they should be replaced**

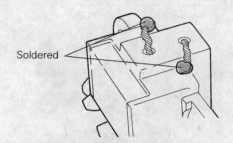

**14.31b If the brushes are being replaced, unsolder and solder the pigtails at the area shown**

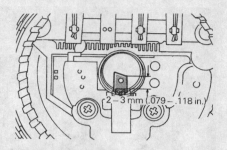

**14.32 When installing new brushes, they should extend out of the holder the proper amount**

When the ignition key is turned to the Start position, the starter solenoid is actuated through the starter control circuit. The starter solenoid then connects the battery to the starter. The battery supplies the electrical energy to the starter motor, which does the actual work of cranking the engine.

The starter motor on models equipped with manual transaxles can only be operated when the clutch pedal is depressed; the starter on models equipped with automatic transaxles can only be operated when the selector lever is in Park or Neutral.

Always observe the following precautions when working on the starting system:

a) *Excessive cranking of the starter motor can overheat it and cause serious damage. Never operate the starter motor for more than 15 seconds at a time without pausing to allow it to cool for at least two minutes.*

b) *The starter is connected directly to the battery and could arc or cause a fire if mishandled, overloaded or shorted out.*

c) *Always detach the cable from the negative terminal of the battery before working on the starting system.*

## 16  Starter motor - in-vehicle check

*Refer to illustration 16.6*

**Note:** *Before diagnosing starter problems, make sure the battery is fully charged.*

1    If the starter motor does not turn at all when the switch is operated, make sure the shift lever is in Neutral or Park (automatic transaxle) or the clutch pedal is depressed (manual transaxle).

2    Make sure the battery is charged and all cables, both at the battery and starter solenoid terminals, are clean and secure.

3    If the starter motor spins but the engine is not cranking, the over-

running clutch in the starter motor is slipping and the starter motor must be replaced. Also, the ring gear on the flywheel or driveplate may be worn.

4    If, when the switch is actuated, the starter motor does not operate at all but the solenoid clicks, the problem lies with either the battery, the main solenoid contacts or the starter motor itself (or the engine is seized).

5    If the solenoid plunger cannot be heard when the switch is actuated, the battery is bad, the fusible link is burned (the circuit is open), a fuse is burned out, the starter-cut relay is defective (manual transaxles) or the solenoid itself is defective. **Note:** *Check the number 15 and the number 18 fuse under the hood in the relay box or the number 9 (7.5A) fuse in the under dash relay box.*

6    To check the starter-cut relay, remove the relay and check for battery voltage **(see illustration)**. There should be battery voltage present.

7    To check the starter solenoid, connect a jumper lead between the battery and the ignition switch wire terminal (the small terminal) on the solenoid. If the starter motor now operates, the solenoid is OK and the problem is in the ignition switch, neutral start switch or the wiring.

8    If the starter motor still does not operate, remove the starter/solenoid assembly for disassembly, testing and repair.

9    If the starter motor cranks the engine at an abnormally slow speed, first make sure that the battery is charged and that all terminal connections are tight. If the engine is partially seized, or has the wrong viscosity oil in it, it will crank slowly.

10    Run the engine until normal operating temperature is reached, then disconnect the coil wire from the distributor cap and ground it on the engine.

11    Connect a voltmeter positive lead to the positive battery post and connect the negative lead to the negative post.

12    Crank the engine and take the voltmeter readings as soon as a steady figure is indicated. Do not allow the starter motor to turn for

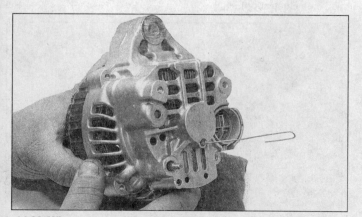

**14.33 When reassembling the two halves of the alternator, use a piece of wire inserted through the rear case and into the brush holder to retain the brushes in the holder**

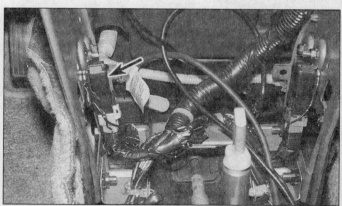

**16.6 Remove the starter cut relay (arrow) from the console area and with the ignition key ON (engine not running) check for battery voltage at the connector**

**17.3  Remove the bolts (arrows) and separate the starter from the transaxle**

**18.8  Remove the bolts that retain the end cover to the gear housing**

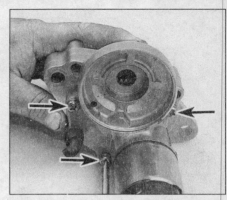

**18.9  Remove the screws (arrows) that retain the gear housing to the gear housing cover**

more than 15 seconds at a time. A reading of nine volts or more, with the starter motor turning at normal cranking speed, is normal. If the reading is nine volts or more but the cranking speed is slow, the motor, solenoid contacts or circuit connections are faulty. If the reading is less than nine volts and the cranking speed is slow, the starter motor is probably bad.

## 17   Starter motor - removal and installation

*Refer to illustration 17.3*

1    Detach the cable from the negative terminal of the battery. **Caution:** *The radio in your vehicle is equipped with an anti-theft system, make sure you have the correct activation code before disconnecting the battery.*

2    Clearly label, then disconnect the wires from the terminals on the starter motor solenoid. Disconnect any clips securing the wiring to the starter.

3    Remove the mounting bolts **(see illustration)** and detach the starter.

4    Installation is the reverse of removal.

## 18   Starter solenoid - removal and installation

1    Disconnect the cable from the negative terminal of the battery. **Caution:** *The radio in your vehicle is equipped with an anti-theft system, make sure you have the correct activation code before disconnecting the battery.*

2    Remove the starter motor (see Section 17).

### *Nippondenso starter/solenoid units*

3    Disconnect the large wire from the solenoid to the starter motor terminal.

4    The solenoid (plunger) is located inside the solenoid housing. Remove the screws which secure the solenoid housing to the starter motor gear housing and detach the solenoid housing from the gear housing.

5    Remove the plunger from the solenoid housing. Be sure to check the contact points inside the solenoid housing for burns, pits or oxidation. Use sandpaper to clean the surfaces if necessary. Check the overrunning clutch assembly and idler gear for broken teeth or obvious damage. If the gear is worn or damaged, replace the complete overrunning clutch assembly (the gear isn't available separately). If the starter gear teeth are damaged, you should also inspect the flywheel or driveplate ring gear for damage.

6    Installation is the reverse of removal.

### *Mitsuba starter/solenoid units*

*Refer to illustrations 18.8, 18.9, 18.10 and 18.11*

7    Disconnect the large wire from the solenoid to the starter motor terminal.

8    Remove the long bolts that secure the end cover to the gear housing **(see illustration)** and remove the armature housing from the assembly.

9    Remove the screws from the gear housing **(see illustration)** and separate it from the gear housing cover

10   Remove the screws from the gear housing **(see illustration)** and separate the solenoid.

11   Installation is the reverse of removal. Be sure to apply a slight amount of grease to the solenoid lever and the plunger before installation **(see illustration)**.

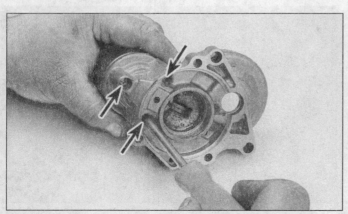

**18.10  Remove the screws (arrows) that retain the solenoid to the gear housing**

**18.11  Apply grease to the lever and plunger (arrow) before assembly**

# Chapter 6
# Emissions and engine control systems

## Contents

## Specifications

### General

Oxygen sensor voltage
Four-cylinder engine
Open loop .............................................. 0.1 to 0.2 volts (100 to 200 millivolts)
Closed loop .......................................... 0.1 to 0.9 volts (100 to 900 millivolts)
CKP sensor resistance
Four-cylinder engine
1994 and 1995
Non-VTEC .......................................... 350 to 700 ohms
VTEC ................................................. 700 to 1,300 ohms
1996 ................................................... 500 to 1,000 ohms
1997 ................................................... 1,850 to 2,450 ohms
V6 engine ............................................... 1,800 to 2,500 ohms
CYP sensor resistance
Four-cylinder engine
1994 and 1995
Non-VTEC .......................................... 350 to 700 ohms
VTEC ................................................. 700 to 1,300 ohms
1996 and later ..................................... 800 to 1,500 ohms
V6 engine ............................................... 1,500 to 3,000 ohms
TDC sensor resistance
Four-cylinder engine
1994 and 1995
Non-VTEC .......................................... 350 to 700 ohms
VTEC ................................................. 700 to 1,300 ohms
1996 ................................................... 500 to 1,000 ohms
1997 ................................................... 1,850 to 2,450 ohms
V6 engine ............................................... 1,500 to 3,000 ohms

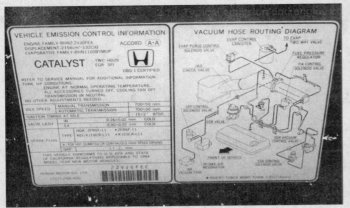

**1.6a  The Vehicle Emission Control Information (VECI) label is located on the underside of the hood and contains information on idle speed adjustment, ignition timing, location of the emission devices on your vehicle, vacuum line routing, etc. (four-cylinder engine shown)**

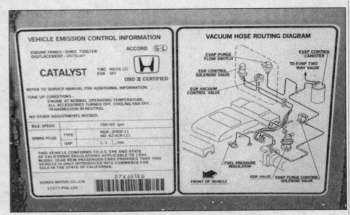

**1.6b  VECI label on the V6 engine**

## 1    General information

*Refer to illustrations 1.6a and 1.6b*

To prevent pollution of the atmosphere from incompletely burned and evaporating gases, and to maintain good driveability and fuel economy, a number of emission control systems are incorporated.

They include the:

    *Self diagnosis system*
    *Electronic engine controls (PGM-FI)*
    *Electronic Load Detector (ELD)*
    *Exhaust Gas Recirculation (EGR) system*
    *Evaporative Emissions Control (EVAP) system*
    *Positive Crankcase Ventilation (PCV) system*
    *Catalytic converter (CAT)*

The Sections in this Chapter include general descriptions, checking procedures within the scope of the home mechanic and

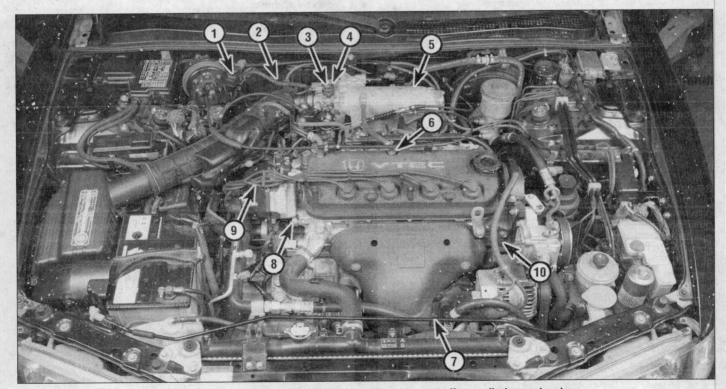

**2.1a  Typical emission and engine control components (four-cylinder engines)**

| | | | |
|---|---|---|---|
| *1* | *Purge Control Solenoid* | *7* | *Oxygen sensor (on lower section of exhaust manifold)* |
| *2* | *Charcoal canister* | *8* | *Coolant temperature sensor* |
| *3* | *MAP sensor* | *9* | *CYP, TDC,CKP sensor (within distributor, 1994 and 1995)* |
| *4* | *Throttle Position Sensor (TPS)* | | *CKP sensor (within distributor, 1996 and later)* |
| *5* | *Intake Air Temperature (IAT) sensor (on backside of plenum)* | *10* | *CYP, TDC sensor (front of oil pump housing, 1996 and later)* |
| *6* | *Positive Crankcase Ventilation (PCV) valve* | | |

component replacement procedures (when possible) for each of the systems listed above.

Before assuming that an emissions control system is malfunctioning, check the fuel and ignition systems carefully. The diagnosis of some emission control devices requires specialized tools, equipment and training. If checking and servicing become too difficult or if a procedure is beyond your ability, consult a dealer service department or other repair shop. Remember, the most frequent cause of emissions problems is simply a loose or broken wire or vacuum hose, so always check the hose and wiring connections first.

This doesn't mean, however, that emissions control systems are particularly difficult to maintain and repair. You can quickly and easily perform many checks and do most of the regular maintenance at home with common tune-up and hand tools. **Note:** *Because of a Federally mandated extended warranty which covers the emissions control system components, check with your dealer about warranty coverage before working on any emissions-related systems. Once the warranty has expired, you may wish to perform some of the component checks and/or replacement procedures in this Chapter to save money.*

Pay close attention to any special precautions outlined in this Chapter. It should be noted that the illustrations of the various systems may not exactly match the system installed on your vehicle because of changes made by the manufacturer during production or from year-to-year.

A Vehicle Emissions Control Information (VECI) label is attached to the underside of the hood **(see illustrations)**. This label contains important emissions specifications and adjustment information. Part of this label, the Vacuum Hose Routing Diagram, provides a vacuum hose schematic with emissions components identified. When servicing the engine or emissions systems, the VECI label and the vacuum hose routing diagram in your particular vehicle should always be checked for up-to-date information.

## 2  Programmed Fuel Injection (PGM-FI) system - general information

*Refer to illustrations 2.1a and 2.1b*

The Programmed Fuel Injection system (PGM-FI) **(see illustrations)** consists of three sub-systems: air intake, electronic control and fuel delivery. The PGM-FI system uses an Engine Control Module (ECM) along with the sensors (Engine Coolant Temperature sensor (ECT), Throttle Position sensor (TP), Manifold Absolute Pressure sensor (MAP) etc.) to determine the proper fuel/air ratio under all operating conditions.

The fuel injection system and the emission control system are closely linked in function and design. For additional information, refer to Chapter 4.

The electronic control system consists of an eight-bit microprocessor (computer), output actuators and various information sensors:

The distributor is driven off the end of the camshaft and, on four-cylinder models, contains three sensors which are an integral part of the distributor assembly. The Crankshaft Position sensor (CKP) determines the timing for the fuel injection and ignition and also detects the rpm of the engine. The Cylinder Position sensor (CYP) detects the position of the no. 1 cylinder as the base for sequential injection; the Top Dead Center (TDC) sensor determines the ignition timing at start-up (when the engine is cranking).

The Manifold Absolute Pressure sensor (MAP) converts manifold pressure readings into electrical voltage signals and sends them to the ECM. This data, along with the data from the TDC and CYL sensors, enables the ECM to determine the duration during which fuel is injected.

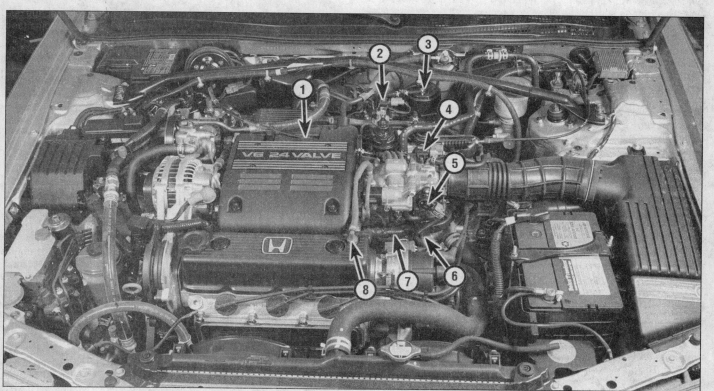

**2.1b  Typical emission and engine control components (V6 engines)**

1   Intake Air Temperature (IAT) sensor (under intake manifold)
2   Purge Control Solenoid
3   Charcoal canister
4   MAP sensor
5   Throttle Position Sensor (TPS)
6   Coolant temperature sensor
7   Distributor
8   Positive Crankcase Ventilation (PCV) valve

**3.1a  The diagnostic connector is located under the passenger side glovebox behind the kick panel. Using a small screwdriver, depress the tangs and push the connector away from the metal bracket**

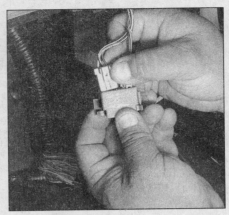

**3.1b  Separate the two wire service check connector from the data link connector**

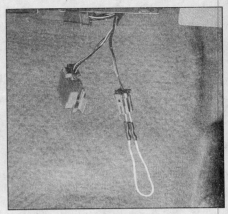

**3.1c To activate the diagnostic codes, remove the two-terminal electrical connector and bridge the terminals with a jumper wire or paper clip, then turn the ignition to the ON position**

ture-dependent resistor (thermistor) to measure differences in the coolant temperature. The resistance of the thermistor decreases with a rise in coolant temperature. The ECM uses this input to increase or decrease the fuel discharge duration.

The Intake Air Temperature sensor (IAT), which is located in the intake manifold, is also a thermistor. In operation, it's similar to the coolant temperature sensor but has a lower thermal capacity for quicker response time.

A Vehicle Speed Sensor (VSS) detects pulses from the front wheels which in turn determines the actual speed the vehicle is moving. This data is sent to the ECM for processing the correct air/fuel ratio delivered from the fuel injectors and the air intake system.

The Throttle Position sensor (TP) is a variable resistor. The sensor is mounted on the side of the throttle body and engages the throttle shaft. As the throttle valve is rotated, the resistance varies, altering the output voltage to the control unit, which in turn alters the fuel discharge duration.

The oxygen sensor monitors the oxygen content in the exhaust gas and sends a variable voltage signal to the ECM, which alters the fuel discharge duration.

When the ignition key is turned to Start, the ignition switch sends a signal to the ECM which increases the amount of fuel injected in accordance with the engine temperature. The amount of fuel injected is gradually reduced once the engine is started. Refer to Chapter 4 for additional information on the fuel injection system and diagnosing the components.

## 3    Self diagnosis system - description and diagnostic trouble codes

*Refer to illustrations 3.1a, 3.1b, 3.1c and 3.3*

**Note 1:** *The 1995 and later V6 and the 1996 and later four-cylinder models are equipped with the new On-Board Diagnostic II (OBDII) diagnostic system. The five character OBD-II codes are accessible only with an OBD-II compatible SCAN tool or Honda PGM tester. However, the two-digit trouble codes, used on previous models, can still be retrieved using the following procedure.*

**Note 2:** *The ECM is located under the dashboard, behind the carpet on the passenger side. The codes can be read by jumping the two-cavity diagnostic connector and reading the CHECK engine light on the instrument panel.*

1    To view self-diagnosis information from the ECM memory, install a jumper wire into the diagnostic terminal **(see illustrations)** located in the far right corner under the dash, then turn the ignition switch to the ON position. The codes are stored in the memory of the ECM and when accessed, blink a sequence on the CHECK ENGINE light on the

**3.3  To clear the codes from the ECM memory, remove the BACK-UP fuse (7.5 amp) from the fuse panel**

instrument panel to relay a number or code that represents a system or component failure.

2    The CHECK ENGINE light will blink a longer blink to represent the first digit of a two digit number and then will blink short for the second digit (for example, 1 long blink then 6 short blinks for the code 16). **Note:** *If the system has more than one problem, the codes will be displayed in sequence then a pause and the codes will repeat.*

3    When the ECM sets a trouble code, the CHECK ENGINE light will come on and a trouble code will be stored in the memory. The trouble code will stay in the ECM memory until the voltage to the ECM is interrupted. To clear the memory, remove the BACK-UP fuse **(see illustration)** from the relay box located in the right side of the engine compartment. **Note:** *Disconnecting the BACK-UP fuse also cancels the radio preset stations and the clock setting. Be sure to make a note of the various radio stations that are programmed into the memory before removing the fuse.*

4    The following table is a list of the typical trouble codes which may be encountered while diagnosing the system. Also included are simplified troubleshooting procedures. If the problem persists after these checks have been made, more detailed service procedures will have to be done by a dealer service department or other repair shop. **Caution:** *To prevent damage to the ECM, the ignition switch must be off when disconnecting or connecting power to the ECM (this includes disconnecting and connecting the battery). The stereo in your vehicle is equipped with an anti-theft system, make sure you have the correct activation code before disconnecting the battery.*

| Trouble code | Circuit or system | Corrective action |
| --- | --- | --- |
| Code 0 | Faulty ECM | Check the ECM electrical connector. If no loose connectors are found, have the ECM diagnosed by a dealer service department. |
| Code 1 | Oxygen sensor | Check the oxygen sensor and circuit (see Section 4). |
| Codes 3 | Manifold Absolute Pressure sensor | Check the MAP sensor and circuit (see Section 4). |
| Code 4 | Crankshaft Position sensor (CKP) | Check the CKP sensor and circuit (see Section 4). |
| Code 6 | Engine Coolant Temperature sensor (ECT) | Check the ECT sensor and circuit (see Section 4). |
| Code 7 | Throttle Position sensor (TP) | Check the TP sensor and circuit (see Section 4). |
| Code 8 | Top Dead Center position sensor (TDC) | Check the TDC sensor and circuit (see Section 4). |
| Code 9 | Cylinder Position sensor (CYP) | Check the CYP sensor and circuit (see Section 4). |
| Code 10 | Intake Air Temperature sensor (IAT) | Check the IAT sensor and circuit (see Section 4). |
| Code 12 | Exhaust Gas Recirculation valve lift sensor | Check the vacuum hoses, the EGR valve lift sensor and the EGR valve (see Section 6). |
| Code 13 | Barometric Pressure sensor (BARO) | The BARO sensor is built into the ECM, have the vehicle checked at a dealer service department. |
| Code 14 | Idle Air Control valve (IAC) | Check the IAC valve and system (see Chapter 4). |
| Code 15 | Ignition output signal | Check the ignition system (see Chapter 5). |
| Code 16 | Fuel injector | Check the fuel injection system and the fuel injectors (see Chapter 4). |
| Code 17 | Vehicle Speed Sensor (VSS) | Check the VSS and circuit (see Section 4). |
| Code 20 | Electronic load detector (ELD) | Check the ELD system (see Section 8). |
| Code 21 | Variable Valve Timing solenoid valve | See Chapter 2A, VTEC solenoid checks. |
| Code 22 | Variable Valve Timing pressure switch | See Chapter 2A, VTEC pressure switch checks. |
| Code 30 | A/T FI signal A (automatic transaxle) | Code 30 indicates a problem between the transmission control module and the ECM, have the vehicle checked at a dealer service department. |
| Code 31 | A/T FI signal B (automatic transaxle) | Code 31 indicates a problem between the transmission control module and the ECM, have the vehicle checked at a dealer service department. |
| Code 41 | Oxygen sensor heater | Check the heater for the proper voltage signal (see Section 4). |
| Code 43 | Fuel supply system | Check the fuel pressure/fuel pressure regulator (see Chapter 4). Also check the oxygen sensor (see Section 4). |
| Code 61 | Oxygen sensor | Check the front oxygen sensor, slow response detected (OBD-II). |
| Code 63 | Oxygen sensor | Check the rear oxygen sensor, voltage out-of-range detected (OBD-II). |
| Code 65 | Oxygen sensor | Check the rear oxygen sensor, circuit malfunction detected (OBD-II). |
| Code 67 | Catalytic converter | Check the catalytic converter, low efficiency detected (OBD-II). |
| Code 70 | Automatic transaxle | Problem detected with the automatic transaxle (OBD-II). |
| Codes 71 through 76 | Cylinder missfire | Cylinder missfire detected (OBD-II). |
| Code 80 | EGR system | Check the EGR system, insufficient EGR flow detected (OBD-II). |
| Code 86 | Engine Coolant temperature sensor (ECT) | Check the ECT sensor and circuit, circuit problem detected (OBD-II). |
| Code 92 | Evaporative emissions system | Check the EVAP system, purge flow problem detected (OBD-II). |

**4.7  Install a pin into the connector and backprobe the oxygen sensor electrical connector white wire (terminal B) to monitor the sensor output signal voltage. Raise the engine rpm and confirm that the voltage signal increases**

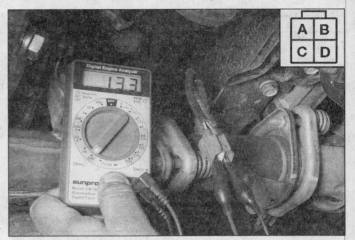

**4.10  Measure the resistance of the oxygen sensor heater. Check terminals C and D, it should be 10 to 40 ohms**

## 4    Information sensors

### *Oxygen sensor*

#### General description

1    The oxygen sensor, which is located in the exhaust manifold, monitors the oxygen content of the exhaust gas stream. The oxygen content in the exhaust reacts with the oxygen sensor to produce a voltage output which varies from 0.1-volt (high oxygen, lean mixture) to 0.9-volts (low oxygen, rich mixture). The ECM constantly monitors this variable voltage output to determine the ratio of oxygen to fuel in the mixture. The ECM alters the air/fuel mixture ratio by controlling the pulse width (open time) of the fuel injectors. A mixture ratio of 14.7 parts air to 1 part fuel is the ideal mixture ratio for minimizing exhaust emissions, thus allowing the catalytic converter to operate at maximum efficiency. It is this ratio of 14.7 to 1 which the ECM and the oxygen sensor attempt to maintain at all times.

2    The oxygen sensor produces no voltage when it is below its normal operating temperature of about 600-degrees F. During this initial period before warm-up, the ECM operates in OPEN LOOP mode.

3    If the engine reaches normal operating temperature and/or has been running for two or more minutes, and if the oxygen sensor is producing a steady signal voltage below 0.45-volts at 1,500 rpm or greater, the ECM will set a Code 1. The ECM will also set a code 41 if it detects any problem with the heater circuit.

4    When there is a problem with the oxygen sensor or its circuit, the ECM operates in the open loop mode - that is, it controls fuel delivery in accordance with a programmed default value instead of feedback information from the oxygen sensor.

5    The proper operation of the oxygen sensor depends on four conditions:

  a)  *Electrical - The low voltages generated by the sensor depend upon good, clean connections which should be checked whenever a malfunction of the sensor is suspected or indicated.*

  b)  *Outside air supply - The sensor is designed to allow air circulation to the internal portion of the sensor. Whenever the sensor is removed and installed or replaced, make sure the air passages are not restricted.*

  c)  *Proper operating temperature - The ECM will not react to the sensor signal until the sensor reaches approximately 600-degrees F. This factor must be taken into consideration when evaluating the performance of the sensor.*

  d)  *Unleaded fuel - The use of unleaded fuel is essential for proper operation of the sensor. Make sure the fuel you are using is of this type.*

6    In addition to observing the above conditions, special care must be taken whenever the sensor is serviced.

  a)  *The oxygen sensor has a permanently attached pigtail and electrical connector which should not be removed from the sensor. Damage or removal of the pigtail or electrical connector can adversely affect operation of the sensor.*

  b)  *Grease, dirt and other contaminants should be kept away from the electrical connector and the louvered end of the sensor.*

  c)  *Do not use cleaning solvents of any kind on the oxygen sensor.*

  d)  *Do not drop or roughly handle the sensor.*

  e)  *The silicone boot must be installed in the correct position to prevent the boot from being melted and to allow the sensor to operate properly.*

#### Check

*Refer to illustrations 4.7, 4.10 and 4.11*

7    Locate the oxygen sensor electrical connector and without disconnecting it, insert a long pin into the oxygen sensor connector terminal B (signal voltage) (white wire) **(see illustration).** Install the positive probe of a voltmeter onto the pin and the negative probe to ground. **Note:** *Also, use terminal A (green wire) for the ground as a double check of the harness ground system.*

8    Apply the parking brake, shift the transaxle into Park (automatic) or Neutral (manual), raise the front of the vehicle and place it securely on jackstands. Start the engine and monitor the voltage signal as the engine warms up. **Caution:** *Be extremely careful of hot exhaust components when performing this procedure.*

9    The oxygen sensor will produce a steady voltage signal at first (open loop) of approximately 0.1 to 0.2 volts with the engine cold. After a period of approximately two minutes, the engine will reach operating temperature and the oxygen sensor should start to fluctuate between 0.1 to 0.9 volts (closed loop). If the oxygen sensor fails to reach the closed loop mode or there is a very long period of time until it does switch into closed loop mode, replace the oxygen sensor.

10    Also inspect the oxygen sensor heater. Disconnect the oxygen sensor electrical connector and connect an ohmmeter between the C and D terminals **(see illustration).** It should measure 10 to 40 ohms.

11    Check for proper supply voltage to the heater. Working on the ECM side of the connector, measure voltage between the yellow/black wire (+) and the green/blue wire (-) on the oxygen sensor electrical connector **(see illustration).** There should be battery voltage with the ignition key ON (engine not running). If there is no voltage, check the circuit between the main relay, the ECM and the sensor.

12    If the oxygen sensor fails any of these tests, replace it with a new part.

4.11 Working on the harness side of the oxygen sensor connector, check for battery voltage on the yellow/black and green/blue wire

4.16 Remove the oxygen sensor from the exhaust manifold with a socket specially designed for this purpose

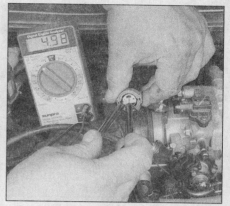

4.24 Using a voltmeter, check for reference voltage to the MAP sensor (yellow/white (+) wire) and the green/white (–) wire. It should be approximately 5.0 volts - depending on the altitude

## Replacement

*Refer to illustration 4.16*

**Note:** *Because it is installed in the exhaust manifold or pipe, which contracts when cool, the oxygen sensor may be very difficult to loosen when the engine is cold. Rather than risk damage to the sensor (assuming you are planning to reuse it in another manifold or pipe), start and run the engine for a minute or two, then shut it off. Be careful not to burn yourself during the following procedure.*

13    Disconnect the cable from the negative terminal of the battery.
**Caution:** *The stereo in your vehicle is equipped with an anti-theft system. Make sure you have the correct activation code before disconnecting the battery.*
14    Raise the vehicle and place it securely on jackstands.
15    Carefully disconnect the electrical connector from the sensor.
16    Carefully unscrew the sensor from the exhaust manifold **(see illustration)**.
17    Anti-seize compound must be used on the threads of the sensor to facilitate future removal. The threads of new sensors will already be coated with this compound, but if an old sensor is removed and reinstalled, recoat the threads.
18    Install the sensor and tighten it securely.
19    Reconnect the electrical connector of the pigtail lead to the main engine wiring harness.
20    Lower the vehicle, take it on a test drive and check to see that no trouble codes set.

## Manifold Absolute Pressure (MAP) sensor

*Refer to illustrations 4.24, 4.25 and 4.26*

### General description

21    The Manifold Absolute Pressure (MAP) sensor monitors the intake manifold pressure changes resulting from changes in engine load and speed and converts the information into a voltage output. The ECM uses the MAP sensor to control fuel delivery and ignition timing. The ECM will receive information as a voltage signal that will vary from 1.0 to 1.5 volts at closed throttle (high vacuum) and 4.0 to 4.5 volts at wide open throttle (low vacuum). The MAP sensor is attached to the throttle body.
22    A failure in the MAP sensor circuit should set a Code 3.

### Check

23    Check the electrical connector at the sensor for a snug fit. Check the terminals in the connector and the wires leading to it for looseness and breaks. Repair as required.
24    Disconnect the MAP sensor connector, turn the ignition key ON (engine not running) and check for voltage on the reference wire (yellow/white wire [+]) and green/white wire (ground) **(see illustration)**. There should be approximately 5 volts.
25    Connect the MAP sensor connector and backprobe the connector. Check for voltage on the signal wire (+) (white/yellow) and ground wire (–) (green/white) with the ignition key ON (engine not running). There should be approximately 1.5 to 3.5 volts. This checks signal voltage from the MAP sensor **(see illustration)**.
26    Start the engine and observe that the voltage from the signal wire increases as the rpm are raised **(see illustration)**. Voltage should

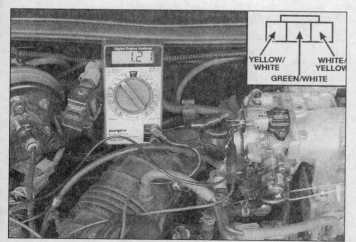

4.25 Check the signal voltage on the white/yellow wire. It should be approximately 1.5 to 3.5 volts - depending on the altitude

YELLOW/WHITE    WHITE/YELLOW    GREEN/WHITE

4.26 Next, start the engine and check for the MAP sensor voltage - it should increase between 2.5 and 4.5 volts (voltage should increase as vacuum decreases).

**4.28a  Lift the MAP sensor from the throttle body (four-cylinder engine shown)**

**4.28b  Removing the screws from the MAP sensor on the V6 engine**

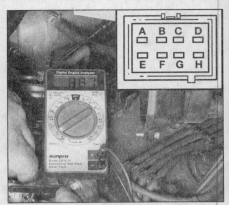

**4.31  Check the CKP sensor resistance by probing terminals B and F with an ohmmeter**

increase as vacuum decreases. If the readings are incorrect, replace the MAP sensor. **Note:** *Manifold vacuum is high when the engine is idling and decreases as the throttle is opened allowing manifold vacuum to become equal to atmospheric levels.*

## Replacement

*Refer to illustrations 4.28a and 4.28b*

27   Disconnect the electrical connector from the MAP sensor.
28   Remove the bolts that retain the MAP sensor to the throttle body and remove the MAP sensor **(see illustrations).**
29   Installation is the reverse of removal.

## *CKP, TDC and CYP sensors*

### General description

30   The crank angle sensor (CKP) determines the timing for the fuel injection and ignition on each cylinder. It also detects engine rpm. The TDC sensor determines the ignition timing at start-up (engine cranking) and the CYP sensor determines the position of the cylinder for sequential fuel injection to each cylinder. On 1994 and 1995 four-cylinder models, all three sensors are built into the distributor. On 1996 and later four-cylinder models, only the CYP is built into the distributor since the CKP and TDC sensors are a separate assembly that is attached to the oil pump housing. Diagnosis for all three sensors is performed by checking for the diagnostic codes (codes 4, 8 and 9) and then checking for proper resistance at the electrical connector. **Note:** *This test procedure does not cover the 1996 and later four-cylinder and V6 models. On these models, it is necessary to use a scan tool to diagnose these types of sensors (the sensors are attached to the front of the engine, under the timing belt cover).*

### Check

*Refer to illustration 4.31*

31   To check the CKP sensor, disconnect the electrical connector at the distributor and probe terminals B and F with an ohmmeter **(see illustration).** Check the resistance listed in this Chapter's Specifications.
32   Check for continuity to ground on each terminal. Continuity should NOT exist. If the test results are incorrect, replace the distributor unit (see Chapter 5).
33   If the test results are all correct, have the system diagnosed by a dealer service department.
34   To check the TDC sensor, disconnect the ignition harness connector at the distributor and probe terminals C and G with an ohmmeter **(see illustration 4.31).** Check the resistance listed in this Chapter's Specifications.
35   Check for continuity to ground on each terminal. Continuity should NOT exist. If the test results are incorrect, replace the distributor unit (see Chapter 5).
36   If the test results are all correct, have the system diagnosed by a dealer service department.
37   To check the CYP sensor, disconnect the ignition harness con-

nector at the distributor and probe terminals D and H with an ohmmeter **(see illustration 4.31).** Check the resistance listed in this Chapter's Specifications.
38   Check for continuity to ground on each terminal. Continuity should NOT exist. If the test results are incorrect, replace the sensor.
39   If the test results are all correct, have the system diagnosed by a dealer service department.

## Replacement

40   Disconnect the negative battery terminal. **Caution:** *The stereo in your vehicle is equipped with an anti-theft system. Make sure you have the correct activation code before disconnecting the battery.*
41   On 1994 and 1995 four-cylinder models, to replace the CKP, TDC and CYP sensors, and on 1996 and later four-cylinder models, to replace the CYP sensor, disconnect the harness connector at the distributor. Remove the distributor (see Chapter 5) and transfer the necessary components to the new distributor. Installation is the reverse of removal.
42   On 1996 and later four-cylinder models, to replace the CKP and TDC sensors, perform Steps 1 through 4, *Crankshaft front oil seal replacement* (see Chapter 2 Part A, Section 12) and remove the sensor assembly. Installation is the reverse of removal
43   On V6 models, to replace the CKP sensor, remove the crankshaft pulley (see Chapter 2 Part B, Section 7). Remove the two mounting bolts and remove the sensor assembly. To remove the TDC and CYP sensor, remove the front camshaft pulley and the back cover (see Chapter 2 Part B, Section 7). Remove the three mounting bolts and remove the sensor assembly. Installation is the reverse of removal.

## *Engine Coolant Temperature (ECT) sensor*

### General description

44   The coolant temperature sensor is a thermistor (a resistor which varies the value of its voltage output in accordance with temperature changes). The change in the resistance values will directly affect the voltage signal from the thermosensor. As the sensor temperature DECREASES, the resistance values will INCREASE. As the sensor temperature INCREASES, the resistance values will DECREASE. A failure in this sensor circuit should set a Code 6. This code indicates a failure in the ECT circuit, so in most cases the appropriate solution to the problem will be either repair of a wire or replacement of the sensor.

### Check

*Refer to illustrations 4.45a, 4.45b and 4.46*

45   To check the sensor, check the resistance value of the coolant temperature sensor while it is completely cold (50 to 80 degrees F = 2,200 to 2,700 ohms) **(see illustrations).** Next, start the engine and warm it up until it reaches operating temperature. The resistance should be lower (180 to 200 degrees F = 280 to 350 ohms). **Note:** *Access to the coolant temperature sensor makes it difficult to position probes of the meter on the terminals. If necessary, remove the sensor*

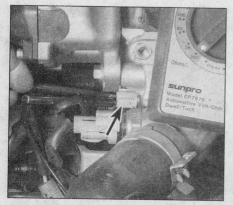

**4.45a  Check the resistance of the coolant temperature sensor with the engine completely cold and then with the engine at operating temperature (four-cylinder engine shown)**

**4.45b  Location of the coolant temperature sensor on the V6 engine (arrow)**

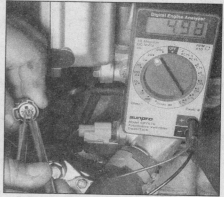

**4.46  Check for reference voltage to the coolant temperature sensor on the red/white wire (+) and the green/blue wire (−). It should be approximately 5.0 volts**

and perform the tests in a pan of heated water to simulate the conditions.

46    Check the reference voltage red/white wire (+) and green/blue wire (−) with the ignition key ON (engine not running). It should be approximately 5.0 volts **(see illustration)**. If not, check for an open circuit in the red/white wire from the sensor to the ECM.

### Replacement

**Warning:** *Wait until the engine has cooled completely before beginning this procedure.*

47    Before installing the new sensor, wrap the threads with Teflon sealing tape to prevent leakage and thread corrosion.

48    To remove the sensor, depress the locking tab, disconnect the electrical connector, then carefully unscrew the sensor. Coolant will leak out when the sensor is removed, so install the new sensor as quickly as possible. **Caution:** *Handle the coolant sensor with care. Damage to this sensor will affect the operation of the entire fuel injection system.*

49    Installation is the reverse of removal.

## Throttle Position (TP) sensor

**Note:** *The TP sensor is not replaceable. In the event of failure, purchase a complete throttle body unit from the dealer parts department*

### General description

50    The Throttle Position (TP) sensor is located on the end of the throttle shaft on the throttle body. By monitoring the output voltage

from the TP sensor, the ECM can determine fuel delivery based on throttle valve angle (driver demand). A broken or loose TP sensor can cause intermittent bursts of fuel from the injector and an unstable idle because the ECM thinks the throttle is moving.

### Check

*Refer to illustrations 4.53a and 4.53b*

51    Follow the wiring harness from the TP sensor to the throttle body and using pins, backprobe the electrical connector. Be very careful not to damage the wiring harness.

52    Using a voltmeter, check the reference voltage from the ECM. Install the probes on the yellow/blue wire (+) and the green/blue wire (−). It should read approximately 5.0 volts.

53    Next, check the TP sensor signal voltage. With the ignition key ON (engine not running), throttle fully closed and TP sensor electrical connector connected, install the probes of the voltmeter onto the red/black wire (+) and green/blue wire (−) **(see illustrations)**. gradually open the throttle valve and observe the TP sensor voltage. With the throttle valve fully closed, the voltage should read approximately 0.5 volts. Slowly move the throttle valve and observe a distinct change in the voltage values as the sensor travels from idle to full throttle. The voltage should increase smoothly to approximately 4.5 volts. If the readings are incorrect, replace the TP sensor.

54    A problem in any of the TP sensor circuits will set a Code 7. Once a trouble code is set, the ECM will use an artificial default value and some vehicle performance will return.

**4.53a  Check the TP sensor voltage signal from the signal wire (yellow/blue) and ground wire (green/blue). First, check the voltage with the throttle completely closed. It should be approximately 0.5 volts**

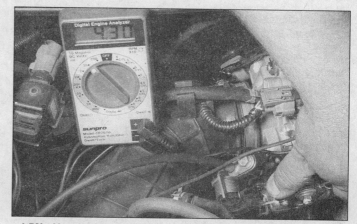

**4.53b  Next, using your hand, rotate the throttle valve until wide open throttle is attained and check the voltage signal. It should be 4.5 volts**

4.55  Check the resistance of the IAT sensor (plenum removed for clarity)

4.56  With the ignition key turned ON (engine not running), check for reference voltage to the IAT sensor

## Intake Air Temperature (IAT) sensor

### Check

*Refer to illustrations 4.55 and 4.56*

55   With the ignition switch ON, disconnect the electrical connector from the IAT sensor, which is located on the intake manifold. Using an ohmmeter, measure the resistance between the two terminals on the sensor. It should be between 1,000 and 4,000 ohms depending upon the temperature **(see illustration)**. Refer to the Specifications listed in this Chapter.

56   With the ignition key ON (engine not running), check for reference voltage at the electrical connector (red/yellow wire) to the sensor **(see illustration)**. It should be approximately 5.0 volts.

57   If the test results in Step 55 are incorrect, replace the IAT sensor.

58   If the sensor checks out okay but there is still a problem, have the vehicle checked at a dealer service department or other qualified repair shop, as the ECM may be defective.

### Replacement

59   Disconnect the electrical connector from the IAT sensor.

60   Remove the IAT sensor from the plenum.

61   Installation is the reverse of removal.

## Vehicle Speed Sensor (VSS)

*Refer to illustration 4.63*

### General description

62   The Vehicle Speed Sensor (VSS) is located on the transaxle. This sensor is a permanent magnetic variable reluctance sensor that produces a pulsing voltage whenever vehicle speed is over 3 mph. These pulses are translated by the ECM and provided for other systems for fuel and transaxle shift control.

### Check

63   To check the vehicle speed sensor, remove the electrical connector at the sensor. Using a voltmeter, check for voltage at the electrical connector (yellow wire) to the sensor **(see illustration)**. The circuit should have battery available. If there is no voltage available, check for an open circuit between the VSS and the fuse box. Using an ohmmeter, check the black wire of the connector for continuity to ground.

64   Raise the front of the vehicle and place it securely on jackstands. Block the rear wheels and place the transaxle in Neutral. Connect the electrical connector to the VSS, turn the ignition to On and backprobe the VSS connector orange wire with a voltmeter positive lead. Connect the negative lead of the meter to body ground. While holding one wheel steady, rotate the other wheel by hand. The voltmeter should pulse between zero and 5 volts. If it doesn't, replace the sensor.

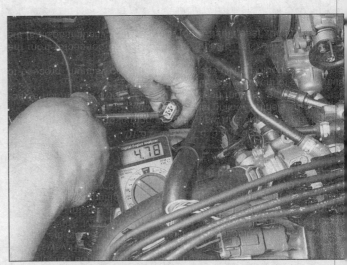

4.63  Checking the VSS on a four-cylinder engine

### Replacement

65   To replace the VSS, disconnect the electrical connector from the VSS.

66   Remove the retaining screws and withdraw the VSS from the transaxle.

67   Installation is the reverse of removal.

## Barometric (BARO) pressure sensor

### General description

68   The barometric pressure sensor is incorporated into the ECM. In the event the self diagnosis system exhibits a code 13, have the system checked by a dealer service department or other qualified repair facility.

## Lock-up Control Solenoid (automatic transaxle only)

### General description

69   The Lock-up Control Solenoid is a computer controlled output actuator that is used to activate the lock-up torque converter on vehicles equipped with the automatic transaxle. Refer to Chapter 7B for additional information.

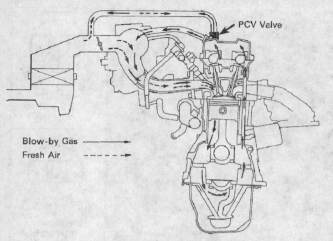

5.1  Gas flow in a typical PCV system

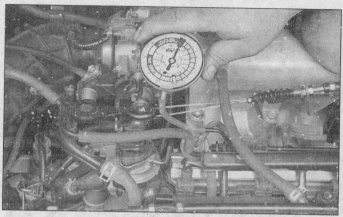

6.4  Check for vacuum to the EGR valve

# 5   Positive Crankcase Ventilation (PCV) system

*Refer to illustration 5.1*

1    The Positive Crankcase Ventilation (PCV) system **(see illustration)** reduces hydrocarbon emissions by scavenging crankcase vapors. It does this by circulating fresh air from the air cleaner through the crankcase, where it mixes with blow-by gases and is then rerouted through a PCV valve to the intake manifold.

2    The main components of the PCV system are the PCV valve, a blow-by filter and the vacuum hoses connecting these two components with the engine.

3    To maintain idle quality, the PCV valve restricts the flow when the intake manifold vacuum is high. If abnormal operating conditions (such as piston ring problems) arise, the system is designed to allow excessive amounts of blow-by gases to flow back through the crankcase vent tube into the air cleaner to be consumed by normal combustion.

4    Checking and replacement of the PCV valve is covered in Chapter 1.

6.6  If there's no vacuum at the EGR valve at idle, disconnect the electrical connector from the EGR control box and check for vacuum again

# 6   Exhaust Gas Recirculation (EGR) system

## General description

1    The EGR system reduces oxides of nitrogen by recirculating exhaust gas through the EGR valve and intake manifold into the combustion chambers.

2    The EGR system consists of the EGR valve, the EGR valve lift sensor, the EGR control solenoid valve, the EGR Vacuum Control Valve, the Electronic Control Module (ECM) and various sensors. The ECM memory is programmed to produce the ideal EGR valve lift for each operating condition. An EGR valve lift sensor detects the amount of EGR valve lift and sends this information to the ECM. The ECM then compares it with the ideal EGR valve lift, which is determined by data received from the other sensors. If there's any difference between the two, the ECM triggers the EGR control solenoid valve to reduce the amount of vacuum applied to the EGR valve.

## Check

*Refer to illustrations 6.4, 6.6, 6.7, 6.8 and 6.10*

3    Start the engine and warm it to its normal operating temperature (wait for the electric cooling fan to come on).

4    Detach the vacuum hose from the EGR valve and attach a vacuum gauge to the hose **(see illustration)**.

5    There should be NO vacuum. If there is no vacuum, proceed to Step 7.

6    If vacuum exists, disconnect the electrical connector from the EGR control box **(see illustration)** and check for vacuum again at the

6.7  Apply vacuum directly to the EGR valve and observe that the valve diaphragm moves up and down freely without any binding - the engine should stall with vacuum applied

EGR vacuum hose. If vacuum does not exist, have the ECM diagnosed by a dealer service department. If vacuum is present, check all the vacuum lines to make sure they are routed properly. If all the hoses are routed properly with no leaks, the EGR control box is probably defective.

7    If there originally was no vacuum, install a hand held vacuum pump to the EGR valve and apply 8 in-Hg of vacuum to the valve and observe that the engine stalls **(see illustration)**. Also, does the EGR

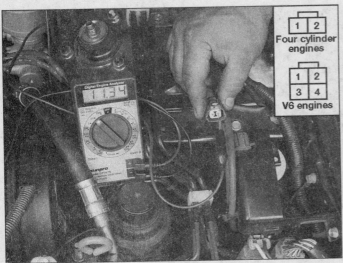

6.8  Check the battery voltage at the black/yellow (+) wire on the
harness side of the connector at the EGR control box

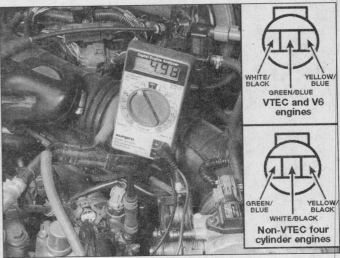

6.10  Check for battery voltage on the yellow/blue wire (+) and the
green/blue wire (–) located on the EGR valve position sensor

valve hold vacuum? If not, replace the EGR valve.

8    Check for battery voltage to the EGR Control Box. Disconnect the
two-pin connector from the control box **(see illustration)** and check
for battery voltage at the black/yellow (+) terminal on the main harness.
There should be battery voltage.

9    Reconnect the vacuum gauge to the EGR valve vacuum hose,
start the engine and allow it to idle. Connect the battery positive cable
with a jumper wire to the number 1 terminal on the two-pin connector
**(see illustration 6.8)**. While observing the vacuum gauge, ground terminal 2 with another jumper wire. Vacuum should increase within one
second. If there is no vacuum, replace the EGR control solenoid. Also
check for voltage to the EGR control solenoid with the ignition key ON
(engine not running)). Battery voltage should exist. **Note:** *The EGR
control solenoid is located in the EGR control box.*

10    Next, check the operation of the EGR valve lift sensor. Disconnect
the three pin electrical connector from the top of the EGR valve (if
equipped) and with the ignition key ON (engine not running), check for
reference voltage on the yellow/blue (+) to terminal and the green/blue
(–) terminal **(see illustration)**. There should be approximately 5.0 volts.

11    Further checking of the EGR control system requires special tools
and equipment.

## *Component replacement*

### EGR valve

*Refer to illustrations 6.13a and 6.13b*

12    Disconnect the electrical connector for the EGR valve lift sensor.

13    Remove the two nuts that secure the EGR valve and detach the
EGR valve **(see illustrations)**.

14    Clean the mating surfaces of the EGR valve and adapter.

15    Install the EGR valve, using a new gasket. Tighten the nuts
securely.

16    Plug in the electrical connector.

### EGR control solenoid

17    Remove the control box located on the firewall and separate the
cover from the main body.

18    Locate the EGR control solenoid and remove the two mounting
screws.

19    Lift the solenoid from the control box.

20    Installation is the reverse of removal.

6.13a  Remove the two nuts (arrows) from the base of the EGR
valve (four-cylinder engines)

6.13b  Location of the EGR mounting nuts (arrows) on
the V6 engine

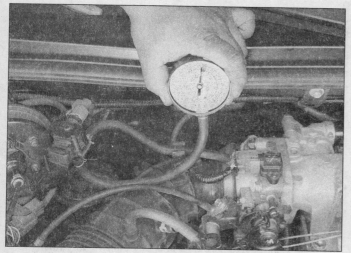

7.8 Remove the vacuum hose from the canister purge valve, attach a vacuum gauge to the hose (arrow) and, with the engine idling (cold engine), there should be no vacuum

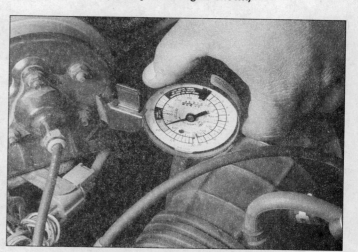

7.10 Check for battery voltage to the canister purge solenoid (four-cylinder engine shown)

## 7   Evaporative emissions control (EVAP) system

### General description

1   The fuel evaporative emissions control system absorbs fuel vapors and, during engine operation, releases them into the engine intake where they mix with the incoming air-fuel mixture.

2   Every evaporative system employs a canister filled with activated charcoal to absorb fuel vapors. The means by which these vapors are controlled, however, varies considerably from one system to another. The following descriptions of a typical system for the models covered by this manual should provide you enough information to understand the system on your vehicle. **Note:** *The following descriptions are not intended as a specific description of the evaporative system on your particular vehicle. Rather, they are intended as a general description of a typical system used on fuel-injected vehicles. Although the following components are most likely all used on your particular system, there may also be other devices, not included here, which are unique to your system. Check with the VECI label and the Vacuum Hose Routing Diagram under the hood.*

3   The fuel filler cap is fitted with a two-way valve as a safety device. The valve vents fuel vapors to the atmosphere if the evaporative control system fails.

4   Another fuel cut-off valve (two-way valve), mounted on the fuel tank, regulates fuel vapor flow from the fuel tank to the charcoal canister, based on the pressure or vacuum caused by temperature changes.

5   After passing through the two-way valve, fuel vapor is carried by vent hoses to the charcoal canister in the engine compartment. The activated charcoal in the canister absorbs and stores these vapors.

6   When the engine is running and warmed to a pre-set temperature, a purge cut-off solenoid valve near the canister closes, allowing a purge control diaphragm valve in the charcoal canister to be opened by intake manifold vacuum. Fuel vapors from the canister are then drawn through the purge control diaphragm valve by intake manifold vacuum.

### Check

*Refer to illustrations 7.8, 7.10, 7.13 and 7.16*
**Note:** *Complete checking of the evaporative emissions control system is beyond the scope of the average home mechanic. Fortunately, the evaporative control system, like all emission control systems, is protected by a Federally-mandated extended warranty (5 years or 50,000 miles at the time this manual was written). The EVAP system probably won't fail during the service life of the vehicle; however, if it does, the*

7.13 With the engine warmed up, check for vacuum at the number 7 hose

*hoses or charcoal canister are usually to blame.*

7   Always check the hoses first. A disconnected, damaged or missing hose is the most likely cause of a malfunctioning EVAP system. Refer to the Vacuum Hose Routing Diagram (attached to the underside of the hood) to determine whether the hoses are correctly routed and attached. Repair any damaged hoses or replace any missing hoses as necessary.

8   Disconnect the vacuum hose from the purge control diaphragm valve (located near the charcoal canister) and connect a vacuum gauge to the hose **(see illustration)**. Start the engine and allow it to idle. There should be NO vacuum present. **Note:** *The temperature of the engine must be below 167-degrees F.*

9   If there is no vacuum present, proceed to Step 13.

10   If there is vacuum present, disconnect the two-pin connector and measure the voltage between the yellow/black (+) terminal and the red (-) terminal. There should be battery voltage **(see illustration)**.

11   If battery voltage is present, replace the purge cut-off solenoid valve.

12   If there is no battery voltage, repair the wiring harness to the ECM and/or the number two fuse.

13   Warm the engine up to normal operating temperature (cooling fan must come on). If there originally was no vacuum on the purge control diaphragm valve, check for vacuum on the number 7 hose **(see illustration)**.

7.16 Remove the purge air hose from the bottom of the charcoal canister, connect a vacuum gauge to the hose and check for vacuum with the engine at 3,500 rpm

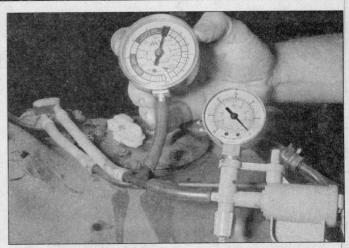

7.18 With the fuel tank removed, check the two-way valve for correct operation first with vacuum applied and then with pressure applied

14    If there is vacuum present, proceed to Step 16.

15    If there is no vacuum present, disconnect the two-pin connector and check for manifold vacuum now. If there is no vacuum, check to make sure the vacuum hoses are routed correctly. If there is vacuum, check for a short in the wiring harness between the two-pin connector and the ECM.

16    If vacuum was originally present, reconnect the number 7 hose and connect a vacuum gauge to the purge air hose **(see illustration)** and raise the engine rpm to 3,500. Vacuum should be present within one minute. If there is vacuum, check the two-way valve.

### Two-way valve

*Refer to illustration 7.18*

17    Remove the fuel tank (see Chapter 4).

18    Detach the vapor line from the fuel tank and connect a T-fitting into a vacuum pump and vacuum gauge **(see illustration)**.

19    Apply vacuum slowly and steadily and observe the gauge. Vacuum should stabilize momentarily at 0.2 to 0.6 in-Hg. If the valve opens (stabilizes) before the correct vacuum, replace it with a new part.

20    Move the hand held vacuum pump over to the pressure fitting (same vacuum line arrangement). Pressurize the line and observe the gauge. Pressure should stabilize at 0.4 to 1.4 in-Hg (valve opens).

21    If the valve opens (stabilizes) before or after the correct vacuum, replace it with a new part.

### 8    Electronic Load Detector (ELD) system

*Refer to illustrations 8.2 and 8.3*

### General information

1    The ELD system detects excess amperage draw (load) on the electrical circuits that govern the headlights, fuel injection, charging system etc. The prime symptom of an electrical overload is a driveability problem, usually occurring when the engine is idling. Any trouble with the ELD system will set a code 20.

### Check

2    Disconnect the electrical connector from the ELD system and measure voltage **(see illustration)** between the black/yellow (+) wire and the black (-) wire (two outside terminals) with the ignition key ON (engine not running). There should be battery voltage. If no voltage is present, check the wiring harness back to the fuse box (under the dash) and the main fuse box (engine compartment).

3    Measure voltage with the ignition key ON (engine not running) between the green/red (+) terminal and the black (-) terminal **(see illustration)**. There should be 4.5 to 5.0 volts. If no voltage is present, check the ELD circuit between the engine and the alternator.

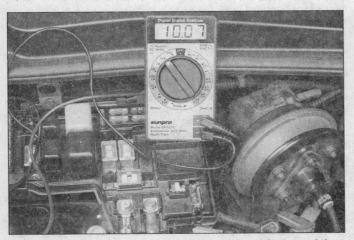

8.2 Measure voltage between the black/yellow (+) wire and the black (-) wire (two outside terminals) with the ignition key ON (engine not running) - there should be battery voltage

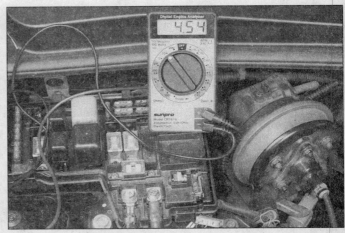

8.3 Measure voltage with the ignition key ON (engine not running) between the green/red (+) terminal (middle terminal) and the black (-) terminal - there should be 4.5 to 5.0 volts

**9.4  Remove the retaining nuts (arrows) from the kick plate and lift the plate out of the passenger compartment to gain access to the ECM**

**9.5  Location of the ECM**

4    Reconnect the three-pin connector to the ELD system. With the ignition key ON (engine not running) and the headlights ON (low beam), measure the voltage on the green/red terminal (+) (middle wire). There should be approximately 2.5 to 3.5 volts.

5    Now, turn the switch to high beam and check the amount of voltage. It should 1.5 to 2.5 volts.

6    If the test results are not correct, replace the ELD unit. This requires changing the entire main fuse box. The ELD unit is not available separately.

## 9    Engine Control Module (ECM) - general information and replacement

*Refer to illustrations 9.4 and 9.5*

**Warning:** *The vehicles covered by this manual are equipped with airbags. Always disable the airbag system before working in the vicinity of the steering column, instrument panel or console to avoid the possibility of accidental deployment of the airbag, which could cause personal injury (see Chapter 12). The yellow wiring harness and connectors routed through the console and instrument panel are used for the airbag system. Do not use electrical test equipment on the system wiring or connectors or tamper with them in any way.*

**Caution:** *The stereo in your vehicle is equipped with an anti-theft system. Make sure you have the correct activation code before disconnecting the battery.*

1    The Engine Control Module (ECM) is located inside the passenger compartment under the dashboard behind the kick panel (right side).

2    Disable the airbag system (see Chapter 12).

3    Remove the carpet from the lower panel assembly and the floor area (see Chapter 11) under the right end of the dash. Place the carpet sufficiently out of the way.

4    Remove the kick plate to expose the relay panel and the ECM **(see illustration)**.

5    Disconnect the electrical connectors from the ECM **(see illustration)**. **Caution:** *The ignition switch must be turned OFF when pulling out or plugging in the electrical connectors to prevent damage to the ECM.*

6    Remove the retaining nut from the ECM bracket.

7    Carefully remove the ECM. **Note:** *Avoid any static electricity damage to the computer by grounding yourself to the body before touching the ECM and using a special anti-static pad to store the ECM on once it is removed.*

## 10    Catalytic converter

**Note:** *Because of a Federally mandated extended warranty which covers emissions-related components such as the catalytic converter, check with a dealer service department before replacing the converter at your own expense.*

### General description

1    The catalytic converter is an emission control device added to the exhaust system to reduce pollutants from the exhaust gas stream. There are two types of converters. The conventional oxidation catalyst reduces the levels of hydrocarbon (HC) and carbon monoxide (CO). The three-way catalyst lowers the levels of oxides of nitrogen (NOx) as well as hydrocarbons (HC) and carbon monoxide (CO).

### Check

2    The test equipment for a catalytic converter is expensive and highly sophisticated. If you suspect that the converter on your vehicle is malfunctioning, take it to a dealer or authorized emissions inspection facility for diagnosis and repair.

3    Whenever the vehicle is raised for servicing of underbody components, check the converter for leaks, corrosion, dents and other damage. Check the welds/flange bolts that attach the front and rear ends of the converter to the exhaust system. If damage is discovered, the converter should be replaced.

4    Although catalytic converters don't break too often, they can become plugged. The easiest way to check for a restricted converter is to use a vacuum gauge to diagnose the effect of a blocked exhaust on intake vacuum.

a)   *Open the throttle until the engine speed is about 2000 rpm.*

b)   *Release the throttle quickly.*

c)   *If there is no restriction, the gauge will quickly drop to not more than 2 in-Hg or more above its normal reading.*

d)   *If the gauge does not show 5 in-Hg or more above its normal reading, or seems to momentarily hover around its highest reading for a moment before it returns, the exhaust system, or the converter, is plugged (or an exhaust pipe is bent or dented, or the core inside the muffler has shifted).*

### Component replacement

*Refer to illustrations 10.5a and 10.5b*

5    Be sure to spray the exhaust nuts on the flange studs before

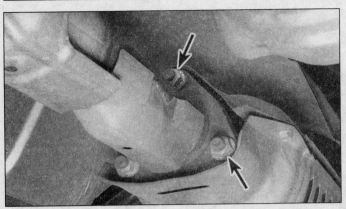

**10.5a  Spray penetrating lubricant onto the threads of the rear mounted studs (arrows) of the catalytic converter**

**10.5b  Forward mounted catalytic converter flange nuts (arrows)**

removing them from the catalytic converter **(see illustrations).**

6    Remove the nuts and separate the catalytic converter from the exhaust system.

7    Installation is the reverse of removal.

# Chapter 7 Part A
# Manual transaxle

## Contents

## Specifications

## Torque specifications

| | Ft-lbs |
|---|---|
| Transaxle-to-engine bolts | 47 |

## 1  General information

The vehicles covered by this manual are equipped with either a five-speed manual transaxle or a four-speed automatic transaxle. Information on the manual transaxle is included in this Part of Chapter 7. Service procedures for the automatic transaxle are contained in Chapter 7, Part B.

The manual transaxle is a compact, two-piece, lightweight aluminum alloy housing containing both the transmission and differential assemblies.

## 2  Driveaxle oil seals - replacement

*Refer to illustrations 2.4 and 2.6*

Oil leaks frequently occur due to wear of the driveaxle oil seals. Replacement of these seals is relatively easy, since the repair can usually be performed without removing the transaxle from the vehicle.

The driveaxle oil seals are located at the sides of the transaxle, where the driveaxles are attached. If leakage at the seal is suspected, raise the vehicle and support it securely on jackstands. If the seal is leaking, lubricant will be found on the sides of the transaxle, below the seals.

Refer to Chapter 8 and remove the driveaxles.

Using a screwdriver or prybar, carefully pry the oil seal out of the transaxle bore (see illustration).

5    If the oil seal cannot be removed with a screwdriver or prybar, a special oil seal removal tool (available at auto parts stores) will be required.

**2.4  Insert the tip of a large screwdriver or prybar behind the oil seal and very carefully pry it out**

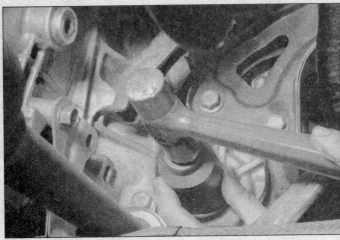

2.6  Using a large socket or a section of pipe, drive the
new seal squarely into the bore

3.3  Remove the cotter pin and washer (left arrow) and detach the
select cable from the change lever linkage, then remove the
self-locking nut and washer (right arrow) and detach
the shift cable from the shift lever

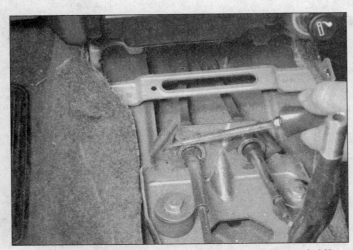

3.4  Pry off the retaining clips and detach the select and shift
cables from the shift lever base plate

3.5  Remove the cotter pins, steel washers and plastic washers
and disconnect the select cable from the select lever (lower
right arrow) and the shift lever from the shift arm lever
(upper right arrow), then pry off the retaining clip
(left arrows) from the cable brackets

6    Using a large section of pipe or a large deep socket (as large as
the outside diameter of the seal) as a drift, install the new oil seal (see
illustration). Drive it into the bore squarely and make sure it's completely seated. Coat the seal lip with transaxle lubricant.
7    Install the driveaxle(s). Be careful not to damage the lip of the new
seal.

3    Select and shift cables - replacement

Refer to illustrations 3.3, 3.4 and 3.5
Warning: The vehicles covered by this manual are equipped with
airbags. Always disable the airbag system before working in the vicinity
of the steering column, instrument panel or console to avoid the possibility of accidental deployment of the airbag, which could cause
personal injury (see Chapter 12). The yellow wiring harness and connectors routed through the console and instrument panel are used for
the airbag system. Do not use electrical test equipment on the system
wiring or connectors or tamper with them in any way.
Caution: The stereo in your vehicle is equipped with an anti-theft system. Make sure you have the correct activation code before
disconnecting the battery.

Note: Even if only one cable is broken, you must replace the select and
shift cables as a single assembly - they're not available separately.
1    Unscrew and remove the shift lever knob.
2    Remove the console (see Chapter 11).
3    Remove the cotter pin and washer and detach the select cable
from the change lever linkage (see illustration). Remove the self-locking nut and washer and detach the shift cable from the shift lever.
4    Remove the retaining clips and detach the cables from the shift
lever base plate (see illustration).
5    Open the hood and locate the forward ends of the cables (see
illustration). Disconnect the select cable from the select lever (the one
on the top of the shift arm cover) and the shift cable from the shift arm
lever (the one on the side). Remove the retaining clips from the cable
bracket.
6    Follow the cables back to the firewall and remove the cable grommet.
7    Pull the cables out.
8    Installation is the reverse of removal. At the shift arm cover, make
sure the plastic washer is between the steel washer and the cable; at the
shift lever, make sure it's between the steel washer and the cotter pin.

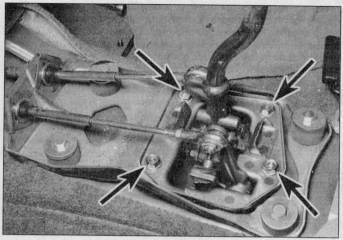

4.4  Shift lever base mounting bolts (arrows)

6.4  To test the back-up light switch, pull up on the dust boot (arrow), unplug the electrical connector and connect an ohmmeter or circuit tester across the two switch terminals - there should be continuity between the two switch terminals with the shift lever in Reverse, but not in any other gear

## 4    Shift lever - removal and installation

**Warning:** *The vehicles covered by this manual are equipped with airbags. Always disable the airbag system before working in the vicinity of the steering column, instrument panel or console to avoid the possibility of accidental deployment of the airbag, which could cause personal injury (see Chapter 12). The yellow wiring harness and connectors routed through the console and instrument panel are used for the airbag system. Do not use electrical test equipment on the system wiring or connectors or tamper with them in any way.*
**Caution:** *The stereo in your vehicle is equipped with an anti-theft system. Make sure you have the correct activation code before disconnecting the battery.*

1    Unscrew and remove the shift lever knob.
2    Remove the console (see Chapter 11).
3    Disconnect the select and shift cables from the shift lever (see Section 3).
4    Remove the shift lever base mounting bolts **(see illustration)**.
5    Remove the shift lever assembly.
6    Installation is the reverse of removal.

## 5    Transaxle mount - check and replacement

1    Insert a large screwdriver or prybar between the mount and the transaxle and try to lever the transaxle up or down.
2    The transaxle should not move more than about 1/2 to 3/4-inch away from the mount. If it does, replace the mount.
3    To replace the mount, support the transaxle with a jack, remove the nuts and bolts and remove the mount. It may be necessary to raise the transaxle slightly to provide enough clearance to remove the mount. **Warning:** *Do not place any part of your body under the transaxle when it's supported only by a jack.*
4    Installation is the reverse of removal.

## 6    Back-up light switch - check and replacement

*Refer to illustration 6.4*

### Check

1    Before testing the back-up light switch, check the fuse in the under-dash fuse box.
2    Place the shift lever in Reverse and turn the ignition switch to On. The back-up lights should go on. Turn off the ignition switch.
3    If the back-up lights didn't go on, check the back-up light bulbs in the tail light assembly.

4    If the fuse and bulbs are both okay, disconnect the electrical connector from the back-up light switch **(see illustration)** and connect an ohmmeter or continuity tester across the two switch terminals.
5    With the shift lever in Reverse, there should be continuity; there should be no continuity with the shifter in any other gear.
6    If the switch fails the above tests, replace the switch (see below).
7    If the switch is OK, check for a poor ground in the circuit; if the grounds are good, look for shorts or opens in the wires.

### Replacement

8    Disconnect the back-up light switch electrical connectors **(see illustration 6.4)**.
9    Unscrew and remove the back-up light switch.
10   Discard the old washer.
11   Using a new washer, install the new switch.
12   Plug in the connectors.

## 7    Manual transaxle - removal and installation

*Refer to illustrations 7.12a, 7.12b, 7.19, 7.22, 7.25, 7.26a and 7.26b*
**Caution:** *The stereo in your vehicle is equipped with an anti-theft system. Make sure you have the correct activation code before disconnecting the battery.*

### Removal

1    Disconnect the negative (first) and positive (last) cables from the battery and remove the battery. Remove the battery tray (see Chapter 5).
2    Remove the air intake hose (see Chapter 4).
3    Disconnect the starter motor cables and remove the starter motor (see Chapter 5).
4    Disconnect the transaxle ground cable, disconnect the back-up light switch connectors (see Section 6) and detach the wiring harness clamp from the transaxle.
5    Shift the transaxle into reverse gear.
6    Disconnect the shift and select cables from the transaxle (see Section 3). It's not necessary to disconnect the cables from the cable stay - simply disconnect the stay itself from the transaxle and leave the cables attached to the stay.
7    Disconnect the electrical connector for the power steering speed sensor, remove the hold-down bolts for the sensor, and remove the sensor, but don't disconnect the power steering fluid hoses.
8    Loosen the front wheel lug nuts, raise the vehicle and support it securely on jackstands. Remove the front wheels.

**7.12a  Remove the front bolts (arrows) . . .**

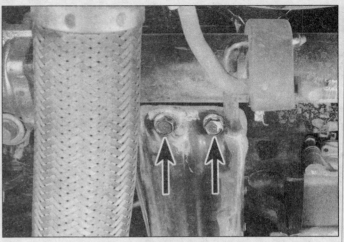

**7.12b  . . . and the rear bolts (arrows) from the center beam, disconnect the exhaust pipe hanger and remove the beam**

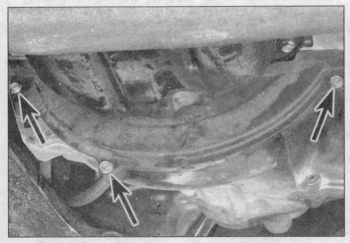

**7.19  Remove the clutch access cover bolts (arrows) and the cover**

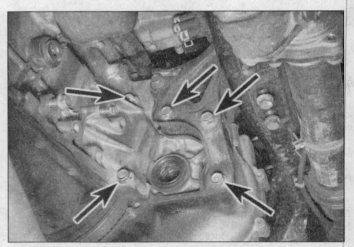

**7.22  Remove the engine-to-transaxle retaining bolts (arrows)**

9    Remove the splash shield, if equipped.
10   Drain the transaxle lubricant (see Chapter 1).
11   Remove the clutch fluid hose-to-clutch fluid pressure line junction, the clutch fluid pressure line, the release cylinder and the release cylinder pushrod (see Chapter 8). **Caution:** *Be careful not to bend or kink the clutch fluid pressure line. And do NOT depress the clutch pedal while the clutch release cylinder is removed. Remove the clutch damper assembly, but don't disconnect the lines. Support it with a piece of wire.*
12   Remove the center beam **(see illustrations)**.
13   Remove the section of exhaust pipe which runs underneath the engine (see Chapter 4).
14   Disconnect the lower control arms from the steering knuckles, then disconnect the damper forks from the lower control arms (see Chapter 10).
15   Pry the left driveaxle out of the intermediate shaft and the right driveaxle out of the transaxle (see Chapter 8). Tie plastic bags over the inner CV joints to keep them clean.
16   Disconnect the bearing support and detach the intermediate shaft from the transaxle (see Chapter 8).
17   Remove the right damper fork pinch bolt and separate the damper fork from the shock absorber (see Chapter 10).
18   Remove the right side radius rod (see Chapter 10).
19   Remove the clutch access cover **(see illustration)**.
20   Remove the exhaust manifold bracket.

21   Remove the three rear engine mount bracket bolts (see Chapter 2, Part A).
22   Remove all five transaxle retaining bolts on the engine side **(see illustration)**.
23   Swivel the right driveaxle inner CV joint forward so that it's out of the way.
24   Place a floor jack under the transaxle and raise the transaxle just enough to take the weight off the mounts.
25   Remove the transaxle mount retaining bolt and loosen the mount bracket retaining nuts **(see illustration)**.
26   Remove the three transaxle housing retaining bolts **(see illustrations)**.
27   Make a final check that all wires and hoses have been disconnected from the transaxle, then carefully pull the transaxle and jack away from the engine.
28   Once the input shaft is clear, lower the transaxle and remove it from under the vehicle.
29   With the transaxle removed, the clutch components are now accessible and can be inspected. In most cases, new clutch components should be routinely installed when the transaxle is removed (see Chapter 8).

*Installation*

30   If removed, install the clutch components (see Chapter 8.)
31   With the transaxle secured to the jack by a chain, raise it into

7.25 Remove the transaxle mount through-bolt (arrow) and loosen the mount bracket retaining nuts (arrows)

7.26a Remove the three transaxle-to-engine retaining bolts: Two of them (arrows) are on top . . .

7.26b . . . and another (arrow) is underneath the starter motor

position behind the engine, then carefully slide it forward, engaging the four dowel pins on the transaxle with the corresponding holes in the block and the input shaft with the clutch plate hub splines. Do not use excessive force to install the transaxle - if the input shaft does not slide into place, readjust the angle of the transaxle so it is level and/or turn the input shaft so the splines engage properly with the clutch plate hub.

32    Install the three transaxle housing-to-engine bolts. Tighten the bolts to the torque listed in this Chapter's Specifications.

33    Install the transaxle mount and mount bracket. Tighten the bolt first, but not too tightly; then tighten the three nuts securely; and, finally, tighten the bolt securely.

34    Install the five engine-to-transaxle housing bolts and tighten them to the torque listed in this Chapter's Specifications.

35    Install the three rear engine bracket mounting bolts and tighten them securely.

36    Install the rear engine mount bracket stay. Install the stay mounting bolt and nut and tighten the bolt and nut securely.

37    The remainder of installation is the reverse of removal.

38    Refill the transaxle with the specified amount of lubricant (see Chapter 1).

39    Bleed the clutch hydraulic system (see Chapter 8).

40    Road test the vehicle for proper operation and check for leaks.

## 8    Manual transaxle overhaul - general information

Overhauling a manual transaxle is difficult for the do-it-yourselfer. Not only must you disassemble and reassemble many small parts, but you must also measure numerous clearances and, if necessary, change them with select-fit shims, thrust washers and spacer collars.

If transaxle problems arise, you can save a lot of money by removing and installing the transaxle yourself. Then buy a rebuilt transaxle (check with your dealer parts department and auto parts stores). The cost for an overhaul almost always exceeds the cost of a rebuilt unit. If rebuilt units aren't available, have the transaxle rebuilt by a dealer or a shop that specializes in rebuilding these units.

# Notes

# Chapter 7  Part B
# Automatic transaxle

## Contents

## Specifications

| | |
|---|---|
| Shift lock solenoid clearance | 5/32 ± 1/64-inch |

## Torque specifications

| | Ft-lbs (unless otherwise indicated) |
|---|---|
| Shift lock solenoid self-locking nuts | 84 in-lbs |
| Transaxle-to-engine bolts | 47 |
| Transaxle mount bracket nuts | 28 |
| Torque converter-to-driveplate bolts | 9 |

## 1  General information

All vehicles covered in this manual come equipped with either a five-speed manual or a four-speed automatic transaxle. All information on the automatic transaxle is included in this Part of Chapter 7. Information for the manual transaxle can be found in Part A of this Chapter.

Due to the complexity of the automatic transaxles covered in this manual and to the specialized equipment necessary to perform most service operations, this Chapter contains only those procedures related to general diagnosis, routine maintenance, adjustment and removal and installation.

If the transaxle requires major repair work, it should be left to a dealer service department or an automotive or transmission repair shop. You can, however, remove and install the transaxle yourself and save the expense, even if the repair work is done by a transmission shop.

## 2  Diagnosis - general

**Note:** *Automatic transaxle malfunctions may be caused by five general conditions: poor engine performance, improper adjustments, hydraulic malfunctions, mechanical malfunctions or malfunctions in the computer or its signal network. Diagnosis of these problems should*

*always begin with a check of the easily repaired items: fluid level and condition (see Chapter 1), shift control cable adjustment and throttle control cable adjustment. Next, perform a road test to determine if the problem has been corrected or if more diagnosis is necessary. If the problem persists after the preliminary tests and corrections are completed, additional diagnosis should be done by a dealer service department or transmission repair shop. Refer to the Troubleshooting section at the front of this manual for information on symptoms of transaxle problems.*

### Preliminary checks

1  Drive the vehicle to warm the transaxle to normal operating temperature.
2  Check the fluid level as described in Chapter 1:
a) *If the fluid level is unusually low, add enough fluid to bring the level within the designated area of the dipstick, then check for external leaks (see below).*
b) *If the fluid level is abnormally high, drain off the excess, then check the drained fluid for contamination by coolant. The presence of engine coolant in the automatic transmission fluid indicates that a failure has occurred in the internal radiator walls that separate the coolant from the transmission fluid (see Chapter 3).*
c) *If the fluid is foaming, drain it and refill the transaxle, then check for coolant in the fluid, or a high fluid level.*

3    Check the engine idle speed. **Note:** *If the engine is malfunctioning, do not proceed with the preliminary checks until it has been repaired and runs normally.*

4    Check the throttle control cable for freedom of movement. Adjust it if necessary (see Section 5). **Note:** *The cable may function properly when the engine is shut off and cold, but it may malfunction once the engine is hot. Check it cold and at normal engine operating temperature.*

5    Inspect the shift control linkage (see Section 4). Make sure that it's properly adjusted and that the linkage operates smoothly.

### Fluid leak diagnosis

6    Most fluid leaks are easy to locate visually. Repair usually consists of replacing a seal or gasket. If a leak is difficult to find, the following procedure may help.

7    Identify the fluid. Make sure it's transmission fluid and not engine oil or brake fluid (automatic transmission fluid is a deep red color).

8    Try to pinpoint the source of the leak. Drive the vehicle several miles, then park it over a large sheet of cardboard. After a minute or two, you should be able to locate the leak by determining the source of the fluid dripping onto the cardboard.

9    Make a careful visual inspection of the suspected component and the area immediately around it. Pay particular attention to gasket mating surfaces. A mirror is often helpful for finding leaks in areas that are hard to see.

10    If the leak still cannot be found, clean the suspected area thoroughly with a degreaser or solvent, then dry the area.

11    Drive the vehicle for several miles at normal operating temperature and varying speeds. After driving the vehicle, visually inspect the suspected component again.

12    Once the leak has been located, the cause must be determined before it can be properly repaired. If a gasket is replaced but the sealing flange is bent, the new gasket will not stop the leak. The bent flange must be straightened.

13    Before attempting to repair a leak, check to make sure that the following conditions are corrected or they may cause another leak. **Note:** *Some of the following conditions cannot be fixed without highly specialized tools and expertise. Such problems must be referred to a transmission shop or a dealer service department.*

### Gasket leaks

14    Check the right side cover periodically. Make sure the bolts are tight, no bolts are missing, the gasket is in good condition and the cover is not damaged.

15    If the leak is from the right side cover area, the bolts may be too tight, the sealing surface of the transaxle housing may be damaged, the gasket may be damaged or the transaxle casting may be cracked or porous. If sealant instead of gasket material has been used to form a seal between the cover and the transaxle housing, it may be the wrong sealant.

### Seal leaks

16    If a transaxle seal is leaking, the fluid level or pressure may be too high, the vent may be plugged, the seal bore may be damaged, the seal itself may be damaged or improperly installed, the surface of the shaft protruding through the seal may be damaged or a loose bearing may be causing excessive shaft movement.

17    Make sure the dipstick tube seal is in good condition and the tube is properly seated. Periodically check the area around the speedometer gear or sensor for leakage. If transmission fluid is evident, check the O-ring for damage.

### Case leaks

18    If the case itself appears to be leaking, the casting is porous and will have to be repaired or replaced.

19    Make sure the oil cooler hose fittings are tight and in good condition.

### Fluid comes out vent pipe or fill tube

20    If this condition occurs, the transaxle is overfilled, there is coolant in the fluid, the case is porous, the dipstick is incorrect, the vent is plugged or the drain-back holes are plugged.

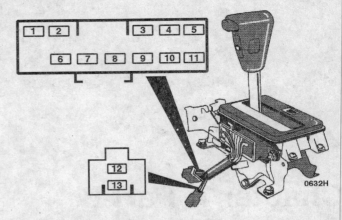

**3.2 Terminal guide for the 2-pin and 12-pin connectors (viewed from the terminal side)**

3    **Shift position console switch - check, adjustment and replacement**

### Check

*Refer to illustrations 3.2 and 3.3*

**Warning:** *The vehicles covered by this manual are equipped with airbags. Always disable the airbag system before working in the vicinity of the steering column, instrument panel or console to avoid the possibility of accidental deployment of the airbag, which could cause personal injury (see Chapter 12). The yellow wiring harness and connectors routed through the console and instrument panel are used for the airbag system. Do not use electrical test equipment on the system wiring or connectors or tamper with them in any way.*

**Caution:** *The stereo in your vehicle is equipped with an anti-theft system. Make sure you have the correct activation code before disconnecting the battery.*

1    Remove the console (see Chapter 11).

2    Disconnect the 2- and 12-pin electrical connectors from the shift position console switch **(see illustration)**.

3    Check for continuity between the indicated terminals in each switch position in accordance with the accompanying table **(see illustration)**. Move the shift lever back and forth without touching the pushbutton at each switch position and check for continuity within the range of shift lever freeplay (about 5/32-inch).

4    If there's no continuity within the range of shift lever freeplay at each shift lever position, adjust the position of the console switch.

### Adjustment

5    Move the shift lever to the Park position and loosen the switch mounting nuts **(see illustration 3.11)**.

6    Slide the switch toward the Drive positions until there's continuity between terminals F and I, within the range of shift lever freeplay (about 5/64-inch).

7    Recheck continuity as described above in Step 3. Make sure the engine starts when the shift lever is in the Neutral position.

8    If there's still no continuity at each shift lever position, inspect the shift lever detent and bracket for damage. If they're undamaged, replace the shift position console switch.

### Replacement

*Refer to illustration 3.11*

9    Remove the console (see Chapter 11).

10    Disconnect the 2- and 12-pin connectors **(see illustration 3.2)**.

11    Remove the two console switch mounting nuts and washers **(see illustration)**.

12    Position the switch slider at the Park position **(see illustration 3.11)**.

| Position | A/T Gear Position Switch | | | | | | | | | Back-up Light Switch | | Neutral Safety Switch | |
|---|---|---|---|---|---|---|---|---|---|---|---|---|---|
| Terminal | *1 | 9 | 2 | 3 | 4 | 5 | 6 | 10 | 11 | 7 | 8 | 12 | 13 |
| 1 | | O— | —O | | | | | | | | | | |
| 2 | O— | O— | | —O | | | | | | | | | |
| D3 | O— | O— | | | —O | | | | | | | | |
| D4 | O— | O— | | | | —O | | | | | | | |
| P | | O— | | | | | —O | | | | | O— | —O |
| R | | O— | | | | | | —O | | O— | —O | | |
| N | | O— | | | | | | | —O | | | O— | —O |

▲ = With cruise control

**3.3 Continuity table for the shift position console switch**

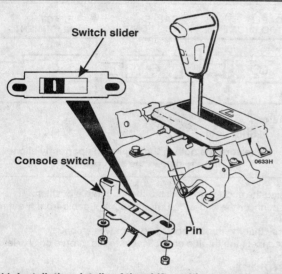

Switch slider

Console switch

Pin

0633H

**3.11 Installation details of the shift position console switch - note the position in which the switch slider must be when installing the switch (Park)**

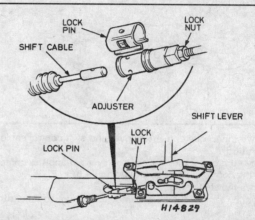

LOCK PIN

LOCK NUT

SHIFT CABLE

ADJUSTER

SHIFT LEVER

LOCK PIN

LOCK NUT

H14829

**4.2 Details of the shift cable, adjuster and retaining clip assembly**

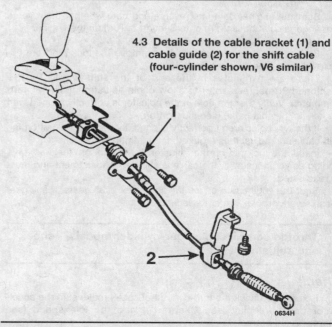

1

2

0634H

**4.3 Details of the cable bracket (1) and cable guide (2) for the shift cable (four-cylinder shown, V6 similar)**

13 Move the shift lever to the Park position, then install the new switch.

14 Attach the new switch with the two nuts and washers.

15 Test the new switch as described above in Step 3. Make sure the engine starts when the shift lever is in the Neutral or Park position.

16 Reconnect the connectors. Clamp the harness.

17 Install the console (see Chapter 11).

## 4 Shift control cable - replacement and adjustment

### Replacement

*Refer to illustrations 4.2, 4.3 and 4.6*

**Warning:** *The vehicles covered by this manual are equipped with airbags. Always disable the airbag system before working in the vicinity of the steering column, instrument panel or console to avoid the possibility of accidental deployment of the airbag, which could cause personal injury (see Chapter 12). The yellow wiring harness and connectors routed through the console and instrument panel are used for the airbag system. Do not use electrical test equipment on the system wiring or connectors or tamper with them in any way.*

**Caution:** *The stereo in your vehicle is equipped with an anti-theft system. Make sure you have the correct activation code before disconnecting the battery.*

1 Remove the front console (see Chapter 11).

2 Remove the lock pin from the cable adjuster **(see illustration)**.

3 Remove the bolts, then remove the cable bracket and cable guide **(see illustration)**.

4 Remove the exhaust pipe (see Chapter 4) and the center beam (see Section 7).

5 Remove the engine stiffener.

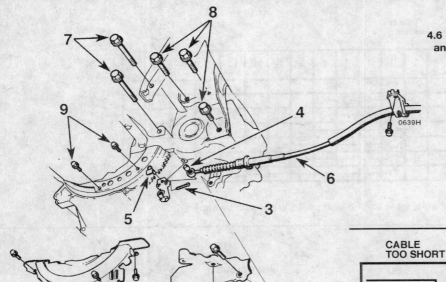

**4.6  Details of the transaxle end of the shift cable and related components (four-cylinder shown, V6 similar)**

1   Torque converter cover
2   Shift control cable holder
3   Cotter pin
4   Control lever bushing
5   Control lever pin
6   Shift control cable
7   Transaxle housing mounting bolts
8   Rear engine mount bracket bolts
9   Torque converter-to-driveplate bolts

**4.13  Make sure the hole in the adjuster is perfectly aligned with the hole in the shift cable**

6   Remove the torque converter cover and shift control cable holder **(see illustration)**.
7   Remove the cotter pin, the control lever pin and the control lever roller from the control lever **(see illustration 4.6)**.
8   Remove the shift cable.
9   Installation is the reverse of removal. Be sure to adjust the shift cable when you're through.

## Adjustment

*Refer to illustration 4.13*
10   Start the engine. Shift into reverse and note whether the reverse gear engages. If it doesn't, refer to Section 2. Turn off the engine.
11   Remove the console (see Chapter 11).
12   Shift to the Neutral position, then remove the lock pin from the cable adjuster **(see illustration 4.2)**.
13   There are two holes in the end of the shift cable. They're positioned 90-degrees apart to allow cable adjustments in 1/4-turn increments. Verify that the hole in the adjuster is perfectly aligned with the hole in the shift cable **(see illustration)**.
14   If the two holes aren't perfectly aligned, loosen the locknut on the shift cable and adjust it as required, then retighten the locknut.
15   Install the lock pin on the adjuster. If the lock pin feels as if it's binding as you reinstall it, the cable is still out of adjustment and must be readjusted.
16   Start the engine and check the shift lever in all gears. If any gear doesn't work properly, refer to Section 2.

## 5   Throttle control cable (four-cylinder models) - check and adjustment

## Check

1   Before you check the throttle control cable, make sure the accelerator cable freeplay (see Chapter 4) and the idle speed (see Chapter 1) are correct.
2   Warm up the engine to its proper operating temperature.
3   Verify that the throttle control lever is synchronized with the throttle linkage while depressing and releasing the accelerator pedal.
4   If the throttle control lever isn't synchronized with the throttle linkage, adjust the throttle control cable (see below).
5   Verify that there's play in the throttle control lever while depressing the accelerator pedal to the full-throttle position.
6   Disconnect the end of the throttle control cable from the throttle control lever.
7   Verify that the throttle control lever moves smoothly.
8   Reconnect the throttle control cable to the throttle control lever.

## Adjustment

*Refer to illustration 5.11*
9   Follow Steps 1 and 2 above.
10   Verify that the throttle linkage is in the fully-closed position.
11   Loosen the lower locknut on the throttle control cable at the throttle control lever **(see illustration)**.
12   While pushing the throttle control lever to the fully-closed position, remove all freeplay from the throttle control cable by tightening the upper locknut.
13   Tighten the lower locknut.
14   After the locknut is tightened, check the synchronization and throttle control lever movement.
15   After tightening the locknuts, check the operation of the throttle control cable.

## 6   Interlock system - description, check and solenoid replacement and adjustment

## Description

1   Vehicles equipped with an automatic transaxle have an interlock system to prevent unintentional shifting. The interlock system consists of two subsystems: a shift lock system and a key interlock system.

### Key interlock system

2   The key interlock system prevents the ignition key from being removed from the ignition switch unless the shift lever is in the Park position. If you insert the key when the shift lever is in any position other than Park, a solenoid is activated, making it impossible for you to remove the key until the shift lever is moved to the Park position.

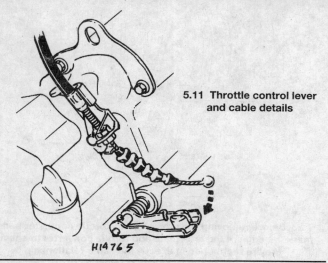

**5.11 Throttle control lever and cable details**

H14765

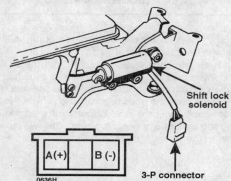

Shift lock solenoid

A(+)    B(-)

0636H

3-P connector

**6.11 Terminal guide for the shift lock solenoid connector (as seen from the terminal side of the connector)**

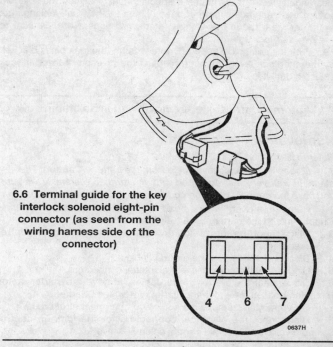

**6.6 Terminal guide for the key interlock solenoid eight-pin connector (as seen from the wiring harness side of the connector)**

4    6    7

0637H

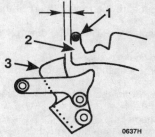

1

2

3

0637H

**6.18 Energize the solenoid, check the clearance between the top of the shift lock lever and the lock pin groove (arrows) and compare your measurement to the clearance listed in this Chapter's Specifications**

## Shift lock system

3    The shift lock system prevents the shift lever from moving from the Park position into the Reverse or Drive positions unless the brake pedal is depressed. Nor can the shift lever be shifted when the brake pedal and the accelerator pedal are depressed at the same time. In the event of a system malfunction, you can release the shift lever by inserting a key into the release slot near the shift lever.

## *Check*

4    The following checks are simple tests of the key interlock solenoid and the shift lock solenoid you can do at home. Further testing of the interlock system should be left to a dealer service department.

### Key interlock solenoid

*Refer to illustration 6.6*

5    Remove the lower instrument panel and knee bolster (see Chapter 11).
6    Disconnect the 8-pin electrical connector from the main wire harness **(see illustration)**.
7    Check for continuity between the terminals in each switch position. With the key pushed in, there should be continuity between terminals 4, 6 and 7; with the key released, there should be continuity between terminals 6 and 7.
8    Verify that the key can't be removed when the battery is connected to the 4 and 7 terminals.
9    If the key can't be removed, the key interlock solenoid is okay; if the key can be removed, the steering lock assembly needs to be replaced (see Chapter 12). The key interlock solenoid isn't available separately.

### Shift lock solenoid

*Refer to illustration 6.11*

10    Remove the console (see Chapter 11).
11    Disconnect the three-pin electrical connector for the shift lock solenoid **(see illustration)** from the dashboard wiring harness.
12    Using a pair of jumper wires, momentarily touch a positive battery lead to the A terminal of the three-pin connector and a negative lead to the B terminal and note whether the solenoid clicks on or not. If it doesn't, replace it. **Caution:** *Make sure you don't connect the battery voltage leads to the wrong connector terminals. Reversing the polarity can damage or destroy the diode inside the solenoid.*
13    Also, while the solenoid is on, check the clearance between the top of the shift lock lever and the lock pin groove (see below).
14    With the solenoid turned off, note whether the lock pin is blocked by the shift lock lever. If it isn't, adjust the position of the shift lock solenoid until it is (see below).

## *Solenoid replacement and adjustment*

*Refer to illustration 6.18*

**Note:** *The following procedure pertains only to the shift lock solenoid. For information on how to replace the key interlock solenoid, refer to the "Ignition switch/key lock cylinder replacement" Section in Chapter 12. The key interlock solenoid isn't available separately.*

15    Remove the E-ring and the solenoid pin.
16    Remove the self-locking nuts and the shift lock solenoid.
17    Installation is the reverse of removal.
18    To adjust the shift lock solenoid, energize the solenoid and check the clearance between the top of the shift lock lever and the lock pin groove **(see illustration)** and compare your measurement to the

clearance listed in this Chapter's Specifications. Position the solenoid so that the clearance is correct, then tighten the new self-locking nuts to the torque listed in this Chapter's specifications. **Note**: *Be sure to use new self-locking nuts.*

19   With the solenoid turned off, note whether the lock pin is blocked by the shift lock lever. If it isn't, readjust the position of the shift lock solenoid until it is.

## 7   Automatic transaxle - removal and installation

### *Removal*

*Refer to illustration 7.23*

1   *Disconnect the negative cable from the battery.* **Caution:** *The stereo in your vehicle is equipped with an anti-theft system. Make sure you have the correct activation code before disconnecting the battery.*

2   Remove the air intake hose and the air cleaner case (see Chapter 4) and the battery case (see Chapter 5).

3   Disconnect the throttle control cable from the throttle control lever (see Section 5).

4   Disconnect the transaxle ground cable.

5   Disconnect the speed sensor electrical connectors.

6   Disconnect the starter motor cables, remove the starter motor mounting bolts and remove the starter motor (see Chapter 5).

7   On V6 models, remove the engine compartment strut brace.

8   Disconnect the electrical connectors for the lock-up control solenoid valve and the shift control solenoid valve.

9   Raise the vehicle and support it securely on jackstands.

10   Remove the splash shield underneath the forward part of the vehicle.

11   Drain the transaxle fluid (see Chapter 1). Reinstall the drain plug. Be sure to use a new washer.

12   Disconnect the transmission fluid cooler hoses.

13   Remove the center beam (the large longitudinal support member running underneath the engine).

14   Disconnect the electrical connector for the oxygen sensor (see Chapter 6).

15   Remove the exhaust pipe (see Chapter 4).

16   Disconnect the lower arms from the steering knuckles (see Chapter 10).

17   Separate the driveaxles from the differential (see Chapter 8). Cover the inner CV joints with plastic bags to keep them clean.

18   Remove the right (four-cylinder models) or left (V6 models) damper fork (see Chapter 10).

19   Remove the right (four-cylinder models) or left (V6 models) radius rod (see Chapter 10).

20   Remove the torque converter access plate **(see illustration 4.6)**.

21   Remove the shift control cable holder.

22   Remove the shift control cable (see Section 4).

23   Mark the relationship of the torque converter to the driveplate so they can be installed in the same position **(see illustration)**.

24   Remove the torque converter-to-driveplate bolts **(see illustration 7.23)**. Turn the crankshaft pulley bolt for access to each bolt.

25   Remove the two rear transaxle housing bolts on the engine side **(see illustration 4.6)**.

26   Remove the bolts from the rear engine mounting bracket **(see illustration 4.6)**

27   Remove the intake manifold bracket (four-cylinder models) or rear mounting bracket (V6 models).

28   Using a floor jack, with a wood block on the jack head to serve as a cushion, support the engine under the oil pan. Position the jack head as close to the transaxle end of the engine as possible. **Caution:** *The pickup for the oil pump is very close to the bottom of the oil pan. If the pan is bent or distorted in any way, engine oil starvation could occur.*

29   Place a transmission jack or a floor jack under the transaxle. Raise the transaxle assembly just enough to take the load off the transaxle mount.

30   Remove the transaxle housing mounting bolts and mounting

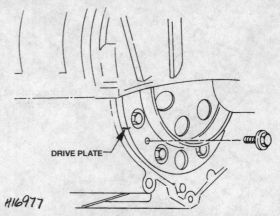

**DRIVE PLATE**

H16977

**7.23 Before removing the driveplate-to-torque converter bolts, mark the edge of the driveplate and torque converter to ensure they're reattached in exactly the same relationship when the transaxle is reinstalled**

bracket nuts.

31   Remove any other chassis or suspension components which might interfere with transaxle removal.

32   Move the transaxle back to disengage it from the engine block dowel pins and make sure the torque converter is detached from the driveplate. Secure the torque converter to the transaxle so it will not fall out during removal. Lower the transaxle from the vehicle. **Note:** *It may be necessary to slowly lower the jack supporting the engine while the jack supporting the transaxle is being lowered. This will provide more clearance between the transaxle and the body.*

### *Installation*

33   The manufacturer recommends flushing the transmission cooler and cooler hoses/lines with solvent whenever the transmission is removed from the vehicle. Use an approved solvent, such as Honda J-35944-20 or equivalent. Flush the lines and fluid cooler thoroughly and make sure no solvent remains in the lines or cooler after flushing.

34   Prior to installation, make sure that the torque converter hub is securely engaged in the pump.

35   With the transaxle secured to the jack, raise it into position. Be sure to keep it level so the torque converter does not slide out.

36   Turn the torque converter to line it up with the driveplate. The white paint mark on the torque converter and the driveplate in Step 23 must line up.

37   Make sure the two dowel pins are still installed, then move the transaxle forward carefully until the dowel pins and the torque converter are engaged.

38   Install the four transaxle housing-to-engine bolts. Tighten them to the torque listed in this Chapter's Specifications. **Caution:** *Don't use the bolts to force the transaxle and engine together. If the transaxle doesn't slide easily up against the engine, find out why before you tighten the bolts.*

39   The remainder of installation is the reverse of removal.

40   Refill the transaxle with fluid to the specified level (see Chapter 1). Note that the transaxle may require more fluid than in a normal fluid and filter change, since the torque converter may be empty (the converter is not drained during a fluid change).

41   Start the engine, set the parking brake and shift the transaxle through all gears three times. Make sure the shift control cable is working properly (see Section 4).

42   Check and, if necessary, adjust the ignition timing (see Chapter 1).

43   Allow the engine to reach its proper operating temperature with the transaxle in Park or Neutral, then turn it off and check the fluid level.

44   Road test the vehicle and check for fluid leaks.

# Chapter 8
# Clutch and driveaxles

## Contents

## Specifications

### General

| | |
|---|---|
| Clutch pedal disengagement height | 3 to 3-1/2 inches |
| Clutch pedal freeplay | 3/8 to 5/8 inch |
| Clutch pedal standard height | 7-1/4 inches |
| Clutch pedal stroke | 5-3/4 inches |

### Driveaxles

Driveaxle length
| | |
|---|---|
| Four-cylinder engine | |
|   Manual transaxle | 19-1/8 to 19-5/16 inches |
|   Automatic transaxle | |
|     Left | 33-15/16 to 33-1/2 inches |
|     Right | 19-1/8 to 19-5/16 inches |
|   V6 engine | |
|     Left | 19-13/16 to 20-3/16 inches |
|     Right | 20-13/64 to 20-13/32 inches |

### Torque specifications

| | Ft-lbs |
|---|---|
| Clutch pressure plate bolts | 19 |
| Driveaxle/hub nut | 181 |
| Intermediate shaft bearing support bolts | |
|   Four-cylinder engine | 28 |
|   V6 engine | 16 |

**3.3 Pinch off the fluid feed hose with a pair of locking pliers to prevent the fluid from running out of the end of the hose when you disconnect it from the clutch master cylinder**

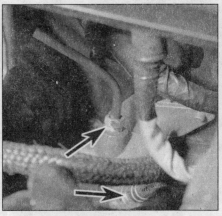

**3.4 To disconnect the clutch fluid lines from the master cylinder, loosen the hose clamp (right arrow) on the feed line and use a flare-nut wrench to loosen the pressure line (left arrow)**

**4.3 Using a flare-nut wrench, disconnect the clutch fluid line at the release cylinder (upper arrow), then remove the two mounting bolts (lower arrows)**

## 1  General information

The information in this Chapter deals with the components from the rear of the engine to the front wheels, except for the transaxle, which is dealt with in the previous Chapter. For the purposes of this Chapter, these components are grouped into two categories - clutch and driveaxles. Separate Sections within this Chapter offer general descriptions and checking procedures for components in each of the two groups.

Since nearly all the procedures covered in this Chapter involve working under the vehicle, make sure it's securely supported on sturdy jackstands or on a hoist where the vehicle can be easily raised and lowered.

## 2  Clutch - description and check

1  All vehicles with a manual transaxle use a single dry-plate, diaphragm-spring type clutch. The clutch disc has a splined hub which allows it to slide along the splines of the transmission input shaft. The clutch and pressure plate are held in contact by spring pressure exerted by the diaphragm in the pressure plate.

2  The clutch release system is operated by hydraulic pressure. The hydraulic release system consists of the clutch pedal, a master cylinder and fluid reservoir, the hydraulic line, a release (or slave) cylinder which actuates the clutch release lever and the clutch release (or throwout) bearing.

3  When pressure is applied to the clutch pedal to release the clutch, hydraulic pressure is exerted against the outer end of the clutch release lever. As the lever pivots the shaft fingers push against the release bearing. The bearing pushes against the fingers of the diaphragm spring of the pressure plate assembly, which in turn releases the clutch plate.

4  Terminology can be a problem when discussing the clutch components because common names are in some cases different from those used by the manufacturer. For example, the driven plate is also called the clutch plate or disc, the clutch release bearing is sometimes called a throwout bearing, the release cylinder is sometimes called the operating or slave cylinder.

5  Other than to replace components with obvious damage, some preliminary checks should be performed to diagnose clutch problems. These checks assume that the transaxle is in good working condition.

   a) *The first check should be of the fluid level in the clutch master cylinder (see Chapter 1). If the fluid level is low, add fluid as necessary and inspect the hydraulic system for leaks. If the master cylinder reservoir has run dry, bleed the system as described in*

*Section 5 and retest the clutch operation.*
   b) *To check "clutch spin-down time," run the engine at normal idle speed with the transmission in Neutral (clutch pedal up - engaged). Disengage the clutch (pedal down), wait several seconds and shift the transmission into Reverse. No grinding noise should be heard. A grinding noise would most likely indicate a problem in the pressure plate or the clutch disc.*
   c) *To check for complete clutch release, run the engine (with the parking brake applied to prevent movement) and hold the clutch pedal approximately 1/2-inch from the floor. Shift the transmission between 1st gear and Reverse several times. If the shift is rough, component failure is indicated. Check the release cylinder pushrod travel. With the clutch pedal depressed completely, the release cylinder pushrod should extend substantially. If it doesn't, check the fluid level in the clutch master cylinder.*
   d) *Visually inspect the pivot bushing at the top of the clutch pedal to make sure there is no binding or excessive play.*
   e) *Crawl under the vehicle and make sure the clutch release lever is solidly mounted on the ball stud.*

## 3  Clutch master cylinder - removal and installation

### Removal

*Refer to illustrations 3.3 and 3.4*

1  *Disconnect the cable from the negative battery terminal.* **Caution:** *The stereo in your vehicle is equipped with an anti-theft system. Make sure you have the correct activation code before disconnecting the battery.*

2  Working under the dashboard, remove the cotter pin from the master cylinder pushrod clevis. Pull out the clevis pin to disconnect the pushrod from the pedal.

3  Clamp a pair of locking pliers onto the clutch fluid feed hose, a couple of inches downstream of the reservoir **(see illustration)**. The pliers should be just tight enough to prevent fluid flow when the hose is disconnected.

4  Disconnect the hydraulic lines at the cylinder **(see illustration)**. Loosen the fluid feed hose clamp and detach the hose from the cylinder. Have rags handy as some fluid will be lost as the line is removed. Cap or plug the ends of the lines (and/or hose) to prevent fluid leakage and the entry of contaminants. **Caution:** *Don't allow brake fluid to come into contact with the paint as it will damage the finish.*

5  Working under the dash, unscrew the two clutch master cylinder retaining nuts and remove the cylinder.

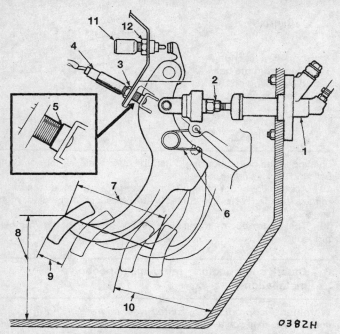

**6.1 Clutch pedal adjustment details**

| | | | |
|---|---|---|---|
| 1 | Clutch master cylinder | 7 | Stroke at pedal |
| 2 | Locknut C | 8 | Clutch pedal height |
| 3 | Locknut A | 9 | Clutch pedal freeplay |
| 4 | Clutch pedal switch A | 10 | Clutch pedal |
| 5 | Pedal in contact with | | disengagement height |
| | switch | 11 | Clutch pedal switch B |
| 6 | Clutch assist spring | 12 | Locknut B |

## Installation

6    Place the master cylinder in position and install the mounting nuts finger tight.

7    Connect the hydraulic lines to the master cylinder. Move the cylinder slightly as necessary to thread the fitting into the cylinder (don't tighten the fitting yet). Attach the fluid feed hose to the cylinder and tighten the hose clamp.

8    Tighten the mounting nuts securely, then tighten the hydraulic line fitting securely.

9    Connect the pushrod to the clutch pedal. Use a new cotter pin to secure the clevis pin.

10    Remove the locking pliers from the feed hose. Fill the clutch master cylinder reservoir with brake fluid conforming to DOT 3 specifications and bleed the clutch system as outlined in Section 5.

## 4    Clutch release cylinder - removal and installation

### Removal

*Refer to illustration 4.3*

1    Disconnect the negative cable from the battery. **Caution:** *The stereo in your vehicle is equipped with an anti-theft system. Make sure you have the correct activation code before disconnecting the battery.*

2    Raise the vehicle and support it securely on jackstands.

3    Disconnect the fluid hose at the release cylinder. Use a flare nut wrench so you don't round-off the fitting **(see illustration)**. Have a small can and rags handy, as some fluid will be spilled as the line is removed.

4    Remove the two release cylinder mounting bolts.

5    Remove the release cylinder.

### Installation

6    Install the release cylinder on the clutch housing, but don't

completely tighten the bolts yet. Make sure the pushrod is seated in the release fork pocket.

7    Connect the hydraulic line to the release cylinder, then tighten the release cylinder mounting bolts securely. Using a flare-nut wrench, tighten the hydraulic fitting securely.

8    Fill the clutch master cylinder with brake fluid conforming to DOT 3 specifications.

9    Bleed the system as described in Section 5.

10    Lower the vehicle and connect the negative battery cable.

## 5    Clutch hydraulic system - bleeding

1    Bleed the hydraulic system whenever any part of the system has been removed or the fluid level has fallen so low that air has been drawn into the master cylinder. The bleeding procedure is very similar to bleeding a brake system.

2    Fill the master cylinder with new brake fluid conforming to DOT 3 specifications. **Caution:** *Do not re-use any of the fluid coming from the system during the bleeding operation or use fluid which has been inside an open container for an extended period of time.*

3    Raise the vehicle and place it securely on jackstands to gain access to the release cylinder, which is located on the front of the transaxle.

4    Remove the dust cap which fits over the bleeder valve and push a length of plastic hose over the valve. Place the other end of the hose into a clear container with about two inches of brake fluid. The hose end must be in the fluid at the bottom of the container.

5    Have an assistant depress the clutch pedal and hold it. Open the bleeder valve on the release cylinder, allowing fluid to flow through the hose. Close the bleeder valve when the flow of fluid (and bubbles) ceases. Once closed, have your assistant release the pedal.

6    Continue this process until all air is evacuated from the system, indicated by a solid stream of fluid being ejected from the bleeder valve each time with no air bubbles in the hose or container. Keep a close watch on the fluid level inside the clutch master cylinder reservoir - if the level drops too far, air will get into the system and you'll have to start all over again.

7    Install the dust cap and lower the vehicle. Check carefully for proper operation before placing the vehicle into normal service.

## 6    Clutch pedal - adjustment

*Refer to illustration 6.1*

1    Loosen locknut A **(see illustration)**, then turn pedal switch A.

2    Loosen locknut C, then turn the pushrod in or out until the stroke and height of the pedal are within the range listed in the Specifications at the beginning of this Chapter.

3    Tighten locknut C.

4    Screw in clutch pedal switch A until it contacts the clutch pedal.

5    Turn the switch another 1/4 to 1/2-turn.

6    Tighten locknut A.

7    Loosen locknut B.

8    Push the clutch to the floor then raise it approximately 3/4-inch.

9    Screw in clutch pedal switch B until it contacts the clutch pedal.

10    Turn the switch another 1/4 to 1/2-turn.

11    Tighten locknut B.

## 7    Clutch release bearing and fork - removal, inspection and installation

**Warning:** *Dust produced by clutch wear and deposited on clutch components may contain asbestos, which is hazardous to your health. DO NOT blow it out with compressed air and DO NOT inhale it. DO NOT use gasoline or petroleum-based solvents to remove the dust. Brake system cleaner should be used to flush the dust into a drain pan. After the clutch components are wiped clean with a rag, dispose of the contaminated rags and cleaner in a labeled, covered container.*

**7.3a  Slide the bearing off the input shaft . . .**

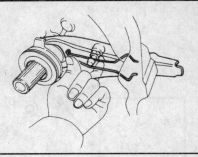

7.3b  . . . then disengage the fork from the ball stud by pulling on the retention spring

## Removal

*Refer to illustrations 7.3a and 7.3b*

1    Unbolt the clutch release cylinder (see Section 4), but don't disconnect the fluid line between the master cylinder and the release cylinder. Suspend the release cylinder out of the way with a piece of wire.
2    Remove the transaxle (see Chapter 7, Part A).
3    Slide the release bearing off the input shaft, lift the clutch release fork off the ball stud and remove the fork **(see illustrations)**.

## Inspection

4    Hold the bearing by the outer race and rotate the inner race while applying pressure. If the bearing doesn't turn smoothly or if it's noisy, replace the bearing/hub assembly with a new one. Wipe the bearing with a clean rag and inspect it for damage, wear and cracks. It's common practice to replace the bearing with a new one whenever a clutch job is performed, to decrease the possibility of a bearing failure in the future. Don't immerse the bearing in solvent - it's sealed for life and to do so would ruin it. Also check the release lever for cracks and bends.
5    If the new bearing is not equipped with a bearing holder (hub), drive the holder from the old bearing and install it to the new one. A seal/bushing driver or an appropriately sized socket can be used to accomplish this.

## Installation

*Refer to illustrations 7.6 and 7.7*

6    Fill the inner groove of the release bearing with high temperature grease. Also apply a light coat of the same grease to the transaxle input shaft splines and the front bearing retainer **(see illustration)**.
7    Lubricate the release fork ball socket, fork ends and release cylinder pushrod socket with high temperature grease **(see illustration)**.
8    Attach the release bearing to the release fork.
9    Slide the release bearing onto the transaxle input shaft front bearing retainer while passing the end of the release fork through the

opening in the clutch housing. Push the clutch release fork onto the ball stud until it's firmly seated.
10    Apply a light coat of high temperature grease to the face of the release bearing where it contacts the pressure plate diaphragm fingers.
11    The remainder of installation is the reverse of the removal procedure.

## 8    Clutch components - removal, inspection and installation

**Warning:** *Dust produced by clutch wear and deposited on clutch components may contain asbestos, which is hazardous to your health. DO NOT blow it out with compressed air and DO NOT inhale it. DO NOT use gasoline or petroleum-based solvents to remove the dust. Brake system cleaner should be used to flush the dust into a drain pan. After the clutch components are wiped clean with a rag, dispose of the contaminated rags and cleaner in a covered, marked container.*

## Removal

*Refer to illustrations 8.5 and 8.6*

1    Access to the clutch components is normally accomplished by removing the transaxle, leaving the engine in the vehicle. If the engine is being removed for major overhaul, check the clutch for wear and replace worn components as necessary. However, the relatively low cost of the clutch components compared to the time and trouble spent gaining access to them warrants their replacement anytime the engine or transaxle is removed, unless they are new or in near-perfect condition. The following procedures are based on the assumption the engine will stay in place.
2    Remove the transaxle from the vehicle (see Chapter 7, Part A). Support the engine while the transaxle is out. Preferably, an engine hoist should be used to support it from above. However, if a jack is used underneath the engine, make sure a piece of wood is positioned between the jack and oil pan to spread the load. **Caution:** *The pickup for the oil pump is very close to the bottom of the oil pan. If the pan is bent or distorted in any way, engine oil starvation could occur.*
3    The clutch fork and release bearing can remain attached to the transaxle housing for the time being.
4    To support the clutch disc during removal, install a clutch alignment tool through the clutch disc hub.
5    Carefully inspect the flywheel and pressure plate for indexing marks. The marks are usually an X, an O or a white letter. If they cannot

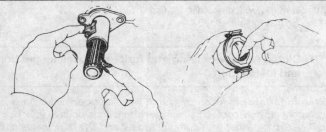

**7.6  Fill the inner groove of the release bearing with high temperature grease and apply a light coat to the transaxle input shaft splines and the front bearing retainer**

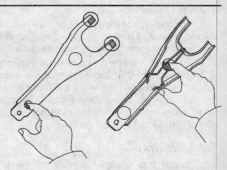

7.7  Lubricate the release fork ball socket, fork ends and release cylinder pushrod socket with high temperature grease

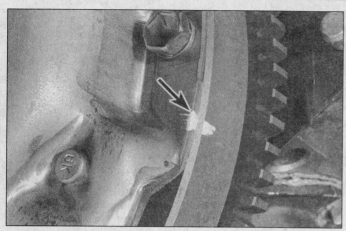

**8.5  Mark the relationship of the pressure plate to the flywheel (if you're going to reuse the old pressure plate)**

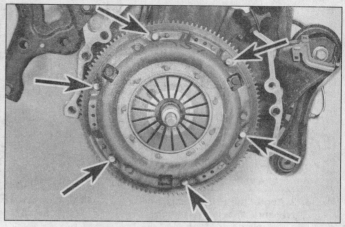

**8.6  Remove the pressure plate bolts (arrows) gradually and evenly in a criss-cross pattern**

be found, scribe or paint marks yourself so the pressure plate and the flywheel will be in the same alignment during installation **(see illustration)**.

6    Turning each bolt a little at a time, loosen the pressure plate-to-flywheel bolts **(see illustration)**. Work in a criss-cross pattern until all spring pressure is relieved. Then hold the pressure plate securely and completely remove the bolts, followed by the pressure plate and clutch disc.

## Inspection

*Refer to illustrations 8.9 and 8.11*

7    Ordinarily, when a problem occurs in the clutch, it can be attributed to wear of the clutch driven plate assembly (clutch disc). However, all components should be inspected at this time.

8    Inspect the flywheel for cracks, heat checking, grooves and other obvious defects. If the imperfections are slight, a machine shop can machine the surface flat and smooth, which is highly recommended regardless of the surface appearance. Refer to Chapter 2 for the flywheel removal and installation procedure.

9    Inspect the lining on the clutch disc. There should be at least 1/16-inch of lining above the rivet heads. Check for loose rivets, distortion, cracks, broken springs and other obvious damage **(see illustration)**. As mentioned above, ordinarily the clutch disc is routinely

replaced, so if in doubt about the condition, replace it with a new one.

10    The release bearing should also be replaced along with the clutch disc (see Section 7).

11    Check the machined surfaces and the diaphragm spring fingers of the pressure plate **(see illustration)**. If the surface is grooved or otherwise damaged, replace the pressure plate. Also check for obvious damage, distortion, cracking, etc. Light glazing can be removed with emery cloth or sandpaper. If a new pressure plate is required, new and factory-rebuilt units are available.

## Installation

*Refer to illustration 8.13*

12    Before installation, clean the flywheel and pressure plate machined surfaces with aerosol brake system cleaner, lacquer thinner or acetone. It's important that no oil or grease is on these surfaces or the lining of the clutch disc. Handle the parts only with clean hands.

13    Position the clutch disc and pressure plate against the flywheel with the clutch held in place with an alignment tool **(see illustration)**.

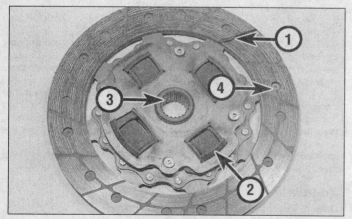

**8.9  The clutch disc**

1    **Lining** - this will wear down in use
2    **Springs or dampers** - check for cracking and deformation
3    **Splined hub** - the splines must not be worn and should slide smoothly on the transaxle input shaft splines
4    **Rivets** - these secure the lining and will damage the flywheel or pressure plate if allowed to contact the surfaces

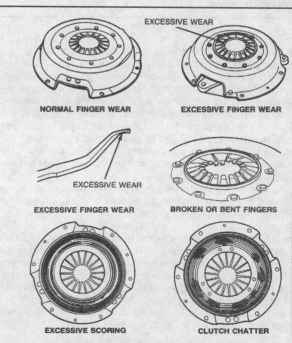

**8.11  Replace the pressure plate if any of these conditions are noted**

**8.13  Center the clutch disc in the pressure plate with a clutch alignment tool**

**10.1  If the driveaxle nut is "staked," use a small chisel to unstake it**

**10.2  To prevent the hub from turning while you're loosening it, place a prybar between two of the wheel studs**

Make sure it's installed properly (most replacement clutch plates will be marked "flywheel side" or something similar - if not marked, install the clutch disc with the damper springs toward the transaxle).
14    Tighten the pressure plate-to-flywheel bolts only finger tight, working around the pressure plate.
15    Center the clutch disc by ensuring the alignment tool extends through the splined hub and into the pocket in the crankshaft. Wiggle the tool up, down or side-to-side as needed to center the disc. Tighten the pressure plate-to-flywheel bolts a little at a time, working in a criss-cross pattern to prevent distorting the cover. After all of the bolts are snug, tighten them to the torque listed in this Chapter's Specifications. Remove the alignment tool.
16    Using high-temperature grease, lubricate the inner groove of the release bearing (see Section 7). Also place grease on the release lever contact areas and the transaxle input shaft bearing retainer.
17    Install the clutch release bearing (see Section 7).
18    Install the transaxle and all components removed previously.

**9    Starter/clutch interlock switch - check, replacement and adjustment**

### Check

1    The starter/clutch interlock switch is located near the upper end of the clutch pedal (pedal switch B in **illustration 6.1**). It has two wires - one coming from the starter relay and one going to ground. When the ignition switch key is turned to the Start position and the clutch pedal is depressed, the starter relay's path to ground is closed by the starter/clutch interlock switch and the starter motor is activated.
2    If the engine won't start when the clutch pedal is depressed, adjust the switch (see Step 6) and try again. If it still won't start, check the switch (see Step 3) and, if necessary, replace it (see Step 5). If the engine starts when the clutch pedal isn't depressed, adjust the switch and try again.
3    If the engine won't start when the clutch pedal is depressed, either there's no voltage from the starter relay to the switch, or there's no continuity between the two terminals on the switch.
4    Check the voltage to the switch with a voltmeter or test light. When you turn the ignition key to the Start position and depress the clutch pedal, there should be voltage in the wire from the starter relay. If there isn't, look for an open or short circuit condition somewhere between the starter relay and the switch. If there is voltage in this wire, check the other side of the switch for voltage (with the pedal depressed). If there's voltage on both sides of the switch, the switch should be operating correctly. Try adjusting it (see Step 6). If voltage isn't present on both sides, the switch is bad.

### Replacement

5    Disconnect the electrical connector, loosen the adjustment nut

and unscrew the switch from its mounting bracket. Installation is the reverse of removal.

### Adjustment

6    Loosen the locknut and turn the switch in or out, as necessary, to provide continuity through the switch when the clutch pedal is depressed.

**10    Driveaxles - removal and installation**

### Removal

*Refer to illustrations 10.1, 10.2, 10.6, 10.7a and 10.7b*
1    Remove the hub cap or lug nut cover. If the driveaxle/hub nut is staked, unstake it with a chisel **(see illustration)**; if it's secured by locking tabs, bend the tabs out. Break the hub nut loose with a socket and large breaker bar. Loosen the wheel lug nuts, raise the front of the vehicle and support it securely on jackstands. Remove the wheel lug nuts and the front wheel.
2    Remove the driveaxle hub nut. To prevent the hub from turning, place a prybar between two of the wheel studs, then loosen the nut **(see illustration)**.
3    Drain the transaxle lubricant (see Chapter 1).
4    Disconnect the damper fork from the shock absorber assembly and the lower control arm (see Chapter 10).
5    Separate the lower control arm from the steering knuckle (see Chapter 10).
6    Swing the knuckle/hub assembly out (away from the vehicle) until the end of the driveaxle is free of the hub **(see illustration)**. Support the outer end of the driveaxle with a piece of wire to avoid unnecessary strain on the inner CV joint.
7    Carefully pry the inner end of the driveaxle from the transaxle or intermediate shaft, using a large screwdriver or prybar positioned between the transaxle or bearing support and the CV joint housing **(see illustrations)**. Support the CV joints and carefully remove the driveaxle from the vehicle. To prevent damage to the intermediate shaft seal or the differential seal, hold the inner CV joint horizontal until the driveaxle is clear of the intermediate shaft or transaxle.

### Installation

*Refer to illustrations 10.8a, 10.8b and 10.9*
8    Pry the old spring clip from the inner end of the driveaxle and install a new one **(see illustrations)**. Lubricate the differential or intermediate shaft seal with multi-purpose grease and raise the driveaxle into position while supporting the CV joints.
9    Insert the splined end of the inner CV joint into the differential side gear or the intermediate shaft and make sure the spring clip locks in its groove **(see illustration)**.
10    Apply a light coat of multi-purpose grease to the outer CV joint

**10.6  Swing the hub/knuckle out (away from the vehicle) and pull the driveaxle from the hub**

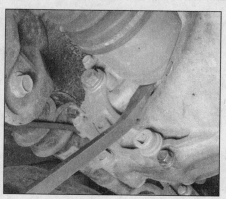

**10.7a  If you're removing the right (passenger's) side driveaxle, use a large screwdriver or a prybar to pop the inner end of the driveaxle from the transaxle, or . . .**

**10.7b  . . . if you're removing the left (driver's) side driveaxle, insert the prybar between the intermediate shaft bearing and the driveaxle to pop it loose**

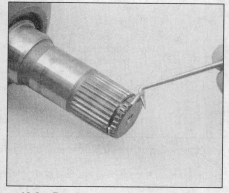

**10.8a  Pry the old spring clip from the inner end of the driveaxle with a small screwdriver or awl**

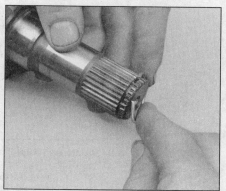

**10.8b  To install the new spring clip, start one end in the groove and work the clip over the shaft end, into the groove**

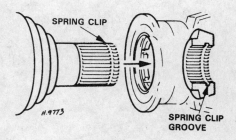

**10.9  When installing the driveaxle, make sure the spring clip pops into place in its groove - if it's seated properly, you shouldn't be able to pull it out by hand**

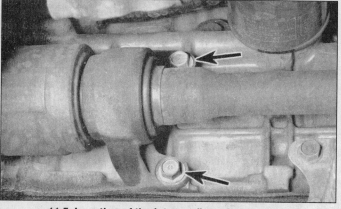

**11.5  Location of the intermediate shaft bearing support bolts (arrows)**

splines, pull out on the strut/steering knuckle assembly and install the stub axle into the hub.

11    Insert the stud of the lower control arm balljoint into the steering knuckle and tighten the nut (see the torque specifications in Chapter 10). Be sure to use a new cotter pin. Install the damper fork (see Chapter 10).

12    Install the hub nut (and, if applicable, a new locking tab washer). Lock the disc as described in Step 2 so it can't turn, then tighten the hub nut securely. Don't try to tighten it to the actual torque specifi-

cation until you've lowered the vehicle to the ground.

13    Grasp the inner CV joint housing (not the driveaxle) and pull out to make sure the driveaxle has seated securely in the transaxle.

14    Install the wheel and lug nuts, then lower the vehicle.

15    Tighten the lug nuts to the torque listed in the Chapter 1 Specifications. Tighten the hub nut to the torque listed in this Chapter's Specifications. Using a hammer and punch, stake the nut to the groove in the driveaxle. If the hub nut uses a locking tab, be sure to bend the tabs up against the nut. Install the wheel cover (if applicable).

16    Refill the transaxle with the recommended type and amount of lubricant (see Chapter 1).

## 11    Intermediate shaft - removal and installation

### Removal

*Refer to illustration 11.5*

1    Loosen the left (driver's side) front wheel lug nuts, raise the front of the vehicle and support it securely on jackstands. Remove the wheel.

2    Drain the transaxle lubricant or automatic transmission fluid (see Chapter 1).

3    Separate the left lower control arm from the steering knuckle (see Chapter 10).

4    Pry the inner CV joint housing from the intermediate shaft. Position the driveaxle out of the way and hang it with a piece of wire. Do not allow it to hang unsupported, as the outer CV joint may be damaged.

5    Unscrew the bearing support-to-engine block bolts **(see illustration)** and slide the intermediate shaft out of the transaxle. Be careful

**12.3a  Cut off the boot clamps and discard them - don't try to reuse old clamps**

**12.3b  Slide the boot down the driveaxle, out of the way**

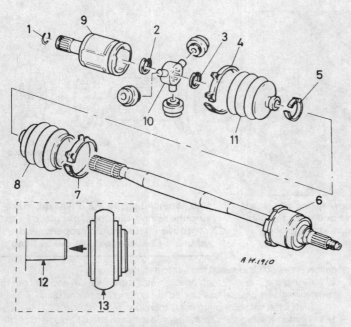

**12.3c  An exploded view of a typical driveaxle assembly**

| | | | |
|---|---|---|---|
| 1 | Spring clip | 8 | Boot |
| 2 | Snap-ring | 9 | Inner CV joint |
| 3 | Stop-ring | | housing/outer race |
| 4 | Boot clamp | 10 | Tri-pot assembly |
| 5 | Boot clamp | 11 | Boot |
| 6 | Outer CV joint assembly | 12 | Tri-pot post |
| 7 | Boot clamp | 13 | Roller bearing |

not to damage the differential seal when pulling the shaft out.

6    Check the support bearing for smooth operation by turning the shaft while holding the bearing. If you feel any roughness, take the bearing support to a dealer service department or other repair shop to have a new bearing installed. To do the job at home you'd need specialized tools.

## Installation

7    Lubricate the lips of the differential seal with multi-purpose grease. Carefully guide the intermediate shaft into the differential side gear then install the mounting bolts through the bearing support. Tighten the bolts to the torque listed in this Chapter's Specifications.

8    Install a new spring clip on the inner CV joint **(see illustrations**

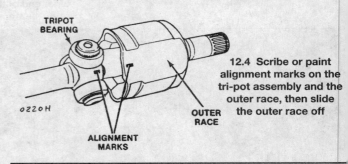

**12.4  Scribe or paint alignment marks on the tri-pot assembly and the outer race, then slide the outer race off**

**10.8a and 10.8b)** and seat the driveaxle into the intermediate shaft splines.

9    Connect the lower control arm to the steering knuckle and tighten the balljoint stud nut to the torque listed in the Chapter 10 Specifications.

10    Install the wheel and lug nuts, lower the vehicle and tighten the lug nuts to the torque listed in the Chapter 1 Specifications.

11    Refill the transaxle with the proper type and amount of lubricant (see Chapter 1).

## 12  Driveaxle boot replacement and constant velocity (CV) joint overhaul

**Note 1:** *If the CV joints are worn, indicating the need for an overhaul (usually due to torn boots), explore all options before beginning the job. Complete rebuilt driveaxles are available on an exchange basis, which eliminates much time and work. If you decide to rebuild a CV joint, check on the cost and availability of parts before disassembling the driveaxle.*

**Note 2:** *Some auto parts stores carry "split" type replacement boots, which can be installed without removing the driveaxle from the vehicle. This is a convenient alternative; however, the driveaxle should be removed and the CV joint disassembled and cleaned to ensure the joint is free from contaminants such as moisture and dirt which will accelerate CV joint wear.*

1    Remove the driveaxle from the vehicle (see Section 10).

2    Mount the driveaxle in a vise. The jaws of the vise should be lined with wood or rags to prevent damage to the driveaxle.

### Inner CV joint and boot

#### Disassembly

*Refer to illustrations 12.3a, 12.3b, 12.3c, 12.4, 12.5 and 12.6*

3    Cut off both boot clamps and slide the boot towards the center of the driveaxle **(see illustrations)**.

4    Scribe or paint alignment marks on the outer race and the tri-pot bearing assembly **(see illustration)** so they can be returned to their original position, then slide the outer race off the tri-pot bearing assembly.

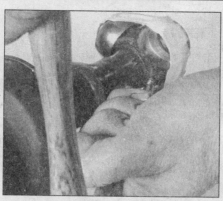

**12.5  Remove the snap-ring from the end of the axleshaft, then mark the relationship of the tri-pot bearing assembly to the axleshaft**

**12.6  Secure the bearing rollers with tape and drive the tri-pot off the shaft with a hammer and brass drift, then remove the stop-ring**

**12.10a  Wrap the splined area of the axleshaft with tape to prevent damage to the boot when installing it**

**12.10b  Install the stop-ring on the axleshaft, making sure it seats in its groove**

**12.12  Install the tri-pot assembly on the axleshaft, making sure the punch marks are lined up, then install the snap-ring**

**12.13  Use plenty of CV joint grease to hold the needle bearings in place when you install the roller assemblies on the tri-pot, and make sure you put each roller in its original position**

**12.14  Pack the outer race with grease and slide it over the tri-pot assembly - make sure the match marks on the outer race and tri-pot line up**

5    Remove the snap-ring from the end of the axleshaft, then mark the relationship of the tri-pot bearing assembly to the axleshaft **(see illustration)**.

6    Secure the bearing rollers with tape, then remove the tri-pot bearing assembly from the axleshaft with a brass drift and a hammer **(see illustration)**. Remove the tape, but don't let the rollers fall off and get mixed up.

7    Remove the stop-ring, slide the old boot off the driveaxle and discard it.

### Inspection

8    Clean the old grease from the outer race and the tri-pot bearing assembly. Carefully disassemble each section of the tri-pot assembly, one at a time so as not to mix up the parts, and clean the needle bearings with solvent.

9    Inspect the rollers, tri-pot, bearings and outer race for scoring, pitting or other signs of abnormal wear, which will warrant the replacement of the inner CV joint.

### Reassembly

*Refer to illustrations 12.10a, 12.10b, 12.12, 12.13, 12.14, 12.15, 12.16, 12.17a and 12.17b*

10   Wrap the splines of the axleshaft with tape to avoid damaging the new boot, then slide the boot onto the axleshaft **(see illustration)**. Remove the tape and slide the inner stop-ring into place **(see illustration)**.

11   Align the match marks you made before disassembly and tap the tri-pot assembly onto the axleshaft with a hammer and brass drift.

12   Install the outer snap-ring **(see illustration)**.

13   Apply a coat of CV joint grease to the inner bearing surfaces to hold the needle bearings in place when reassembling the tri-pot assembly **(see illustration)**. Make sure each roller is installed on the same post as before. **Note:** *If the rollers are equipped with a flat, rectangular shaped surface, make sure the flat sides are positioned closest to the driveaxle.*

14   Pack the outer race with half of the grease furnished with the new boot and place the remainder in the boot. Install the outer race **(see illustration)**. Make sure the marks you made on the tri-pot assembly and the outer race are aligned.

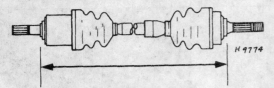

H 9774

**12.15  Before tightening the boot clamps, adjust the driveaxle length to the dimension listed in this Chapter's Specifications**

**12.17a  To install the new clamps, bend the tang down . . .**

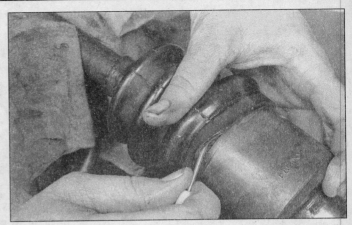

**12.16  Equalize the pressure inside the boot by inserting a small, dull screwdriver between the boot and the outer race**

**12.17b  . . . and flatten the tabs to hold it in place**

**12.23  After the old grease has been rinsed away and the solvent has been blown out with compressed air, rotate the outer joint assembly through its full range of motion and inspect the bearing surfaces for wear and damage - if any of the ball bearings, the race or the cage look damaged, replace the driveaxle and outer joint assembly**

15    Seat the boot in the grooves in the outer race and the axleshaft, then adjust the driveaxle to the proper length **(see illustration)**.

16    With the driveaxle set to the proper length, equalize the pressure in the boot by inserting a blunt screwdriver between the boot and the outer race **(see illustration)**. Don't damage the boot with the tool.

17    Install and tighten the new boot clamps **(see illustrations)**.

18    Install the driveaxle assembly (see Section 10).

## Outer CV joint and boot

### Disassembly

19    Following Steps 3 through 7, remove the inner CV joint from the driveaxle and disassemble it.

20    If the driveaxle is equipped with a dynamic damper, scribe or paint a location mark on the axleshaft along the outer edge of the damper (the side facing the outer CV joint), cut the retaining clamp and slide the damper off.

21    Cut the boot clamps from the outer CV joint. Slide the boot off the shaft. **Note:** *The outer CV joint can't be disassembled or removed from the shaft.*

### Inspection

*Refer to illustration 12.23*

22    Thoroughly wash the inner and outer CV joints in clean solvent and blow them dry with compressed air, if available. **Warning:** *Wear eye protection when using compressed air.* **Note:** *Because the outer joint can't be disassembled, it is difficult to wash away all the old grease and to rid the bearing of solvent once it's clean. But it is imperative that the job be done thoroughly, so take your time and do it right.*

23    Bend the outer CV joint housing at an angle to the axleshaft to expose the bearings, inner race and cage **(see illustration)**. Inspect the bearing surfaces for signs of wear. If the bearings are damaged or worn, replace the driveaxle.

### Reassembly

24    Slide the new outer boot onto the axleshaft. It's a good idea to wrap tape around the splines of the shaft to prevent damage to the boot **(see illustration 12.10a)**. When the boot is in position, add the specified amount of grease (included in the boot replacement kit) to the outer joint and the boot (pack the joint with as much grease as it will hold and put the rest into the boot). Slide the boot on the rest of the

way and install the new clamps **(see illustrations 12.17a and 12.17b)**.

25    Slide the dynamic damper, if equipped, onto the shaft. Make sure its outer edge is aligned with the previously applied mark. Install a new retaining clamp.

26    Clean and reassemble the inner CV joint by following Steps 8 through 17, then install the driveaxle as outlined in Section 10.

# Chapter 9  Brakes

## Contents

## Specifications

### General

| | |
|---|---|
| Brake pedal | |
|   Height | |
|     Manual transaxle | 7-1/2 inches |
|     Automatic transaxle | 7-1/2 inches |
|   Freeplay | 1/16 to 13/64 inch |
| Parking brake lever travel | |
|   Disc | 7 to 11 clicks |
|   Drum | 4 to 8 clicks |
| Power brake booster pushrod-to-master cylinder | |
|   Piston clearance (with a vacuum of 20 in-Hg applied to booster) | 0.0 to 0.020 inch |

### Disc brakes

| | |
|---|---|
| Brake pad minimum thickness | See Chapter 1 |
| Disc minimum thickness | Refer to minimum thickness cast into disc |
| Thickness variation (parallelism) | No more than 0.0006 inch |
| Runout limit | 0.004 inch |

### Drum brakes

| | |
|---|---|
| Brake lining minimum thickness | See Chapter 1 |
| Drum diameter | Refer to maximum diameter cast into drum |

## Torque specifications

**Ft-lbs** (unless otherwise indicated)

### General

| | |
|---|---|
| Brake hose-to-caliper banjo bolt (front or rear) | 25 |
| Master cylinder mounting nuts | 132 in-lbs |
| Brake booster mounting nuts | 108 in-lbs |

### Front disc brake

| | |
|---|---|
| Caliper mounting bolts | 54 |
| Caliper mounting bracket bolts | 80 |
| Driveaxle nut | See Chapter 8 |
| Steering knuckle-to-hub bolts | 33 |
| Hub-to-disc bolts | 40 |

### Rear disc brake

| | |
|---|---|
| Caliper mounting bolts | 17 |
| Caliper mounting bracket bolts | 28 |

### Rear drum brake

| | |
|---|---|
| Wheel cylinder nuts | 84 in-lbs |

## 1    General information

### General

All vehicles covered by this manual are equipped with hydraulically operated, power-assisted brake systems. All front brake systems are disc type. Some models use drum type brakes at the rear, others are equipped with rear disc brakes.

All brakes are self-adjusting. The front and rear disc brakes automatically compensate for pad wear, while the rear drum brakes incorporate an adjustment mechanism which is activated as the brakes are applied, either through the pedal or the parking brake lever.

The hydraulic system is a split design, meaning there are two separate circuits that control the brakes. If one circuit fails, the other circuit will remain functional and a warning indicator will light up on the dashboard when a substantial amount of brake fluid is lost, showing that a failure has occurred.

### Master cylinder

The master cylinder is bolted to the power-brake booster, which is mounted on the driver's side of the firewall. To locate the master cylinder, look for the large fluid reservoir on top. The fluid reservoir is a removable plastic cup, secured to the master cylinder by a clamp.

The master cylinder is designed for the "split system" mentioned earlier and has separate piston assemblies for each circuit.

### Proportioning valve

The proportioning-valve assembly is located near the front left wheel well. On vehicles equipped with the Anti-lock Brake System (ABS), it's an integral part of the modulator/solenoid unit, which is located just in front of the left front wheel well. The proportioning valve is really two separate valves - one valve for each circuit.

The proportioning valve regulates the hydraulic pressure to the rear brakes during heavy braking to eliminate rear wheel lock-up. Under normal braking conditions, it allows full pressure to the rear brake system until a predetermined pedal pressure is reached. Above that point, the pressure to the rear brakes is limited.

The proportioning valve is not serviceable - if a problem develops with the valve, it must be replaced as an assembly.

### Power brake booster

The power brake booster, which uses engine manifold vacuum and atmospheric pressure to provide assistance to the hydraulically operated brakes, is mounted on the firewall in the engine compartment.

### Parking brake

A parking-brake lever inside the vehicle operates a rod attached to a pair of rear cables, each of which is connected to its respective rear brake. When the parking-brake lever is pulled up on drum brake models, each rear cable pulls on a lever attached to the brake shoe assembly, causing the shoes to expand against the drum. When the lever is pulled on models with rear disc brakes, the rear cables pull on levers that are attached to screw-type actuators in the caliper housings, which apply force to the caliper pistons, clamping the brake pads against the brake disc.

### Precautions

There are some general cautions and warnings involving the brake system on these vehicles:

a) *Use only brake fluid conforming to DOT 3 specifications.*

b) *The brake pads and linings may contain asbestos fibers, which are hazardous to your health if inhaled. Whenever you work on brake system components, clean all parts with brake system cleaner. Do not allow the fine dust to become airborne, and wear a filter/mask over your nose and mouth when cleaning or servicing brakes.*

c) *Safety should be paramount whenever any servicing of the brake components is performed. Do not use parts or fasteners which are not in perfect condition, and be sure that all clearances and torque specifications are adhered to. If you are at all unsure about a certain procedure, seek professional advice. Upon completion of any brake system work, test the brakes carefully in a controlled area before putting the vehicle into normal service.*

d) *If a problem is suspected in the brake system, don't drive the vehicle until it's fixed.*

## 2    Anti-lock Brake System (ABS) - general information

In a conventional braking system, if you press the brake pedal too hard, the wheels can "lock up" (stop turning) and the vehicle can go into a skid. If the wheels lock up, you can lose control of the vehicle. The Anti-lock Brake System (ABS) prevents the wheels from locking up by modulating (pulsing on and off) the pressure of the brake fluid at each caliper.

The Anti-lock Brake System has two basic subsystems: One is an electrical system and the other is hydraulic. The electrical half has four "gear pulsers", four wheel sensors, a computer and an electrical circuit connecting all the components. The hydraulic part of the system consists of a modulator unit, the disc brake calipers and the hydraulic fluid lines between the modulator unit and the calipers.

The modulator unit incorporates a pump, solenoid valves pressure switches, pistons and an accumulator. The pump pressurizes the fluid which is stored in the accumulator. There are two chambers within the accumulator, one containing the fluid and the other containing pressurized nitrogen gas that keeps the accumulated fluid pressurized.

**3.5  Using a large C-clamp, push the piston back into the caliper - note that one end of the clamp is on the back side of the caliper and the other end (screw end) is pressing on the outer brake pad**

**3.6a  Before removing anything, spray the caliper and brake pads with brake system cleaner to remove the dust produced by brake pad wear - DO NOT blow the dust off with compressed air!**

In principle, the system is pretty simple: Each wheel has a wheel sensor monitoring a gear pulser (a ring with evenly spaced raised ridges cast into its circumference). The wheel sensor "counts" the ridges of the gear pulser as they pass by, converts this information into an electrical output and transmits it back to the computer. The computer constantly "samples" the voltage inputs from all four wheel sensors and compares them to each other. As long as the gear pulsers at all four wheels are rotating at the same speed, the Anti-lock Brake System is inactive. But when a wheel locks up, the voltage signal from that wheel sensor deviates from the signals coming from the other wheels. So the computer "knows" the wheel is locking up. It sends an electrical signal to the solenoid/modulator assembly, which releases the brake fluid pressure to the brake caliper at that wheel. As soon as the wheel unlocks and resumes turning at the same rate of speed as the other wheels, its wheel sensor voltage output once again matches the output of the other wheels and the computer deactivates the signal to the solenoid/modulator.

In reality, the Anti-lock Brake System is far more complex than it sounds, so we don't recommend that you attempt to diagnose or service it. If the Anti-lock Brake System on your vehicle develops problems, take it to a dealer service department or other qualified shop.

## 3    Disc brake pads (front) - replacement

*Refer to illustrations 3.5, 3.6a through 3.6h and 3.7*
**Warning:** *Disc brake pads must be replaced on both front wheels at the same time - never replace the pads on only one wheel. Also, the dust created by the brake system may contain asbestos, which is harmful to your health. Never blow it out with compressed air and don't inhale any of it. An approved filtering mask should be worn when working on the brakes. Do not, under any circumstances, use petroleum-based solvents to clean brake parts. Use brake system cleaner only!*

1    Remove the cap from the brake fluid reservoir.
2    Loosen the front wheel lug nuts, raise the front of the vehicle and support it securely on jackstands.
3    Remove the front wheels. Work on one brake assembly at a time, using the assembled brake for reference if necessary.
4    Inspect the brake disc carefully as outlined in Section 7. If machining is necessary, follow the information in that Section to remove the disc, at which time the calipers and pads can be removed as well.
5    Push the piston back into the bore to provide room for the new brake pads. A large C-clamp can be used to accomplish this **(see illustration)**. As the piston is depressed to the bottom of the caliper bore, the fluid in the master cylinder will rise. Make sure it doesn't overflow. If necessary, siphon off some of the fluid.
6    Follow the accompanying illustrations, beginning with 3.6a, for the pad removal procedure. Be sure to stay in order and read the caption under each illustration. When you're done, proceed to the next Step.

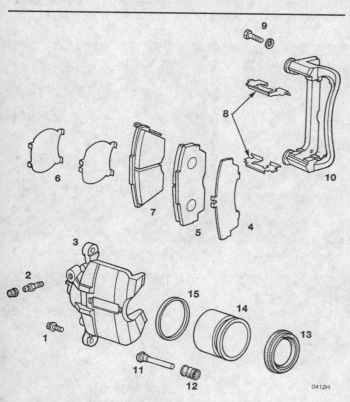

**3.6b  An exploded view of a typical front brake caliper assembly**

| | | | |
|---|---|---|---|
| 1 | Caliper mounting bolt (some models use longer bolts and don't have item 11) | 8 | Pad retainers |
| | | 9 | Caliper bracket bolts |
| 2 | Bleeder screw | 10 | Caliper bracket |
| 3 | Caliper body | 11 | Caliper pin (not all models) |
| 4 | Outer pad shim | 12 | Pin dust boot |
| 5 | Outer brake pad | 13 | Piston boot |
| 6 | Inner pad shim | 14 | Piston |
| 7 | Inner brake pad | 15 | Piston seal |

7    Apply a thin coat of disc brake anti-squeal compound, in accordance with the manufacturer's recommendations, on the backing plates of the new pads **(see illustration)**.

8    Install the shims onto their respective pads.

9    Install the pad retainers in the caliper mounting bracket. Lubricate the retainers with a thin film of silicone grease.

10    Install the new pads and shims to the caliper mounting bracket.

11    Install the caliper and caliper mounting bolt(s) and tighten them to the torque listed in this Chapter's Specifications, then proceed to the next Step.

12    Install the wheel and lug nuts, lower the vehicle and tighten the lug nuts to the torque listed in the Chapter 1 Specifications.

13    Check the brake fluid level and add fluid, if necessary (see Chapter 1).

14    Apply and release the brake pedal several times to bring the pads into contact with the brake discs. Check the operation of the brakes in an isolated area before driving the vehicle in traffic.

3.6c  If you're going to overhaul the caliper, disconnect the brake hose banjo fitting (arrow). To remove the brake pads, remove the lower mounting bolt as shown . . .

## 4    Disc brake caliper (front) - removal, overhaul and installation

**Warning:** *Dust created by the brake system may contain asbestos, which is harmful to your health. Never blow it out with compressed air and don't inhale any of it. An approved filtering mask should be worn when working on the brakes. Do not, under any circumstances, use petroleum-based solvents to clean brake parts. Use brake system cleaner only!*

**Note:** *If an overhaul is indicated (usually because of fluid leakage) explore all options before beginning the job. New and factory rebuil calipers are available on an exchange basis, which makes this job quite easy. If you decide to rebuild the calipers, make sure a rebuild kit is available before proceeding. Always rebuild the calipers in pairs - neve rebuild just one of them.*

3.6d . . . swing the caliper up . . .

3.6e . . . remove the outer pad shim . . .

3.6f . . . remove the outer brake pad . . .

3.6g . . . remove the inner pad shims (there are two, so note the order in which they are removed, because they're different . . .

3.6h . . . and remove the inner brake pad - if you're also removing the caliper mounting bracket and/or the brake disc, note how the upper and lower pad retainers (arrows) are installed in the bracket, then remove them

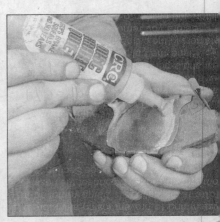

3.7  Before installing the brake pads, appl a coat of disc brake anti-squeal compound to the backing plates of the pads - follow the manufacturer's instructions on the label

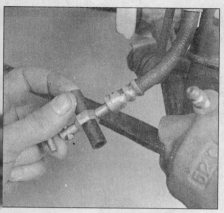

**4.2 Using a short piece of rubber hose of the appropriate diameter, plug the brake line banjo fitting like this**

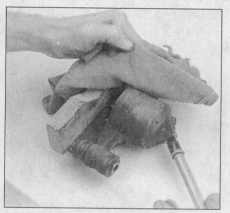

**4.5 With the caliper padded to catch the piston, use compressed air to force the piston out of its bore - make sure your hands and fingers are not between the piston and the caliper**

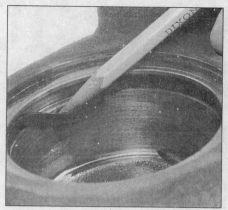

**4.7 The piston seal should be removed with a plastic or wooden tool to avoid damage to the bore and seal groove - a pencil will do the job**

## Removal

*Refer to illustration 4.2*

1    Loosen - but don't remove - the lug nuts on the front wheels. Raise the front of the vehicle and place it securely on jackstands. Remove the front wheels.

2    Disconnect the brake line **(see illustration 3.6c)** from the caliper and plug it **(see illustration)** to keep contaminants out of the brake system and to prevent losing any more brake fluid than is necessary. **Note:** *If the caliper is being removed just to gain access to other components, don't disconnect the hose.*

3    Remove the caliper (see Section 2).

## Overhaul

*Refer to illustrations 4.5, 4.7 and 4.12*

**Note:** *In addition to the illustrations accompanying this Section, refer to illustration 3.6b. The models covered by this book include two different caliper assemblies. They're only slightly different in design, but when you buy a caliper rebuild kit, be sure to tell your dealer or auto parts store the year and exact model of your vehicle so you don't get the wrong kit.*

4    Place the caliper on a clean workbench. If there are any pad retainers in the caliper, note how they're installed, then remove them.

5    Before you remove the piston, place a wood block between the piston and caliper to prevent damage as it is removed. To remove the

piston from the caliper, apply compressed air to the brake fluid hose connection on the caliper body **(see illustration)**. Use only enough pressure to ease the piston out of its bore. **Warning:** *Be careful not to place your fingers between the piston and the caliper, as the piston may come out with some force. Wear eye protection, as some brake fluid may also spray out.* Remove the piston boot.

6    Inspect the mating surfaces of the piston and caliper bore wall. If there is any scoring, rust, pitting or bright areas, replace the complete caliper unit with a new one.

7    If these components are in good condition, remove the piston seal from the caliper bore using a wooden or plastic tool **(see illustration)**. Metal tools may damage the cylinder bore.

8    Remove the dust boots from the caliper mounting bracket **(see illustration 3.6b)**.

9    Wash all the components in brake system cleaner.

10    Submerge the new piston seal in brake fluid and install it in the lower groove in the caliper bore.

11    Install the piston boot in the upper groove in the caliper bore.

12    Lubricate the piston with clean brake fluid, carefully slide it through the new boot, position it squarely in the caliper bore and apply firm (but not excessive) pressure to bottom it in the bore. Make sure the piston boot seats in the groove in the piston **(see illustration)**.

13    If equipped, install the dust boots in the caliper mounting bracket, lubricate the caliper pins with silicone grease and install the pins in the bracket.

## Installation

14    Install the caliper by reversing the removal procedure. Remember to replace the copper sealing washers on either side of the brake line banjo fitting (they should be included with the rebuild kit).

15    Bleed the brake system (see Section 13).

16    Install the wheels and lug nuts, remove the jackstands and lower the vehicle. Tighten the wheel lug nuts to the torque listed in the Chapter 1 Specifications.

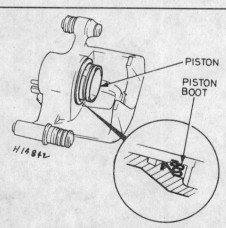

PISTON

PISTON BOOT

H14842

**4.12 With the piston boot positioned in the caliper bore, stretch the boot over the bottom of the piston and push the piston into the bore - the folds of the boot should be even, with no distortion or twist**

## 5    Disc brake pads (rear) - replacement

*Refer to illustrations 5.6a through 5.6f and 5.11*

**Warning:** *Disc brake pads must be replaced on both rear wheels at the same time - never replace the pads on only one wheel. Also, the dust created by the brake system may contain asbestos, which is harmful to your health. Never blow it out with compressed air and don't inhale any of it. An approved filtering mask should be worn when working on the brakes. Do not, under any circumstances, use petroleum-based solvents to clean brake parts. Use brake system cleaner only!*

1    Remove the cap from the brake fluid reservoir.

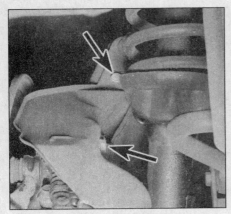

5.6a  Remove the caliper shield bolts and the shield

5.6b  Remove the two caliper mounting bolts (arrows) . . .

5.6c  . . . and lift the caliper from its mounting bracket - hang the caliper out of the way with a piece of wire - don't let it hang by the brake hose

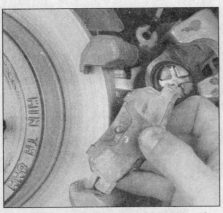

5.6d  Remove the outer shim and pad

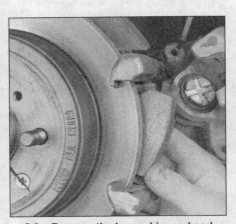

5.6e  Remove the inner shim and pad

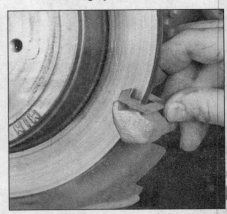

5.6f  Remove the brake pad retainers from the caliper (lower retainer shown, upper retainer identical)

2    Loosen the rear wheel lug nuts, raise the rear of the vehicle and support it securely on jackstands.
3    Remove the rear wheels. Work on one brake assembly at a time, using the assembled brake for reference if necessary.
4    Inspect the brake disc carefully as outlined in Section 7. If machining is necessary, follow the service information in that Section.
5    Before you remove anything, spray the caliper and brake pads with brake cleaner to remove the dust produced by brake pad wear **(see illustration 3.6a)**.
6    Follow **illustrations 5.6a through 5.6f** for the pad removal procedure. Be sure to stay in order and read the caption under each illustration. When those Steps have been completed, proceed to Step 7.
7    Apply a thin coat of disc brake anti-squeal compound, in accordance with the manufacturer's recommendations, on the backing plates of the new pads **(see illustration 3.7)**.
8    Install the shims onto their respective pads.
9    If you removed them, install the pad retainers in the caliper mounting bracket. Lubricate the retainers with a thin film of silicone grease.
10    Install the new pads and shims into the caliper mounting bracket. The inboard pad should be installed with its wear indicator facing down.
11    Retract the piston by engaging the tips of a pair of needle-nose pliers with two of the grooves in the top of the piston and turning it clockwise until it bottoms out **(see illustration)**. Now, rotate the piston out until one of its grooves is aligned with the tab on the inner brake pad when you install the caliper. You may have to lubricate the boot with rubber lubricant to keep the boot from twisting. Adjust the piston

position by turning it back and forth until the tab fits. If the piston dust boot becomes distorted when the piston is turned, turn the piston in the opposite direction to restore the shape of the boot, but make sure the cut-out still lines up.

5.11  To provide enough clearance between the caliper piston and the disc, back the piston into the caliper bore by rotating it with a pair of needle-nose pliers

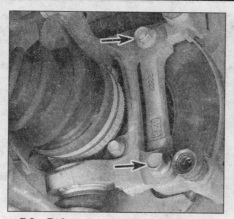

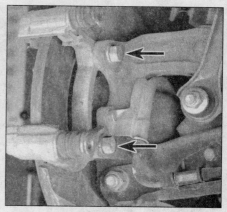

6.2  The parking brake cable is attached to the rear caliper by a clevis pin that is secured by a cotter pin

7.2a  Before you can remove the front disc, you'll have to remove these caliper mounting bracket-to-steering knuckle bolts (arrows) and the bracket

7.2b  To remove the rear disc, remove these caliper-to-spindle bolts (arrows) and the brackets

12   Install the caliper mounting bolts and tighten them to the torque listed in this Chapter's Specifications.
13   Install the caliper shield.
14   Install the wheel and lug nuts, lower the vehicle and tighten the lug nuts to the torque listed in the Chapter 1 Specifications.
15   Check the brake fluid level and add fluid, if necessary (see Chapter 1).
16   Apply and release the brake pedal and the hand brake lever several times to bring the pads into contact with the brake discs. Check the operation of the brakes in an isolated area before driving the vehicle in traffic.

## 6   Disc brake caliper (rear) - removal and installation

Refer to illustration 6.2
**Warning:** *Dust created by the brake system may contain asbestos, which is harmful to your health. Never blow it out with compressed air and don't inhale any of it. An approved filtering mask should be worn when working on the brakes. Do not, under any circumstances, use petroleum-based solvents to clean brake parts. Use brake system cleaner only!*

### Removal

1   Loosen - but don't remove - the lug nuts on the rear wheels. Raise the rear of the vehicle and place it securely on jackstands. Remove the rear wheels.

7.3  The brake pads on this vehicle were obviously neglected, as they wore down to the rivets; the rivets then cut deep grooves into the disc, and now the disc must be replaced

2   Remove the caliper shield **(see illustration 5.6a)**, remove the cotter pin from the clevis pin that connects the parking brake cable to the parking brake lever **(see illustration)**, pull out the pin and detach the cable.
3   Disconnect the brake hose fitting from the caliper and plug it to keep contaminants out of the brake system and to prevent losing any more brake fluid than is necessary **(see illustration 4.2)**.
4   Remove the caliper mounting bolts and lift the caliper off its mounting bracket (see Section 5).
5   Disassembly of the rear caliper requires special tools not generally available to the home mechanic. If the rear caliper needs to be overhauled, take it to a dealer service department or other repair shop or obtain a rebuilt unit from an auto parts store or dealer service department.

### Installation

6   Install the caliper by reversing the removal procedure. Remember to install new copper sealing washers on either side of the brake line banjo fitting.
7   Bleed the brake system (see Section 13).
8   Install the wheels and lug nuts, remove the jackstands and lower the vehicle. Tighten the lug nuts to the torque listed in the Chapter 1 Specifications.

## 7   Brake disc - inspection, removal and installation

**Note:** *This procedure applies to both the front and (on vehicles so equipped) rear brake discs.*

### Inspection

Refer to illustrations 7.2a, 7.2b, 7.3, 7.4a, 7.4b, 7.5a and 7.5b
1   Loosen the wheel lug nuts, raise the vehicle and support it securely on jackstands. Remove the wheel and, if you're checking the rear brake disc, install two lug nuts with 3 mm thick washers under them to hold the disc in place (if the two disc retaining screws are still in place, this will be unnecessary). If you're checking the rear disc, release the parking brake.
2   Remove the brake caliper (see Section 4 or 6). It isn't necessary to disconnect the brake hose. After removing the caliper bolts, suspend the caliper out of the way with a piece of wire. Remove the two caliper mounting bracket-to-steering knuckle bolts **(see illustration)** or, on rear calipers, the bracket-to-spindle bolts **(see illustration)**, and remove the mounting bracket.
3   Visually inspect the disc surface for scoring or damage **(see illustration)**. Light scratches and shallow grooves are normal after use and may not always be detrimental to brake operation, but deep scoring (over 0.015 inch) requires refinishing by an automotive machine shop. Be sure to check both sides of the disc.

**7.4a Make sure the disc retaining screws or lug nuts are tight, then rotate the disc and check the runout with a dial indicator - if the reading exceeds the maximum allowable runout limit, the disc will have to be machined or replaced**

4    If you've noted pulsation during braking, suspect disc runout. To check disc runout, place a dial indicator at a point about 1/2-inch from the outer edge of the disc **(see illustration)**. Set the indicator to zero and turn the disc. The indicator reading should not exceed the

specified allowable runout limit. If it does, have the disc refinished by an automotive machine shop. **Note 1:** *Professionals recommend that the discs be resurfaced regardless of the dial indicator reading, as this will impart a smooth finish and ensure a perfectly flat surface, eliminating any brake pedal pulsation or other undesirable symptoms related to questionable discs. At the very least, if you elect not to have the discs resurfaced, remove the glazing from the surface with emery cloth or sandpaper using a swirling motion* **(see illustration). Note 2:** *The manufacturer recommends that the discs be refinished while installed on the vehicle. Most shops specializing in brake repair will have the equipment necessary to do this.*

5    It is absolutely critical that the disc not be machined to a thickness less than the minimum allowable thickness. The minimum wear (or discard) thickness is cast into the disc **(see illustration)**. The disc thickness can be checked with a micrometer **(see illustration)**.

## Removal

*Refer to illustration 7.6a, 7.6b and 7.11*
**Caution:** *The driveaxle CV joints (the parts covered by the rubber boots) can be damaged if they are over-extended. Be very careful not to pull the halves of either joint away from each other, which will damage the boot or the joint itself.*

6    On models equipped with ABS, remove the wheel-sensor wire bracket, then remove the wheel sensor from the knuckle **(see illustrations)**. **Note:** *Do not remove the wire connector from the wheel sensor.*

### Front disc

7    Remove the driveaxle hub nut. To prevent the hub from turning, place a prybar between two of the wheel studs, then loosen the nut.

**7.4b Using a swirling motion, remove the glaze from the disc with emery cloth or sandpaper**

**7.5a The minimum allowable thickness is cast into the disc (typical)**

**7.5b A micrometer is used to measure disc thickness**

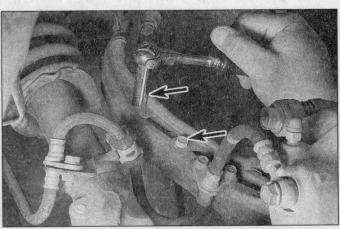

**7.6a Remove these two bolts (arrows) retaining the ABS wheel-sensor wire harness, which is protected by this metal tube**

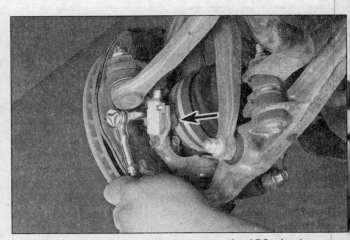

**7.6b Remove these two bolts to remove the ABS wheel sensor (arrow) from the knuckle**

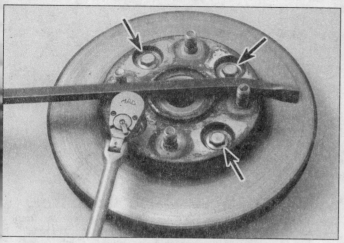

7.11  Remove the four bolts that hold the hub assembly
to the brake disc (arrows)

8.2  If the drum is hard to pull off, thread a pair of 8 mm bolts into
the holes provided and press the drum off

8    Remove the cotter pin and loosen the lower balljoint nut about
three turns. Don't remove the nut completely. Separate the lower
control arm from the steering knuckle using a two-jaw puller (see
Chapter 10).
9    Swing the knuckle/hub assembly out (away from the vehicle) and
push the driveaxle through the hub assembly until the end of the
driveaxle is free of the hub. The shaft on the end of the driveaxle is
frequently difficult to dislodge from the hub, so it may be necessary to
tap the outer end of the shaft with a brass mallet until it pulls easily out
of the hub. If you tap on the shaft end, be very careful not to damage
the threads. After the hub and axle are separated, support the outer
end of the driveaxle with a piece of wire to avoid unnecessary strain on
the inner CV joint.
10    Remove the four bolts that hold the hub and brake disc assembly
to the steering knuckle and remove hub and disc assembly (see
Chapter 10).
11    To prevent the hub assembly from turning while you're loosening
it, place a prybar between two of the wheel studs, then remove the four
bolts that hold the disc to the hub assembly and remove the brake disc
(see illustration).

### Rear disc

12    Remove the two screws securing the disc to the hub, then slide
the disc off.

## Installation

### Front disc

13    Place the hub assembly onto the brake disc and install the four
bolts. Place the disc and hub assembly onto the steering knuckle and
tighten the four bolts. Now tighten all eight bolts to the torque listed in
this Chapter's Specifications. Place a prybar through the wheel studs
when tightening the hub-to-disc bolts.
14    Install the driveaxle through the hub assembly and insert the stud
of the lower balljoint into the lower control arm. Tighten the balljoint nut
to the torque listed in this Chapter's Specifications. Be sure to use a
new cotter pin.
15    Install the hub nut. Hold the disc as described in Step 6 so it can't
turn, then tighten the hub nut securely. Don't try to tighten it to the
actual torque specification until you've lowered the vehicle to the
ground.

### Rear disc

16    Slide the disc over the wheel studs on the hub, then install the
two screws and tighten them securely.

### Front or rear disc

17    If equipped, reattach the ABS wheel sensor to the knuckle and

secure the wheel sensor wire bracket.
18    Install the caliper mounting bracket, brake pads and caliper over
the disc. Tighten the mounting bracket and caliper bolts to the torque
listed in this Chapter's specifications.
18    Install the wheel, then lower the vehicle to the ground and tighten
the driveaxle hub nut to the torque listed in the Chapter 8 Specifications. Tighten the lug nuts to the torque listed in the Chapter 1
Specifications. Stake the hub nut to the driveaxle. Depress the brake
pedal a few times to bring the brake pads into contact with the disc.
Bleeding of the system will not be necessary unless the fluid hose was
disconnected from the caliper. Check the operation of the brakes
carefully before placing the vehicle into normal service.

## 8    Drum brake shoes - replacement

*Refer to illustrations 8.2, 8.4a through 8.4o and 8.5*
**Warning:** *Drum brake shoes must be replaced on both wheels at the
same time - never replace the shoes on only one wheel. Also, the dust
created by the brake system may contain asbestos, which is harmful to
your health. Never blow it out with compressed air and don't inhale any
of it. An approved filtering mask should be worn when working on the
brakes. Do not, under any circumstances, use petroleum-based
solvents to clean brake parts. Use brake system cleaner only!*
**Caution:** *Whenever the brake shoes are replaced, the return and hold-
down springs should also be replaced. Due to the continuous
heating/cooling cycle that the springs are subjected to, they lose their
tension over a period of time and may allow the shoes to drag on the
drum and wear at a much faster rate than normal.*
1    Loosen the wheel lug nuts, raise the rear of the vehicle and
support it securely on jackstands. Block the front wheels to keep the
vehicle from rolling. Remove the rear wheels. Release the parking
brake.
2    Remove the brake drum. It should simply pull straight off the hub.
If the drum won't come off, tap it carefully with a soft-faced mallet, or
screw a couple of 8.0 mm bolts into the tapped holes (see illustration). If it still won't budge, the shoes have probably carved wear
grooves into the drum. To get the drum off, you'll have to retract them.
Remove the rubber plug in the backing plate. Use one screwdriver
inserted through the hole in the backing plate to hold the self-adjuster
lever away from the adjuster bolt, then use another screwdriver to
rotate the adjuster bolt until the drum can be removed.
3    Replacing the shoes is a lot easier if you remove the rear wheel
bearing cap, spindle nut and washer, and slide off the hub unit (see
Chapter 10).
4    Follow **illustrations 8.4a through 8.4o** for the inspection and
replacement of the brake shoes. Be sure to stay in order and read the

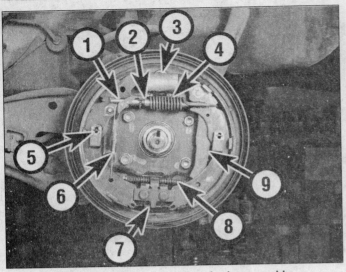

**8.4a Details of the rear drum brake assembly**

| | | | |
|---|---|---|---|
| 1 | Self adjuster lever | 6 | Self adjuster spring |
| 2 | Adjuster assembly | 7 | Lower return spring |
| 3 | Wheel cylinder | 8 | Parking brake cable |
| 4 | Upper return spring | 9 | Parking brake lever |
| 5 | Retainer spring | | |

**8.4b Push down on the retainer spring with a screwdriver, then turn the pin to align its blade with the slot - the spring should pop off (repeat this on the other side)**

**8.4d Remove the adjuster/spring assembly from the leading brake shoe**

caption under each illustration. All four rear brake shoes must be replaced at the same time, but to avoid mixing up parts, work on only one brake assembly at a time.

5      Before reinstalling the drum it should be checked for cracks, score marks, deep scratches and hard spots, which will appear as small discolored areas. If the hard spots cannot be removed with fine emery cloth or if any of the other conditions listed above exist, the drum must be taken to an automotive machine shop to have it

**8.4c Pull the upper return spring back while supporting the brake shoe and unhook the spring from the shoe (a pair of diagonal cutting pliers are being used here because they grip the spring well, but care must be taken so as not to damage the spring)**

**8.4e Detach the lower return spring . . .**

**8.4f . . . and remove the self adjuster lever and spring**

**8.4g Remove the parking brake lever retaining clip; be careful not to lose the wave washer that is under the clip**

**8.4h** Lubricate the brake shoe contact areas on the backing plate with high-temperature grease

**8.4i** Clean the adjuster bolt and clevis, then lubricate the threads and ends with high-temperature grease

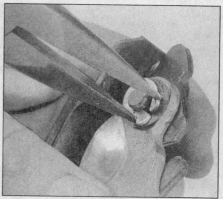

**8.4j** Put the new trailing shoe on the lever, place the wave washer over the pin, then install the retaining clip; crimp the ends of the clip together with a pair of needle-nose pliers

**8.4k** Install the adjusting lever and spring on the new leading shoe

**8.4l** Install the lower return spring

**8.4m** Install the adjuster assembly . . .

...achined. **Note:** *Professionals recommend resurfacing the drums whenever a brake job is done. Resurfacing will eliminate the possibility of out-of-round drums.* If the drums are worn so much that they can't be resurfaced without exceeding the maximum allowable diameter (stamped into the drum) **(see illustration)**, then new ones will be required. At the very least, if you elect not to have the drums resurfaced, remove the glazing from the surface with sandpaper or emery cloth using a swirling motion.

Install the hub and bearing unit, the washer and a new spindle nut if removed previously (see Chapter 10). Tighten the nut to the torque listed in the Chapter 10 Specifications. Install the brake drum.

7    Mount the wheel, install the lug nuts, then lower the vehicle. Tighten the lug nuts to the torque listed in the Chapter 1 Specifications.

8    Make a number of forward and reverse stops to adjust the brakes until satisfactory pedal action is obtained.

9    Check brake operation before driving the vehicle in traffic. **Warning:** *Do not operate the vehicle if you are in doubt about the effectiveness of the brake system.*

**8.4n** . . . and connect the upper return spring

**8.4o** Install both retainer springs

**8.5** The maximum allowable diameter is cast into the drum (typical)

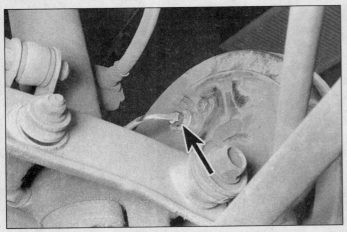

**9.4  Unscrew the brake line fitting (arrow), then
remove the two bolts**

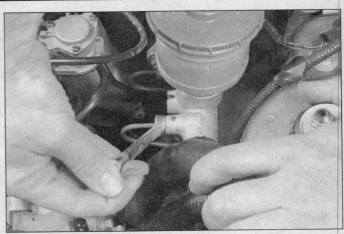

**10.4  Use a flare-nut wrench to remove the threaded fittings at the
master cylinder - a regular wrench can round off the corners**

**9   Wheel cylinder - removal and installation**

**Note:** *If the wheel cylinders leak, they must be replaced with new ones
- the manufacturer does not recommend rebuilding them.*

## Removal

*Refer to illustration 9.4*

1    Raise the rear of the vehicle and support it securely on
jackstands. Block the front wheels to keep the vehicle from rolling.
2    Remove the brake shoe assembly (see Section 8).
3    Remove all dirt and foreign material from around the wheel
cylinder.
4    Unscrew the brake line fitting **(see illustration)**. Don't pull the
brake line away from the wheel cylinder.
5    Remove the wheel cylinder mounting bolts.
6    Detach the wheel cylinder from the brake backing plate. Immediately plug the brake line to prevent fluid loss and contamination. Golf
tees or rubber vacuum caps work well for plugging or capping flared
metal lines. **Note:** *If the brake shoe linings are contaminated with brake
fluid, install new brake shoes and clean the drums with brake system
cleaner.*

## Installation

7    Apply silicone sealant to the mating surface of the wheel cylinder
and the brake backing plate, place the cylinder in position and connect
the brake line. Don't tighten the fitting completely yet.
8    Install the mounting bolts, tightening them securely. Tighten the
brake line fitting. Install the brake shoe assembly.
9    Bleed the brakes (see Section 13).
10    Check brake operation before driving the vehicle in traffic.
**Warning:** *Do not operate the vehicle if you are in doubt about the
effectiveness of the brake system.*

**10   Master cylinder - removal and installation**

*Refer to illustrations 10.4 and 10.6*
**Note:** *If the master cylinder is defective, it must be replaced with a new
one - the manufacturer does not recommend rebuilding it.*

## Removal

1    The master cylinder is located in the engine compartment,
mounted to the power brake booster.
2    Remove as much fluid as you can from the reservoir with a
syringe, such as an old turkey baster.
3    Place rags under the fluid fittings and prepare caps or plastic
bags to cover the ends of the lines once they are disconnected.

**Caution:** *Brake fluid will damage paint. Cover all body parts and be
careful not to spill fluid during this procedure.*
4    Loosen the fittings at the ends of the brake lines where they enter
the master cylinder **(see illustration)**. To prevent rounding off the
corners on these nuts, the use of a flare-nut wrench, which wraps
around the nut, is preferred.
5    Pull the brake lines slightly away from the master cylinder and
plug the ends to prevent contamination.
6    Disconnect the electrical connector at the master cylinder, then
remove the nuts attaching the master cylinder to the power booster **(see
illustration)**. Pull the master cylinder off the studs and out of the engine
compartment. Again, be careful not to spill the fluid as this is done.

## Installation

7    Before installing the new master cylinder it should be bench bled.
Because it will be necessary to apply pressure to the master cylinder
piston and, at the same time, control flow from the brake line outlets, it
is recommended that the master cylinder be mounted in a vise, with
the jaws of the vise clamping on the mounting flange.
8    Insert threaded plugs into the brake line outlet holes and snug
them down so there will be no air leakage past them, but not so tight
that they cannot be easily loosened.
9    Fill the reservoir with brake fluid of the recommended type (see
Chapter 1).
10    Remove one plug and push the piston assembly into the master
cylinder bore to expel the air from the master cylinder. A large Phillips
screwdriver can be used to push on the piston assembly.
11    To prevent air from being drawn back into the master cylinder, the
plug must be replaced and snugged down before releasing the
pressure on the piston assembly.
12    Repeat the procedure until only brake fluid is expelled from the
brake line outlet hole. When only brake fluid is expelled, repeat the
procedure with the other outlet hole and plug. Be sure to keep the
master cylinder reservoir filled with brake fluid to prevent the intro-
duction of air into the system.
13    Since high pressure is not involved in the bench bleeding
procedure, an alternative to the removal and replacement of the plugs
with each stroke of the piston assembly is available. Before pushing in
on the piston assembly, remove the plug as described in Step 10.
Before releasing the piston, however, instead of replacing the plug,
simply put your finger tightly over the hole to keep air from being
drawn back into the master cylinder. Wait several seconds for brake
fluid to be drawn from the reservoir into the piston bore, then depress
the piston again, removing your finger as brake fluid is expelled. Be
sure to put your finger back over the hole each time before releasing
the piston, and when the bleeding procedure is complete for that
outlet, replace the plug and snug it before going on to the other port.
14    Install the master cylinder over the studs on the power brake

10.6 To detach the master cylinder from the brake booster, remove the two nuts (only one nut is visible in this photo)

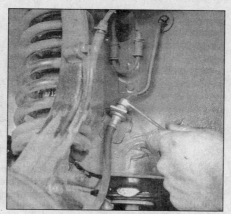

12.4a Use a flare-nut wrench to break loose the brake line-to-hose fitting . . .

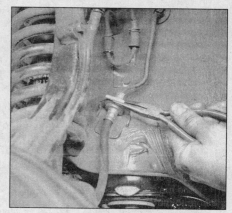

12.4b . . . then remove the clip and slide the hose out of the bracket

booster and tighten the attaching nuts only finger tight at this time.

15   Thread the brake line fittings into the master cylinder. Since the master cylinder is still a bit loose, it can be moved slightly in order for the fittings to thread in easily. Do not strip the threads as the fittings are tightened.

16   Fully tighten the mounting nuts, then the brake line fittings.

17   Fill the master cylinder reservoir with fluid, then bleed the master cylinder and the brake system as described in Section 13. To bleed the cylinder on the vehicle, have an assistant pump the brake pedal several times slowly and then hold the pedal to the floor. Loosen the fitting nut to allow air and fluid to escape. Repeat this procedure on both fittings until the fluid is clear of air bubbles. **Caution:** *Have plenty of rags on hand to catch the fluid - brake fluid will ruin painted surfaces.*

18   Test the operation of the brake system carefully before placing the vehicle into normal service. **Warning:** *Do not operate the vehicle if you are in doubt about the effectiveness of the brake system.*

## 11   Proportioning valve - general information, removal and installation

1   The proportioning valve is mounted on the front of the master cylinder, near the left wheel well. Its purpose is to limit hydraulic pressure to the rear brakes under heavy braking conditions to prevent rear wheel lockup.

2   The valve is not serviceable; if you suspect it's malfunctioning, have it checked by a dealer service department or repair shop equipped with the necessary pressure gauges.

3   If the valve is defective, replace it by unscrewing the brake lines (using a flare-nut wrench, if available) and unbolting the valve from its mounting bracket. After the new valve is installed, bleed the complete brake system as described in Section 13.

## 12   Brake hoses and lines - inspection and replacement

*Refer to illustrations 12.4a and 12.4b*

1   About every six months the flexible hoses which connect the steel brake lines with the rear brakes and front calipers should be inspected for cracks, chafing of the outer cover, leaks, blisters, and other damage.

2   Replacement steel and flexible brake lines are commonly available from dealer parts departments and auto parts stores. Do not, under any circumstances, use anything other than genuine steel brake lines or approved flexible brake hoses as replacement items.

3   When installing the brake line, leave at least 3/4-inch clearance between the line and any moving or vibrating parts.

4   To disconnect a hose and line, use a flare-nut wrench **(see illustration)**. Then remove the clip and slide the hose out of the bracket **(see illustration)**.

5   When disconnecting two hoses, use normal wrenches on the hose fittings. When connecting two hoses, make sure they are not twisted or strained.

6   Steel brake lines are usually retained along their span with clips. Always remove these clips completely before removing a rigid brake line. Always reinstall these clips, or new ones if the old ones are damaged, when replacing a brake line, as they provide support and keep the lines from vibrating, which can eventually break them.

7   When replacing brake lines be sure to use the correct parts. NEVER use copper tubing! Purchase steel brake lines from a dealer or auto parts store.

8   When installing a steel line, make sure it's securely supported in the brackets and has plenty of clearance between moving or hot components.

9   After installation, check the fluid level in the master cylinder and add fluid as necessary. Bleed the brake system as described in Section 13 and test the brakes carefully before driving the vehicle in traffic. **Warning:** *Do not operate the vehicle if you are in doubt about the effectiveness of the brake system.*

## 13   Brake hydraulic system - bleeding

*Refer to illustration 13.12*

**Warning:** *Wear eye protection when bleeding the brake system. If the fluid comes in contact with your eyes, immediately rinse them with water and seek medical attention.*

1   Bleeding the hydraulic system is necessary to remove any air that manages to find its way into the system when it's been opened during removal and installation of a hose, line, caliper or master cylinder. It will be necessary to bleed the system at the modulator and all four brakes if air has entered the system due to low fluid level, or if the brake lines have been disconnected at the master cylinder.

2   If a brake line was disconnected only at a wheel, then only that caliper or wheel cylinder must be bled.

3   If a brake line is disconnected at a fitting located between the modulator unit and any of the brakes, that part of the system served by the disconnected line must be bled, in addition to the modulator.

### *Bleeding the ABS modulator unit*

4   Check the brake fluid reservoir, adding fluid as necessary to bring it to the appropriate (MAX) level. Remove the rubber cap from the bleeder screw on the modulator, attach a hose to it and place the other end of the hose in a container partially filled with clean brake fluid.

5   Place a wrench on the bleeder screw, hold the hose with your other hand and slowly loosen the bleeder screw until fluid begins to flow out. If the modulator is completely drained, no fluid will flow out. **Warning:** *Don't loosen the bleeder screw quickly or excessively, since the brake fluid is under high pressure.*

6    Have an assistant start the engine to activate the ABS pump motor. When bubble-free fluid begins to flow from the bleeder, tighten the bleeder screw securely.

7    Stop the engine and check the fluid level, adding fluid if necessary to bring it to the MAX marking on the reservoir. If the ABS indicator light on the dash comes on and the pump motor stops, start the engine again and repeat Steps 5 and 6. Now, proceed to bleed the rest of the system.

### Bleeding the remainder of the system

8    Remove any residual vacuum from the power brake booster by applying the brake several times with the engine off.

9    Remove the master cylinder reservoir cover and fill the reservoir with brake fluid. Reinstall the cover. **Note:** *Check the fluid level often during the bleeding operation and add fluid as necessary to prevent the fluid level from falling low enough to allow air bubbles into the master cylinder.*

10    Have an assistant on hand, as well as a supply of new brake fluid, a clear container partially filled with clean brake fluid, a length of 3/16-inch clear plastic, rubber or vinyl tubing to fit over the bleed screw and a wrench to open and close the bleed screw.

11    Beginning at the right rear wheel, loosen the bleed screw slightly, then tighten it to a point where it is snug but can still be loosened quickly and easily.

12    Place one end of the tubing over the bleed screw and submerge the other end in brake fluid in the container **(see illustration)**.

13    Have the assistant pump the brakes slowly a few times to get pressure in the system, then hold the pedal firmly depressed.

14    While the pedal is held depressed, open the bleed screw just enough to allow a flow of fluid to leave the screw. Watch for air bubbles to exit the submerged end of the tube. When the fluid flow slows after a couple of seconds, close the screw and have your assistant release the pedal.

15    Repeat Steps 13 and 14 until no more air is seen leaving the tube, then tighten the bleed screw and proceed to the left front wheel, the left rear wheel and the right front wheel, in that order, and perform the same procedure. Be sure to check the fluid in the master cylinder reservoir frequently.

16    Never use old brake fluid. It contains moisture which will cause the fluid to boil, rendering the brakes inoperative.

17    Refill the master cylinder with fluid at the end of the operation.

18    Check the operation of the brakes. The pedal should feel solid when depressed, with no sponginess. If necessary, repeat the entire process. **Warning:** *Do not operate the vehicle if you are in doubt about the effectiveness of the brake system.*

---

### 14    Power brake booster - check, removal and installation

---

### Operating check

1    Depress the brake pedal several times with the engine off and make sure there is no change in the pedal reserve distance.

2    Depress the pedal and start the engine. If the pedal goes down slightly, operation is normal.

### Airtightness check

3    Start the engine and turn it off after one or two minutes. Depress the brake pedal several times slowly. If the pedal goes down farther the first time but gradually rises after the second or third depression, the booster is airtight.

4    Depress the brake pedal while the engine is running, then stop the engine with the pedal depressed. If there is no change in the pedal reserve travel after holding the pedal for 30 seconds, the booster is airtight.

### Removal

*refer to illustration 14.10 and 14.11*

5    Power brake booster units should not be disassembled. They require special tools not normally found in most automotive repair stations or shops. They are fairly complex and because of their critical

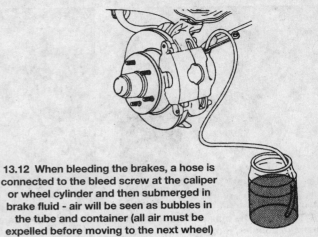

**13.12 When bleeding the brakes, a hose is connected to the bleed screw at the caliper or wheel cylinder and then submerged in brake fluid - air will be seen as bubbles in the tube and container (all air must be expelled before moving to the next wheel)**

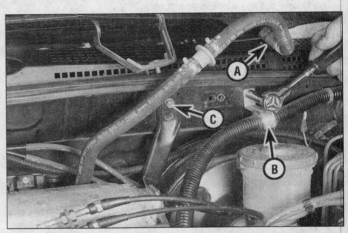

**14.10 To clear the way for booster removal, remove the vacuum line (A), unbolt and pull away the wiring harness (B), and unbolt the throttle cable bracket (C)**

relationship to brake performance it is best to replace a defective booster unit with a new or rebuilt one.

6    To remove the booster, first remove the brake master cylinder as described in Section 10.

7    Locate the pushrod clevis pin connecting the booster to the brake pedal. This is accessible from under the dash panel in front of the driver's seat.

8    Loosen the pushrod locknut, remove the cotter pin with pliers, and pull out the clevis pin.

9    Disconnect the vacuum hose leading from the engine to the booster. Be careful not to damage the hose when removing it from the booster fitting.

10    Unbolt and move away the throttle control cable bracket and unbolt and pull away the wiring harness near the booster **(see illustration)**.

11    Remove the four nuts and washers holding the brake booster to the firewall. You may need a light to see these, as they are up under the dash area **(see illustration)**.

12    Slide the booster straight out from the firewall until the studs clear the holes and pull the booster, brackets and gaskets from the engine compartment area.

### Installation

*Refer to illustrations 14.14a and 14.14b*

13    Installation procedures are basically the reverse of those for removal. Tighten the booster mounting nuts to the torque listed in this Chapter's Specifications. Also, be sure to use a new cotter pin on the clevis pin.

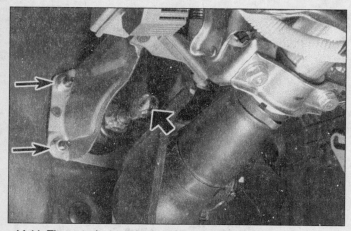

14.11 The nuts (arrows indicate two in camera's view, there are two more) for the booster mount are up under the dash - remove the clevis (larger arrow) first

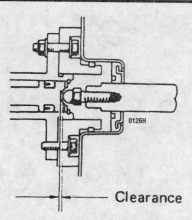

14.14a The booster pushrod-to-master cylinder clearance must be as specified - if there is interference between the two, the brakes may drag; if there is too much clearance, there will be excessive brake pedal travel

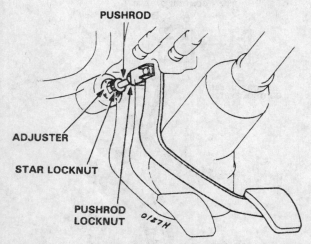

14.14b To adjust the length of the booster pushrod, loosen the star locknut and turn the adjuster in or out, as necessary, to achieve the desired setting

15.4 The adjusting nut (1) is on the equalizer assembly - when removing a cable, unscrew the clamp bolts (2) and lift off the clamp

14   If a replacement power booster unit is being installed, the clearance between the master cylinder piston and the pushrod in the vacuum booster must be measured. Using a depth micrometer or vernier calipers, measure the distance from the seat (recessed area) in the master cylinder piston to the master cylinder mounting flange. Next, apply a vacuum of 20 in-Hg to the booster (using a hand-held vacuum pump) and measure the distance from the end of the vacuum booster pushrod to the mounting face of the booster (including gasket, if used) where the master cylinder mounting flange seats. Subtract the two measurements to get the clearance **(see illustration)**. If the clearance is more or less than listed in this Chapter's Specifications, loosen the star locknut and turn the adjuster on the power booster pushrod until the clearance is within the specified limit **(see illustration)**. After adjustment, tighten the locknut.
15   After the final installation of the master cylinder and brake hoses and lines, bleed the brakes as described in Section 13.

## 15   Parking brake - adjustment

*Refer to illustration 15.4*
1   Refer to Chapter 11 and remove the console trim around the parking brake lever.

2   Remove the center console.
3   Block the front wheels, raise the rear of the vehicle and support it securely on jackstands. Apply the parking brake lever until you hear one click.
4   Turn the adjusting nut on the equalizer **(see illustration)** clockwise while rotating the rear wheels. Stop turning the nut when the brakes just start to drag on the rear wheels.
5   Release the parking brake lever and check to see that the brakes don't drag when the rear wheels are turned. When properly adjusted, the travel on the parking brake lever should be as listed in this Chapter's Specifications.
6   Lower the vehicle and reinstall the console or cover.

## 16   Parking brake cable(s) - replacement

*Refer to illustrations 16.4a and 16.4b*
1   Block the front wheels and loosen the rear wheel lug nuts. Raise the rear of the vehicle and support it securely on jackstands.
2   On vehicles with rear drum brakes, remove the brake drum(s) (see Section 8).
3   Following the procedure in the previous Section, loosen the cable adjusting nut. Remove the cable clamp from the cable housing **(see illustration 15.4)**. Unhook the cable from the equalizer.

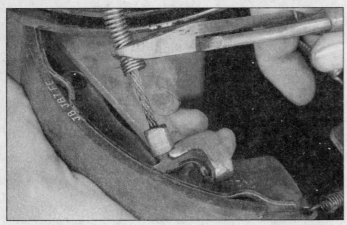

**16.4a To detach the parking brake cable from a drum brake, remove the brake shoe and grab the cable end with a pair of pliers and pull it out of its slot in the parking brake lever . . .**

4    On models with rear drum brakes, remove the brake shoes (see Section 8) and disconnect the cable end from the lever on the trailing brake shoe **(see illustration)**. Depress the tangs on the cable housing retainer and pass the cable through the backing plate. You can do this by passing an offset 12 mm box end wrench over the end of the cable and onto the retainer **(see illustration)**. This compresses all the tangs simultaneously. **Note:** *If you do not have this wrench, you can also use a small screw-type hose clamp. Tighten the clamp around the tangs about 3/8-inch behind the hole in the backing plate, start the cable through the hole and remove the hose clamp.*

5    On models with rear disc brakes, remove the clip and clevis to disconnect the cable end from the actuator lever on the caliper (see Section 6), then remove the spring clip to free the cable housing from the support bracket.

6    Unbolt the cable housing clamps from the underbody, noting how the cable is routed, then remove the cable from the vehicle. It may be necessary to remove the exhaust pipe heat shield bolts at the rear to allow cable removal.

7    If both cables are to be removed, repeat the above steps to remove the remaining cable.

8    Installation is the reverse of the removal procedure. After the cable(s) are installed, be sure to adjust them according to the procedure described in Section 15.

## 17   Brake light switch - check, replacement and adjustment

*Refer to illustration 17.3*

### Check

1    To check the brake light switch, push on the brake pedal and verify that the brake lights come on.

2    If they don't, check the brake light fuse (see Chapter 12 or check your owner's manual for fuse locations). Also check the brake light bulbs in both tail light assemblies (don't forget to check the high-mount brake light).

3    Locate the brake light switch at the top of the brake pedal **(see illustration)**.

4    Unplug the switch connector.

5    Check for continuity across switch terminals A and B with an ohmmeter (between B and C on cruise-control-equipped models). When the brake pedal is depressed, there should be continuity; when it's released, there should be no continuity. If the switch doesn't operate as described, replace it.

### Replacement

6    Disconnect the electrical connector from the switch, if you

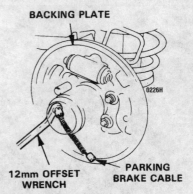

**16.4b . . . then compress the tangs on the retainer by sliding a 12 mm offset box wrench over the end of the cable onto the retainer, and pull the cable out of the backing plate**

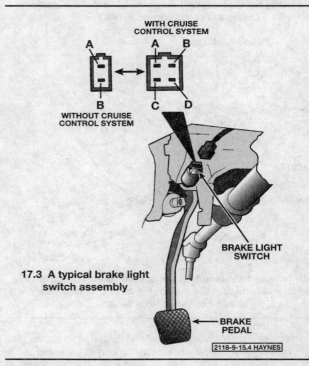

**17.3 A typical brake light switch assembly**

haven't already done so.

7    Remove the locknut on the pedal side of the switch and unscrew the switch from the bracket.

8    Installation of the brake light switch is the reverse of the removal procedure.

### Adjustment

9    Loosen the brake light switch locknut and back off the brake light switch until it's not touching the brake pedal.

10    Loosen the pushrod locknut and screw the pushrod in or out with pliers until the pedal height from the floor is correct (as listed in this Chapter's Specifications). **Note:** *Measure from the top face of the pedal pad to the floor (not the carpet).*

11    Tighten the locknut securely.

12    Screw in the brake light switch until its plunger is fully depressed (threaded end touching the pad on the pedal arm), then back off the switch 1/2-turn and tighten the locknut securely.

13    Depress the pedal with your hand and measure the pedal freeplay. It should be within the dimensions listed in this Chapter's Specifications. Make sure the brake lights operate when the pedal is depressed and go off when the pedal is released.

# Chapter 10
# Suspension and steering systems

## Contents

## Specifications

### General
Power steering fluid type...................................................................... See Chapter 1

### Torque specifications
**Ft-lbs**
#### Front suspension
| | |
|---|---|
| Damper fork pinch bolt | 32 |
| Damper fork-to-lower control arm through bolt/nut | 47 |
| Lower control arm inner pivot bolt | 40 |
| Radius rod-to-crossmember nut | 32 |
| Radius rod-to-lower control arm bolts | 76 |
| Shock absorber-to-body mounting nuts | 28 |
| Shock absorber damper rod upper nut | 22 |
| Steering knuckle (lower) balljoint nut | 40 |
| Upper control arm assembly-to-body mounting nuts | 47 |
| Upper control arm pivot bolt/nut | 22 |
| Upper control arm balljoint nut | 32 |

## Torque specifications

Ft-lbs

### Rear suspension

| | |
|---|---|
| Front lower arm inner pivot bolt/nut | 40 |
| Front/rear lower arm-to-knuckle through bolt/nut | 47 |
| Rear lower arm inner pivot bolt | 47 |
| Hub nut | 134 |
| Shock absorber damper rod nut | 22 |
| Shock absorber-to-knuckle bolt | 40 |
| Shock absorber upper mounting nuts | 28 |
| Trailing arm bracket-to-body bolts | 47 |
| Trailing arm-to-bracket pivot bolt | 47 |
| Trailing arm-to-knuckle bolts | 26 |
| Upper control arm balljoint-to-knuckle nut | 32 |
| Upper control arm inner mounting bolts | 28 |

### Steering system

| | |
|---|---|
| Steering wheel nut | 36 |
| Steering gear mounting bolts | |
|     Left (driver's side) | 32 |
|     Right (passenger's) side | 28 |
| Tie-rod end-to-steering knuckle nut | 32 |

## 1    General information

*Refer to illustrations 1.1 and 1.2*

The front suspension is a fully independent design with upper and lower control arms, shock absorber/coil spring assemblies and a stabilizer bar **(see illustration)**.

The rear suspension uses trailing arms, two unequal length lower control arms, an upper control arm, shock absorber/coil spring units and a stabilizer bar **(see illustration)**.

All models use a power-assisted rack-and-pinion steering gear. The power steering system employs an engine-driven pump connected by hoses to the steering gear.

Frequently, when working on the suspension or steering system components, you may come across fasteners which seem impossible to loosen. These fasteners on the underside of the vehicle are continually

**1.1 Front suspension and steering components**

| | | | | | |
|---|---|---|---|---|---|
| *1* | *Radius rod* | *4* | *Stabilizer bar* | *7* | *Damper fork* |
| *2* | *Shock absorber/coil spring assembly* | *5* | *Lower control arm* | *8* | *Steering knuckle* |
| *3* | *Steering gear* | *6* | *Tie-rod end* | *9* | *Upper control arm* |

**1.2  Rear suspension components**

| | | | | | |
|---|---|---|---|---|---|
| 1 | Rear lower arm | 3 | Trailing arm | 5 | Rear knuckle |
| 2 | Front lower arm | 4 | Shock absorber/coil spring assembly | 6 | Upper arm |

subjected to water, road grime, mud, etc., and can become rusted or "frozen," making them extremely difficult to remove. In order to unscrew these stubborn fasteners without damaging them (or other components), be sure to use lots of penetrating oil and allow it to soak in for a while. Using a wire brush to clean exposed threads will also ease removal of the nut or bolt and prevent damage to the threads. Sometimes a sharp blow with a hammer and punch is effective in breaking the bond between a nut and bolt threads, but care must be taken to prevent the punch from slipping off the fastener and ruining the threads. Heating the stuck fastener and surrounding area with a torch sometimes helps too, but isn't recommended because of the obvious dangers associated with fire. Long breaker bars and extension, or "cheater," pipes will increase leverage, but never use an extension pipe on a ratchet - the ratcheting mechanism could be damaged. Sometimes, turning the nut or bolt in the tightening (clockwise) direction first will help to break it loose. Fasteners that require drastic measures to unscrew should always be replaced with new ones.

Since most of the procedures that are dealt with in this Chapter involve jacking up the vehicle and working underneath it, a good pair of jackstands will be needed. A hydraulic floor jack is the preferred type of jack to lift the vehicle, and it can also be used to support certain components during various operations. **Warning:** *Never, under any circumstances, rely on a jack to support the vehicle while working on it. Whenever any of the suspension or steering fasteners are loosened or removed they must be inspected and, if necessary, be replaced with new ones of the same part number or of original equipment quality and design. Torque specifications must be followed for proper reassembly and component retention. Never attempt to heat or straighten any suspension or steering component. Instead, replace any bent or damaged part with a new one.*

## 2  Shock absorber/coil spring assembly (front) - removal and installation

### *Removal*

*Refer to illustrations 2.4, 2.5a, 2.5b and 2.6*

1    Loosen the wheel lug nuts, raise the vehicle and support it securely on jackstands. Remove the wheel.

2    Unbolt the brake hose from the shock absorber assembly.

3    Disconnect the stabilizer bar from the lower control arm (see Section 6).

4    Place a floor jack under the lower control arm to support it when the shock absorber assembly is removed. Remove the damper fork pinch bolt **(see illustration)**.

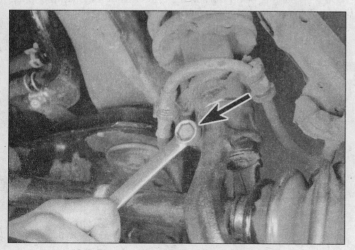

**2.4  Remove the damper fork pinch bolt**

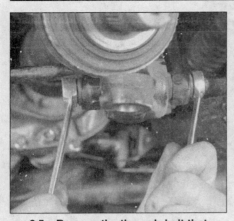

**2.5a Remove the through-bolt that connects the damper fork to the lower control arm**

**2.5b Detach the damper fork from the shock absorber**

**2.6 Remove these three nuts (arrows) from the shock absorber mounting studs**

5    Remove the damper fork-to-lower control arm bolt and remove the fork **(see illustrations)**. It may be necessary to tap the fork from the shock absorber.

6    Support the shock absorber and coil spring assembly and remove the three upper mounting nuts **(see illustration)**. Remove the unit from the fenderwell.

## *Installation*

7    Guide the shock absorber assembly up into the fenderwell and insert the three upper mounting studs through the holes in the body. Once the studs protrude from the holes, install the nuts so the assembly won't fall back through, but don't tighten the nuts completely yet. The shock absorber is heavy and awkward, so get an assistant to help you, if possible.

8    Insert the lower end of the shock absorber into the damper fork. Make sure the aligning tab on the back of the shock body enters the slot in the damper fork.

9    Connect the damper fork to the lower control arm, tightening the self-locking nut to the torque listed in this Chapter's Specifications. Now tighten the damper fork pinch bolt to the torque listed in this Chapter's Specifications.

10    Attach the brake hose to its bracket and tighten the bolt securely.

11    Install the wheel and lug nuts, lower the vehicle and tighten the lug nuts to the torque listed in the Chapter 1 Specifications.

12    Tighten the upper mounting nuts to the torque listed in this Chapter's Specifications.

## 3    Shock absorber or coil spring - replacement

*Refer to illustrations 3.5 and 3.6*

1    Remove the shock absorber/coil spring assembly (see Section 2 or 11).

2    Check the shock absorber for leaking fluid, dents, cracks or other obvious damage. Check the coil spring for chips or cracks which could cause premature failure and inspect the spring seats for hardness or general deterioration. The shock absorber assemblies, complete with the coil springs, are available on an exchange basis which eliminates much time and work. So, before disassembling your shock to replace individual components, check on the availability of parts and the price of a complete rebuilt unit. **Warning:** *Disassembling a shock absorber/coil spring assembly is a potentially dangerous undertaking and utmost attention must be directed to the job, or serious injury may result. Use only a high quality spring compressor and carefully follow the manufacturer's instructions furnished with the tool.* After removing the coil spring from the shock absorber, set it aside in a safe, isolated area.

3    Mount the shock absorber assembly in a vise. Line the vise jaws

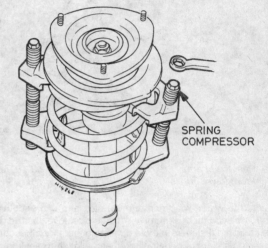

SPRING COMPRESSOR

**3.5 Install the spring compressor according to the tool manufacturer's instructions and compress the spring until all pressure is relieved from the mounting base**

with wood or rags to prevent damage to the unit and don't tighten the vise excessively.

4    Mark the relationship of the damper mounting base to the spring (or if the spring is being replaced, put the mark on the damper unit). This will ensure correct positioning of the mounting base when the unit is reassembled.

5    Following the tool manufacturer's instructions, install the spring compressor (which can be obtained at most auto parts stores or equipment yards on a daily rental basis) on the spring and compress it sufficiently to relieve all pressure from the damper mounting base **(see illustration)**.

6    Remove the damper cap **(see illustration)**. Unscrew the self-locking nut while holding the damper shaft with an Allen wrench to prevent it from turning. Remove the parts from the upper part of the shock and lay them out in the exact order in which they're removed.

7    Carefully lift the compressed spring from the assembly and set it in a safe place. **Warning:** *Keep the ends of the spring facing away from your body!*

8    Slide the rest of the parts off of the damper shaft and lay them out in the exact order in which they're removed.

9    Install the bump stop, bump stop plate (if equipped), dust cover and dust cover plate onto the new damper unit. Extend the damper shaft as far as it will go and slide the components down to the damper body.

10    Carefully place the coil spring onto the shock absorber body, with

**3.6  Exploded view of a typical front shock absorber/coil spring assembly**

  1   *Damper cap*
  2   *Self-locking nut*
  3   *Damper mounting washer*
  4   *Upper mounting rubber*
  5   *Seal*
  6   *Damper mounting collar*
  7   *Damper mounting base*
  8   *Lower mounting rubber*
  9   *Spring mounting rubber*
  10  *Spring*
  11  *Dust cover plate (if equipped)*
  12  *Dust cover*
  13  *Bump stop plate*
  14  *Bump stop*
  15  *Damper unit*

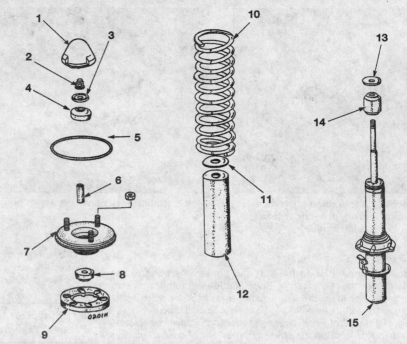

**4.7  Swing the hub/knuckle out (away from the vehicle) and pull the driveaxle from the hub**

**4.8  Remove the four bolts that hold the hub and disc assembly to the steering knuckle (arrows)**

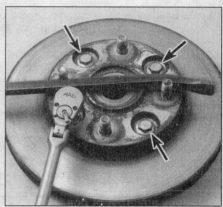

**4.9  Remove the four bolts (arrows) that hold the hub assembly to the brake disc**

the end of the spring resting in the lowest part of the seat.

11  Install the spring mounting rubber, lower mounting rubber, damper mounting collar, damper mounting base, seal, upper mounting rubber, damper mounting washer and a new self-locking nut. Before tightening the nut, align the previously applied marks on the mounting base and the spring (or damper body).

12  Tighten the self-locking nut securely, again using the Allen wrench to prevent the shaft from turning. Remove the spring compressor. Install the damper cap.

13  Install the shock absorber/coil spring assembly (see Section 2 or 11).

---

## 4   Steering knuckle and hub assembly - removal and installation

*Refer to illustrations 4.7, 4.8 and 4.9*

### Removal

1  Remove the wheel cover, if equipped. Loosen the driveaxle/hub nut (see Chapter 8). Loosen the wheel lug nuts, raise the front of the

vehicle and support it securely on jackstands. Remove the wheel and the driveaxle/hub nut.

2  Unbolt the brake hose bracket from the steering knuckle. Unbolt the brake caliper, hang it out of the way with a piece of wire, then remove the caliper mounting bracket (see Chapter 9).

3  Disconnect the tie-rod end from the steering knuckle (see Section 16).

4  Separate the lower control arm from the balljoint in the bottom of the steering knuckle (see Section 8).

5  Remove the ABS sensor (see Chapter 9).

6  Separate the upper end of the knuckle from the upper control arm balljoint (see Section 8).

7  Carefully pull the knuckle and hub assembly along with the brake disc off of the driveaxle **(see illustration)**. Support the driveaxle with a piece of wire to prevent damage to the inner CV joint.

8  Remove the four mounting bolts that retain the brake disc/hub assembly to the steering knuckle **(see illustration)**.

9  Separate the brake disc from the hub assembly **(see illustration)**. If the wheel bearing is in need of replacement, take the hub assembly to a dealer service department or an automotive machine shop to have the old wheel bearing pressed out and a new one pressed in.

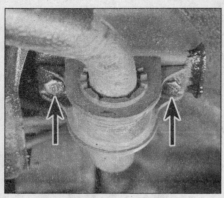

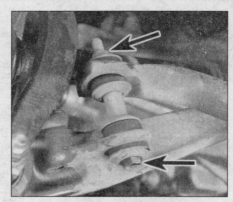

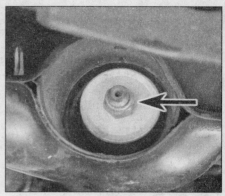

**6.2 Stabilizer bar bracket (driver's side bracket shown, passenger side bracket similar)**

**6.3 Stabilizer bar link bolt assembly**

**7.3 To detach the front end of the radius rod, remove the plug in the plastic splash shield, then remove this nut from the rod**

## Installation

10   Attach the brake disc to the hub and tighten the bolts to the torque listed in the Chapter 9 Specifications. Install the hub assembly/brake disc to the steering knuckle and install the bolts, tightening them to the torque listed in this Chapter's Specifications.

11   Apply a light coat of wheel bearing grease to the driveaxle splines. Insert the driveaxle through the splined bore of the hub while guiding the steering knuckle into position.

12   Connect the upper end of the knuckle to the upper control arm balljoint (see Section 9). Tighten the balljoint stud nut to the torque listed in this Chapter's Specifications.

13   Connect the balljoint on the bottom of the knuckle to the lower control arm (see Section 8).

14   Install the caliper mount and caliper, tightening the bolts to the proper torque (see Chapter 9). Attach the brake hose to its bracket.

15   Install the driveaxle nut and tighten it securely.

16   Install the wheel and lug nuts, lower the vehicle and tighten the lug nuts to the torque listed in the Chapter 1 Specifications.

17   Tighten the driveaxle nut to the torque listed in the Chapter 8 Specifications.

18   Drive the vehicle to an alignment shop and have the front end alignment checked and, if necessary, adjusted.

## 5   Hub and bearing assembly (front) - removal and installation

1   Remove the steering knuckle assembly from the vehicle and separate the hub assembly from the brake disc (see Section 4).

2   Due to the special tools and expertise required to press the hub

and bearing from the steering knuckle, the assembly should be taken to a dealer service department or other qualified repair shop to have the bearing replaced if it is worn.

## 6   Stabilizer bar and bushings (front) - removal and installation

*Refer to illustrations 6.2 and 6.3*

1   Apply the parking brake. Loosen the front wheel lug nuts, raise the front of the vehicle and support it securely on jackstands. Remove the wheels.

2   Remove the bolts which attach the stabilizer bar brackets to the underside of the vehicle **(see illustration)**.

3   Detach the stabilizer bar link bolts from the lower control arms **(see illustrations)**. Note the order in which the spacers, washers and bushings are arranged on the link bolt.

4   Remove the bar from under the vehicle.

5   Pull the brackets off the stabilizer bar and inspect the bushings for cracks, hardness and other signs of deterioration. If the bushings are damaged, replace them.

6   Installation is the reverse of removal.

## 7   Radius rod - removal and installation

*Refer to illustrations 7.3 and 7.4*

1   Loosen the wheel lug nuts, raise the front of the vehicle and place it securely on jackstands. Remove the wheel.

2   Remove the plug from the plastic splash shield.

**7.4 To detach the rear end of the radius rod, remove the two bolts (arrows) that attach the radius rod to the lower control arm**

**8.5 Separate the lower control arm from the steering knuckle balljoint with a two-jaw puller**

**8.6 To remove the lower control arm, remove the pivot bolt from the inner end of the arm**

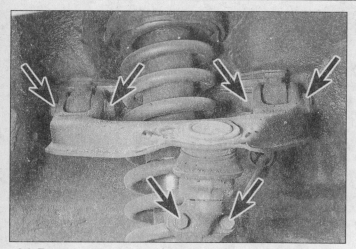

**9.2 To remove the upper control arm, remove the balljoint stud protector (lower arrows), separate the knuckle from the upper control arm and remove the two pivot bolts and nuts**

3    Remove the nut from the front end of the radius rod in the front crossmember **(see illustration)**.
4    Remove the bolts that attach the rear end of the radius rod to the lower control arm **(see illustration)** and remove the rod.
5    Installation is the reverse of removal. Be sure to tighten all fasteners to the torque values listed in this Chapter's Specifications.
6    Drive the vehicle to an alignment shop and have the front end alignment checked and, if necessary, adjusted.

## 8    Lower control arm - removal and installation

*Refer to illustrations 8.5 and 8.6*
1    Loosen the front wheel lug nuts, raise the vehicle, place it securely on jackstands and remove the wheel.
2    Detach the damper fork from the shock absorber (see Section 2).
3    Detach the radius rod from the lower control arm (see Section 7).
4    Detach the stabilizer bar from the lower control arm (see Section 6).
5    Remove the cotter pin from the castle nut on the lower balljoint stud. Loosen the nut, but don't remove it yet. Using a two-jaw puller, separate the lower control arm from the balljoint in the steering knuckle **(see illustration)**. Remove the nut.
6    Remove the pivot bolt from the inner end of the lower control arm **(see illustration)** and remove the arm.
7    Installation is the reverse of removal.

## 9    Upper control arm - removal and installation

*Refer to illustration 9.2*
1    Loosen the front wheel lug nuts, raise the vehicle, place it securely on jackstands and remove the wheel. Support the lower control arm with a floor jack.
2    Remove the two bolts and detach the balljoint stud protector from the steering knuckle **(see illustration)**. Remove the cotter pin and loosen, but do not remove, the castle nut from the upper balljoint stud. The nut will prevent the upper control arm and the steering knuckle from separating violently in the next step.
3    Separate the upper control arm from the steering knuckle with a two-jaw puller. Don't let the top of the steering knuckle fall out. If necessary, secure it to the shock absorber with a piece of wire.
4    Remove the upper control arm pivot nuts and bolts **(see illustration 9.2)** and the balljoint nut, then remove the upper control arm. Note that the heads of the pivot bolts face toward each other - be sure to install them the same way.
5    If the inner pivot bushings are worn, remove the anchor bolts from the inner fenderwell, mount the anchor bolts in a vise and drive the bushings out with an appropriately-sized drift. Press the new ones in with the jaws of the vise.
6    Installation is the reverse of removal. Be sure to tighten all of the fasteners to the torque values listed in this Chapter's Specifications.

## 10    Balljoints - replacement

1    The front suspension uses two balljoints. The upper balljoint, located in the upper control arm, can't be removed. If it's worn or damaged, replace the upper control arm (see Section 9).
2    The lower balljoint, located in the steering knuckle, can be removed, but special tools are needed. If it's worn or damaged, remove the knuckle (see Section 4) and take it to a dealer service department or other repair shop to have it replaced.

## 11    Shock absorber/coil spring assembly (rear) - removal and installation

*Refer to illustration 11.2, 11.3 and 11.4*
1    Loosen the rear wheel lug nuts, raise the vehicle, place it securely on jackstands and remove the rear wheels.
2    Remove the rear seat. On Coupe models, also remove the trim panel covering the upper mount of the shock absorber **(see illustration)**.
3    Remove the shock absorber upper mounting nuts **(see illustration)**.
4    Remove the shock absorber lower mounting bolt **(see illustration)**.

**11.2 On Coupe models, remove the rear seat back and the trim panel for access to the shock absorber upper mount**

**11.3 Remove the rear shock absorber upper mounting nuts (arrows)**

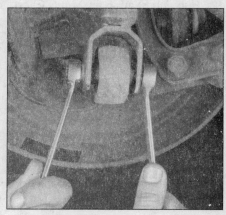

**11.4 Removing the lower mounting bolt from the rear shock absorber assembly**

12.3  Using a hammer and chisel, remove the dust cover

12.4  Unstake the hub nut

12.5  Stake the hub nut back into place

13.2  To disconnect the stabilizer bar from the trailing arm, remove the stabilizer bar-to-link bolt and nut (arrow) (right side shown)

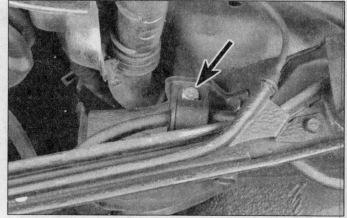

13.3  To detach the stabilizer bar from the body remove this bolt (arrow) from each bracket (left side shown)

5     Pull the rear knuckle down and remove the shock absorber/coil spring assembly.
6     To inspect or replace the shock absorber or coil spring, see Section 3.
7     Installation is the reverse of removal. Be sure to tighten all fasteners to the torque values listed in this Chapter's Specifications.

## 12  Hub and bearing assembly (rear) - removal and installation

*Refer to illustrations 12.3, 12.4 and 12.5*
**Note:** *The rear hub and bearing are combined into a single assembly. The bearing is sealed for life and requires no lubrication or attention. If the bearing is worn or damaged, replace the entire hub and bearing assembly.*
1     Loosen the rear wheel lug nuts, raise the vehicle, place it securely on jackstands and remove the rear wheel.
2     Remove the brake drum or caliper and disc (see Chapter 9).
3     Remove the dust cover **(see illustration)**.
4     Unstake the hub retaining nut **(see illustration),** unscrew the nut and remove the thrust washer then remove the hub assembly.
5     Install the new hub assembly and thrust washer, tighten the new nut to the torque listed in this Chapter's Specifications, then stake its edge into the groove in the spindle **(see illustration)**.
6     Install the dust cover by tapping lightly around the edge until it is seated.
7     The remainder of installation is the reverse of removal.

## 13  Stabilizer bar and bushings (rear) - removal and installation

*Refer to illustrations 13.2 and 13.3*
1     Loosen the rear wheel lug nuts, raise the rear of the vehicle, place it securely on jackstands and remove the rear wheels.
2     Remove the stabilizer bar-to-link nuts and bolts **(see illustration)**.
3     Remove the stabilizer-to-body clamp bolts **(see illustration)** and remove the stabilizer bar.
4     Pull the brackets off the stabilizer bar and inspect the bushings for cracks, hardness and other signs of deterioration. If the bushings are damaged, replace them.
5     Installation is the reverse of removal.

## 14  Suspension arms (rear) - removal and installation

1     Loosen the rear wheel lug nuts, raise the vehicle, place it securely on jackstands and remove the wheel.

### *Upper arm*

*Refer to illustration 14.2*
2     To disconnect the outer end of the upper arm from the knuckle, remove the nut from the balljoint stud at the knuckle **(see illustration)**, install a small two-jaw puller and separate the arm from the knuckle.
3     Remove the two mounting bolts that attach the inner end of the upper arm to the chassis.
4     Remove the upper arm.

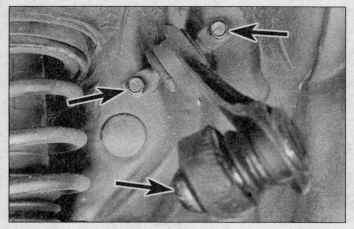

14.2  To remove the upper arm, remove the nut on the balljoint stud (lower arrow), separate the balljoint stud from the knuckle with a two-jaw puller and remove the two mounting bolts from the inner end of the arm (upper arrows)

14.7  To disconnect the outer ends of the lower control arms from the knuckle, remove this through bolt - you'll need to use a back-up wrench

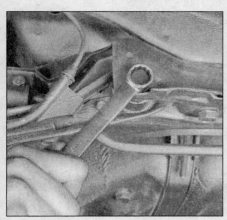

14.8  To disconnect the inner ends of the lower control arms from the chassis, remove the pivot bolts (bolt for rear arm shown)

14.12  Detach the brake hose bracket (two upper arrows) and the parking brake cable bracket (lower arrow) from the trailing arm

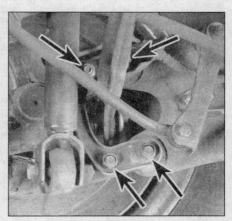

14.14  To disconnect the rear end of the trailing arm and its bracket from the knuckle, remove these four bolts (arrows)

5    Inspect the bushing at the inner end of the arm for cracks. Inspect the balljoint at the outer end of the arm for excessive freeplay. If either is worn, replace it.
6    Installation is the reverse of removal. Be sure to tighten all fasteners to the torque values listed in this Chapter's Specifications.

## Lower arms

*Refer to illustrations 14.7 and 14.8*
7    Remove the through bolt that attaches the lower arms to the knuckle **(see illustration)**.
8    Disconnect any brake hoses or cables from the lower arms. Mark the position of the adjustment cam on the rear lower arm to its bracket. Remove the pivot bolts that attach the inner ends of the lower arms to the chassis **(see illustration)**.
9    Remove the lower arms.
10   Inspect the lower arm bushings for cracks and deterioration. If any of them are worn, replace the arm.
11   Installation is the reverse of removal. Be sure to tighten all fasteners to the torque values listed in this Chapter's Specifications.

## Trailing arm

*Refer to illustrations 14.12 and 14.14*
**Note:** *The trailing arm bushing on V6 models is a hydraulic type. The interior of the bushing is divided into four hydraulic chambers*

*connected by a series of orifices. Do not attempt to change the trailing arm bushing - instead, replace the trailing arm as a single unit.*
12   Disconnect the brake hose and the parking brake cable brackets from the trailing arm **(see illustration)**.
13   Disconnect the stabilizer bar link from the trailing arm (see Section 13).
14   Remove the four bolts that attach the trailing arm bracket to the knuckle **(see illustration)**.
15   Remove the bolts that attach the trailing arm bracket to the chassis.
16   Remove the trailing arm.
17   Inspect the bushing at the forward end of the arm. If they're cracked or deteriorated, replace the arm.
18   Installation is the reverse of removal. Be sure to tighten all fasteners to the torque listed in this Chapter's Specifications.

---

## 15   Steering wheel - removal and installation

**Warning 1:** *These models have airbags. Always disable the airbag system before working in the vicinity of the steering column, instrument panel or console to avoid the possibility of accidental deployment of the airbag, which could cause personal injury (see Chapter 12). The yellow wiring harnesses and connectors routed through the console and instrument panel are for this system. Do not use electrical test equipment on the system wiring or connectors or tamper with them in any way.*

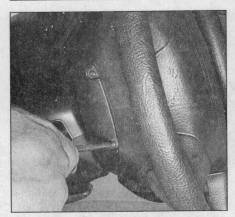

**15.2a  Remove the two screws and lift the access plate from the steering column**

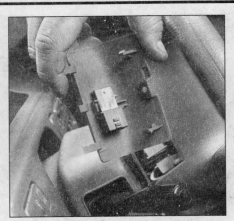

**15.2b  The short connector is stowed on the inside of the access plate**

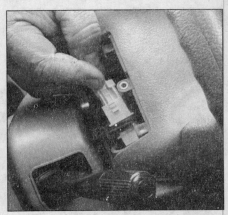

**15.2c  Unplug the yellow connector for the airbag module**

**Warning 2:** *On models equipped with airbags, make sure the steering shaft is not turned while the steering wheel is removed or you could damage the airbag system. To prevent the shaft from turning, position the wheels straight ahead, turn the ignition key to the lock position and remove the key before beginning work. Due to the possible damage to the airbag system, we recommend only experienced mechanics attempt this procedure.*

### Removal

*Refer to illustrations 15.2a, 15.2b, 15.2c, 15.2d, 15.3a, 15.3b, 15.4 and 15.6*

1    Disconnect the cable from the negative battery terminal, then disconnect the positive battery cable. **Caution:** *The stereo in your vehicle is equipped with an anti-theft system. Make sure you have the correct activation code before disconnecting the battery.* Wait three minutes before proceeding to the next step to allow the airbag's backup power supply to be depleted.

2    Remove the access plate from the lower steering column cover and remove the short connector from the access plate **(see illustrations)**. Unplug the airbag module-to-cable reel connector and plug the short connector into the airbag module side of this connector to disable the airbag module **(see illustrations)**.

3    Remove the access panels from each side of the steering wheel cover. Remove both Torx screws retaining the airbag module to the steering wheel **(see illustrations)**.

4    Pull off the module **(see illustration)** and carefully set the module aside with the trim side facing up.

5    Unplug the electrical connectors for the horn and, if equipped, the cruise control system.

6    Remove the steering wheel retaining nut. Paint or scribe a mark indicating the relationship of the steering wheel hub to the steering shaft **(see illustration)**.

7    Remove the steering wheel using a steering wheel puller. **Warning:** *While the steering wheel is removed, DO NOT turn the steering shaft. If you do so, the airbag reel could be damaged.*

### Installation

*Refer to illustration 15.9*

8    Make sure the front wheels are pointed straight ahead.

9    Make absolutely sure that the cable reel is centered with the arrow on the cable reel pointing up **(see illustration)**. This shouldn't be a problem as long as you have not turned the steering shaft while the wheel was removed. If for some reason the shaft was turned, center the cable reel as follows:

a) *Rotate the cable reel clockwise until it stops.*

b) *Rotate the cable reel counterclockwise about two turns until the arrow on the cable reel points straight up. On 1994 and 1995 models, make sure the yellow gear tooth lines up with the mark on the cover.*

10    Be sure to align the index mark on the steering wheel hub with the mark on the shaft when you slip the wheel onto the shaft. Make sure the locating pins on the steering column engage the holes in the backside of the steering wheel. Install the mounting nut and tighten it to the torque listed in this Chapter's Specifications.

11    Plug in the horn connector and, if equipped, the cruise control connector.

12    Reattach the airbag module with NEW Torx bolts and tighten the bolts securely. Install the Torx bolt access panels.

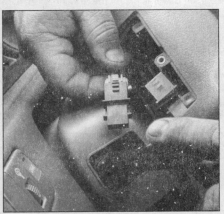

**15.2d  Plug the short connector into the airbag module connector**

**15.3a  Remove the left Torx screw (arrow) that attaches the airbag module to the steering wheel**

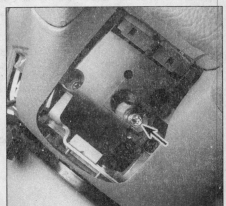

**15.3b  Remove the right Torx screw (arrow)**

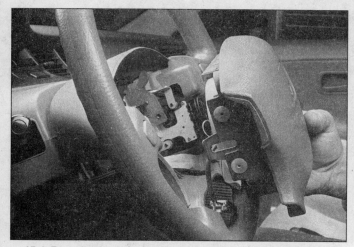

15.4  Remove the airbag module from the steering wheel and set it aside (always store the airbag module with the trim side facing UP)

15.6  After removing the steering wheel nut, mark the relationship of the steering wheel to the shaft

13   Unplug the short connector from the airbag connector.
14   Plug the airbag and cable reel connector halves together.
15   Secure the short connector to the access plate and install the access plate.

## 16   Tie-rod ends - removal and installation

### Removal

*Refer to illustrations 16.2a, 16.2b and 16.4*

1   Loosen the wheel lug nuts. Raise the front of the vehicle, support it securely on jackstands and remove the wheel.
2   Hold the tie-rod end with a backup wrench and loosen the jam nut enough to mark the position of the tie-rod end in relation to the threads **(see illustrations)**.
3   Remove the cotter pin and loosen the nut on the tie-rod end stud. Don't completely remove the nut.
4   Separate the tie-rod from the steering knuckle arm with a puller **(see illustration)**. Remove the nut and detach the tie-rod.
5   Unscrew the tie-rod end from the tie-rod.

### Installation

6   Thread the tie-rod end on to the marked position and insert the tie-rod stud into the steering knuckle arm. Don't tighten the jam nut yet.

15.9  Before installing the steering wheel, make sure the front wheels are pointed straight ahead and the "TOP" mark points straight up on the cable reel for the airbag system; also, on 1994 and 1995 models, note the yellow gear tooth at 7 o'clock is lined up with its mark on the cover

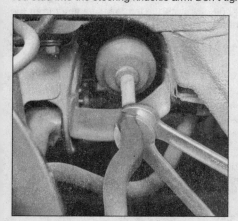

16.2a  Using a backup wrench to prevent the tie-rod end from turning, loosen the jam nut

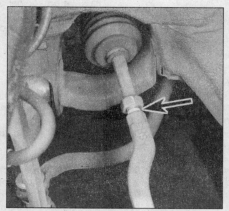

16.2b  Make an alignment mark on the exposed threads, along the edge of the tie-rod end, so the new tie-rod end will be installed in the exact same position

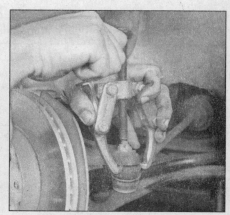

16.4  Use a two-jaw puller to separate the tie-rod end from the steering knuckle arm

**18.1 Pop off the upper and lower clamps (left arrow points to lower clamp; upper clamp not visible in this photo) and slide off the cover - when you put it back on, make sure the two nibs (arrows) on the flange at the lower end are pushed into the holes in the floor**

7    Install the nut on the stud and tighten it to the torque listed in this Chapter's Specifications. Install a new cotter pin.
8    Tighten the jam nut securely.
9    Install the wheel and lug nuts. Lower the vehicle and tighten the lug nuts to the torque listed in the Chapter 1 Specifications.
10    Have the alignment checked by a dealer service department or an alignment shop.

## 17  Steering gear boots - replacement

1    Loosen the lug nuts, raise the front of the vehicle and support it securely on jackstands. Remove the wheel.
2    Remove the tie-rod end and jam nut (see Section 16).
3    Remove the steering gear boot clamps and slide off the boot.
4    Before installing the new boot, wrap the threads and serrations on the end of the tie-rod with a layer of tape so the small end of the new boot isn't damaged.
5    Slide the new boot into position on the steering gear until it seats in the groove in the steering rod and install new clamps.
6    Remove the tape and install the tie-rod end (see Section 16).
7    Install the wheel and lug nuts. Lower the vehicle and tighten the lug nuts to the torque listed in the Chapter 1 Specifications.

## 18  Steering gear - removal and installation

*Refer to illustrations 18.1, 18.2 and 18.10*
**Warning 1:** *The vehicles covered by this manual have airbags. Always disable the airbag system before working in the vicinity of the steering column, instrument panel or console to avoid the possibility of accidental deployment of the airbag, which could cause personal injury (see Chapter 12). The yellow wiring harnesses and connectors routed through the console and instrument panel are for this system. Do not use electrical test equipment on the system wiring or connectors or tamper with them in any way.*
**Warning 2:** *Make sure the steering shaft is not turned while the steering gear or box is removed or you could damage the airbag system. To prevent the shaft from turning, position the wheels straight ahead, turn the ignition key to the lock position and remove the key before beginning work or run the seat belt through the steering wheel and clip the seat belt into place. Due to the possible damage to the airbag system, we recommend only experienced mechanics attempt this procedure.*

**18.2 Mark the relationship of the intermediate shaft to the steering gear input shaft and remove the pinch bolt (arrow)**

**Caution:** *The stereo in your vehicle is equipped with an anti-theft system. Make sure you have the correct activation code before disconnecting the battery.*

### Removal

1    Working under the dash, remove the steering joint cover **(see illustration)**.
2    Mark the relationship of the intermediate shaft universal joint to the steering gear input shaft **(see illustration)** and remove the pinch bolt.
3    Raise the front of the vehicle and support it securely on jackstands. Apply the parking brake.
4    Drain the power steering system fluid (see Chapter 1).
5    Place a drain pan under the steering gear. Disconnect the power steering fluid pressure and return lines and cap them to prevent contamination and loss of fluid. **Note:** *Don't disconnect the fittings on the lines that lead to the steering gear pressure cylinder.*
6    Separate the tie-rod ends from the steering knuckle arms (see Section 16).
7    Remove the oxygen sensor (see Chapter 6) and the catalytic converter from the exhaust system.
8    Disconnect the shift linkage (see Chapter 7).
9    Remove the stiffener plate from the chassis and steering gear.
10    Support the steering gear and remove the mounting bolts **(see illustration)**. Lower the unit, separate the intermediate shaft from the steering gear input shaft and remove the steering gear from the vehicle. It will be necessary to angle the steering gear slightly to clear the right side beam.

### Installation

11    Raise the steering gear into position and connect the intermediate shaft, aligning the marks.
12    Install the steering gear mounting bolts and washers and tighten them securely.
13    Connect the tie-rod ends to the steering knuckle arms (see Section 16).
14    Install the intermediate shaft pinch bolt and tighten it securely.
15    Install the steering joint cover and clamps. Make sure the two tabs on the flange at the lower end of the shield are aligned with holes in the floor.
16    Connect the power steering hoses/lines to the steering gear and fill the power steering pump reservoir with the recommended fluid (see Chapter 1).
17    Install the steering gear shield.
18    Lower the vehicle and bleed the steering system (see Section 20).

**18.10  Remove these bolts (arrows) from the right (passenger side) steering gear mounting clamp and remove the clamp (left [driver's side] clamp similar)**

**19.2a  Remove the mounting nut and bolt (arrow) . . .**

**19.2b  . . . and then remove the adjuster bolt (arrow)**

## 19  Power steering pump - removal and installation

*Refer to illustrations 19.2a and 19.2b*

1   Disconnect the fluid hoses at the pump. Note the difference between the pressure and the return hoses; the return hose is held to the pump with a spring type clamp, and the pressure line has two bolts holding it to the pump body. Cap or plug both hoses to prevent leakage or contamination. Install a new O-ring on the end of the pressure line when reassembling.

2   Remove the pump mounting bolt and adjuster bolt **(see illustrations)**.

3   Remove the upper pivot bolt and remove the pump from the engine.

4   Installation is the reverse of removal. Be sure to bleed the power steering system (see Section 20) and adjust the drivebelt tension (see Chapter 1).

## 20  Power steering system - bleeding

1   Following any operation in which the power steering fluid lines have been disconnected, the power steering system must be bled to remove all air and obtain proper steering performance.

2   With the front wheels in the straight ahead position, check the power steering fluid level (see Chapter 1). If it's low, add fluid until it reaches the lower mark on the reservoir.

3   Start the engine and allow it to run at fast idle. Recheck the fluid level and add more if necessary to reach the Cold mark on the dipstick.

4   Bleed the system by turning the wheels from side-to-side, without hitting the stops. This will work the air out of the system. Keep the reservoir full of fluid as this is done.

5   When the air is worked out of the system, return the wheels to the straight ahead position and leave the vehicle running for several more minutes before shutting it off.

6   Road test the vehicle to be sure the steering system is functioning normally and noise free.

7   Recheck the fluid level to be sure it is up to the Hot mark on the reservoir while the engine is at normal operating temperature. Add fluid if necessary (see Chapter 1).

## 21  Wheels and tires - general information

*Refer to illustration 21.1*

All vehicles covered by this manual are equipped with metric-sized fiberglass or steel belted radial tires **(see illustration)**. Use of other size or type of tires may affect the ride and handling of the vehicle. Don't mix different types of tires, such as radials and bias belted, on the same vehicle as handling may be seriously affected. It's recommended that tires be replaced in pairs on the same axle, but if only one tire is being replaced, be sure it's the same size, structure and tread design as the other.

Because tire pressure has a substantial effect on handling and wear, the pressure on all tires should be checked at least once a month or before any extended trips (see Chapter 1).

Wheels must be replaced if they are bent, dented, leak air, have elongated bolt holes, are heavily rusted, out of vertical symmetry or if the lug nuts won't stay tight. Wheel repairs that use welding or peening are not recommended.

Tire and wheel balance is important to the overall handling, braking and performance of the vehicle. Unbalanced wheels can adversely affect handling and ride characteristics as well as tire life. Whenever a tire is installed on a wheel, the tire and wheel should be balanced by a shop with the proper equipment.

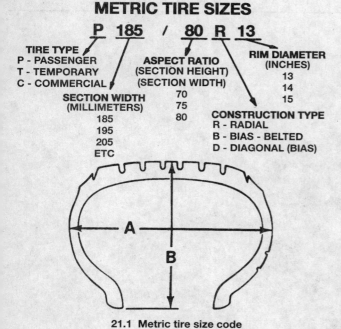

# METRIC TIRE SIZES

## P  185  /  80  R  13

**TIRE TYPE**
P - PASSENGER
T - TEMPORARY
C - COMMERCIAL

**ASPECT RATIO (SECTION HEIGHT) (SECTION WIDTH)**
70
75
80

**RIM DIAMETER (INCHES)**
13
14
15

**SECTION WIDTH (MILLIMETERS)**
185
195
205
ETC

**CONSTRUCTION TYPE**
R - RADIAL
B - BIAS - BELTED
D - DIAGONAL (BIAS)

**21.1  Metric tire size code**

1   A = Section width          2   B = Section height

## 22   Wheel alignment - general information

*Refer to illustration 22.1*

A wheel alignment refers to the adjustments made to the wheels so they are in proper angular relationship to the suspension and the ground. Wheels that are out of proper alignment not only affect steering control, but also increase tire wear. Toe-in and caster can be adjusted on the front wheels, and the rear toe-in can also be adjusted. The front and rear camber angle, and rear caster should be checked to determine if any of the suspension components are worn out or bent **(see illustration)**.

Getting the proper wheel alignment is a very exacting process, one in which complicated and expensive machines are necessary to perform the job properly. Because of this, you should have a technician with the proper equipment perform these tasks. We will, however, use this space to give you a basic idea of what is involved with wheel alignment so you can better understand the process and deal intelligently with the shop that does the work.

Toe-in is the turning in of the wheels. The purpose of a toe specification is to ensure parallel rolling of the wheels. In a vehicle with zero toe-in, the distance between the front edges of the wheels will be the same as the distance between the rear edges of the wheels. The actual amount of toe-in is normally only a fraction of an inch. At the front end, toe-in is controlled by the tie-rod end position on the tie-rod. At the rear it is adjusted by moving the rear lower arm, in or out, within its bracket on the body. Incorrect toe-in will cause the tires to wear improperly by making them scrub against the road surface.

Camber is the tilting of the wheels from the vertical when viewed from the front or rear of the vehicle. When the wheels tilt out at the top, the camber is said to be positive (+). When the wheels tilt in at the top the camber is negative (-). The amount of tilt is measured in degrees from the vertical and this measurement is called the camber angle. This angle affects the amount of tire tread which contacts the road and compensates for changes in the suspension geometry when the vehicle is cornering or traveling over an undulating surface. Camber isn't adjustable on these vehicles.

Caster is the tilting of the top of the steering axis from the vertical. A tilt toward the rear is positive caster and a tilt toward the front is negative caster. The caster on the front end is adjustable by installing shims of different thicknesses on the radius rod.

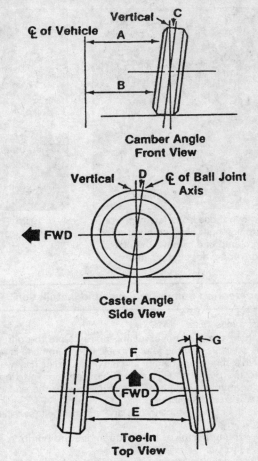

**Camber Angle Front View**

**Caster Angle Side View**

**Toe-In Top View**

**22.1  Front end alignment details**

1   *A minus B = C (degrees camber)*
2   *E minus F = toe-in (measured in inches)*
3   *G = toe-in (expressed in degrees)*

# Chapter 11  Body

## Contents

## 1    General information

These models feature a "unibody" layout, using a floor pan with front and rear frame side rails which support the body components, front and rear suspension systems and other mechanical components.

Certain components are particularly vulnerable to accident damage and can be unbolted and repaired or replaced. Among these parts are the body moldings, bumpers, the hood and trunk lid (or liftgate) and all glass.

Only general body maintenance practices and body panel repair procedures within the scope of the do-it-yourselfer are included in this Chapter.

## 2    Body - maintenance

1    The condition of your vehicle's body is very important, because the resale value depends a great deal on it. It's much more difficult to repair a neglected or damaged body than it is to repair mechanical components. The hidden areas of the body, such as the wheel wells, the frame and the engine compartment, are equally important, although they don't require as frequent attention as the rest of the body.

2    Once a year, or every 12,000 miles, it's a good idea to have the underside of the body steam cleaned. All traces of dirt and oil will be removed and the area can then be inspected carefully for rust, damaged brake lines, frayed electrical wires, damaged cables and other problems.

3    At the same time, clean the engine and the engine compartment with a steam cleaner or water soluble degreaser.

4    The wheel wells should be given close attention, since under-coating can peel away and stones and dirt thrown up by the tires can cause the paint to chip and flake, allowing rust to set in. If rust is found, clean down to the bare metal and apply an anti-rust paint.

5    The body should be washed about once a week. Wet the vehicle thoroughly to soften the dirt, then wash it down with a soft sponge and plenty of clean soapy water. If the surplus dirt is not washed off very carefully, it can wear down the paint.

6    Spots of tar or asphalt thrown up from the road should be removed with a cloth soaked in solvent.

7    Once every six months, wax the body and chrome trim. If a chrome cleaner is used to remove rust from any of the vehicle's plated parts, remember that the cleaner also removes part of the chrome, so use it sparingly.

These photos illustrate a method of repairing simple dents. They are intended to supplement *Body repair - minor damage* in this Chapter and should not be used as the sole instructions for body repair on these vehicles.

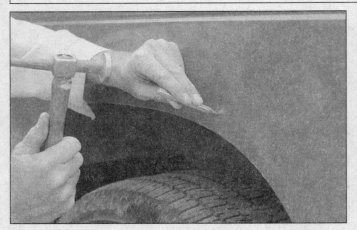

1   If you can't access the backside of the body panel to hammer out the dent, pull it out with a slide-hammer-type dent puller. In the deepest portion of the dent or along the crease line, drill or punch hole(s) at least one inch apart . . .

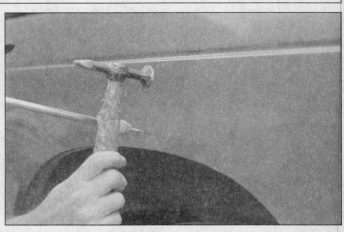

2   . . . then screw the slide-hammer into the hole and operate it. Tap with a hammer near the edge of the dent to help 'pop' the metal back to its original shape. When you're finished, the dent area should be close to its original contour and about 1/8-inch below the surface of the surrounding metal

3   Using coarse-grit sandpaper, remove the paint down to the bare metal. Hand sanding works fine, but the disc sander shown here makes the job faster. Use finer (about 320-grit) sandpaper to feather-edge the paint at least one inch around the dent area

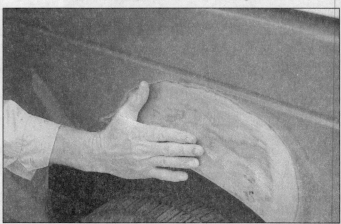

4   When the paint is removed, touch will probably be more helpful than sight for telling if the metal is straight. Hammer down the high spots or raise the low spots as necessary. Clean the repair area with wax/silicone remover

5   Following label instructions, mix up a batch of plastic filler and hardener. The ratio of filler to hardener is critical, and, if you mix it incorrectly, it will either not cure properly or cure too quickly (you won't have time to file and sand it into shape)

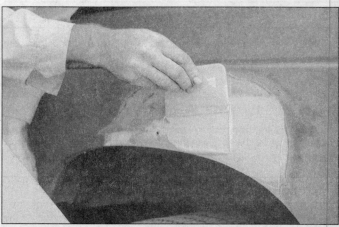

6   Working quickly so the filler doesn't harden, use a plastic applicator to press the body filler firmly into the metal, assuring it bonds completely. Work the filler until it matches the original contour and is slightly above the surrounding metal

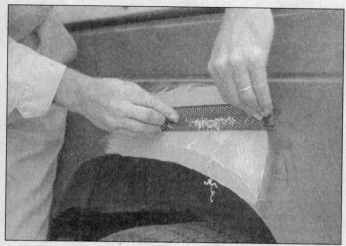

7   Let the filler harden until you can just dent it with your fingernail. Use a body file or Surform tool (shown here) to rough-shape the filler

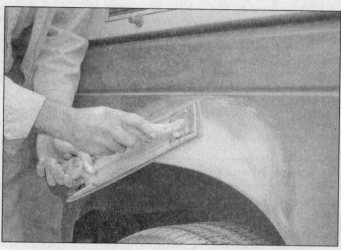

8   Use coarse-grit sandpaper and a sanding board or block to work the filler down until it's smooth and even. Work down to finer grits of sandpaper - always using a board or block - ending up with 360 or 400 grit

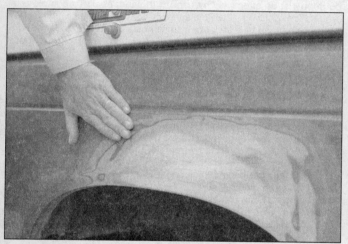

9   You shouldn't be able to feel any ridge at the transition from the filler to the bare metal or from the bare metal to the old paint. As soon as the repair is flat and uniform, remove the dust and mask off the adjacent panels or trim pieces

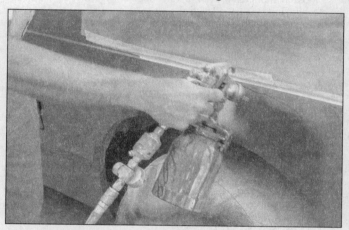

10   Apply several layers of primer to the area. Don't spray the primer on too heavy, so it sags or runs, and make sure each coat is dry before you spray on the next one. A professional-type spray gun is being used here, but aerosol spray primer is available inexpensively from auto parts stores

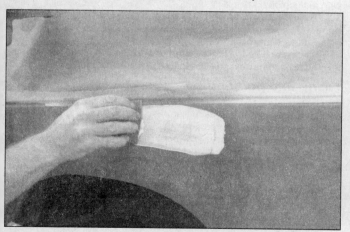

11   The primer will help reveal imperfections or scratches. Fill these with glazing compound. Follow the label instructions and sand it with 360 or 400-grit sandpaper until it's smooth. Repeat the glazing, sanding and respraying until the primer reveals a perfectly smooth surface

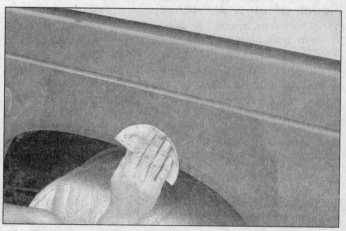

12   Finish sand the primer with very fine sandpaper (400 or 600-grit) to remove the primer overspray. Clean the area with water and allow it to dry. Use a tack rag to remove any dust, then apply the finish coat. Don't attempt to rub out or wax the repair area until the paint has dried completely (at least two weeks)

## 3   Vinyl trim - maintenance

Don't clean vinyl trim with detergents, caustic soap or petroleum based cleaners. Plain soap and water works just fine, with a soft brush to clean dirt that may be ingrained. Wash the vinyl as frequently as the rest of the vehicle.

After cleaning, application of a high quality rubber and vinyl protectant will help prevent oxidation and cracks. The protectant can also be applied to weather stripping, vacuum lines and rubber hoses, which often fail as a result of chemical degradation, and to the tires.

## 4   Upholstery and carpets - maintenance

1    Every three months remove the floormats and clean the interior of the vehicle (more frequently if necessary). Use a stiff whisk broom to brush the carpeting and loosen dirt and dust, then vacuum the upholstery and carpets thoroughly, especially along seams and crevices.
2    Dirt and stains can be removed from carpeting with basic household or automotive carpet shampoos available in spray cans. Follow the directions and vacuum again, then use a stiff brush to bring back the "nap" of the carpet.
3    Most interiors have cloth or vinyl upholstery, either of which can be cleaned and maintained with a number of material-specific cleaners or shampoos available in auto supply stores. Follow the directions on the product for usage, and always spot-test any upholstery cleaner on an inconspicuous area (bottom edge of a backseat cushion) to ensure that it doesn't cause a color shift in the material.
4    After cleaning, vinyl upholstery should be treated with a protectant. **Note:** *Make sure the protectant container indicates the product can be used on seats - some products may make a seat too slippery.* **Caution:** *Do not use protectant on vinyl-covered steering wheels.*
5    Leather upholstery requires special care. It should be cleaned regularly with saddlesoap or leather cleaner. Never use alcohol, gasoline, nail polish remover or thinner to clean leather upholstery.
6    After cleaning, regularly treat leather upholstery with a leather conditioner, rubbed in with a soft cotton cloth. Never use car wax on leather upholstery.
7    In areas where the interior of the vehicle is subject to bright sunlight, cover leather seating areas of the seats with a sheet if the vehicle is to be left out for any length of time.

## 5   Body repair - minor damage

*See photo sequence*

### Repair of minor scratches

1    If the scratch is superficial and does not penetrate to the metal of the body, repair is very simple. Lightly rub the scratched area with a fine rubbing compound to remove loose paint and built up wax. Rinse the area with clean water.
2    Apply touch-up paint to the scratch, using a small brush. Continue to apply thin layers of paint until the surface of the paint in the scratch is level with the surrounding paint. Allow the new paint at least two weeks to harden, then blend it into the surrounding paint by rubbing with a very fine rubbing compound. Finally, apply a coat of wax to the scratch area.
3    If the scratch has penetrated the paint and exposed the metal of the body, causing the metal to rust, a different repair technique is required. Remove all loose rust from the bottom of the scratch with a pocket knife, then apply rust inhibiting paint to prevent the formation of rust in the future. Using a rubber or nylon applicator, coat the scratched area with glaze-type filler. If required, the filler can be mixed with thinner to provide a very thin paste, which is ideal for filling narrow scratches. Before the glaze filler in the scratch hardens, wrap a piece of smooth cotton cloth around the tip of a finger. Dip the cloth in thinner and then quickly wipe it along the surface of the scratch. This will ensure that the surface of the filler is slightly hollow. The scratch can now be painted over as described earlier in this Section.

### Repair of dents

4    When repairing dents, the first job is to pull the dent out until the affected area is as close as possible to its original shape. There is no point in trying to restore the original shape completely as the metal in the damaged area will have stretched on impact and cannot be restored to its original contours. It is better to bring the level of the dent up to a point which is about 1/8-inch below the level of the surrounding metal. In cases where the dent is very shallow, it is not worth trying to pull it out at all.
5    If the back side of the dent is accessible, it can be hammered out gently from behind using a soft-face hammer. While doing this, hold a block of wood firmly against the opposite side of the metal to absorb the hammer blows and prevent the metal from being stretched.
6    If the dent is in a section of the body which has double layers, or some other factor makes it inaccessible from behind, a different technique is required. Drill several small holes through the metal inside the damaged area, particularly in the deeper sections. Screw long, self tapping screws into the holes just enough for them to get a good grip in the metal. Now the dent can be pulled out by pulling on the protruding heads of the screws with locking pliers.
7    The next stage of repair is the removal of paint from the damaged area and from an inch or so of the surrounding metal. This is easily done with a wire brush or sanding disk in a drill motor, although it can be done just as effectively by hand with sandpaper. To complete the preparation for filling, score the surface of the bare metal with a screwdriver or the tang of a file or drill small holes in the affected area. This will provide a good grip for the filler material. To complete the repair, see the Section on filling and painting.

### Repair of rust holes or gashes

8    Remove all paint from the affected area and from an inch or so of the surrounding metal using a sanding disk or wire brush mounted in a drill motor. If these are not available, a few sheets of sandpaper will do the job just as effectively.
9    With the paint removed, you will be able to determine the severity of the corrosion and decide whether to replace the whole panel, if possible, or repair the affected area. New body panels are not as expensive as most people think and it is often quicker to install a new panel than to repair large areas of rust.
10   Remove all trim pieces from the affected area except those which will act as a guide to the original shape of the damaged body, such as headlight shells, etc. Using metal snips or a hacksaw blade, remove all loose metal and any other metal that is badly affected by rust. Hammer the edges of the hole in to create a slight depression for the filler material.
11   Wire brush the affected area to remove the powdery rust from the surface of the metal. If the back of the rusted area is accessible, treat it with rust inhibiting paint.
12   Before filling is done, block the hole in some way. This can be done with sheet metal riveted or screwed into place, or by stuffing the hole with wire mesh.
13   Once the hole is blocked off, the affected area can be filled and painted. See the following subsection on filling and painting.

### Filling and painting

14   Many types of body fillers are available, but generally speaking, body repair kits which contain filler paste and a tube of resin hardener are best for this type of repair work. A wide, flexible plastic or nylon applicator will be necessary for imparting a smooth and contoured finish to the surface of the filler material. Mix up a small amount of filler on a clean piece of wood or cardboard (use the hardener sparingly). Follow the manufacturer's instructions on the package, otherwise the filler will set incorrectly.
15   Using the applicator, apply the filler paste to the prepared area. Draw the applicator across the surface of the filler to achieve the desired contour and to level the filler surface. As soon as a contour that approximates the original one is achieved, stop working the paste. If you continue, the paste will begin to stick to the applicator. Continue to add thin layers of paste at 20-minute intervals until the level of the filler is just above the surrounding metal.

**9.2  Scribe or draw alignment marks around the hood hinges to ensure proper alignment of the hood when it's reinstalled**

16   Once the filler has hardened, the excess can be removed with a body file. From then on, progressively finer grades of sandpaper should be used, starting with a 180-grit paper and finishing with 600-grit wet-or-dry paper. Always wrap the sandpaper around a flat rubber or wooden block, otherwise the surface of the filler will not be completely flat. During the sanding of the filler surface, the wet-or-dry paper should be periodically rinsed in water. This will ensure that a very smooth finish is produced in the final stage.
17   At this point, the repair area should be surrounded by a ring of bare metal, which in turn should be encircled by the finely feathered edge of good paint. Rinse the repair area with clean water until all of the dust produced by the sanding operation is gone.
18   Spray the entire area with a light coat of primer. This will reveal any imperfections in the surface of the filler. Repair the imperfections with fresh filler paste or glaze filler and once more smooth the surface with sandpaper. Repeat this spray-and-repair procedure until you are satisfied that the surface of the filler and the feathered edge of the paint are perfect. Rinse the area with clean water and allow it to dry completely.
19   The repair area is now ready for painting. Spray painting must be carried out in a warm, dry, windless and dust free atmosphere. These conditions can be created if you have access to a large indoor work area, but if you are forced to work in the open, you will have to pick the day very carefully. If you are working indoors, dousing the floor in the work area with water will help settle the dust which would otherwise be in the air. If the repair area is confined to one body panel, mask off the surrounding panels. This will help minimize the effects of a slight mismatch in paint color. Trim pieces such as chrome strips, door handles, etc., will also need to be masked off or removed. Use masking tape and several thickness of newspaper for the masking operations.
20   Before spraying, shake the paint can thoroughly, then spray a test area until the spray painting technique is mastered. Cover the repair area with a thick coat of primer. The thickness should be built up using several thin layers of primer rather than one thick one. Using 600-grit wet-or-dry sandpaper, rub down the surface of the primer until it is very smooth. While doing this, the work area should be thoroughly rinsed with water and the wet-or-dry sandpaper periodically rinsed as well. Allow the primer to dry before spraying additional coats.
21   Spray on the top coat, again building up the thickness by using several thin layers of paint. Begin spraying in the center of the repair area and then, using a circular motion, work out until the whole repair area and about two inches of the surrounding original paint is covered. Remove all masking material 10 to 15 minutes after spraying on the final coat of paint. Allow the new paint at least two weeks to harden, then use a very fine rubbing compound to blend the edges of the new paint into the existing paint. Finally, apply a coat of wax.

## 6   Body repair - major damage

1   Major damage must be repaired by an auto body shop specifically equipped to perform unibody repairs. These shops have the specialized equipment required to do the job properly.
2   If the damage is extensive, the body must be checked for proper alignment or the vehicle's handling characteristics may be adversely affected and other components may wear at an accelerated rate.
3   Due to the fact that all of the major body components (hood, fenders, etc.) are separate and replaceable units, any seriously damaged components should be replaced rather than repaired. Sometimes the components can be found in a wrecking yard that specializes in used vehicle components, often at considerable savings over the cost of new parts.

## 7   Hinges and locks - maintenance

Once every 3000 miles, or every three months, the hinges and latch assemblies on the doors, hood and trunk (or liftgate) should be given a few drops of light oil or lock lubricant. The door latch strikers should also be lubricated with a thin coat of grease to reduce wear and ensure free movement. Lubricate the door and trunk (or liftgate) locks with spray-on graphite lubricant.

## 8   Windshield and fixed glass - replacement

Replacement of the windshield and fixed glass requires the use of special fast-setting adhesive/caulk materials and some specialized tools and techniques. These operations should be left to a dealer service department or a shop specializing in glass work.

## 9   Hood - removal, installation and adjustment

### Removal and installation
*Refer to illustration 9.2*
**Note:** *The hood is heavy and somewhat awkward to remove and install - at least two people should perform this procedure.*
1   Use blankets or pads to cover the fenders and cowl areas. This will protect the body and paint as the hood is lifted off.
2   Scribe or draw alignment marks around the bolt heads to ensure proper alignment during installation **(see illustration)**.
3   Disconnect any cables or wire harnesses which will interfere with removal. Also disconnect the windshield washer hoses at the Y-junction.
4   Have an assistant support the weight of the hood. On V6 models, detach the support struts (see Section 12). Remove the hinge-to-hood bolts and any shims, if installed. If there are any shims, make sure you keep the shims for each side with their respective bolts. Don't mix them up.
5   Lift off the hood.
6   Installation is the reverse of removal. If you fit the hood so that the hinges fit within the scribe marks you made before loosening the bolts - and if you install the shims, if any, in the same number and location they were in prior to removal, then the hood should still be aligned. Of course, if you're installing a new hood, or forgot to scribe the hinge positions, or mixed up the shims, etc. then you'll need to readjust the hood position.

### Adjustment
*Refer to illustrations 9.10 and 9.11*
7   You can adjust the hood fore-and-aft and right-and-left by means of the elongated holes in the hinges.
8   Scribe a line around the entire hinge plate so you can judge the amount of movement.

9    Loosen the bolts and move the hood into correct alignment. Move it only a little at a time. Tighten the hinge bolts or nuts and carefully lower the hood to check the alignment.

10   If necessary after installation, the entire hood latch assembly can be adjusted up-and-down as well as from side-to-side on the upper radiator support so the hood closes securely and is flush with the fenders **(see illustration)**. To do this, scribe a line around the hood latch mounting bolts to provide a reference point. Then loosen the bolts and reposition the latch assembly as necessary. Following adjustment, retighten the mounting bolts.

11   Adjust the vertical height of the leading edge of the hood by screwing the edge cushions in or out so that the hood, when closed, is flush with the fenders **(see illustration)**. Finally, adjust the rear edge of the hood until it's flush with the fenders by using shims (available at a Honda dealer parts department) between the hood and the hinge plates.

12   The hood latch assembly, as well as the hinges, should be periodically lubricated with white lithium-base grease to prevent sticking and wear.

## 10   Trunk lid - removal, installation and adjustment

*Refer to illustration 10.3*

### Removal and installation

1    Open the trunk lid and cover the edges of the trunk compartment with pads or cloths to protect the painted surfaces when the lid is removed.

2    Unplug the electrical connectors for the license plate lights and the brake lights, and remove the wire harness from the trunk lid. Tie string or wire to the cables so they can be pulled back into the body when the trunk lid is reinstalled.

3    Scribe or draw alignment marks around the hinge-to-trunk lid bolt heads **(see illustration)**.

4    Remove the hinge-to-trunk lid bolts from both sides and lift off the trunk lid.

5    Installation is the reverse of removal. Be sure to align the hinge bolt flanges with the marks made during removal.

### Adjustment

6    After installation, close the lid and see if it's in proper alignment with the adjacent body surfaces. Fore-and-aft and side-to-side adjustments of the lid are controlled by the position of the hinge bolts in the slots. To adjust it, loosen the hinge bolts, reposition the lid and retighten the bolts.

7    The height of the rear of the lid in relation to the surrounding body panels when closed can be adjusted by loosening the lock striker bolts (you'll need a Torx R-T30 bit) and adding or removing adjusting shims

**9.10  To adjust the hood latch horizontally or vertically, loosen these bolts (arrows)**

(available from a Honda dealer parts department) between the strike and the body and re-tightening the bolts.

8    Finally, you can fine-tune the height of the trailing edge of th trunk lid by turning the trunk lid edge cushions **(see illustration 9.11** in or out to lower or raise the trunk as necessary.

## 11   Liftgate (station wagon models) - removal, installatio and adjustment

### Removal and installation

1    Open the liftgate and cover the upper body area around th opening with pads or cloths to protect the painted surfaces when th liftgate is removed.

2    Remove all trim panel screws, pry off all trim panel clips an remove the upper and lower liftgate trim panels.

3    Unplug all electrical connectors and pull the wire harness out c the liftgate (tie string or wire to the cables so they can be pulled bac into the body when the liftgate is reinstalled).

4    Detach the headliner for access to the hinge-to-body retainin nuts.

5    While an assistant supports the liftgate, detach the support struj (see Section 12).

6    Remove the hinge nut and detach the liftgate from the vehicle.

7    Installation is the reverse of removal. Be extremely careful wit the wire harness when threading it back into the liftgate or you coul cut it on a metal edge.

**9.11  To adjust the vertical height of the leading edge of the hood so that it's flush with the fenders, turn each edge cushion clockwise (to lower the hood) or counterclockwise (to raise the hood)**

**10.3  Draw around the trunk hinges with a marking pen before loosening the bolts to ensure proper alignment of the trunk lid when it's reinstalled**

**12.2  Loosen the hood strut upper and lower nuts (arrows)**

**12.5  Remove C-clip (arrow) and detach the lower end of the strut**

**12.6  Remove the strut upper end nut (arrow)**

**13.2  Remove these five screws from the top of the grille to detach it from the radiator support/upper crossmember**

## Adjustment

After installation, close the liftgate and make sure it's in proper alignment with the surrounding body panels.

If the liftgate needs to be adjusted, loosen the bolts and slightly reposition the striker, repeating the procedure as necessary.

10  You can also adjust the liftgate position in relation to the adjacent fender panels by screwing the liftgate edge cushions in (to depress the liftgate) or out (to raise it).

## 12  Support struts - replacement

### Hood (V6 models only)

*Refer to illustration 12.2*

Open the hood and support it.

Loosen the nuts at each end and detach the strut from the vehicle (see illustration).

Installation is the reverse of removal.

### Trunk

*Refer to illustrations 12.5 and 12.6*

Support the trunk lid in the open position.

Pry off the plastic cover from the lower end of the strut with a small screwdriver. Pry off the clip and detach the lower end of the strut (see illustration).

Remove the nut and detach the strut (see illustration).

Installation is the reverse of removal.

### Tailgate

8  Open and support the tailgate.

9  Loosen the single locknut at the upper end of each strut. Remove the two mounting bolts at the lower end of each strut, then unscrew the stud at the upper end from the liftgate.

10  Installation is the reverse of removal. Tighten all fasteners securely.

## 13  Radiator grille - removal and installation

*Refer to illustrations 13.2, 13.3a and 13.3b*

1  Open the hood.

2  Remove the five screws along the top of the grille (see illustration).

3  Insert a flat-blade screwdriver down from the top of each end of the grille, push down on the clip that attaches the grille to the bumper (see illustrations) and remove the grille.

4  Installation is the reverse of removal.

## 14  Bumpers - removal and installation

### Front bumper

*Refer to illustrations 14.2a, 14.2b, 14.2c and 14.4*

1  Open the hood.

2  From under the vehicle, remove the bumper retaining bolts (see illustrations), followed by the retaining screws and clips from the underside of the bumper.

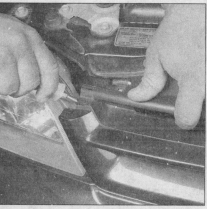

**13.3a  Insert a flat-bladed screwdriver down past the grille ends . . .**

**13.3b  . . . and push down the center of each locking clip that secures the grille to the bumper**

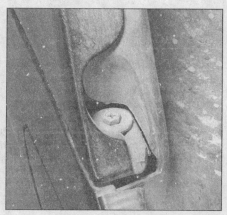

**14.2a  Remove the fender to bumper bolts, . . .**

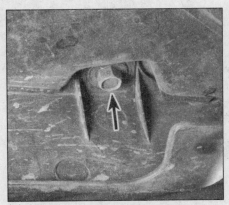

**14.2b ... the bolts at the lower edge of the bumper ...**

**14.2c ... as well as those at the middle of the bumper**

**14.4 Remove the retaining bolts (arrows) from inside the turn signal recesses - (left side shown, two more bolts are located inside the right turn signal recess)**

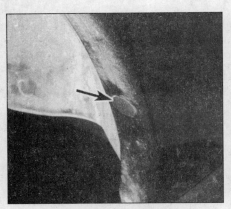

**14.7 Pry out the rear bumper to fender well clips**

**14.8a Remove the five plastic screws along the top of the bumper and ...**

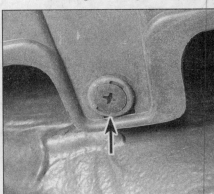

**14.8b ... the four screws along the bottom**

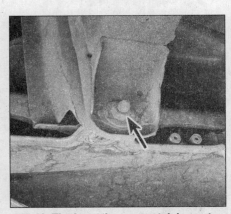

**14.10 The lower bumper retaining nuts (arrow) on each side are accessible from under the vehicle**

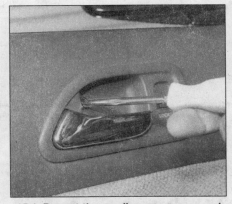

**15.1 Pry out the small access cover and remove the inside door handle screw(s)**

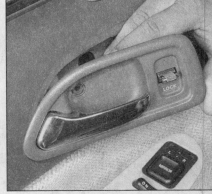

**15.2 Rotate the handle away from the door and disconnect the lock rods**

3   Remove the front turn signal lights (see Chapter 12).

4   Remove the four retaining bolts (two on each side, located inside the turn signal recesses) **(see illustration)**.

5   Lift the bumper, slide it forward and remove it.

6   Installation is the reverse of removal.

### Rear bumper

*Refer to illustrations 14.7, 14.8a, 14.8b and 14.10*

7   Remove the four clips retaining the forward ends of the bumper to the fender wells **(see illustration)**.

8   Remove the plastic screws retaining the bumper cover to th[e] body **(see illustrations)**.

9   Remove the side marker lights (see Chapter 12).

10   From under the vehicle, remove the two lower bumper retainin[g] nuts **(see illustration)**.

11   From inside the vehicle, detach the trim panels and remove uppe[r] retaining nuts.

12   Slide the bumper to the rear and remove it.

13   Installation is the reverse of removal.

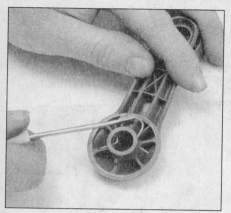

16.1 On models equipped with a manual window regulator, remove the window crank handle by pulling this clip off with a wire hook (handle removed for clarity)

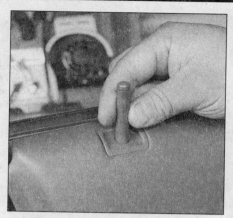

16.2 Unscrew the door lock knob

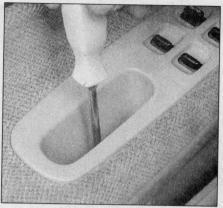

16.5a Remove the screw from inside the door pull/switch assembly

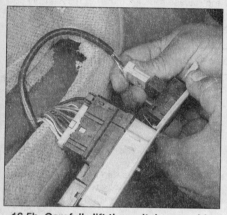

16.5b Carefully lift the switch assembly out of the trim panel and rotate it out far enough to disconnect the electrical connectors

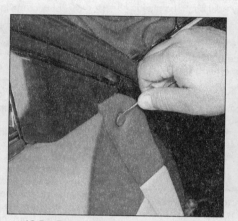

16.5c Pry off the protective cap and remove the front upper trim panel retaining screw

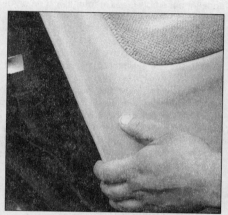

16.6a Carefully pry loose the retaining clips, then grasp the rear of the panel and . . .

## 15 Inside door handle - removal and installation

*Refer to illustrations 15.1 and 15.2*

1   Remove the inside door handle retaining screw **(see illustration)**.
2   Carefully pull the door handle assembly out of the door trim panel **(see illustration)**.
3   Use a small screwdriver to disconnect the release rod from the handle lever and remove the handle.
4   Installation is the reverse of removal.

## 16 Door trim panel - removal and installation

*Refer to illustrations 16.1, 16.2, 16.5a, 16.5b, 16.5c, 16.6a, 16.6b and 16.7*

## *Removal*

1   On manual window regulator equipped models, remove the window crank handle **(see illustration)**.
2   Remove the door lock knob **(see illustration)**.
3   Remove the inside door handle (see Section 15).
4   Pry out the outside mirror cover (see Section 20).
5   Remove the door trim panel retaining screws and the screw in the door arm rest **(see illustrations)**, then carefully pry loose the retaining clips with a trim pad remover or a putty knife between the trim panel and the door. Work slowly and carefully around the outer edge of the

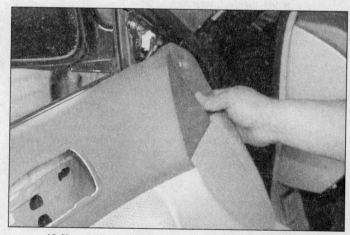

16.6b . . . the front of the panel and lift it straight up

trim panel until it's free.
6   Once all of the clips are disengaged, pull the trim panel up, unplug any wiring harness connectors and remove the panel **(see illustrations)**.
7   For access to the door outside handle or the door window regulator inside the door, raise the window fully, remove the power

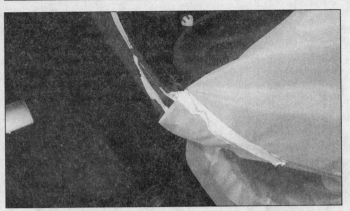

16.7  Carefully peel back the plastic watershield

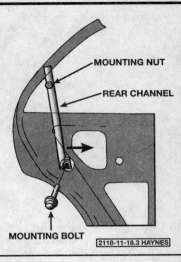

17.3  On rear doors, you'll have to move the rear glass channel for access to the outer door handle bolts

MOUNTING NUT

REAR CHANNEL

MOUNTING BOLT

2118-11-18.3 HAYNES

window control unit (if equipped), the door panel bracket and the speaker assembly (see Chapter 12), then carefully peel back the plastic watershield (see illustration).

## Installation

8    Prior to installation of the door trim panel, be sure to reinstall any clips in the panel which may have come out when you removed the panel.

9    Plug in the wire harness connectors for the power door lock switch and the power window switch, if equipped, and place the panel in position in the door. Press the door panel into place until the clips are seated. Install the two trim panel retaining screws and the armrest retaining screw. Install the power door lock switch assembly, if equipped. Install the manual regulator crank handle or power window switch assembly.

## 17   Door outside handle, lock cylinder and latch - removal and installation

### Outside door handle

*Refer to illustration 17.3*

1    Remove the inside door handle, door trim panel and plastic watershield (see Sections 15 and 16).

2    Apply tape around the handle opening to protect the paint.

3    Remove the screw and detach the anti-theft lock rod protector. On rear doors, it will be necessary to first detach the door lock bell crank and then move the rear glass channel out of the way for access. This is accomplished by loosening the upper channel mounting nut and removing the lower mounting bolt, then move the lower end of the channel forward (see illustration).

4    Remove the door handle retaining bolts.

5    Pry the lock rod loose with a small flat-bladed screwdriver, pull the handle out from the door, mark the number of threads showing above the lever pin and rotate the handle to unscrew it from the release rod.

6    Installation is the reverse of removal.

### Lock cylinder

7    Remove the outside door handle (see above).

8    Remove the retaining clip and detach the lock cylinder from the handle. Be careful not to damage the clip when working in the tight confines around the anti-theft shield.

9    Installation is the reverse of removal.

### Latch

*Refer to illustration 17.11*

10    Disconnect the lock and inner handle rod from the latch.

11    Remove the door latch retaining screws (see illustration) and maneuver the latch out of the door. **Caution:** *Make sure you don't bend the rods.*

12    Disconnect the lock and release rods from the latch assembly and switch them over to the new latch unit.

13    Installation is the reverse of removal.

## 18   Door window glass - removal and installation

*Refer to illustrations 18.3 and 18.4*

1    Remove the door trim panel and plastic watershield (see Section 16).

2    Remove the inside door handle (see Section 15).

3    On two-door models, peel off the sash guide cover and remove the mounting screws, then remove the center sash guide from the door (see illustration).

4    Lower the window so the mounting bolts can be reached through the access hole in the door, then remove the bolts (see illustration).

5    Lift the door glass up and out of the door window slot, then tilt and remove it from the door.

6    Installation is the reverse of removal.

## 19   Window regulator - removal, installation and adjustment

### Removal and installation

1    Remove the inside door handle (see Section 15).

2    Remove the door trim panel and plastic watershield (see Section 16).

17.11  Remove the door latch retaining screws (arrows) and remove the door latch and rods (make sure you don't bend the rods)

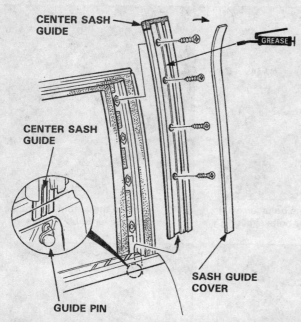

18.3  On two door models, peel off the sash guide cover and remove the mounting screws, then remove the center sash guide from the door

3    Remove the door window glass (see Section 18).
4    Scribe or mark a line around the four bolts to ensure proper reassembly. Remove the two upper and two lower retaining bolts and remove the regulator assembly through the hole in the center of the door. On power window models, unplug the electrical connector.
5    Prior to installation, lubricate all contact surfaces with multi-purpose grease.
6    Installation is the reverse of removal.

## Adjustment

7    To adjust the glass position it evenly in the opening, loosen the glass and regulator mounting bolts. Raise the window as far as possible, making sure it's centered in its channel, then tighten the mounting bolts securely.
8    On rear doors, adjustment can also be made by moving the position of the rear glass channel (see illustration 17.3).

## 20  Outside mirrors - removal and installation

*Refer to illustrations 20.1a, 20.1b, 20.2 and 20.3*
1    On manual mirrors, remove the cap and screw **(see illustrations)** and pull off the knob.
2    Pry off the cover panel **(see illustration)**.
3    Remove the three retaining nuts **(see illustration)** and lift the mirror off. On models equipped with power mirrors, unplug the electrical connector.
4    Installation is the reverse of removal.

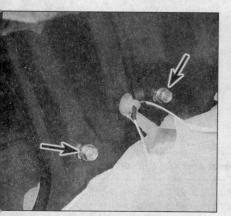

18.4  Remove the two bolts (arrows) and detach the glass

20.1a  On vehicles with manual mirrors, remove the cap . . .

20.1b  . . . remove the screw (arrow) and pull off the knob

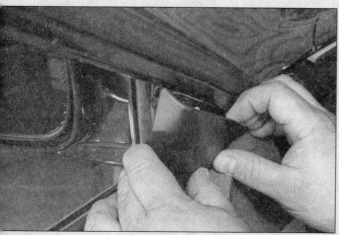

20.2  Detach the mirror cover

20.3  To remove the mirror, remove these three nuts (arrows) - if the vehicle has power mirrors, unplug the electrical connector

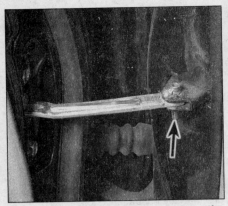

21.4a  To remove the door, disconnect the
check-strap pin (arrow) . . .

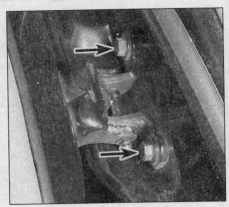

21.4b  . . . and the door hinge bolts (arrows)
(upper bolts shown, lower bolts similar)

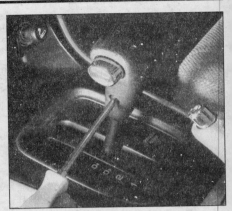

22.1  Remove the automatic transaxle
shift lever knob screws

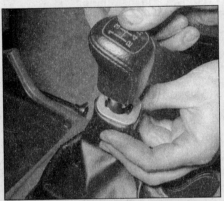

22.2  To remove the shift lever knob on
models with a manual transaxle, pinch the
retaining clips (inside the top of the boot)
together like this, slide the boot down and
unscrew the knob from the shift lever

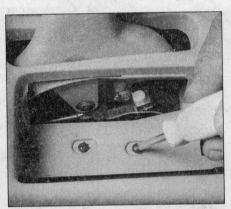

22.3a  Detach the cup holder, then remove
these two screws and . . .

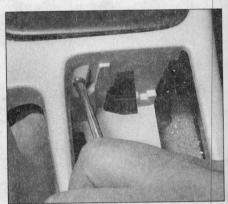

22.3b  . . . the front screw

## 21  Door - removal, installation and adjustment

*Refer to illustrations 21.4a and 21.4b*

### Removal and installation

1    Remove the door trim panel (see Section 16). Disconnect any wire harness connectors and push them through the door opening so they won't interfere with door removal.
2    Place a jack or jackstand under the door or have an assistant on hand to support it when the hinge bolts are removed. **Note:** *If a jack or jackstand is used, place a rag between it and the door to protect the door's painted surfaces.*
3    Scribe alignment marks around the door hinges.
4    Remove the check-strap pin and hinge-to-door bolts **(see illustrations)**, then carefully lift off the door.
5    Installation is the reverse of removal.

### Adjustment

6    Following installation of the door, check the alignment and adjust it if necessary as follows:
  a)  *Up-and-down and forward-and-backward adjustments are made by loosening the hinge-to-body bolts and moving the door as necessary.*
  b)  *The door lock striker can also be adjusted both up-and-down and sideways to provide positive engagement with the lock mechanism. This is done by loosening the mounting bolts and moving the striker as necessary.*

## 22  Console - removal and installation

*Refer to illustrations 22.1, 22.2, 22.3a, 22.3b, 22.5, 22.6a and 22.6b*
**Warning:** *The vehicles covered by this manual are equipped with airbags. Always disable the airbag system before working in the vicinity of the steering column, instrument panel or console to avoid the possibility of accidental deployment of the airbag, which could cause personal injury (see Chapter 12). The yellow wiring harness and connectors routed through the console and instrument panel are used for the airbag system. Do not use electrical test equipment on the system wiring or connectors or tamper with them in any way.*
**Caution:** *The stereo in your vehicle is equipped with an anti-theft system. Make sure you have the correct activation code before disconnecting the battery.*
1    On models with an automatic transaxle, remove the two shift lever knob retaining screws **(see illustration)** and pull off the knob and slider.
2    On models with a manual transaxle, simply unscrew and remove the shifter knob **(see illustration)**.

### Rear console

3    Remove the two screws on the sides of the console. Open the storage compartment lid, pry open the access cover on the bottom of the compartment and remove the two screws. Pull the parking brake lever up, remove the cup holder and remove the three retaining screws **(see illustrations)**. Lift the console up and to the rear, detaching the hooks at the front. Lift the rear console over the parking brake lever and remove it from the vehicle.
4    Installation is the reverse of removal.

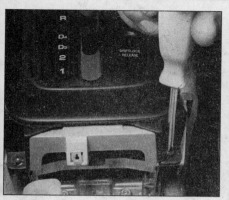

**22.5  Remove the two screws from the trim plate (arrow)**

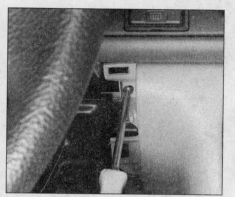

**22.6a  Remove the screws from the left side of the console . . .**

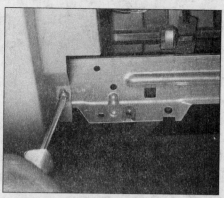

**22.6b  . . . remove the screws from the right side of the console and lift the console from the vehicle**

**23.7a  Remove the instrument panel screws (2 of 6 shown)**

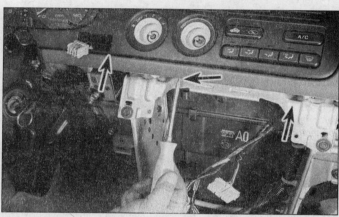

**23.7b  Remove the three screws (arrows) along the lower right side of the bezel**

## Front console

5    Remove the ashtray and the screw behind it. Remove the two screws at the rear of the trim plate **(see illustration)**. Lift the trim plate off the console, detaching the retaining clips. Disconnect any electrical connectors from the trim plate and set it aside.

6    Remove the radio (see Chapter 12), the lower instrument panel cover and the glove box (see Sections 24 and 26). Remove the retaining screws and lift the console out of the vehicle **(see illustrations)**.

7    Installation is the reverse of removal.

## 23   Instrument cluster bezel - removal and installation

*Refer to illustrations 23.7a, 23.7b and 23.8*

**Warning:** *The vehicles covered by this manual are equipped with airbags. Always disable the airbag system before working in the vicinity of the steering column, instrument panel or console to avoid the possibility of accidental deployment of the airbag, which could cause personal injury (see Chapter 12). The yellow wiring harness and connectors routed through the console and instrument panel are used for the airbag system. Do not use electrical test equipment on the system wiring or connectors or tamper with them in any way.*

**Caution:** *The stereo in your vehicle is equipped with an anti-theft system. Make sure you have the correct activation code before disconnecting the battery.*

Pry the cruise control master switch/sunroof switch assembly, if equipped, from the dashboard and unplug the electrical connectors.

Pry the instrument panel brightness controller, the hazard warning switch and the rear window defogger switch out of the dashboard and unplug their electrical connectors.

**23.8  Unplug the bezel electrical connectors**

3    Remove the ashtray and ashtray holder. The holder is attached to the underside of the pocket below the stereo by three screws.

4    Remove the console (see Section 22).

5    Remove the radio (see Chapter 12).

6    Remove the center and left side air vents.

7    Remove all 6 cluster bezel retaining screws **(see illustrations)**.

8    Grasp the instrument cluster bezel securely and pull out sharply to detach the clips, then unplug the electrical connectors and remove the bezel **(see illustration)**.

9    Installation is the reverse of removal.

**25.2 Remove the three screws and separate the steering column cover halves**

**26.4 Remove the four bolts (one at each corner) and remove the knee bolster**

**27.1 Typical front seat track retaining bolt (arrow) (left bolt shown, right bolt identical)**

## 24 Glove box - removal and installation

**Warning:** *The vehicles covered by this manual are equipped with airbags. Always disable the airbag system before working in the vicinity of the steering column, instrument panel or console to avoid the possibility of accidental deployment of the airbag, which could cause personal injury (see Chapter 12). The yellow wiring harness and connectors routed through the console and instrument panel are used for the airbag system. Do not use electrical test equipment on the system wiring or connectors or tamper with them in any way.*
**Caution:** *The stereo in your vehicle is equipped with an anti-theft system. Make sure you have the correct activation code before disconnecting the battery.*
1    Open the glove box and remove the glove box damper screw.
2    Remove the two screws from the underside of the glove box and remove the glove box.
3    Installation is the reverse of removal.

## 25 Steering column cover - removal and installation

*Refer to illustration 25.2*
**Warning:** *The vehicles covered by this manual are equipped with airbags. Always disable the airbag system before working in the vicinity of the steering column, instrument panel or console to avoid the possibility of accidental deployment of the airbag, which could cause personal injury (see Chapter 12). The yellow wiring harness and connectors routed through the console and instrument panel are used for the airbag system. Do not use electrical test equipment on the system wiring or connectors or tamper with them in any way.*
**Caution:** *The stereo in your vehicle is equipped with an anti-theft system. Make sure you have the correct activation code before disconnecting the battery.*
1    On tilt steering columns, move the column to the lowest position. Remove the instrument panel lower cover (see Section 26).
2    Remove the three screws, then separate the halves and remove the covers **(see illustration).**
3    Installation is the reverse of the removal procedure.

## 26 Instrument panel lower cover and knee bolster - removal and installation

*Refer to illustration 26.4*
**Warning:** *The vehicles covered by this manual are equipped with*

*airbags. Always disable the airbag system before working in the vicinity of the steering column, instrument panel or console to avoid the possibility of accidental deployment of the airbag, which could cause personal injury (see Chapter 12). The yellow wiring harness and connectors routed through the console and instrument panel are used for the airbag system. Do not use electrical test equipment on the system wiring or connectors or tamper with them in any way.*
**Caution:** *The stereo in your vehicle is equipped with an anti-theft system. Make sure you have the correct activation code before disconnecting the battery.*

### Lower cover

1    Remove the coin holder and bolt.
2    Grasp the edges securely, detach the clips and lower the cover from the dash.
3    Installation is the reverse of the removal procedure.

### Knee bolster

4    Remove the bolts at each corner and lower the metal knee bolster from the dash **(see illustration).**
5    Installation is the reverse of removal.

## 27 Seats - removal and installation

*Refer to illustration 27.1*
1    Remove the front and rear seat track retaining bolts and remove the seat **(see illustration).** Unplug any electrical connectors.
2    Installation is the reverse of removal, making sure to apply thread locking compound to the bolts.

## 28 Seat belt check

1    Check the seat belts, buckles, latch plates and guide loops for obvious damage and signs of wear.
2    Check that the seat belt reminder light comes on when the key is turned to the Run and Start positions. A chime should also sound.
3    The seat belts are designed to lock up during a sudden stop or impact, yet allow free movement during normal driving. Check that the retractors return the belt against your chest while driving and rewind the belt completely when the buckle is unlatched.
4    If any of the above checks reveal problems with the seat belts, replace parts as necessary.

# Chapter 12
# Chassis electrical system

## Contents

## 1  General information

The electrical system is a 12-volt, negative ground type. Power for the lights and all electrical accessories is supplied by a lead/acid-type battery which is charged by the alternator.

This Chapter covers repair and service procedures for the various electrical components not associated with the engine. Information on the battery, alternator, distributor and starter motor can be found in Chapter 5. It should be noted that when portions of the electrical system are serviced, the negative battery cable should be disconnected from the battery to prevent electrical shorts and/or fires. **Caution:** *The stereo in your vehicle is equipped with an anti-theft system. Refer to the information at the front of this manual before detaching the battery cables.*

## 2  Electrical troubleshooting - general information

**Warning:** *The vehicles covered by this manual have airbags. Always disable the airbag system before working in the vicinity of the steering column, instrument panel or console to avoid the possibility of accidental deployment of the airbag, which could cause personal injury (see Section 25). The yellow wiring harnesses and connectors routed through the console and instrument panel are for this system. Do not use electrical test equipment on the system wiring or connectors or tamper with them in any way.*
**Caution:** *The stereo in your vehicle is equipped with an anti-theft system. Make sure you have the correct activation code before disconnecting the battery.*

A typical electrical circuit consists of an electrical component, any

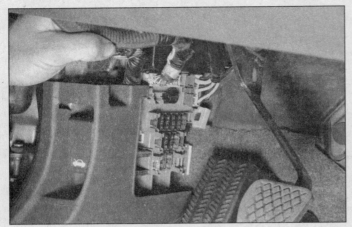

**3.1a  The interior fuse box is located under the left (driver's side) of the instrument panel, under a cover**

**3.1b The engine compartment fuse box is located in the right rear corner of the engine compartment**

switches, relays, motors, fuses, fusible links or circuit breakers related to that component and the wiring and connectors that link the component to both the battery and the chassis. To help you pinpoint an electrical circuit problem, wiring diagrams are included at the end of this book.

Before tackling any troublesome electrical circuit, first study the appropriate wiring diagrams to get a complete understanding of what makes up that individual circuit. Trouble spots, for instance, can often be narrowed down by noting if other components related to the circuit are operating properly. If several components or circuits fail at one time, chances are the problem is in a fuse or ground connection, because several circuits are often routed through the same fuse and ground connections.

Electrical problems usually stem from simple causes, such as loose or corroded connections, a blown fuse, a melted fusible link or a bad relay. Visually inspect the condition of all fuses, wires and connections in a problem circuit before troubleshooting it.

If testing instruments are going to be utilized, use the diagrams to plan ahead of time where you will make the necessary connections in order to accurately pinpoint the trouble spot.

The basic tools needed for electrical troubleshooting include a circuit tester or voltmeter (a 12-volt bulb with a set of test leads can also be used), a continuity tester, which includes a bulb, battery and set of test leads, and a jumper wire, preferably with a circuit breaker incorporated, which can be used to bypass electrical components. Before attempting to locate a problem with test instruments, use the wiring diagram(s) to decide where to make the connections.

## Voltage checks

Voltage checks should be performed if a circuit is not functioning properly. Connect one lead of a circuit tester to either the negative battery terminal or a known good ground. Connect the other lead to a connector in the circuit being tested, preferably nearest to the battery or fuse. If the bulb of the tester lights, voltage is present, which means that the part of the circuit between the connector and the battery is problem free. Continue checking the rest of the circuit in the same fashion. When you reach a point at which no voltage is present, the problem lies between that point and the last test point with voltage. Most of the time the problem can be traced to a loose connection. **Note:** *Keep in mind that some circuits receive voltage only when the ignition key is in the Accessory or Run position.*

## Finding a short

One method of finding shorts in a circuit is to remove the fuse and connect a test light or voltmeter in its place to the fuse terminals. There should be no voltage present in the circuit. Move the wiring harness from side-to-side while watching the test light. If the bulb goes on, there is a short to ground somewhere in that area, probably where the

insulation has rubbed through. The same test can be performed on each component in the circuit, even a switch.

## Ground check

Perform a ground test to check whether a component is properly grounded. Disconnect the battery and connect one lead of a self-powered test light, known as a continuity tester, to a known good ground. **Caution:** *If the radio in your vehicle is equipped with an anti-theft system. Make sure you have the correct activation code before disconnecting the battery.* Connect the other lead to the wire or ground connection being tested. If the bulb goes on, the ground is good. If the bulb does not go on, the ground is not good.

## Continuity check

A continuity check is done to determine if there are any breaks in a circuit - if it is passing electricity properly. With the circuit off (no power in the circuit), a self-powered continuity tester can be used to check the circuit. Connect the test leads to both ends of the circuit (or to the "power" end and a good ground), and if the test light comes on the circuit is passing current properly. If the light doesn't come on, there is a break somewhere in the circuit. The same procedure can be used to test a switch, by connecting the continuity tester to the switch terminals. With the switch turned On, the test light should come on.

## Finding an open circuit

When diagnosing for possible open circuits, it is often difficult to locate them by sight because oxidation or terminal misalignment are hidden by the connectors. Merely wiggling a connector on a sensor or in the wiring harness may correct the open circuit condition. Remember this when an open circuit is indicated when troubleshooting a circuit. Intermittent problems may also be caused by oxidized or loose connections.

Electrical troubleshooting is simple if you keep in mind that all electrical circuits are basically electricity running from the battery, through the wires, switches, relays, fuses and fusible links to each electrical component (light bulb, motor, etc.) and to ground, from which it is passed back to the battery. Any electrical problem is an interruption in the flow of electricity to and from the battery.

## 3    Fuses - general information

*Refer to illustrations 3.1a, 3.1b, 3.1c and 3.3*

1    The electrical circuits of the vehicle are protected by a combination of fuses and circuit breakers. The two fuse blocks are located under the instrument panel and on the right side of the engine compartment **(see illustrations)**. The fuse block for the Anti-lock

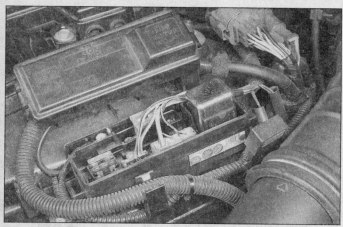

**3.1c  The ABS system fuse block is located on the right side of the engine compartment**

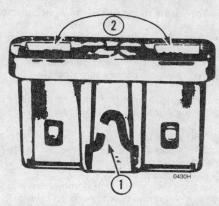

**3.3  To test for a blown fuse you can pull it out and inspect it for a broken element (1) or, with the circuit activated, use a test light between ground and each of the terminals (2) (if there's power to one terminal but not the other, the fuse is blown)**

Brake System (ABS) is on the right side of the engine compartment, near the fender **(see illustration)**.

2    Each of the fuses is designed to protect a specific circuit (or circuits), and the various circuits are identified on the fuse panel itself.

3    Miniaturized fuses are employed in the fuse block. These compact fuses, with blade terminal design, allow fingertip removal and replacement. If an electrical component fails, always check the fuse first. To check the fuses, turn the ignition key to the On position and, using a test light, probe each exposed terminal of each fuse. If the test light glows on both terminals of a fuse, the fuse is good. If power is available on one side of the fuse but not the other, the fuse is blown. When removed, a blown fuse is easily identified through the clear plastic body. Visually inspect the element for evidence of damage **(see illustration)**.

4    Be sure to replace blown fuses with the correct type. Fuses of different ratings are physically interchangeable, but only fuses of the proper rating should be used. Replacing a fuse with one of a higher or lower value than specified is not recommended. Each electrical circuit needs a specific amount of protection. The amperage value of each fuse is molded into the fuse body.

5    If the replacement fuse immediately fails, don't replace it again until the cause of the problem is isolated and corrected. In most cases, the cause will be a short circuit in the wiring caused by a broken or deteriorated wire.

6    All models are equipped with a main fuse (either an 80A or 100A) which protects all the circuits coming from the battery. If these circuits are overloaded, the main fuse blows, preventing damage to the main wiring harness. The main fuse consists of a metal strip which will be visibly melted when overloaded. Always disconnect the battery before replacing a main fuse (available from your dealer). **Caution:** *The stereo in your vehicle is equipped with an anti-theft system. Make sure you have the correct activation code before disconnecting the battery.*
The main fuse is located in the engine compartment fuse block. It's very similar in appearance to standard fuses and is replaced in the same way. If you have to replace a main fuse, make sure you install a replacement unit that's equivalent to the old fuse. In other words, if the old main fuse is an 80A unit, replace it with an 80A fuse; if it's a 100A unit, replace it with a 100A fuse. Don't switch amperage ratings on the main fuse!

## 4    Circuit breakers - general information

Circuit breakers protect components such as sunroof motors, power window motors and airbag inflator resistors.

On some models the circuit breaker resets itself automatically, so an electrical overload in a circuit breaker protected system will cause the circuit to fail momentarily, then come back on. If the circuit does

not come back on, check it immediately. Once the condition is corrected, the circuit breaker will resume its normal function. Some circuit breakers must be reset manually.

## 5    Relays - general information

Several electrical accessories such as the rear window defogger, the blower motor, the cooling fan and the anti-lock brake system use relays, which are remote switches that allow a small amount of current in one circuit to open or close a switch in a circuit with more current. If the relay is defective, the circuit it controls won't operate properly.

Relays are located in both main fuse boxes (see Section 3):

**Interior fuse box** (under left side of instrument panel):
   *Rear window defogger relay*
   *Sunroof open and close relays*
   *Blower motor relay*
   *Turn signal/hazard relay*

**Engine compartment fuse box** (right rear corner of engine compartment):
   *Rear window defogger relay*
   *Headlight relay*

**They're also located in various other locations** throughout the vehicle:

   *Anti-lock brake motor relay - anti-lock brake fuse box on right side of engine compartment*
   *Condenser fan relay - front left corner of the engine compartment*
   *Air conditioner compressor clutch relay - front left corner of the engine compartment next to condenser fan relay*
   *PGM-FI main relay - in center of dashboard*
   *Starter relay - in center dashboard, next to PGM-FI relay*
   *Cigarette lighter relay - in right side of center console*
   *Horn relay - in left side of center console*
   *If you suspect a faulty relay, remove it and have it tested by a dealer service department or a repair shop. Defective relays must be replaced - they can't be serviced.*

## 6    Hazard/turn signal flashers - check and replacement

**Warning:** *The vehicles covered by this manual have airbags. Always disable the airbag system before working in the vicinity of the steering column, instrument panel or console to avoid the possibility of accidental deployment of the airbag, which could cause personal injury* (see Section 25). *The yellow wiring harnesses and connectors routed through the console and instrument panel are for this system. Do not use electrical test equipment on the system wiring or connectors or tamper with them in any way.*

**Caution:** *The stereo in your vehicle is equipped with an anti-theft system. Make sure you have the correct activation code before disconnecting the battery.*

1    The hazard/turn signal flasher is a small square relay located in the upper left corner of the interior fuse block under the left side of the instrument panel.

2    If the flasher unit is functioning properly, you can hear an audible clicking sound when it's operating. If the turn signals fail on one side or the other and the flasher unit doesn't make its characteristic clicking sound, look for a faulty turn signal bulb.

3    If both turn signals fail to blink, the problem may be due to a blown fuse (in the engine compartment fuse box), a faulty flasher unit, a broken switch or a loose or open connection. If a quick check of the fuse box indicates that the turn signal fuse has blown, check the wiring for a short before installing a new fuse.

4    To replace the flasher, simply pull it out of the fuse block.

5    Make sure that the replacement unit is identical to the original. Compare the old one to the new one before installing it.

6    Installation is the reverse of removal.

## 7   Combination switches - check and replacement

**Warning:** *The vehicles covered by this manual have airbags. Always disable the airbag system before working in the vicinity of the steering column, instrument panel or console to avoid the possibility of accidental deployment of the airbag, which could cause personal injury (see Section 25). The yellow wiring harnesses and connectors routed through the console and instrument panel are for this system. Do not use electrical test equipment on the system wiring or connectors or tamper with them in any way.*

**Caution:** *The stereo in your vehicle is equipped with an anti-theft system. Make sure you have the correct activation code before disconnecting the battery.*

### Check

*Refer to illustrations 7.3a, 7.3b, 7.4a, 7.4b and 7.4c*

1    Remove the instrument panel lower cover and knee bolster (see Chapter 11).

2    Remove the steering column covers (see Chapter 11).

3    Unplug the twenty-pin electrical connector (headlight/dimmer/passing and turn signal switch) or the seven-pin electrical

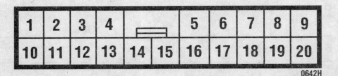

**7.3a  Terminal guide for the lighting/dimmer/passing/ turn signal and rear wiper/washer switch (backside of connector shown)**

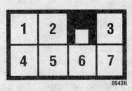

**7.3b  Terminal guide for the front wiper/washer switch (backside of connector shown)**

## Lighting/Dimmer/Passing Switch

| Position \ Terminal | | 20 | 17 | 18 | 5 | 6 |
|---|---|:---:|:---:|:---:|:---:|:---:|
| **Headlight switch** | OFF | ● | | | | ● |
| | LOW | ● | | ● | ● | ● |
| | HIGH | ● | ● | ● | ● | ● |
| **Passing switch (Headlight switch "OFF")** | OFF | | | | | |
| | ON | | ● | ● | ● | |
| **Passing switch (Headlight switch "●")** | OFF | | | ● | ● | |
| | ON | | ● | ● | ● | |

## Turn Signal Switch

| Position \ Terminal | 7 | 8 | 9 |
|---|:---:|:---:|:---:|
| R | ● | | ● |
| NEUTRAL | | | |
| L | | ● | ● |

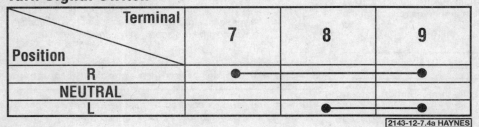

**7.4a  Continuity table for the lighting/dimmer/passing switch and turn signal switch**

2143-12-7.4a HAYNES

| Terminal / Position | 1 | 2 | 3 | 4 | 5 | 6 | 7 |
|---|---|---|---|---|---|---|---|
| OFF | | | | | ●— | | —● |
| INT | | ●— | —● | | ●— | | —● |
| LO | ●— | | | | | | —● |
| HI | ●— | | | —● | | | |
| Mist switch "ON" | ●— | | | —● | | | |
| Washer switch "ON" | | ●— | | | | —● | |

0645H

**7.4b  Continuity table for the windshield wiper/washer switch**

| Terminal / Position | 1 | 3 | 10 | 11 | 12 |
|---|---|---|---|---|---|
| Washer Switch "ON" | ●— | —● | | ●— | —● |
| OFF | | | | ●— | —● |
| ON | | | ●— | | —● |
| Washer Switch "ON" | ●— | —● | ●— | | —● |

0646H

**7.4c  Continuity table for the rear wiper/washer switch**

**7.6  Locations of the retaining screws for the combination switches (steering wheel removed for clarity)**

connector (windshield wiper/washer switch) **(see illustrations)**.

4    Check the connector for continuity between the indicated terminals with the switch in each position **(see illustrations)**. If the continuity is not as specified, replace the switch.

## Replacement

5    Remove the steering column covers, if not already done. Turn the steering wheel as required for access to the switch screws.

### Turn signal/headlight/dimmer switch

*Refer to illustration 7.6*

6    Remove the two retaining screws **(see illustration)**, detach the switch, unplug the electrical connector and remove the switch from the housing.

7    Installation is the reverse of removal.

### Windshield wiper/washer switches

8    Remove the two retaining screws, then use a small screwdriver to carefully detach the switch from the housing and unplug the electrical connector.

9    Installation is the reverse of removal.

## 8    Ignition switch/key lock cylinder - check and replacement

**Warning:** *The vehicles covered by this manual have airbags. Always disable the airbag system before working in the vicinity of the steering column, instrument panel or console to avoid the possibility of accidental deployment of the airbag, which could cause personal injury (see Section 25). The yellow wiring harnesses and connectors routed through the console and instrument panel are for this system. Do not use electrical test equipment on the system wiring or connectors or tamper with them in any way.*

**Caution:** *The stereo in your vehicle is equipped with an anti-theft system. Make sure you have the correct activation code before disconnecting the battery.*

1    Remove the steering column covers, instrument panel lower cover and knee bolster (see Chapter 11).

## Switch

*Refer to illustrations 8.4a and 8.4b*

2    Disconnect the negative battery cable, then the positive battery cable (see Caution and Warning above).

3    Trace the wire harness for the ignition switch/key lock cylinder assembly to the fuse box under the left side of the dash, then unplug the connectors from the fuse box.

4    Check the connector for continuity between the indicated terminals with the key in each position **(see illustrations)**.

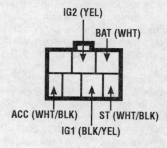

IG2 (YEL)
BAT (WHT)
ACC (WHT/BLK)    ST (WHT/BLK)
IG1 (BLK/YEL)

**8.4a  Terminal guide for the seven-pin connector for the ignition switch (trace the wires from the ignition switch to the fuse box to find the connector)**

0648H

| Terminal<br>Position | White/<br>Black<br>(ACC) | White<br>(BAT) | Black/<br>Yellow<br>(IG1) | Yellow<br>(IG2) | Black/<br>White<br>(ST) |
|---|---|---|---|---|---|
| 0 | | | | | |
| 1 | ● | ● | | | |
| 2 | ● | ● | ● | ● | |
| 3 | | ● | ● | | ● |

0647H

**8.4b   Continuity table for the ignition switch terminals**

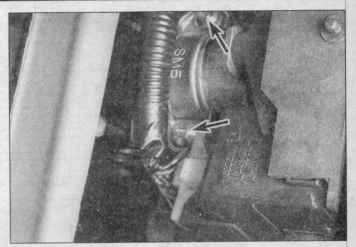

**8.10   Drill out the heads of these two bolts (arrows) or cut grooves in them with a chisel and use a screwdriver to remove them, then separate the clamp halves**

**9.1   Carefully pry the defogger switch out of the dash with a small screwdriver**

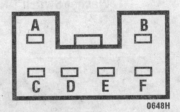

0648H

**9.2   Terminal guide for the rear window defogger switch**

5   If the continuity is not as specified, replace the switch by simply unplugging it and removing the three retaining screws, after first removing the column lock assembly (see below).

### Lock cylinder and steering column lock assembly

*Refer to illustration 8.10*

6   Check the lock cylinder in each position to make sure it isn't worn or loose and that the key position corresponds to the markings on the housing. If the lock cylinder is faulty, the entire steering column lock assembly will have to be replaced.

7   Disconnect the negative battery cable, then the positive battery cable (see Caution and Warning above).

8   Remove the steering column cover and lower instrument panel (see Chapter 11).

9   Remove the retaining nuts and lower the steering column.

10   The lock assembly is clamped to the steering column by two shear-head bolts **(see illustration)**. Use a center punch to make a dimple in the head of each bolt, then drill them out with a 3/16-inch bit. Separate the clamp and remove the assembly from the steering column.

11   Place the new switch in position without the key inserted and tighten the bolts until they are snug.

12   Insert the key and check the lock cylinder for proper operation.

13   Tighten the bolts until their heads break off.

14   The remainder of installation is the reverse of removal.

15   Connect the positive battery cable, followed by the negative cable.

## 9   Rear window defogger switch - check and replacement

*Refer to illustrations 9.1 and 9.2*

1   Using a small screwdriver, carefully pry the switch from the dashboard, then unplug it from the connector **(see illustration)**.

2   Check for continuity between the indicated terminals of the connector **(see illustration)** as follows: with the button pushed, there should be continuity between terminals D and F; with the button released, there should be continuity between terminals A and C and between terminals B and E. **Note:** *If there is no continuity between A and C or between B and E, the light bulb in the circuit between those terminals may be burnt out.*

3   If the continuity isn't as indicated, replace the switch.

## 10   Rear window defogger - check and repair

1   The rear window defogger consists of a number of horizontal elements baked onto the glass surface.

2   Small breaks in the element can be repaired without removing the rear window.

### Check

*Refer to illustration 10.4*

3   Turn the ignition switch and defogger system switches On.

4   Ground the negative lead of a voltmeter to terminal B and the positive lead to terminal A **(see illustration)**.

5   The voltmeter should read between 10 and 15 volts. If the reading is lower there is a poor ground connection.

6   Connect the negative lead to a good body ground. The reading

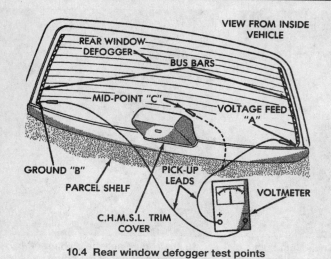

10.4  Rear window defogger test points

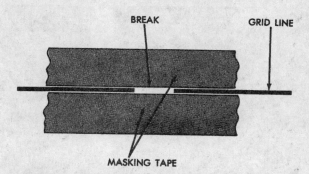

10.14  To repair a broken grid, first apply a strip of masking tape to either side of the grid to mask off the area

11.6  Remove the screws, pull the speaker out and unplug it

should stay the same.

7  Connect the negative lead to the ground bus bar (point "B"), then touch each grid line at the mid-point with the positive lead.

8  The reading should be approximately six volts. If the reading is 0, there is a break between the mid-point "C" and the battery voltage bus bar point "A".

9  A 10 to 14 volt reading is an indication of a break between mid-point "C" and ground.

10  Move the lead toward the break; the voltage will change when the break is crossed.

## Repair

*Refer to illustration 10.14*

11  Repair the break in the line using a repair kit specifically recommended for this purpose. Included in this kit is plastic conductive epoxy.

12  Prior to repairing a break, turn off the system and allow it to de-energize for a few minutes.

13  Lightly buff the element area with fine steel wool, then clean it thoroughly with rubbing alcohol.

14  Use masking tape to mask off the area being repaired **(see illustration)**.

15  Mix the epoxy thoroughly, following the instructions provided with the repair kit.

16  Apply the epoxy material to the slit in the masking tape, overlapping the undamaged area about 3/4-inch on either end.

17  Allow the repair to cure for 24 hours before removing the tape and using the system.

## 11  Stereo and speakers - removal and installation

**Warning:** *The vehicles covered by this manual have airbags. Always disable the airbag system before working in the vicinity of the steering column, instrument panel or console to avoid the possibility of accidental deployment of the airbag, which could cause personal injury (see Section 25). The yellow wiring harnesses and connectors routed through the console and instrument panel are for this system. Do not use electrical test equipment on the system wiring or connectors or tamper with them in any way.*

**Caution:** *The stereo in your vehicle is equipped with an anti-theft system. Make sure you have the correct activation code before disconnecting the battery.*

## Stereo

1  Detach the cable from the negative terminal of the battery, then

detach the positive cable (see the Caution and Warning above).

2  Remove the front console panel and ashtray (see Chapter 11).

3  Reach under the radio and remove the two retaining screws. Pull out the stereo, unplug the electrical connector and antenna lead, then remove the stereo.

4  Installation is the reverse of removal.

## Speakers

### Front speakers

*Refer to illustration 11.6*

5  Remove the door trim panel (see Chapter 11).

6  Remove the speaker mounting screws, pull out the speaker and unplug the electrical connector **(see illustration)**.

7  Installation is the reverse of removal.

### Rear speakers

8  Working in the trunk, remove the three speaker cover screws.

9  Working inside the vehicle detach the speaker cover, remove the three bolts, lift the speaker out, unplug the connector and remove the speaker.

10  Installation is the reverse of removal.

## 12  Antenna - removal and installation

## Fixed antenna

*Refer to illustration 12.2*

1  Open the trunk lid or liftgate and remove the left side inner trim panel for access to the antenna assembly.

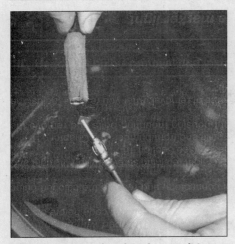

**12.2  After removing the trim panel, trace the lead down from the antenna and unplug this connector**

**13.3a  To remove the headlight bulb, rotate the bulb holder retaining collar counterclockwise . . .**

**13.3b . . . then pull the bulb assembly straight out of the housing**

2    Trace the lead from the antenna down to the connector and unplug it **(see illustration)**. *Caution: Pull on the metal terminals when separating this connector. Do not pull on the cable or damage to the cable may result.*
3    Remove the locknut, spacer and rubber washer from the base of the antenna and pull the antenna assembly and lead through the hole in the fender.
4    Installation is the reverse of removal.

### Power antenna

5    Remove the locknut, spacer and rubber washer.
6    Turn on the radio. As the antenna extends, withdraw it and the antenna drive cable from the fender.
7    Carefully insert the cable of the new antenna into the hole with the drive teeth facing toward the rear of the vehicle. You can verify that the cable teeth are properly engaged with the antenna motor drive gear by carefully moving the cable up and down.
8    Turn off the radio and let the antenna motor pull the drive cable into the antenna housing.
9    Clean the antenna housing threads and insert the antenna into the housing. Install the bushing, spacer and locknut. Tighten the locknut securely.
10    Verify that the antenna fully extends and retracts when the stereo is turned on and off, respectively. If the antenna sticks, the locknut my be over-tightened. Loosen it until the antenna can move up and down freely.

## 13  Headlight bulb - removal and installation

*Refer to illustrations 13.3a, 13.3b and 13.3c*
**Warning:** *Halogen gas-filled bulbs are under pressure and may shatter if the surface is scratched or the bulb is dropped. Wear eye protection and handle the bulbs carefully, grasping only the base whenever possible. Do not touch the surface of the bulb with your fingers because the oil from your skin could cause it to overheat and fail prematurely. If you do touch the bulb surface, clean it with rubbing alcohol.*
1    Open the hood.
2    If you're removing a right-side bulb, remove the coolant reservoir (see Chapter 3).
3    Reach behind the headlight assembly, grasp the bulb holder retaining collar, turn it counterclockwise, then pull out the bulb/holder assembly **(see illustrations)**. To disconnect the electrical connector, simply press the release tab and pull it straight out of the holder **(see illustration)**.

**13.3c  Press the release tab and disconnect the electrical connector**

4    Insert the new bulb assembly into the housing and rotate the retaining collar in a clockwise direction to lock the holder into place. Plug in the electrical connector.

## 14  Headlights - adjustment

*Refer to illustrations 14.1a and 14.1b*
**Note:** *The headlights must be aimed correctly. If adjusted incorrectly they could temporarily blind the driver of an oncoming vehicle and cause an accident or seriously reduce your ability to see the road. The headlights should be checked for proper aim every 12 months and any time a new headlight is installed or front end body work is performed. It should be emphasized that the following procedure is only an interim step which will provide temporary adjustment until the headlights can be adjusted by a properly equipped shop.*
1    Headlights have spring-loaded adjusting screws for controlling up-and-down and left-and-right movement **(see illustrations)**.
2    There are several methods of adjusting the headlights. The simplest method requires a blank wall 25 feet in front of the vehicle and a level floor.
3    Position masking tape vertically on the wall in reference to the vehicle centerline and the centerlines of both headlights.
4    Position a horizontal tape line in reference to the centerline of all

**14.1a  To make horizontal adjustments insert a Phillips screwdriver into the geared housing adjuster**

**14.1b  The headlight vertical adjustment screw (arrow) is located at the upper corner of the headlight assembly**

the headlights. **Note:** *It may be easier to position the tape on the wall with the vehicle parked only a few inches away.*

5     Adjustment should be made with the vehicle sitting level, the gas tank half-full and no unusually heavy load in the vehicle.

6     Starting with the low beam adjustment, position the high intensity zone so it is two inches below the horizontal line and two inches to the right of the headlight vertical line. Adjustment is made by turning the vertical adjusting screw. The horizontal adjusting screw should be used to move the beam left or right.

7     With the high beams on, the high intensity zone should be vertically centered with the exact center just below the horizontal line. **Note:** *It may not be possible to position the headlight aim exactly for both high and low beams. If a compromise must be made, keep in mind that the low beams are the most used and have the greatest effect on driver safety.*

8     Have the headlights adjusted by a dealer service department or service station at the earliest opportunity.

## 15   Composite headlight housing replacement

*Refer to illustration 15.4*
**Warning:** *The vehicles covered by this manual have airbags. Always disable the airbag system before working in the vicinity of the steering*

column, instrument panel or console to avoid the possibility of accidental deployment of the airbag, which could cause personal injury (see Section 25). The yellow wiring harnesses and connectors routed through the console and instrument panel are for this system. Do not use electrical test equipment on the system wiring or connectors or tamper with them in any way.*
**Caution:** *The stereo in your vehicle is equipped with an anti-theft system. Make sure you have the correct activation code before disconnecting the battery.*

1     Unplug the electrical connectors, and remove the halogen bulbs (see Section 13).

2     Remove the side marker light retaining screw, pull off the light and unplug the electrical connector (see Section 16).

3     Remove the radiator grille and front bumper (see Chapter 11).

4     Remove the headlight housing mounting bolts and remove the housing **(see illustration)**.

5     Installation is the reverse of removal. After you're done, adjust the headlights (see Section 14).

## 16   Bulb replacement

### Front parking/side marker light

*Refer to illustrations 16.1a, 16.1b, 16.2 and 16.3*

1     Open the hood and remove the screw that secures the parking/marker light housing, then pull the housing straight forward **(see illustrations)**.

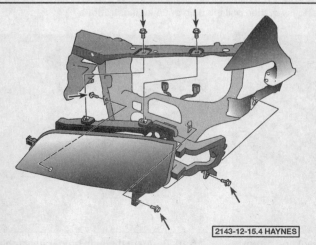

**15.4  After removing the bumper, remove the five retaining bolts and detach the composite headlight housing**

**16.1a  Remove the front parking/side marker light retaining screw . . .**

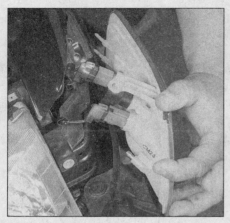

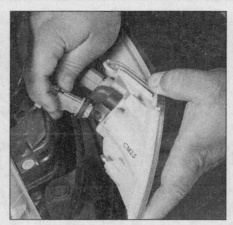

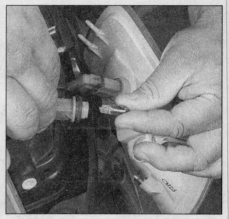

**16.1b** . . . and push the housing forward to detach it

**16.2  Rotate the bulb holder counterclockwise to remove it**

**16.3  Pull the bulb straight out**

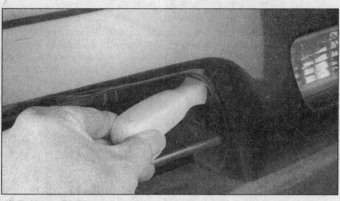

**16.5  Use a Phillips screwdriver to remove the parking light screw**

**16.7  Remove the screw and detach the side marker light housing from the fender**

2    Turn the bulb holder counterclockwise and pull it out of the housing **(see illustration)**.
3    Pull the bulb out of the holder **(see illustration)**.
4    Installation is the reverse of removal.

### Front turn signal
*Refer to illustration 16.5*
5    Working through the bumper air intake, remove the Phillips head retaining screw and rotate the signal housing out for access to the bulb holder **(see illustration)**.

6    Turn the holder counterclockwise, pull it out of the housing, then pull the bulb straight out.

### Rear side marker bulb
*Refer to illustrations 16.7 and 16.8*
7    Remove the screw and pull the side marker housing out **(see illustration)**.
8    Rotate the bulb holder 1/8-turn counterclockwise and pull it out of the housing, then pull the bulb out **(see illustration)**.

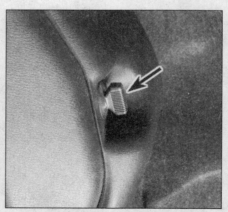

**16.8  After removing the holder, pull the bulb straight out**

**16.9  Rotate the knob (arrow) and remove the bulb housing cover**

**16.10  Remove the bulb holder assembly by rotating it counterclockwise, then push the bulb into the holder and rotate it counterclockwise to remove it**

**16.21  To remove an instrument cluster light bulb, depress it and turn it counterclockwise to release it**

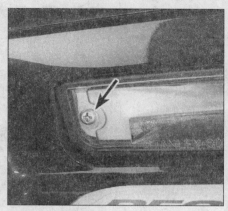

**16.24  Remove the screw (arrow) at each corner, then remove the license plate light bulb housing**

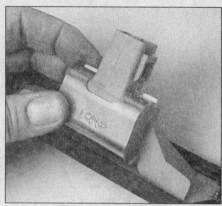

**16.25  Detach the bulb cover . . .**

**16.26  . . . and pull the bulb straight out**

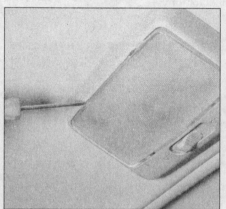

**16.31  To remove the lens for the interior lights, simply pry it out with a small screwdriver like this (but be careful not to scratch the plastic)**

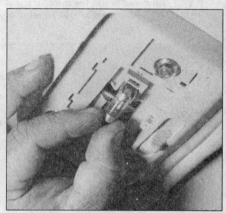

**16.32  Pull the bulb straight out of the clips at each end - if it is necessary to pry it out, pry only at the metal ends**

## Tail light bulb

*Refer to illustrations 16.9 and 16.10*

9  Remove the cover for the tail light bulb housing **(see illustration)**.
10  Turn the bulb holder 1/8-turn counterclockwise and pull it out of the housing **(see illustration)**.
11  Push in on the bulb and turn it counterclockwise, then pull it out of the bulb holder.
12  Installation is the reverse of removal.

## High-mounted brake light

### Coupe/Sedan models

13  Working in the trunk, unplug the electrical connector and remove the two brake light housing retaining nuts.
14  Inside the vehicle, remove the light housing and twist the bulb holder counterclockwise to remove it, then pull the bulb straight out of the holder.
15  Installation is the reverse of removal.

### Station wagon models

16  Open the liftgate, press in on the center of the cover clips, then detach the cover.
17  Twist the bulb holder 1/8-turn counterclockwise and pull it out of the housing.
18  Pull the bulb straight out of the holder.
19  Installation is the reverse of removal.

## Instrument panel lights

*Refer to illustration 16.21*

20  To gain access to the instrument panel lights, the instrument cluster will have to be removed first (see Section 18).
21  Rotate the bulb holder counterclockwise and remove it from the instrument cluster **(see illustration)**.
22  Pull the bulb straight out of the holder.
23  Installation is the reverse of removal.

## License plate lights

### Coupe/sedan

*Refer to illustrations 16.24, 16.25 and 16.26*

24  Remove the two screws and pull out the lens **(see illustration)**.
25  Remove the bulb holder cover **(see illustration)**.
26  Pull the bulb straight out of the holder **(see illustration)**.
27  Installation is the reverse of removal.

### Station wagon

28  Remove the two screws and detach the bulb lens/housing.
29  Pull the holder out of the housing and remove the bulb.
30  Installation is the reverse of removal.

## Dome/cargo/trunk lights

*Refer to illustrations 16.31 and 16.32*

31  Carefully pry the lens off **(see illustration)**.
32  Remove the bulb from the terminals. It may be necessary to pry the bulb out - if this is the case, pry on the ends of the glass (otherwise the glass may shatter) **(see illustration)**.
33  Installation is the reverse of removal.

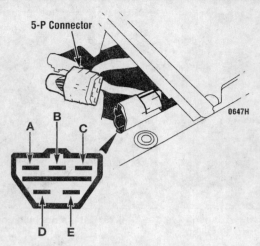

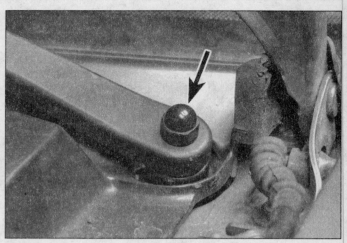

**17.2  Terminal guide for the electrical connector for the windshield wiper motor**

**17.4  To remove a wiper arm, remove this acorn nut and pull the arm straight off its splined shaft**

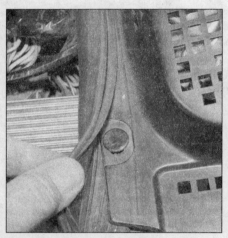

**17.5a  Pull the weatherstripping away for access, and remove the plastic retaining clips from the front edge of the hood seal**

**17.5b  Remove the plastic screws at the rear edge of the cowl panel**

**17.9  Remove the nut and three wiper motor mounting bolts (arrows) to separate the motor from the linkage**

## 17  Wiper motor - check and replacement

### *Windshield wiper motor*

#### Check

*Refer to illustration 17.2*

1    Disconnect the electrical connector from the wiper motor assembly.

2    Using a pair of jumper wires, apply battery voltage to the D terminal and ground the A terminal (Hi) **(see illustration)**. The wiper should operate at high speed. Then connect the battery positive terminal to the D terminal again and the negative terminal to the B terminal. The wiper motor should operate at low speed.

3    If the motor fails to run at low or high speed, replace it.

#### Replacement

*Refer to illustrations 17.4, 17.5a, 17.5b and 17.9*

4    Detach the wiper arms **(see illustration)**.

5    Remove the hood seal and cowl panel by prying off the trim clips and removing the screws **(see illustrations)**.

6    Unplug the electrical connector.

7    Remove the three wiper motor and linkage frame-to-body

mounting bolts.

8    Turn the frame assembly over for access to the motor and linkage.

9    Remove the retaining nut, detach the linkage from the motor, then remove the three motor-to-frame mounting bolts and separate the motor from the wiper linkage **(see illustration)**.

10    Installation is otherwise the reverse of removal. Before installing the new motor assembly, lubricate the contact points of the wiper linkage with multi-purpose grease.

### *Rear wiper motor*

#### Check

*Refer to illustration 17.13*

11    Open the liftgate and remove the trim panel.

12    Disconnect the electrical connector from the wiper motor assembly.

13    Using a pair of jumper wires, apply battery voltage to the D terminal and ground the C terminal **(see illustration)**. The motor should run smoothly.

14    If the motor fails to run, replace it.

#### Replacement

15    Detach the wiper arm and remove the rubber seal, shaft nut

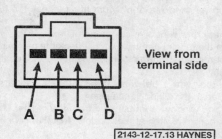

View from terminal side

A  B  C  D

2143-12-17.13 HAYNES

**17.13  Terminal guide for the electrical connector for the rear wiper motor**

and washer.

16    Open the liftgate, remove the wiper motor cover and unplug the electrical connector.

17    Support the motor with one hand while removing the three retaining bolts, then lower the wiper motor from the vehicle.

18    Installation is the reverse of removal.

## 18    Instrument cluster - removal and installation

*Refer to illustrations 18.3a and 18.3b*

**Warning:** *The vehicles covered by this manual have airbags. Always disable the airbag system before working in the vicinity of the steering column, instrument panel or console to avoid the possibility of accidental deployment of the airbag, which could cause personal injury (see Section 25). The yellow wiring harnesses and connectors routed through the console and instrument panel are for this system. Do not use electrical test equipment on the system wiring or connectors or tamper with them in any way.*

**Caution:** *The stereo in your vehicle is equipped with an anti-theft system. Make sure you have the correct activation code before disconnecting the battery.*

1    Disconnect the negative cable from the battery, followed by the positive cable. Review the Warning and Caution above.

2    Remove the instrument cluster bezel (see Chapter 11).

3    Remove the instrument cluster screws, pull out the cluster and unplug the electrical connectors **(see illustrations)**.

4    Installation is the reverse of removal. Be sure to connect the positive cable to the battery first, then the negative cable.

## 19    Horn - check and replacement

**Warning:** *The vehicles covered by this manual have airbags. Always disable the airbag system before working in the vicinity of the steering column, instrument panel or console to avoid the possibility of accidental deployment of the airbag, which could cause personal injury (see Section 25). The yellow wiring harnesses and connectors routed through the console and instrument panel are for this system. Do not use electrical test equipment on the system wiring or connectors or tamper with them in any way.*

**Caution:** *The stereo in your vehicle is equipped with an anti-theft system. Make sure you have the correct activation code before disconnecting the battery.*

1    Remove the radiator grille (see Chapter 11).

2    Unplug the electrical connector from the horn.

3    To test the horn, connect battery voltage to the two terminals with a pair of jumper wires. If the horn doesn't sound, replace it. If it does sound, the problem lies in the switch, relay or the wiring between the components.

4    To replace the horn, unplug the electrical connector and remove the bracket bolt.

5    Installation is the reverse of removal.

6    Install the radiator grille (see Chapter 11).

## 20    Cruise control system - description and check

*Refer to illustration 20.5*

1    The cruise control system maintains vehicle speed with a vacuum actuated servo motor located in the engine compartment, which is connected to the throttle linkage by a cable. The system consists of the servo motor, brake switch, control switches, a relay, the vehicle speed sensor and associated vacuum hoses. Cruise controls all work by the same basic principles; however, the hardware used varies considerably depending on model and year of manufacture. Listed below are some general procedures that may be used to locate common problems.

2    Locate and check the fuse (see Section 3).

3    Have an assistant operate the brake lights while you check their operation (voltage from the brake light switch deactivates the cruise control).

4    If the brake lights don't come on or don't shut off, correct the problem and retest the cruise control.

5    Inspect the cable linkage between the cruise control actuator and

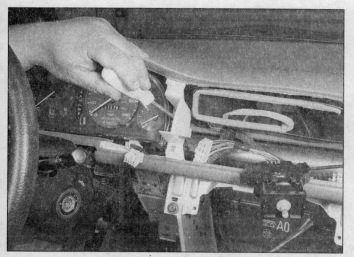

**18.3a  Remove the instrument cluster screws**

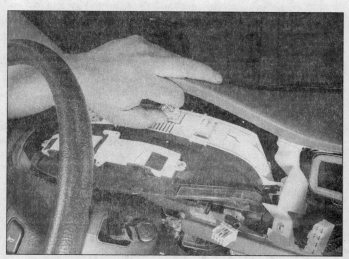

**18.3b  Pull the cluster out of the dash, turn it over and unplug the electrical connectors from the backside**

**20.5  The cruise control servo (arrow) is located in the rear of the engine compartment**

the throttle linkage. The cruise control servo is located on the firewall on the right (passenger) side of the engine compartment **(see illustration)**.

6    Visually inspect the vacuum hose(s) and wires connected to the cruise control actuator and replace as necessary.

7    The vehicle speed sensor is located on top of the transaxle. Raise the front of the vehicle and support it on jackstands. Unplug the electrical connector and touch one probe of a digital voltmeter to the orange wire of the connector and the other to a good ground. With the vehicle in Neutral and key On, measure the voltage while rotating one wheel with the other one blocked. If the voltage doesn't vary as the wheel rotates, the sensor is defective.

8    Test drive the vehicle to determine if the cruise control is now working. If it isn't, take it to a dealer service department or an automotive electrical specialist for further diagnosis and repair.

## 21    Power window system - description and check

**Warning:** *The vehicles covered by this manual have airbags. Always disable the airbag system before working in the vicinity of the steering column, instrument panel or console to avoid the possibility of accidental deployment of the airbag, which could cause personal injury (see Section 25). The yellow wiring harnesses and connectors routed through the console and instrument panel are for this system. Do not use electrical test equipment on the system wiring or connectors or tamper with them in any way.*
**Caution:** *The stereo in your vehicle is equipped with an anti-theft system. Make sure you have the correct activation code before disconnecting the battery.*

1    The power window system consists of the control switches, the motors, glass mechanisms (regulators), and associated wiring.

2    Power windows are wired so they can be lowered and raised from the master control switch by the driver or by remote switches located at the individual windows. Each window has a separate motor which is reversible. The position of the control switch determines the polarity and therefore the direction of operation. The system is equipped with a relay that controls current flow to the motors.

3    The power window system operates when the ignition switch is ON. In addition, these models have a window lockout switch at the master control switch which, when activated, disables the switches at the rear windows and, sometimes, the switch at the passenger's window also. Always check these items before troubleshooting a window problem.

4    These procedures are general in nature, so if you can't find the problem using them, take the vehicle to a dealer service department or other qualified repair shop.

5    If the power windows don't work at all, check the fuse or circuit breaker.

6    If only the rear windows are inoperative, or if the windows only operate from the master control switch, check the rear window lockout switch for continuity in the unlocked position. Replace it if it doesn't have continuity.

7    Check the wiring between the switches and fuse panel for continuity. Repair the wiring, if necessary.

8    If only one window is inoperative from the master control switch, try the other control switch at the window. **Note:** *This doesn't apply to the drivers door window*.

9    If the same window works from one switch, but not the other, check the switch for continuity.

10    If the switch tests OK, check for a short or open in the wiring between the affected switch and the window motor.

11    If one window is inoperative from both switches, remove the trim panel from the affected door and check for voltage at the motor while the switch is operated.

12    If voltage is reaching the motor, disconnect the glass from the regulator (see Chapter 11). Move the window up and down by hand while checking for binding and damage. Also check for binding and damage to the regulator. If the regulator is not damaged and the window moves up and down smoothly, replace the motor (see Chapter 11). If there's binding or damage, lubricate, repair or replace parts, as necessary.

13    If voltage isn't reaching the motor, check the wiring in the circuit for continuity between the switches and motors. Check that the relay is grounded properly and receiving voltage from the switches. Also check that the relay sends voltage to the motor when the switch is turned on. If it doesn't, replace the relay.

14    Test the windows after you are done to confirm proper repairs.

## 22    Power door lock system - description and check

**Warning:** *The vehicles covered by this manual have airbags. Always disable the airbag system before working in the vicinity of the steering column, instrument panel or console to avoid the possibility of accidental deployment of the airbag, which could cause personal injury (see Section 25). The yellow wiring harnesses and connectors routed through the console and instrument panel are for this system. Do not use electrical test equipment on the system wiring or connectors or tamper with them in any way.*
**Caution:** *The stereo in your vehicle is equipped with an anti-theft system. Make sure you have the correct activation code before disconnecting the battery.*

1    Power door lock systems are operated by bi-directional solenoids located in the doors. The lock switches have two operating positions: Lock and Unlock. These switches activate a relay which in turn connects voltage to the door lock solenoids. Depending on which way the relay is activated, it reverses polarity, allowing the two sides of the circuit to be used alternately as the feed (positive) and ground side.

2    Always check the circuit protection first. Some vehicles use a combination of circuit breakers and fuses.

3    Operate the door lock switches in both directions (Lock and Unlock) with the engine off. Listen for the faint click of the relay operating.

4    If there's no click, check for voltage at the switches. If no voltage is present, check the wiring between the fuse panel and the switches for shorts and opens.

5    If voltage is present but no click is heard, test the switch for continuity. Replace it if there's not continuity in both switch positions.

6    If the switch has continuity but the relay doesn't click, check the wiring between the switch and relay for continuity. Repair the wiring if there's no continuity.

7    If the relay is receiving voltage from the switch but is not sending voltage to the solenoids, check for a bad ground at the relay case. If the relay case is grounding properly, replace the relay.

8    If all but one lock solenoid operates, remove the trim panel from

the affected door (see Chapter 11). and check for voltage at the solenoid while the lock switch is operated. One of the wires should have voltage in the Lock position; the other should have voltage in the unlock position.

9   If the inoperative solenoid is receiving voltage, replace the solenoid.

10   If the inoperative solenoid isn't receiving voltage, check for an open or short in the wire between the lock solenoid and the relay. **Note:** *It's common for wires to break in the portion of the harness between the body and door (opening and closing the door fatigues and eventually breaks the wires).*

## 23   Power seats - description and check

1   Power seats allow you to adjust the position of the seat with little effort. The optional power seats on these models adjust forward and backward, up and down and tilt forward and backward.

2   The power seat system consists of a motor, a switch on the seat and a relay and fuse in the engine compartment fuse block.

3   Look under the seat for any objects which may be preventing the seat from moving.

4   If the seat won't work at all, check the fuse .

5   With the engine off to reduce the noise level, operate the seat controls in all directions and listen for sound coming from the seat motor(s).

6   If the motor runs or clicks but the seat doesn't move, the integral the seat drive mechanism is damaged and the motor assembly must be replaced.

7   If the motor doesn't work or make noise, check for voltage at the motor while an assistant operates the switch.

8   If the motor is getting voltage but doesn't run, test it off the vehicle with jumper wires. If it still doesn't work, replace it.

9   If the motor isn't getting voltage, check for voltage at the switch. If there's no voltage at the switch, check the wiring between the fuse panel and the switch. If there's voltage at the switch, obtain the wiring diagrams for the vehicle and check the switch for continuity in all its operating positions. Replace the switch if there's no continuity.

10   If the switch is OK, check for a short or open in the wiring between the switch and motor. If there's a relay between the switch and motor, check that it's grounded properly and there's voltage to the relay. Also check that there's voltage going from the relay to the motor when the when the switch is operated. If there's not, and the relay is grounded properly, replace the relay.

11   Test the completed repairs.

## 24   Electric rear view mirrors - description and check

1   Electric rear view mirrors use two motors to move the glass; one for up-and-down adjustments and one for left-to-right adjustments.

2   The control switch has a selector portion which sends voltage to the left or right side mirror. With the ignition ON but the engine OFF, roll down the windows and operate the mirror control switch through all functions (left-right and up-down) for both the left and right side mirrors.

3   Listen carefully for the sound of the electric motors running in the mirrors.

4   If the motors can be heard but the mirror glass doesn't move, there's probably a problem with the drive mechanism inside the mirror. Remove and disassemble the mirror to locate the problem.

5   If the mirrors don't operate and no sound comes from the mirrors, check the fuse (see Section 3).

6   If the fuse is OK, remove the mirror control switch from its mounting without disconnecting the wires attached to it. Turn the ignition ON and check for voltage at the switch. There should be voltage at one terminal. If there's no voltage at the switch, check for an open or short in the wiring between the fuse panel and the switch.

7   If there's voltage at the switch, disconnect it. Check the switch for

continuity in all its operating positions. If the switch does not have continuity, replace it.

8   Re-connect the switch. Locate the wire going from the switch to ground. Leaving the switch connected, connect a jumper wire between this wire and ground. If the mirror works normally with this wire in place, repair the faulty ground connection.

9   If the mirror still doesn't work, remove the cover and check the wires at the mirror for voltage with a test light. Check with ignition ON and the mirror selector switch on the appropriate side. Operate the mirror switch in all its positions. There should be voltage at one of the switch-to-mirror wires in each switch position (except the neutral "off" position).

10   If there's not voltage in each switch position, check the wiring between the mirror and control switch for opens and shorts.

11   If there's voltage, remove the mirror and test it off the vehicle with jumper wires. Replace the mirror if it fails this test (see Chapter 11).

## 25   Airbag - general information

### *Description*

1   All models are equipped with a Supplemental Restraint System (SRS), more commonly known as an airbag. There are two airbags, one for the driver and one for the front seat passenger. The SRS system is designed to protect the driver (and on later models, the passenger as well) from serious injury in the event of a head-on or frontal collision.

2   The SRS system consists of an SRS unit - which contains a safing sensor, self-diagnosis circuit and a back-up power circuit - located under the dash, right in front of the floor console, two impact sensors, one on each side of the dashboard, an airbag assembly in the center of the steering wheel and a second airbag assembly for the front seat passenger, located in the top of the dashboard right above the glove box.

### *Operation*

3   For the airbag(s) to deploy, one or both impact sensors and the safing sensor must be activated. When this condition occurs, the circuit to the airbag inflator is closed and the airbag inflates. If the battery is destroyed by the impact, or is too low to power the inflator, a back-up power unit inside the SRS unit provides power.

### *Self-diagnosis system*

4   A self-diagnosis circuit in the SRS unit displays a light when the ignition switch is turned to the On position. If the system is operating normally, the light should go out after about six seconds. If the light doesn't come on, or doesn't go out after six seconds, or if it comes on while you're driving the vehicle, there's a malfunction in the SRS system. Have it inspected and repaired as soon as possible. Do not attempt to troubleshoot or service the SRS system yourself. Even a small mistake could cause the SRS system to malfunction when you need it.

### *Servicing components near the SRS system*

5   Nevertheless, there are times when you need to remove the steering wheel, radio or service other components on or near the dashboard. At these times, you'll be working around components and wire harnesses for the SRS system. The SRS wiring harnesses are easy to identify: They're all bright yellow. Do not unplug the connectors for these wires. And do not use electrical test equipment on yellow wires; it could cause the airbag(s) to deploy. **ALWAYS DISABLE THE SRS SYSTEM BEFORE WORKING NEAR THE SRS SYSTEM COMPONENTS OR RELATED WIRING.**

### *Disabling the SRS system*

*Refer to illustrations 25.8 and 25.12*

**Warning:** *Any time you are working in the vicinity of airbag wiring or components, DISABLE THE SRS SYSTEM.*

6   Disconnect the battery negative cable, then disconnect the

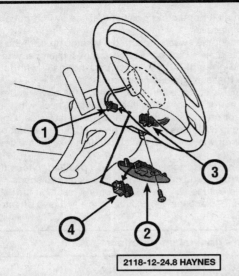

**25.8  To prevent the possibility of accidental deployment of the driver's side airbag, remove the two screws from the maintenance lid under the steering wheel, pull off the lid, remove the short connector, unplug the three-pin connector between the airbag and the cable reel and plug the short connector into the airbag side of the three-pin connector**

| | | | |
|---|---|---|---|
| 1 | Airbag connector | 3 | Cable reel connector |
| 2 | Access cover | 4 | Short connector (red) |

positive cable and wait three minutes. **Caution:** *The stereo in your vehicle is equipped with an anti-theft system. Make sure you have the correct activation code before disconnecting the battery.*

7    Connect the short (red) connectors to the airbag side of the connectors as described in the following steps.

### Driver's side airbag

8    Remove the access panel below the airbag and remove the short (red) connector **(see illustration)**.
9    Unplug the three-pin connector between the airbag and the cable reel.
10    Plug the short (red) connector into the airbag side of the three-pin connector.

### Passenger's side airbag

11    Remove the glove box (see Chapter 11).
12    Unplug the electrical connector between the passenger side airbag and the SRS main wiring harness. Install the red short connector on the airbag side of the connector **(see illustration)**.

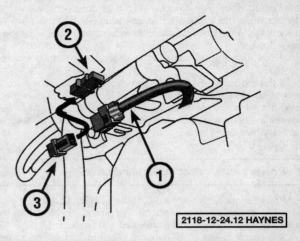

**25.12  When disabling the passenger's side airbag, unplug the airbag electrical connector from the SRS main harness and install the red short connector to the airbag electrical connector**

| | | | |
|---|---|---|---|
| 1 | SRS main harness | 3 | Front passenger's airbag |
| 2 | Short connector (red) | | three-pin connector |

### Either airbag

13    After you've disabled the airbag and performed the necessary service, unplug the short connector from the airbag connector and plug in the three-pin airbag connector into the three-pin cable reel connector (driver's side) or the SRS main harness (passenger's side) attach the short connector to its holder and reinstall the lid to the underside of the steering wheel or reinstall the glove box.
14    Reattach the positive (first) and negative (last) battery cables.

### 26  Wiring diagrams - general information

Since it isn't possible to include all wiring diagrams for every year and model covered by this manual, the following diagrams are those that are typical and most commonly needed.

Prior to troubleshooting any circuits, check the fuse and circuit breakers (if equipped) to make sure they're in good condition. Make sure the battery is properly charged and check the cable connections (see Chapter 1).

When checking a circuit, make sure that all connectors are clean, with no broken or loose terminals. When unplugging a connector, do not pull on the wires. Pull only on the connector housings themselves.

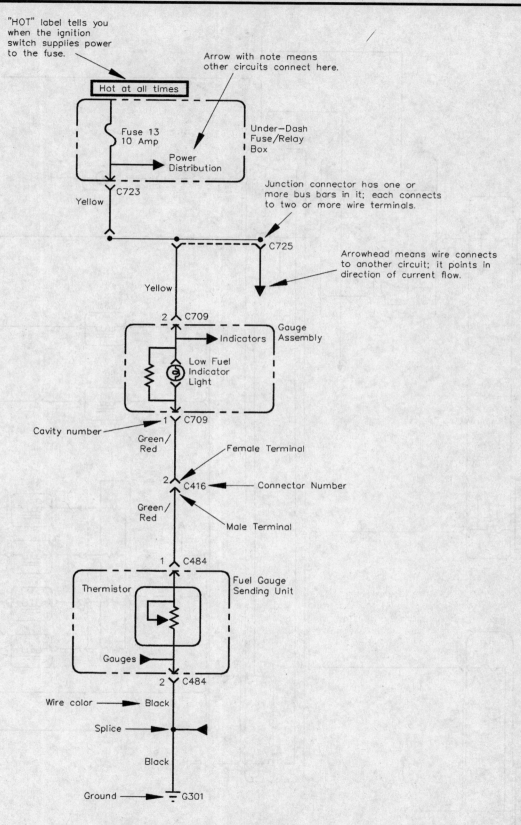

**Key to circuit diagrams**

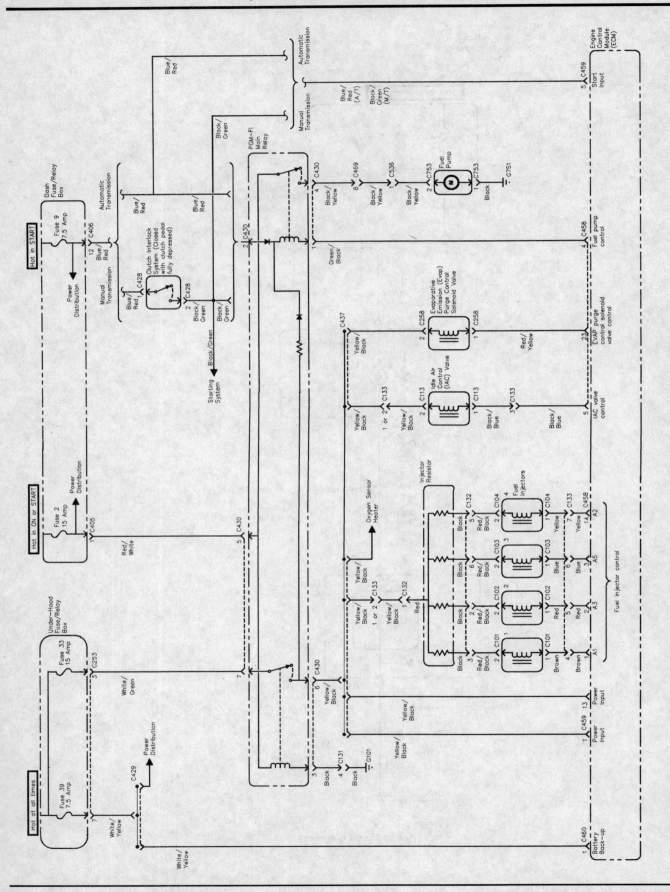

**Typical four-cylinder model PGM-FI fuel control circuit**

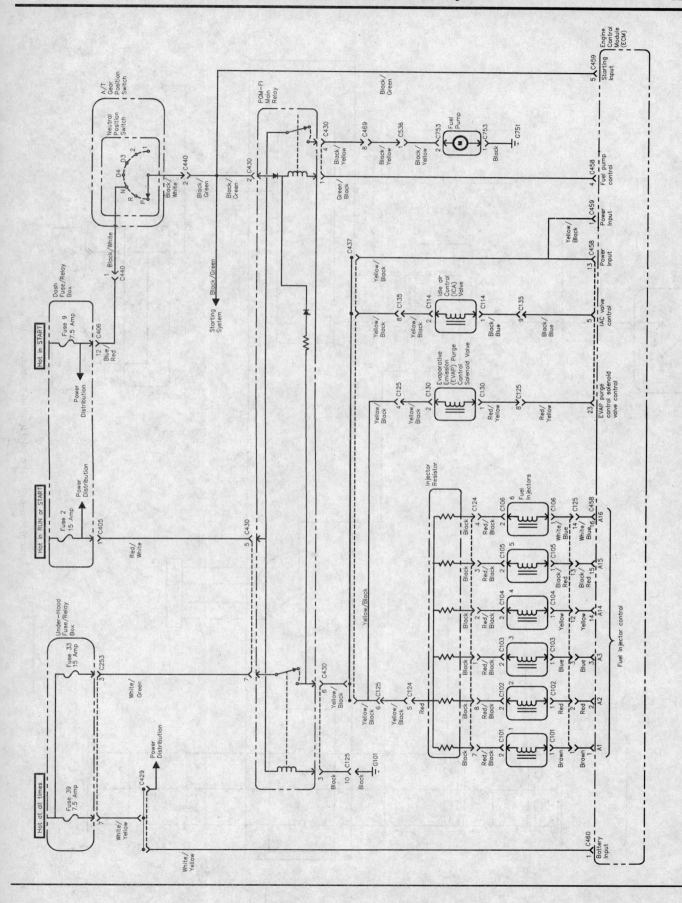

**Typical V6 model PGM-FI fuel control circuit**

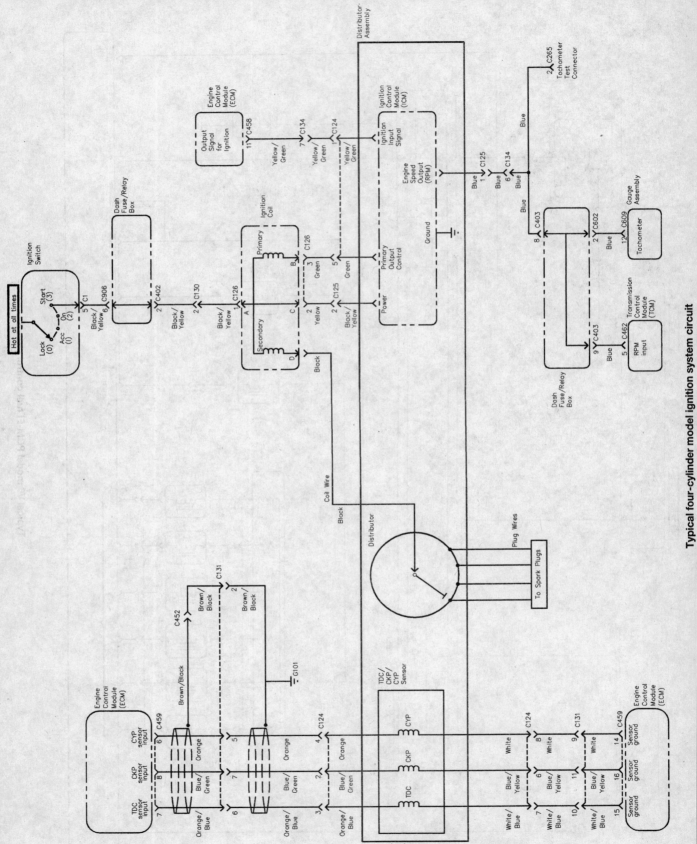

**Typical four-cylinder model ignition system circuit**

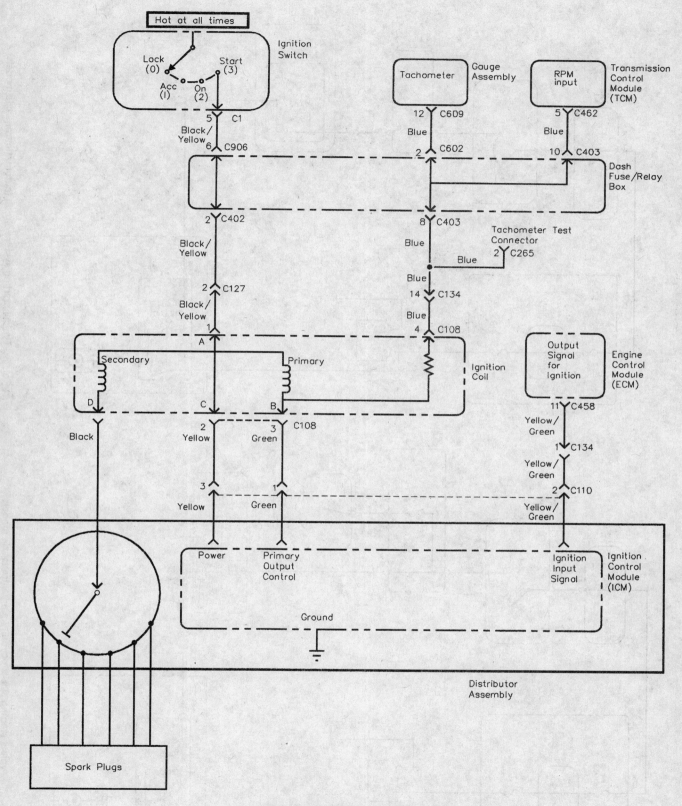

**Typical V6 model ignition system circuit**

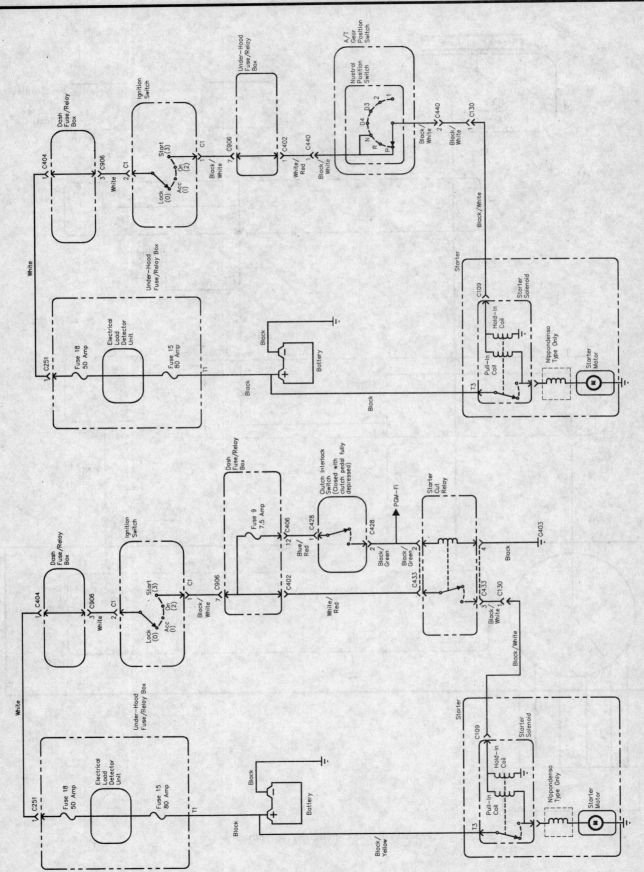

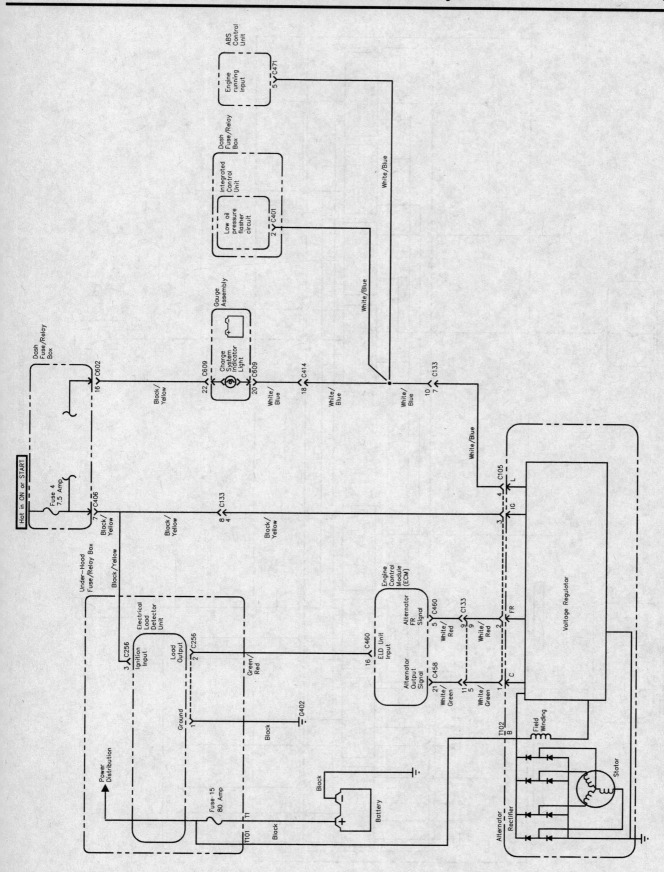

Typical charging system circuit

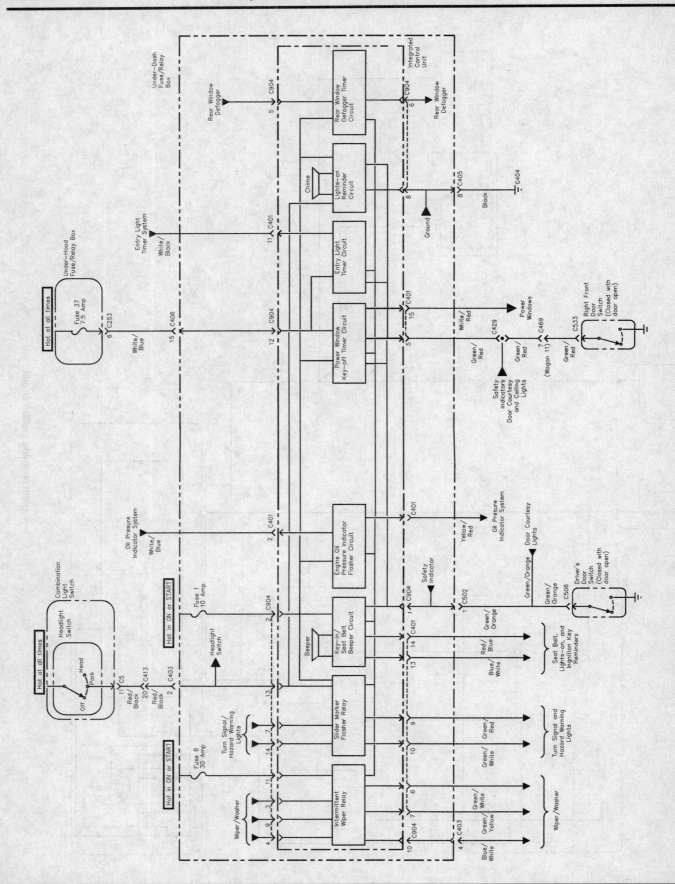

**Typical integrated control unit circuit**

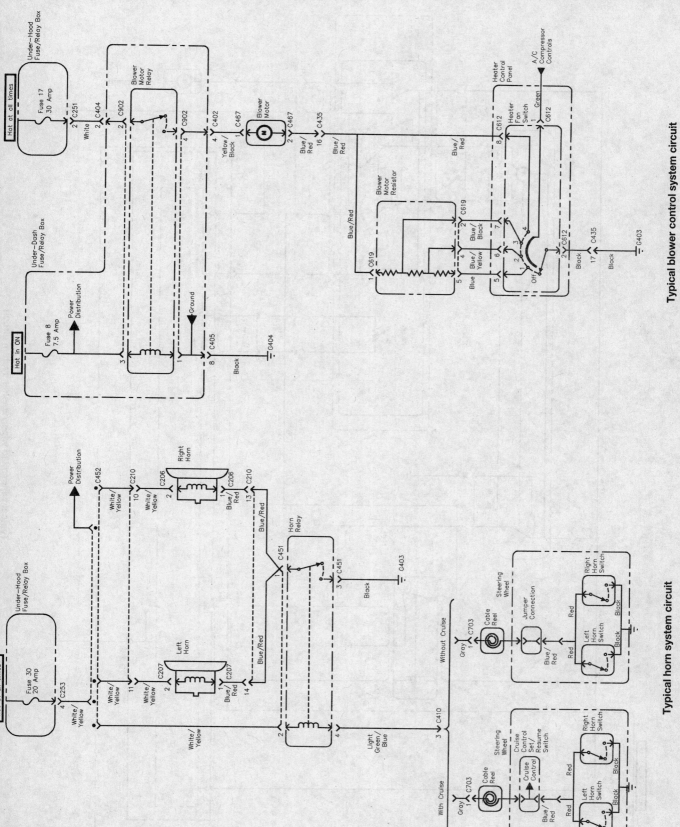

Typical blower control system circuit

Typical horn system circuit

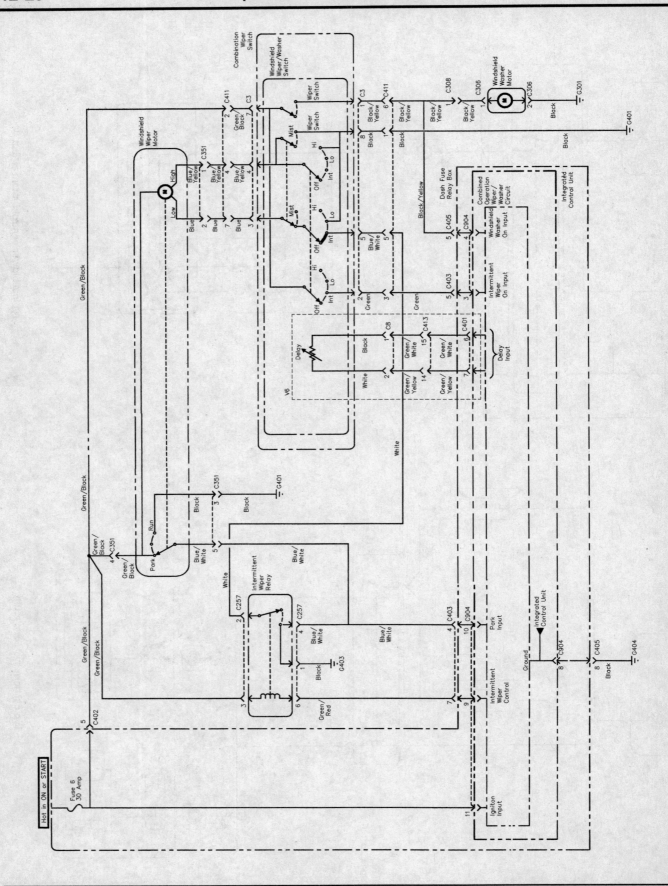

**Typical windshield wiper/washer system circuit**

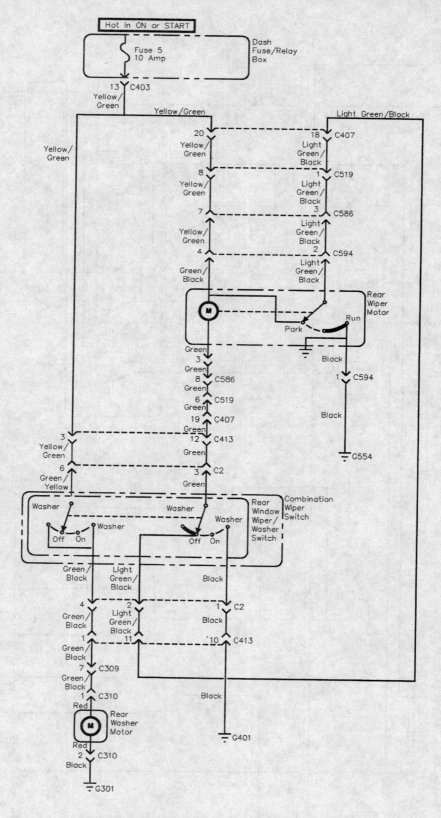

**Typical rear window wiper/washer system circuit**

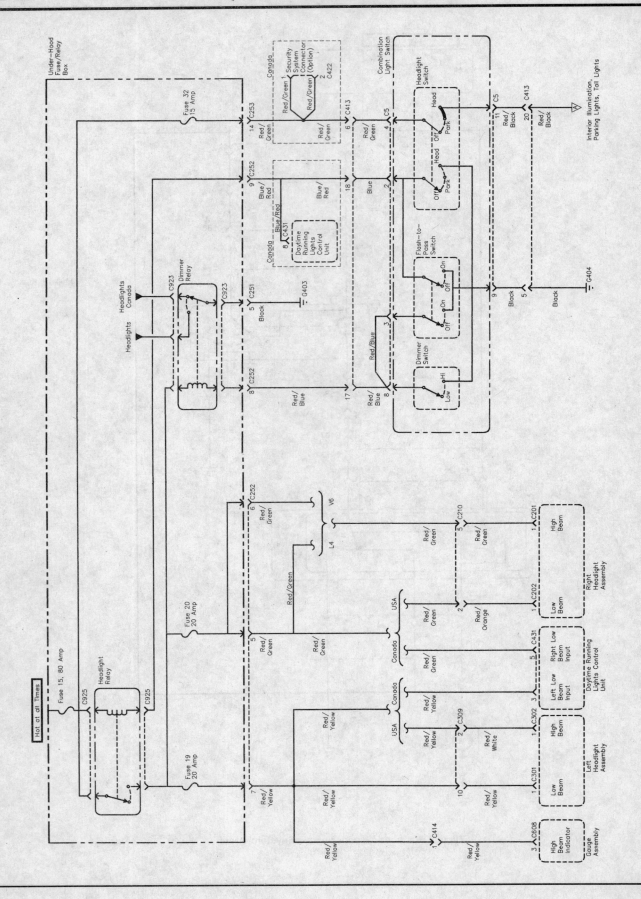

**Typical headlight switch circuit**

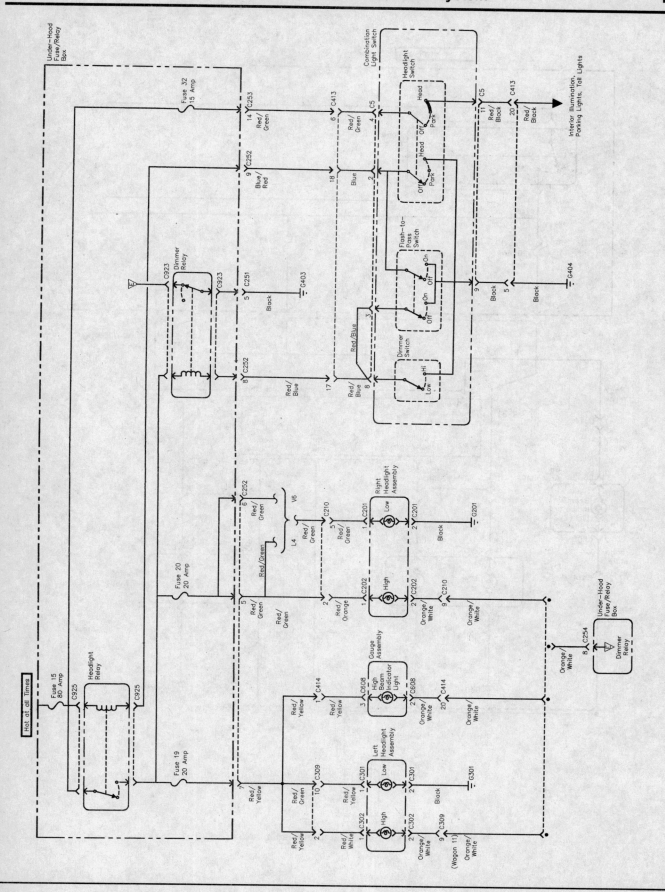

Typical headlight system circuit (US models)

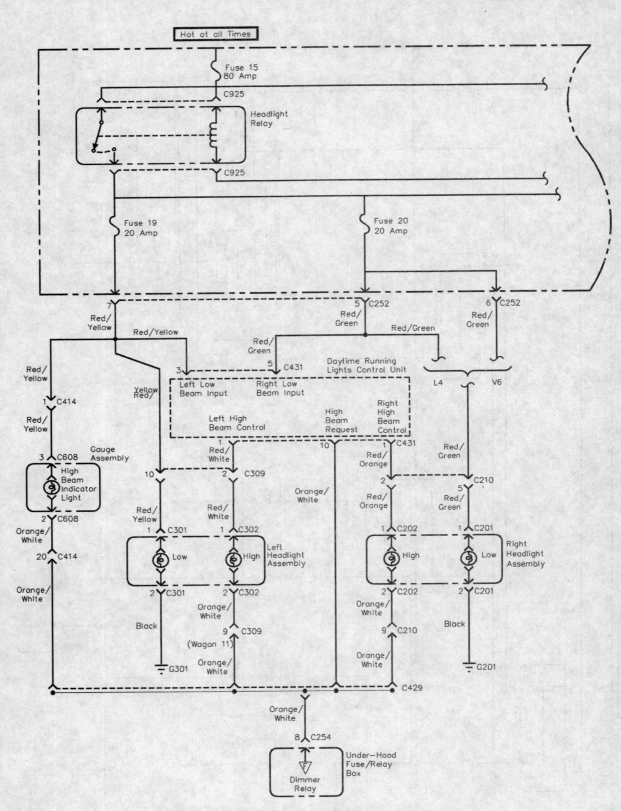

**Typical headlight system circuit (Canadian models) (1 of 3)**

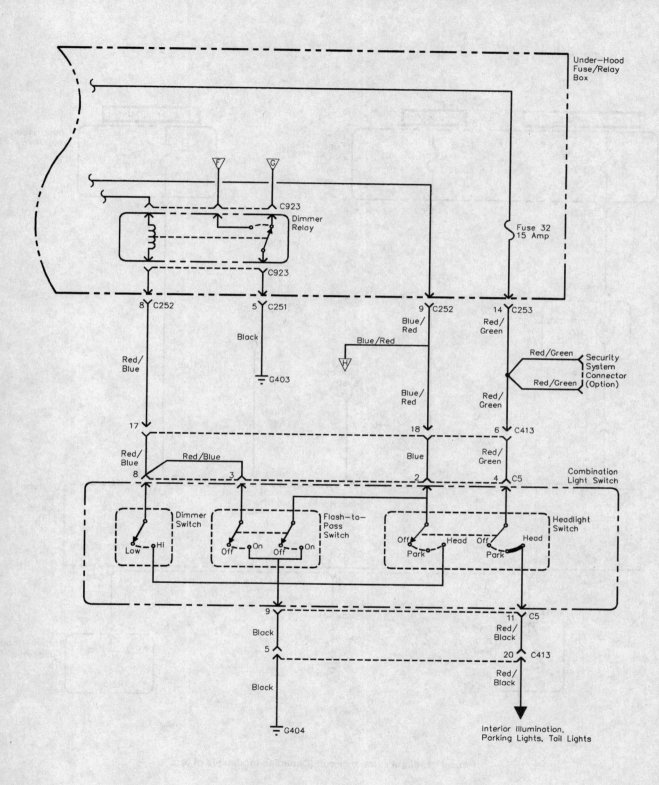

**Typical headlight system circuit (Canadian models) (2 of 3)**

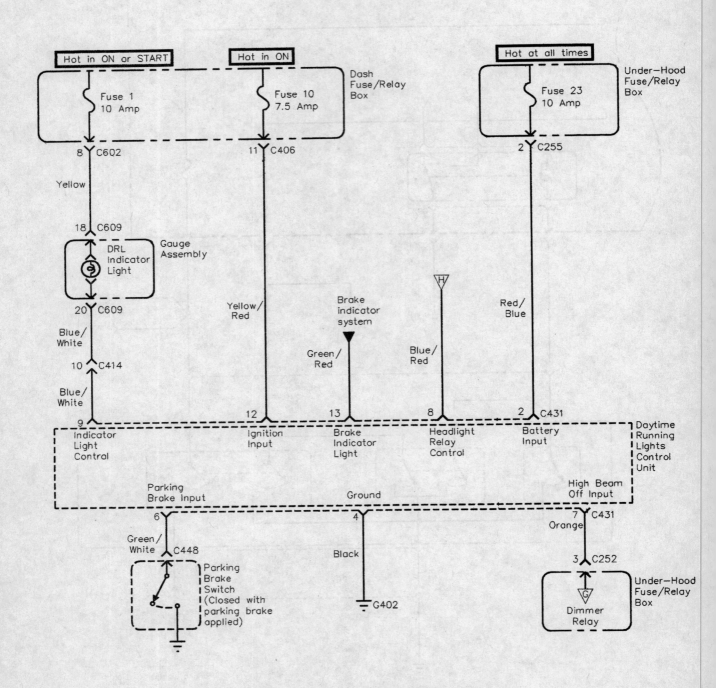

**Typical headlight system circuit (Canadian models) (3 of 3)**

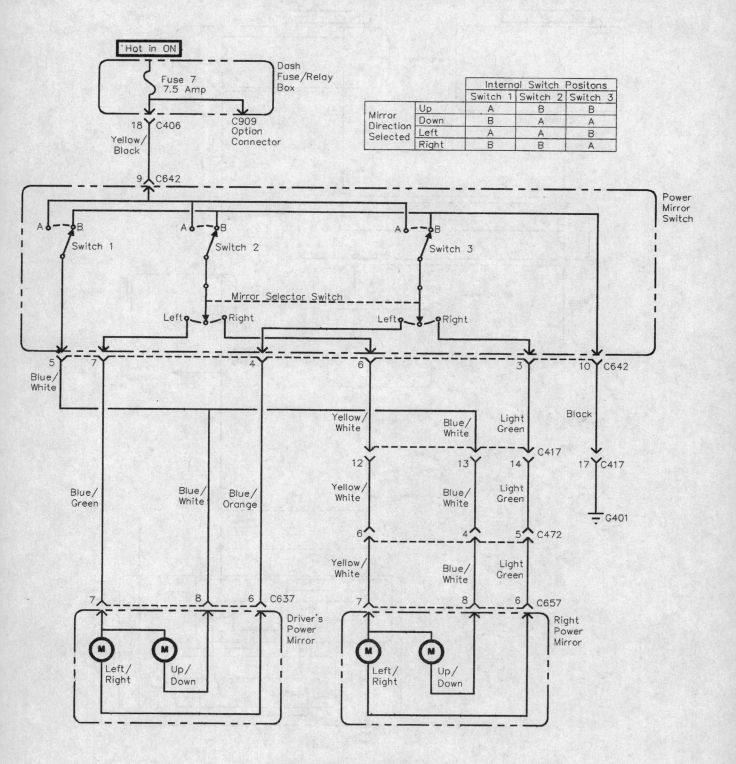

| | | Internal Switch Positons | | |
|---|---|---|---|---|
| | | Switch 1 | Switch 2 | Switch 3 |
| Mirror Direction Selected | Up | A | B | B |
| | Down | B | A | A |
| | Left | A | A | B |
| | Right | B | B | A |

**Typical power mirror system circuit**

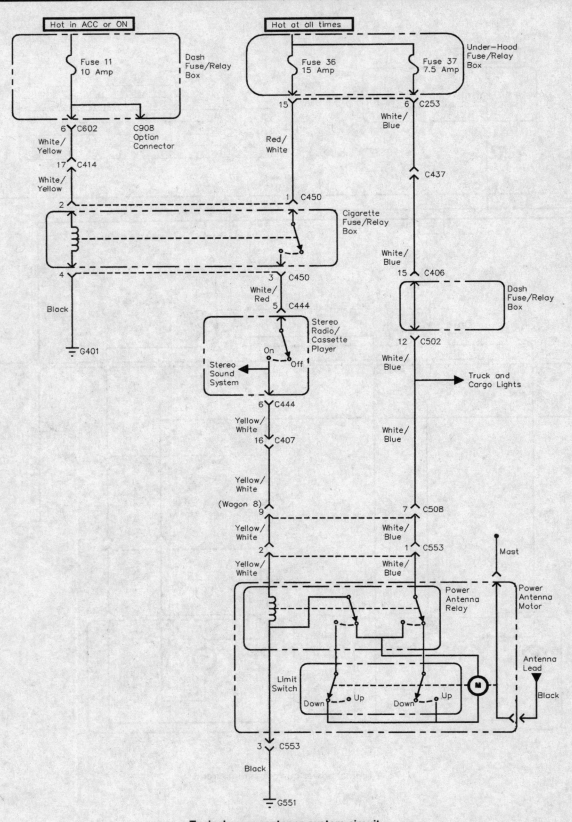

**Typical power antenna system circuit**

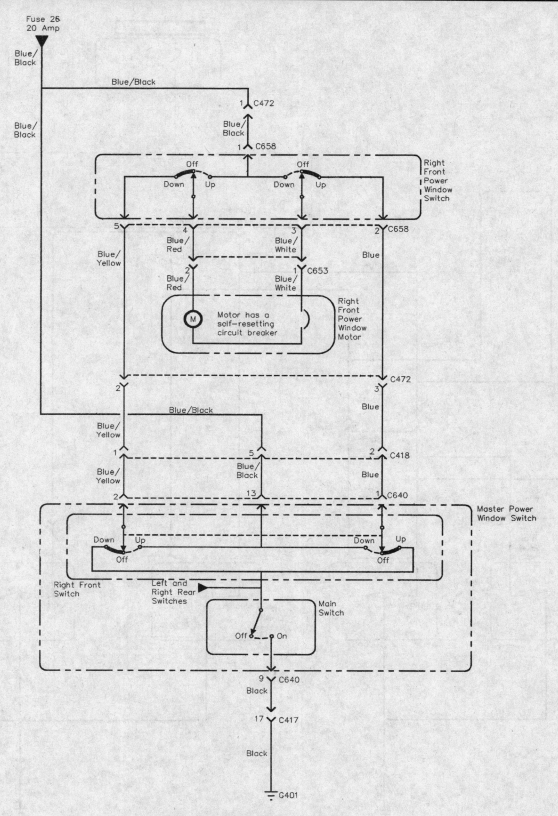

**Typical power window circuit**

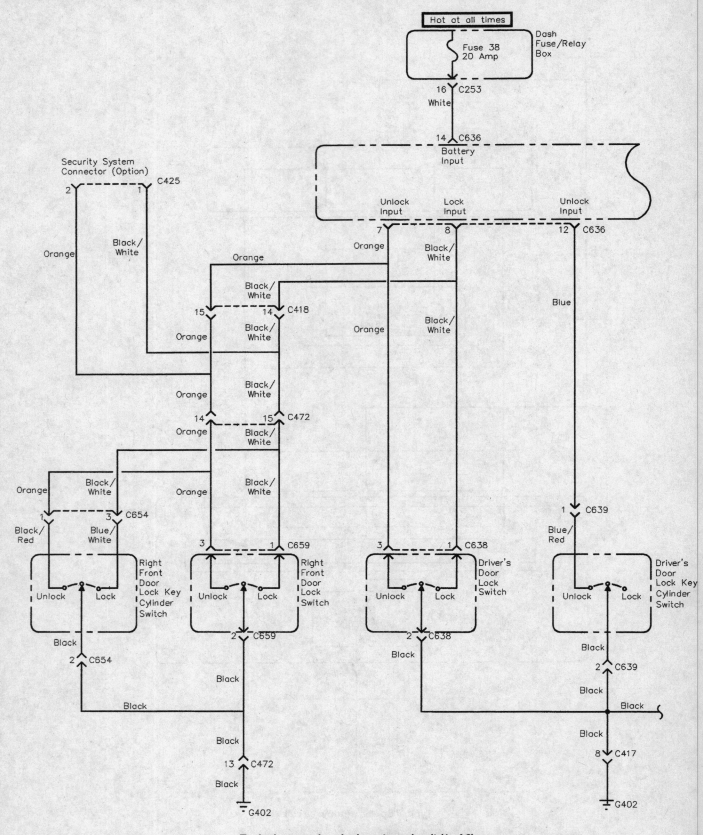

**Typical power door lock system circuit (1 of 2)**

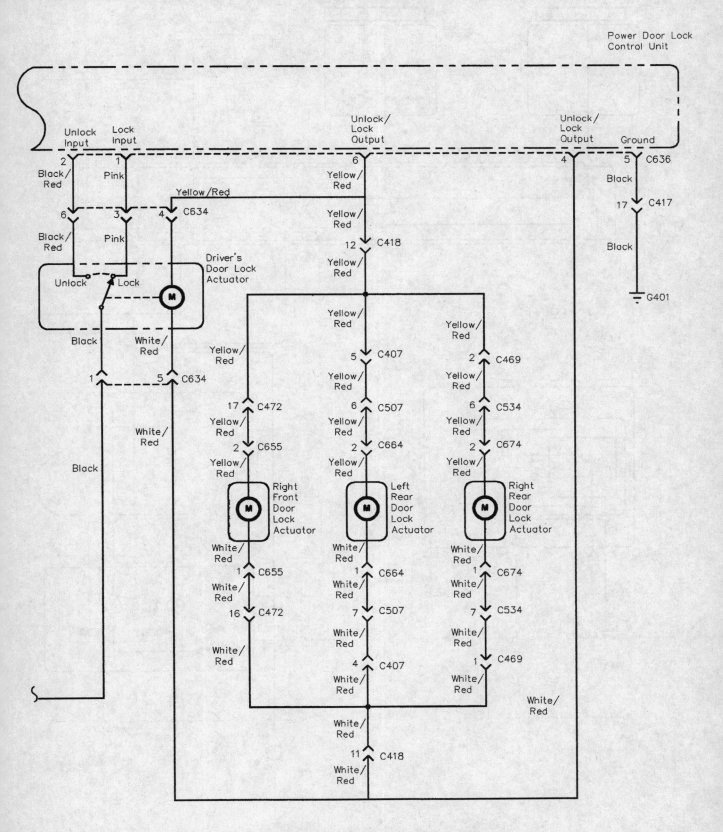

**Typical power door lock system circuit (2 of 2)**

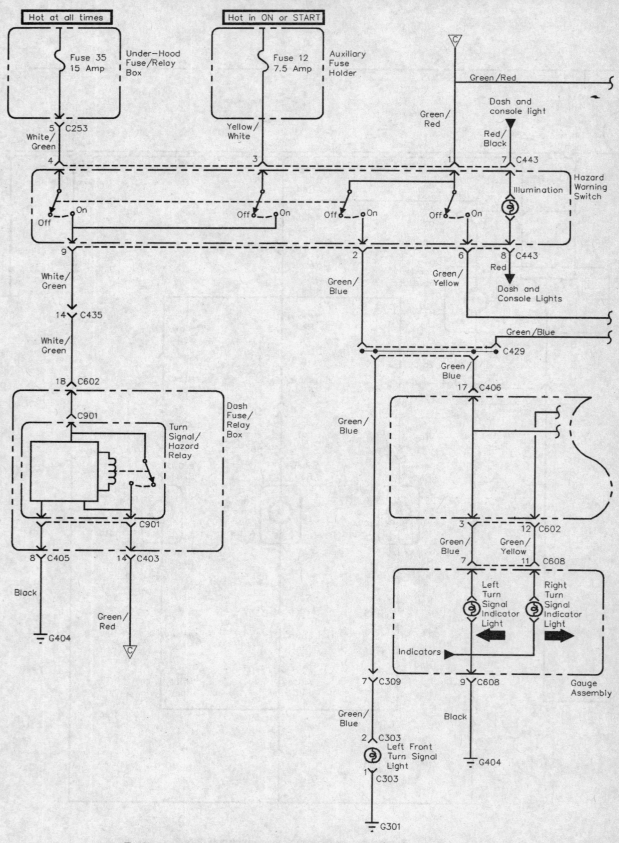

**Typical turn signal and hazard warning light system circuit (1 of 2)**

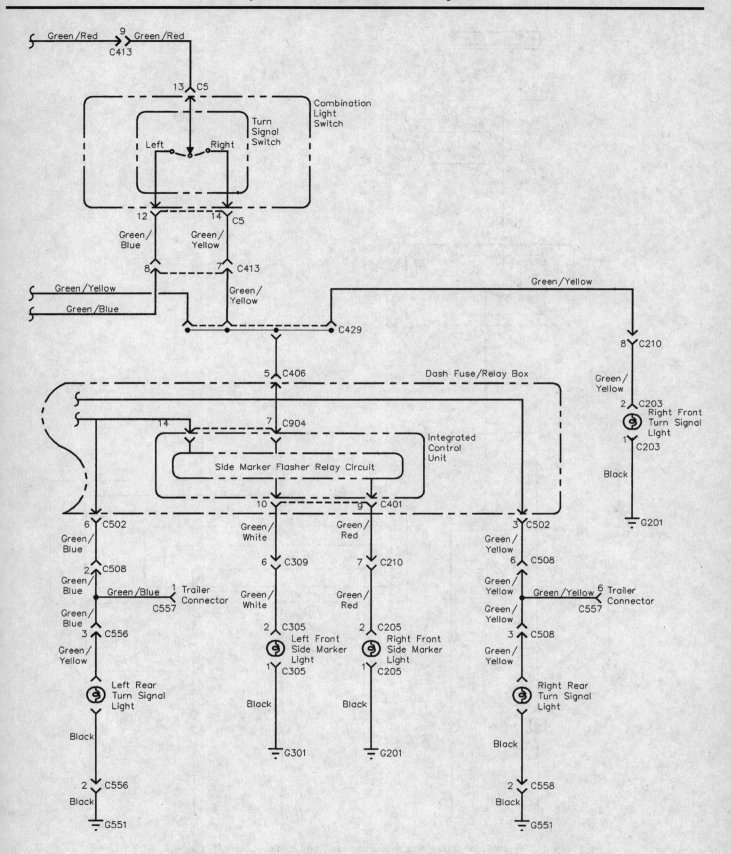

**Typical turn signal and hazard warning light system circuit (2 of 2)**

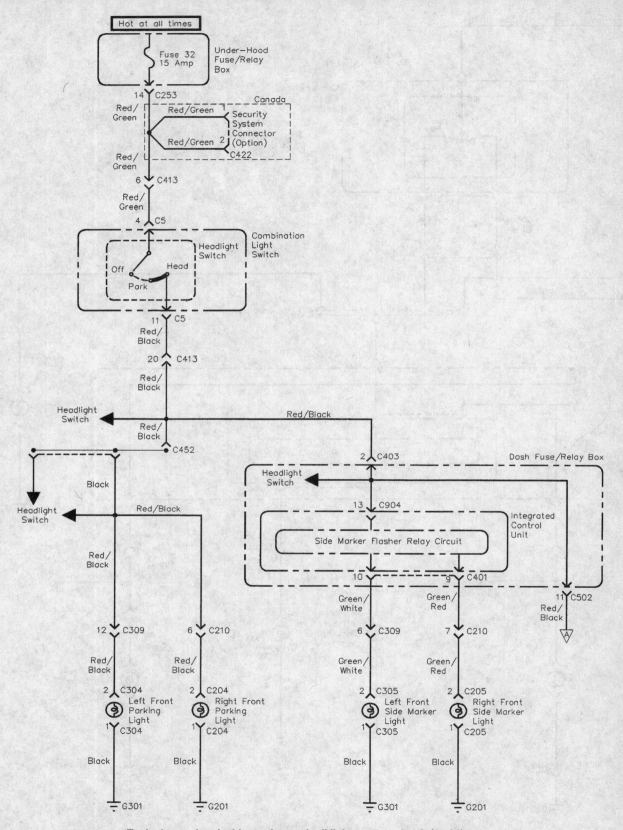

**Typical turn signal, side marker and tail light system circuit (1 of 2)**

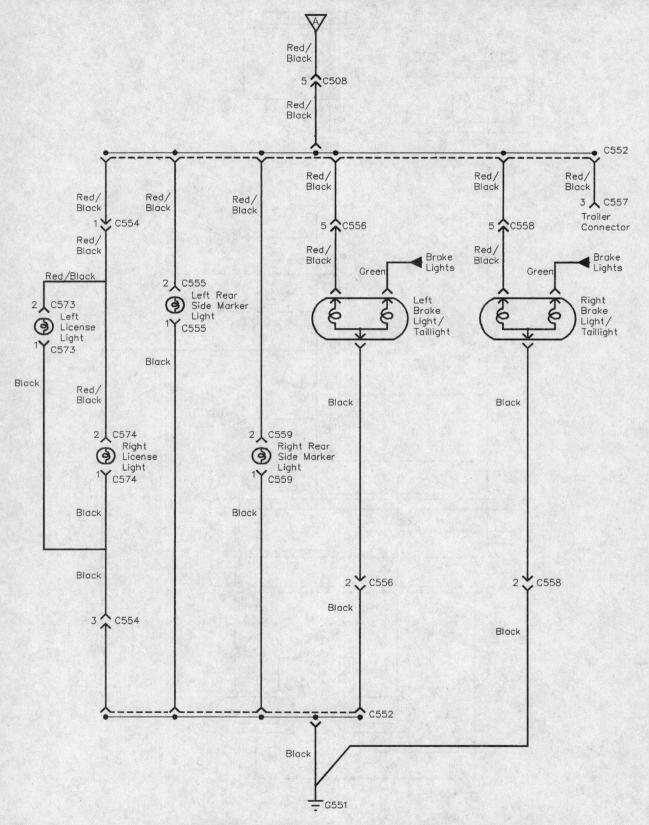

**Typical turn signal, side marker and tail light system circuit (2 of 2)**

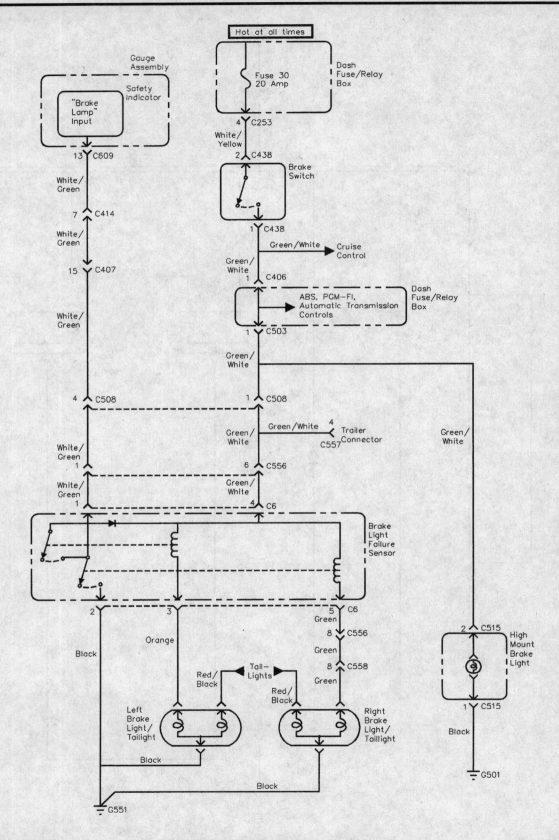

**Typical brake light system circuit**

# Index

# Haynes Automotive Manuals

NOTE: New manuals are added to this list on a periodic basis. If you do not see a listing for your vehicle, consult your local Haynes dealer for the latest product information.

## ACURA
12020 Integra '86 thru '89 & Legend '86 thru '90
12021 Integra '90 thru '93 & Legend '91 thru '95

## AMC
    Jeep CJ - see JEEP (50020)
14020 Concord/Hornet/Gremlin/Spirit '70 thru '83
14025 (Renault) Alliance & Encore '83 thru '87

## AUDI
15020 4000 all models '80 thru '87
15025 5000 all models '77 thru '83
15026 5000 all models '84 thru '88

## AUSTIN
    Healey Sprite - see MG Midget (66015)

## BMW
*18020 3/5 Series '82 thru '92
18021 3 Series including Z3 models '92 thru '98
18025 320i all 4 cyl models '75 thru '83
18050 1500 thru 2002 except Turbo '59 thru '77

## BUICK
*19010 Buick Century '97 thru '02
    Century (FWD) - see GM (38005)
*19020 Buick, Oldsmobile & Pontiac Full-size (Front wheel drive) '85 thru '02
19025 Buick Oldsmobile & Pontiac Full-size (Rear wheel drive) '70 thru '90
19030 Mid-size Regal & Century '74 thru '87
    Regal - see GENERAL MOTORS (38010)
    Skyhawk - see GM (38030)
    Skylark - see GM (38020, 38025)
    Somerset - see GENERAL MOTORS (38025)

## CADILLAC
21030 Cadillac Rear Wheel Drive '70 thru '93
    Cimarron, Eldorado & Seville - see GM (38015, 38030, 38031)

## CHEVROLET
10305 Chevrolet Engine Overhaul Manual
*24010 Astro & GMC Safari Mini-vans '85 thru '03
24015 Camaro V8 all models '70 thru '81
24016 Camaro all models '82 thru '92
    Cavalier - see GM (38015)
    Celebrity - see GM (38005)
24017 Camaro & Firebird '93 thru '02
24020 Chevelle, Malibu, El Camino '69 thru '87
24024 Chevette & Pontiac T1000 '76 thru '87
    Citation - see GENERAL MOTORS (38020)
24032 Corsica/Beretta all models '87 thru '96
24040 Corvette all V8 models '68 thru '82
24041 Corvette all models '84 thru '96
24045 Full-size Sedans Caprice, Impala, Biscayne, Bel Air & Wagons '69 thru '90
24046 Impala SS & Caprice and Buick Roadmaster '91 thru '96
    Lumina '90 thru '94 - see GM (38010)
*24048 Lumina & Monte Carlo '95 thru '03
    Lumina APV - see GM (38035)
24050 Luv Pick-up all 2WD & 4WD '72 thru '82
    Malibu - see GM (38026)
24055 Monte Carlo all models '70 thru '88
    Monte Carlo '95 thru '01 - see LUMINA
24059 Nova all V8 models '69 thru '79
24060 Nova/Geo Prizm '85 thru '92
24064 Pick-ups '67 '87 - Chevrolet & GMC, all V8 & in-line 6 cyl, 2WD & 4WD '67 thru '87; Suburbans, Blazers & Jimmys '67 thru '91
24065 Pick-ups '88 thru '98 - Chevrolet & GMC, all full-size models '88 thru '98; C/K Classic '99 & '00; Blazer & Jimmy '92 thru '94; Suburban '92 thru '99; Tahoe & Yukon '95 thru '99
*24066 Pick-ups '99 thru '02 - Chevrolet Silverado & GMC Sierra '99 thru '02; Suburban/Tahoe/Yukon/Yukon XL '00 thru '02
24070 S-10 & GMC S-15 Pick-ups '82 thru '93
*24071 S-10, Gmc S-15 & Jimmy '94 thru '01
*24072 Chevrolet TrailBlazer & TrailBlazer EXT, GMC Envoy & Envoy XL, Oldsmobile Bravada '02 and '03
24075 Sprint '85 thru '88, Geo Metro '89 thru '01
24080 Vans - Chevrolet & GMC '68 thru '96

## CHRYSLER
10310 Chrysler Engine Overhaul Manual
25015 Chrysler Cirrus, Dodge Stratus, Plymouth Breeze, '95 thru '98
25020 Full-size Front-Wheel Drive '88 thru '93
    K-Cars - see DODGE Aries (30008)
    Laser - see DODGE Daytona (30030)
25025 Chrysler LHS, Concorde & New Yorker, Dodge Intrepid, Eagle Vision '93 thru '97
*25026 Chrysler LHS, Concorde, 300M, Dodge Intrepid '98 thru '03
25030 Chrysler/Plym. Mid-size '82 thru '95
    Rear-wheel Drive - see DODGE (30050)
*25035 PT Cruiser all models '01 thru '03
*25040 Chrysler Sebring/Dodge Avenger '95 thru '02

## DATSUN
28005 200SX all models '80 thru '83
28007 B-210 '73 thru '78
28009 210 all models '78 thru '82
28012 240Z, 260Z & 280Z Coupe '70 thru '78
28014 280ZX Coupe & 2+2 '79 thru '83
    300ZX - see NISSAN (72010)
28016 310 all models '78 thru '82
28018 510 & PL521 Pick-up '68 thru '73
28020 510 all models '78 thru '81
28022 620 Series Pick-up all models '73 thru '79
    720 Series Pick-up - NISSAN (72030)
28025 810/Maxima all gas models, '77 thru '84

## DODGE
    400 & 600 - see CHRYSLER (25030)
30008 Aries & Plymouth Reliant '81 thru '89
30010 Caravan & Ply. Voyager '84 thru '95
*30011 Caravan & Ply. Voyager '96 thru '02
30012 Challenger/Plymouth Saporro '78 thru '83
    Challenger '67-'76 - see DART (30025)
30016 Colt/Plymouth Champ '78 thru '87
30020 Dakota Pick-ups all models '87 thru '96
*30021 Durango '98 & '99, Dakota '97 thru '99
30025 Dart, Challenger/Plymouth Barracuda & Valiant 6 cyl models '67 thru '76
30030 Daytona & Chrysler Laser '84 thru '89
    Intrepid - see Chrysler (25025, 25026)
*30034 Dodge & Plymouth Neon '95 thru '99
*30035 Omni & Plymouth Horizon '78 thru '90
30040 Pick-ups all full-size models '74 thru '93
*30041 Pick-ups all full-size models '94 thru '01
*30045 Ram 50/D50 Pick-ups & Raider and Plymouth Arrow Pick-ups '79 thru '93
30050 Dodge/Ply./Chrysler RWD '71 thru '89
30055 Shadow/Plymouth Sundance '87 thru '94
30060 Spirit & Plymouth Acclaim '89 thru '95
*30065 Vans - Dodge & Plymouth '71 thru '03

## EAGLE
    Talon - see MITSUBISHI (68030, 68031)
    Vision - see CHRYSLER (25025)

## FIAT
34010 124 Sport Coupe & Spider '68 thru '78
34025 X1/9 all models '74 thru '80

## FORD
10355 Ford Automatic Transmission Overhaul
10320 Ford Engine Overhaul Manual
36004 Aerostar Mini-vans '86 thru '97
    Aspire - see FORD Festiva (36030)
36006 Contour/Mercury Mystique '95 thru '00
36008 Courier Pick-up all models '72 thru '82
*36012 Crown Victoria & Mercury Grand Marquis '88 thru '00
36016 Escort/Mercury Lynx '81 thru '90
36020 Escort/Mercury Tracer '91 thru '00
    Expedition - see FORD Pick-up (36059)
36022 Ford Escape & Mazda Tribute '01 thru '03
*36024 Explorer & Mazda Navajo '91 thru '01
36025 Ford Explorer & Mercury Mountaineer '02 and '03
36028 Fairmont & Mercury Zephyr '78 thru '83
36030 Festiva & Aspire '88 thru '97
36032 Fiesta all models '77 thru '80
*36034 Focus all models '00 and '01
36036 Ford & Mercury Full-size '75 thru '87
36044 Ford & Mercury Mid-size '75 thru '86
36048 Mustang V8 all models '64-1/2 thru '73
36049 Mustang II 4 cyl, V6 & V8 '74 thru '78
36050 Mustang & Mercury Capri '79 thru '86
*36051 Mustang all models '94 thru '03
36054 Pick-ups and Bronco '73 thru '79
36058 Pick-ups and Bronco '80 thru '96
*36059 Pick-ups, Expedition & Lincoln Navigator '97 thru '02
*36060 Super Duty Pick-up, Excursion '97 thru '02
36062 Pinto & Mercury Bobcat '75 thru '80
36066 Probe all models '89 thru '92
36070 Ranger/Bronco II gas models '83 thru '92
*36071 Ford Ranger '93 thru '00 &
    Mazda Pick-ups '94 thru '00
36074 Taurus & Mercury Sable '86 thru '95
36075 Taurus & Mercury Sable '96 thru '01
36078 Tempo & Mercury Topaz '84 thru '94
36082 Thunderbird/Mercury Cougar '83 thru '88
36086 Thunderbird/Mercury Cougar '89 thru '97
36090 Vans all V8 Econoline models '69 thru '91
*36094 Vans full size '92 thru '01
*36097 Windstar Mini-van '95 thru '03

## GENERAL MOTORS
10360 GM Automatic Transmission Overhaul
38005 Buick Century, Chevrolet Celebrity, Olds Cutlass Ciera & Pontiac 6000 '82 thru '96
*38010 Buick Regal, Chevrolet Lumina, Oldsmobile Cutlass Supreme & Pontiac Grand Prix front wheel drive '88 thru '02
38015 Buick Skyhawk, Cadillac Cimarron, Chevrolet Cavalier, Oldsmobile Firenza Pontiac J-2000 & Sunbird '82 thru '94
*38016 Chevrolet Cavalier/Pontiac Sunfire '95 thru '04
38020 Buick Skylark, Chevrolet Citation, Olds Omega, Pontiac Phoenix '80 thru '85
38025 Buick Skylark & Somerset, Olds Achieva, Calais & Pontiac Grand Am '85 thru '98
*38026 Chevrolet Malibu, Olds Alero & Cutlass, Pontiac Grand Am '97 thru '00
38030 Cadillac Eldorado & Oldsmobile Toronado '71 thru '85, Seville '80 thru '85, Buick Riviera '79 thru '85
*38031 Cadillac Eldorado & Seville '86 thru '91, DeVille & Buick Riviera '86 thru '93, Fleetwood & Olds Toronado '86 thru '92
38032 DeVille '94 thru '02, Seville '92 thru '04
38035 Chevrolet Lumina APV, Oldsmobile Silhouette & Pontiac Trans Sport '90 thru '96
*38036 Chevrolet Venture, Olds Silhouette, Pontiac Trans Sport & Montana '97 thru '01
    General Motors Full-size Rear-wheel Drive - see BUICK (19025)

## GEO
    Metro - see CHEVROLET Sprint (24075)
    Prizm - see CHEVROLET (24060) or TOYOTA (92036)
40030 Storm all models '90 thru '93
    Tracker - see SUZUKI Samurai (90010)

## GMC
    Vans & Pick-ups - see CHEVROLET

## HONDA
42010 Accord CVCC all models '76 thru '83
42011 Accord all models '84 thru '89
42012 Accord all models '90 thru '93
42013 Accord all models '94 thru '97
*42014 Accord all models '98 thru '02
42020 Civic 1200 all models '73 thru '79
42021 Civic 1300 & 1500 CVCC '80 thru '83
42022 Civic 1500 CVCC all models '75 thru '79
42023 Civic all models '84 thru '91
42024 Civic & del Sol '92 thru '95
*42025 Civic '96 thru '00, CR-V '97 thru '00, Acura Integra '94 thru '00
    Passport - see ISUZU Rodeo (47017)
42026 Civic '01 thru '04, CR-V '02 thru '04
*42040 Prelude CVCC all models '79 thru '89

## HYUNDAI
*43010 Elantra all models '96 thru '01
43015 Excel & Accent all models '86 thru '98

## ISUZU
    Hombre - see CHEVROLET S-10 (24071)
*47017 Rodeo '91 thru '02, Amigo '89 thru '02, Honda Passport '95 thru '02
47020 Trooper '84 thru '91, Pick-up '81 thru '93

## JAGUAR
49010 XJ6 all 6 cyl models '68 thru '86
49011 XJ6 all models '88 thru '94
49015 XJ12 & XJS all 12 cyl models '72 thru '85

## JEEP
50010 Cherokee, Comanche & Wagoneer Limited all models '84 thru '01
50020 CJ all models '49 thru '86
*50025 Grand Cherokee all models '93 thru '03
50029 Grand Wagoneer & Pick-up '72 thru '91
*50030 Wrangler all models '87 thru '00
50035 Liberty '02 thru '04

## LEXUS
    ES 300 - see TOYOTA Camry (92007)

## LINCOLN
    Navigator - see FORD Pick-up (36059)
*59010 Rear Wheel Drive all models '70 thru '01

## MAZDA
61010 GLC (rear wheel drive) '77 thru '83
61011 GLC (front wheel drive) '81 thru '85
61015 323 & Protegé '90 thru '00
*61016 MX-5 Miata '90 thru '97
61020 MPV all models '89 thru '94
    Navajo - see FORD Explorer (36024)
61030 Pick-ups '72 thru '93
    Pick-ups '94 on - see Ford (36071)
61035 RX-7 all models '79 thru '85
61036 RX-7 all models '86 thru '91
61040 626 (rear wheel drive) '79 thru '82
61041 626 & MX-6 (front wheel drive) '83 thru '91
61042 626 '93 thru '01, & MX-6/Ford Probe '93 thru '97

## MERCEDES-BENZ
63012 123 Series Diesel '76 thru '85
63015 190 Series 4-cyl gas models, '84 thru '88
63020 230, 250 & 280 6 cyl sohc '68 thru '72
63025 280 123 Series gas models '77 thru '81
63030 350 & 450 all models '71 thru '80

## MERCURY
64200 Villager & Nissan Quest '93 thru '01
    All other titles, see FORD listing.

## MG
66010 MGB Roadster & GT Coupe '62 thru '80
66015 MG Midget & Austin Healey Sprite Roadster '58 thru '80

## MITSUBISHI
68020 Cordia, Tredia, Galant, Precis & Mirage '83 thru '93
68030 Eclipse, Eagle Talon & Plymouth Laser '90 thru '94
*68031 Eclipse '95 thru '01, Eagle Talon '95 thru '98
68035 Mitsubishi Galant '94 thru '03
68040 Pick-up '83 thru '96, Montero '83 thru '93

## NISSAN
72010 300ZX all models incl. Turbo '84 thru '89
72015 Altima all models '93 thru '04
72020 Maxima all models '85 thru '92
*72021 Maxima all models '93 thru '01
72030 Pick-ups '80 thru '97, Pathfinder '87 thru '95
*72031 Frontier Pick-up '98 thru '01, Xterra '00 & '01, Pathfinder '96 thru '01
72040 Pulsar all models '83 thru '86
72050 Sentra all models '82 thru '94
72051 Sentra & 200SX all models '95 thru '99
72060 Stanza all models '82 thru '90

## OLDSMOBILE
*73015 Cutlass '74 thru '88
    For other OLDSMOBILE titles, see BUICK, CHEVROLET or GM listings.

## PLYMOUTH
    For PLYMOUTH titles, see DODGE.

## PONTIAC
79008 Fiero all models '84 thru '88
79018 Firebird V8 models except Turbo '70 thru '81
79019 Firebird all models '82 thru '92
79040 Mid-size Rear-wheel Drive '70 thru '87
    For other PONTIAC titles, see BUICK, CHEVROLET or GM listings.

## PORSCHE
80020 911 Coupe & Targa models '65 thru '89
80025 914 all 4 cyl models '69 thru '76
80030 924 all models incl. Turbo '76 thru '82
80035 944 all models incl. Turbo '83 thru '89

## RENAULT
    Alliance, Encore - see AMC (14020)

## SAAB
*84010 900 including Turbo '79 thru '88

## SATURN
*87010 Saturn all models '91 thru '02
87020 Saturn all L-series models '00 thru '04

## SUBARU
89002 1100, 1300, 1400 & 1600 '71 thru '79
89003 1600 & 1800 2WD & 4WD '80 thru '94

## SUZUKI
90010 Samurai/Sidekick/Geo Tracker '86 thru '01

## TOYOTA
92005 Camry all models '83 thru '91
92006 Camry all models '92 thru '96
*92007 Camry/Avalon/Solara/Lexus ES 300 '97 thru '01
92015 Celica Rear Wheel Drive '71 thru '85
92020 Celica Front Wheel Drive '86 thru '99
92025 Celica Supra all models '79 thru '92
92030 Corolla all models '75 thru '79
92032 Corolla rear wheel drive models '80 thru '87
92035 Corolla front wheel drive models '84 thru '92
92036 Corolla & Geo Prizm '93 thru '02
92040 Corolla Tercel all models '80 thru '82
92045 Corona all models '74 thru '82
92050 Cressida all models '78 thru '82
92055 Land Cruiser FJ40/43/45/55 '68 thru '82
92056 Land Cruiser FJ60/62/80/FZJ80 '80 thru '96
92065 MR2 all models '85 thru '87
92070 Pick-up all models '69 thru '78
92075 Pick-up all models '79 thru '95
*92076 Tacoma '95 thru '00, 4Runner '96 thru '00, T100 '93 thru '98
*92078 Tundra '00 thru '02, Sequoia '01 thru '02
92080 Previa all models '91 thru '95
*92082 RAV4 all models '96 thru '02
92085 Tercel all models '87 thru '94

## TRIUMPH
94007 Spitfire all models '62 thru '81
94010 TR7 all models '75 thru '81

## VW
96008 Beetle & Karmann Ghia '54 thru '79
*96009 New Beetle '98 thru '00
96016 Rabbit, Jetta, Scirocco, & Pick-up gas models '74 thru '91 & Convertible '80 thru '92
96017 Golf, GTI & Jetta '93 thru '98, Cabrio '95 thru '02
*96018 Golf, GTI, Jetta & Cabrio '99 thru '02
96020 Rabbit, Jetta, Pick-up diesel '77 thru '84
96023 Passat '98 thru '01, Audi A4 '96 thru '01
96030 Transporter 1600 all models '68 thru '79
96035 Transporter 1700, 1800, 2000 '72 thru '79
96040 Type 3 1500 & 1600 '63 thru '73
96045 Vanagon air-cooled models '80 thru '83

## VOLVO
97010 120, 130 Series & 1800 Sports '61 thru '73
97015 140 Series all models '66 thru '74
97020 240 Series all models '76 thru '93
97025 260 Series all models '75 thru '82
97040 740 & 760 Series all models '82 thru '88

## TECHBOOK MANUALS
10205 Automotive Computer Codes
10210 Automotive Emissions Control Manual
10215 Fuel Injection Manual, 1978 thru 1985
10220 Fuel Injection Manual, 1986 thru 1999
10225 Holley Carburetor Manual
10230 Rochester Carburetor Manual
10240 Weber/Zenith/Stromberg/SU Carburetor
10305 Chevrolet Engine Overhaul Manual
10310 Chrysler Engine Overhaul Manual
10320 Ford Engine Overhaul Manual
10330 GM and Ford Diesel Engine Repair
10340 Small Engine Repair Manual
10345 Suspension, Steering & Driveline
10355 Ford Automatic Transmission Overhaul
10360 GM Automatic Transmission Overhaul
10405 Automotive Body Repair & Painting
10410 Automotive Brake Manual
10415 Automotive Detailing Manual
10420 Automotive Eelectrical Manual
10425 Automotive Heating & Air Conditioning
10430 Automotive Reference Dictionary
10435 Automotive Tools Manual
10440 Used Car Buying Guide
10445 Welding Manual
10450 ATV Basics

## SPANISH MANUALS
98903 Reparación de Carrocería & Pintura
98905 Códigos Automotrices de la Computadora
98910 Frenos Automotriz
98915 Inyección de Combustible 1986 al 1999
99040 Chevrolet & GMC Camionetas '67 al '87
99041 Chevrolet & GMC Camionetas '88 al '98
99042 Chevrolet Camionetas Cerradas '68 al '95
99055 Dodge Caravan/Ply. Voyager '84 al '95
99075 Ford Camionetas y Bronco '80 al '94
99077 Ford Camionetas Cerradas '69 al '91
99088 Ford Modelos de Tamaño Mediano '75 al '86
99091 Ford Taurus & Mercury Sable '86 al '95
99095 GM Modelos de Tamaño Grande '70 al '90
99100 GM Modelos de Tamaño Mediano '70 al '88
99110 Nissan Camioneta '80 al '96, Pathfinder '87 al '95
99118 Nissan Sentra '82 al '94
99125 Toyota Camionetas y 4-Runner '79 al '95

Nearly 100 Haynes motorcycle manuals also available

2-05

*Listings shown with an asterisk (*) indicate model coverage as of this printing. These titles will be periodically updated to include later model years - consult your Haynes dealer for more information.*